American Sociological Theory

A CRITICAL HISTORY

American Sociological Theory

A CRITICAL HISTORY

Robert Bierstedt
University of Virginia

ACADEMIC PRESS
A Subsidiary of Harcourt Brace Jovanovich, Publishers
New York London Toronto Sydney San Francisco

ACADEMIC PRESS, INC.
111 Fifth Avenue, New York, New York 10003

United Kingdom Edition published by
ACADEMIC PRESS, INC. (LONDON) LTD.
24/28 Oval Road, London NW1 7DX

Library of Congress Cataloging in Publication Data

Bierstedt, Robert, Date.
American sociological theory.

Bibliography: p.
Includes indexes.
1. Sociology--United States--History. 2. Sociologists --United States--Biography. I. Title.
HM22.U5B45 301'.0973 81-10820
ISBN 0-12-097480-0 AACR2
ISBN 0-12-097482-7 (pbk.)

PRINTED IN THE UNITED STATES OF AMERICA

81 82 83 84 9 8 7 6 5 4 3 2 1

This book is for Betty

Contents

CHAPTER 4

Edward Alsworth Ross 131

CHAPTER 5

Florian Znaniecki 185

CHAPTER 6

Robert Morrison MacIver 243

CHAPTER 7

Pitirim A. Sorokin 299

Preface

As its title indicates, this book is a history of American sociological theory. It is not, however, a comprehensive or detailed history. It is, instead, a selective and critical account of ten writers whose names loom large on the continuum of the discipline, whose contributions have won them a prominence that may or may not be permanent, and who belong on the roster of those who achieved some stature and significance during their active careers.

Selections, of course, are always arbitrary and, therefore, always debatable. Why did Lewis Coser exclude William Graham Sumner from his superior history of sociological thought? And why did he include Robert E. Park who, however great his influence upon his Chicago students, exhibited little interest in sociological theory? Why did Raymond Aron in his incisively written story of sociology include de Tocqueville who, however perceptive as an observer of the human and especially the American scene, was not an orthodox sociologist in any Comtean or Spencerian sense? And why, on the other hand, did he exclude Spencer and Simmel and give us no Americans at all? Why did Ronald Fletcher, in his magisterial volumes, elevate Mill and Hobhouse to places of distinction when they have no chapters of their own in Coser and Aron? And why, to end these illustrations, did Harry Elmer Barnes in his much earlier *Introduction to the History of Sociology*, a book containing forty-seven chapters on more than that many sociologists, include Benjamin Kidd and leave Karl Marx out in the cold?

There is, in the history of sociology, as in the history of other disciplines, a pantheon, a building dedicated not to the gods but to the illustrious dead. Statues are commissioned and placed in the Great Hall for all to see and admire. The population of this pantheon, however, is constantly changing. Some of the statues fail, after a while, to attract their share of visitors, so they are removed to the basement to make room for others. We thus have the phenomenon of the depopulated pantheon. Sometimes there is a renewal of interest. The statue is dusted off, retrieved from storage, and restored to its former place of honor. Herbert Spencer is an example. Once one of the most celebrated of Englishmen, he lived to see his fame diminish and almost disappear. But he had his place in the sociologists' pantheon until Crane Brinton, with Talcott Parsons' approval, consigned him to oblivion in 1933 with the question "Who now reads Spencer?" Later, it was, paradoxically, Parsons himself who, with his historical and comparative studies of societies, restored him to his former place. It may be a permanent place, but predictions are precarious. Inevitably, a sociologist would come along and ask in print, "Who now reads Parsons?" It happened in 1979.

Consider also the instructive cases of Emile Durkheim and Max Weber. For many years—until the mid-1930s—their statues were not in the American pantheon at all. Indeed, Pitirim Sorokin, in his *Contemporary Sociological Theories* of 1928, devoted more than twice as much space to Frédéric Le Play as he did to Durkheim and Weber combined. Now, in 1981, Le Play is in the basement while tour guides sing the praises of the former two to sightseers and serious students alike.

The point of the figure is that any selection of sociological theorists to be included in a book of this kind is bound to be arbitrary. If I am asked, therefore, why I include Sumner but not Small, Znaniecki but not Thomas, MacIver but not Park, Lundberg but not Mills (and why I relegate Giddings, once an imperial figure in the field, to a brief appendix), the best answer is that my choices are entirely personal. On the other hand, I am not altogether bereft of defenses. I could say, for example, that Small's major contributions were made in academic administration, that Park and Thomas were not seriously interested in general theory, and that Mills, like Veblen before him, was an outstanding publicist rather than a sociological theorist. I have no doubt that many will disagree and consider my choices not only arbitrary but possibly irresponsible. The men included here, however, happen to have written the kind of sociological theory that attracted my attention to a degree that others did not. They are the writers who, in their own times, addressed the central issues of sociology.

Considerations of another kind apply to my stopping place. No one doubts that important contributions to sociological theory have been made since Merton wrote his *Social Theory and Social Structure*. But a time line is needed, a place to write *finis*, and to say that the book is big enough. I have, therefore, omitted all sociologists of my own cohort with confidence that their names will find a place in other books by other authors.

If the selections are arbitrary, so also is their number. In this respect, every author of a book like this finds himself playing a game he cannot win. A book of a given size can be devoted to a thousand writers or to one, with an entire spectrum of possibilities in between. At one extreme, we would have an annotated bibliography; at the other, a study of a single sociologist. Two desiderata are always in conflict—scope and depth. One of them can be purchased only at the price of the other. I have thus chosen to treat ten American sociologists at greater length rather than twenty say, at half the length, or forty at a quarter. Again, the decision is an arbitrary one.

Another deliberate limitation requires a word of comment. I have not treated the entire corpus of the sociologists included, but only their sociological theory. In some cases, of course, almost all of their work falls under this rubric. But I have neglected Sumner on banking, Ward on botany, Znaniecki on nationalities, MacIver on government, Lundberg on social research, Parsons on the family, and, except for a few words, Merton on science.

It should be apparent that this book is also limited to writers whose principal concerns were general sociological theory. Those who have a repute, however high, in other areas of sociological inquiry—race relations, stratification, social psychology, demography, research methods, criminology, and so on—are all perforce omitted. One does not, of course, denigrate the significance of work in these other sectors of sociology simply because attention is directed elsewhere.

My treatment of each writer is a traditional one—in full awareness of the fact that to some the adjective is pejorative. Each chapter begins with a biographical sketch, continues with substantive exposition of major works, and concludes with a critical evaluation. I know full well—the issue is discussed in the text—of Merton's demand that the history of sociology be written sociologically, that is, with an effort to relate ideas to the social and economic conditions of the society on which they arise. I am also aware of Coser's brilliant advocacy of this point of view. It is an issue, however, on which I have to disagree with Merton and Coser and agree instead with Parsons. In my opinion, ideas are relatively autonomous in the stream of history and are more dependent upon antecedent ideas than they are upon the social, economic, or political circumstances prevailing at the time of their appearance. It is doubtless true that every thinker is in some sense a child of his time and place. In societies far apart in time, like those of Plato, William of Occam, and Immanuel Kant, connections between sociocultural conditions and systems of thought can doubtless be discerned. But when the temporal distances are shortened, the connections become a bit tenuous and tend to disappear.

Bertrand Russell once suggested that John Dewey's pragmatic instrumentalism was a "natural" reflection of the booming industrial economy of the United States in the last half of the nineteenth century. Dewey replied, with some irritation, that one might, with comparable cogency, attribute the dualism characteristic of French philosophy to the Frenchman's custom of keeping both a wife and a mistress. Less facetiously, I have no doubt whatever that Kant's *Critique of Pure Reason* is better explained by the antecedent epistemologies of Locke, Berkeley, and Hume than by the economy of Königsberg at the time it was written. It seems to me nothing less than clotted nonsense to suppose that propositions in Etruscan archaeology, topological mathematics, or pure sociology are affected by the price of wool or the prime interest rates prevailing at the time of their publication.

This book, as its subtitle indicates, is a critical history. I have not been content with a rehearsal of the theories of my American writers but have introduced critical comments throughout, sometimes in the expositions of their major works and always in concluding summaries and evaluations. I trust that these criticisms, often severe and perhaps especially so in the cases of Sorokin, Parsons, and Lundberg, are not unfair. I would contend, as Sorokin did before me, that criticism is of the essence of scholarship and that the vigor of a discipline depends upon positions taken, advanced, defended, lost, and won again in the eternal dialectic that is the life of the mind.

Prefaces normally conclude with a list of persons to whom the author is indebted. I have one important debt to pay. My good friend, Charles H. Page, read the chapter on Parsons and gave it the benefit of his considerable editorial talents. But all of the opinions in this book, however perverse, belong to me.

American Sociological Theory

A CRITICAL HISTORY

CHAPTER 1

William Graham Sumner

It is vain to imagine that "a scientific man" can divest himself of prejudice or previous opinion, and put himself in an attitude of neutral independence towards the mores.

—*Folkways*, No. 102.

William Graham Sumner, the first American sociologist, was born in Paterson, New Jersey, on October 30, 1840. His father, Thomas Sumner, was a member of the working class who had immigrated to this country from England and who had married another English immigrant, Sarah Graham, who died when William was eight years old. William was educated in the public schools of Hartford, Connecticut, an education interrupted by two years of work in a dry-goods establishment. His father, in a period of relative prosperity, managed to give him $1000 for higher education (later subtracted from his inheritance), and this sum was enough to see him through four years of Yale College, where the tuition was $45 a year. An eager student, he was graduated in 1863 with many curricular and extracurricular honors.[1]

Shortly before graduation Sumner received his draft induction notice into the army, but he accepted from Henry C. Whitney, the older brother of a classmate, sufficient funds to purchase a substitute.[2] He did not attend the

1. The curriculum at that time was a narrow one. For the first three years it consisted almost entirely of Latin, Greek, mathematics, and rhetoric, although the juniors had an additional choice between a modern language and mineralogy. Seniors were offered instruction also in history, the Constitution of the United States, moral and political philosophy, the history of philosophy, theology, astronomy, and chemistry. For these and other facts, see the splendid biography by Harris E. Starr, *William Graham Sumner* (New York: Henry Holt & Co., 1925). The author of this indispensable book was a Congregational clergyman and associate editor of the *Dictionary of American Biography*. The best brief treatment of Sumner's life and work is Maurice R. Davie, *William Graham Sumner* (New York: Thomas Y. Crowell Co., 1963).

2. Little or no social stigma attached to this practice. The first conscription act for the Civil War was passed by Congress on March 3, 1863. It provided that a draftee could avoid a particular call by the payment of $300 or gain exemption for the entire war by providing a substitute who would agree to serve for three years. Sumner's substitute cost $250.

commencement exercises of his class because he was enroute to Europe to continue his education, again using funds provided by his classmate's brother and later supplemented by his father and his own brother Joseph. He spent the first year abroad at Geneva, where he studied French and Hebrew. The following two years found him at Göttingen studying ancient languages, history, and "Biblical science," all in preparation for a career in the ministry. The professors of this last subject made an impression upon the young scholar because of the rigor of the methods they employed—methods in Sumner's opinion comparable in every way with those employed in the natural sciences. Furthermore, they were the only group of men he had met who were willing to sacrifice wealth, political distinction, preferment, and popularity for what he called the truth of science.

In May 1866 Sumner went to Oxford to study theology. While there he became acquainted with the work of Henry Thomas Buckle, whose great book *The History of Civilization in England*[3] was then a topic of conversation among his colleagues. In this book, Buckle criticized historians on the ground that they were too much interested in biography and in political and military history and failed to seek universal principles or laws.[4] Of course, they lacked the statistical materials that would enable them to do so, but Buckle was confident that it was possible to construct a science of society on the basis of inductions from history. The difficulty was practical, not theoretical; it concerned the sheer quantity of materials that would have to be mastered. Buckle's book is a brilliant effort to find regularities in social phenomena and historical events and to find something in nature that can explain these regularities. His thesis, in short, was that human society is a product of natural forces and is therefore susceptible to a natural explanation. It is easy to understand why it had such a stimulating effect upon Sumner.[5] Actually, as we shall presently see, it was Herbert Spencer who became the dominating influence upon Sumner's thought, but it was Buckle who planted the seed.[6]

Sumner returned from Oxford in the fall of 1866 to take up an unsolicited appointment as tutor in mathematics and Greek at Yale. Yale at that time was "squalidly poor," possessed of ill-equipped classrooms and a "miserably inadequate" library. It was also squarely facing the past, and

3. 2 vols. (London: Parker, Son, and Bourn, 1857–1861).

4. Recall, for example, the famous remark of Edward Augustus Freeman: "History is past politics, and politics present history."

5. Indeed, as Floyd Nelson House suggests, it had a similar effect upon many of the rising young social scientists in the latter part of the century. House, *The Development of Sociology* (New York: McGraw-Hill, 1936), p. 143.

6. Buckle's book, incidentally, was used by the economist Thomas Nixon Carver in his course in sociology at Harvard long before Harvard had a department of sociology.

Sumner became a leader in the "Young Yale" movement agitating for reform. He had not surrendered his ministerial ambitions, however, and resigned his appointment in 1869 in order to become assistant to the rector of Calvary Church (Episcopal) in New York City. During his year there he also edited a religious periodical, *The Living Church,* and was offered—and declined—the chair of Hebrew at the General Theological Seminary.[7] In 1870 he became rector of the Church of the Redeemer in Morristown, New Jersey, where for two years he preached two sermons every Sunday. In these sermons he stressed without surcease the Puritan virtues of hard work, self-reliance, self-denial, frugality, prudence, and perseverance.

Sumner was, in fact, a veritable avatar of the Puritan ethic. Wasting time was to him a serious sin. Hard work was the key to a satisfactory and successful life. Frivolity disgusted him; deceit and dishonesty aroused his wrath. There was a wide streak of intolerance in him—intolerance above all of folly and stupidity. He sought out evil in order to denounce it. Throughout his life he suffered the consequences of those who claimed to be more righteous than their neighbors.

On April 17, 1871, Sumner married Jeannie Whittemore Elliott, the daughter of a New York business man. They had two sons and, although the biographer is sparing of detail, enjoyed a long and happy marriage, marred only by the fact that in later years Mrs. Sumner was a semi-invalid.[8]

It may be said that Sumner spent his entire life as a preacher of sermons. He preferred the classroom to the pulpit, however, and so was permanently lost to the ministry when he accepted appointment at Yale in 1872 as professor of political and social science, a post he held until his retirement in 1909. Although he never consciously surrendered his religious beliefs, it was about that time, as he said, that he put them in a drawer, and when he later came to open it there was nothing there. On the other hand, he never formally severed his religious ties. He attended Trinity Church in New Haven regularly until the last ten years of his life and occasionally after that, served as a member of the vestry, performed the baptismal ceremony for a grandson, and, shortly before his death, took Communion.[9]

7. In addition to Greek, Latin, Hebrew, French, and German, all of which he learned in his youth, Sumner taught himself in later years to read Dutch, Spanish, Portuguese, Italian, Russian, Polish, Danish, and Swedish.

8. A few more glimpses of Sumner's family life may be found in Albert Galloway Keller, *Reminiscenses (Mainly Personal) of William Graham Sumner* (New Haven, Conn.: Yale University Press, 1933).

9. Although Sumner, like Weber and Durkheim, came to be, in Weber's phrase, "religiously unmusical," he never failed to appreciate the role of religion in social life. Indeed, the second volume of *The Science of Society* is devoted almost entirely to the sociology of religion. At the

About the time Sumner joined the Yale faculty he began to read with growing enthusiasm the writings of Herbert Spencer. Spencer's essays were appearing periodically, essays that were later published in a volume entitled *The Study of Society*, and they offered Sumner exactly what he was looking for and what had been only adumbrated in Buckle, namely, a science of society, a notion of society operating under natural forces. It seemed to him to represent a new and inspiring kind of inquiry and one destined to have an exciting and important future.[10] He formed a class for reading and discussing Spencer's ideas, and this, in 1875, was one of the first courses in sociology in the United States, if not in the world.[11]

Sumner's acceptance of Spencer's evolutionary doctrine marked a transition in his thought. In his sermons, a few years earlier, he had rejected such modern notions as rationalism, individualism, materialism, evolutionism, and skepticism and held fast to an orthodox cosmology. He was finally converted by Professor Othniel C. Marsh. Marsh, the first director of the Peabody Museum of Natural History at Yale, had arranged an exhibit of fossil horses that illustrated the evolution of the toe from multiple to single; this evidence was difficult to ignore. The intellectual stimulus, however, came from Spencer. If Buckle had given Summer the goal, it was Spencer who gave him the means to reach it, namely, the evolutionary principle. In

---

end of the volume Sumner notes both the services and disservices of religion, agrees with Lippert that religion is a means of continuing the struggle for existence beyond the grave, and invites attention to the various and even contrary practices that religion has sanctioned:

> It has favored both war and peace, wealth and poverty, diligence and idleness, virginity and prostitution, humility and ostentation, indulgence and austerity. It has prescribed game-laws, cannibalism, human sacrifice, the killing of the old, suicide, incest, polyandry, polygyny, slavery, and the levirate; has guaranteed all forms of property-holding, of inheritance, and of government; has both favored and proscribed commerce and the taking of interest; it has been forced to bend to new vices. It has therefore offered no absolute standard of morality for there is none, but has sanctioned what lay in the mores of the time and place—or, often, what lay in the mores of the place at some previous time.

The Science of Society, 4 vols. (New Haven, Conn.: Yale University Press, 1927–1928), vol. 2, p. 1463.

10. Interestingly enough, Sumner had been entirely unimpressed by Spencer's *First Principles.* Although he does not say so, Spencer's "Unknowable" was doubtless too metaphysical a conception to suit his tastes.

11. It was probably not, however, the very first. George Frederick Holmes, who taught at the University of Virginia from 1857 to 1897, purchased Comte's *Cours de philosophie positive* in May 1848 and, as his marginal notes attest, read it the same year. In 1852 he published two papers on Comte, both in the *Methodist Quarterly Review.* Comte, in turn, considered Holmes his most worthy American critic. See Richard L. Hawkins, *Auguste Comte and the United States, 1816–1853* (Cambridge, Mass.: Harvard University Press, 1936), pp. 99–142. In 1884 Holmes printed privately a series of lectures entitled *The Science of Society*, and it is conceivable that he began giving these lectures to his students some years earlier. In the book he is both appreciative and critical of Comte and Spencer, recognizes that there is order in society, and proclaims the necessity of inquiring into "the essential motions of humanity" under some such name as sociology, social science, or the science of society. There

an 1852 essay entitled "A Theory of Population," published in the *Westminster Review*, Spencer had used the expressions "struggle for existence" and "survival of the fittest"—expressions that appeared as chapter titles in Darwin's *The Origin of Species* (1859) and that became the twin slogans of the most influential movement of thought in the nineteenth century. Social Darwinism became the name of a doctrine that has been called "the great extrapolation," an extension of the natural selection that Darwin had discovered in the world of biological species to the world of human societies. It was a doctrine that had percussive consequences—in sociological and political theory—and that achieved such dominance and potency that even its critics, so to speak, were members of the school.[12] It was embraced with enthusiasm by Sumner, who believed that sociology, "if it borrowed the theory of evolution in the first place, would speedily render it back again enriched by new and and independent evidence."[13]

Evolution was the immediate issue in a controversy in which Sumner became embroiled in 1879, a controversy that had important consequences for the future of academic freedom in the United States. To Sumner's astonishment, Noah Porter, then president of Yale, demanded that he abandon the use of Spencer's *The Study of Sociology* (1873) in his courses.[14] Sumner was astonished both because of the infringement of a professor's freedom that the "order" implied and because Porter had been

---

is a copy of this book in the Alderman Library, University of Virginia. See House, *Development of Sociology*, p. 219. See also Frederick E. Salzillo, Jr., "The Development of Sociology at the University of Virginia: The First 100 Years, 1873–1973" (Unpublished manuscript: University of Virginia, 1974), where the work of Holmes is treated in detail.

There are two earlier American books with the word "sociology" in their titles: *Sociology for the South*, by George Fitzhugh of Virginia (Richmond, 1854), and *A Treatise on Sociology*, by Henry Hughes of Mississippi (Philadelphia, 1854). These are proslavery tracts.

12. See "The Social Darwinists," in Robert Bierstedt, *Power and Progress: Essays on Sociological Theory* (New York: McGraw-Hill, 1974). Although it is doubtless of minor interest now, we may recall Spencer's definition of evolution, his key to the cosmos, a sesquipedalian definition about which he was in dead earnest: "Evolution is an integration of matter and concomitant dissipation of motion; during which the matter passes from an indefinite, incoherent homogeneity to a definite, coherent heterogeneity; and during which the retained motion undergoes a parallel transformation" (Herbert Spencer, *First principles* [New York: D. Appleton and Company 1897], p. 407). The mathematician T. P. Kirkman, a contemporary of Spencer, "translated" this definition as follows: "Evolution is a change from a no-howish untalkaboutable all-alikeness to a somehowish and in general talkaboutable not-all-alikeness by continuous sticktogetherations and somethingelsefications."

13. *Essays of William Graham Sumner*, ed. Albert Galloway Keller and Maurice R. Davie (New Haven, Conn.: Yale University Press, 1934), 2 vols., 2, p. 10.

14. Porter, who occupied the presidency from 1871 to 1886, was a distinguished psychologist and moral philosopher, among whose works were *The Human Intellect* (1868) and *The Elements of Moral Science* (1885). For an appreciation of Porter's place as a psychologist, see Jay Wharton Fay, *American Psychology before William James* (New Brunswick, N. J.: Rutgers University Press, 1939), pp. 147–150.

using Spencer in his own classes—although only, to be sure, as an example of pernicious doctrine. At this time the debate between the evolutionists and their opponents was at its height, and the question whether a Darwinian was qualified for a professorship in an American university was the subject of an intense and emotional struggle.[15] Porter had no objection to Darwinian theory in the natural sciences but objected strenuously to its importation into the moral and social sciences.[16]

Sumner's defense did not go to the merits of Spencer, nor did it dwell upon the evidence supporting evolutionary theory in general. Instead, it questioned the authority of a university president to dictate to a professor the books he might use in his classes. No such exercise of authority could be tolerated in the academy:

> His [Porter's] position was that the students might better get no sociology than run the risk of getting agnosticism in getting sociology, and he even seems to maintain that they might better get no sociology than get it from a book by Spencer. I resisted this and maintained that they should have sociology anyhow, from the best means available, and I would not submit to a restraint the motive of which was consideration for metaphysical and theological interests. This is the only issue to which I have been a party.[17]

There were misunderstandings on both sides. It appears that Sumner wrested from the president a reluctant acquiescence in his use of the book,

---

15. See Richard Hofstadter and Walter P. Metzger, *The Development of Academic Freedom in the United States* (New York: Columbia University Press, 1955), pp. 320–366 (this section was written by Metzger). The Sumner–Porter dispute is treated in detail in Starr, *William Graham Sumner*, pp. 345–372.

16. Porter to Sumner, December 6, 1879:

> The use of Spencer's 'Study of Sociology' as a textbook has made a great deal of talk and is likely to make still more. When the subject has been brought to my notice I have been able to reply that I have used his First Principles and his Psychology in my graduate classes with very great advantage. I cannot, however, think that this is or ought to be satisfactory, for the reason that the capacity of an undergraduate student when introduced to the elements of a science, to discriminate between the valid and the invalid is much below that of a graduate. A much more cogent reason is that the book itself is written very largely in a pamphleterring style, which is very unlike most of Spencer's more solid treatises. The freedom and unfairness with which it attacks every Theistic Philosophy of society and of history, and the cool and yet sarcastic effrontery with which he assumes that material elements and laws are the only forces and laws which any scientific man can recognize, seem to me to condemn the book as a textbook for a miscellaneous class in an undergraduate course. I ought to have examined the book sooner, but I feel assured that the use of the book will bring intellectual and moral harm to the students, however you may strive to neutralize or counteract its influence, and that the use of it will inevitably and reasonably work serious havoc to the reputation of the college. Having these opinions, I can do nothing else than express them, and as I am presumed to authorize the use of every textbook, I must formally object to the use of this.

Quoted in Starr, *William Graham Sumner*, pp. 346–347.

17. From a communication addressed by Sumner to the members of the Corporation and to the permanent officers of Yale College, June 1881, quoted *ibid.*, p. 360.

and it appears also that Sumner withdrew it on the ground that the controversy had impaired its usefulness. At one point Sumner planned to resign because the matter involved "rights and interests which no honest teacher ever ought to concede" but was dissuaded from doing so by his faculty colleagues. Passions finally subsided. There can be no doubt, however, that presidential interference with a professor's bibliography ceased to be an issue at Yale and that Sumner struck a hard blow in defense of academic freedom in the United States.

During his long tenure at Yale Sumner found time to exercise the responsibilities of citizenship. In 1873 he was elected to the Board of Aldermen for the city of New Haven and served for three years. He participated in Republican party politics and was said to have written the state platform of 1874. He was a frequent speaker at meetings sponsored by the Chamber of Commerce, usually on behalf of free trade and "sound money." He supported Tilden in the Hayes–Tilden campaign of 1876 and attracted criticism for doing so—criticism he rejected by announcing that, although his first responsibility was to the university, he was free nevertheless, as an independent man, to assume those political duties that were incumbent upon every citizen. In 1882 he became a member of the Board of Education of the state of Connecticut and served in that capacity until his death. Academic administration, on the other hand, had no appeal for him. He scorned the notion, once seriously put forward, that he might become president of Yale. "Nothing on earth would induce me to give up the freedom of a professorship for such a job as college president." Indeed, with the possible exception of the physicist Willard Gibbs, he became the most famous professor in the history of the university and a legend in his lifetime.

William Lyon Phelps, himself a popular professor of English at Yale and once Sumner's student, recalled that Sumner entered the classroom with "the air of a conqueror." To him the classroom was the most important place on earth. He scorned the manuals of pedagogy in use at the time, but so widespread was his fame as a teacher that James B. Angell, president of the University of Michigan, wrote him in 1878 seeking the secret of his success. Nicholas Murray Butler, later and for a long time president of Columbia University, attended one Sumner's classes in 1883 in order to discover methods that would be helpful to him as a newly appointed instructor in logic in Columbia College. Sumner lectured not only on sociology but also on "the sort of opinions that ought to be held on things in general by a Yale man."[18] He nurtured his prejudices until they grew formidable. He had nothing but contempt for sentimentality, fallacious reasoning, and for the designs, however well intentioned, of social reformers, whom he regarded

18. Albion W. Small, "Fifty Years of Sociology in the United States," *American Journal of Sociology* 21 (May 1916): 732, n. 3.

as idiots. He assured his upper-class students, the scions of an American business aristocracy, that they were right to seek the fruits of free enterprise. Their efforts would be in harmony with the nature of the universe and their success another proof of the survival of the fittest.

Except for a serious illness in his fiftieth year, which deprived him of his beloved classroom for a time, Sumner's later career was uneventful. In 1909 his own university awarded him the honorary degree of Doctor of Laws in a ceremony broken both before and after the presentation by the ovations of several generations of alumni fathers and sons, most of whom he had taught. In December of that year, in New York City to deliver his presidential address to the American Sociological Society, he suffered a third and fatal paralytic stroke. He died in Englewood Hospital, New Jersey, on April 12, 1910.

Sumner on Sociology

In Sumner's view every science begins its life by emancipating itself from metaphysics and from all a priori assumptions. Sociology is no exception. It is not, however, necessary to quarrel with the metaphysicians. It is necessary instead to contribute positively to the advancement of this new and important field of inquiry. This is what Sumner proposed to do. Although sociology was still in its infancy, he was sure that it would become a science of the highest utility to the human race. Sociology for him was, quite simply, "the science of life in society":

> It investigates the forces which come into action wherever a human society exists. It studies the structure and functions of the organs of human society, and its aim is to find out the laws in subordination to which human society takes its various forms and social institutions grow and change. Its practical utility consists in deriving the rules of right social living from the facts and laws which prevail by nature in the constitution and functions of society. It must, without doubt, come into collision with all other theories of right living which are founded on authority, tradition, arbitrary invention, or poetic imagination.[19]

Several aspects of this conception merit attention. In the first place, Sumner's emphasis upon structure and function requires special notice.

---

19. "Sociology," in William Graham Sumner, *War and Other Essays*, ed. Albert Galloway Keller (New Haven, Conn.: Yale University Press, 1911), pp. 167–168. This article appeared originally in the Princeton Review (November 1881): 303–323.

Secondly, Sumner stated that the laws of society prevail "by nature," thus regarding society as a natural phenomenon and thus placing the discipline squarely in the domain of the natural sciences. In the third place, Sumner was sure, as we no longer are, that sociology could provide prescriptions for "right living." For Sumner, sociology is thus different from religion because the theories of religion are authoritative and final. Novelists, utopians, and socialists also make easy work of the complex phenomena with which sociology has to deal.

Sociology is, in fact, a difficult kind of inquiry because social phenomena are always complex. It is always difficult to interpret them. They are three or four steps removed from their causes, and it is therefore impossible to use the technique of experimentation. A special method is involved, one that requires arduous training, skill, and sagacity. Sumner supplies no details of this method, except to assert and reassert the importance of trained judgment and critical thinking. Although he occasionally taught a course entitled "The Logic and Method of the Social Sciences," he was methodologically unsophisticated. As Høffding said of Comte, he never felt the sting of the epistemological problem, and philosophy in general was a discipline for which he had nothing but contempt.[20] It is fair to say, however, that he appreciated the importance of classification in his assemblage of facts, in order not to be overwhelmed by them, and the importance also of cross-cultural surveys, in order to escape the limitations of his own culture. It is necessary to say that he was a consistent protagonist of scientific and objective methods in sociology, methods that would win the confidence of other men engaged in the pursuit of truth. Like Spencer, he was a gatherer of facts, cabinet after cabinet of facts, and it may be, as Spencer said of Buckle, that he "took in" more than he was able to organize.

On the question of Sumner's method, Charles Horton Cooley had the following observation:

> What strikes me most strongly when I consider this question is that *Folkways* does not conform to any of the current canons of methodology. It is not *quantitative;* it does not proceed by *statistical* method; it is not made up of *case*

---

20. At a faculty meeting considering the appointment of a professor of philosophy, Sumner denounced it as follows:

> Philosophy is in every way as bad as astrology. It is a complete fake. Yale has a great opportunity now to announce that she will take the lead and banish the study of philosophy from the curriculum on the ground that it is unworthy of serious consideration. It is an anachronism. We might just as well have professors of alchemy or fortune-telling or palmistry.

Quoted in William Lyon Phelps, Introduction, in William Graham Sumner, *Folkways* (New York: New American Library, Mentor edition, 1940), p. xiii.

> *studies;* it is not *psychoanalytic,* nor yet *behavioristic,* according to the doctrine of the sect that goes by that name, since much of the material it uses is based on sympathetic imagination. Moreover, it is not in any great measure a work of direct observation at all! It is almost all secondhand. And, last and worst, its objectivity is open to question.[21]

Cooley, of course, was paying Sumner a compliment. Precisely because his method did not merit the adjectives Cooley italicized, Cooley regarded *Folkways* as the most successful piece of sociological research produced in the United States. Whether methodologically sophisticated or not, Sumner always, as Davie remarks, went to the heart of a matter, gleefully exposing to public view the fragility of cherished notions and traditional ideas.

Finally, Sumner had little faith in systematic works on sociology. There is a reference to Gumplowicz's *Grundriss der Soziologie* in Sumner's essay on war, but for the most part he seems to have avoided intellectual contact with other pioneers in the discipline. He announced, in fact, that sociology was too new a science for extended theorizing and ambitious systematization. His faith in the potentialities of the science itself, however, never wavered. Although he discarded the word *sociology* for *the science of society,* he had great hopes for it, under whatever name.[22] Admitting that such a science was still in a tentative and inchoate state, he nevertheless insisted that social phenomena were subject to laws, laws as definite as the laws of physics. Sumner was honest enough to say that these laws had not yet been discovered but that discovery was only a matter of time. Ultimately the science of society would supply the answers to all social questions.

Sumner's Social Darwinism

For Sumner, society is any group that engages itself in a cooperative effort to earn subsistence and to perpetuate the race. It can be of any size. Thus, a family constitutes a society, as does a nation. An army, however, is not a society because it fails to satisfy the second of his two criteria. The

21. "Sumner and Methodology," in *Sociological Theory and Social Research* (New York: Holt, Rinehart, and Winston, 1930), p. 325. For similar observations, which include de Tocqueville's *Democracy in America* and Veblen's *The Theory of the Leisure Class* as well as Sumner's *Folkways,* see Robert Redfield, "The Art of Social Science," *American Journal of Sociology* 54 (November, 1948): 181–190.

22. He experimented for a while with *societology.* His students, of course, called it "Sumnerology."

division of labor found in the family is a normal division inasmuch as it is prescribed by biology. Human societies develop in a sequence of stages, from hunting to herding to agriculture—and in this respect Sumner is an orthodox Social Darwinist.[23]

He modifies the orthodoxy, however, in one respect. He adds to the struggle for existence another kind of struggle that he calls a competition of life. The first is the struggle of man with other species for survival in a natural universe, a struggle that is in essence a biological phenomenon. The competition of life, on the other hand, is the struggle of man with man for survival in a social universe, a struggle that is in essence a social phenomenon. The latter depends upon what Sumner calls the man–land ratio, which introduces a demographic factor into the social equation. Where men are few and land is plentiful there is no need for competition. Newcomers are assistants, not competitors; no one will work for another when he can be his own master; and no man will want to own more land than he can cultivate by his own labor. When men are many, on the other hand, and where land is scarce, the opposite situation obtains. Now the newcomers are competitors, and the struggle increases in intensity. There is only so much food to go around, and the relation of numbers to sustenance thus becomes the basic and primordial "footing" for social organization. Progress itself has no meaning except in terms of the law of population, and when the man–land ratio becomes unfavorable we meet the "iron spur" that accounts not only for social organization but for all the other achievements of the human race. Democracy itself depends upon the man–land ratio. When men are few and land abundant, it is easy for all men to be equal. When the competition of life intensifies, the stronger will inevitably move in front of the weaker.

The error of the socialists and the sentimentalists is that they blame society and its organization for stresses that should be attributed to the creator of the universe. The struggle for existence is inevitable. Society therefore is not to be blamed for those natural ills that flesh is heir to. Let us not burden those who have conquered these ills to do the same all over again for someone else. In a powerful and often quoted passage, Sumner declaims as follows:

> The law of the survival of the fittest was not made by man and cannot be abrogated by man. We can only, by interfering with it, produce the survival of the unfittest. If a man comes forward with any grievance against the order of society so far as this is shaped by human agency, he must have patient hearing and full redress; but if he addresses a demand to society for relief from the

23. It is of some interest to note that a portrait of Darwin hung in Sumner's study.

> hardships of life, he asks simply that somebody else should get his living for him. In that case he ought to be left to find out his error from hard experience.[24]

Seldom have the social consequences of Social Darwinism been so vividly exposed. It was a doctrine that obviously led, in Sumner as in Spencer, to an extreme kind of laissez-faire. All state interference is folly because it cannot succeed against the ineluctable laws of nature. Indeed, attempts to interfere, whether by government or by sentimental reformers, can only produce results that are worse than the diseases they are intended to cure.[25] Although Sumner defended the ruthless competition of the marketplace and approved of the concentration of wealth in private hands,[26] as simple expressions of the struggle for existence and the survival of the fittest, he also consistently incurred the hostility of the captains of industry by his opposition to the protective tariff, which he similarly considered to be an interference with the natural laws of society. Indeed, it was a matter of patriotism and of civic duty to resist the intrusion of the state at all levels.[27] Should the state interfere, however, in order to secure industrial peace? On the contrary, industrial peace is not even desirable. What is needed is industrial war because industrial war is a sign of vigor in a society. It ensures a just distribution between capital and labor and, in any event, it is not possible to stop it.[28]

Sumner was not only a defender but indeed a protagonist of the capitalist system of economic organization. Devoid, in public at least, of all humanitarian sentiment, he had no sense of the oppression to which the working class was subject, no sense of the exploitation that an entirely free enterprise entailed. He had no use for the proletariat, among whose ranks he discerned those who have nothing to lose, the discontented, the hotheaded, and the ill balanced.[29] He insisted that the class of unskilled and skilled laborers in the United States was better off with respect to diet, clothing, housing, furniture, fuel, the advantages its members could give to

---

24. "Sociology," in *War and Other Essays*, p. 177.

25. Sumner was fully aware of the unanticipated consequences of purposive social action: "It would be hard to find a single instance of a direct assault by positive effort upon poverty, vice, and misery which has not either failed or, if it has not failed directly and entirely, has not entailed other evils greater than the one which it removed." *Ibid.*, p. 186. Indeed, this is a recurring theme in his essays.

26. One of his essays is entitled "Justification of Wealth." *Independent* 54 (May 1902): 1036–1040.

27. "State Interference," in *War and Other Essays*, pp. 213–226, especially p. 225.

28. "Do We Want Industrial Peace?" *ibid.*, pp. 229–243.

29. "What is the Proletariat?" in *The Challenge of Facts and Other Essays*, ed. Albert Galloway Keller (New Haven, Conn.: Yale University Press, 1914), pp. 161–165.

their children, and their chances of accumulating capital than any previous working class in history.[30]

If Sumner had no use for the proletariat, he had great concern indeed for the "Forgotten Man." The Forgotten Man is the man who is prudent, thrifty, and industrious, the man who attends to his own affairs, the man who bears his burdens without complaint, the man who exemplifies the virtues of the Puritan ethic. Unfortunately, there are always others who want to mind his business for him, who decide that after he has solved his own problems of existence he must come to the support of others less prudent. It is A and B who dream up schemes that determine what C must do for the benefit of D and it is C, of course, who is the Forgotten Man. As for public welfare, the state cannot give a cent to one man without taking it from another, the man who has produced and saved it, and again it is the latter who is the Forgotten Man. If poverty is of no concern of the state, neither is vice:

> Almost all legislative effort to prevent vice is really protective of vice, because all such legislation saves the vicious man from the penalty of his vice. Nature's remedies against vice are terrible. She removes the victims without pity. A drunkard in the gutter is just where he ought to be, according to the fitness and tendency of things. Nature has set up in him the process of decline and dissolution by which she removes things which have survived their usefulness.[31]

Furthermore, all sumptuary legislation is a fallacy. A and B, for example, are teetotalers. They decide that C, who drinks in moderation, must be deprived of his pleasure because of D, who drinks too much. Once again, C is the Forgotten Man. Tramps, outcasts, criminals, the poor, the weak, the ignorant, the illiterate—all of these attract Sumner's contumely. Sumner—proud, confident, haughty, and successful—had nothing but disdain for the losers in the battle of life. From sentiments like these one easily infers that Sumner lacked the gift of *caritas.* Two things, perhaps, may be said in partial exoneration. The first is that, as we are assured by both Starr and Davie, Sumner was generous in his private charities. Indeed, he wrote a defense of private, in contrast to public, charity. The second is that these sentiments are entirely consistent with the Social Darwinism of which he was so redoubtable a champion. As Herbert Spencer also wrote, "The ultimate result of shielding men from the effects of folly is to fill the world with fools."[32]

30. "The Absurd Effort to Make the World Over," in *War and Other Essays,* pp. 195–210.
31. "On the Case of a Certain Man Who Is Never Thought of," *ibid.,* pp. 247–253.
32. *An Autobiography,* 2 vols. (London: Watts, 1904), vol. 2, p. 5.

In the entire corpus of Sumner's writings there is, so far as the writer has discovered, not a single reference to Karl Marx. Sumner appears throughout his essays as a staunch champion of free enterprise, intolerant of its critics, and contemptuous of socialism in all its varieties and degrees. And yet, paradoxically, he expresses opinions that are quite in harmony with Marxist doctrine and, still more paradoxically, he does so in an essay entitled "The Absurd Effort to Make the World Over." Consider the following two effusions, both from the essay in question: "Indeed, in any true philosophy, it must be held that in the economic forces which control the material prosperity of a population lie the real causes of its political institutions, its social-class adjustments, its industrial prosperity, its moral code, and its world-philosophy."[33] And again: "Now the next conflict which must inevitably come is that between the middle capitalist class and the proletariat."[34] Finally, in close relation both to Marx on alienation and Weber on bureaucracy:

> The movement of industry has been all the time toward promptitude, punctuality, and reliability. It has been attended all the way by lamentations about the good old times; about the decline of small industries; about the lost spirit of comradeship between employer and employee; about the narrowing of the interests of the workman; about his conversion into a machine or into a 'ware;' and about industrial war. These lamentations have all had reference to unquestionable phenomena attendant on advancing organization. In all occupations the same movement is discernible—in the learned professions, in schools, in trade, commerce, and transportation.[35]

Sumner's social philosophy is now entirely clear. It is a Social Darwinism in so extreme a sense as to make the label pejorative—and to do harm to Darwin, who had no responsibility for it. Spontaneous forces are at work in society, forces only slightly amenable to human alteration and design. Indeed, human interference is mostly folly because of the evil and unanticipated consequences that result. Evolution is a natural process and therefore an ineluctable one, and only fools, idiots, schemers, and dreamers would try to bend it to their own desires. Laissez-faire once meant, to a group of French businessmen in conference with a newly elected mayor, a plea to the municipal government to let business alone. In Sumner, as before in Spencer, it means for everyone, and especially the legislators, to let nature alone. And, since society is a part of nature, it

33. In *War and Other Essays*, p. 205.

34. *Ibid.*, p. 204. The conflict preceding the next one to which Sumner refers was that in which feudalism was overthrown. Note also the use of the word *inevitably*.

35. *Ibid.*, p. 198.

means as well to let society alone. Society has its own laws—inexorable and inevitable—which will defeat any effort to tamper with them.

Folkways

Sumner's bibliography, including both books and articles, runs to around 300 items. It is seldom mentioned that not all of his writings are devoted to sociology, the science he did so much to create. Indeed, he wrote also on economics, politics, and public affairs. He was a historian as well.[36] It is his sociological work, however, that has given him an enduring reputation and, above all, it is *Folkways* that has assumed the stature of a classic in the literature of sociology.

In his courses at Yale on the origins of social institutions, Sumner expressed the view that institutions could all be traced back to usages and customs. To usages and customs, therefore, he intended to devote the first chapter of a comprehensive text on sociology, a book he began to write in 1899. He had more to say, however, than he could include within a single chapter, and the result was a book of almost 600 pages, published in 1906 and later reissued in several editions. *Folkways* is almost entirely concrete and descriptive rather than abstract and theoretical. As a system builder Sumner could not compete with his contemporaries on both sides of the Atlantic. Indeed, he had no desire to do so. *Folkways* is deficient in organization and, although the style is lucid and straightforward, it induces a kind of tedium when its chapters are read seriatim.[37] Sumner's genius

36. Books devoted to subjects other than sociology include *A History of American Currency* (1874), *Andrew Jackson as a Public Man* (1882), *Alexander Hamilton* (1890), *The Financier and the Finances of the American Revolution* (2 vols., 1891), and *A History of Banking in the United States* (1896).

37. Albert Galloway Keller, Sumner's able colleague and loyal disciple, describes it as follows:

> *Folkways*, except for the first chapters, reveals the writer as aged and weary. Though significant for general enlightenment far beyond anything else he did, it succeeds by reason of its deep insight and massive evidence, rather than because of its style, form, or arrangement. Compared with the essays that ran like hot, impetuous metal from the crucible, *Folkways* is hard, unexciting reading; and his manuscript fragments on *The Science of Society* were not dissimilar.

Reminiscences, p. 77. *The Science of Society*, to which Keller refers, was published in four volumes, by Yale University Press, New Haven, Conn., 1927–1928. The first three carry the names of Sumner and Keller on the title page; the fourth, a "Case-Book" of 1331 pages, carries in addition the name of Maurice R. Davie, then associate professor of the science of society at Yale, and later chairman of the department. The facts amassed in these volumes were collected by Sumner but the formulations are almost entirely Keller's. The book has no independent theoretical significance.

expressed itself not in system building, and decidedly not in the methodological foundations of sociological theory, but rather in his sharp insights into the nature of society and in his ability to label these insights with words that have since become an integral part of the language of sociology.

"Men begin with acts, not with thoughts," says Sumner at the outset. They have needs to satisfy, but few instincts to help them do it. Their efforts, therefore, are of a trial and error variety, often clumsy and uncertain, but finally, under the guidance of pain and pleasure, ways are found and followed.[38] These ways are the folkways, and this is the manner in which they arise. Children learn them by tradition, imitation, and authority.[39] They become fixed in a society; they are uniform, imperative, and almost invariable. With the passage of time they become a societal force. This is a social process and requires no psychological faculty except the ability to distinguish between pleasure and pain.

No one plans the folkways. No one notices them until they become fixed by repetition. They are not purposeful creations or the result of rational reflection. In the course of time they become coercive and universal in a group or a society. It is thus that folkways come to control the daily lives of human beings. They are so deeply embedded that only the topmost layer is susceptible to modification by philosophy, ethics, and religion. They exhibit two qualities, the first of which is a strain toward improvement, and the second, a strain toward consistency. The former is self-explanatory; the latter reduces friction and contributes to cultural integration. Oriental and Occidental cultures, for example, are consistent within themselves and yet different from each other. If the origins of the folkways are lost in mystery, there is in their development something Sumner calls "the aleatory element"[40]—the element of chance that affects the fortunes of men in ways impossible to predict. And so it is with the folkways. The most rational attempt to satisfy a need may fail, the most irrational succeed. There are goblins in the lives of primitive peoples and gremlins (their first cousins) in the lives of the civilized. The folkways are the product of chance and cir-

38. One is reminded of Jeremy Bentham's famous statement: "Nature has placed mankind under the governance of two sovereign masters, pain and pleasure."

39. On imitation, see Gabriel Tarde, who also lacks a reference in *Folkways.*

40. From *alea,* 'luck' or 'chance'. Caesar, considering what to do, heard a stranger playing upon a pipe and decided to cross the Rubicon with the cry *"Alea jacta est!"* ('The die is cast!'). Suppose the stranger had not been there. See Mark Twain's delightful description of this episode in his essay "The Turning Point in My Life" in *What Is Man? And Other Essays* (New York: Harper Brothers, 1935). The "turning point," of course, the event that caused him to become a writer, was Caesar's crossing of the Rubicon.

cumstance. They are almost wholly nonrational. Error, accident, and luck are the factors that create the structures of human societies.[41]

The Mores

Sumner's coinage of the word *folkways* was a stroke of genius.[42] He introduced in addition, however, the concept of the mores. This word is Latin for *customs* and is plural. The singular, *mos*, is not used in sociology.[43] Sumner makes a number of attempts to define the mores. In the Preface to *Folkways* he says that it is the best word he could find for his purpose: "I mean by it the popular usages and traditions, when they include a judgment that they are conducive to societal welfare, and then they exert a coercion on the individual to conform to them, although they are not coordinated by any authority." In another section (34) he again says that when elements of truth and right develop into doctrines of welfare, the folkways are raised to another plane; then we call them mores. In Section 43 he writes that mores are folkways that have connotations of right and truth in respect to welfare. Finally, in Section 66, he offers his "more complete" definition: "They are the ways of doing things which are current in a society to satisfy human needs and desires, together with the faiths, notions, codes, and standards of well living which inhere in those ways, having a genetic connection with them." Like the folkways, the mores develop without conscious reflection and without conscious planning.

---

41. Late in his career W. I. Thomas became enamored with the role of chance in individual lives. He once told the writer that his decision to resign from Oberlin College, where he was teaching English, and go to the University of Chicago was stimulated by an unexpected rent increase imposed upon him by his landlady. Suppose she had not done so. The girl one meets at a party and later marries—suppose she had not been there. The book one serendipitously finds in the library stacks that determines one's choice of a career—suppose it had not been there. For that matter, there is Pascal's suggestion that if Cleopatra's nose had been an inch longer than it was, all subsequent history would have been different. Nothing could be more delightful—or more idle—than speculations such as these. It may be, however, that the aleatory element will defeat the efforts of the philosophers of history to penetrate the arcanum in which Clio keeps her secrets. Every event is a determinate consequent of preceding events in a linear causal chain. But there is an infinite number of causal chains, and the points at which they happen to intersect may be indeterminate. The intersections may be aleatory rather than causal and thus alter the linearity.

42. In Webster's Unabridged Dictionary the sole attribution is to Sumner. Webster's New International Dictionary of the English Language, 2nd ed., unabridged (Springfield, Mass.: G. & C. Merriam Company, Publishers, 1961), p. 980.

43. There is an instance of it, however, in Sumner and Keller, *Science of Society*, vol. 1, sec. 20.

The distinction between folkways and mores is blurred in the following passage, from Section 68 of *Folkways*. It is important nevertheless because it emphasizes the importance of the mores in the life of the individual:

> The mores are social ritual in which we all participate unconsciously. The current habits as to hours of labor, meal hours, family life, the social intercourse of the sexes, propriety, amusements, travel, holidays, education, the use of periodicals and libraries, and innumerable other details of life fall under this ritual. Each does as everybody does. For the great mass of mankind as to all things, and for all of us for a great many things, the rule to do as all do suffices. We are led by suggestion and association to believe that there must be wisdom and utility in what all do. The great mass of the folkways give us discipline and the support of routine and habit. If we had to form judgments as to all these cases before we could act in them, and were forced always to act rationally, the burden would be unendurable. Beneficent use and wont save us this trouble.

In this passage, as can be seen, Sumner begins by discussing the mores and ends by treating the folkways, as if the two were synonymous, thus sacrificing the distinction he has drawn between them. He also relates the mores to some of the minor concerns of life, such as amusements and meal hours, that have little to do with societal welfare or with right and wrong. The function of the folkways, however, is clear. They are guides to conduct; they relieve the individual of what would otherwise be an intolerable burden of decision. Without them, one would have to decide what to do in every situation. Most of the things we do, we do without reflection and without conscious attention, and it is important that we have the social capacity to do so. It is the folkways and the mores that provide this capacity. The philosopher Alfred North Whitehead might have had Sumner's folkways in mind—but probably did not—when he observed that the advice to think about what we are doing is nonsense when applied to the ordinary affairs of life. The more things we can do without thinking, the better off we are.[44] This insight is Sumner's most important lesson and a major contribution to sociology.

There is much more to say about folkways and mores. Instead of following Sumner's book in detail, I shall treat selectively most of his "fundamen-

---

44. The jingle attributed to Mrs. Edward Craster (1871) is also relevant:

The centipede was happy quite
Until a toad in fun
Said, "Pray, which leg goes after which?"
That worked her mind to such a pitch,
She lay distracted in a ditch,
Considering how to run.

tal notions" and then exhibit his observations on various social phenomena.

Supplementary Concepts

TABOOS

On the negative side, the mores can be viewed as taboos. Taboos also contain judgments as to social welfare and indeed arise to protect a society against any number of threats to its continued existence. The mores, in fact, consist in large part of taboos of both mystical and utilitarian origin, in the former case prohibiting actions that would displease the ghosts,[45] and in the latter protecting against the ordinary perils of life—pain, loss, disease, and death. Actions are inhibited by taboo because they are regarded as injurious to the group. In this category Sumner places the mores regulating the sexes, property, war, and, again, ghosts and suggests that they all have something to do with philosophy. Philosophy itself, by which Sumner means a generalized view of the world, has its source in the folkways:

> World philosophy, life policy, right, rights, and morality are all products of the folkways. They are reflections on, and generalizations from, the experience of pleasure and pain which is won in efforts to carry on the struggle for existence under actual life conditions. The generalizations are very crude and vague in their germinal forms. They are all embodied in folklore, and all our philosophy and science have been developed out of them.[46]

Taboos are of two types—protective and destructive. Sumner recognizes that taboos, like folkways and mores, can sometimes be harmful, despite that they arise to satisfy needs. The destruction of a person's property at death, for example, is no boon to the survivors.[47] Men starve in the midst of plenty because there is a taboo on eating certain animals, especially the totem animal. Similarly harmful are taboos that prevent the killing of

45. Like Spencer, Sumner was impressed by the role of ghosts, and of ghost-fear, among primitive peoples.

46. *Folkways*, sec. 31. For a similar but more profound treatment of the origin of science, see Durkheim, *The Elementary Forms of the Religious Life*, trans. J. W. Swain (New York, Macmillan, 1915).

47. "With this custom we must class all the expenditure of labor and capital on graves, temples, pyramids, rites, sacrifices, and support of priests, so far as these were supposed to benefit the dead." *Folkways*, sec. 29.

crocodiles, cobras, pythons, and other dangerous creatures. Sumner thought that the culture of India was especially rich in harmful mores.

NEEDS

When Sumner tried to explain the kinds of needs that were to be satisfied by the growth of folkways and mores, he put forth the notion of four basic needs—hunger, love (or "sex passion"), vanity, and fear. The problem of needs, of course, has attracted the attention of a host of sociologists, both before and after Sumner, and it is one that is by no means solved. Whether the basic springs of human action are called motives, drives, instincts, prepotent reflexes, interests, needs, or wishes, the problem is compounded by the necessity to classify them, an exercise that usually exposes their defects. It is difficult, for example, to maintain a consistent *fundamentum divisionis*, to treat them on a single level of abstraction, and to keep them in the same universe of discourse. Sumner's hunger, sex, and fear are physiological phenomena, but it is doubtful if there is a physiological need to be vain. In any event, he gives the subject only a one-paragraph treatment.[48]

CONVENTIONALIZATION

Sumner is not entirely clear about what he means by this concept, and indeed it did not become a part of the sociological vocabulary. Conventionalization seems to mean the continued use, under specified conditions, of folkways that would otherwise be tabooed. Thus, words in the Bible or in Shakespeare that would offend current sensibilities are nevertheless relieved of sanctions because of their source. The taboo becomes inoperative.

---

48. The list of sociologists who have tried to classify interests would include the names of Ratzenhofer, Small, and MacIver. This volume is not the place to tell the story of the rise and fall of instinct theory. It will suffice to say that it foundered on its own excesses. It began to explain too much—that is, for every item of behavior that required explanation it was easy, too easy, to posit an instinct, and in no time at all the number of instincts became large and unmanageable—thus illustrating the methodological principle that a theory that explains too much is as useless as one that explains too little. Sociologists came to realize that the word *instinct*, to borrow an expression, was one of the fig leaves used to conceal the nudity of our ignorance. In the literature of the 1920s the four "wishes" of W. I. Thomas came to be prominent. These wishes were for response, recognition, security, and new experience. Curiously enough, in view of Thomas's early appreciation of the importance of the sexual factor, sex is missing from his list, and none of his wishes has a physiological correlate, base, or locus. On the subject of instinct in general, see L. L. Bernard, *Instinct: A Study in Social Psychology* (New York: Henry Holt & Co., 1924); for a more recent and resourceful effort to resurrect the concept, see Ronald Fletcher, *Instinct in Man* (London: Allen & Unwin, 1957).

The folkways, although unconscious in origin, may sometimes become the subject of rational and critical examination and, if this is so, they can be judged to be gross, absurd, or inexpedient. They need not, however, be rejected or replaced on these grounds. They may, in fact, be treated as permissible fictions, just as in the world of fable animals are permitted to speak. The drama is full of instances. Similarly, the illustrations in a textbook of anatomy, if reproduced in other places, would offend the mores of propriety, but they are tolerated there. Sumner sees these examples as inconsistencies in the mores but he regards them as quite important. Bathing suits and theatrical costumes are protected by conventionalization. By conventionalization "there may be nakedness without indecency, and tales of adultery without lewdness."[49]

Sumner is not clear on this point, and his illustrations are not helpful. The conventions of the theater, for example, are also part of the folkways and mores, and if they are permissive it is because the mores are differentially applied and not because a taboo receives a special kind of suspension. This phenomenon, however, is important for another reason. In all societies the norms are often felt to be oppressive, and all societies therefore institutionalize occasions when violation produces neither censure nor other negative sanction. Sumner mentions the ancient Saturnalia and the modern carnival—times of license in which the ordinary taboos are relaxed. He also mentions the Fourth of July, a day on which we endure noise, risk, and annoyance that we would not tolerate at other times. This is a useful insight. Relaxation of the norms on certain occasions, however, implies no departure from them but is a process that is itself institutionalized in the societies in which it occurs.[50]

SYNCRETISM

Syncretism is the process by which the divergent mores of subgroups become reconciled and the entire group becomes homogeneous. Groups with different folkways frequently come into contact with one another, through intermarriage, social intercourse, conquest, immigration, or slavery. In these cases one of the dominant subgroups sets the standards, and the inferior groups begin to imitate them and finally to absorb them. After a time the folkways and mores of the other subgroups become obsolete and ultimately disappear. Christian mores, for example, were

49. *Folkways,* sec. 74. See also sec. 599.

50. Individual rebellion against the norms is a different process. Thus, George F. Babbitt, in Sinclair Lewis's novel *Babbitt,* wakes up one morning, goes to the bathroom, and intentionally wipes his hands on the guest towel!

formed by syncretism of Jewish and pagan mores, and such practices as slavery, concubinage, demonism, and "base amusements" succumbed to the strain toward consistency. In a similar way such "inferior mores" as polygamy, infanticide, and idolatry disappeared from Western Christian mores and became obsolete.

THE STRAIN TOWARD CONSISTENCY

Closely related to syncretism is another phenomenon that Sumner calls a strain toward consistency in the folkways. Societies find it difficult to support contrary folkways, and thus there is less friction and antagonism when the folkways are consistent and mutually supportive. This is a process that occurs in societies simultaneously with a strain toward improvement.

ANTAGONISTIC COOPERATION

Although the struggle for existence and the competition of life can be fierce and although they set man against man and group against group, it is nevertheless the case that they often find that it is to their common interest to combine their efforts and cooperate with one another. This combination, when otherwise prevailing antagonisms are set aside, Sumner calls antagonistic cooperation. It is a most productive form of combination in a "high civilization," and it is especially visible in the political process. In political parties, for example, the differences among the members are suppressed during an election campaign when "all good men come to the aid of the party."

IN-GROUP AND OUT-GROUP

One of the most important of the concepts that Sumner introduced is the concept of the in-group or, more generally, the in-group–out-group distinction. The in-group is the we-group—ourselves—the out-group is everyone else. Members of the in-group have sentiments for one another that permit them to enjoy peace, comradeship, order, law, government, and industry. The relation of an in-group to an out-group, on the contrary, is one of suspicion and hostility, often of war and plunder, "except so far as agreements have modified it." War with an out-group reduces the discords within the in-group. War outside, peace inside—these are facets of the same phenomenon, the in-group–out-group relation.

ETHNOCENTRISM

A corollary of the in-group–out-group distinction is ethnocentrism, again one of Sumner's most creative concepts. This is the tendency, all too human, to regard one's own group as the center and focus of all concern. It is the tendency to measure all mores by the rules of one's own. It is the tendency to regard the name of one's own tribe or nation as a synonym for mankind, to devise derisory epithets for barbarians beyond the pale, to regard one's own nation as the summit of civilization. In modern states it assumes the form of patriotism, which has become a civic duty and is regarded as a noble and necessary sentiment. The masses, Sumner thinks, are always patriotic and are eager to exhibit jealousy, vanity, truculence, and superiority to all foreigners. Patriotism, when excessive, degenerates into chauvinism. Sumner is suspicious of both. The notion that "we" are good and "they" are bad is never true. Indeed, "The patriotic bias is a recognized perversion of thought and judgment against which our education should guard us."[51] Sumner concedes, however, that ethnocentrism is a force that strengthens the folkways.

INSTITUTIONS AND LAWS

An institution, for Sumner, consists of a concept and a structure; by concept he means an idea, notion, doctrine, or interest. Institutions, like laws, grow out of the folkways and mores. One gathers that they are more definite and specific than folkways and mores. They are an apparatus. Institutions may be either crescive or enacted. Property, marriage, and religion—the primary institutions—have grown slowly out of the mores and thus are examples of the former. The banking system and the electoral college in the United States, on the other hand, are the result of rational reflection and thus are examples of the latter. Laws also grow out of the mores, but they, like enacted institutions, are the products of reflection and criticism. They are, quite simply, the enactments of legislatures. If they are to be strong, they must be consistent with the mores. Although institutions and laws grow out of the mores, they nevertheless differ from the mores in that the elements of faith and sentiment that characterize the latter are absent in the former, which are more rational, practical, mechanical, and utilitarian. Actions under the laws and institutions are conscious and voluntary, under the folkways and mores, unconscious and involuntary.[52]

51. *Folkways*, sec. 20.
52. *Ibid.*, secs. 61–64.

THE MORES CAN MAKE ANYTHING RIGHT

"The mores can make anything right and prevent condemnation of anything"—such is the ringing title of one of Sumner's chapters. It is a proposition upon which he insists, which he dogmatically defends, and to which he returns again and again. When it comes to the folkways and the mores, whatever is, is right. The folkways and the mores are always right because what is right is defined by them. There is no external or objective standard by which they can be judged. "When we come to the folkways we are at the end of our analysis."[53]

The morality of a group at a given time is, simply, the sum of its prescriptions and taboos. Thus, it is idle to condemn usages that seem offensive—infanticide, slavery, and witchcraft, for example—because they were "right" in their time and place. Of course, the folkways and mores change over the course of time, but only slowly, and only in response to changing life conditions. We do not study the mores of other societies and other times in order to approve them or condemn them, but only to understand them. There are "good" mores and "bad" mores, but only in the sense that they are well adapted or ill adapted to the circumstances in which they obtain. Sumner is dedicated to the principle of cultural relativity.

Miscellaneous Observations

Sumner treats his concepts (or "fundamental notions") and the topics that attract his attention in no logical, or even recognizable, order; his discussion therefore lacks all organization and continuity. In this section I helplessly succumb to Sumner's careless practices and briefly recount some of the more interesting of his miscellaneous observations.

MORES AND LAWS

The relationship between the mores and the laws, of course, is an ancient question and is far from resolved in sociological theory. It is part of the conventional wisdom of the discipline that the answer to the question posed by Tacitus— "*Quid leges sine moribus*?"—is "Nothing," that not even the awesome authority of the state can enforce a law that lacks the support of the mores. Indeed, Aristotle observed earlier than Tacitus that "a law derives all of its strength from custom."[54] The history of sumptuary

53. *Ibid.*, sec. 31.

54. *Politics*, 1269a. Durkheim also had something to say on this subject: "Law expresses customs, and if it acts against them, it is with a force that it has borrowed from them." *The Division of Labor in Society*, trans. George Simpson (Glencoe, Ill.: Free Press, 1933), p. 146.

legislation supplies many examples. On the other hand, such legislation appears to have been effective in certain places and under certain conditions, for example, in theocracies such as John Calvin's Geneva, John Knox's Edinburgh, and Cotton Mather's Massachusetts.[55] What does Sumner contribute to this intriguing question? His views, although unsystematic, are clear. He approaches the subject briefly when he discusses the differences between mores and laws, remarking that the latter are strong when they are consistent with the mores, and in brief allusions in other passages. In discussing the relationships between blacks and whites in Southern society, Sumner, who did not believe that blacks should be given the vote and thought that they could be quite happy as slaves if they were not separated from their families, contends that before the Civil War blacks and whites had learned how to get along with one another and had lived in peace and concord, going their traditional and customary ways. After the war the two races had to learn new ways, ways not established. Indeed, times of social confusion and discord are not conducive to the establishment of new mores. In any event, efforts to fix the new order by legislation are entirely vain because laws cannot make the mores.[56] This view is wholly in accord with Sumner's Social Darwinism. Laws are forms of tampering with natural processes, almost, one might say, with the laws of the universe, and it is folly therefore to expect them to do more than fix and seal the processes already set in motion by the folkways and mores.[57]

SOCIAL CHANGE

Sumner recognizes that the mores contribute inertia and rigidity to the social order and are thus conservative factors in the life of a society. They are brakes on the processes of social change but they are nevertheless

55. See J. M. Vincent, "Sumptuary Legislation," in Edwin-R. A. Seligman, ed., *Encyclopedia of the Social Sciences*, 15 vols. (New York: Macmillan), vol. 14, pp. 464-466, where he observes, "The eighteenth century with its doctrines of individual liberty and its leanings toward economic freedom finally sealed the doom of sumptuary law." On a related issue—not whether the law can but whether the law should be used to legislate morality—see H.L.A. Hart, *The Concept of Law* (London and New York: Oxford University Press, 1961), and *Punishment and Responsibility: Essays in the Philosophy of Law* (London and New York: Oxford University Press, 1969); and Sir Patrick Devlin, *The Enforcement of Morals* (London and New York: Oxford University Press, 1965). Devlin takes the view that the law is indeed an appropriate instrument for the enforcement of morals, whereas Hart maintains, on the contrary, that it is important to distinguish between crime and sin, that is, between acts that harm individuals and those that only offend them, and that the latter are no business of the law.

56. *Folkways*, sec. 81.

57. Meanwhile, the organic analogy slips into Sumner's discussion. He observes that the mores, unrecorded and unknown to conscious reflection, "grow up, gain strength, become corrupt, decline, and die, as if they were organisms." *Ibid.*, sec. 82.

susceptible to change. One kind of change is generational; children do not carry on the mores exactly in the way they have received them from their parents. They change also because conditions change. The mores suitable for a tribal village or small community may not be well adapted to a large city. Sometimes it is possible to change them by artifice or device, not suddenly and not to any great degree but by minute variations over the course of time. Changes that are consistent with current mores, of course, can be brought about more easily than changes that run counter to them. So far as conscious social change is involved, however, any politician or philosopher who imagines that he will be able to manipulate changes in social institutions is operating on the basis of a fallacy as radical as it is mischievous. For that matter, not even scientists can free themselves from the presuppositions contained in the mores of their society: "It is vain to imagine that 'a scientific man' can divest himself of prejudice or previous opinion, and put himself in an attitude of neutral independence towards the mores. He might as well try to get out of gravity or the pressure of the atmosphere."[58]

Sumner does not seem to notice that his own political and social doctrines are also products of the mores. In discussing the "capricious interest of the masses," for example, he suggests that whether the masses will regard certain things as reasonable and sensible or ridiculous and fantastic depends upon the convictions and feelings that are dominant in the mores. That his own strong views in opposition to the protective tariff, the abuses of the civil service system, and public welfare might have a similar determination does not occur to him. Nor, when speaking of the masses—not always, it must be said, without contempt—does he remember that the mores can make anything right.

In relation to social change again, Sumner raises the question of the degree to which "societal administration" can influence and change the mores. The answer, consistent with his general position, is not very much. The mores are social, not political, phenomena; they belong to society, not to the state. If social administration or legislation tries to alter them, the attempt will almost certainly fail. Publicists, statesmen, and reformers succeed only when they understand new forces that are working in the mores themselves and are able to grasp and utilize them.[59] Crises occur in society when new forces meet the resistance of the old. He writes:

> It behooves us by education and will, with intelligent purpose, to criticise and judge even the most established ways of our time, and to put courage and labor into resistance to the current mores when we judge them wrong. It would

58. *Ibid.*, sec. 102.
59. *Ibid.*, sec. 121.

> be a mighty achievement of the science of society if it could lead up to an art of societal administration which should [*sic*] be intelligent, effective, and scientific.[60]

It is not legislation, therefore, but sociological knowledge that will ultimately change the mores.[61]

LANGUAGE

One of the best illustrations of changes in the folkways and mores is the growth and development of languages. Both arise and change without conscious invention; in both there is an absence of reflection and intention. No one, with artificial exceptions, deliberately plans to invent or improve a language. The norms of grammar, like other folkways, are rules to which people more or less conform. Nevertheless, language changes over the course of time, as do other folkways. Sometimes, indeed often, slang expressions enter and are retained. Words become obsolete and disappear. Different groups have different ways of speaking, and thus dialects and, finally, different languages arise. Furthermore, different ways of thinking are embedded in different languages. They represent stages in the evolution of thought. It is in these linguistic processes that we can see clearly the ways in which folkways and mores change.[62]

MONEY

The growth of the use of money and of monetary exchange provides another illustration of the folkways and mores. Sumner, who as a political economist had written on currency problems and on the institution of banking, indulges in *Folkways* in a long disquisition on money, on intragroup and intergroup exchange, on different forms of money (including such materials as salt, metal, skins, cotton, glass, tobacco, coffee beans, shells, and beads), on the relation of property and trade to the medium of exchange, on token money, on the plutocratic effects of money, on the evolution of money, and on many other monetary phenomena. Again, like

60. *Ibid.*

61. Sumner does not reveal, unfortunately, how this knowledge will be applied or who will apply it. Furthermore, if not even a scientific man can escape the mores of his time, as Sumner claims, and if the mores can make anything right, it is difficult to see how we can judge the current mores to be wrong.

62. *Ibid.*, secs. 137–141.

the folkways and mores, money does its work impersonally and mechanically, but no ethical function can be ascribed to it.[63]

LABOR AND WEALTH

On these subjects Sumner observes that in all stages of society a general philosophy of labor emerges and that this philosophy too is a part of the mores. He writes that most religions approve of productive labor and disapprove of idleness, except that some surcease from toil is often recommended. Also, most labor, required as it is in the struggle for existence, is irksome and painful. It is absurd, however, to glorify labor on the one hand and to decry wealth on the other, because the latter is the result of the former. It is one more sign of the survival of the fittest.[64]

FADS AND FASHIONS

Inasmuch as fads and fashions are also folkways, it can come as no surprise that Sumner gives them a full treatment. On this subject he is again conscious of the principle of cultural relativity. The Japanese, unbothered by nudity and even given to mixed bathing facilities, wear clothing that conceals the lines of the figure. The Americans, who have a taboo on nudity, wear clothing that exposes the figure. Sumner is also aware that ideals of feminine beauty are carried in the folkways and are as relative as fashions in dress. He knows that fashion governs almost every sphere of human activity. Indeed, it rules tools, utensils, weapons, boats, architecture, painting, poetry, fiction, education, dancing, eating, drinking, deportment, language, faith, ideals, and many more. On this subject he quotes Erasmus, "Nothing is so ridiculous that usage may not make it pass."[65] That some folkways are harmful can be seen in that fashion sometimes requires the deformation of the body. Finally, he recognizes that fashion is not a trivial phenomenon; indeed, it marks the dominion of the group over the individual.[66]

---

63. *Ibid.*, secs. There is no reference to Simmel's *Philosophie des Geldes,* which was published in 1900.

64. See *Folkways,* chap. 4. Sumner's views on these subjects represent a complete fusion of Social Darwinism and the Protestant ethic.

65. *Ibid.*, sec. 190.

66. One is reminded in this connection of Gabriel Tarde's observation that in conforming to custom we are imitating our ancestors and in conforming to fashion we are imitating our contemporaries. Although there are useful insights such as this, sociology still lacks an acceptable theory of fashion and its fluctuations.

IDEALS AND SLOGANS

Sumner exhibits his iconoclasm again in his treatment of ideals and slogans. He regards ideals as entirely unscientific and as unworthy of serious discussion. Indeed, he suggests that they are escapes from the necessity of dealing with hard, intractable facts. "Who does the thinking?" Sumner asks. The notion that the group thinks and sets its ideals is not only fallacious but also one of the "great freaks of philosophy." The thinking for any society is done only by its elites. On the other hand, where manias, delusions, fads, fashions, and affectations are involved, it is the crowd that always dominates the individual.[67] For slogans, epithets, "watchwords," and "catchwords," Sumner similarly has little use. Among them are such expressions as Americanism, patriotism, humanity, citizenship, slavery, "peace with honor," and "all men are created equal." Democracy itself he regards as "the pet superstition of the age." That slogans like these are powerful influences in society, however, Sumner fully appreciates. The slogan "Fifty-four forty or fight" nearly provoked a war in 1844, partly because of its alliteration. "Forty-nine thirty or fight" would have been much less effective.[68]

SLAVERY

Sumner, no humanitarian, has some favorable things to say about slavery. On the premise that no one would do any hard work if he could possibly avoid it, slavery proved to be the schoolmaster that taught the race to do it. Those who were defeated learned to submit, and it was their work that helped the whole of society to a higher status, a process that also profited the slaves.[69] Slavery exhibits the tendency of stronger groups to exploit weaker ones in the struggle for existence; it is one way in which the survival of the fittest is brought about. Slavery differs from other folkways in an important respect. Most folkways arise unconsciously in random efforts to satisfy needs. Slavery, on the contrary, owes its origin to ill feeling for the members of an out-group, the desire to get something for nothing, the love of dominion over others (which is a species of vanity), and as mentioned above the hatred of hard labor.[70]

Sumner devotes an entire chapter to the institution of slavery. It is an extended catalogue of practices in North and South America, Polynesia and Melanesia, the East Indies, Asia, Japan, Greece and Rome, the late Roman

67. *Ibid.*, secs. 203–208.
68. *Ibid.*, secs. 171–177.
69. *Ibid.*, sec. 271.
70. *Ibid.*, sec. 270.

Empire, the Germanic nations, Italy, France, and England, and in Christianity and Islam. As we wander through this mass of material, as through the corridors of a vast museum, we appreciate again the depth and strength of Sumner's Social Darwinism. Is it right, he asks, to permit an inferior civilization to imperil a superior one? Whatever the answer—and his is clearly implied although not expressly stated—we cannot surrender to the sentiments of humanitarians. He concedes, however, that despite the "good work" that slavery has done, it is not an institution that need endure forever.

ON THE SEXES

Reading Sumner on the sexes is a fascinating exercise. He regards the sex mores as the most important of all. As in the case of other mores, when institutions and laws come to be concerned with the subject they only ratify what has long been ordained. Sexual equality is an impossibility. Because of the division of reproductive labor, so to speak, the sexes can be independent and complementary, but not equal. Women bear an unequal burden with respect to the duties of reproduction; men, with respect to the duties of property, war, and politics. Men are polygamous by instinct and powerful in ways that women cannot be. Women are superior in adaptability and tact, inferior in muscular strength. They have quicker perceptions and a lack of egoism. Men are more combative and courageous, with nervous systems more stable. Physical and mental variation are greater in the male than in the female; there are more giants and dwarfs among them, more idiots and geniuses. The interests of the sexes, except in reproduction, are antagonistic. A continuing relationship between man and woman cannot be explained by the sexual need. It is only the need to care for offspring that can explain the relationship. As has been said, sex can explain mating but not marriage, and it is clear that Sumner agrees. All regulations concerning endogamy and exogamy, polygyny and polyandry, matriarchy and patriarchy, and capture and purchase are products of the mores.

One may suppose that Sumner has something original to say on this subject as he does on so many others. The supposition is fulfilled. Monogamy, or "pair marriage" as he calls it, works a hardship on those who are excluded from it, and a particular hardship on women. Unmarried women are condemned to lead an aimless life and are handicapped in the struggle for existence. They are victims of a system by which their married sisters profit.

On the future of marriage, Sumner suggests that the mores, as always, are susceptible to change, and it may be that women will some day rise in revolt and do away with it. Always the realist, he is suspicious of romantic love:

> The more poetical and elevated the ideas which are clustered around marriage, the more probable it is that experience will produce disappointment. If one spouse enters wedlock with the belief that the other is the most superlative man or woman living, the cases must be very few in which disappointment and disillusion will not result. Moreover, pair marriage, by its exclusiveness, risks the happiness of the parties on a very narrow and specific condition of life. The coercion of this arrangement for many persons must become intolerable.[71]

For this reason no society has existed, nor can exist, in which divorce is not allowed.

Finally, Sumner's extensive discussion of the social codes pertaining to such matters as chastity, modesty, propriety, and decency is a storehouse of illustrations of cultural relativity and one in which he takes an almost malicious delight.

RELIGION AND THE MORES[72]

When Sumner discusses the relationship between religion and the mores, he notices that they are sometimes out of phase. Religion, however, is never an independent force operating outside the mores. The mores grow not out of religion but out of the conditions of life as a whole. In this process they sometimes become contrary and even antagonistic to religion, and in these cases it is religious notions that succumb to the changing mores.[73] In Section 593 he suggests that "morals" and "the mores" are synonymous expressions, although in an earlier section he had said that the mores and morality may change together, thus implying that they are different phenomena. In the earlier passage, however, he had also said that the word *immoral* never means anything except "contrary to the mores."

Sumner insists throughout that philosophy has nothing to do with the mores. They do not develop in a logical or any other kind of sequence. Furthermore, there are no ethical forces in history, and no group ever has an

71. *Ibid.*, sec. 394. As we shall see, Lester Frank Ward expressed similar sentiments.

72. Sumner's presidential address to the American Sociological Society, delivered in New York City in December 1909, a few months before his death, carries this title.

73. Sumner often expresses opinions that are hostile to Christian, and especially Catholic, practices and taboos. Missionaries, for example, have unwittingly done great harm to "nature people" by inducing them to wear clothes. Mendicant orders present a history of "wrong-headedness." The notion that poverty is a virtue is "an inversion of common sense." Sacerdotal celibacy is a rule that was never obeyed and was the source of vice, hypocrisy, corruption, and moral turpitude. *Ibid.*, secs. 696–697.

ethical ideal it strives to achieve. Ethics simply grow out of the mores and are never antecedent to them:

> The men, women, and children who compose a society at any time are the unconscious depositaries and transmitters of the mores. They inherited them without knowing it; they are molding them unconsciously; they will transmit them involuntarily. The people cannot make the mores. They are made by them.[74]

Although the mores are impressive in their office as instruments of social control, they sometimes fail. This happens when dogma interferes with them, when dogma rather than experience determines them.[75]

SPORT

It merits only a brief mention that Sumner was a pioneer in the treatment of what has come to be called the sociology of sport. It is apparent to him that relaxation and amusement are important needs and that the mores have a great deal to do with the manner in which they are satisfied. These amusements, however, require the control of "good judgment" because history shows that "good mores" can sometimes be lost and "evil" ones prevail.[76]

EDUCATION

That Sumner did not hesitate to attack the conventional wisdom of his time is evident again in his pronouncements on education. Education, like democracy, is one of the superstitions of the age. We regard illiteracy, for some reason, as an abomination and we expect book learning "to form character, make good citizens, keep family mores pure, elevate morals, establish individual character, civilize barbarians, and cure social vice and disease."[77] It can do none of these things. Our faith in it is entirely misplaced. Feelings, not the intellect, are the springs of action. Education can do harm. It can strain the brain, especially in women and youth, and it sometimes leads to insanity, nervous disease, crime, and suicide.[78] Further-

74. *Ibid.*, sec. 507.

75. *Ibid.*, sec. 676.

76. *Ibid.*, chap. 17, "Popular Sports, Exhibitions, and Drama." Note the inconsistency in Sumner's characterization of the mores as good or evil.

77. *Ibid.*, sec. 699.

78. One is reminded of the German proverb *Je gelehrter jesto verkehrter* ('The more learned one is the crazier he is').

more, it molds men and women into a single pattern. The schools teach that the facts that constitute knowledge are unchanging and universal; instead, they are subject to unlimited variation and revision.[79] On the other hand, the schools can be used as an agency both to transmit the folkways and to criticize them. Intelligent study of the mores can help to rejuvenate them, keep them fresh, and adapt them to changing circumstances.

HISTORY

Sumner is finally skeptical of history. No historian can escape the mores of his own society; none can deal fairly with societies other than his own; all succumb to the kind of patriotism that warps the judgment. A knowledge of history may be an accomplishment, but ignorance of it is no hindrance to success in life.

Summary and Evaluation

Sumner is easy to criticize. A catalogue of his inconsistencies and confusions would require many pages. It would also require an amount of space that could be devoted to more fruitful enterprises. It is necessary nevertheless to mention his serious inability to maintain a distinction between folkways and mores. The subtitle of *Folkways* itself alerts us to this difficulty. It is "A Study of the Sociological Importance of Usages, Manners, Customs, Mores, and Morals." Are we to assume that all of these phenomena are examples of folkways, that *folkways* is the generic term of which the others are examples? Sumner himself, as we have seen, attempts to distinguish between folkways and mores by characterizing the latter as conducive to societal welfare, an attribute lacking in the former. It is a distinction that he fails to maintain. Indeed, he frequently uses them as synonyms, sometimes uses one and sometimes the other in the same paragraph and in discussions of the same phenomenon. He apparently recognized this himself when he (or Keller?) said in *The Science of Society* that although the distinction between them is a real one, it belongs to the laboratory rather than to actual practice.[80] His confusion is more than semantic; it is also substantive. That is, if the folkways arise to satisfy needs, then they too permit an implication of welfare.

79. These opinions, it may be noticed, stem from a man who served for many years on the Connecticut Board of Education.

80. Sec. 20.

Moreover, it is difficult to find a line that will separate "conducive to welfare" from "not conducive to welfare." How do we distinguish between customs that benefit individuals and those that merely please them, between customs that harm individuals and those that merely offend them? Where, for example, should be put the taboo against bigamy? It is possible that the practice of polygamy among the Mormons contributed a great deal to their welfare. Offering tips for services rendered may not seem important to the welfare of a society, but it may indeed contribute to the welfare of the recipients. It is difficult, in short, to consider any custom and to say that it does or does not contribute to welfare. It may be that Sumner could not support the distinction on the ground he chose because it is impossible to do so. As we shall have occasion to see, it can, however, be supported on different grounds.[81]

Nor is there anything in Sumner's treatment that tells us whether customs and mores are both folkways, whether folkways and mores are both customs, or whether all three are usages. The confusion is complete. Furthermore, the subtitle of *Folkways* suggests that mores and morals are different phenomena—since they are both listed—and indeed he often treats them as different. The only clue to the difference, however, is the assertion that "the 'morals' of an age are never anything but the consonance between what is done and what the mores of the age require."[82] It is possible that he is here consigning morals to what we would today call the real culture pattern and the mores to the ideal culture pattern. On the other hand, the thrust of his doctrine is that morals and the mores are identical, that there is no "outside standpoint" from which to judge whether or not they are right, and that any attempt to find one is a delusion. Indeed, this is the central thesis of Sumner's book. More than that, it is an important contribution to sociology.[83]

Although, as has been said, the situation is semantically unsatisfactory, we cannot regard it as a serious fault. As Emerson said, "A foolish con-

81. Contributions to welfare, of course, may vary in degree. Prohibitions against murder, theft, and adultery, for example, may seem more important than prohibitions against alcohol, tobacco, and marijuana, and these, in turn, more important that prohibitions against eating meat on Friday, working on the Sabbath, and wearing scanty dress in the cathedral. But the difficulty of graduating the seriousness of virtues and vices was well known to the moral philosophers. Distinctions of degree were denied by some of the utilitarians, for example William Paley (*Moral Philosophy*, 1785, bk. 1, chap. 6) and Bentham (*The Principles of Morals and Legislation*, 1789, vol. 1, no. 8), the latter of whom wrote, "Quantity of pleasure being equal, pushpin is as good as poetry."

82. *Folkways*, sec. 232.

83. In a similar way, Sumner frequently forgets his own distinction between the struggle for existence and the competition of life and uses the two expressions interchangeably.

sistency is the hobgoblin of little minds, adored by little statesmen and philosophers and divines." Furthermore, no serious consequences ensue from it. A neat and clean conceptual scheme is always to be preferred, of course, to one in which the categories are blurred and the distinctions hazy. But Sumner's intentions at least are usually clear. His prose, however, seldom rises to the level of excellence. It is almost always slovenly. It is also dogmatic, humorless, sarcastic, and truculent. It is the writing of a proud and arrogant man who entertained no doubt whatever of his own success in the struggle for existence.[84]

A second, obvious, criticism of Sumner is his almost total lack of organization. As Robert G. McCloskey observes, "His logical power was not great; even the short essays are often discursive and lacking in cohesion [and] the *sequiturs* are hard to find."[85] Sumner inundates the reader with facts, offered with no particular order or arrangement, as his table of contents testifies. As another example, in the final chapter of the study he treats without any recognizable continuity such subjects as life policy, oaths, the clever hero, the lack of historical sense among Christians, success policy in the Italian Renaissance, divergences between convictions and conduct, the fad of classical learning, the humanists, individualism, the perverted use of words, the extravagance of the passions, the sex relation and the position of women, the cult of success, literature on the mores, and moral anarchy. There is no summary, no conclusion, no effort to reach generalizations about the vast mass of material he has surveyed. He simply stops writing, as if the ink in his pen has suddenly given out.

It may be, as Sumner contended, that it was too early in the history of the discipline to construct a system of sociology. One suspects, however, that he had no sense of what a systematic sociological theory might be. His thinking was entirely concrete and descriptive, not abstract or theoretical. He tells us that it is the duty of sociology to study the mores. But to what end? In both *Folkways* and the four volumes of *The Science of Society* we are subjected to an avalanche of facts about the folkways and mores, in societies both primitive and civilized, Eastern and Western, ancient and recent. But facts like these do not constitute a system of sociology. The most comprehensive and accurate collection of facts—for example, the telephone

---

84. The only suspicion of humor in *Folkways* is Sumner's reference to a Moslem woman in the street looking like "a bundle of bedclothes" (sec. 446), and even that suspicion may be unwarranted. The adjectives *sarcastic* and *truculent* were used by L. L. Bernard in "The Social Science Theories of William Graham Sumner," *Social Forces* 19 (December 1940): 153–175.

85. Robert G. McCloskey, *American Conservatism in the Age of Enterprise: A Study of William Graham Sumner, Stephen J. Field, and Andrew Carnegie* (Cambridge, Mass.: Harvard University Press, 1951), p. 39.

directory of New York City—is not to be confused with a science. Something more is required.[86] Similarly, the Human Relations Area Files, for the compilation of which Sumner's work gave a primary stimulus, cannot themselves constitute a theory of the structure of society. The level of abstraction is too low. Facts require arrangement, organization, continuity, logical connections, and these Sumner fails to supply. He provides no generalizations, no causal propositions, no principles, no laws. His genius remains, but it is a stranger to the notion of systems.

Finally, Sumner, like Laocoön, is hopelessly entangled by serpents—not the serpents of the sea but the serpents of the sociology of knowledge. He claims that it is vain to suppose that even a scientific man is independent of the mores of his time and place. He tells us that "the mores contain the norm by which, if we should discuss the mores, we should have to judge the mores." He writes that "criticism of the mores is like criticising one's ancestors for the physique one has inherited, or one's children for being, in body and mind, one's children."[87] And he tells us, in a late statement, that we cannot criticize the mores because they are our "law of right," that we cannot rise above them to pass judgment upon them.[88] He insists that they are not only "right" but also "true." *Autres temps, autres moeurs* (Sumner does not use the apothegm)—that is the end of the story. And yet Sumner incessantly indulges in his own judgments of the mores. They can be

86. The proposition that facts alone do not and cannot constitute a science is now an almost elementary methodological principle. John Dewey, for example, always insisted that facts are never given. They are taken. And they are taken in connection with some purpose, some design, some hypothesis, some conceptual scheme. Among sociologists, Lester Frank Ward cautioned:

> Another reef to be shunned is the notion that was formerly quite prevalent and which is still continually coming into view, that science consists in the discovery of facts. There is not a single science of which this is true, and a much more correct definition would be that science consists in reasoning about facts.

Pure Sociology, chap. 1, p. 6. Emile Durkheim wrote, "It is a vain delusion to believe that the best way to prepare for the advent of a science is first to accumulate patiently all the materials it will use, for one can know what these needed materials are only if there is already some presentiment of its essence and its needs." *Division of Labor*, p. 37. Ferdinand Tönnies, in his presidential address to the first meeting of the German Sociological Society, noted that sociology is mainly concerned with concepts and that "it is not so much its task to perceive facts but to construct the most convenient, the most useful implements for their perception: a task of supreme importance, which is, frequently to their own disadvantage, not much appreciated by the mere empiricist." Wege und Ziele der Soziologie," *Soziologische Studien und Kritiken* 2 (Jena, 1926): 131. For an elaboration of this theme, see Robert Bierstedt, "A Critique of Empiricism in Sociology," *Power and Progress*, pp. 133–149.

87. *Folkways*, secs. 80, 507.

88. "The Mores of the Present and the Mores of the Future," *War and Other Essays*, p. 151. This essay was written in 1909, the year before his death.

"gross," "absurd," "inexpedient," "corrupt." They can be good or evil. The colonial custom of bundling has been abolished by "better taste." The lupanars of the medieval cities illustrate the power of the mores to sanction "an evil thing." We must learn to criticize and judge the mores; indeed, this is one of the functions of education.

The trouble with these propositions, of course, is that they are executed by their own logic. Like Archimedes, Sumner has a very long lever but no place to stand, no vantage point outside the mores from which to judge them. If the mores can make anything right can the lupanars be wrong? Sumner's moral opinions are themselves creatures of the mores—the mores of his own time and place. Furthermore, if the mores define what is right, then the proposition that they can make anything right is a simple tautology. Finally, if not even a man of science can extricate himself from the mores, then a science of society becomes impossible. The objectivity that such a science would require is unattainable.[89]

The laissez-faire doctrine, to which Sumner gives extreme expression, sinks him in a sea of paradox. Let society alone! Do not tamper with it! Do not try to force changes upon it! All efforts to do good, by legislation or otherwise, almost always have evil as their unintended consequences. What good can one do when what one does does none? Why then did Sumner bother to write his books and essays? And why did he believe that the science of sociology, then in its infancy, would have any more effect upon the natural processes of society than the foolish schemes of the reformers? Why not sit back and enjoy the show, as a kind of Olympian spectator? Here, of course, he is caught in the Humean problem. Hume may have been skeptical about the validity of the category of causation, but he doubtless intended his views to have some effect and thus attributed to them, if only unconsciously, some causal efficacy.[90] Here again, Sumner places in jeopardy the very science he endeavored so strenuously to advance. Although he was vaguely aware of some of his contradictions, he was apparently unembarrassed by them. As for the puzzles of logic—and

89. Karl Mannheim tried to solve this problem by removing intellectuals from the constrictions of the class structure altogether, thus freeing their propositions from what would otherwise be a class-induced and class-limited "truth," making them, in Alfred Weber's words, a *freischwebende Intelligenz*. See Mannheim, *Ideology and Utopia*, trans. Louis Wirth and Edward Shils (New York: Harcourt, Brace & Co., 1936), pp. 136–146. See also his *Essays on the Sociology of Knowledge*, trans. Paul Kecskemeti (London and New York: Oxford University Press, 1952).

90. As MacIver has observed, "If Hume convinced me that he was right about the lack of evidence on which to base the concept of causation, he would have proved himself wrong, since it was his reasoning that caused me to change my mind." *Social Causation* (Boston: Ginn & Co., 1942), p. 59.

especially the paradox of double implication[91]—he would have regarded them as "freaks" and not as genuine problems. In Sumner's defense it must be said that the discipline of logic fell far outside the provinces of his interests.

If it is easy to criticize Sumner, so also is it easy to praise him. His defects are balanced—indeed, overbalanced—by his virtues. His first major contribution consists almost certainly in his vigorous insistence upon the principle of cultural relativity. He did not originate the principle; it can be traced as far back as the Greek philosophers and playwrights, and it receives express articulation in Boethius.[92] Sumner, however, lived in the nineteenth century, a Victorian century in the English-speaking world, in which moral standards were fixed and stable and permanent. They were the result of "innate, intuitive, instinctive perception."[93] They were firmly grounded in the Christian religion. They were part of the nature of the universe, and of human society. Of course, as in all societies, there were deviations from them, but they were deviations from standards that were not open to question.[94] Sumner, however, challenged the notion that there was anything absolute about ethical standards. He was not alone in doing so. The rise of the new science of anthropology had a similar influence. Reports of travelers and missionaries from the far corners of the earth disclosed the existence of "savage" and "immoral" peoples, who wore no clothes and who procreated without benefit of clergy. If the missionaries

---

91. There is class of propositions whose truth implies their falsity and whose falsity implies their truth. An example is Oliver Wendell Holmes's proposition, "Every man worth his salt endeavors to form general propositions and no general proposition is worth a damn." The latter half of the sentence, of course, is itself a general proposition and one that, if true, is false. Bertrand Russell made a brilliant but possibly unsuccessful assault upon this problem in the Introduction to *Principia Mathematica.* Russell and Alfred North Whitehead, *Principia Mathematica,* 3 vols. (Cambridge, Eng.: At the University Press, 1910), vol. 1.

92. "The customs and laws of diverse nations do so much differ the one from the other, that the same thing which some commend as laudable, others condemn as deserving punishment." *De Consolatione Philosophiae,* Loeb Classical Library, vol. 2, p. 215. For earlier statements see Abraham Edel, *Ethical Judgment* (New York: Free Press of Glencoe, 1955).

93. W.E.H. Lecky, for example, writes in 1869 about the sexual appetite:

> The feeling of all men and the language of all nations, the sentiment which though often weakened is never wholly effaced, that this appetite, even in its most legitimate gratification, is a thing to be veiled and withdrawn from sight, all that is known under the names of decency and indecency, concur in proving that we have an innate, intuitive, instinctive perception that there is something degrading in the sensual part of our nature, something to which a feeling of shame is naturally attached, something that jars with our conception of perfect purity, something we could not with any propriety ascribe to an all-holy being.

History of European Morals, 3d ed. rev. (New York: D. Appleton & Co., 1913), pp. 104–105.

94. On deviations, especially deviations from sexual morality, see the illuminating study by Steven Marcus, *The Other Victorians* (New York: Basic Books, 1966).

wanted to clothe them and convert them, the anthropologists on the contrary wanted only to study them. And when they did, they learned to ask not how well their conduct conformed to Victorian standards but how well it conformed to their own. Thus, in the social sciences at least, the principle of cultural relativity supplanted the notion of ethical absolutism. Sumner's contribution to this development was a major one. In ringing terms he declares:

> For every one the mores give the notion of what ought to be. This includes the notion of what ought to be done, for all should coöperate to bring to pass, in the order of life, what ought to be. All notions of propriety, decency, chastity, politeness, order, duty, right, rights, discipline, respect, reverence, coöperation, and fellowship, especially all things in regard to which good and ill depend entirely on the point at which the line is drawn, are in the mores. The mores can make things seem right and good to one group or one age which to another seem antagonistic to every instinct of human nature.[95]

The syntax leaves something to be desired, but the emphasis is unmistakable. Once again, the mores can make anything right.

It should be said that this principle has encountered renewed skepticism—and from sociologists themselves. Theodore Caplow, for example, suggests that there are cultural universals after all, that all peoples probably respond in much the same way to social snubs, dirty jokes, and political speeches.[96] And Alvin W. Gouldner, in an important paper, has nominated the norm of reciprocity as a candidate for universal status.[97] Fortunately or unfortunately, these considerations reintroduced into sociology one of the ancient issues of ethical theory. What is the nature of obligation, of which reciprocity is an instance, and what is its source? Does it rest in society (as Durkheim insisted), in conscience (which Cicero called the god within us), in nature (the natural law), in utility (as Bentham thought), in the Kantian imperative, in the decrees of God (as the world's theistic religions suppose), or in some innate moral faculty that requires us to acknowledge it even when we fail to act upon it?[98] Again, Sumner does not examine the problem in the context of ethical theory. But *Folkways* was a remarkable correction of an earlier kind of conventional wisdom, one

95. *Folkways,* sec. 232. Expressions like this are too numerous to count.

96. *Elementary Sociology* (Englewood Cliffs, N. J.: Prentice-Hall, 1971), p. 112. The title is misleading; Caplow's sociology is far from elementary.

97. "The Norm of Reciprocity," *American Sociological Review* 25 (April 1960): 161–178. See also the brief discussion of hospitality in Robert Bierstedt, *The Social Order*, 4th ed. (New York: McGraw-Hill, 1974), p. 180.

98. An adequate treatment of this subject would also require attention to a distinction between what is absolute and what is merely universal.

supported by all the resources of church and state. And this, as has been said, is a major contribution to sociology.

A second, rather considerable, contribution of Sumner's is his emphasis upon the range and significance of nonlogical actions in human life—a contribution usually credited to Pareto. As a result of the Pareto cult that flourished at Harvard in the 1930s, and as a result too of the prominent place that Parsons gave to Pareto in his *Structure of Social Action* in 1937, many have considered Pareto to be the originator and foremost protagonist of a sociology that would take such actions into account. Unlike utilitarian ethical theory and classical economics, both of which treated human action in the context of rational choice—the first to maximize pleasure and minimize pain and the second to increase gain and decrease loss—Pareto suggested that such logical choices, or logical actions, were in reality only a small part of all actions, the much larger number of which were in fact nonlogical. Pareto insisted, in fact, that apart from town planning, penology, and military tactics, most human actions are nonlogical.[99] For this insistence he received extraordinary accolades and assumed a place, now more modestly evaluated, in the pantheon of sociological heroes.[100] None of this would have been news to Sumner. Indeed, Sumner insists at the outset that men begin with acts, not thoughts, and that these acts have little or nothing to do with rationality. The folkways and mores develop in random and unplanned fashion, as ways of satisfying human needs. No one notices their origin, no one watches them grow, no one sees them change. Their history—until crystallized in institutions—contains no trace of rational reflection. Some irrational folkways may be effective, in fact, and some rational ones, ineffective. This again is a major achievement and one by which Sumner anticipated Pareto by more than a decade. There is no reference to Sumner and few references to other American writers in Pareto, but if priority is the candle for which the game is played, as Merton and others suggest, Sumner must surely enjoy its light. If he did not develop this insight in any "logical," "rational," or systematic form, neither did Pareto. Indeed, Sumner's folkways and mores, although inadequately distinguished, are clear, and clearly understood. Pareto's residues and derivations are clouded with uncertainty. It is difficult, incidentally, to decide which of the two was the more slovenly in the organization of his materials. Both swoop down like bats from a rafter on any subject, and any

99. All three of his exceptions are questionable.

100. Bernard De Voto, for example, wrote: "A good many men whose opinion is entitled to consideration asset that the *Traité* is the most important intellectual achievement of the twentieth century," and "In the opinion of these men, Pareto has made possible exact knowledge about society for the first time in the history of thought." "Sentiment and the Social Order: An Introduction to the Teachings of Pareto," *Harper's Magazine* 167 (October, 1933): 569.

illustration that attracts their attention, without regard to connection or continuity. Few, in truth, have read verbatim and seriatim either *The Science of Society* of Sumner and Keller or *The Mind and Society* of Pareto,[101] both in four volumes. One is tempted to quote the English reviewer who observed that he did not know if the author of the book under review was a good writer, but he did know that anyone who managed to finish it was a good reader.

Finally, I observe that it is given to few sociologists to contribute new concepts to a discipline and to fewer still to contribute new words to the common language. Sumner did both. The quartet of hunger, love, vanity, and fear, "in-group and out-group," the "man-land ratio," "the strain toward consistency," and "ethnocentrism" are firmly lodged in the vocabulary of sociology. *Folkways* and *mores* are now common coin and belong to the English language itself. This is no mean achievement. It is one that places us all in Sumner's debt.

Appreciation of Sumner, however, is by no means universal. At one end of the spectrum he has suffered the criticism of silence. Lewis A. Coser, for example, fails to mention him, except incidentally and in series with other writers, in an otherwise outstanding book.[102] Much earlier, Howard Odum gave him the same silent treatment.[103] Parsons ignores him in *The Structure of Social Action*, but that work, of course, is not a history of sociological theory, and it is almost entirely devoid of American names. We should not expect Sumner to have attracted the attention of Raymond Aron, because Aron is concerned with only a few figures in the European tradition.[104] Helmut Schoeck, in a comprehensive history, mentions Sumner only once, and then in series with others.[105] On the other hand, Sumner receives condign discussions in most of the American texts and in the two American encyclopedias of the social sciences. And, in England, Ronald Fletcher devotes a long chapter to Sumner in his magisterial history and says that he

---

101. Except, of course, Arthur Livingston, the English translator of Pareto—a translation so accomplished that someone has remarked that it is superior to the original work.

102. *Masters of Sociological Thought* (New York: Harcourt Brace Jovanovich, 1971). Coser devotes separate chapters to Comte, Mark, Spencer, Durkheim, Simmel, Weber, Veblen, Cooley, Mead, Park, Pareto, and Mannheim. Sumner is omitted also from the second edition, 1977, which contains, in addition to the above, chapters on Sorokin, Thomas and Znaniecki, and one on Recent Trends.

103. *American Masters of Social Science* (New York: Henry Holt & Co., 1927).

104. Montesquieu, Comte, Marx, Tocqueville, Durkheim, Pareto, Weber. *Main Currents in Sociological Thought*, 2 vols., trans. Richard Howard and Helen Weaver (New York: Basic Books, 1965–1967).

105. There is, however, a brief biographical note. *Die Soziologie und die Gesellschaften: Problemsicht und Problemlösung vom Beginn bis zur Gegenwart*, 2nd ed. (Munich: Verlag Karl Alber, 1964).

"was undoubtedly one of the most important American scholars contributing to the making of sociology towards the end of the nineteenth century."[106]

Some critics have been hostile. Albion W. Small, for example, referred to Sumner as "a moving picture of what a sociologist should not be" and was surprised and shocked by Sumner's election to the presidency of the American Sociological Society in 1909.[107] Small's Chicago colleague George E. Vincent adopted a relatively neutral stance, praising Sumner for his citations of more than 700 authors in *Folkways* and for his "clearness, vigor, and frequently convincing force" but referring to him also as a "folk psychologist."[108] L. L. Bernard regarded Sumner as a transitional figure between "social science" and "sociology" but called him nevertheless "the most versatile of all American social scientists."[109]

At the far end of the spectrum, Harry Elmer Barnes expresses the opinion, "Of this work [*Folkways*] it is not inaccurate to say that it is unsurpassed as a sociological achievement by any single volume in any language and that it has made the sociological treatment of usages, manners, customs, mores, and morals essentially a completed task."[110] Barnes, of course, is given to hyperbole. At the same end of the spectrum we find Albert Galloway Keller, Sumner's younger colleague. Keller submerged his own career almost entirely in Sumner's and devoted his life not only to writing *The Science of Society* with the mountain of data that Sumner had collected but also to the publication and advertisement of Sumner's works.[111] This observation is less true of Keller's younger colleague, Maurice R. Davie, who worked on the last volume of *The Science of Society* (a 1331-page "Case-Book"). Davie concedes that Sumner was "essentially a nineteenth-century figure" but nevertheless pays him high tribute (perhaps too high) for introducing the scientific method into the study of society. Davie writes in addition:

> He had the ability to ask fundamental questions and the courage to pursue their investigation wherever it might lead and however many cherished and traditional notions it might trample underfoot. He always went directly to the heart of a matter and kept his eye on the main issue.[112]

---

106. *The Making of Sociology*, 2 vols. (London: Michael Joseph, 1971), vol. 1, p. 502.

107. Albion W. Small, "Fifty Years of Sociology in the United States," p. 732, Sumner was the second president of the society, Small the fourth.

108. "Review of *Folkways*," *American Journal of Sociology* 13 (November 1907): 414–419.

109. "Social Science Theories of William Graham Sumner."

110. "William Graham Sumner: Spencerianism in American Dress," ed. Harry Elmer Barnes, *An Introduction to the History of Sociology* (Chicago: University of Chicago Press, 1948), p. 157.

111. Keller wrote an independent book, *Societal Evolution* (New York: Macmillan, 1915). but it is entirely Sumnerian in flavor.

112. *William Graham Sumner*, p. viii.

Davie says simply that Sumner was a great figure in the history of social science. The sheer presence of Harris E. Starr's magnificent biography is another kind of evaluation. We have earlier quoted Cooley's praise of Sumner's scientific method, which Cooley regarded as nothing but common sense, refined and perfected, and Cooley did not hesitate to compare *Folkways* with *The Origin of Species.*

Clearly, as Richard Hofstadter says, Sumner was a commanding figure in American life.[113] His name appears in general histories of the United States (in Charles A. Beard's and Samuel Eliot Morison's, for example), as well as in histories of sociology. As a publicist Sumner's importance can hardly be denied. He lent the sanctions of the Puritan ethic and Social Darwinism to the free and competitive exercise of capitalistic endeavor. He wrote the apologia for the economic views that prevailed in the United States until the Great Depression and for the laissez-faire philosophy that the Supreme Court itself protected until the second term of Franklin D. Roosevelt's administration.[114] Darwin and Spencer were right because the struggle for existence is the law of the universe. American entrepreneurial capitalism needed no further justification.

As a sociologist Sumner was a pioneer in winning disciplinary autonomy for the study of society. Much of what he had to say about the folkways and mores seems to be only common sense. But in his day it was uncommon sense. If we now pay him less than is his due it is because we now take his views for granted. They are part of the stuff and substance—indeed the very vocabulary—of sociology. Someone had to give them first expression and it was Sumner's role to do so. His philosophy was shallow, his "system" nonexistent. But in his emphasis upon the nonrational actions that constitute the folkways and mores, in his identification (if frequently inconsistent) of the morals of an age with its mores, and in his insistence that social processes are natural processes, he was a beacon that continues to shed a powerful beam in the American tradition of sociological inquiry.

113. Hofstadter's chapter, though brief, is indispensable. See *Social Darwinism in American Thought*, rev. ed. (Boston: Beacon Press, 1955), pp. 51–66. See also the much longer, and important, treatment in McCloskey, *American Conservatism*, where pages 30–71 are devoted to Sumner. See also Kurt Samuelsson, *Religion and Economic Action: A Critique of Max Weber* [1957], trans. E. Geoffrey French (New York: Harper & Row, Harper Torch books, 1964), pp. 71–79, who calls Sumner "the chief ideological hero of the captains of industry." For the entire period 1865–1918, see Joseph Dorfman, *The Economic Mind in American Civilization*, 5 vols. (New York: Viking Press, 1949), vol. 3.

114. Indeed, it was not until 1937 that the Court upheld the constitutionality of such legislation as a minimum wage law for women in the state of Washington, the National Labor Relations Act, and the Social Security Act. Sumner would have been appalled.

CHAPTER 2

Lester Frank Ward

It is the misfortune of all truly great minds to be wedded to errors as well as to truths.

—*Dynamic Sociology*, vol. 1, p. 83.

Lester Frank Ward was born on June 18, 1841, in Joliet, Illinois, near the site of what is now the Illinois State Penitentiary. He was the tenth and last child of Justus and Silence Rolph Ward. His father, a man of migratory tendencies, raised the family in various places, moving from western New York to Illinois and then to Iowa in a small covered wagon. In Iowa he had been given 160 acres for his services as a fife major in the War of 1812. He earned his living, such as it was, as a handyman, jack-of-all-trades, sawmill operator, and towpath builder. It was a precarious existence, and the family was always in straitened circumstances. Frank, as he was known to the family, received the rudiments of an education at Saint Charles, Illinois, on the Fox River, where the family lived until he was nine years old. He spent his childhood roaming the prairies, swimming, fishing, hunting birds and small game, and trying to satisfy a limitless curiosity about the insects and flowers that he saw, often, with no knowledge of entomology or botany, coining his own names for them.[1]

1. There are several sources of biographical detail: Ward's own "Personal Remark," in his *Glimpses of the Cosmos*, 6 vols. (New York: G. P. Putnam's Sons, 1913–1918), vol. 1, pp. lvii–lxxxix, and Emily Palmer Cape, *Lester F. Ward, A Personal Sketch* (New York: G. P. Putnam's Sons, 1922). Worshipful in tone, Cape tells of their work together on *Glimpses of the Cosmos* and prints a number of Ward's letters to her. Samuel Chugerman, *Lester Frank Ward, The American Aristotle* (Durham, N.C.: Duke University Press, 1939), although useful as a full-length treatment of Ward and his work, is, as its subtitle suggests, foolishly adulatory and frequently mistaken on matters of fact. Indeed, with respect to the first of these faults, Chugerman writes that Ward was superior even to Aristotle, that he had fewer opportunities and greater abilities than Abraham Lincoln, that he was the "master of system builders," and that "many philosophers have furnished beads for sociology, but it remained for Ward to string them into an immortal necklace [p. 209]." He asserts that *Glimpses of the Cosmos* "forms one of the most amazing symposia of knowledge ever written [p. 60]." Seldom has a man's work been so suffocated by superlatives. With respect to unreliability, Chugerman uses incorrect titles of books, misspells names, and complains that the *Encyclopedia of the Social Sciences*

Ward's father died when Frank was sixteen, whereupon the family returned to Illinois from Iowa. For a brief time he became a farmhand to a French Canadian, in whose house he found a French grammar. He studied it thirstily and by his own effort attained enough proficiency to be able to write his diary in that language—ostensibly to practice the language but also to conceal from alien eyes the details of his romantic activities with the girl he was to marry. For reasons that defy explanation he developed an almost fanatical attachment to books and used whatever few pennies he could accumulate in order to purchase them.

In 1858, when he was seventeen, Ward and his brother Erastus hiked across the country to join an older brother, Cyrenus Osborn Ward, in Myersburg, Pennsylvania, where Cyrenus owned and operated a factory producing wagon hubs.[2] After work Frank burrowed into textbooks of physiology and into grammars of the Greek, Latin, French, and German languages. Unfortunately, the factory failed after two years, and Frank was on his own. By working on a farm in the summer and teaching school in the winter, he managed to earn enough to enroll, at the age of twenty, in the Susquehanna Collegiate Institute of Towanda, Pennsylvania, and briefly received his first formal schooling above the elementary level. To his surprise he discovered that he knew more Greek and Latin than anyone there.

In 1860, at age nineteen, Ward began to keep a diary, written, as stated earlier, in French.[3] It is an interesting document that provides a glimpse of the life of an impecunious young man in rural Pennsylvania in the seventh decade of the nineteenth century and of the folkways of that time and place. It is also artless, callow, candid, prosaic, and dull. A typical entry is the second one, written on July 9, 1860:

"does not recognize Ward's pioneering labors as the founder of sociology in America, and only in a few of the introductory articles is he included 'among those present'" (p. 69). There is an article on Ward in that publication. It was written by Bernhard J. Stern and begins with the observation that Ward, along with Comte and Spencer, is one of the founders of sociology. *Encyclopedia of the Social Sciences*, 15 vols. (New York: Macmillan, 1937), vol. 15, pp. 353–354.

2. Cyrenus achieved a measure of fame as the author of two tracts, *A Labor Catechism of Political Economy* and *The Ancient Lowly: A History of the Working People*, which he set in type and printed himself and which won favorable notice from such worthies as Horace Greeley, Charles A. Dana, and Henry George. The second of these apparently grew into a book by C. Osborne Ward, entitled, *A History of the Ancient Working People* (Washington, D.C.: Press of the Craftsman, 1889.) There is a copy in the Alderman Library, University of Virginia.

3. *Young Ward's Diary*, ed. Bernhard J. Stern and trans. Elizabeth N. Nichols (New York: G. P. Putnam's Sons, 1935).

> I cultivated corn this morning for the first time this year. I was a little annoyed with the horse's not keeping to the row.
>
> In the afternoon I gathered and bound the sheaves.
>
> When night came I had a fine time playing on the violin while Baxter played the tambourine. My heart was very light regarding the girl whom I loved, and whom I no longer esteem.
>
> But everyone has gone to bed, and I must wash my feet before going myself.[4]

Another, February 26, 1861, reads: "We had a debate but not a very good one last evening. Ridgeway was fined for disorder. I am in the third book in Geometry, and through the fables in Latin, almost through the first book of the *Anabasis*, and almost at the end of the Algebra."[5] The diary, which runs through 1869, tells little about the development of Ward's ideas and indeed has little intellectual content. It has several major concerns. The first is his romance with Elizabeth Vought, the girl he married in 1862, five days before going off to war. (They had one son, who died before his first birthday.) The second is his finances and financial transactions. We learn, for example, that on one day his total worth was $1.14, that on another he paid a debt of 21 cents, that he broke his watch and had it repaired for 35 cents; that his salary at Standing Stone, where he taught school, was $17 a month, that he bought a suit of clothes for $7. In one entry he writes, "We have saved more than ten dollars since we bought the frying pan." The third concern is his health. He mentions every cold he caught and every boil he lanced. It was warm in Washington one week, and therefore he took several baths. The fourth is an account of the books he read and the studies he pursued, but with no intimations of his views, favorable or unfavorable, of these books or estimate of their importance. Finally, he relates the debates in which he participated, both in Towanda and later in Washington, sometimes winning and sometimes losing.[6]

Ward continued his diary until his death. Unfortunately, the continuation is not available. His beloved wife, Lizzie, died in 1871, casting a pall over his life that he thought he could not endure. However, he married a widow, Rose Asenath Simons Pierce, two years later, and she destroyed the later diaries, written in English and covering the years from 1870 to his

---

4. *Ibid.*, p. 3.

5. *Ibid.*, p. 38.

6. The subjects of these debates have a certain fascination. For example: Resolved, that pleasure has a much greater influence upon men than sorrow; Resolved, that Alexander was a greater general than Hannibal; Resolved, that father and mother are under more obligations to their children than the children are to their parents; Resolved, that women exercise more influence over men than money does; Resolved, that there is more happiness in the world than misery.

death in 1913. There is a hint that she did so because they contained admissions of "lapses of loyalty" to her.

Ward served in the Union army for twenty-seven months and was wounded in both legs at the Battle of Chancellorsville. At first an intense and even bloodthirsty patriot, he soon came to realize that the soldiers on the other side were helplessly caught in the same horror as he was himself. After his discharge he had difficulty finding employment—even importuning President Lincoln himself, in a letter reproduced in the diary—but finally found a job in government service as supervisor of a ward in the Fairfax Seminary Hospital, outside of Washington. In May 1865 he achieved what he regarded as a victory, namely, an appointment as a clerk in the Treasury Department, an appointment that initiated his long career in the government. His advancement was rapid. He moved two years later to the Division of Navigation and Immigration and then became librarian of the United States Bureau of Statistics. In 1881 he moved again to the United States Geological Survey and in 1892 became chief paleontologist in that bureau.

In Washington Ward found time to attend classes at the Columbian (now George Washington) University, from which he was graduated in 1869 with an A.B. degree. In 1871 he received the degree of LL.B. and was admitted to the bar of the District of Columbia. The following year he was awarded an A.M. degree and in 1897 the honorary degree of LL.D. He also earned a diploma in medicine. He never practiced either of these two professions.[7] In Washington also he formed with others the National Liberal Reform League and edited its paper, *The Iconoclast*, dedicated to refuting the false claims of religion and to advancing the cause of reason and science over faith and theology. Early on he began to attend the meetings of scientific societies and contributed, and published, an impressive number of papers on a wide variety of subjects, especially geology, botany, and paleontology. He was a fellow of the American Association for the Advancement of Science, the Anthropological, Biological, and Geological societies of Washington, serving several of them as president, and a member of the American Philosophical Society, the American Economic Association, and the International Geological Congress. From 1900 to 1903 he served as president of L'Institut International de Sociologie and in 1906

7. In *Pure Sociology* Ward explains why he did not practice law: "I used to smile when I heard good and simple country dames say that lawyers lived by lying, and I 'studied law,' acquired that profession, and was duly admitted to the bar. But long before the end I had learned that the good country dames were right and I was wrong. I was openly taught by the senior professor that my business was to gain my case, and that I was not to be the judge of the justice of the case. That was matter for the judge. I need scarcely add that I have never pleaded a case" *Pure Sociology*, 2nd ed. (New York: Macmillan, 1903), p. 488.

became the first president of the American Sociological Society. Late in his career he was invited to membership in Phi Beta Kappa but declined the invitation on the ground that he had all the honors anyone could want. He read Greek, Latin, French, German, Italian, Spanish, and Russian and contributed to both the *Century Dictionary* and Webster's *International Dictionary.*

Although Ward lectured at various times, and for short terms, at the universities of West Virginia, Chicago, Johns Hopkins, Harvard, Stanford, Wisconsin, and Columbia, he did not realize his ambition to hold a regular academic appointment until 1906 when, after forty years of government service and at the age of sixty-five, he became professor of sociology at Brown University, a post he held until his death. During the last five years, with his wife bedridden in Washingon, he lived alone in a student dormitory. On a visit to her in the spring of 1913, he died; the date was April 13 and his age was seventy-two.

Physically, and despite numerous protestations to the contrary, Ward enjoyed good health until after his seventieth year. His colleague at Brown, James Q. Dealey, described him:

> He was in height fully six feet, broad shouldered, deep chested, and muscular from the experiences of early years, showing no tendency towards stoutness. Even in his sixties he was able to walk without apparent fatigue fifteen to twenty miles on a stretch, absorbed in the botanical or geological phenomena about him. In complexion he was blond, but tanned by much exposure to the sun, and had brown hair and the bluish-gray eyes of his race. In older years he acquired a "scholarly stoop" that detracted somewhat from his real height. He smoked with great moderation and rarely drank except on social occasions. His abounding health enabled him to work hard and long, day after day, with very brief intervals for rest or social intercourse, since he found his happiness, not in play or amusement, but in the contact of mind with mind or in reflection in his study or on the long jaunts away from the city into the country.[8]

He was a shy and lonely man. In demeanor he was modest, except when writing, at his publisher's request, advertisments for his books and when he suspected that other writers were using his ideas without giving him appropriate credit.[9] He was well traveled and knew personally such European

8. Dealey, "Lester Frank Ward," *American Masters of Social Science*, ed. Howard W. Odum (New York: Henry Holt & Co., 1927), p. 65. See Dealey's entire chapter, pp. 61–96.

9. He was especially upset by Henri Bergson's *Creative Evolution:*

> Sometimes an author of high standing and great eminence comes forward with a work that focuses the attention of the thinking world, in which, along with much, of course that is new and original, and often with considerable that is questionable or positively untrue, these ideas upon which I have been ringing the changes for thirty years, are served up as something wholly new to the world.

Glimpses of the Cosmos, vol. 1, p. lxxxiii.

contemporaries as Ernest Haeckel, Ludwig Gumplowicz, Gustav Ratzenhofer, Edward B. Tylor, and Herbert Spencer. He attended a dinner in honor of Spencer in New York in 1882,[10] visited Haeckel in Jena in 1911, and presided over the World Congress of L'Institut International de Sociologie in 1905, where he delivered his address in French. Tylor and Spencer both wrote him complimentary letters on the publication of his *Dynamic Sociology.* A number of his successors to the presidency of the American Sociological Society, including Edward A. Ross, Franklin H. Giddings, Ulysses G. Weatherly, Charles A. Ellwood, Frank W. Blackmar, and Albion W. Small, paid him obituary tribute in the *American Journal of Sociology.*[11]

Ward's contributions to sociology are contained in five books: *Dynamic Sociology,* in two volumes, 1883; *The Psychic Factors of Civilization,* 1893; *Outlines of Sociology,* 1898; *Pure Sociology,* 1903;[12] and *Applied Sociology,* 1906. They were published in translation in seven languages (although not all in each), German, French, Spanish, Italian, Russian, Polish, and Japanese. The Russian translation of *Dynamic Sociology* was burned on order of the council of Ministers in 1891.[13] It remains to mention *Glimpses of the Cosmos,* published in six volumes beginning in 1913.[14] In these volumes he gathered together everything of less than book length that he had ever published—except annual reports of the United States Geological Survey. The collection, beginning with "The Spaniard's Revenge," a tale published in the *Saint Charles* (Ill.) *Argus* a few months before his seventeenth birthday, is curious, fascinating, and even bizarre. *Glimpses of the Cosmos* is appropriately named. It is breathtaking in its range. Although there are no papers on medicine or jurisprudence, it contains papers on philosophy, philology, theology, botany, geology, meterology, paleontology, chemistry, biology, psychology, statistics, economics, political science, anthropology, and sociology, together with

10. For which he prepared, but did not deliver, a letter of tribute. See *ibid.*, vol. 3, pp. 112–117.

11. Vol. 19 (July 1913): 61–78. See also Bernhard J. Stern, "Giddings, Ward and Small: An Interchange of Letters," *Social Forces* 10 (1932–1933): 305–318, and "The Letters of Albion Small to Lester F. Ward," *ibid.* 12 (1933): 163–173, "The Letters of Ludwig Gumplowicz to Lester F. Ward," in *Sociologus* (Leipzig) 1 (1933), and "The Ward-Ross Correspondence (1891–1896)," *American Sociological Review* 3 (June 1938): 362–401.

12. *A Text Book of Sociology,* 1905, written with James Q. Dealey, is largely a condensation of this book.

13. For the story of this episode, see Ward's Preface to the second edition of *Dynamic Sociology,* pp. xii–xxii. George Kennan, then American ambassador to Russia, informed him that the Council of Ministers decided that "the book is saturated with the rankest materialism." *The Psychic Factors of Civilization,* however, was published in Russian, albeit with references to *Dynamic Sociology* deleted.

14. All published by G. P. Putnam's Sons, New York.

papers that fit into no known category, such as, for example, "Who Destroyed the Alexandrian Library?"[15] It invites us to apply to Ward such labels as polymath and polyhistor. We smile at his presumption in offering a course at Brown University entitled "A Survey of All Knowledge." We are uncomfortable with Chugerman's reference to him as "The American Aristotle."[16] Yet, one must confess to awe and amazement at the astonishing variety of subjects that Ward discussed with lucidity and sophistication. It is time, however, to turn to his sociology.[17]

15. The papers, editorials, and reviews are arranged chronologically rather than in categories. A small sample of some 563 items includes the following: Rapidity of Progress, Science vs. Theology, Abraham Lincoln's Religion, Christianity and Civilization, Religion and Progress, What Is the Positive Philosophy, The Atonement, Transubstantiation, Immigration Statistics, The Immaculate Conception, Comparative Theology, Mental vs. Physical Liberty, Rocky Mountain Flora, Winter-Blooming Jessamine, Eccentricity of the Pith of Rhus Toxicodendron, A New Fir of the Rocky Mountains, The Local Distribution of Plants, Evolution in Biology and Philology, Haeckel's Genesis of Man, Timber-Trees of the Dismal Swamp, Cosmic and Organic Evolution, The Province of Statistics, On the Genealogy of Plants, Texas Plants, On the Natural Succession of the Dicotyledons, Timber Trees and Grasses of Utah, Sexual Differentiation in Epigae Repens, Feeling and Function as Factors in Human Development, The World's Supply of Live Stock, Evolution of the Chemical Elements, Pre-Social Man, Savage and Civilized Orthoëpy, The Animal Population of the Globe, On the Cause of the Absence of Trees on the Great Plains, Guide to the Flora of Washington and Vicinity, Kant's Antinomies, Darwin as a Botanist, Vowel Systematization, Origin of the Arabic Numerals, The Organic Compounds in Their Relations to Life, The Postage Question, Proterogyny in Sparganium Eurycarpum, Classification of Organisms, Marsh and Aquatic Plants of the Northern United States, Darwin's View of Christianity, Society as a Domain of Natural Forces, Prof. Sumner's Social Classes, The Claims of Political Science, The Upper Missouri River System, Irrigation in the Upper Missouri and Yellowstone Valleys, Mind as a Social Factor, The Fossil Flora of the Globe, Our Knowledge of Fossil Plants, The Ginkgo-Tree, A Convenient System of River Nomenclature, A National University, Sketch of Paleobotany, Notes on the Flora of Eastern Virginia, On the Determination of Fossil Dicotyledonous Leaves, The Use and Abuse of Wealth, False Notions of Government, The Frequency of Coincidences, Civil Service Reform, Evidence of the Fossil Plants as to the Age of the Potomac Formation, American Weather, Some Social and Economic Paradoxes, Carboniferous Glaciation, Geographical Distribution of Fossil Plants, The Course of Biologic Evolution, Origin of the Plane-Trees, The Transmission of Culture, The Science and Art of Government, Geographic Nomenclature of the Rock Creek Region, The Psychologic Basis of Social Economics, and Weissman's Theory of Heredity.

16. E. A. Ross indulged in the same comparison:

> When one considers the vast range of Ward's intellectual interests, the number and variety of his original contributions to science and his great power of generalization, one feels that if Aristotle had by chance been born in Illinois about the middle of the nineteenth century, his career would have resembled that of Lester F. Ward more than that of any other American of our time. Had I had the privilege of intimate association with Aristotle, he would not have made upon me a greater impression of vast knowledge and intellectual force than did Lester F. Ward.

Quoted in Chugerman, *Lester Frank Ward*, p. 14.

17. For more recent treatments of Ward, see bibliography, *ibid*, pp. 559–560; Harold Pfautz, "Lester Frank Ward," *International Encyclopedia of the Social Sciences*, ed. David L.

Dynamic Sociology

Ward began writing his *Dynamic Sociology* in 1869, finished it in 1880, and after having serious difficulty finding a publisher, saw it in print in 1883.[18] It fell, as the saying goes, stillborn from the press. The almost total absence of a reception, favorable or otherwise, so discouraged him that he considered abandoning sociology altogether. Albion W. Small, then president of Colby College, began to use the book, however, in his course in 1890 and more or less launched it on its career. Ward's original title for it—because of its emphasis upon the importance of education—was "The Great Panacea," but something induced him to use the word *sociology* instead. He conceded that *sociology* was then a forbidding word, "snarled at by petty purists as illegitimate," and that the adjective *dynamic* was even more obscure.[19]

The title Ward finally chose is too narrow for his purpose. Indeed, the book, like the work of Comte and Spencer, is a positive philosophy, a synthetic philosophy, even a cosmic philosophy. He begins, however, with the observation that social phenomena exhibit uniformity and regularity and are therefore susceptible to scientific study. The classification of the sciences is important, and to this task he devotes attention. Science is moving in two principal directions: the first bringing more and more distantly related phenomena into some kind of a unified system, and the second establishing a hierarchy of the sciences. In the latter respect Ward follows Comte and places sociology at the top as the science that is most dependent upon the others, which in turn are least dependent upon it. There is no suggestion of reductionism in this arrangement; rather, sociology is the capstone of the sciences and the synthesis of them all.

If Sumner believed that men begin with acts, not thoughts, Ward gave the distinction of the *primum mobile* to feelings, not ideas. Men are moved by the power of sentiment, not intellect, and the religious sentiment is the most powerful of all. If religious reformers have been successful, it is due to their emotional nature, not to their intellectual supremacy.[20]

Sills (New York: Macmillan and the Free Press, 1968); ed. Henry Steele Commager, *Lester Ward and the Welfare State* (Indianapolis: Bobbs-Merrill, 1967); Alan F. Nelson, *The Development of Lester Ward's World View* (Fort Worth, Tex. Branch-Smith, 1968), and "Lester Ward's Conception of the Nature of Science," *Journal of the History of Ideas* 33 (October–December 1972): 633–638; and Charles H. Page, *Class and American Sociology: From Ward to Ross*, rev. ed (New York: Schocken Books, 1969).

18. 2 vols. (New York: D. Appleton & Co.). A second edition appeared in 1897. All page references in the text are to the second edition.

19. *Glimpses of the Cosmos*, vol. 3, p. 135; a history of the writing of the book, together with remarks by a few reviewers, appears at pp. 146–231.

20. Ward will later iron out an apparent inconsistency between this view and the importance that he ascribed to the "psychic factors in civilization."

> What I desire to draw attention to here is the remarkable fact that not only has the world been thus far ruled by passion and not by intellect, but that the true rulers of the world have had to be, in order to win that distinction, not merely enthusiasts and fanatics, but, in the majority of cases, insane persons, in a certain legitimate acceptation of that term.[21]

Intellect directs; it does not impel. It is feeling alone that drives "the social train," and all sociology must be informed by that ineluctable fact. This fact is nevertheless a paradoxical one. Religious feeling has moved the world but it has signally failed to improve it. It has produced an enormous amount of evil but only a small amount of demonstrable good. True progress can come only from the side of intellect, through the processes of natural selection that have preserved the highest and best. The problem now is to substitute artificial selection for natural selection, and what Ward means by this, one of his central theses, will become clear in the sequel.[22] What is really required, he says, is knowledge—defined as "truth apprehended by the intellect"—diffused throughout the masses of men by education. It is education, therefore, and scientific education that will teach us to utilize the forces of nature.

Early on Ward makes his famous distinction between the genetic forces of nature and the telic forces of man. It is his first sharp break with the Social Darwinism of Spencer and Sumner. The genetic forces of nature move too slowly and imperceptibly to be of much use in the improvement of society.[23] To them must be added the telic forces, the forces of human design. They are not antagonistic to the natural forces, but are rather a supplement to them. Natural forces can be neither created nor destroyed, but they can be controlled by human agency. Indeed, all that we call civilization is a result of such control. And here is the mistake made by those who defend the doctrine of laissez-faire. It is not true that society does better when it is left alone. Every mechanical invention is a supplement to a natural force and every act of legislation is an effort to control a natural force. The error is not only practical but it is also a logical contradiction. Those who decry governmental interference with the natural forces of

21. *Dynamic Sociology*, vol. 7, pp. 11–12.

22. If Ward had little use for the influence of a religious priesthood in the world, his skepticism extended also to an industrial or scientific "priesthood." Saint-Simon's Council of Newton was not for him.

23. As Richard Hofstadter observes in this connection:

> There is a certain touching irony in the thought that, while writers like these [Spencer and Sumner] preached slow change and urged men to adapt to the environment, the very millionaires whom they took to be the "fittest" in the struggle for existence were transforming the environment with incredible rapidity and rendering the values of the Spencers and Sumners of this world constantly less and less fit for survival.

Social Darwinism in American Thought, rev. ed. (Boston: Beacon Press, 1955), p. 12.

society on the ground that such interference only does harm are in fact conceding that such interference can do *something*, that it is not without an effect. Of course, much legislation has been harmful, and much government has been a failure. But that is because legislators have been "bunglers," ignorant of the laws of society, ignorant of the forces they sought to control. The remedy is sociology:

> No legislator is qualified to propose or vote on measures designed to affect the destinies of millions of social units until he masters all that is known of the science of society. Every true legislator must be a sociologist, and have his knowledge of that most intricate of all sciences founded upon organic and inorganic science. For the organic world is a product of the inorganic, and in its most general aspects is governed by the same laws, and man is at best but a highly organized animal, and is as fully under the dominion of biological laws as is the humblest worm. Society is ruled by the simple resultant of all the physical and physiological forces which control its members. How profound, then, and comprehensive, must be the science of sociology![24]

Dynamic sociology is thus synonymous with applied social science.

That society itself belongs to the domain of law seems to Ward to be something of a paradox:

> Last of all must we add the paradox that society itself is the domain of law, and that its movements, so far from being sporadic, irregular, and incapable of classification or prediction, are the strict determinable products of antecedent causes, which can be studied and known by man in the same way that the causes of physical phenomena have been studied and learned by him—by the scientific method. Although, when we consider particular acts of individuals or of communities, they seem to have emanated from their own arbitrary free will, and therefore, so far as science is concerned, to be purely fortuitous and incalculable, yet, when vast numbers of such acts are collected, co-ordinated, and tabulated, they are found to fall readily under a few general laws more or less modified by numerous special laws; proving that even this great field of nature belongs to Science the moment she sees fit to claim it.[25]

Thus society is a natural object, its motions determined by antecedent causes, its explanation susceptible to statement in general laws.[26] To this view, of course, all sociologists subscribe. Otherwise, there could be no

24. *Dynamic Sociology*, vol. 1, pp. 37–38.
25. *Ibid.*, pp. 50–51.
26. One is reminded of Gabriel Tarde's even more eloquent affirmation of this faith:

> When we travese the gallery of history, and observe its motley succession of fantastic paintings—when we examine in a cursory way the successive races of mankind, all different and constantly changing, our first impression is apt to be that the phenomena of social life are incapable of any general expression or scientific law, and that the attempt to found a system of sociology is wholly chimerical. But the first herdsmen who scanned the starry heavens, and the first tillers of the soil who essayed to discover the secrets of plant life, must have been impressed in much the same way

disciplined inquiry known as sociology, no science of society. Although it seems acceptable to us today, it was less so to the majority of Ward's contemporaries. Comte had launched a new kind of inquiry upon the world—a positive and therefore a scientific approach to society—and it was an inquiry that Ward, along with Spencer, was privileged to carry forward.

Why then should those who are best able to appreciate this view, who in fact have propounded it themselves, been so zealous in their addiction to laissez-faire? Surely one acquires knowledge of the physical universe in order to apply it to the benefit of mankind. The same can be said of knowledge of the social universe. Knowledge is acquired in order to be used. If we let society alone, there would be no such things as fire departments, post offices, public schools, or courts. For that matter, there would be no such thing as government. Competition itself can be free only when the monopolistic tendencies of private enterprise are restrained by government. Here, in short, is Ward's answer to Sumner, and it is a theme to which he returns again and again.

Even intellect is unsafe when left to itself. The barren systems of the metaphysicians provide ample proof. The intellect must be fortified with knowledge, not knowledge of thoughts but knowledge of things, and the only important knowledge therefore is scientific knowledge. Ward does not dismiss erudition, but it is education that rises to significance in his mind. Intelligence is more important than intellect; science, more than art; and knowledge, more than culture.[27] All progress is artificial, but *artificial* is a word to be praised, not demeaned. It means the application of sociological knowledge to the natural processes of society. That application is the task and destiny of the great science that is dynamic sociology. To predict in order to control, as Comte insisted, is the essence of science.

Despite Ward's respect for Comte, he finds his system full of fundamental and obtrusive errors, and to these he devotes a chapter.[28] Comte's style is voluminous, verbose, and unattractive. He provides no adequate account of what he means by "positive," as the last of his three stages. He is

---

> by the sparkling disorder of the firmament, with its manifold meteors, as well as by the exuberant diversity of vegetable and animal forms. The idea of explaining sky or forest by a small number of logically concatenated notions, under the name of astronomy or biology, had it occurred to them, would have appeared in their eyes the height of extravagance. And there is no less complexity—no less real irregularity and apparent caprice—in the world of meteors and in the interior of the virgin forest, than in the recesses of human history.

Social Laws, trans. Howard C. Warren (New York: Macmillan, 1899), pp. 1-2.

27. By *culture* Ward means refinement in art and letters and not the phenomena that wear that label in contemporary sociology.

28. "It is the misfortune of all truly great minds to be wedded to errors as well as to truths." *Dynamic Sociology,* vol. 1, p. 83.

disinclined to search for causes. He fails to perceive any difference between final causes and efficient causes. As a result of his "obstinate blindness" he multiplies problems beyond the finite capacities of men to solve them. He pays no attention to modern science and denies that the chemical constitution of the planetary bodies can be known even while Kirchhoff and Fraunhofer are discovering it. His classification of the sciences requires the kind of elaboration that he does not supply. He is insufficiently appreciative of the advances of biological science. He omits psychology entirely and confuses it with phrenology.[29] On the other hand, it was the great merit of Comte to make the discerning distinction between order and progress and to note the tension that obtains between them, that is, those who prefer order belittle progress and vice versa. Negatively again, Comte's views on the position of women in society are "simply execrable." Ward has a summary judgment, as follows:

> As the founder of the science of sociology, as the first to establish the true principle of the natural dependence of all the sciences, as the man who has thus far alone undertaken to classify the history of human thought according to the fundamental conditions of the mind, and to assign a generic name to all those intellectual processes which converge to develop the scientific method, and, finally, as the great pioneer champion of universal education, the one form of modification of social phenomena certain to result in benefits which can be scientifically predicted, the world is surely under heavy and lasting obligations to this somewhat erratic philosopher.[30]

Spencer also receives fairly high marks from Ward. There is no question that he is England's greatest philosopher, and England's best is almost always the world's best. It is Spencer's merit to have demonstrated the universality of evolution and to have made it the basis of all inquiry. Ward discusses *First Principles, The Principles of Biology, The Principles of Psychology,* and *The Data of Ethics. The Principles of Sociology* was unfinished at the time Ward was writing, and he is therefore able to describe the contents of only the first volume. This he does with appreciation, although he does not refrain from judging Spence's philosophy as a whole to be unsystematic, nonconstructive, and nonprogressive. He does not in this place criticize Spencer's doctrine of laissez-faire.

---

29. Ward regards phrenology as "systematic jugglery" and "itinerant charlatanism." Psychology also failed to win Ward's approval: "Psychology, on the other hand, besides being identified in its composition with all that is vague and unreal in human thought, is scarcely as yet emancipated from the fogs of mysticism, scholasticism, and metaphysical speculation." *Ibid.*, p. 124. It is useful to remember that Ward wrote these words before psychology won its independence from mental philosophy more than a decade before William James published his *Principles of Psychology* in 1890. In his later work he changed his mind about psychology and even contributed to the subject himself.

30. *Ibid.*, pp. 137–138.

The greater part of *Dynamic Sociology* is devoted to Ward's own cosmic and evolutionary philosophy. The key is aggregation, of which there are three degrees—primary, secondary, and tertiary. The first degree includes cosmogeny, or the genesis of matter; the second, biogeny, or the genesis of organic forms, psychogeny, or the genesis of mind, and anthropogeny, or the genesis of man. The third, sociogeny, or the genesis of society, is the continuation and culmination of the great process of aggregation. Society "in its literal or primary sense, is simply an association of individuals."[31] That man is by nature a social being, or was so originally, may be doubted. It is more likely that ancestral man was a creature of antisocial tendencies and of "irascible and quarrelsome disposition." Like other animals, he was in fierce rivalry with others for the possession of females. The race was perpetually embroiled in war, and man was indeed, in Hobbes's phrase, the wolf among men (*homo homini lupus est*). When he became a social being it was for the purpose of protection against others of his kind. There are four stages in the development of society—and here Ward's predilection for neologisms becomes apparent—(*a*) the solitary, or autarchic; (*b*) the constrained aggregate, or anarchic; (*c*) the national, or politarchic; and (*d*) the cosmopolitan, or pantarchic. The first of these is largely theoretical, and the last ideal. The second is a transitional stage, and thus the human race through most of its history has occupied the third, or politarchic, stage, possessed of government but still divided into nations. One may hope that some day there will be a universal government, that the fourth stage will be attained, but unfortunately diversities of language and nationalistic prejudice will delay its consummation.

Ward is now ready to discuss the social forces and produces a classification that today has only an antiquarian interest. He uses it so often, however, that we reproduce it here:

The Social Forces Are

- Essential Forces
  - Preservative Forces
    - Positive, gustatory (seeking pleasure)
    - Negative, protective (avoiding pain)
  - Reproductive Forces
    - Direct. The sexual and amative desires
    - Indirect. Parental and consanguineal affections
- Non-Essential Forces
  - Aesthetic Forces
  - Emotional (moral) Forces
  - Intellectual Forces[32]

---

31. *Ibid.*, p. 460.

32. This classification appears *ibid.*, p. 472. For a discussion, see Floyd Nelson House, "Ward's Classification of Social Forces," *American Journal of Sociology* 31 (1925–1926): 156–172.

This classification merits two comments. In the first place, it is neatly logical and thus conveys an aesthetic satisfaction. In the second place, Ward posits, or discovers, a physiological seat, locus, or base, for his forces. The locus of the nutritive appetites in the tongue, palate, and stomach is obvious, and so also the locus of the sexual appetite. The seat of the aesthetic forces is in the eye, ear, and nose; of the emotional forces (more difficult, as he concedes), in the nervous system; and of the intellectual forces, in the brain. Nutrition and sex are absolutely necessary, the one contributing to the survival of the individual and the other to the survival of the race. It is through the operation of these forces that society originates.

Of more than transitory interest is Ward's discussion of the three types of codes that arise in society—the civil, the social, and the moral. The civil code, obviously, is the law, including the edicts of despots and kings, the statutes of legislatures, and the decisions of courts. The social code consists of those limitations society imposes upon its members for the sake of propriety. Because of the importance of the social code I will quote Ward's view of the matter:

> What I understand by the *social code* is, that body of rules, limitations, and conditions which society has gradually built up to cause its members to observe *propriety* in all their acts. It embraces all the forms and conventionalities of society, covers the whole field of fashion and appearances, and aims to enforce uniformity, regularity, and consistency between the acts and the circumstances, and to abolish all eccentricity and indecency. Although a *lex non scripta*, it is, if possible, more inexorable than the edicts of despots or the statutes of states. The feeling experienced in its violation is more intolerable than any corporal punishment or personal confinement. It prevails in all countries and all forms of society, although so whimsical and irrational is it that often what is violation of it in one country or age is obedience to it in another. Although supposed to be confined to indifferent actions, its boundaries often encroach so far over upon the territory of civil law on the one hand, and moral law on the other, that it should not be omitted in a consideration of the self-imposed limitations of society. Actions are constantly passing backward and forward from one to another of these three codes, according to the age and degree of intelligence of the society in which they are performed.[33]

These, of course, are Sumner's folkways. His mores Ward describes as follows:

> The *moral code* is designed to limit the members of society in the commission of actions which tend to cause pain or deprive of pleasure. All unwritten as it is, it has assumed the most definite form, and acquired a powerful binding

33. *Dynamic Sociology*, vol. 1, p. 515.

force. Like both the others, it has been a growth, and has arisen out of the wants and necessities of society, and like the social code it is exceedingly capricious, changing, and irrational in many of its mandates. That it is not a natural system, owing its sanction to an unerring monitor called conscience, I shall hereafter endeavor to show.[34]

Like Sumner, Ward fails to distinguish adequately between the social code and the moral code, except that the first has to do with eccentricity and indecency, and the second with pain and pleasure. Both are crescive, to use Sumner's word, both are unwritten, and both, to use a more modern idiom, exhibit the principle of cultural relativity. In both, the sanctions applied to nonconformity are clear.

How then, despite the operation of the codes, does it happen that inequities and injustices arise among men? Why does poverty increase among the many while property accumulates in the hands of the few?[35] The part that indolence can play is very small; indeed, it is the poorest people in the world who are the most industrious. Nor can the difference be attributed to the superior intelligence of the rich. The ability to accumulate wealth is in fact one of the "coarsest and cheapest of all mental attributes," and the pleasure it confers is a sordid one. One might be inclined to attribute it to avarice, which is one of the preservative forces and thus a natural force. But what is natural is not necessarily ethical. The answer to the problem of inequity must be sought in another place. It resides in the inequalities of circumstance, in bare fortuity and accidental coincidence, including the accident of birth. Nature itself is unfeeling, in this situation as in others:

> No merit which may be supposed to inhere in superiority of mind, not even of the sordid passion and talent of money-getting; nay, not even the questionable merit of superior brute-force, can enter here to palliate the state of things. We see only the cold, feelingless fingers of natural law as it rides in its icy chariot through the universe. We get a foretaste of the inexorable character of Nature, and find ourselves more ready to believe her capable of blotting out our central source of light and warmth and life, and quenching, in her slow,

34. *Ibid.*, pp. 515–516.

35. *Ibid.*, p. 517n:

> Under the natural, or spontaneous, system of society, the accumulation of wealth proceeds in a manner exactly the reverse of that best suited to the true advancement of social and individual welfare. Instead of its equitable distribution in proportion to the amount each contributes to its production, it tends to concentrate in the hands of those who produce least. Equity would require that the difficulty in obtaining wealth should increase in some direct ratio to the amount obtained. In fact, the difficulty rapidly diminishes as the amount increases. Equity would require that the extra burdens produced by unforeseen events should be chiefly borne by those who have already an abundance. They are ultimately borne by the laborer who has little or nothing. In most countries even taxation, which one would suppose must necessarily be drawn from capital, is in great part drawn directly from labor in the form of duties, or imposts, on articles of universal consumption.

> imperial way, all the vitality, feeling, thought, and intelligence which have been evolved. When we reflect upon these immense sociological facts, we realize more and more that there is a dark side to the picture presented by the operations of the preservative force, we see more and more clearly that in its grand career of development civilization has left a blackened trail and smoking ruins in the domain of feeling.[36]

Thus eloquently does Ward warm to one of his major themes. Nature, when let alone, produces neither justice nor equity. He seizes the opportunity to criticize Spencer's distinction between militant and industrial societies. Even the so-called militant societies require industry. He also, without reference to Marx, gives direct expression to a labor theory of value: "Civilization is the result of human labor, guided by thought," and "All value is the result of labor."[37]

Throughout his discussion Ward expresses angry opinions about those who through cunning or other means amass wealth and live in luxury. They are parasites upon society. To this same parasitic class he assigns the priesthood.[38] There is no more successful mode of acquisition than the ecclesiastical, and most of the world is a victim of this "costly superstition." Ward is especially irked that those who enjoy the products of labor, without themselves contributing, consider themselves a superior class and look down upon the humble artisan and peasant. The power that produces inequality is of four kinds—military, political, sacerdotal, and speculative—by the last of which Ward means the power that results in monopoly. Thus arise the evils of society. It is the task of sociology to find the remedy, to use such measures as will prevent the advancement of a small class at the expense of a larger one. So much for the operation of the preservative forces of society.

If the preservative forces serve the individual, the reproductive forces serve the species; the one operates for the present, the other for the future. Ward apologizes for having to treat the subject of reproduction, but science (even an infant science such as sociology) cannot defer to delicate sentiments. His system would not be complete without it, and furthermore all truth is dignified. What is Darwin's *The Descent of Man* but a treatise on the sexual relations of mankind, and no one deems his treatment to be im-

---

36. *Ibid.*, pp. 523–524.
37. *Ibid.*, p. 542.
38. *Ibid.*, p. 589:

> The reign of this parasitic hierarchy still continues all over the world; and still, to-day, the hard labor of the masses, just saving a subsistence, is paying its tithes to the support of this great non-industrial class, and for the erection of costly edifices which the state exempts from taxation, and which serve no other purpose than to be opened once in each week that honors may be paid and anthems sung to imaginary deities.

proper. Thus, Ward is able to tell us that the organs of reproduction may be considered under two aspects, one as the seat of a special kind of desire and the other as the means of continuing the race. These two functions are independent and distinct. "There is even less relation discernible between the sexual desire and the procreative function than between taste and digestion."[39] Sexual love, a sentiment diffused in man throughout the nervous system, can never be impure, however, because it is indissolubly connected with the perpetuation of life. Sexual selection, exercised by the female in the animal kingdom and originally by the female also in the human species, has been reversed in the latter, and now it is male selection that rules. It is Ward's hope that woman will be able to regain her "lost scepter" and once more dominate the male in this important domain of activity. This is one of his repeated assertions, one that encourages him to demand sexual equality and to attribute superiority to the female of the species. Modesty has its source in fear, fear that male rivals for the sexual favors of the female will interfere with the consummation of the sexual act. Of course it is now overlaid by custom and supports the idea of propriety. "The essence of propriety is conformity to custom,"[40] but there is no necessary relation, in human society, between custom and either reason or justice. It is the sentiment of modesty and the sanction of shame that accounts for the origin of clothing. Variations in the latter, however, are so great that when we enter the realm of fashion we are subjected to a reign that is despotic because it can condemn anything or sanction anything in independence of reason.

Ward was disturbed by the inequalities between the sexes—inequalities that operate to the detriment of women. He discusses these inequalities under four rubrics: inequality of dress,[41] inequality of duties,[42] inequality of education,[43] and inequality of rights.[44] Discrimination on the ground of

39. *Ibid.*, p. 602.

40. *Ibid.*, p. 636.

41. "The dress of men is not in all respects what it should be, but that of women is certainly the disgrace of civilization." *Ibid.*, p. 643.

42. "If we grant that there is a certain natural connection between the bearing of offspring and the care of the household, which is probably true, there remains a chasm to be filled in order to equalize the duties of the two sexes"; "If this vicious dogma that woman's place is in the house is persisted in for a few more centuries, there can be no escape from a general physical and intellectual degeneracy of the whole human race." *Ibid.*, pp. 643–644, 645.

43. "Not content with shutting woman out of all opportunities for gaining knowledge by experience, society has seen fit to debar her also from the knowledge acquired by instruction"; if men seem to be superior in intellectual achievement, it is because in women "the spirit has been crushed and the opportunity denied." *Ibid.*, p. 645, 646.

44. "In all civilized societies women have been discriminated against and they are banned altogether from matters relating to law and government. They are without voice, vote, or representation." *Ibid.*, p. 646.

sex is a scandal that deserves the attention of every thoughtful student of society. The relationship between the sexes has become a castelike relationship, with men undeservedly in the superior position. Ward is eloquent on this subject:

> The broad recognition of the social equality of the sexes has never been distinctly and practically made. All pretensions to it have been contradicted by the treatment of women, by their exclusion from the most honorable forms of labor, and by withholding from them social, civil, and political rights. To affirm that women are the recognized social equals of men is to betray the prevalent incapacity to see the plainest facts in a rational or abstract light, the inability to see them in any but a conventional light.[45]

He looks forward to the time, therefore, when men and women will wear more nearly the same kind of clothing, perform the same kinds of work, reap the benefits of the same kind of education, and enjoy the same civil rights (including the control of their own bodies). The emancipation of women is long overdue. Civilization demands it.

Ward gives less space to the nonessential social forces—the aesthetic, the moral, and the intellectual. They give him an opportunity, however, to discuss the visual arts (sculpture, painting, landscape gardening, and architecture), music, parental love, consanguineal love, patriotism, philanthropy, and fear (of violence, of man, of animals, of inanimate nature, of spiritual beings, of disease, and of death). The doctrine of immortality, incidentally, is a pernicious one, and one that has retarded the progress of thought. In his concluding remarks, Ward laments the condition of sociology in which the discovery of principles has fallen so far behind the accumulation of facts. Finally, the time has come when human foresight must gain control over the blind forces of nature. This must happen if civilization itself is not to be imperiled. And it is the task of a dynamic sociology.

In his second volume Ward devotes separate chapters to such subjects as happiness, progress, dynamic action, dynamic opinion, education, and knowledge. It would be a mistake to think that there is no logical connection between them. On the contrary, happiness is the purpose of conation; progress, the means to happiness; dynamic action, the means to progress; dynamic opinion, the means to dynamic action; knowledge, the means to dynamic opinion; and education, the means to knowledge. These, in essence, are the "theorems" he intends to establish. It is not necessary to pursue him in their establishment because they have a certain musty, not to

45. *Ibid.*, p. 650.

say archaic, character. I shall, however, mention points on which he is especially incisive or those, including the former, that have an especial relevance to current concerns in sociological theory.

At the outset he demands that society take seriously the artificial improvement of its condition. Here again it is necessary to note that he is using the word *artificial* in a now obsolete sense. He means not something fictitious, factitious, supposititious, spurious, inauthentic, or, as in Shakespeare's "artificial tears," an imitation of reality. He means something produced by human artifice, human skill, human labor, and human knowledge. Without mentioning John Stuart Mill, he nevertheless agrees with him that everything that mankind has accomplished is a result not of submission to nature but of a victory over nature.[46] The attitude that man should assume toward nature is not one of awe and wonder but one that disposes him to rule, direct, and control its forces.[47] Civilization itself is the artificial adjustment of natural objects in a way to produce results beneficial to man.[48]

Ward adopts a Benthamite view of the importance of pleasure and pain. Indeed, "feeling" is the foundation stone of the social sciences. "What function is to biology, feeling is to sociology." The five primary stimuli to progress in the human race are the pleasures associated with nutrition, reproduction, physical exercise, taste, and the uses of the intellect. Taken together they may be subsumed under the general term "happiness."[49] It is

46. Mill's *Auguste Comte and Positivism* (1866) is mentioned in Ward's bibliography, but his essay "Nature," which was written some time between 1850 and 1858 and published in 1873, is not. In this essay Mill uses the word *artificial* in the same sense. Thus, "if the artificial is not better than the natural, to what end are all the arts of life? To dig, to plough, to build, to wear clothes, are direct infringements of the injunction to follow nature," and "the sentiment of justice is entirely of artificial origin." See "Nature," in *Three Essays on Religion* (New York: Henry Holt & Co., 1874), pp. 20, 52.

47. Here Ward encourages us to accept his opposition to any theistic view of the universe. He expresses his approval of Laplace who when asked how he could write so great a work as *Mécanique Célèste* without mentioning the Author of the universe replied, "Je n'avais pas besoin de cette hypothèse-là" *Dynamic Sociology*, vol. 2, p. 7n. Indeed, Ward uses the word *religionists* with contempt. *Ibid.*, p. 114. For a long, learned, and hostile disquisition on religion, see *ibid.*, pp. 252–306.

48. *Ibid.*, p. 205.

49. *Ibid.*, p. 123.

> There is an apparent incongruity between the doctrine, on the one hand, that progress consists essentially and solely in the elevation of the feelings, the increase of pleasure, the elimination of pain, the intensification of sentiment, the creation and diffusion of new enjoyments, the encouragement of natural emotions, the gratification of the normal instincts, the satisfaction of desire, and the general pursuit of happiness; and the doctrine, on the other hand, that progress is to be attained solely through the cultivation of the intellect, the acquisition of knowledge, and the thorough and universal dissemination and enforced adoption of educational measures for the elevation and systematic development of the cold, objective faculties of the mind. To bring these two seemingly incoherent and incongruous doctrines into harmony, and to show the true

clearly in the nature of the universe that men should aim their endeavors at happiness rather than virtue, although the latter may be assigned a role in the attainment of the former. Ward has two definitions of progress, both of which are of more than incidental interest. The first is "success in harmonizing natural phenomena with human advantage," and the second, italicized, "whatever increases the sum total of human happiness."[50] He believes further that a state of stagnation is impossible. Every society is either advancing or receding. In anticipation of a future thesis, he asserts that social phenomena differ from biological phenomena in that a new force—an intellectual force—supervenes. Religion and government (especially laissez-faire government) are nonprogressive forces in society, whereas language, literature, the mechanical arts, and the exact sciences are progressive. The fine arts, however enjoyable in themselves, do not contribute to progress and thus belong "entirely to the department of social statics."[51] Ward expresses a certain skepticism about necessary and inevitable stages in the evolution of mankind, a thesis accepted by many if not most of the Social Darwinists:

> The great diversity now known to exist among the various low races of men still inhabiting certan parts of the globe has greatly shaken faith in the chronological order in which early writers assumed that man had successively sought his subsistence, viz., the existence of the hunting, pastoral, and agricultural stages.[52]

Inasmuch as Ward lists government among the nonprogressive forces of society, his remarks on this subject merit a modicum of attention. Members of the human race, unlike other gregarious animals, require protection against themselves. Their insatiable efforts to satisfy their desires infringe upon the similar efforts of others. Thus, government has three functions—protection, accommodation, and amelioration. Protection is self-explanatory. By accommodation Ward means the use of government to conduct the business of society. This, in brief, is a management function. As to amelioration, this is a function that government has so far failed to

---

> mechanical dependence of the one upon the other, as cause and effect, is one of the primary objects of this work.

Ibid., pp. 129–130. The manner in which he does this is, as Ward says, diffused throughout the work. Here he is content to suggest that the end of both individual and collective being is to administer to the feelings, but this can be accomplished only through the cultivation of the intellect.

50. *Ibid.*, pp. 108, 161.
51. *Ibid.*, p. 192.
52. *Ibid.*, p. 196.

perform. Society itself, incidentally, has nothing to do with protection. Society is "simply the gregarious condition of the human race, enbued with their natural passions and affections." Ward dismisses entirely the "noble savage" notions of Rousseau and Fénelon and dismisses also Aristotle's affirmation that man is a social being. "Civilized man is undoubtedly a social being, but this quality has been the result of a long and severe experience by which a great change has been produced in his constitution. Not only so, but he is utterly incapable of social existence in a native state, unless protected in his life, his liberty, and his property by an artificial system of government."[53] Unfortunately, the function of protection has too often been assumed—even usurped—by those who claim to be public benefactors but whose only interest is the exercise of power. And here is the paradox of government—that an institution whose original and ostensible function was protection has so often destroyed the liberties of those it presumed to protect. An ideal government would be the exact opposite of all existing ones. All governments, furthermore, have been "andrarchies," excluding one-half of the human race from participation. "It would be far better were every second individual excluded without regard to sex, since then there would be equilibrium."[54] It is time, in any event, for government to utilize scientific knowledge in order to harness the natural forces for the good of society.

In view of the fact that progress can be brought about only by actions, Ward finds it necessary to classify them in a chapter devoted to the subject. Inasmuch as, in a later period, Znaniecki and Parsons also laid strong emphasis upon actions, although from an entirely different perspective, the classification is of some contemporary interest. Ward's classification is reproduced in Figure 2.1. It is ingenius but not, it must be said, useful.[55] His detailed discussion includes disquisitions on virtue and vice, guilt and innocence, and reward, punishment, and responsibility. His treatment includes both moral actions and those devoid of moral quality. There is no evidence that Sorokin consulted Ward for his work on altruism (a word, incidentally, coined by Comte), but Ward has several sophisticated observations on the subject: "There is a certain *luxury of altruism* in which some persons indulge to the verge of dissipation," and it can become a "morbid sentiment" that deprives individuals of the "wholesome egoistic pursuits

53. *Ibid.*, pp. 219, 221.

54. *Ibid.*, p. 23.

55. For Znaniecki's classification, see *Social Actions* (New York: Farrar & Rinehart, 1936). See also Leopold von Wiese, "A Systematic Classification of Interhuman Action Patterns," in *Systematic Sociology*, adapted and amplified by Howard Becker (New York: John Wiley & Sons, 1932), pp. 123–138 and chart on p. 124. For Sorokin's classification, see *Society, Culture, and Personality* (New York: Harper & Row, 1947), pp. 43–47.

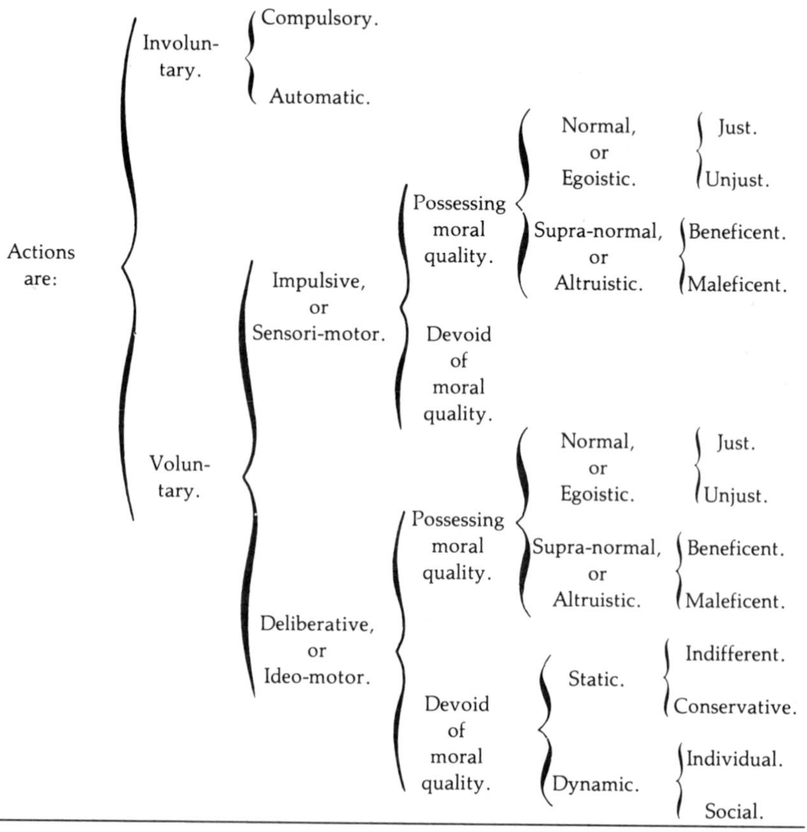

Figure 2.1. Ward's classification of actions. (Reproduced from *Dynamic Sociology*, vol. 2, p. 314.)

which nature properly demands of them."[56] Ethical codes are a product of society, and they are supported by automatic sanctions:

> Even the least deviation from the path of rectitude is, in developed social centers, a signal for ostracism, the withdrawal of esteem, systematic avoidance, and all the other forms of punishment which render life intolerable, and demonstrate the completely compulsory character of the ethical code. It is a code which enforces itself, and therefore requires no priesthood and no manual. And strangely enough, here, where alone *laissez faire* is sound doctrine, we find the *laissez faire* school calling loudly for "regulation."[57]

56. *Dynamic Sociology*, vol. 2, p. 370n.
57. *Ibid.*, p. 373.

Attention is especially invited to the last sentence—a point also elaborated upon by MacIver.

On another ethical matter, Ward considers the obligations that children owe to their parents.[58] His answer is that they owe none whatever. They were conceived, after all, in gratification of a sensual desire, with no thought of the consequences. His criticism of the Ten Commandments induces reflection even today. He indulges in it without iconoclasm but only to indicate that all but three of them are religious rather than ethical in character and to suggest that it is easy to confound the two. Confusion also exists between the codes of convention and of morality (etiquette being an example of the former), and yet they are so related that the distinction gradually disappears. The only test is "to determine if possible whether injury has really been done to any one, a test which is usually very difficult of application."[59]

In his chapter on "Knowledge" Ward is constrained to argue, among many other things, that there are no class differences in intelligence and that such differences as may be discerned in knowledge are entirely due to differences in opportunity. The same conclusion can be reached about urban–rural differences. The progress that civilization has exhibited is due not to any increase in the capacity for knowledge but to an increasingly correct interpretation of experience. The criteria for the importance of knowledge are two—generality and practicality. "To know one's environment is to possess the most real, the most practical, the most useful of all kinds of knowledge, and, properly viewed, this class of information constitutes the only true knowledge."[60] His pragmatic stance—although he does not use the adjective—is apparent in his insistence that the only object of knowledge is in what it enables us to do. Philosophy, which should be constituted of the most general and useful kind of knowledge, is for the most part nothing but "intellectual gymnastic." On a methodological matter, Ward asks himself how truth can be distinguished from error. The answer is that no proposition can be accepted that is not subject to verification. The verification proceeds from two sources: the senses on the one hand and reason on the other.[61] The remainder of the chapter deals with such subjects as ethical knowledge, dynamic knowledge, the principles of

58. This, it will be remembered, was one of the subjects that he debated in his youth.

59. *Ibid.*, p. 456.

60. "While we were not present when the upheavals took place which raised the strata of the Alps to their present position, rational deductions from a thousand facts converge so irresistibly to the theory of their submarine origin that it must be regarded as a verified truth." *Ibid.*, p. 417.

61. *Ibid.*, p. 496.

certitude, the difference between deductive and inductive knowledge, the nature of judgment, and the distribution of knowledge.

The final chapter of the book, on education, is a condensation of a longer treatise that Ward wrote on the subject in 1873. Inasmuch as the final end of man is the increase and organization of happiness, it is now necessary to substitute successful means for the unsuccessful means used in the past. The ultimate means to the more equal distribution of knowledge is education. Education, which has been inadequately defined by such writers as Bain, Mill, and Spencer, is "a system for extending to all the members of society such of the extant knowledge of the world as may be deemed important."[62] There are five kinds of education: (*a*) education of experience; (*b*) education of discipline; (*c*) education of culture; (*d*) education of research; and (*e*) education of information.[63] Along the way, Ward indulges in a defense of theory as opposed to practical research:

> Contrary to the received opinion, the tendency of the mind is to original research and practical application. So great is this mental bias, that such research and application are being constantly undertaken without due preparation. The superficiality which should be complained of is that which narrows down to practical things before a sufficient foundation has been laid in theoretical preparation. . .
>
> It is this same false conception of the practical which causes society to regard the mere collectors of scientific facts as the true scientific men, while treating the organizers of those facts and those alone who put them to any use as theorists to be looked upon with suspicion.[64]

So far as research is concerned, Ward is opposed to the "detailed elaboration of every conceivable subject and the pursuit of minutiae," which are characteristic of the German university.

The system of education to be constructed must be public and not private. Private education is worse than useless because it increases rather than reduces the inequalities that exist in society. In public education nothing matters—not birth, rank, or station—except the quality of the pupil's mind itself, and thus the "lowest gamin of the street" can meet the "pampered son of opulence" in a situation of strict equality. Ward is thus a

62. *Ibid.*, p. 569.

63. Without especially noting it, Ward here takes a reductionist position on psychology:

> Rigidly defined, psychology and physiology are one, and that one is physiology. But practically they are distinct. So doubtless every intellectual process is a physiological one, and every registered impression results from an alteration more or less permanent of the matter of the organ of thought.

Ibid., pp. 563–564. There is no mention of David Hartley's great work, *Observations on Man, His Frame, His Duty, and His Expectations* (1746), although Ward does refer to Hartley in another connection in *Pure Sociology*, p. 153.

64. *Dynamic Sociology*, vol. 2, pp. 552–553.

champion of universal, free, and public education.[65] And once more he denies, with emphasis, that there are class differences in intelligence. There is no excellence without opportunity, and it is opportunity that the state must provide. "It is just this initial circumstance, this vision of the promised land, that education is specially adapted to furnish to those naturally bright minds whom fortune has restricted to dark and narrow regions." It is unfortunately necessary to add that universal education means the education of women as well as men. "The position of women in human society is so absurdly anomalous that whatever is intended to include them must have this particularly expressed, else it will be apt to be inferred that they are excluded."[66]

Ward cannot discuss the matter, means, and methods of education in these "already swollen volumes," but he manages to indulge in a few observations on all three. With respect to matter, for example, we have the earnest, although sensibly qualified, sentiment that "every thing that has been known by man should be made known to all men." With respect to means, the emphasis is upon reading, writing, and calculation. They are the doors to all else. And with respect to method, it is necessary to create a demand for education, a desire to know. Finally, and once again in answer to the laissez-faire doctrines of the Social Darwinists:

> All social progress is artificial. It is the consequence of teleological foresight, design, and intellectual labor, which are processes diametrically opposed in principle to the processes of nature. If in learning the law of evolution we must apply it to society, it would have been better to have remained ignorant of that law. In passing from the policy of inaction due to the belief that Providence is alone able to act, to the policy of inaction due to the belief that Nature is alone able to act, we have gained nothing. As well worship the old god as the new one.[67]

This is the theme he reiterates in his conclusion.[68]

---

65. He anticipates a criticism of his work in that he deals so little with economic problems. The reason is that an equal distribution of knowledge is the initial means to achieve an equal distribution of wealth. "It is high time for socialists to perceive that, as a rule, they are working at the roof instead of at the foundation of the structure which they desire to erect." *Ibid.*, p. 597.

66. *Ibid.*, pp. 613, 614.

67. *Ibid.*, p. 628.

68. Needless to say, Spencer did not agree. In a letter to Ward of July 2, 1883, acknowledging receipt of the two volumes of *Dynamic Sociology*, he noted that Ward had more faith in a constructive social philosophy than he had and that he regarded progress as a matter of character rather than of knowledge or enlightenment. The letter is reprinted in *Glimpses of the Cosmos*, vol. 3, pp. 213–214. For additional correspondence with Spencer, see the exchange of letters twelve years later reprinted in *Pure Sociology*, pp. 66–69, this time a disagreement about the classification of the sciences.

The Psychic Factors of Civilization

This second of Ward's books appeared in 1893.[69] It occurred to him that in *Dynamic Sociology* he had underestimated the importance of psychology, and he now wanted to repair the defect. He regarded it as an essential part of his system of "social philosophy" (his label) and wanted to emphasize again the superiority of the telic over the genetic processes of society. He expresses the general intent:

> If it cannot be shown that society is a domain of true natural forces the claim to the possibility of a social science must be abandoned. Supposing such a claim to be sustained, if it cannot be shown that social phenomena can be controlled as physical phenomena are controlled by a knowledge of the laws according to which they occur, the hope of improving the social condition of man as his physical condition has been improved must be given up.[70]

It might be said that these two sentences contain the essence of Ward's sociological theory.

The book, however, is inferior in quality to *Dynamic Sociology.* Most of its thirty-eight chapters are quite brief, and in no case do they present an exhaustive—or even a satisfactory—analysis of the subjects with which they deal. All except the last six are concerned with psychology, and the treatment as a whole cannot stand comparison with William James's great *Principles of Psychology,* published three years earlier, in 1890.[71] He attends to such matters as might fall variously under the rubrics of epistemology, mental philosophy, and psychology, including the nature of mind, sensations, perceptions, the conative faculty,[72] pleasure and pain, the soul,[73] desire, the will, pessimism, happiness, feeling, judgment, invention, and genius. The influence of Schopenhauer is heavy in Ward's treatment of the will.

The brief chapter on "Social Action" is typical of the book. It begins with the observation that the history of man is the history of what man has done. It is therefore the history of action and, since man is social, of social

---

69. All references are to the second edition (Boston: Ginn & Co., 1906).

70. *Psychic Factors,* p. 2.

71. There is no reference to James in the book, but references to him appear in Ward's later writings.

72. It may be recalled that psychology before William James was the study of the mind and its three "faculties"—the intellect, the emotions, and the will.

73. Ward is not using this concept in any theological or metaphysical sense. He defines it as "the collective feelings of organic beings and their resultant efforts." *Ibid.,* p. 46. One is reminded of a now forgotten book, the title page of which contains these words: "The Human Soul: With 128 diagrams and illustrations."

action. The laws and principles of action belong to sociology. Man, inferior to the other animals in most respects, has nevertheless been able to transform his environment and attain mastery because of the superiority of his mind. Civilization can be achieved only through the actions of individuals. Society itself, as yet, has no end; the soul of society is not yet born. Society is only an idea—a Platonic idea—and it exists only for the good of the individual. No one personifies society, or endows it with wants and passions; nevertheless, it is proper to speak of improving society, which means improving the conditions of its individual members. The evils that individuals suffer can legitimately be attributed to the "constitution" of society. Social reformers are therefore necessary, indeed "natural" products of every age, and those who scorn them are guilty of absurdity.[74]

The title of the book—and Ward's thesis—becomes clear when he informs us that the mind is the motor force of social change and that the social forces are essentially psychic. That is why sociology must be based upon psychology, and not, as many writers assume, on biology, where the dynamics are in vital rather than in psychic forces. Comte and Spencer are the writers to whom Ward refers. In sum:

> Upon biology it [sociology] can only rest unconformably [uncomfortably?[75]] and precariously, since it is felt that there is a causal hiatus between them, but upon psychology it rests naturally and safely, since, as has been shown, the dynamic department of psychology becomes also that of sociology the moment we rise from the individual to society. The social forces are the psychic forces as they operate in the collective state of man.[76]

These passages are interesting because not only Comte and Spencer but also Durkheim, more dogmatically, denied the relevance of psychology to the explanation of social phenomena.[77]

---

74. Here he catches Sumner in a paradox, not to say a contradiction:

> In his severe condemnation of the "friends of humanity," as he sneeringly calls all who believe in the attainment through human effort of a higher social state, he seems to forget that these very troublesome persons are merely products of society and *natural.* To hear him, remembering his premises, one would suppose that these men either had invaded the world from some outer planet or had artificially created themselves. But they belong to society as much as the hated paupers and worthless invalids whom he would turn over to nature. Why then not let them alone? Why meddle with the natural course of things? In fact what is the *raison d'être* of this earnest book that wants to have so much done? On his own theory, the author should let his deluded victims alone.

From Ward's review of Sumner's *What Social Classes Owe to Each Other, ibid.*, p. 100n.

75. In tribute to Ward and his publishers, it must be said that his many volumes are almost entirely free of typographical errors. Indeed, this is the only one the writer has noticed.

76. *Ibid.*, p. 123.

77. With respect to Comte and Spencer:

> Comte recognized the influence of mind in society and placed psychology in its proper position in his hierarchy of the sciences, but he refused to regard it as a distinct science, and treated it under

The third and last part of *Psychic Factors* is called "Social Synthesis of the Factors"; in this Ward breaks sharply with the Social Darwinists in denying a basic point that in the struggle for existence only the fittest survive. This may be true in the economics of animal development, where it is better expressed as the best adapted structures survive, but on the human level it is wholly false. "The effect of competition is to prevent any form from attaining its maximum development, and to maintain a certain comparatively low level of development for all forms that succeed in surviving."[78] Because of the rhythmic character of natural phenomena, what is gained in the flood tide is lost in the ebb. Protected plants, liike cereals and fruit trees, and domestic animals, gain more than the wild of their kind. Competition therefore not only involves enormous waste but also prevents maximum development. On this Ward is expansive and insistent:

> All human institutions—religion, government law, marriage custom—together with innumerable modes of regulating social, industrial, and commercial life, are, broadly viewed, only so many ways of meeting and checkmating the principle of competition as it manifests itself in society. And finally, the ethical code and the moral law of enlightened man are nothing else than the means adopted by reason, intelligence, and refined sensibility for suppressing and crushing out the animal nature of man—for chaining the competitive egoism that all men have inherited from their animal ancestors.[79]

In no sense—once mind is applied to nature—do only the fittest of human organisms survive.

Without making much of a point of it, Ward essays a distinction between two kinds of groups in society. The first kind is such organized groups as corporations, companies, associations, sects, and churches, distinguished by the fact that they do not include all of the inhabitants of a given territory. The second, which he calls universal or complete, include all of the inhabitants in a given territory. The former kind are heterogeneous in purpose; the latter have the single function of promoting the general good of

---

the name of "transcendental biology." Nevertheless, in his discussions he gave considerable weight to it, and laid stress on the elements of prevision and the control of social phenomena. Spencer, on the contrary, while he treated psychology at length and assigned it the same position, namely, between biology and sociology, failed to make it in any proper sense the basis of either his sociology or his ethics, both of which are made to rest squarely upon biology. His psychology, therefore, which indeed was written before his biology, and largely from the standpoint of metaphysics, stands isolated and useless in his system of synthetic philosophy.

Ibid., pp. 242–243. Durkheim's views are expressed most emphatically in his *The Rules of Sociological Method* (1895).

78. *Psychic Factors*, p. 260.

79. *Ibid.*, p. 262.

their members. The prime and perhaps the sole example of the latter is government, although, as he says, the words *state* or *nation* may be substituted. And here he slips intentionally into the biological analogy, which permits him to discuss "the social will" and "the social intellect."[80]

The last chapter in *Psychic Factors* is entitled "Sociocracy." Sociocracy, of course, is for Ward a form of government superior to all others. He repeats his criticisms of laissez-faire, which he regards as practically a kind of anarchy. Present governments, whether democracies or monarchies, have done little except to serve as the guardians of the rights of property and to encourage the concentration of wealth into fewer and fewer hands. Meanwhile, social evils increase—starvation, drudgery, misery, squalor, disease, and premature death for those who labor. It is a "vast theater of woe," which government ignores. "The ignoring of great evils while so violently striking at small ones is the mark of an effete civilization, and warns us of the approaching dotage of the race."[81] Sociocracy will change all that. The individual has ruled long enough. It is now time for society to take charge.

Outlines of Sociology

Ward published his *Outlines of Sociology* in 1898 and dedicated it to Albion W. Small, who, he says, was the first to draw attention to his philosophy.[82] It consists of a series of 12 lectures that he gave at the Hartford Society for Education Extension in 1894 and 1895, each of which was published in successive issues of the *American Journal of Sociology*, beginning with its first issue in July 1895. The first six lectures, under the title of "Social Philosophy," treat of such matters as the place of sociology among the sciences, the relation of sociology to cosmology, biology, anthropology, psychology, and the data of sociology. The second six, under the title of "Social Science," treat the social forces, the mechanics of society, the purpose of sociology, social genesis, individual telesis, and collective telesis.

The book contains little that Ward has not said before. We need to note only a few points. He adopts the classification of the sciences used by

80. Once more, as in Sumner, we find an appreciation of the unintended consequences of purposive social action: "Laws are enacted which do not accomplish their purpose; some of them have effects which are the opposite of those which were intended. Numbers of them have to be repealed because they are found injurious." *Ibid.*, p. 301.

81. *Ibid.*, p. 320.

82. Quotations are from the reprint edition of 1899 (New York: Macmillan).

Comte, namely, a logical procession of astronomy, physics, chemistry, biology, and sociology. Like Spencer, however, he places psychology between biology and sociology. By the data of sociology he appears to mean the knowledge furnished by the sciences, and especially psychology. He adheres, somewhat inconsistently, to the notion of stages in human evolution—savagery, barbarism, civilization. He used the word *institutions* to include language, customs, governments, religions, industries, art, and literature and remarks that the study of these constitutes "real history," as contrasted with the study of battles, migrations, and "the vicissitudes of empire." He distinguishes between the natural history of man and the history of culture and uses the latter word in its contemporary sense. Sociology is a general, not a special, social science. The special social sciences provide data for sociology, which is the synthesis of them all. Inasmuch as the pursuit of sociology requires so much prior knowledge, it is best to consider it a postgraduate course, or at least not to introduce it before the final year of the undergraduate curriculum.

Although Ward retains some skepticism about the efficacy of mathematics and mathematical methods as applied to such complex phenomena as mind, life, and society, he nevertheless believes that scientific laws attain perfection when they are expressed in mathematical form. Once again he follows Comte in distinguishing between social statics and social dynamics—the former treats social order; the latter, social progress. The book ends with a paean to sociocracy, by which, as we have seen, he means the scientific control of the social forces by the collective mind of society. If individualism creates artificial inequalities, and socialism artificial equalities, sociocracy, different from both, recognizes natural inequalities and aims to abolish artificial inequalities. Finally, "sociocracy would confer benefits in strict proportion to merit, but insists upon *equality of opportunity* as the only means of determining the degree of merit."[83] One can hardly imagine a more benign social philosophy.

Pure Sociology[84]

Ward began writing *Pure Sociology* on January 1, 1901, and therefore dedicated it "To the Twentieth Century." He conceived of it, together with *Applied Sociology*, as a system of sociology, and the entire corpus of his

83. *Ibid.*, p. 293.

84. Published in 1903; second edition, 1907; reprinted 1909, 1911, and 1925. All references are to the 1911 reprint edition (New York: Macmillan, 1911).

work as a comprehensive system of social philosophy. Long before the followers of Max Weber gave currency to the word *Wertfreiheit,* Ward insisted that pure science neither praises nor blames, neither extols nor condemns, and indeed quotes Comte and Gumplowicz to the same effect. Pure sociology, accordingly, takes as its canon *nil admirari.* It has no concern with what ought to be; it is directed solely to the pursuit of truth. Of course, science itself rests upon certain matters of faith—faith in the validity of the category of causation, faith that everything that is, is worth knowing, and faith that the discovery of truth will have a beneficial effect. Nor is science to be construed simplistically as the discovery of facts. There is not a single science of which this is true. Science consists also in the logical organization and arrangement of facts. Finally, those men in the history of thought who have created and elaborated one idea have contributed the most:

> The notion has always been prevalent that men of one idea are useless or worse than useless. The fact is that they are the most useful of all men. I do not refer to such as are afflicted with the pathological *idée fixe,* but to those who are, as it were, possessed and consumed by some single thought, some favorite hypothesis, some heuristic conception, which grows larger and more all-comprehensive, until it impels them to pursue it untiringly to its last logical conclusion and to work into it great fields of truth.[85]

Ward is not generally known as a "functionalist" in sociology, but that is how he describes himself. Sociology is concerned not with what men are but with what they do. It is physiology, not anatomy. Structure is the means; function, the end. Most systems of sociology—including Ward's—take their departure from a single phenomenon, conception, or unit. Ward pays tribute to Ratzenhofer, for example, for the term *interests,* which he regards as synonymous with his own *social forces.* For Ward, however, the basic word appears to be *achievement,* the result of human action, and it is achievement therefore that is the subject matter of sociology. A synonymous word is *institution.* In the same way that life consists of existing forms, so society consists of existing institutions. Sociology differs from anthropology in that the latter deals with the uncivilized races, whose societies are useful for illustration or comparison but do not properly enter the sphere of sociology itself. Sociology can become a science only when it is recognized that social phenomena exhibit regularities and are the effects

85. *Pure Sociology,* p. 12. This is the phenomenon, with sociologists like Comte, Spencer, Marx, Buckle, and Durkheim in mind, that the present writer has called "the theoretic bias." See "Sociology and Humane Learning," in *Power and Progress: Essays on Sociological Theory* (New York: McGraw-Hill, 1974), pp. 309–321.

of causes. They are due to actions, but unfortunately "there lurks in the word *actions* the ghost of the old doctrine of free will."[86] If it were true that men could act otherwise than they do, there would be no science of action, no philosophy of history, no sociology. The scientific view is that social phenomena have the same general character as other natural phenomena, although they are more difficult to study because they are more complex.

Ward realizes that the level of abstraction on which sociology operates is relatively high. Sociology deals with generalizations and is unable to predict local and particular events. He also conceives of sociology as a general, not a special, social science, as the following passage indicates:

> It is the function of methodology in social science to classify social phenomena in such a manner that the groups may be brought under uniform laws and treated by exact methods. Sociology then becomes an exact science. In doing this, too, it will be found that we have passed from chaos to cosmos. Human history presents a chaos. The only science that can convert the milky way of history into a definite social universe is sociology, and this can only be done by the use of an appropriate method, by using the data furnished by all the special sciences, including the great scientific trunks of psychology, biology, and cosmology, and generalizing and coördinating the facts and groups of facts until unity is attained.[87]

Although true, it is not enough to say that sociology is a synthesis of the special sciences. It is a new compound, the last term in the genesis of science, and consequently the *scientia scientiarum.*[88]

In his discussion of social statics Ward introduces the concept of synergy. He begins with social energy, remarking that it "surges through society in all directions" and must therefore be restrained and controlled. If energy is ruthless and destructive, synergy, on the contrary, is creative and constructive. Ward means by it a combination of energy and mutuality, a working together of the otherwise antithetical forces of nature.[89] Without it society could not have arisen. Synergy, like the Hegelian dialectic to which Ward refers in this connection, is the synthesis of all antinomies, the principle that explains all structures. Function is the way that structure is utilized; the two are related as dependent and independent variables. Social struc-

86. *Pure Sociology*, p. 57.

87. *Ibid.*, p. 62.

88. The notion that chemical combination results in products unlike their components elicits from Ward a favorable reference to Durkheim. *Ibid.*, p. 80. In this connection he does not hesitate to talk about a "social mind," which he defines as the creative synthesis of individual minds. He also refers to a "group reason" and a "group instinct" in discussing the origin of social control. The references, however, are brief and superficial, and Ward accords them no importance. *Ibid.*, pp. 133–134.

89. *Ibid.*, p. 171.

tures are realized in social institutions, which, in turn, are both primary and secondary. Marriage, for example, is a primary institution; the family, a secondary. Religion is primary; the church, secondary. Law is primary; the court, secondary. Institutions and social structures are almost synonymous:

> They are all the result of some form of struggle among the social forces whereby the centrifugal and destructive character of each force acting alone is neutralized and each is made to contribute to the constructive work of society. In forming these structures the various forces are equilibrated, conserved, commuted, and converted into energy and power. The structures once created become reservoirs of power, and it is through them alone that all the work of society is performed. All these structures are interrelated and the performance of their functions brings them into contact or even conflict with one another. This mild struggle among social structures has the same effect as other struggles, and leads to general social organization. The final result is the social order, or society itself as an organized whole—a vast magazine of social energy stored for use by human institutions.[90]

The struggle of the races, which is the "true key" to the origin of society, is also the foundation of the edifice of sociology—and on this point Ward pays tribute to Gumplowicz and Ratzenhofer. This struggle also produces nations and patriotism, and for this latter sentiment Ward, like Sumner, has little regard.[91] It is a kind of collective egoism. It does, however, have one virtue. Its rise marks the end of race struggle, because the nation is then well formed and antagonistic forces have spent themselves. In a rare contradiction, he asserts in a later passage that war, however horrible, is the leading condition of human progress, that when race struggle ceases, progress ceases, and that peace is equivalent to stagnation.[92] He hopes that the moral forces are now gaining strength to mitigate the severity of struggle, but he is not optimistic. And furthermore, those who agitate for peace are ignorant of cosmic facts.

Ward finds three principles of social dynamics: difference of potential (illustrated by karyokinesis[93] and sexual exogamy), innovation (which he equates with Veblen's "instinct of workmanship"), and conation (by which he means social effort). From these abstract principles, Ward turns again, as he did in *Psychic Factors*, to the social forces and their classification,

90. *Ibid.*, p. 193.

91. He expresses the opinion, however, that the United States is the most civilized nation of the globe. *Ibid.*, p. 368.

92. *Ibid.*, pp. 212, 238.

93. By this word he means the process of amalgamation that occurs when a superior race confronts an inferior one. The references are to Lilienfeld, Gumplowicz, and Ratzenhofer.

discussing them under the rubrics ontogenetic, phylogenetic and sociogenetic. Under the first we have treatments of slavery,[94] labor, and property; under the second, his "gynaecocentric theory,"[95] gynaecocracy, androcracy, and love; and under the third, the moral, aesthetic, and intellectual forces. Again and again he asserts the superiority of the female over the male, as in such expressions as "While female superiority is a perfectly natural condition, male development requires explanation." The superiority of the male in size and strength is due entirely to female sexual selection, in man and throughout the animal kingdom. On the human level it is the factor of rationality—the ability to reason—that has given men dominion over women. At some dim point in history it dawned upon men that some causal connection obtains between sexual intercourse and the birth of a child. "It was this simple act of ratiocination that literally reversed the whole social system."[96] In discovering his paternity man discovered his power. Andreclexis, or male sexual selection, then succeeded gyneclexis, and androcracy supplanted gynaecocracy.[97]

Ward classifies the phylogenetic forces in five categories—natural love, romantic love, conjugal love, maternal love, and consanguineal love—and on all of them he has interesting things to say. He has a quite contemporary view of "natural love," by which he means, of course, sexual love. He deplores the tendency of many philosophers "to condemn the only act by which the race can be preserved." He frowns upon the tendency to underestimate the importance of sex in society, to push it into the background, and to keep the youth of both sexes ignorant of it.[98] Sexual love is indeed "the most vital of all the subjects of human contemplation," and sexual satisfaction is a social necessity.[99]

On romantic love, a derivative of sexual love, Ward advances the notion

---

94. Slavery, like war, had its uses. It at least marked an advance over extermination and cannibalism. *Ibid.*, p. 269.

95. *Ibid.*, p. 296. This theory Ward regards with pride because it is wholly his own.

> The gynaecocentric theory is the view that the female sex is primary and the male secondary in the organic scheme, that originally and normally all things center, as it were, about the female, and that the male, though not necessary in carrying out the scheme, was developed under the operation of the principle of advantage to secure organic progress through the crossing of strains.

96. *Ibid.*, pp. 323, 335, 341.

97. One is inclined to smile at Ward's Greek neologisms. His use of them, however, is not excessive. On the other hand, it was probably unnecessary for him to call romantic love "ampheclexis."

98. *Ibid.*, p. 379. W. I. Thomas also came to an early appreciation of the importance of sex in society, publishing a series of papers on the subject, beginning with his Ph.D. dissertation of 1897. In 1907, the same year in which *Pure Sociology* appeared, he published *Sex and Society: Studies in the Social Psychology of Sex* (Chicago: University of Chicago Press).

99. *Pure Sociology*, pp. 381, 389.

that it is a late development in history (sometime in the Middle Ages) and that it is largely confined to "the Aryan race," or at most to Europeans wherever they have settled.[100] The difference between romantic love and natural love is that the former is satisfied with presence, the latter only with possession. One additional observation merits quotation:

> It is a curious fact that there is always a touch of the illicit in all the romances of great geniuses—Abelard and Heloise, Dante and Beatrice, Petrarch and Laura, Tasso and Eleonora, Goethe and Charlotte von Stein, Wilhelm von Humboldt and Charlotte Diede, Comte and Clotilde de Vaux—and the romantic literature of the world has for one of its chief objects to emphasize the fact that love is a higher law that will and should prevail over the laws of men and the conventions of society. In this it is in harmony with the teachings of biology and with those of a sound sociology.[101]

Conjugal love is an entirely different sentiment. If romantic lovers imagine that their "wild, violent, tumultuous passion" will continue after marriage, they are almost certainly mistaken:

> Marriage takes place. What follows? The tumultuous billows of romantic love are quickly calmed; the confused and undistinguishable but all-absorbing hopes and fears vanish never to return; the longings, yearnings, cravings of temporary separation disappear; but neither is that leaping, throbbing, exultant joy at meeting any longer felt as such. The prolonged warring of passion is over and peace supervenes. The pair are lovers no longer.[102]

Conjugal love has rewards of its own, but it is hard to find descriptions of it in fiction and poetry.

Ward's treatment of maternal love requires no comment, except to say that he regards it as biologically based in mammals (in the mammary glands) and as therefore different from merely parental love. As for consanguineal love, it is distinct from maternal love, although frequently felt also by the mother, and it is probably related to "consciousness of kind," an expression that Ward uses in this connection. If jealousy is one of the negative consequences of natural, romantic, and conjugal love, race hatred is the negative consequence of consanguineal love. It is also—and both—the principal cause of war and one of the prime factors of social

100. *Ibid.*, p. 393:

> If I have read my Homer, Aeschylus, Virgil, and Horace to any purpose they do not reveal the existence in ancient Greece and Rome of the sentiment of romantic love. . . . Nothing in their literature conclusively proves that love with them meant more than the natural demands of the sexual instinct under the control of strong character and high intelligence.

101. *Ibid.*, p. 400.

102. *Ibid.*, p. 404.

progress.[103] Ward, of course, entertained no doubts whatever about the reality of progress.[104]

The third and final section of *Pure Sociology* is devoted to the doctrine of telesis, and here we have already been apprised of Ward's view. It is clearly expressed, however, in the following sentences:

> If, then, we take a comprehensive view of all the phenomena of society we will see that they fall under two radically distinct classes, and we shall have the purely spontaneous or natural phenomena of society, on the one hand, produced by the dynamic agent, and the phenomena that result from intention or design, on the other hand, which are the products of the directive agent in the sense that but for the directive agent they would not have taken place.[105]

The difference is that between the drift of an iceberg and the directed movement of an ocean liner. So also it is in human societies. Left to themselves the social forces would result in aimless drift. They must be harnessed and directed for the good of mankind.[106]

It remains for Ward to extol the virtues of the state. It is fashionable to dwell upon its abuses. Writers such as Ratzenhofer, Simmel, Gumplowicz, de Greef, and even Spencer, in an early and forgotten essay (forgotten even by him), however, have recognized that its institution was the most important step taken in the control of social forces. The state is genetic in origin but telic in method. Its sole purpose is the welfare of society. Although an instrument of restraint, it is also the source and guarantor of freedom.[107] The role of the state in education is clear and advantageous. In a prophetic vein he applauds the founding of state universities and intimates that although their future is hard to predict, it is altogether possible that they will someday supersede the private universities. Indeed, whatever the defects of public education, it "is undoubtedly the most promising form thus far taken by collective achievement." These words appear in the final paragraph of *Pure Sociology*.

Applied Sociology

Applied Sociology, which Ward published in 1906, completes his system of sociology. It is, in the words of its subtitle, "A Treatise on the Conscious

103. *Ibid.*, p. 416. Writing at the time he did, Ward believed that a code of "civilized warfare" had developed. *Ibid.*, p. 451.

104. See especially *Ibid.*, pp. 448–454.

105. *Ibid.*, p. 465.

106. Ward does not hesitate to use the concept of final causes and to compare them with efficient causes. In the operation of the former intelligence is added to instinct. Telesis is the adjustment of means to ends, whereas genesis is mere trial and error.

107. *Ibid.*, pp. 549–555.

Improvement of Society by Society." Its purpose is to counteract the counsel of despair that characterized the laissez-faire dogmas of the Social Darwinists, to affirm the efficacy of human effort, and to "remove the embargo laid upon human activity by a false interpretation of scientific determinism."[108] Pure sociology is a scientific inquiry into the nature of society. It deals with facts, causes, and principles. It answers the questions What, Why, and How. Applied sociology, on the other hand, deals with objects, ends, and purposes. It answers the question What for. Pure sociology is theoretical; applied, practical. The first deals with achievement; the second, with improvement. Applied sociology, however, is not an art; it is a science. It does not itself apply sociological principles, but it instead shows how they may be applied. Neither is it government, politics, or social reform. Social reform movements, whether the socialism of Fourier of that of Marx, belong to politics, not to science. Thus clearly and directly does Ward state his position.

His thesis is now so clear, in fact, that it is not necessary to pursue it through the chapters of *Applied Sociology.* Some of his observations, however, have sufficient interest to detain our attention. In discussing "world views," for example, he asserts that there are two—and presumably only two—interpretations of history: the economic interpretation of history, an expression he attributes to de Greef and to Seligman in 1900 and 1901, respectively, and the ideological interpretation of history. He attempts to reconcile the two interpretations by using such words as *interest, belief,* and *desire.* All interests are essentially economic, and economics is based on desire and its satisfaction. A belief, or idea, is not a social force; it is desire that moves the world. Economic conditions create feelings, which in turn determine ideas, which are then transformed into impulses and become "true idea forces." Ward's argument on this subject is less than clear, and it is therefore best to quote his conclusion: "Now although the economic impulses—desires, wants, feelings—necessarily precede the ideas—opinions, beliefs, world conceptions—still it is the latter that determine action, and the purely economic interpretation of history is utterly inadequate."[109] There is no mention of Marx in this discussion.

A large part of *Applied Sociology* is devoted to the question of heredity and environment and their respective roles in the production of "great men." The question is important because Ward, with some inconsistency, believes that the agents of civilization are men of thought, not men of action. He is accordingly intent upon refuting the views of Galton on the hereditary character of genius and upon emphasizing instead the role of opportunity. As indicated earlier, Ward is sure that intellectual ability is

108. *Applied Sociology* (Boston: Ginn & Co., 1906), p. iii.
109. *Applied Sociology*, p. 48.

equally distributed among the social classes, that all men are equally capable of learning "practical truths," and that the problem is one of maximizing opportunity. The error of Galton, and those who support his view, is that he failed to consider those who might have risen to great heights of intellectual and scientific achievement had their educational environment been favorable. Great men are produced by both heredity and environment, but Ward is intent upon emphasizing the latter. What is needed is quite simple. All that it is necessary to do is to extend to all the members of society an equal opportunity to exercise their mental powers. The notion that genius will create its own opportunity is false. Genius without opportunity is impotent.

Ward recognizes that he has not presented a detailed program for the improvement of society and admits that some may be disappointed that he has not done so. All he wants to say is that such a program is not a utopian dream but is instead a practical matter. He is not omniscient and cannot supply the details, which in any event will be worked out as a matter of trial and error.[110] If education, however, is the panacea and the sine qua non of progress, he considers it necessary to say in what it should consist. And here he produces his own *scala intellectualis,* which from the point of view of logical dependence consists of astronomy, physics, chemistry, biology, psychology, and sociology, in reverse order. These are the subjects that would constitute the curriculum. Like Comte, he is skeptical of the virtues of mathematics. Mathematics does not in fact strengthen either reason or judgment but, when too intensely pursued, destroys them both. The same may be said of history, which he defines as "a record of exceptional phenomena." The only faculty that the study of history can strengthen is memory. History therefore is a kind of luxury, a form of amusement. "The only kind of history that could exercise the reason and the judgment would be that which studies the conditions underlying social phenomena and their relations of coexistence and sequence—in a word their causal relations. But this is sociology."[111]

It is apparent that *Applied Sociology* does not deal with applied sociology in any of the senses in which that term is currently used. It has nothing to do with the application of sociological principles to the solution of social problems, such as crime, delinquency, divorce, prostitution, narcotics addiction, and poverty. Nor does it concern the application of such principles to the arts of social work, diplomacy, and administration. It is concerned instead with producing a society where the equality of oppor-

110. He has previously said that the telic processes, unlike the genetic, are not a matter of trial and error.

111. *Ibid.*, p. 312.

tunity is realized and the intelligence of the members of all social classes utilized. This is the great social problem, and upon its solution depends the solution of all others. On the details of the latter Ward confesses he has little to offer. He concludes once more with the firm assertion that the human intellect, on the social level, has done away with the struggle for existence on the biological level. "On this higher plane competition takes the form of honorable emulation."[112]

Summary and Evaluation

Ward's principal themes have now become so clear that a summary can be brief. It should be noted, first of all, that he was a protagonist—indeed, one of the progenitors—of the view that society itself was amenable to scientific modes of inquiry and that such inquiry would constitute a science of sociology—a great science of sociology. In this respect he was greatly influenced by Comte and Spencer, and especially by Comte. Sociology was not only a positive science, but also the synthesis and culmination of the other sciences.

Secondly, Ward placed himself squarely in the tradition of Social Darwinism, which was the reigning social philosophy of the late nineteenth and early twentieth centuries. He believed in the operation of natural forces in society and, of course, in the validity and importance of causal inquiry. From the view that the course of history was determined by God he begged to dissent. Society too is a natural object, and subject to natural law. He supported the notion of the struggle for existence but believed that the struggle was softened as civilization advanced. Although he deplored the horrors of war, he nevertheless thought that it was a useful institution in the evolutionary process. With respect to stages in the development of human societies, he was inconsistent, first denying and then accepting that the stages were regular—from savagery to barbarism to civilization. When taxed for inconsistency, however, he was content to answer that he was not a mule tied to a post.

To one tenet of Social Darwinism, however, he took strong exception and in doing so made his most notable contribution to sociology. This was the doctrine of laissez-faire. On this issue he deplored the views of both Spencer and Sumner.[113] It is not enough to leave things alone on the theory that all social phenomena are natural phenomena, determined by natural

112. *Ibid.*, p. 321.

113. He was particularly incensed by Sumner's contention that the favors of this world are distributed according to merit and that poverty, therefore, is the natural result of indolence and vice.

causes, and that any effort to interfere with them is doomed to fail. This may be true with respect to genetic processes, but there are telic processes as well, and therefore man can take a hand in his own evolution. If society in its evolution exhibits natural achievement, it also leaves room for artificial improvement. Indeed, civilization itself is artificial.

The great engine to be applied to the telic process is education. The notion that the upper classes have a monopoly on intelligence is a false and despicable doctrine. Intelligence is distributed equally in all social classes, and if the working classes have so far failed to contribute their share to the welfare of society, the sole reason is that they have been denied the opportunity—through deprivation of education—to do so. One-half of the human race—women—have also been denied the opportunity, and this is the greatest scandal of an otherwise civilized society. Finally, as social philosophies, neither individualism nor socialism, neither natural inequality nor contrived equality, can benefit the race. The answer rests in sociocracy, a philosophy that maximizes the opportunity of every man to realize his full potential and to become the director of his own destiny.

We have already mentioned the obituary tributes paid to Ward by his contemporaries in American sociology—Ross, Giddings, Weatherly, Ellwood, Blackmar, and Small. James Q. Dealey, his colleague at Brown University, was a disciple, as Keller was of Sumner. Hobhouse acknowledged his obligation to Ward in the Preface of his *Mind in Evolution* (1901).[114] Bernhard J. Stern appreciatively edited Ward's diary and correspondence and ranked him with Comte and Spencer as a founder of sociology—a credit that everyone concedes.[115] Harry Elmer Barnes says that Ward produced the most impressive and comprehensive system of sociology in the American record and that no one excelled him in his possession of the scientific knowledge of his day.[116] Ronald Fletcher echoed Barne's opinion twenty three years later, praising Ward for his "passionate concern for the radical reform of industrial society as he knew it," for his "broad, detailed, profound and admirable erudition," and for maintaining in all his writing "the very highest standards of excellence."[117]

114. Without mentioning Ward, Morris Ginsberg gave almost exact expression to his view: "The conception of a self-directed humanity is new, and as yet vague in the extreme. To work out its full theoretical implications, and, with the aid of other sciences, to inquire into the possibilities of its realization, may be said to be the ultimate object of sociology." *Sociology* (London and New York: Oxford University Press, 1934), p. 244.

115. See his article in the *Encyclopedia of the Social Sciences* and the appended bibliography. See also "The Liberal Views of Lester F. Ward," *The Scientific Monthly* 71 (August 1950): 102-104.

116. "Lester Frank Ward," in ed. Harry Elmer Barnes, *An Introduction to the History of Sociology* (Chicago: University of Chicago Press, 1948), p. 173.

117. *The Making of Sociology*, 2 vols. (London: Michael Joseph, 1971), vol. 1, pp. 459-501.

American historians have also paid tribute to Ward and his work, among them Charles A. Beard, Ralph H. Gabriel, Henry Steele Commager, and Richard Hofstadter. Beard said that he "was high among the giants of his time" and ranked him as superior to Spencer. Gabriel wrote of him, "More than any other single individual, Ward formulated the basic pattern of the American concept of the planned society." Commager regarded him as a thinker equal in rank to William James, John Dewey, and Oliver Wendell Holmes, and superior to Henry Adams and Thorstein Veblen.[118] Hofstadter called his work "a bold pioneering stroke" and wrote that he "suffered much undeserved neglect partly for the very reason that he was so far in advance of the rest of his generation."[119]

Ward, of course, had his critics as well, among them Small, Hayes, House, Gillette, and Bristol.[120] The most negative criticism comes from John C. Burnham, who regards his psychology as untenable, his science unacceptable, his neologisms barbarous, and his dogmatism offensive; who writes that the burden of proof is upon those who see him as an influential figure; and who even begrudges him his reputation as a paleobotanist.[121] John Dewey reviewed his *Psychic Factors* favorably, with some reservations about his psychology; there is, however, no reference to Ward in the works or the letters of William James. Sumner, who succeeded him as second president of the American Sociological Society, fails to mention him,

118. The views of Beard, Gabriel, and Commager are mentioned in John C. Burnham, "Lester Frank Ward in American Thought," *Annals of American Sociology* (Washington, D.C.: Public Affairs Press, 1956), p. 1. For an extended treatment of Commager's views, see his Introduction to *Lester Ward and the Welfare State*, pp. xi–xxxvii.

119. *Social Darwinism in American Thought*, pp. 67–84.

120. Small, who said that he would "rather have written *Dynamic Sociology* than any other book that has ever appeared in America," nevertheless subjected *Pure Sociology* to a searching examination in the *American Journal of Sociology* 9 (1903–1904): 404–407, 567–575, 703–707. Edward Cary Hayes, "The Social Forces Error," *ibid.* 16 (1910–1911): 613–625; Floyd Nelson House, "The Concept 'Social Forces' in American Sociology," *ibid.* 31 (1925–1926): 145, 347, 507, 632; J. M. Gillette, "Critical Points in Ward's Pure Sociology," *ibid.* 20 (1914–1915): 31–67; and Lucius Moody Bristol, *Social Adaptation* (Cambridge, Mass.: Harvard University Press, 1915). pp. 232–236.

121. Burnham, "Ward in American Thought," pp. 1–31. Burnham concludes:

> Ward systematized when he should have experimented; he speculated when he should have observed; he tried to embrace all knowledge in a world turning increasingly to specialization. Because of his failure to adapt to the rapid changes in his own intellectual environment, he became an anachronism; he represented a part of the nineteenth century surviving into the twentieth. Today a reader might be interested in some of the insights and some of the dynamic spirit buried in Ward's massive prose, but his pretentious works will never become classics. The devotion of a few followers and the efforts of early sociologists to deal tactfully with a well-meaning old man and to invent a history for themselves, together with a certain political appeal, created a self-perpetuating Ward tradition in sociology that spilled over into history. Ward was in a sense a prophet of a modern positive philosophy of government, but he played an insignificant role in the thinking of his own day and after [p. 22].

either in *Folkways* or in *The Science of Society*. On the other hand, his work made its mark on Roscoe Pound and his school of sociological jurisprudence.

A contemporary critic would surely find deficiencies in Ward's sociology. Society may be the product of the synergy of social forces, but he had no clear conception of its structure. To him achievement, institutions, and social structures are synonymous expressions, and there is no attempt to subject them to serious classification and analysis. He has sensible comments on the social codes and the sanctions that support them, but they are not central to his work. We have no treatment of groups except the almost incidental observation that some of them, notably the state, include all of the inhabitants of a given territory and that others do not. The difference between organized and unorganized groups did not occur to him, and indeed he paid no attention to organization as such. One gains from him no sense of the social order and its component parts. Nor, apart from his acceptance of evolution and his commitment to progress, is there a sustained effort to construct a theory of social change and to sort out the factors involved. His biology overwhelmed his sociology.

Some of the propositions in which Ward takes pride are trivial and in any case difficult to relate to anything else. In *Psychic Factors*, for example, he arrives at three "conclusions," which, for emphasis, he offers twice: "(1) The object of Nature is Function; (2) The object of Man is Happiness; (3) The object of Society is Action."[122] They would seem to belong only to a banal and primitive philosophy. Finally, as Ward himself is uncomfortably aware, there is no program for social action—except the cry for equality of opportunity. One does not ordinarily demand of a sociologist that he supply prescriptions for social policy. But Ward's insistence upon the importance of the telic almost requires him to do so. It is not enough to ask for more education and more government. The specifics are missing.

It is nevertheless easy to agree with those who have assigned to Lester Frank Ward a place of eminence in the history of sociology. Few writers in the discipline have exhibited a comparable erudition. He was perhaps the only—and perhaps the last—sociologist to be thoroughly conversant with both the biological and the social sciences. To read him is an intellectual treat, to enjoy total immersion in the intellectual issues of his time and place. He had a logical and lucid mind and produced, whatever its deficiencies, a system of social thought. A critic of Spencer and Sumner, he was nevertheless a Social Darwinist. So pervasive was Darwinian doctrine in his time that even its critics were Social Darwinists.[123] But his emphasis

122. Pp. 80, 130.

123. Hofstadter observes that despite Ward's criticism of Spencer, "the Spencerian virus remained in his blood." *Social Darwinism in American Thought*, p. 84. See the entire chapter on Ward.

upon the capacity of society to direct its own evolution—the doctrine of telesis—was a unique, if flawed, contribution.

Ward, like Horatio Alger, knew that talent was not confined to the aristocracy and could flower from the prairies of Iowa and Illinois, as well as from the cities of Boston and New York. He himself was proof of that. Nor could he share the distrust of goverment so common in his day and ours. He spent most of his life as a government servant and knew that government could be a force for good, as well as for evil. It may be overly generous to call him, as Henry Steele Commager does, "the philosophical architect of the modern welfare state." The lines of influence are not so easily traced. But when Oliver Wendell Holmes, in protest against the heartlessness of a laissez-faire Supreme Court, exclaimed that the Fourteenth Amendment does not enact Spencer's *Social Statics* into law, he could have found support—and more—in the sociology of Lester Frank Ward.

And yet, a problem remains. As the twentieth century wanes, Ward has no disciples. No one attends to him except the antiquarians who write the history of sociology. The simple truth is that his system is now archaic. It belongs in large part to cosmology, or cosmic philosophy, rather than to sociology. The notion that human societies, like the flora and fauna of the planet, are susceptible to scientific inquiry has long been accepted. The notion that sociology stands at the apex of the *scala intellectualis* and is the synthesis of all the sciences has been abandoned for more modest interpretations of its mission. The hopes that this "Nestor of sociology" had for it have not been satisfied.

CHAPTER 3

Charles Horton Cooley

Self and society are twin-born, we know one as immediately as we know the other, and the notion of a separate and independent ego is an illusion.

—*Social Organization,* p. 5.

In a brief biography of Charles Horton Cooley, his nephew Robert Cooley Angell writes, "Scholars are known to posterity by their writings. Charles Horton Cooley was largely so known even to his contemporaries."[1] It appears to be an apposite observation about a thoughtful, gentle, kind, and unassuming man who was almost pathologically shy, who was uncomfortable in company of any kind (except perhaps his graduate students), and who did not hesitate to refer to himself as an intellectual recluse.[2] Early meetings of the American Sociological Society, which he served as its eighth president in 1918, were painful occasions for him, and it was only after he became an elder statesman of the discipline that he began to take a modicum of pleasure in attending them. He lived a quiet life on the edge of the University of Michigan campus, traveled little, and was content to dedicate his ruminations to his books and his journals. The journals he kept for forty-seven years and, as his biographer remarks, they "provided him with a pleasant retreat from a social world whose vicissitudes often proved too much for his delicate sensitivity."[3]

He was born in 1864, the fourth of six children. His father, Thomas McIntyre Cooley, was the leading constitutional lawyer of his time. He wrote books on the law and served at various times as dean of the University of Michigan Law School, justice of the Supreme Court of Michigan, and first chairman of the Interstate Commerce Commission in Washington. Cooley's own childhood was marked by psychological insecurity and physical illness and accordingly it took him seven years to earn his bac-

1. Introduction to *The Two Major Works of Charles H. Cooley (Social Organization* and *Human Nature and the Social Order)* (Glencoe, Ill.: Free Press, 1956), p. v.

2. Edward C. Jandy, *Charles Horton Cooley, His Life and Social Theory* (New York: Dryden Press, 1942), p. 39.

3. *Ibid.*, p. 35.

calaureate degree at the University of Michigan, which he entered at the age of sixteen. During his undergraduate years he traveled and worked in several places, including Colorado and North Carolina, and in his eighteenth year he traveled and studied in Europe.

After his graduation from the university Cooley took an additional year there studying mechanical engineering. A year as a draftsman in Bay City, Michigan, convinced him that he would be happier in another line of work. About this time he discovered Herbert Spencer and began to buy and to read his works as they fell from the press. Although he finally found Spencer's system uncongenial he was nevertheless impressed by what it was that Spencer was trying to do. When he sought the advice of James Burrill Angell, then president of the University of Michigan, as to his future, Angell persuaded him to consider an academic career. Before attending graduate school, however, and at the behest of his father, he went to Washington, where he stayed for two years, working first for the Interstate Commerce Commission and then for the Bureau of the Census. Sometime in these two years he wrote a paper entitled "The Social Significance of Street Railways," which he read at the 1890 meeting of the American Economic Association. It was there that he met Franklin Henry Giddings and Lester Frank Ward; both men encouraged him to study sociology and to prepare himself for an academic appointment in what was then a new discipline.[4] Accordingly, he accepted a half-time instructorship in the Department of Political Economy at Michigan and prepared for his doctoral degree in economics with a minor in sociology. He finished in 1894, at the age of thirty, having produced a dissertation entitled "The Theory of Transportation".[5] About his examination he later wrote, "My examination came off in June, 1894, the questions in sociology being sent from Columbia by Professor Giddings. They are now before me, and are divided into three groups: Society and Social Evolution, the Family, and Philanthropy. My answers are with the questions and I doubt whether any one ever read them."[6] However that may be, he now possessed the passport to an academic career.

Cooley became a full-time instructor in 1895 and was promoted to assistant professor in 1899, associate professor in 1904, and full professor in

---

4. About Giddings Cooley wrote, "It was he more than any other who led me to believe that sociology might become a university subject, and myself a teacher of it"; about Ward, "I had and have the greatest respect for Ward, and concur heartily as to the high rank assigned to him in American sociology, but it would be untrue to say that his writings had any large part in forming my own conceptions of the subject." "The Development of Sociology in Michigan," *Sociological Theory and Social Research* (New York: Henry Holt & Co., 1930), pp. 3–14.

5. The dissertation is reprinted in its entirety, *ibid.*, pp. 17–118.

6. *Ibid.*, p. 6.

1907. In 1890 he married Elsie Jones, the daughter of the dean of the Medical School at the University of Michigan, and three children were born to them. Largely under the influence of G. Stanley Hall, child psychology grew to be a popular discipline in the United States during the first decade of the century, and Cooley often studied his own children, especially with respect to the development of the pronouns *I, me, my* and *mine.*[7]

A life as uneventful as Cooley's requires few words to describe. He spent his days with his manuscripts and journals, quite content to observe the world at a distance. He took his bride on a six-month tour of Europe, during which they explored particularly the hill towns of Italy. Afterwards, except for a few trips to Washington, New York, and other cities to attend meetings of the American Sociological Society, he was happy to remain in Ann Arbor. Giddings once offered him an appointment at Columbia University, but the thought of living in New York City terrified him. He was acutely uncomfortable in the presence of others, especially during his late adolescence, when his father seriously worried about him, and then again after the age of forty, when he became increasingly deaf. His intellectual companions were Emerson, Thoreau, and Goethe. Spencer, Darwin and Schäffle were to influence him in different ways,[8] and for Darwin especially he had the highest respect. To Comte he paid no attention. Baldwin, James, and Dewey all contributed to his thought, and often, in later years, he quoted from the works of Jane Addams, the famous founder of the Hull Street Settlement House in Chicago. Academic administration interested him not at all; indeed, he regarded administration and scholarship as contradictory activities. He even disliked dealing with administrators. Jandy reports that he always returned from a conference with one in a nervous, exhausted, and agitated state.[9]

By the end of World War I Cooley had become a legend at Michigan, and it was traditional for students to take at least one course with him. By 1928 he was lecturing to some 450 students in his introductory class in sociology. Jandy paints a vignette of him in the lecture hall:

> On the platform he made a striking appearance. His tall, aesthenic build, his neatly-trimmed, almost silver Van Dyke, his quietness, all made for an unmistakable dignity. Here indeed was a *professor!* While his students settled

7. See "A Study of the Early Use of Self-Words by a Child," *Psychological Review* 15 (November 1908): 339–357; reprinted in *Sociological Theory and Social Research,* pp. 229–247.

8. See "Reflections on the Sociology of Herbert Spencer," *American Journal of Sociology* 26 (September 1920): 129–145; reprinted in *Sociological Theory and Social Research,* pp. 263–279.

9. *Charles Horton Cooley,* p. 63.

> down, he would wipe his glasses and adjust them carefully. When a slender, slightly nervous hand would push the notes he had placed on the long table away from him, it was the first sign that he was about to start lecturing. He would take one step forward, give his notes another little flip away from him, cup his left hand behind his left ear—he was slightly deaf—clear his throat with vehemence several times, and begin. His voice was in harmony with his aesthenic [sic] form—thin, somewhat weak, slightly feminine; it was as hard to control as his emotions. There was a nervous, strained quality to it, as if it threatened each moment to break completely. His words were carefully chosen, his sentences short, and his transitions easy; the subject matter was connected and amply studded with illustrations. It was not the lectures at which one could direct criticisms, but rather at these mannerisms, which an unsympathetic undergraduate might find irksome. To most of this large audience of students this nervous frightened-looking professor must have seemed extremely academic and unchallengeable.[10]

His graduate students, to whom he gave devoted attention when he thought them worthy of it, nevertheless had to shift largely for themselves. He could sometimes be caustic in his criticism of their work and often, in seminar, he heard only what he wanted to hear. Although he was not, as a single individual, a match for the great University of Chicago department during this period, he nevertheless supervised the doctoral dissertations of a number of men, including Walton Hamilton, Read Bain, Robert Cooley Angell, and William Albig, who later achieved positions of prominence in American social science.

Cooley's final years were happy ones. His health was good; he enjoyed walking, swimming, and boating at his summer cabin in northern Michigan; and he felt a serene satisfaction in the work that he had accomplished. He, his wife, and his younger daughter, Mary, spent the summer of 1928 traveling in France, but once more he found travel a bit irksome and was happy to return to his routine in Ann Arbor. Early in the following year an increasing indisposition was diagnosed as cancer; he died of that disease on May 7, 1929, a few months short of his sixty-fifth birthday.

Human Nature and the Social Order[11]

Cooley begins his first book with one of the most profound and difficult questions of social philosophy—the relationship between the individual and

10. *Ibid.*, pp. 63–64.

11. (New York: Charles Scribner's Sons, 1902); rev. ed., 1922. All page references are to the 1956 edition, *Human Nature and the Social Order.*

society.[12] He writes that in fact this is the subject of the whole book and not merely that of its initial chapter. The matter to him seems fairly simple: "A separate individual is an abstraction unknown to experience, and so likewise is society when regarded as something apart from individuals."[13] Society and the individual are not separate phenomena but are simply collective and distributive aspects of the same thing. The difference, if any, is in our point of view when we look at them:

> Just as there is no society or group that is not a collective view of persons, so there is no individual who may not be regarded as a particular view of social groups. He has no separate existence; through both the heredity and the social factors in his life a man is bound into the whole of which he is a member, and to consider him apart from it is quite as artificial as to consider society apart from individuals.[14]

It is therefore a fallacy to set the individual and society against each other. Not even the word *social* can mean anything that is opposite to the word *individual.* In fact, the word *social* has three different meanings: (*a*) in the first sense, which is somewhat vague, it refers to the collective aspect of humanity; (*b*) in the second, what pertains to immediate intercourse or interaction among people; and (*c*) in the third, conducive to the collective welfare. In the last sense, for example, crime is antisocial. But in none of these senses can we regard society as somehow set apart from the individual. If there is some opposition between an individual and society—and Sorokin makes the same point—it is really an opposition between one individual and various other individuals. The notion that individuals somehow antecede society is altogether incorrect. Shakespeare from one

12. To the second edition he added an introduction that deals with heredity and instinct. Despite advances that have been made in genetics since his time, it is still worth reading. He tries to distinguish what the individual receives in his germ plasm and what he receives from social transmission or, as we would say today, from culture. He notices that identical Chinese twins could be quite different, except in appearance, if one were brought to the United States immediately after birth and raised to adulthood in this country. He accepts the Darwinian view that acquired traits are not inherited and also the principle of natural selection. Individuals with heritable defects should be prevented from having children. "Progress, as ordinarily understood, does not require any change in heredity, but is a development of knowledge, arts, and institutions that takes place in the social process with little or no alteration of the germ-plasm." *Ibid.*, p. 14. We cannot give quantitative weights to the contributions made by hereditary factors on the one hand and social factors on the other. The word *instinct* probably should be avoided in the explanation of human behavior. To attribute war to the instinct of pugnacity, for example, reveals little; the same observation may be made about the so-called gregarious instinct as an explanation of society. Finally, the expression "human nature" has several meanings that ought to be clearly distinguished.

13. *Ibid.*, p. 36.

14. *Ibid.*, p. 38.

point of view is a unique and transcendent individual; from another, a splendid expression of the collective life of mankind.[15] And finally, if a football team cannot exist without a quarterback, neither can a quarterback without a team.

SOCIETY IS MENTAL

Two of Cooley's leading ideas are that society is mental and that the mind is social. The former proposition may strike the reader as unusual, and it therefore requires for its explanation words from Cooley himself:

> Society, then, in its immediate aspect, *is a relation among personal ideas.* In order to have society it is evidently necessary that persons should get together somewhere; and they get together only as personal ideas in the mind. Where else? What other possible *locus* can be assigned for the real contact of persons, or in what other form can they come in contact except as impressions or ideas formed in this common *locus?* Society exists in my mind as the contact and reciprocal influence of certain ideas named "I," Thomas, Henry, Susan, Bridget, and so on. It exists in your mind as a similar group, and so in every mind.[16]

Cooley seems surprised that this is not obvious to everyone. The degree to which it is not he attributes to "vague modes of speech," which it is necessary to discard. He concludes, therefore, "that the imaginations which people have of one another are the *solid facts* of society, and that to observe and interpret these must be a chief aim of sociology."[17]

It follows from this—and Cooley makes a pleasing point of it—that not only the dead, when we think of them, are "real people," but so are the characters in the novels that we read and the dramas that we see. Caesar and Hamlet, for example, are members of our society, persons we all know and whose lives we vicariously share. "What, indeed, would society be, or what would any of us be, if we associated only with corporeal persons and insisted that no one should enter our company who could not show his power to tip the scales and cast a shadow?"[18] Even corporeal persons, for that matter, become members of our society only when they are imagined. The habit of thinking otherwise, of thinking that personality is a physical rather than a social fact, is responsible for all sorts of fallacious conclusions in ethics and politics.[19]

15. *Ibid.*, p. 46.
16. *Ibid.*, p. 119.
17. *Ibid.*, p. 121.
18. *Ibid.*, p. 123.
19. For beneficent influences upon his ideas in this respect Cooley expresses appreciation to James Mark Baldwin and William James.

Personalities interpenetrate one another, and what is part of one is also part of another. This property is entirely lacking to physical bodies, which are mutually exclusive. The self is not altogether distinct from other persons. "*Self and others do not exist as mutually exclusive social facts*, and phraseology which implies that they do, like the antithesis egoism versus altruism, is open to the objection of vagueness, if not of falsity."[20] And here he anticipates his "looking-glass" theory of the self: "We do not think 'I' except with reference to a complementary thought of other persons."[21] Cooley insists that there is nothing unreal or fantastic or impractical about conceiving of people as facts of our imagination. "On the contrary, the fantastic, unreal, and practically pernicious way is the ordinary and traditional one of speculating upon them as shadowy bodies, without any real observation of them as mental facts."[22] Cooley thus arrives, from this personal direction, at a conception of society:

> According to this view of the matter society is simply the collective aspect of personal thought. Each man's imagination, regarded as a mass of personal impressions worked up into a living, growing whole, is a special phase of society; and Mind or Imagination as a whole, that is human thought considered in the largest way as having a growth and organization extending throughout the ages, is the *locus* of society in the widest possible sense.[23]

Society, in short, is life regarded from the point of view of personal intercourse. "And personal intercourse may be considered either in its primary aspects, such as are treated in this book, or in secondary aspects, such as groups, institutions, or processes. Sociology, I suppose, is the science of these things."[24]

The reader of Cooley will soon learn that he is as much a moralist as he is a sociologist and that the line between ethics and sociology is never

---

20. *Ibid.*, p. 126. In a footnote to this page Cooley mentions Spencer as guilty of this phraseology.

> The trouble is, as with his whole system, that the physiological aspect of life is expounded and assumed, apparently, to be the only aspect that science can consider. Having ventured to find fault with Spencer, I may be allowed to add that I have perhaps learned as much from him as from any other writer. If only his system did not appear at first quite so complete and final, one might more easily remain loyal to it in spite of its deficiencies. But when these latter begin to appear its very completeness makes it seem a sort of a prison-wall which one must break down to get out.

See also Cooley's article on Spencer, *American Journal of Sociology* 26 (September 1920): 129–145; reprinted in *Sociological Theory and Social Research*, pp. 263–279.

21. *Human Nature and the Social Order*, p. 127.

22. *Ibid.*, p. 133.

23. *Ibid.*, p. 134.

24. *Ibid.*, p. 135.

clearly drawn. Indeed, he would have had no desire to do so. Accordingly, he freely uses such words as *good* and *bad, right* and *wrong,* and even *goodness* and *badness.* He writes of anger, grief, fear, and love in a manner reminiscent of Emerson's essays, and indeed Emerson's influence is apparent throughout Cooley's writings. He devotes entire chapters to such subjects as sympathy, hostility, emulation, and conscience. He uses the word *sympathy,* however, not in the sense of compassion or pity but rather in the sense of "sharing a mental state with," feeling of oneness with, understanding, or personal insight—something for which the word *empathy* is now used.[25] In any event, sympathy (or understanding) is for Cooley an aspect of society—the society that to him exists in the mind or the imagination. He points out, for example, that social experience is a matter of imaginative, not material, contacts and thus people who live in the world of books, so to speak, can have a much wider range of social experience than those who do not. "The idea that seeing life means going from place to place and doing a great variety of obvious things is an illusion natural to dull minds."[26] So speaks Cooley, who, as we have seen, was not fond of traveling. His antiurban bias appears in his opinion that one finds more "openness" of sympathy in the country than in the city. In any event, it is a person's sympathies that reflect the social order of which he is a part. "Every group of which he is really a member, in which he has any vital share, must live in his sympathy; so that his mind is a microcosm of so much of society as he truly belongs to."[27] Again, in the diversified life of contemporary society, "A man may be regarded as the point of intersection of an indefinite number of circles representing social groups, having as many arcs passing through him as there are groups."[28]

The diversification of modern life induces Cooley to indulge in a few unsystematic observations on the division of labor. He is interested in specialization in the factory not from the point of view of the moral integration of society, as Durkheim was, but rather from that of what meaningless routines can do to the mind of the worker. He does not believe that there is any necessary opposition between specialization and breadth of vision and entertains the optimistic view that despite the mechanization of factory labor broader visions will prevail. Indeed, only those who specialize can appreciate the larger, the general, view.[29] One wonders if he

25. The trouble with *sympathy,* despite its etymology, is that it suggests condescension, a certain superiority on the part of the one who sympathizes. Hobbes defined it as feeling felt for oneself at the sight of another's distress.

26. *Ibid.,* p. 140.

27. *Ibid.,* p. 144.

28. *Ibid.,* p. 148.

29. "Has a student less general knowledge because he is familiar with a specialty, or is it not rather true that in so far as he knows one thing well it is a window through which he sees things in general?" *Ibid.,* p. 150.

would have retained this optimism if he had seen an assembly line fifty years after his words were written.

THE MIND IS SOCIAL

If the notion that society is mental is one of Cooley's basic notions, so also is the notion that the mind is social. Indeed, the self itself is social, and to this contention he devotes two chapters of his book. So firmly is Cooley's name associated with this notion that it may come as a surprise to some to realize that he also regarded the self, as Wundt did, as a feeling, a feeling, moreover, that is instinctive. "It seems to exist in a vague though vigorous form at the birth of each individual, and, like other instinctive ideas or germs of ideas, to be defined and developed by experience."[30] We cannot deny the child a self even in the first weeks of life. In any case, it is clear that when we use the word *I* we seldom have in mind our material body. True, the body may be the locus of the self, but only rarely, perhaps no more than once in ten times, is the body the reference of the pronoun *I*. The references instead are to opinions, purposes, desires, claims, and so on, matters in which all thought of the body is absent.[31] Cooley finally arrives at a definition: "The social self is simply any idea, or system of ideas, drawn from the communicative life, that the mind cherishes as its own."[32] Emphasis upon the communicative life is important. The *I* of common speech always contains some reference to others because it is a word, and words are phenomena of language, which is in turn a phenomenon of the communicative life. Without society there would be no communication; without communication, no language; and without language, no *I*. As Cooley says, to think of the self apart from society is a palpable absurdity.

In an interesting insight Cooley notices that the word *I* refers not only to the self but also to inanimate objects with which the self is associated in the

30. *Ibid.*, p. 171.

31. One does not ordinarily think of Cooley as a man who turned his hand to empirical research. Nevertheless, there is an example of it, and it appears in connection with this discussion:

> I had the curiosity to attempt a rough classification of the first hundred "I's" and "me's" in Hamlet, with the following results. The pronoun was used in connection with perception, as "I hear," "I see," fourteen times; with thought, sentiment, intention, etc., thirty-two times; with wish, as "I pray you," six times; as speaking—"I'll speak to it"—sixteen times; as spoken to, twelve times; in connection with action, involving perhaps some vague notion of the body, as "I came to Denmark," nine times; vague or doubtful, ten times; as equivalent to bodily appearance—"No more like my father than I to Hercules"—once. Some of the classifications are arbitrary, and another observer would doubtless get a different result; but he could not fail, I think, to conclude that Shakespeare's characters are seldom thinking of their bodies when they say "I" or "me." And in this respect they appear to be representative of mankind in general.

Ibid., pp. 176–177.

32. *Ibid.*, p. 179.

relationship that we call "mine." Thus, it is perfectly normal for us to remark, "I am in the long grass down by the third tee," or (about the game of croquet), "I am in position for the middle arch," or (a boy flying a kite), "I am higher than you." In an earlier footnote Cooley quotes William James, "A man's self is the sum total of all he can call his, not only his body and his psychic powers, but his clothes and his house, his wife and children, his ancestors and friends, his reputation and works, his lands and horses and yacht and bank-account. All these things give him the same emotions."[33] Cooley is now ready to offer his famous "looking-glass" conception of the self, one of the most famous ideas in American sociological theory. He begins with the couplet:

Each to each a looking-glass
Reflects the other that doth pass.

and proceeds with a paragraph that merits quotation in full:

> A self-idea of this sort seems to have three principal elements: the imagination of our appearance to the other person; the imagination of his judgment of that appearance, and some sort of self-feeling, such as pride or mortification. The comparison with a looking-glass hardly suggests the second element, the imagined judgment, which is quite essential. The thing that moves us to pride or shame is not the mere mechanical reflection of ourselves, but an imputed sentiment, the imagined effect of this reflection upon another's mind. This is evident from the fact that the character and weight of that other, in whose mind we see ourselves, makes all the difference with our feeling. We are ashamed to seem evasive in the presence of a straightforward man, cowardly in the presence of a brave one, gross in the eyes of a refined one, and so on. We always imagine, and in imagining share, the judgments of the other mind. A man will boast to one person of an action—say some sharp transaction in trade—which he would be ashamed to own to another.[34]

In other words, I am not what I think I am; I am not what you think I am; I am what I think you think I am.[35]

Much of what follows has to do with the development of the self-concept

33. *Ibid.*, p. 170n. For the present writer's reflections on the self as subject and the self as object, see Robert Bierstedt, *The Social Order*, 4th ed. (New York: McGraw-Hill, 1974), pp. 192–202.

34. *Ibid.*, pp. 184–185, see also p. 387.

35. This conception raises problems of reflexivity and infinite regression to which, in another context, Anthony Giddens devotes attention in his *New Rules of Sociological Method* (London: Hutchinson, 1976). See, for example, his treatment of what he calls "the double hermeneutic." See also Robert Bierstedt's "review essay" of this book, *Scottish Journal of Sociology* 1 (April 1977): 183–193.

as Cooley observed it in his own three children—a boy and two girls. Again he remarks that the pronouns of the first person are "names which the race has learned to apply to an instinctive attitude of mind."[36] He is quite sure that there are sex differences in the development of the social self and proceeds to indulge in the kind of sex typing that would arouse the ire of a later generation of women's liberationists. Girls, for example, have more sensibility than boys and care more for their social image. Boys are more interested in muscular activity and with building things and in general are more interested in things than they are in persons. In addition, "There can be no doubt that women are as a rule more dependent upon immediate personal support and corroboration than are men."[37] Opinions such as these, of course, were all but universal in the time in which Cooley was writing although, as we have seen, they were not shared by Lester Frank Ward. The chapter concludes with a brief treatment of the fact that the group self, the "we," is simply an "I" that includes other persons. Just as the individual self is felt only in relation with other persons, so the group self is felt only in relation with a larger society. The "we" of nationhood, the patriotic "we," "can and should be a self of real honor, service, and humane aspiration."[38] The words are quoted to illustrate the flavor of Cooley's prose which, as I have suggested, is both ethical and sociological, and gently hortatory as would become a Christian moralist of his era. Indeed, in the following chapter he discusses such unhealthy and evil traits as selfishness, egotism, pride, and vanity.

> So far as there is any agreement in judgments regarding selfishness it arises from common standards of right, fairness, and courtesy which all thoughtful minds work out from their experience, and which represent what the general good requires. The selfish man is one in whose self, or in whose style of asserting it, is something that falls below these standards. He is a transgressor of fair play and the rules of the game, an outlaw with whom no one ought to sympathize, but against whom all should unite for the general good.[39]

There is little one can do with this so far as sociological theory is concerned. There is in Cooley, here and throughout his work, a total absence of cosmopolitan sophistication. We are told, as another example, that healthy, balanced minds keep to the middle road between self-respect and reasonable ambition.[40]

36. *Human Nature and the Social Order*, p. 189.
37. *Ibid.*, pp. 202–203.
38. *Ibid.*, p. 210.
39. *Ibid.*, p. 216.
40. *Ibid.*, p. 245. Cooley's view of psychoanalysis is appended as a footnote at the end of

CONFORMITY AND NONCONFORMITY

Conformity, for Cooley, is one of three kinds of emulation, the other two being rivalry and hero-worship. He defines it as "the endeavor to maintain a standard set by a group," a voluntary imitation of prevalent modes of action.[41] It is intentional rather than mechanical. Thus, there is no conformity in the act of speaking our own language but there may be if we choose one pronunciation of a word rather than another. The reason we conform is primarily because of the inconvenience of nonconformity. We dislike being pointed out as singular or peculiar in any way. Every profession, trade, church, circle, and fraternity has its standards that it expects its members to meet. "It is not at all essential that there should be any deliberate purpose to set up these standards, or any special machinery for enforcing them. They spring up spontaneously, as it were, by an unconscious process of assimilation, and are enforced by the mere inertia of the minds constituting the group."[42] Although he does not use Sumner's terminology of folkways and mores in this connection, his view that standards arise spontaneously is consistent with Sumner's contention that they are crescive rather than enacted. Cooley also has some praise for nonconformity. It means exploration, enterprise, adventure, innovation. "Conflict is a necessity of the active soul, and if a social order could be created from which it were absent, that order would perish as uncongenial to human nature. 'To be a man is to be a non-conformer.' "[43] And again, "How much of Anglo-Saxon history is rooted in the intrinsic cantankerousness of the race!"[44] Furthermore, what may superficially appear to be nonconformity may in reality be conformity to another group that is a part of our actual or historical environment: "The group to which we give allegiance, and to

---

his second chapter on the social self. It is reprinted here without comment as a matter of intrinsic interest:

> The modern study, aspiring to become a science, called Psychoanalysis, endeavors in a more or less systematic way to investigate the history and working of the self, with a view especially to understanding its maladies and finding a cure for them. There can be no doubt of the need for such a study, or of its great practical use, even if it does not yield enough definite and settled results to establish it as a science. The human mind is indeed a cave swarming with strange forms of life, most of them unconscious and unilluminated. Unless we can understand something as to how the motives that issue from this obscurity are generated, we can hardly hope to foresee or control them. The literature of psychoanalysis is suggestive and stimulating, but the more general theories to be found in it are perhaps only provisional. A sociologist will note especially the tendency to work too directly from supposed instincts, without allowing for the transforming action of social institutions and processes.

Ibid., pp. 262–263.

41. *Ibid.*, p. 293.
42. *Ibid.*, pp. 295–296.
43. *Ibid.*, p. 300.
44. *Ibid.*, p. 299.

whose standards we try to conform, is determined by our own selective affinity, choosing among all the personal influences accessible to us; and so far as we select with any independence of our palpable companions, we have the appearance of non-conformity."[45] Conformity and nonconformity are normal and complementary modes of human activity.[46] As Cooley says, concluding his discussion of this subject:

> Society, like every living, advancing whole, requires a just union of stability and change, uniformity and differentiation. Conformity is the phase of stability and uniformity, while non-conformity is the phase of differentiation and change. The latter cannot introduce anything wholly new, but it can and does effect such a reorganization of existing material as constantly to transform and renew human life.[47]

The remainder of the chapter is devoted to rivalry and hero-worship.

LEADERSHIP, JUDGMENT, AND CONSCIENCE

In a chapter on leadership, largely filled with Emersonian reflections, Cooley asks himself one of the enduring questions in the philosophy of history. What is the role of great men? Do men make history or are they only the surface manifestations of deeper trends and tendencies that would have prevailed even if all famous men had died in infancy? Cooley answers:

> If one accepts the view of the relation between particular individuals and society as a whole already stated in various connections, the answer to these questions must be that the individual *is* a cause, as independent as a cause can be which is part of a living whole, that the leader does lead, and that the course of history must have been notably different if a few great men had been withdrawn from it.[48]

It is false, in short, to set something called general tendencies against individuals. It is only through individuals that general tendencies can begin or persist. "Not one of us floats quite inert upon the general stream of tendency." As individuals we have an effect upon the world.[49]

---

45. *Ibid.*, p. 301. Compare with Merton's "reference groups."

46. In the course of this discussion Cooley has a footnote on Tarde's *Les Lois d'Imitation*. He regards it as a brilliant work but suggests that the social process might also be described in terms of other kinds of activity, such as communication, competition, differentiation, adaptation, or idealization. Imitation is one glimpse among many. *Ibid.*, p. 302n.

47. *Ibid.*, pp. 304–305.

48. *Ibid.*, p. 354.

49. *Ibid.*, p. 355.

In a chapter entitled "The Social Aspect of Conscience," Cooley is concerned with moral judgment. He equates the right with the rational in the largest sense and avers that judgments of right and wrong differ only in degree and not in kind from other judgments:

> The slightest scrutiny of experience shows, it seems to me, that the sharp and absolute distinction often assumed to exist between conscious and other mental activities does not hold good in life. There are gradual transitions from judgments which no one thinks of as peculiarly moral, through others which some would regard as moral and others would not, to those which are universally so regarded.[50]

If the right is the rational—by which Cooley means much more than the result of formal reasoning—the wrong is the irrational. When we do something wrong or immoral, we disturb the order and harmony of the mind, we become less of a person, we become uncomfortable, and indeed we begin to disintegrate. Cooley perceives the mind, in its moral aspect, as a field of battle where various impulses and passions strive for supremacy. "Instinctive passions, like love, ambition, and revenge; the momentum of habit, the need of change, personal ascendencies, and the like, all have their bearing upon the final synthesis, and must either be conciliated or suppressed."[51]

Cooley has no doubt that there is such a thing as conscience and that it serves as the highest criterion of what is right. Is it the Puritan in him or some other quality that induces him to equate the right also with a sense of striving, a sense of "onward," a moving equilibrium? As Emerson said, the good self must be a crescive self, and he is so quoted. Cooley continues:

> The right, then, is not merely the repressive discipline with which we sometimes identify it, but is also something warm, fresh, and outward-looking. That which we somewhat vaguely and coldly call mental development is, when at its best, the revelation of an expanding, variegating, and beautiful whole, of which the right act is a harmonious member.[52]

Cooley also appreciates the role of habit in the determination of what is right, and indeed what we know as a principle is a habit of conscience. But this role must not, of course, be restrictive.

Nor must one regard the right as somehow social in the sense of being opposed to the individual. Here as elsewhere Cooley thinks of the individual and the social as two faces of the same coin and rejects any effort

50. *Ibid.*, p. 359.
51. *Ibid.*, p. 362.
52. *Ibid.*, p. 368.

to separate them. The way he expresses this point with respect to ethical judgment, however, is not altogether clear:

> The consideration of other persons usually enters largely into questions of right and wrong; but the ethical decision is distinctly an assertion of a private, individualized view of the matter. Surely there is no sound general principle in accordance with which the right is represented by the suggestions of the social environment, and the wrong by our more private impulses.[53]

Even a strong sense of duty, of obligation, is something that is mine, something that *I* feel, related to something that *I* owe or ought to do. Once more Cooley concentrates upon the relation between the individual and the group:

> The individual and the group are related in respect to moral thought quite as they are everywhere else; individual consciences and the social conscience are not separate things, but aspects of one thing, namely, the moral Life, which may be regarded as individual by fixing our attention upon a particular conscience in artificial isolation, or as general by attending to some collective phrase, like public opinion upon a moral question.[54]

The separation between the individual conscience and the social conscience is "purely artificial." If we are intent upon opposing something to the social, we should oppose not the individual but the sensual. Although Cooley has insisted that an ethical decision is an assertion of a private view, he also asserts, in three brief paragraphs, that the right always reflects a social group and that conscience is always a group conscience. By this, however, he means a circle of other persons and not anything resembling Durkheim's *conscience collective.* There is, incidentally, no reference to Durkheim in the book. The social factor in conscience may indeed take the form of ideal persons whom we use as standards of our own conduct. Thus, Emerson in his diary refers to one Osman, who is his ideal self, a more perfect Emerson.

At the end of his chapter Cooley touches, but only briefly, upon Sumner's contention that the mores can make anything right—the proposition that opens the door to moral relativism. One would not expect that Cooley would agree with it, and the expectation, or lack of it, is correct. He is favorably inclined in general to Sumner's view. He knows and appreciates that the same things are commended in some societies and condemned in others. But there are, after all, ideas of right that are practically universal. He lists three principles to which all peoples subscribe: loyalty to

53. *Ibid.*, p. 373.
54. *Ibid.*, p. 377.

the group, kindness to members of the group, and adherence to the customs of the tribe. "These are universal because they spring from universal conditions of social life. . . . Morals are profoundly functional, and beneath many strange divergences there is found a core of likeness corresponding to a similarity in the life-process itself."[55]

Cooley's penultimate chapter, on "Personal Degeneracy," requires little comment. Here he is interested in what distinguishes the righteous from the wicked, the virtuous from the vicious, the good from the bad. Once more, heredity and environment cannot be separated in dealing with these questions. Obviously, congenital idiocy by definition is hereditary; crime, on the other hand, may be due to a bad social environment. So far as the treatment of degeneracy is concerned, "As the social surroundings of a person can be changed and his hereditary bias cannot, it is expedient, in that vast majority of cases in which causation is obscure, to assume as a working hypothesis that the social factor is at fault, and to try by altering it to alter the person."[56] In one passage he comes close to anticipating Sutherland's differential association theory of crime. He says that the degenerative individual is a *socius* like the rest of us, that the group forms his conscience "and what it countenances or admires will not seem wrong to him, no matter how the rest of society may regard it. If it becomes traditional for the members of a college fraternity to drink, gamble, and cheat their way through examinations, the freshman will fall into these practices as a matter of course."[57] "In fact," he continues, "the great wrongs are done mainly by people of normal capacity who believe they are doing right. Their consciences are supported by the mores, or collective moral feeling of a group."[58]

The final chapter deals with freedom, which Cooley defines not only as the absence of restraint but also as "opportunity for right development, for development in accordance with the progressive ideal of life that we have in conscience."[59] He perceives, in his own lifetime, a gradual increase in freedom in society's institutions—in the family, the school, the church, the government, in the armed services, in prisons, and even in the industrial system. Freedom permits the individual to become the best that he is naturally fitted to become.

In summary, Cooley has worked assiduously in this book to erase the separateness that ordinary language would attribute to individual and society. They are only distributive and collective aspects of the same entity.

55. *Ibid.*, p. 401.
56. *Ibid.*, p. 410.
57. *Ibid.*, p. 416.
58. *Ibid.*, p. 417.
59. *Ibid.*, p. 423.

Neither has an existence independent of the other. The locus of society, in fact, is in the mind. Cooley sees society not as a network of relationships, and not as a structure of norms and statuses, but rather as something made up of other people, both the living and the dead, both the real and the fictional, as they present themselves to the imagination. If society is mental in this sense so also is the mind social. And thus we have the looking-glass conception of the self. It is a brilliant idea, both simple and apposite, and, even if presented briefly and inconsistently, a major contribution to psychology.

On the whole, this early book of Cooley's is a curious performance. It is more of a homily, a moral lecture, than a treatise on sociology. It resembles more than anything else the essays of Ralph Waldo Emerson, an observation that Cooley would have regarded as a compliment.[60] Like Emerson, he writes from a position of moral and intellectual security. He knows what is right and what is true and what is good. He has a quiet confidence in the superiority of the Anglo-Saxon race and the Christian religion. He is sure that intemperance needs to be suppressed and the heathen converted. He is a "good" man, self-reliant and kind, and is here sharing his goodness with his reader.

Social Organization

Subtitled "A Study of the Larger Mind," *Social Organization* is the second of Cooley's major works.[61] In the Preface he emphasizes again his holistic or organic point of view and says that if in his earlier book he tried to see society in the social nature of man, here he intends to take the larger view, to see society in terms of its organization, with the individual, although still visible, receding a bit into the background. Again, however, he intends to treat the subject from the mental rather than the material side. The book itself is organized into six major divisions: (*a*) primary aspects of organization; (*b*) communication; (*c*) the democratic mind; (*d*) social classes; (*e*) institutions; and (*f*) the public will.

The first two chapters deal with social and individual aspects of the

60. "I wore out a set of his [Emerson's] works when I was young, and even now I carry about a thin book of extracts to which I resort when I need to find a little more glamour on life." *Life and the Student: Roadside Notes on Human Nature, Society, and Letters* (New York: Alfred A. Knopf, 1927), p. 66. "Glamour" somehow does not seem quite the right word to associate with Emerson.

61. (New York: Charles Scribner's Sons, 1909). All page references are to the 1956 edition in *Social Organization.*

mind, and the first paragraph merits quotation because in three sentences Cooley captures the essence of his views on the subject:

> Mind is an organic whole made up of cooperating individuals, in somewhat the same way that the music of an orchestra is made up of divergent but related sounds. No one would think it necessary or reasonable to divide the music into two kinds, that made by the whole and that of particular instruments, and no more are there two kinds of mind, the social mind and the individual mind. When we study the social mind we merely fix our attention on larger aspects and relations rather than on the narrower ones of ordinary psychology.[62]

He regards this view of the matter as consistent with the general standpoint of modern science and seems unaware that it might present difficulties of a metaphysical kind, that is, difficulties pertaining to part-whole relationships in general. His definition of social organization also appears at the beginning. It is the "differentiated unity of mental or social life, present in the simplest intercourse but capable of infinite growth and adaptation."[63] Here also appears the often quoted sentence: "Self and society are twin-born, we know one as immediately as we know the other, and the notion of a separate and independent ego is an illusion."[64]

All views that would ascribe primacy to self-consciousness over social consciousness are incorrect, and Descartes was a principal offender in this respect. His search for the "I" in the "*Cogito, ergo sum*" is defective in two respects: (*a*) it implies that the "I" consciousness is part of all consciousness when instead it belongs to an advanced stage of development; and (*b*) it emphasizes the individual "I" and excludes the social "we," which is equally original with it.[65] Although introspection is necessary, "the introspection of Descartes was, in this instance, a limited, almost abnormal, sort of introspection—that of a self-absorbed philosopher doing his best to isolate himself from other people and from all simple and natural conditions of life."[66] In any event, sympathetic introspection is not only necessary but it is also the principal method of social psychology—the method that enables the social psychologist to understand the child, the idiot, the criminal, the

62. *Ibid.*, p. 3.

63. *Ibid.*, p. 4.

64. *Ibid.*, p. 5.

65. Sometimes, although not often, it is difficult to grasp the meaning of a contention of Cooley's. His first objection is an example. Another is: "And although the growth of social consciousness is perhaps the greatest fact of history, it has still but a narrow and fallible grasp of human life." *Ibid.*, p. 5.

66. Cooley has misconstrued the Cartesian enterprise. Sitting in a warm and sheltered hut in a village near Ulm in 1619, Descartes was searching not for a self but rather for certainty, a proposition so certain that before it all doubt would crumble, a proposition moreover that could be reached by reason alone, without the help of observation or experience.

rich and the poor, the conservative and the radical, and indeed everyone else.

Cooley's first objection to Descartes becomes a little clearer when he explains that children do not achieve a consciousness of self until around the age of two. When it appears it is inseparable from consciousness of others, and indeed there are not, so to speak, two consciousnesses then, but only one. The social consciousness and the self consciousness are intermingled and inseparable. "There is then no mystery about social consciousness. The view that there is something recondite about it and that it must be dug for with metaphysics and drawn forth from the depths of speculation, springs from a failure to grasp adequately the social nature of all higher consciousness."[67] Cooley does not deny that the individual is a "differentiated center" of thought but insists instead that the separation of self and society is a perversion into which we are led by ordinary modes of speech. Our social ideas are so closely connected with the ideas of others that they all make up a common whole which Cooley calls a public consciousness or, in fact, a public opinion.[68] "There are, then, at least three aspects of consciousness which we may usefully distinguish: self-consciousness, or what I think of myself; social consciousness (in its individual aspect), or what I think of other people; and public consciousness, or a collective view of the foregoing as organized in a communicating group. And all three are phases of a single whole."[69]

THE PRIMARY GROUP

If the looking-glass conception of the self is one of Cooley's major contributions to sociology, the other is his conception of the primary group. On the definition of primary groups it is important to have his own words:

> By primary groups I mean those characterized by intimate face-to-face association and cooperation. They are primary in several senses, but chiefly in that they are fundamental in forming the social nature and ideals of the individual. The result of intimate association, psychologically, is a certain fusion

---

67. *Ibid.*, p. 10.

68. In elaboration of this point Cooley writes:

> The consciousness of the American House of Representatives, for example, is by no means limited to the common views, if there are any, shared by its members, but embraces the whole consciousness of every member so far as this deals with the activity of the House. It would be a poor conception of the whole which left out the opposition, or even one dissentient individual. That all minds are different is a condition, not an obstacle, to the unity that consists in a differentiated and cooperative life.

Ibid., p. 11.

69. *Ibid.*, p. 12.

> of individualities in a common whole, so that one's very self, for many purposes at least, is the common life and purpose of the group. Perhaps the simplest way of describing this wholeness is by saying that it is a "we"; it involves the sort of sympathy and mutual identification for which "we" is the natural expression. One lives in the feeling of the whole and finds the chief aims of his will in that feeling.[70]

Intimacy, of course, is the criterion to emphasize. That primary group relations need be "face-to-face" is almost certainly a mistake that Cooley himself would have recognized. We all have many face-to-face relations that are not primary group relations—with barbers and bank tellers and ticket sellers, for example. And, on the other hand, we have primary group relations that are not face-to-face—with old friends, for example, whom we have not seen for many years and with whom we now exchange only a Christmas message. Most important is the "we" feeling, the sense of intimacy. It is not to be supposed, however, as Cooley himself makes clear, that primary group relations are always friendly. As has often been observed, one has to know another person fairly well in order to dislike him, and some of the most hostile relations of all are those between brothers.

So far as actual groups are concerned, Cooley has in mind the family, the play group, the gang, the neighborhood, and a community of the elderly. That the family and the neighborhood are preeminent in the time of childhood makes them preeminent as primary groups. "Primary groups are primary in the sense that they give the individual his earliest and completest experience of social unity, and also in the sense that they do not change in the same degree as more elaborate relations, but form a comparatively permanent source out of which the latter are ever springing."[71] Here one is troubled by "social unity." Does it have a meaning of some sociological kind, or is it only a pious expression? In any event, primary groups are the "springs of life" from which, as Cooley's mood indicates, all blessings flow.

In his discussion of primary groups Cooley has occasion to discourse upon human nature, by which he means "those sentiments and impulses that are human in being superior to those of lower animals, and also in the sense that they belong to mankind at large, and not to any particular race or time."[72] Again, in this connection, he takes a position contrary to cultural relativism: "Always and everywhere men seek honor and dread ridicule, defer to public opinion, cherish their goods and their children, and admire courage, generosity, and success."[73] The generic likeness of peoples

70. *Ibid.*, p. 23.
71. *Ibid.*, pp. 26–27.
72. *Ibid.*, p. 28.
73. *Ibid.*

all over the world is illustrated also by the pleasure we take in their folktales no matter how remote they are from us in time or space. Furthermore, human nature is closely linked to the primary group; as Cooley says is an important paragraph:

> The view here maintained is that human nature is not something existing separately in the individual, but a *group-nature or primary phase of society*, a relatively simple and general condition of the social mind. It is something more, on the one hand, than the mere instinct that is born in us—though that enters into it—and something less, on the other, than the more elaborate development of ideas and sentiments that makes up institutions. It is the nature which is developed and expressed in those simple, face-to-face groups that are somewhat alike in all societies; groups of the family, the playground, and the neighborhood. In the essential similarity of these is to be found the basis, in experience, for similar ideas and sentiments in the human mind. In these, everywhere, human nature comes into existence. Man does not have it at birth; he cannot acquire it except through fellowship, and it decays in isolation.[74]

In this paragraph we have the essence of Cooley's sociological theory. Everything social is the outgrowth of the primary group.

The primary group, in addition, is the source of all of our ideals—ideals of love, justice, loyalty, truth, service, kindness, and freedom. They are not always pleasant or righteous, but they are the ground from which the pleasant and righteous spring. Cooley does not mean to deprecate the "self-assertive passions." Competition and the survival of the fittest are as righteous as some of the ideals he mentions. When we come to such passions as lust, greed, revenge, and the pride of power, however, we are talking about animal nature, and no longer human nature. In any event, the primary group nurtures all of the finer sentiments. Cooley's simple faith is nowhere more apparent than in sentences such as the following:

> In every village and township in the land, I suppose, there are one or more groups of predatory boys and hoydenish girls whose mischief is only the result of ill-directed energy. If each of these could receive a little sympathetic attention from kindred but wiser spirits, at least half of the crime and vice of the next generation would almost certainly be done away with.[75]

With this sentiment he concludes his chapter on primary ideals.

DEMOCRACY

If all of our virtues have their origin in the primary group so also do those larger systems of ideals that we call democracy and Christianity. The

74. *Ibid.*, pp. 29–30.
75. *Ibid.*, p. 50.

former can be traced to the village community life of the Teutonic tribes of northern Europe, the latter to the family life of a Judean carpenter. Cooley is aware, of course, that we do not always live up to our ideals, and for that reason his prose often becomes softly hortatory. Society is a moral organism, created progressively through experiment and struggle.

It is not necessary to follow Cooley through his long discussion of communication. He emphasizes its importance, traces its growth in preverbal forms and development in speech and writing, gives the prodigious effect of the invention of printing its due, treats of the nonverbal arts and their role in communication, discusses "recent" changes in communication, asks how and in what manner communication fosters individuality, and concludes with some remarks on certain pathological effects (superficiality and strain) in modern communication. He fully appreciates the role of the railroad, the telegraph, the telephone, and the daily newspaper, and one can only wonder what he would have had to say about radio and television. He shares Henry James's jaded view of the newspaper and says that although it promotes sociability and a sense of community, it is also little more than "organized gossip," it fosters superficiality, and it "is, of course, the antithesis of literature and of all high or fine spiritual achievement."[76] The importance of communication to the democratic form of government goes without saying.

Cooley begins his long treatment of the democratic mind with a chapter entitled "The Enlargement of Consciousness." Democracy began, as mentioned above, in the Teutonic tribes before they became acquainted with Roman civilization. In the Germanic family, clan, and village group were found the simple virtues of sympathy, loyalty, honor, and congenial intercourse that provided the soil for the growth of the larger mind and ultimately for democracy. He quotes the English historian J. R. Green who, in his *History of the English People,* discusses the village assemblies of these tribes, where "the men from whom Englishmen were to spring learned the worth of public opinion, of public discussion, the worth of the agreement, the 'common-sense' to which discussion leads, as of the laws which derive their force from being expressions of that general conviction."[77] Cooley treats this passage from Green with a total lack of skepticism. Something of the spirit of these primitive assemblies, he says, remains in those festal evenings where, around a campfire, we sing songs and tell stories that are known to all. Democracy is simply the general or public phase of this larger consciousness, this public mind and public opinion. Democracy is the application on a larger scale of those principles that are felt to be right in the smaller group. Finally, "An ideal democracy is in its nature religious, and

76. *Ibid.*, p. 85.
77. *Ibid.*, p. 108.

its true sovereign may be said to be the higher nature, or God, which it aspires to incarnate in human institutions."[78] For Cooley the entire world is moving in the direction of democracy, not only in government but also in religion, industry, education, philanthropy, and the family. It is also moving in the direction of humanism and all of its companion virtues—justice, truth, kindness, brotherhood, and service. In our time—that is, Cooley's time—truth will survive and falsehood perish.

PUBLIC OPINION

Public opinion for Cooley is not a matter of poll taking. He has his own definition: "Public opinion is no mere aggregate of separate individual judgments, but an organization, a cooperative product of communication and reciprocal influence. It may be as different from the sum of what the individuals could have thought out in separation as a ship built by a hundred men is from a hundred boats each built by one man."[79] If an individual can make up his mind so can a group make up its mind. The thoughts of individual minds are "poured into the general stream," and the minds thus become an organic whole. "Their unity is not one of identity, but of life and action, a crystallization of diverse but related ideas."[80] As before, Cooley gives no indication of recognizing that there might be serious metaphysical difficulties with this view. In any event, by an organic whole he does not imply agreement but rather "a certain ripeness and stability of thought resulting from attention and discussion."[81] One also has to distinguish between a true and mature opinion on the one hand and a mere popular impression on the other. The latter is apt to be facile, shallow, transient, fickle, and fatuous. There is all the difference in the world between this and a sound, mature, aroused social judgment.[82] Cooley contends not that group opinion is always moral but only that it is effective. A mob, for example, is morally inferior even when no one can doubt that it is effective.

Public opinion is not an average opinion, and statistical measures are therefore useless in studying it. One mind with a "right judgment" can in-

78. *Ibid.*, p. 205. Cooley's last book, *Life and the Student*, is full of pieties of this kind. It contains, however, one sharp observation: "Institutions and genius are in the nature of things antithetical, and if a man of genius is found living contentedly in a university it is peculiarly creditable to both [p. 184]."

79. *Social Organization*, p. 121.

80. *Ibid.*, p. 122.

81. *Ibid.*

82. Here is an example of what I have called "the fallacy of illicit comparison." Something sound and mature, no matter what it is, is obviously to be preferred to anything that is shallow and fatuous.

duce many others to agree. This in fact is the way in which right social judgments are made in the realms of science, philosophy, literature, and art. We all agree, for example, on the worth of Plato, Dante, Leonardo, Michelangelo, Beethoven, Newton, and Darwin, and this is an example of public opinion at work. These, in addition, are democratic judgments. Everyone has a right to participate in them. But public opinion is not necessarily uniform; indeed, it has many differentiations. There is what might be called a general public opinion, in which all, or almost all, participate, and there also are special or class opinions—of the family, the club, the party, the union. It is upon these special opinions that we rely for the guidance of general opinion. We need the advice of economists, for example, on what to think about the currency. Cooley has little faith in the referendum as a device for discovering public opinion on political questions. If too many are submitted to the people, they will only become confused or indifferent. The distinction between general and special public opinion is not as clear as it might be, except that specialists of all sorts—masons, soldiers, chemists, lawyers, bankers—are governed by the opinion of their own groups.

In one chapter the masses or the common people engage Cooley's attention, and he has nothing but praise for them. Indeed, it was the masses, not people of wealth and distinction, who made the American Revolution possible; it may be the deprived masses of our cities who will initiate new and higher ideals for our civilization; and it is the strength of the masses that makes democracy work.

> The common people, as a rule, live more in the central current of human experience than men of wealth or distinction. Domestic morality, religious sentiment, faith in man and God, loyalty to country and the like, are the fruit of the human heart growing in homely conditions, and they easily wither when these conditions are lost. To be one among many, without individual pretension, is in one way a position of security and grandeur. One stands, as it were, with the human race at his back, sharing its claim on truth, justice, and God.[83]

It is clear that Cooley himself would like to be counted among the common people. But too often, as in this instance, he wanders over the line that separates sentiment from sentimentality. Much of the chapter is written in a vein appropriate to the pulpit but out of place in the classroom.[84]

---

83. *Ibid.*, pp. 136–137.

84. I cannot refrain from quoting two more examples: "Some tendency to isolation and spiritual impoverishment is likely to go with any sort of distinction or privilege," and "Wealth which is not dominated by noble tradition or by rare personal inspiration falls into vulgarity because it permits the inflation of those crude impulses which are much kept down in the poor by the discipline of hardship." *Ibid.*, pp. 138, 139.

Cooley is concerned to show, in opposition to the views of Macauley and Lecky, that democracy does not mean mob rule or the rule of the ignorant many over the knowledgeable few. Surely the example of the United States is enough to show that democracy does not mean rule by an irresponsible crowd. Cooley considers the crowd mind and disagrees with Sighele and Le Bon that the man in the crowd is somehow different from the man in isolation—or maintains at least that these writers exaggerated the difference. "The peculiarity of the crowd-mind is mainly in the readiness with which any communicable feeling is spread and augmented."[85] The man in the crowd is at once excited and intimidated and may thus be led to indulge in reckless action. If the French seem to participate in crowd action more than the English or the Americans, it is because of "race traits" and perhaps because they came to democracy through revolution.

Are democracy and distinction incompatible—especially distinction in science, art, and letters? Cooley devotes some thought to this question and answers it, as we would expect, in the negative. Confusion is the enemy of distinction, and there are some elements of unrest in democracy. On the whole, however, we need not necessarily associate democracy with confusion. He quotes de Tocqueville, "In modern society everything threatens to become so much alike that the peculiar characteristics of each individual will soon be entirely lost in the general aspect of the world," and disagrees. The United States of America is proof that democracy does not suppress "salient personality." He does, however, see a certain uniformity, a certain sameness, on the American landscape as contrasted with the European. It is also, because of advertising and newspapers, a *loud* time in America, and "the whispers of the gods are hard to catch." And yet, it may be after all that democracy and distinction are uncongenial. "I notice," says Cooley, "among the choicest people I know—those who seem to me most representative of the inner trend of democracy—a certain generous contempt for distinction and a passion to cast their lives heartily on the general current."[86]

SOCIAL CLASS

The conception of social class entertained by Cooley is rather different from that which ordinarily obtains in the literature today. He appears to mean by it any persistent social group except the family. "Individuals never achieve their life in separation, but always in cooperation with a group of

85. *Ibid.*, p. 150.
86. *Ibid.*, p. 175.

other minds, and in proportion as these cooperating groups stand out from one another with some distinctness they constitute social classes."[87] When a class is "strictly hereditary" he calls it a caste. As to the explanation of these phenomena, he finds two factors—inheritance and competition. Natural ability is important, but opportunity is perhaps equally so.[88] So far as occupational classes are concerned there is perhaps a natural tendency for sons to follow their fathers as the most convenient path, and thus society comes to be "vaguely divided" into hereditary strata. In any event, an impulse to caste formation seems to Cooley to be inherent in human nature.

Three conditions favor or oppose the growth of caste:

> These are, first, likeness or unlikeness in the constituents of the population; second, the rate of social change (whether we have to do with a settled or shifting system), and finally, the state of communication and enlightenment. Unlikeness in the constituents, a settled system and a low state of communication and enlightenment favor the growth of caste, and *vice versa*. The first provides natural lines of cleavage and so makes it easier to split into hereditary groups; the second gives inheritance time to consolidate its power, while the third means the absence of those conscious and rational forces which are its chief rivals.[89]

The kinds of unlikeness, in turn, are three: race, differences attributable to immigration or conquest, and differences that arise gradually in the differentiation of social functions. That whites and blacks in the United States form different castes seems altogether natural to Cooley. The argument that the two races are distinct organisms "is perhaps better sociology than the view that every one should be considered solely on his merits as an individual."[90] Nevertheless, caste arrogance is to be deplored. "The matter of unequal ability, in races as in individuals, is quite distinct from that sharing in a common spirit and service from which no human being can rightly or Christianly be excluded. The idea that he is fundamentally a man like the rest of us cannot and should not be kept from the Negro any more than from other lowly orders of people."[91] That expressions like these convict Cooley himself of caste arrogance is a notion that would not have occurred to him.

With respect to the future, two contrary tendencies are at work. With the

87. *Ibid.*, p. 209.

88. "I would not have it supposed, however (because I dwell thus upon opportunity), that I agree with those whose zeal for education and training leads them to depreciate natural differences. I do not know how to talk with men who believe in native equality: it seems to me that they lack common sense and observation." *Ibid.*, p. 214.

89. *Ibid.*, p. 217.

90. *Ibid.*, p. 219.

91. *Ibid.*, pp. 219–220.

probability of more settled conditions, the likelihood of caste increases. With the probability of sharper differentiation of functions, however, the likelihood decreases. Although recognition of descent is a wholesome sentiment we should not, in this country, encourage an emphasis on inheritance at the expense of equal opportunity. The abolition of all extrinsic inequalities is part of the democratic ideal. Social democracy must assure that all will have an equal opportunity to enjoy the fruits of progress. Nevertheless, Cooley cannot help but admire the English aristocracy, with its "high traditions of culture and public service," and seems to feel that something important and precious would be lost to the world if this caste should disappear. There are, however, other means than caste for preserving traditions. Voluntary associations might serve the purpose equally well.

In much of the preceding discussion Cooley seems to be using the words *class* and *caste* interchangeably. When he addresses himself specifically to open classes, however, he raises the question whether there is or ought to be class consciousness in a democratic society. Here again his answer is ambivalent:

> If we mean a division of feeling that goes deeper than the sense of national unity and separates the people into alien sections, then there is no such thing in the United States on any important scale (leaving aside the race question), and we may hope there never will be. But if we mean that along with an underlying unity of sentiment and ideals there are currents of thought and feeling somewhat distinct and often antagonistic, the answer is that class-consciousness in this sense exists and is more likely to increase than to diminish.[92]

The discussion of class and of class consciousness, incidentally, proceeds without reference to Marx, of whom there is no mention in any of Cooley's books.[93] He says that "only under conditions of caste would a class war of the sort predicted by some theorists be likely to come to pass,"[94] and it is conceivable that he thought of Marx as one of those theorists. But it is inconceivable to Cooley that there could be such a class war in the United States, any more than there could be a literal war between Republicans and Democrats. For his conclusion on this point he finds an Aristotelian mean: "If there is no class-consciousness men become isolated, degraded and ineffective; if there is too much, or the wrong kind, the group becomes separate and forgets the whole."[95]

92. *Ibid.*, p. 241.

93. There is, however, reference to "Marxian socialism" in *Social Process* (Carbondale, Ill.: Southern Illinois University Press, 1966), p. 44.

94. *Ibid.*, p. 242.

95. *Ibid.*, p. 242.

On the whole, classes in this country overlap one another, and there are as many classes as there are classifiers. Here again Cooley seems to be using class as synonymous with group. The most conspicuous kinds of class divisions are those based upon occupation, wealth, and culture, but the most important and independent of these is virtue. "The real upper class, that which is doing the most for the onward movement of human life, is not to be discerned by any visible sign. The more inward or spiritual a trait is the less it is dependent upon what are ordinarily understood as class distinctions."[96] Sometimes Cooley's piety is suffocating.

All men seek power, and wealth is a form of power. It is a relatively low form, however, and it is one that, in Cooley's view, is not quite respectable. Christianity is not opposed to industrial prosperity, but the scramble for money on the part of individuals, unless they are poor, is unseemly and un-Christian. The capitalist class represents the survival of the fittest but Cooley is careful to add that the fittest are not always the best. They are not even the ablest, except in the facility with which they make money. Some are righteous, some are not; some are of the highest character, others are the reverse. Business, in fact, is of great value to our civilization, and its successful pursuit requires the virtues of energy, tenacity, labor, and prudence. Sometimes, of course, it takes on predatory forms and in this guise is to be condemned as wicked. Most of the time, too, it is autocratic, and the system should be replaced by one of industrial democracy. This means that cooperation, in labor unions, governmental regulation, and even public ownership will increasingly make their appearance on the American scene. Opinions like these would have been considered "radical," possibly even dangerous, in Cooley's day. His biographer suggests that he encountered no trouble on this score because of the distinction and conservative reputation of his family. Unlike Dewey and Ross, however, he indulged in no extracurricular activities on behalf of social reform.

In his discussion of social power—something Cooley concedes to be a vague notion—he gets off on the wrong foot. He regards its essence as spiritual, the power that one mind exerts over another by use of the symbols of communication. This is "live, human power," and it is the power exercised by poets, prophets, philosophers, inventors, and men of science.[97] If these examples are taken seriously, however, they are examples of influence, not power, and it is important to maintain the distinction.[98] Cooley's approach is the more puzzling because he also includes, among those already mentioned, political, military, and religious organizations

96. *Ibid.*, p. 250.

97. The extension of the concept of power to this degree also appears in MacIver.

98. On this subject, see Robert Bierstedt, "An Analysis of Social Power," *Power and Progress: Essays on Sociological Theory* (New York: McGraw-Hill, 1974), pp. 220–241.

and captains of industry and commerce. These latter are surely instruments of power in ways that the former are not. A more tangible form of power for Cooley depends upon organizing ability, the ability to manage men, and utilizes tact, skill, and tenacity. This he refers to as leadership, and again he misses an important distinction. Leadership is persuasive whereas power is coercive. In any event, this ability to operate human machinery commands high prices and there is always a market for it. There is no question that the capitalist class possesses power but the rich are devoid of any "pregnant spiritual leadership, theirs being a pedestrian kind of authority."[99] Here for a third time Cooley misses a necessary distinction. Authority is closely related to power but it is not synonymous with it. Authority is institutionalized power, power legitimized in organized groups.[100] Throughout his treatment Cooley treats power interchangeably with leadership, authority, prestige, and influence. It is quite possible that these finer distinctions would only delay his argument. He is not, in fact, interested in sociological analysis but rather in getting a message to his reader, namely, that the owner of wealth exercises power and, like the feudal chieftain of the medieval world, is the ruler of a social system. That legislatures—federal, state, and local—are often subservient to pecuniary power can only be deplored. The rich exercise their influence and power not only over the professions—law, medicine, education—but also over the newspapers, which are dependent upon advertising for their existence. The power of wealth, in short, can hardly be denied.

Cooley is so interested in this subject that he devotes another chapter to it. Here he speaks of the influence of ambitious young men who, one would think, are anxious to rise in the world and therefore are inimical to class and caste.

> But it by no means follows that they are opposed to the ascendency of an upper class based on wealth and position. This becomes evident when one remembers that their aim is *not to raise the lower class, but to get out of it.* The rising young man does not identify himself with the lowly stratum of society in which he is born, but, dissatisfied with his antecedents, he strikes out for wealth, power or fame. In doing so he fixes his eyes on those who have these things, and from whose example he may learn how to gain them; thus tending to accept the ideals and standards of the actual upper class.[101]

University students, when they are ambitious, are thus confronted with a conflict between their social idealism on the one hand and their desire to

99. *Social Organization,* p. 268.

100. See, in addition to the citation in n. 98, Robert Bierstedt, "The Problem of Authority," in *Power and Progress,* pp. 242–259.

101. *Social Organization,* pp. 273–274. Compare Merton's "reference group."

rise on the other. The dominant class in a society like that of the United States is apt to be stable because it is relatively open and can fill its openings with men of ambition and energy from the lower classes. At the same time the process depletes the lower classes of leadership ability. These classes consequently suffer the evils of the industrial system—bad housing, insecurity, deadening work, child labor, and the rest.[102] There is no reason to ignore these evils. Their solution is to be found in increasing the class consciousness of the "hard-working" classes, in increasing the effectiveness of labor unions, and in socialism. By this last Cooley means "that wider, vaguer, more philosophical or religious movement" which is practically synonymous with the democratic spirit. It may have taken some courage, writing at the time he did, for Cooley to write so favorably about labor unions. Indeed, collective bargaining seems to him to be essential, and "self-assertion through voluntary organization is of the essence of democracy."[103]

In his discussion of class Cooley suggests that if we use income as a basis of division we shall probably have five classes—paupers, the poor, the comfortable, the well-to-do, and the rich. Later, in a treatment of poverty, he says that the poor "are not a class in the sense of having a distinct psychical organization."[104] Indeed, they are too discouraged to cooperate effectively on their own behalf. By the poor, incidentally, he means those who have insufficient income to maintain their health and efficiency. The question whether poverty is due to personal or to social causes suffers from the familiar confusion of trying to treat self and society as separate entities. The laziness, shiftlessness, and vice attributed to the poor are more likely the effect than the cause of their condition. The principal cause of poverty appears to be some maladjustment between individual or family and the wider social group—a maladjustment that interferes with the realization of maximum potential.

Without mentioning Spencer or Sumner, Cooley attends to the notion that the poor are poor because they are unfit in some Malthusian or Darwinian sense. The notion is erroneous because there is no evidence of a hereditary deficiency in the poor. Their plight arises instead from deficiencies in nurture, training, and opportunity. The solution therefore is social—"reform of housing and neighborhood conditions, improvement of the schools, public teaching of trades, abolition of child-labor and the humanizing of industry."[105] If we give the children of the poor the right start in life they will be able to help themselves when they become adults.

102. Cooley explains that agitators against the rich are unlikely to be successful in the United States and that we have no reason to fear the onset of anarchy. *Ibid.*, pp. 276–278.

103. *Ibid.*, p. 288.

104. *Ibid.*, p. 291.

105. *Ibid.*, p. 296.

Cooley concludes his discussion of class with the question of class hostility. He decides that there is less hostility where the classes are clearly separated in a rigid structure and more where the idea of equality prevails. In the latter situation even slight differences will be resented and feeling become most bitter.[106] To reduce the bitterness in a democracy it is necessary to instill in all classes the ideal of service, a growing sense of social responsibility, and an increase in community sentiment.

INSTITUTIONS

Cooley begins with a definition: "An institution is simply a definite and established phase of the public mind, not different in its ultimate nature from public opinion, though often seeming, on account of its permanence and the visible customs and symbols in which it is clothed, to have a somewhat distinct and independent existence."[107] Language, government, the church, the laws and customs of property and of the family, and systems of industry and education are examples of institutions. They are all a working out of the permanent needs of human nature, crystallized forms of the organization of human thought, organized attitudes of the public mind. And again, "An institution is a mature, specialized and comparatively rigid part of the social structure."[108] Immediately after this sentence Cooley confounds us a bit by saying that institutions are made up of persons, but not of whole persons. Thus, it is the legal part of the lawyer, the business part of the merchant, and so on, that enter institutions. Institutions are always partial; it is the person who is whole. We have to be on our guard against institutions because they purchase efficiency at the price of humanity. Moral progress always begins in opposition to institutions. Progress in general results from the interaction of personality and institutions.

Cooley makes an interesting distinction, inspired by Tarde, between tradition and convention. "Tradition comes down from the past, while convention arrives, sidewise as it were, from our contemporaries."[109] Tradition belongs to time, convention to space. The former, for example, may appear in a small and local area, the latter endure only for a day. On the other hand, one must not exaggerate the difference; tradition is also convention in the group in which it operates. But one can use the adjectives to characterize societies themselves. Thus, the society of medieval Europe was a traditional society; that of our own time a conventional one.

106. This is an anticipation, of course, of Stouffer's concept of relative deprivation, discussed with penetration and insight by Merton.

107. *Ibid.*, p. 313.

108. *Ibid.*, p. 319.

109. *Ibid.*, p. 335n.

Still under the rubric of institutions, Cooley discusses social disorganization—disorganization in the family, the church, the economic system, education, higher culture, and the fine arts. Disorganization in the family—a phenomenon he attributes to an increasing permissiveness[110]—takes the form of a declining birth rate (especially among the "comfortable classes"), an increasing lack of discipline and respect in children (when the spirit of choice is in the air children will be sure to inhale it), a growing independence of women (which leads to neglect of the family), and an increase in divorce. As we have seen, Cooley agrees with the estimation of sex differences that was almost universal in his time, namely, men are the more rational sex, women, the more emotional. He concludes his chapter on the family by—surprisingly—finding something good in divorce:

> For divorce, though full of evils, is associated with a beneficent rise in the standing of women, of which it is to a certain degree the cause. The fact that law and opinion now permit women to revolt against the abuse of marital power operates widely and subtly to increase their self-respect and the respect of others for them, and like the right of workman to strike, does most of its good without overt exercise.[111]

Disorganization in the church takes the form of an increasing disregard for tradition and structure, the loss of the truths of creeds, and the substitution of external symbolism and ceremony for the internal virtues of kindness, hope, reverence, humility, and courage. As in the family and the church, disorganization in the economic system, in education, and in the arts is attributable to the confusion and inefficiency that accompany the breaking up of old structures and their replacement with new ones. The old legal and ethical relations of industry have broken down, and the craftsman has lost control of his tools. We see new freedom and vigor in education, but with them comes anarchy. In higher education we see the breakdown of classical discipline and classical learning so that our students at graduation can no longer be presumed to have a common knowledge of Latin, Greek, history, and literature.[112] In art, tradition has given way to experimentation.

110. By permissiveness Cooley means something many degrees away from what it came to mean later in the century. Permitting young people to choose their own marital partners, permitting them to dissolve the marital tie when it no longer gives them gratification, and permitting them to refuse to bear more children than they want are all forms of permissiveness for him.

111. *Ibid.*, p. 371.

112. *Ibid.*, p. 389:

> I suspect that we may be participating in the rise of a new type of culture which shall revise rather than abandon the old traditions, and whose central current will perhaps be a large study of the principles of human life and of their expression in history, art, philanthropy and religion. And the belief that the new discipline of sociology (much clarified and freed from whatever crudeness and pretension may now impair it) is to have a part in this may not be entirely a matter of special predilection.

THE PUBLIC WILL

In the concluding chapters of his book, Cooley talks about the public will (another phase of the democratic mind), government, and the larger will in the context of the method and possibility of social betterment. By public will he means something that he defines simply as "the deliberate self-direction of the group." It has the same nature as public opinion and it appears when some measure of a steadfast policy has been achieved. It can be found in many "savage" tribes, in the Jews in the time of Moses, in the medieval church, and in the Venetian aristocracy. The public will trancends the individual will and may display a kind of rationality that was never planned or purposed by anyone. In such a process we see the growth, for example, of the British colonial empire and the growth of the civil law. Public will is superior to unconscious adaptation, just as private will is superior to instinct and habit. It represents a higher principle of coordination and adaptation. It appears to be Cooley's idea here that for the most part the movement of history has been blind, unplanned, and the result of partial endeavors. It is time to enlist the public will in the intelligent planning of larger goals and larger plans of social action. (For the most part social ills have also been unplanned.) Cooley is not confident that an adequate public will will appear in the near future but thinks he can detect a trend in this direction.

The public will is not to be identified with government. The work of a single scientist, if it shows a public spirit, is also an act of public will. The public will is a diversified whole, "embracing the thought and purpose of all institutions and associations, formal and informal, that have any breadth of aim."[113] Government is well fitted to do some things and unfitted to do others.[114] It has certain advantages, in power and reach, not given to other institutions and it is, in a democracy, responsible to the people. It also has certain defects; it tends to be mechanical, rigid, costly, and unhuman. As "the most institutional of institutions" it also exhibits an undesirable formalism. In the United States, of course, there are spheres of government—federal, state, and local—and it is difficult to doubt that Cooley has a preference, indeed an affection, for the last of these. "There are few things that would be more salutary to the life of our people than a lively and effective civic consciousness in towns, villages and rural communities."[115] Cooley hopes that this consciousness is increasing.

The final word on the public will must be given to Cooley himself. It is the last paragraph of his book:

113. *Ibid.*, p. 403.

114. This, as we shall see, is one of MacIver's central theses.

115. *Ibid.*, p. 408.

The guiding force back of public will, now as ever, is of course human nature itself in its more enduring characteristics, those which find expression in primary groups and are little affected by institutional changes. This nature, familiar yet inscrutable, is apparently in a position to work itself out more adequately than at any time in the past.[116]

We see here again, as throughout his work, Cooley's quiet moral optimism.

Social Process

Social Process, which Cooley published in 1918, does not rank as high in the estimation of his critics and disciples as the two works discussed in the preceding sections. Indeed, it was reprinted ten years after the other two.[117] In a thoughtful Introduction to the reprint edition, Roscoe C. Hinkle points out that, with the exception of Sumner's *Folkways,* these three books of Cooley's are the only works of the earlier American sociologists that have been reprinted in their entirety. If *Social Process* seems even less well organized than *Social Organization,* the reason may be that it resembles a series of essays rather than a systematic work.[118] As Hinkle notes, if has a "diffuse structure," and Robert Gutman refers to it as "the most uneven and disappointing work in Cooley's trilogy."[119] We shall accordingly give it less space than the others.

At the beginning Cooley again professes his faith in the onward movement of life—a movement animated by such different forms of energy as men, factions, tendencies, doctrines, and institutions. Some of these, of course, are personal, others impersonal. A fashion or a myth, or a spoken language, cannot exist without persons. But similarly, personality would not exist if fashion, myth, language, and other institutions were taken away.[120] The personal and the impersonal, like self and society, overlap and blend into a single organic unity. Groups also have lives of their own,

116. *Ibid.*, p. 419.

117. Social Process. All references are to 1966 edition. (Originally published, New York: Scribner's Sons, 1918.) As indicated, the other two books are reprinted in *Two Major Works.*

118. Cooley's *Sociological Theory and Social Research,* a collection of essays, was published posthumously in 1930. Like his *Life and the Student,* published in 1927, it has not been reprinted.

119. "Cooley: A Perspective," *American Sociological Review* 23 (June 1958): 253.

120. "A language or a myth is verily alive; its life is human life; it has the same flesh and blood and nerves that you and I have, only the development of these is organized along lines other than those of personal consciousness." *Social Process,* p. 6. The analogy seems a bit extravagant.

whether they are as small as the family or as large as a nation. Every group, institution, idea—indeed, any form of human life—has a character of its own, a "correlation of complex tendencies," which helps to explain its organic history and how it will grow in the future. In the same way a book that an author is writing sometimes seems to take on a life of its own and move in unanticipated directions. These processes, "deep-rooted, organic, obscure," are poorly understood and cannot be reduced to a formula.

Cooley accepts the view that the movements of history, the social processes, are cyclical. "Every form of organization has its growth, its vicissitudes, and sooner or later, probably, its decline and disappearance. The mob assembles and disperses, fashions come in and go out, business prosperity rises, flourishes, and gives way to depression, the Roman Empire, after centuries of greatness, declines and falls."[121] Not only is this a sociological observation but it also pertains to life in general. These cycles, however, do not move in any predetermined, mechanical, or predictable way. No one knows when the next fashion will take hold, when the next economic depression will occur. Predictions based upon supposed laws governing these phenomena almost always turn out to be false. Cooley nevertheless retains his perennial optimism: "I take it that life as a whole is not a series of futile repetitions, but an eternal growth, an onward and upward development, if you please, involving the continual transformation or elimination of details. Just as humanity lives on while individuals perish, so the social organization endures while particular forms of it pass away."[122] The "onward and upward" theme is never far from Cooley's thoughts.

In society, however, as in life, conflict is inevitable. One can only hope that it will take on ever more humane and rational forms. Even the best marriage is a kind of strife. "The sexes are as naturally antagonistic as they are complementary, and it is precisely in their conflict that a passionate intimacy is found."[123] Cooley recognizes the in-group–out-group principle, without using Sumner's language, when he observes that cooperation within a group is brought about by opposition of the group as a whole to outside forces. Cooperation and conflict are not two separate processes but are only different phases of one process. Even in war enemies can develop mutual interest in and respect for one another. (In Cooley's era chivalry was not yet dead.) It does not follow from these considerations that conflict

121. *Ibid.*, p. 30. "Where institutions, like Christianity, have survived for a millennium or two, it is commonly not their organization that has endured, but a very general idea or sentiment which has vitalized successive systems, each of which has had its cycle of prosperity and decay [p. 31]."

122. *Ibid.*, p. 34.

123. *Ibid.*, p. 36.

is itself an index of progress. Some conflict fails to produce a greater degree of cooperation and is thus a waste. But in general progress is to be sought not in repressing conflict but in bringing it under rational control.

Cooley devotes a chapter to the refutation of something he calls intellectual particularism, by which he means any doctrine opposed to the view of organic process to which he subscribes. Here he has an opportunity to reject single-factor theories of social change, including the geographic and the economic.[124] No matter what factor one chooses, a little reflection will show that it is only a part of an organic whole. The organic view is not merely a theory but a concrete and verifiable fact. Recognition of this fact, however, should not prevent the study of society from particular points of view—the economic, the political, the military, the religious. One has to distinguish between the particularist and the specialist. "The latter is a man you can work with, while the former tries to rule the rest of us off the field."[125] Particularism is the result of something Cooley calls the illusion of centrality. Any factor can appear to be central if one so considers it.[126]

Particularism is also responsible for the failure of much social reform. Reformers tend to think that one kind of reform—the kind to which they are addicted—will solve the ills of society. Thus, the temperance reformers think that drink is the root of all evil, the socialists, that an unjust distribution of wealth is the root, and so on. It is necessary here also to take an organic view of the matter. Degeneration is part of the general process of life. Efforts to find "the cause" of any social phenomena are almost always fallacious. The use of statistics in these matters—for example, to say that 60% of insanity is due to alcohol, 30% to venereal disease—does not contribute to the precision of thought and instead often impairs it.

Two long sections, one entitled "Personal Aspects of Social Process" and the other "Degeneration," are useless for sociological purposes. They offer little more than moral preachments of the most pious and sentimental kind. A chapter devoted to the theory of success, which Cooley calls a sociological subject, is almost pure treacle. Some of his opinions are painful to read: On opportunity: "Opportunity cannot be realized without the ungrudging expenditure of money and spirit in the shape of devoted and well-equipped teachers, working without strain." On travel: "We travel to see the world; but one who stays at home with a spirit-building task will see more of it than one who travels without one." On service: "The merg-

124. On economic determinism see also the long note to p. 255 in *Social Organization*.

125. *Social Process*, p. 49.

126. "I have little hope of converting hardened particularists by argument; but it would seem that the spectacle of other particularists maintaining by similar reasoning views quite opposite to their own must, in time, have some effect upon them." *Ibid.*, p. 51.

ing of himself in the willing service of a greater whole raises man to the higher function of human nature." On religion: "The essence of religion, I suppose, is the expansion of the soul into the sense of a Greater Life; and the way to this is through that social expansion which, however less in extent, is of the same nature." On success: "Success is self-development in social service." More on success: "No matter what a man's external fortunes may be, how slender his purse or how humble his position, if he feels that he is living his real life, playing his full part in the general movement of the human spirit, he will be conscious of success." On God: "God is a builder; to be something we must build with him; understanding the plan if we can, but building in any case." On the spirit of a man: "The spirit of a man is the most practical thing in the world. You cannot touch or define it; it is an intimate mystery; yet it makes careers, builds up enterprises, and draws salaries." On helping: "Most of us who fail to help the world along do so not because we do not mean well, but because we lack force and persistency in well-doing." On anarchy: "Where there is anarchy in thought there will be anarchy in conduct." On striving: "Our civilization, whatever its promise, is far from having solved the problem of maintaining an upward striving in all its members."[127] These little nuggets of wisdom and uplift are perhaps characteristic of Cooley's time, and they are woefully characteristic of Cooley. They were evidently not embarrassing for him to write but they have now become embarrassing to read. Cooley, like Calvin Coolidge's preacher, is against sin.

When he turns to social factors in biological survival he again treats the subject of heredity and environment in much the same way that he had done earlier. It is a mistake to treat them separately because both are important. He places more emphasis upon heredity than has, until the rise of sociology perhaps, become customary, and he is sensitive to the need for social arrangements that will help to preserve and procreate superior stock. In order to preserve the general level of the race it is necessary that superior people have at least four children.[128] Furthermore, "if we find people living in a degeneracy which cannot clearly be ascribed to anything exceptional in the environment, we ought to hold the stock suspect, and prevent its propagation if we can."[129] Although it seems contrary to the democratic spirit, we need a revival of pride in ancestry, a resuscitation of the old ideal of the family line. "Only eugenic ideals and conduct can save from depletion those stocks which share most fully in the currents of progress," and it is

127. *Ibid.*, pp. 63, 70, 72, 75, 88, 94, 96, 170, 187, 192.

128. "A family of three children or less, where the parents are of good descent and, physically and as regards income, capable of having more, must be reckoned a 'race-suicide' family, not doing its share in keeping up the stock." *Ibid.*, p. 211.

129. *Ibid.*, p. 205.

for this reason, of course, that marital selection is so important. Marriage is never to be hasty or frivolous, or entered into for personal gratification. Although women have acquired more freedom and power than they have learned to use responsibly, Cooley is encouraged by the reflection that "there is no reason to believe that women will, in the long run, reject any real wisdom that the male mind may be able to contribute."[130]

Cooley is sure that conflict is ubiquitous in social life and that the struggle for existence, when not carried on under brutal or degrading conditions, is an essential guarantee against degeneracy. The notion of conflict itself leads him into a discussion of international relations, and here he has World War I much on his mind. Although he is in favor of international cooperation and even international organization, he nevertheless feels that the nation is an important entity, to which we dedicate our patriotism, and should be preserved. "Sound theory calls for a type of organism intermediate between the individual or the family and the world-whole which we hope to see arise."[131] Even intermittent war would be better than the demise of the national state. He notes that neither class conflict nor class consciousness is able to subordinate the spirit of nationalism.

The material in *Social Process* resembles a series of essays on separate subjects rather than a systematic work. They exhibit no continuity or logical development. There is an essay on "Social Science," for example, in which Cooley indulges in some quite elementary observations. He distinguishes between biology and sociology on two grounds: first, that social processes are much more rapid than biological ones, and second, that students of society are a conscious part of the process and can view it with sympathetic participation. Furthermore, social science is unique and requires methods independently contrived. "The sooner we cease circumscribing and testing ourselves by the canons of physical and physiological science the better."[132] Statistical methods may contribute precision but precision is no guarantee of truth. Throughout his writing, in fact, Cooley takes mild umbrage at statistics. Durkheim's study of suicide—and this is his only reference to Durkheim—is notable not for its statistics but for the notion of a type of suicide that is altruistic. Included among the qualifications for a sociologist are a patient love of truth and the fullest sympathy and participation in the currents of life. "At bottom any science is simply a more penetrating perception of facts, gained largely by selecting those that are more universal and devoting intensive study to them."[133] In

130. *Ibid.*, p. 216.
131. *Ibid.*, p. 256.
132. *Ibid.*, p. 397.
133. *Ibid.*, p. 403.

endowment at least Goethe was almost the ideal sociologist, and no sharp line should be drawn between science and art.

Summary and Evaluation

Cooley's general sociological views are quickly summarized. Throughout his work he emphasized something he called the organic view of things—a holism in which self and society are inseparable. Indeed, he was an opponent of all particularisms and entertained a deep suspicion of anyone who would attend to this or that aspect of a phenomenon in preference to seeing it as a whole. He approved of specialized interests only if they served as a window on the world. He could not abide a single-factor theory of society or of social change. There is a wholeness about society, a whole that includes the self, and only those who can comprehend this whole can measure up to his standards as a sociologist.

He touched on many if not most of the major concerns of the sociology of his time. He had something to say about institutions, social class, public opinion, the virtues and vices of mankind, and the onward and upward movement of the race. He was a social reformer in thought although not in deed. If his voice lacked vigor his heart nevertheless beat steadily in favor of the betterment of humanity.

As a sociological theorist Cooley contributed two ideas—one more than necessary perhaps—that earned him immortality in the literature of his discipline. They are, of course, the looking-glass conception of the self and the idea of the primary group.

"Self and society are twin-born"—we hear it again. The self is social, and without society it could never come to be. It matters not that Cooley fell into a minor inconsistency, that he first attributed a consciousness of self to the realm of instinct and then suggested that it has a social origin in the second year of life. The emphasis is on the social provenience of what is ineffably our own—our consciousness of ourselves. Our selves arise in juxtaposition with others; thus, the looking-glass conception of the self. We are not what we think we are, but what we think others think we are. One problem with this theory is that it creates too many selves—as many as there are mirrors in which we see ourselves reflected—that is, as many as there are persons with whom we interact. This problem, however, was solved by George Herbert Mead. Mead agreed with Cooley that the self is without any doubt a social product and a social phenomenon. It is not dozens of others, however, in whom we find dozens of selves, but it is rather a "generalized other" which saves us from multiplication and guarantees our integrity as a single self. In the simplest possible terms, we do not have to find ourselves in a multiplicity of others because there is a generalized other. What will people think if I do this or that? It is a question that we all often ask ourselves, even if often subliminally. The "people" here is the generalized other and it is thus to Mead that Cooley's theory owes a debt. It is a debt that he would gladly have acknowledged.[134]

Cooley's second major idea is the idea of the primary group. It is a concept that now belongs to the literature of sociology and one that is doubtless destined for immortality. Although Cooley himself never mentioned anything resembling a secondary group, we can place him too among those sociologists—practically all of them—who distinguished between personal relations on the one hand and impersonal relations on the other and even characterized entire societies in terms of the predominance of one of these kinds over the other. Impersonal relations, or status relations, are especially the mark of a complex society—a society whose members no longer know one another personally, who interact outside of their primary groups in accordance with the norms attached to statuses.[135] But it is the primary group to which belong our lovers and friends, our parents and children, our brothers and sisters, our playmates and colleagues. And it is Cooley who first appreciated its sociological significance and gave it a name.

A third idea of Cooley's, one that he did not satisfactorily develop, is the idea that society is mental. The degree to which he would want to claim, therefore, that its locus is in the mind is a question whose answer cannot be found in Cooley himself. Clearly it has the virtue of including, in our societies, those who once lived and those who exist only in the literature we read. But it presents complex and possibly insurmountable metaphysical problems. If society is mental it is difficult to avoid the inference that the physical world too is mental. And once this position is adopted the last barrier to solipsism falls away. Cooley, however, had no bent for metaphysics. He always contrasted it with "common sense," the latter greatly to be preferred, and it is doubtful that he was aware of the metaphysical implications of the position he had taken.[136]

---

134. See George Herbert Mead, *Mind, Self, and Society* (Chicago: University of Chicago Press, 1934), pp. 135–226. Mead was a suggestive but not a systematic thinker, and his interests lay in social psychology rather than in sociology. See Anselm Strauss (ed.), *George Herbert Mead on Social Psychology*, rev. ed. (Chicago: University of Chicago Press, 1964); Arnold M. Rose (ed.), *Human Behavior and Social Process* (Boston: Houghton Mifflin Co., 1962); and Herbert Blumer, *Symbolic Interactionism: Perspective and Method* (Englewood Cliffs, N.J.: Prentice-Hall, 1969). Lewis A. Coser has splendid chapters on both Cooley and Mead in his *Masters of Sociological Thought*, 2nd ed. (New York: Harcourt Brace Jovanovich, 1977).

135. See the treatment of norms, statuses, and groups in Bierstedt, *Social Order*.

136. In one of his journals he wrote, "Metaphysics—even such a genial sort as Pollock's

Finally, Cooley was a man of faith—faith in God, faith in society, and faith in progress. He shared fully in the pervasive optimism that characterized the American scene of his time and place. The new century opened up vistas for him, vistas of peace and plenty and an onward and upward movement in which virtue would triumph and evil would meet defeat. Not even the Great War could shatter his hopes for the future of mankind.

The reputation of Charles Horton Cooley would seem to be secure. Although one lacks the quantitative measure that would serve as evidence, it is conceivable that he has received more beneficent references in the literature than any other American sociologist. His humanism and his romanticism win the applause of those who, like Cooley himself, entertain a suspicion of systematic thinking. Philip Rieff, who regards him as "a village intellectual," nevertheless says that he possessed "the aesthetic gift," a gift he used "to compel the reader to share in his uniting and serene vision of the self lying peacefully in the maternal bed of society."[137] It was Cooley who wanted to preserve the virtues of a rural society at a time of vast industrial expansion. Even the urbane and sophisticated Rieff, conscious of Cooley's pieties, regards the two major works of Cooley as classic texts in American sociology—classic because they reflect something of importance about American society. In the opinion of Robert Gutman, Cooley is much more for us today than an "atavistic concern." His work possesses an immediacy that belies the time in which it was published. Indeed, "he is almost contemporary in his concern with the decline of individualism in American life, the difficulties involved in maintaining primary ideals such as loyalty in a bureaucratized society, the strains on individual personalities produced by mass organizations, and the disorganization of family life." Gutman presents the somewhat perverse thesis that Cooley was an anomaly in his own time because he speaks so directly to us.[138]

Cooley has also been given sensitive and faithful treatments by Roscoe C. Hinkle and Richard Dewey.[139] Hinkle's tribute we have already mentioned. Dewey pays tribute to Cooley as a writer of depth and sanity, one who "escaped from the passionate, but unscientific, enthusiasm of the advocate of social reform, on the one hand, and from the all too frequent narrowness and technicality of the laboratory psychologist and statistical sociologist, on the other." He is relatively sparing of praise, however, as is

Spinoza—is a strain to me, and I feel somewhat bloodless and purblind to the real world afterward." Quoted in Jandy, *Charles Horton Cooley*, p. 82.

137. Introduction to Cooley's *Social Organization* (New York: Schocken Books, 1962), p. xi.

138. "Cooley: A Perspective," pp. 251–256.

139. Hinkle, "Introduction," *Two Major Works;* and Dewey, "Charles Horton Cooley: Pioneer in Psychosociology," in ed. Harry Elmer Barnes, *An Introduction to the History of Sociology* (Chicago: University of Chicago Press, 1948), pp. 833–852.

Charles H. Page, who concludes a discussion of Cooley on class with the observation that those who share his general outlook "will find solace in his class ideas," but the "rigorous demands of a modern, more exacting social science will send many of us elsewhere."[140] Lewis A. Coser, who honors Cooley with a chapter of his own among only fifteen "masters of sociological thought," both European and American, writes that "none would deny that he should receive credit, along with such major figures as William James, Sigmund Freud, Emile Durkheim, and George H. Mead, for having succeeded in destroying the Cartesian disjunction between mind and the external social world."[141] Coser is induced to remark, however, that Cooley wrote little on the social structure and was not sensitive to the variables of which it is composed. One can go only so far, in short, in the direction of holistic synthesis without sacrificing the logical penetration that only particularistic analysis can provide. Jandy, like Coser, has no difficulty placing Cooley in the company of William James, George Herbert Mead, and John Dewey.[142] Finally, Willard Waller ranks Cooley with those "few men in history who have raised themselves above their fellows, not by deeds, but by their ability to know and to express what goes on in the human mind," and writes, in addition, that he "was one of the great men of his generation and possibly one of the great minds of all time."[143]

Waller's admiration is not universally shared. Cooley is a pleasant and unassuming companion as one discovers him in his books, but he is also given to platitude and to tedious exhortation. He was not a profound thinker or a sophisticated one, and although he used the expression in the title of his first book, he had no enduring sense of the social order. One must conclude nevertheless that his place in the pantheon of sociological heroes is a permanent one. He told us that the self is social at a time when we might have doubted it, if indeed it had occurred to us, and he told us too that of all groups the primary group—the group that is close and personal—plays a more important role than any other in the theater of human life.

140. *Class and American Sociology: From Ward to Ross,* rev. ed. (New York: Schocken Books, 1969), p. 209.

141. Coser, *Masters of Sociological Thought,* p. 310. Coser does not consider the possibility that the destruction was a mistake and that the disjunction is something that it is necessary to restore.

142. Jandy, *Charles Horton Cooley,* p. 269.

143. Introduction to *ibid.,* pp. 1–2.

CHAPTER 4

Edward Alsworth Ross

The endeavor to establish in each sphere of social life a single, typical sequence of changes is bound to fail.

—*Foundations of Sociology*, p. 62.

Edward Alsworth Ross was born in Virden, Illinois, on December 12, 1866, the son of William Carpenter Ross and Rachel Alsworth Ross. His father, who had prospected unsuccessfully for gold in California, moved his family often, from Virden to Centralia, Kansas, and to farms near Davenport and finally Marion, Iowa. He contributed antislavery letters to local newspapers but is otherwise unknown to history. Ross's mother taught in the high school in Marion. Edward was her second son by a second marriage. She succumbed to tuberculosis in 1874, when Edward was eight years old, and his father, an earlier victim of a paralytic stroke, died eighteen months later in 1876. The Ross family, however, enjoyed comparatively comfortable circumstances, and Edward's inheritance covered most of his school expenses through to his Ph.D. degree. During his orphaned childhood he was taken care of by a variety of relatives and finally found a home for five years with a farmer and justice of the peace, John Beach, and his younger second wife, Mary, who lived four miles from Marion. Edward's relationship to his foster mother was a warm one, as the abundance of correspondence, continuing until her death in 1904, can readily testify.[1]

At age fifteen Ross entered the preparatory division of Coe College, in Cedar Rapids, Iowa, a small Presbyterian school from which he was graduated less than five years later. There were fourteen students in his freshman class and six in his senior. There was only one curriculum, which included Greek and Latin, rhetoric, moral science, science and religion, and Christian Evidences. There was, of course, no smoking, dancing, liquor, or

1. This correspondence can be found in the Ross Papers, Archives-Manuscript Division, State Historical Society of Wisconsin, Madison, Wis. Biographical information is easily available in Ross's autobiography, *Seventy Years of It* (New York: D. Appleton-Century Co. 1936), and in Julius Weinberg, *Edward Alsworth Ross* (Madison, Wis.: State Historical Society of Wisconsin, 1972).

levity; daily recitations were required, and the students attended chapel twice a day. Despite the size of the college, the constrictions of the curriculum, and the rigidity of the discipline, Ross never felt ill prepared in comparison with those who received their undergraduate instruction in more illustrious citadels of education.[2]

After graduation he taught for two years at a two year Presbyterian college in Fort Dodge, Iowa, for a salary of $50 a month the first year and $60 the second. The teaching load was seven to eight classes a day; he taught English composition, American literature, German, physiology, physics, logic, psychology, and commercial law. He also taught Sunday school at the Presbyterian church. During these years he was reading widely and voraciously—Carlyle, Goethe, Mommsen, Prescott, Bancroft, Froude, Stubbs, Matthew Arnold, Darwin, Spencer, Draper, Fiske, Turgenev, Tolstoy, De Quincey, Coleridge, Kant, Fichte, and Hegel, among others—and was especially impressed by Carlyle. By this time he was fluent in German and used two summer sessions at Cornell College in Mount Vernon, Iowa, to learn French and Spanish. His gift for languages was such that for a time he hoped to pursue a career in comparative literature. Even before he left Coe College his Presbyterian faith began to waver. After reading Darwin's *The Descent of Man* he wrote to Mary Beach that he had become a "thoroughgoing evolutionist," wrote in his journal that religion was "hollow sham" and "beyond the bounds of logic," and sustained an accusation by a cousin that he was "tinctured with the skepticism of Spencer." He was quite willing to banish God to Spencer's realm of the Unknowable.

In the fall of 1888 Ross, like many American scholars before him, went to Germany, where he matriculated at the University of Berlin. There he attended Zeller's lectures on Greek philosophy and Paulsen's on Kant, was thrown into a period of despondency by Schopenhauer and von Hartmann, and read Kuno Fisher's five-volume *Geschichte der Neuern Philosophie.* Hegel convinced him that German philosophy was overly speculative and he was glad to return to the firm ground of British empiricism.[3] Among his

2. Coe College gave him an honorary degree in 1911.

3. On Hegel: "In my overweening self-confidence I tackled the toughest nut in German philosophy, Hegel's *Phänomenologie des Geistes.* I extracted some meaning up to page 185; at that point the trail dwindled and faded out." *Seventy Years of It,* p. 29. On philosophy in general:

> I have confidence only in that philosophy which begins by renouncing philosophy. Philosophy is an inquiry into the causes of things and the basis of their existence. This is an idle question leading to nothing but failure and despair. The philosophy that sets as its task the determination of the regular time-and-space order of groups of similar phenomena is the only one that is not doomed to disappoint.

Ibid., p. 32.

friends at Berlin were Julian W. Mack, later a judge of the United States Circuit Court; W. A. Heidel, later professor of Greek philosophy at Wesleyan University; Frank Thilly, later professor of philosophy at Cornell University, E. W. Scripture, later director of the Phonetic Institute at the University of Vienna; Frank Sharp, later professor of ethics at the University of Wisconsin; J. A. Morehead, later a high official in the Lutheran church; Frederic Hamilton, later chancellor of American University in Washington; and R. R. Marett, later the distinguished anthropologist and rector of Exeter College, Oxford.[4]

After a walking tour of central and southern Europe in the fall of 1889, Ross returned to the United States and enrolled for more graduate study at Johns Hopkins University. Modeled after the German university, Johns Hopkins was the leading graduate school in the country. Of the graduate students there at the time, as Ross notes, two-thirds achieved distinction in their careers. Among his teachers were such notables as Richard T. Ely, Woodrow Wilson, James Bryce, Herbert Baxter Adams, and Simon Newcomb. The most important influence, however, was Lester Frank Ward, whose two-volume *Dynamic Sociology* he read while at Johns Hopkins. Ross formed "a little band of Wardians," met the great man himself at a meeting of the American Economic Association in Washington in 1890, and two years later, on June 16, 1892, married Rosamond C. Simons, a niece of Ward's second wife. As Weinberg observes, "Ward had no more articulate a disciple among American sociologists than Ross, nor more ardent an admirer."[5] Ross dedicated his first book, *Social Control*, to Ward and named two of his sons after him; the two men carried on a voluminous correspondence until Ward's death in 1913.[6] It was Ward also, along with Richard T. Ely, who helped to turn the younger scholar's interests from economics to sociology. At Johns Hopkins he had taken political economy as a major, with minors in history and philosophy, and wrote his doctoral dissertation on "sinking funds," a technique for funding the public debt.[7]

In the spring of 1891 David Starr Jordan, then president of Indiana University, came to Baltimore looking for an economist, and Ely advised him to offer the appointment to Ross. The times were propitious for young professors. It took Ross only three years to rise from instructor to full professor. He went to Bloomington in the fall of 1891 with a salary of $1500,

4. From Ross's journal: "He [Marett] is the first chap I have met near my own age who is at every point intellectually a match for me and at some my superior." *Ibid.*, p. 37.

5. *Edward Alsworth Ross*, p. 31.

6. The Ward-Ross correspondence, edited by Bernhard J. Stern, appears in *American Sociological Review*, vols. 3, 11–14, 1938, 1946–1949.

7. *Sinking Funds* (Baltimore, Md.: Guggenheim, Weil, and Co., 1892).

and by the end of the following calendar year he had offers from Jordan, who had become president of Stanford University, at $2250, and from Cornell University and Northwestern University, at $2500. He accepted the Cornell offer—an associate professorship—but remained at Ithaca only one semester before going to Stanford in 1893 as a full professor with a salary of $3500 a year. Even as late as 1920 a salary of this size enabled its fortunate possessor to keep at least one domestic servant and to travel with his family to Europe during the long summer vacation.

The classroom was too cramped an enclosure to contain a man of Ross's energy and size. Physically, he stood 6 feet, 6 inches, a mountain among men, and he had an intellectual vigor to match. During the year at Indiana he gave a series of public lectures in Indianapolis on current economic problems and also gave lectures at Rochester, New York, the following year, all of which were well reported in the press and established a pattern that continued for the rest of his life. He had a fondness for the lectern and accordingly became a public figure in all the states in which he taught. He was a Populist and a reformer, one who was convinced of the chicanery of industrialists and capitalists, the sins of the trusts, the abuses of the monetary system, the perils of the gold standard, and the oppressions visited upon the farmer and the working man. His extension course in Rochester brought an audience of 175 persons, and he talked on such subjects as "Signs and Causes of Social Discontent," "The Good Side of the Industrial Revolution," "The Bad Side of the Industrial Revolution," "The Workingman as Plaintiff," "The Farmer as Plaintiff," "The Consumer as Plaintiff," and, in four separate lectures, on the history, nature, strength, and weakness of socialism.[8] He also produced a continuous stream of articles in the national magazines, on such subjects as "The Standard of Deferred Payments," "A New Canon of Taxation," "The Total Utility Standard of Deferred Payments," "The Shifting and Incidence of Taxation," "The Tendencies of Natural Values," and "The Principles of Economic

8. The Rochester *Union and Advertiser* commented as follows:

> The fifteen lectures he has delivered before his class during the past four months have been listened to with deep interest and they have made for him a large circle of friends and admirers. However much one may differ from him, it cannot be denied that he is a profound student, a clear thinker and a stimulating teacher. He has the rare faculty of presenting abstruse questions in a concrete and practical way that brings his lectures within the easy comprehension of the untrained and uninformed mind. Then again he has the rare trait of fairness and impartiality; that is, he always tries to be fair and treat opponents and opposing views with consideration. He is likewise considerate of every effort of his pupils to seek enlightenment. He answers their questions, whether trivial or not, fully and without impatience. It was because of these traits that his class parted with him so reluctantly last evening for the last time.

Quoted in *Seventy Years of It*, pp. 49–50.

Legislation." In addition, he "secretly" wrote the verse for some light opera. In this last endeavor, however, he did not enjoy his customary success. During the year 1892–1893 he also served as secretary of the American Economic Association.

Stanford in 1893 would seem to have been an idyllic place for a young professor to build a career. It was there, in the sunshine of California, that Ross conceived the idea of *Social Control*, published first as a series of twenty articles in the *American Journal of Sociology*, at the invitation of Albion W. Small. It was there too that he wrote the article "Mob Mind,"[9] which contained the germ of his *Social Psychology*, which he published in 1908. Nevertheless, there was something about the place that he distrusted. His friend David Starr Jordan was too thoroughgoing an evolutionist for Ross's taste, and Jordan's course on the subject seemed to give Stanford an official ideology. Social Darwinism, moreover, was an ideology that seemed to justify the brutally competitive practices of big business, for which Ross had an outspoken antipathy. Leland Stanford had founded the university in 1891 in memory of his son, who died in his fifteenth year. He was himself a big businessman, builder and president of railroads, a governor of California, and, at his death, a United States Senator. There is some doubt whether Ross ever referred to him as a "robber," but Mrs. Leland Stanford, who "inherited" the university from her husband, thought he did, and that was enough to arouse her hostility. Futhermore, Ross appeared almost eager to instigate an academic freedom case—with himself as victim and martyr—in his tireless public advocacy of free silver, curbs on trusts, the regulation of railroads, and public ownership of utilities, together with his support of Eugene V. Debs and of the Pullman strikers and his appearance as a speaker to the Socialist Club of Oakland. These activities, which incidentally cost him the presidency of the University of Washington, culminated in a lecture on May 7, 1900, in San Francisco in which he expressed strong opposition to continued "coolie" immigration to the United States.[10] When Mrs. Stanford, then in Europe, read a newspaper

9. *Popular Science Monthly*, July 1897.

10. Ross's sentiments were quite strong. In this lecture he was accused of saying, "Should the worst come to the worst it would be better for us to train our guns on every vessel bringing Japanese to our shores rather than to permit them to land." He was also opposed to the immigration of people from southern and eastern Europe. For a "certified liberal" he was astonishingly reactionary—even racist—on this issue. Weinberg writes: "As a liberal-minded Progressive, Ross was a social optimist, an environmentalist, and a believer in the equality of all peoples; as a nativist, he was fearful about the country's future, hereditarian in many of his explanations of human behavior, and elitist in his attitude toward non-Anglo-Saxons." *Edward Alsworth Ross*, p. 149; see the entire chapter, "The Sociologist as Nativist," pp. 149–176. Ross could even be condescending to the English: "I came to be very fond of the English. It is amaz-

account of the lecture, she demanded that Ross's appointment be terminated. She was particularly upset because the young professor had drawn distinctions "between man and man—all laborers, and equal in the sight of God."[11]

David Starr Jordan, president of the university, was now uncomfortably in the middle, with Mrs. Stanford, the generous benefactor and indeed "owner" of the university on the one side, and Ross, his longtime friend (whose views on Japanese immigration he apparently shared) on the other. He tried for some months to persuade Mrs. Stanford to change her mind and, failing in the effort, accepted Ross's resignation on November 11, 1900. The case became a cause célèbre. Reactions came immediately from over 800 daily newspapers, most of them in support of Ross. Organized labor came to his support; the presidents of Harvard (Charles W. Eliot) and Yale (Arthur Twining Hadley) made statements in favor of academic freedom; seven members of the Stanford faculty resigned in protest; and James D. Phelan, champion of the working man and mayor of San Francisco, gave a formal dinner in his honor. Two formal investigations of the matter were undertaken, one by the Stanford Alumni Association, which concluded that the university had not violated Ross's academic freedom, and the other by a special committee of the American Economic Association, which concluded the reverse. The association committee was chaired by Edwin R. A. Seligman of Columbia, and its report was signed by, in addition to Seligman and others, Franklin Henry Giddings and John Bates Clark of Columbia, Richard T. Ely of Wisconsin, Henry Carter Adams of Michigan, and Frank William Taussig of Harvard. Weinberg concludes his excellent account of the affair by saying, "The final resolution of the controversy favored Ross in almost every way. Ross emerged from the fracas a martyr to the cause of academic freedom and a hero to Progressives throughout the country. Stanford's reputation for many decades was tarnished."[12]

---

ing how many of them are really civilized." *Seventy Years of It*, p. 59. Late in life he renounced the racist views he had earlier expressed with such enthusiasm, saying,

> Difference of race means far less to me now than once it did. Starting on my explorations with the *naive* feeling that only my own race is right, all other races are more or less "queer," I gained insight and sympathy until my heart overleapt barriers of race. . . . Far behind me in a ditch lies the Nordic Myth, which had some fascination for me forty years ago.

Ibid., p. 276.

11. Letter of Jane Lathrop Stanford to David Starr Jordan, May 9, 1900, quoted in Weinberg, *Edward Alsworth Ross*, p. 48.

12. *Ibid.*, p. 54. Ross's own account which includes both reports mentioned above, appears on pages 64–86 of *Seventy Years of It.* See also Richard Hofstadter and Walter P. Metzger, *The Development of Academic Freedom in the United States* (New York: Columbia University

The spring semester of 1901 found Ross at the University of Nebraska, where he taught three courses—Social Psychology, Education and Society, and Cities. His appointment was made permanent in June of that year, and he taught there for five "contented" years until 1906, when he moved to the University of Wisconsin, there to remain for thirty years, until his retirement in 1937, a distinguished member of a distinguished faculty, which included such men as Richard T. Ely and John R. Commons in economics, Max B. Otto in philosophy, and Frederick Jackson Turner in history. It was a progressive university in a progressive state, and Ross and his colleagues became the intellectual leaders of the Progressive movement in the United States.

In 1910 Ross began his career as a world traveler, an avocation he was to pursue with zest for the remainder of his life. He had discovered that by teaching two summer sessions without pay he could take a semester off with pay once every three years. His travels—to China, South America, Russia, Africa, India, Mexico, Europe, and other places around the world—resulted in a spate of books and articles that were widely read and admired in their time and place.[13] Despite certain reservations, he approved of the Russian revolution, seeing in it the realization of some of his Populist and Progressive ideas. His travels and his constant writing and lecturing on popular platforms indubitably interfered with his strictly sociological production and possibly with his sociological creativity. As Weinberg says, "Had Ross shunned the popular essays and lecture series, the commencement lecture and the foreign jaunt, his contribution to American sociology would have been more significant and his place in the history of American sociology more secure and important."[14]

Ross retired from the University of Wisconsin in 1937, at the age of seventy. He was to enjoy fifteen more years of life until his death on July 22, 1951. His first wife, Rosamond, died while he was on a tour of rest and relaxation in Tahiti in 1932, and in 1940 he married Helen Forbes, a former assistant to Dr. John Harvey Kellogg, a surgeon and medical writer of Battle Creek, Michigan. He continued his vigorous activities for at least another decade, enjoying his reputation both as an elder statesman in

---

Press, 1955), pp. 436–445. Lester Frank Ward commented, "I hardly know what to say about the affairs at Stanford. What a disgrace it is that the opinions of professors are made the ground for hunting them about from place to place! The inevitable effect is to make sycophants of all that remain and drive out all that have merit or character." Ward to Ross, October 26, 1900, quoted in *American Sociological Review* 11 (December 1946): 742–743.

13. The books include *The Changing Chinese* (1910), *South of Panama* (1915), *Russia in Upheaval* (1918), *The Russian Bolshevik Revolution* (1921), *The Russian Soviet Republic* (1923), *The Social Revolution in Mexico* (1923), and *World Drift* (1928).

14. *Edward Alsworth Ross*, p. 201.

sociology and as a public figure. One remembers him at sessions of the American Sociological Society (as it then was), sitting in the front row, his hand cupped to his ear, his huge figure straining to hear the words of the speaker. He had been honored with the presidency of the society in 1914 and was the last man to be elected to a second year in that office.

As a public figure he continued to write and speak on behalf of liberal and reformist causes. He supported Franklin Delano Roosevelt and the social legislation of the New Deal. He was a devoted member of the American Association of University Professors and took an active role in a number of academic freedom cases. He joined the American Civil Liberties Union in 1921, became a member of its board of directors in 1925, and served as chairman of the board from 1940 to 1950.[15] He was, as his biographer says, a man in constant motion almost to the day of his death. Once again I quote Weinberg:

> No sociologist in the nation acquired the fame enjoyed by Ross during the Progressive Era and the decade that followed. Many of his colleagues were hard-working and competent scholars; some made contributions of greater significance to the development of American sociology; none possessed his influence on public opinion, his breadth of interests, his flair for publicizing a well-turned phrase, or his entrepreneurial skill in converting an inherently cloistered profession into a lucrative, exciting, and practical vocation.[16]

All in all, he was a likable giant on the American scene.

Social Control

Although Ross wrote twenty-nine books, his sociological theory is contained in only four—*Social Control, Foundations of Sociology, Social Psychology,* and *The Principles of Sociology.*[17] The idea for *Social Control* came to him one day while he was working in the library at Stanford University and much of the book was published as separate papers in the

15. The story of these activities is well told by Weinberg in chap. 10, "The Declining Years, 1931–1951," *ibid.*

16. *Ibid.*, p. 222. See also John L. Gillin, "The Personality of E. A. Ross," *American Journal of Sociology* 42 (January, 1937): 534–542.

17. For a bibliography of Ross from his doctoral dissertation in 1891 to his last paper in 1948, see J. O. Hertzler, "Edward Alsworth Ross: Sociological Pioneer and Interpreter," *American Sociological Review* 16 (October 1951): 609–613. The article itself, pp. 597–613, is an excellent brief summary of Ross's contributions.

American Journal of Sociology between the years 1896 and 1901.[18] Ross writes in his Preface that the book belongs to a narrow sector of sociology, the sector denominated as social psychology, which, in turn, has two branches, the first of which, social ascendancy, deals with the domination of society over the individual, and the second, individual ascendancy, deals with the domination of the individual over society. Unlike Cooley, Ross appears at the outset to be making a sharp distinction between the individual and society, seeing them, as it were, as two separate entities. In any event, social ascendancy is divided further into social influence and social control—the former exerted in unintended, the latter in intended, ways. The subject of social control is thus only one subdivision of social psychology, which is itself a subdivision of sociology.

When he began his inquiry Ross was inclined to believe that social order was a phenomenon that could be explained only by society and that the individual contributed little to it. He goes on to say:

> Further investigation, however, appears to show that the personality freely unfolding under conditions of healthy fellowship may arrive at a goodness all its own, and that order is explained partly by this streak in human nature and partly by the influence of social surroundings. As I now conceive it my task is, therefore, first, to separate the individual's contribution to social order from that of society, and, second, to bring to light everything that is contained in this social contribution.[19]

Thus, for Ross there is apparently a "streak in human nature" that is separate from society and for which society is not responsible.

Ross elaborates upon the problem in his first chapter. A group of pedestrians or vehicles in constant collision with one another would clearly indicate an absence of order. But there is no order either in a group of pedestrians or vehicles all going in the same direction at the same pace. In the latter situation there is no need for order because there is no interference, collision, or conflict. In other words, order appears only in situations that would, so to speak, be disorderly if there were no rules. This is a splendid insight, and the reader begins at once to associate the ideas of social order and social control with norms—although Ross seldom uses this last word and does not elevate it to the status of a concept. Similarly, there is a difference between order and peace. The weaker of two hunters, who surrenders to the stronger the stag that both of them have brought down,

18. The full title is *Social Control: A Survey of the Foundations of Order* (New York: Macmillan, 1901). It was reprinted in 1929, and a photo-offset of the 1929 reprint was published in 1969 by Case Western Reserve University Press, Cleveland and London. Subsequent page references are to the 1929 edition.

19. *Ibid.*, p. viii.

has achieved peace but not order. If they substitute a rule that "first struck" deserves the game, then we have the introduction of order. The highest expression of order appears in a complex division of labor where multifarious activities are nicely coordinated.

The reaction of individuals to order, however, depends upon their "mental make-up." Some are peaceable and readily respond to it; some are pugnacious and do not. If there are individual differences here, so also are there racial: "In a passive race, once order is established, the individual keeps to his prescribed orbit from sheer inertia. In an aggressive race order is perpetually endangered by the unruliness of the individual, and can be maintained only through the unremitting operation of certain social forces."[20] The Teuton is more self-assertive than the docile Slav or the quiescent "Hindoo," and the American is "more strong-willed and unmanageable than even the West-European."[21] Accordingly, Ross sees it as his problem to explain why men of the Western European "breed," the "restless, striving, doing Aryan," have managed to achieve some discipline and order.

Ross observes that many would fail to see order as a problem, that to them disorder is the phenomenon that requires attention. Social order, however, is a human achievement and we must learn how violence among men has been subdued, and struggle controlled. In a slight inconsistency with his earlier statement, Ross says that the notion that order can be explained by the individual's inherited equipment is a delusion. The commandments that produce order are not "etched upon the soul." Ants, beavers, and prairie dogs also exhibit order in their living arrangements and it is possible therefore that social instincts could explain the order of human society as well. The order of human society, however, is not a mere hive or herd order; "it seems to be a *fabric* rather than a *growth*."[22] To ascertain the nature of this fabric we have to consider the moral capital of the person and especially the roles of sympathy, sociability, the sense of justice, and resentment in the establishment of order.

SYMPATHY AND SOCIABILITY

Ross's explanation of the rise of sympathy and sociability in the human species is a Darwinian one. There is a weeding-out process. The quarrelsome are eliminated, the disorderly are "drained away," and the orderly become preponderant. Of course the gentle may also succumb to the

20. *Ibid.*, p. 3.
21. *Ibid.*
22. *Ibid.*, p. 5.

violent, or be self-eliminated "by a mistaken celibacy." But it is likely that social selection removes those at both extremes—the gentle and the ferocious—and it may not be certain after all that the net effect is one that raises the level of sympathy. In short, Ross is not sure that the Darwinian explanation works, especially when it is recognized that social selection adapts to earlier rather than to current conditions. What we have to reflect upon is the enormous range of moral variety in the human species and the variations that different races exhibit in this regard. Sympathy cannot explain the existence of social order, primarily because of the great inequalities that still remain among men. "It is *obedience* that articulates the solid, bony framework of social order; *sympathy* is but the connective tissue. As well build a skeleton out of soft fibre as construct social order out of sympathies":

> Not friendly aid, but reliable conduct, is the corner-stone of great organization. Now, sympathy will stay the hand of the wife-beater, but it will not spurn the bribe or spare the lie. It will snatch a child from trampling hoofs, but it will not keep the watchman awake, or hold the contractor to the terms of his agreement. It will nerve the rescuing fireman, but it will not stimulate the official to do his duty. It will relieve the beggar, but it will not stop the adulteration of goods. It will man the lifeboat, but it will not lead men to give just weight, to make true returns of their property, or to slay their country's enemies.[23]

Sympathy thus has its limits as an explanation of social order. It may explain a great deal of the harmony that appears in the primary group—although Ross does not use Cooley's concept—but it has little relevance to the larger society.

In addition to sympathy, human nature exhibits certain gregarious instincts that contribute to social order. They do not, however, contribute much because their roots do not run deep. "Those enthusiasts, then, who draw charming lessons from the study of gregarious animals and of social insects, not only fail to give us the clew to human association, but are very apt to lead us quite astray as to the real causes of social order."[24] It is a paradox of anthropology, incidentally, that some of the most peaceful and orderly of societies can be found on the lowest levels of culture. The savage, so-called, is not necessarily savage at all—and Ross supplies numerous illustrations. On the contrary, "primitive folks show in unusual degree the traits that make order a matter of course." It is the Teuton, the Anglo-Saxon, and the American (that "most Westerly decanting of the Germanic race") who is the most ferocious and aggressive, and if social

23. *Ibid.*, p. 12.
24. *Ibid.*, pp. 14–15.

organization finally appears in these fierce people it is for economic rather than ethical reasons. It is intellect, not instinct, that teaches the virtue and advantage of association. If the groupings of primitive men are natural societies, those of civilized men are artificial societies.[25] It is interlacing interests, not sociable instinct, that create the latter.

SOCIAL ORIGINS

Ross appears to reject Giddings's "consciousness of kind" and to find, with Gumplowicz and Ratzenhofer, the origin of the state in force and conquest:

> If we take up, one by one, the forms of union that are mighty and spreading in these days, we can see that each of them owes its existence to something else than the charm of like for like. It is a commonplace of history that the unceasing agglomeration of communities has never been due to the mutual attraction of peoples, but always to conquest or to combination for defence. Not sentiment, but invariably force or the dread of force, has called into being that most extensive of co-operations, the State.[26]

If illustration be needed, consider the modern city, surely the work of economic man, not social man. The "long-skull Teuton," now building the cities of central Europe, is the least sociable of men, albeit the most energetic, ambitious, and hardy. And it is in the city that social order most definitely parts company with the sociable impulse. If further evidence be needed, consider the high repute and persistence of fighting in Western societies—the pugnacity of boys, the custom of the duel, the fistic encounters of the lower classes, the popularity of hunting. Furthermore, Western man is averse to physical intimacy and therefore lives apart from his fellows, in separate domiciles.[27] "With us society is a cunning piece of joinery reared above the devouring waves of self-interest."[28] If sociability is not the basis of social order, it nevertheless performs its services. It stimulates the formation of circles, clubs, and fraternities, and encourages the sentiments of friendship and brotherhood.

The sense of justice, which Ross tries to explain by the concern that ego has for alter, is far more intellectual than sympathy. The sense of fair play

25. As in the case of Ward, the use of the word *artificial* in this context is entirely devoid of pejorative connotations.

26. *Ibid.*, p. 18.

27. This aloofness Ross attributes to the Anglo-Saxon character and refers to the curious book of Edmond Demolins, *Anglo-Saxon Superiority*, which appeared in its English edition in 1898, translated from the tenth French edition. (London: The Leadenhall Press, 1898.)

28. *Social Control*, p. 21.

appears both in war and in sport—even in business and politics. It is a virtue that belongs only to men, since women do not participate in the egoistic struggle. "The social group, by drilling its members to observe certain forbearances toward one another, *manufactures* conscience."[29] What reconciles men—even violent men—to one another is not affection but a sense of fairness. It is this sense, alternatively called the sense of justice, that the great conquering and civilizing races possess, a sense that is not at all incompatible with greed, lust, and brutality. This is the virtue, and these the vices, of warriors. "In the sense of fair play," furthermore, "we detect the first superior endowment of the Teutonic peoples for social order. While the long-skulled blond of central and northwestern Europe is mediocre in power of sympathy and weak in sociability, he is strong in that most important of political aptitudes—the will to justice."[30] Unfortunately, the remainder of this discussion of the sense of justice degenerates into racial comparisons between Teutons and such inferior peoples as Egyptians, Chinese, Byzantines, and Saracens. Ross does not pretend that he knows that answer to the differences but suggests that climate may have something to do with it: "A northern climate spares only those who 'look before and after,' while the kindly sun of the warmer lands lets the careless and improvident live."[31] Is the sense of justice or fair play then responsible for the social order? The answer, like the answer to the role of sympathy, is again in the negative. The sense of justice can sustain an order that is in existence, but it cannot generate it. "The bare predilection for justice does not, of itself, give us the secret of a perfected social order."[32]

After sympathy, sociability, and the sense of justice, a fourth factor enters into Ross's calculation. He calls it variously the dread of retaliation, the resentment of the person acted upon, and individual reaction, and it is more than a mere defensive reflex. It is the egoistic side of the sense of injustice:

> The more one recoils from *doing* an unjust action, the more he resents *suffering* such an action. On its altruistic side, the sense of justice lessens aggression

29. *Ibid.*, p. 28. Although it is awkwardly expressed, Ross has an interesting observation: "The fittest to survive when the competition is man-wise, may be eliminated when the competition is group-wise [p. 29]." Although we had not mentioned it earlier, perhaps because it seemed unnecessary, the premises of Ross's discussion are firmly lodged in Social Darwinism.

30. *Ibid.*, p. 32.

31. *Ibid.*, p. 33. "And that capacity for reflection so necessary to conscience? Did the early Western man get it from the long cold of his winters, which by depriving him of the outdoor, sensuous life of the South threw him back upon his thoughts? We do not know." Shades of Montesquieu!

32. *Ibid.*, p. 35. Ross's procedure here is like that of Durkheim in *Suicide*, as he ticks off factors that are not the cause of social order.

> by inspiring respect for the claims of others. On its egoistic side, it lessens aggression by prompting to the energetic assertion of one's own claims.[33]

Resentment, like the other sentiments mentioned, is a moral quality.[34] We thus have four natural pillars of a social order—sympathy, sociability, the sense of justice, and resentment. As can be seen, Ross wavers in his estimate of their importance. He seems to suggest, in spite of his treatment of them in separate chapters, that they do not quite explain what he wants them to explain. In any event, he confesses that he does not know how much of the control that society exercises over the individual is natural and how much is artificial. He sees a natural order arising when men come together from different societies and form a new aggregate.[35]

The Arcadian days of peace in the new aggregate, however, cannot last. Economic equality turns into economic inequality, and the differentiation that the latter represents turns sooner or later into an inequality of property:

> Private property is, in fact, a great transforming force which acts almost independently of the human will. It has an evolution of its own, and the time comes at last when it violently thrusts men apart, in spite of all their vows to draw closer together. As it warps society farther and farther from the pristine equality that brings out the best in human nature, there is need of artificial frames and webs that may hold the social mass together in spite of the rifts and seams that appear in it. Property is, therefore, the thing that calls into being *rigid* structures. It is the reagent that precipitates hard crystals, the lime that changes gristle into bone.[36]

The laws pertaining to the inheritance of property force a serious dilemma upon society—either let each person start the race with equal resources or deny to some the fruits of the victory for which they have struggled. Institutions are thus not shaped by single ethical principles but rather encompass contradictions of one sort or another. It is the contradictions that show the need for control. It is possible, of course, that a natural order could arise and belie the need for an artificial order. But it is not likely and, in any event, it would be a crude and imperfect order. Men are in constant need of an order more reliable than that which their natural moral motives can provide. Most of us, fortunately, are born with a certain "fitness" for order. "Ages of social weathering have allowed a mantle of soft green to creep over the flint of animal ferocity and selfishness. But this layer of soil is too thin. The abundant fruits of righteousness we need to-day must grow

33. *Ibid.*, p. 37.

34. It is not altogether clear why Ross should view determined (and physical) resistance to aggression as one of the foundations of order, but this nevertheless is his contention.

35. An example would be the men who thronged to the mining camps of California in 1848.

36. *Ibid.*, p. 53.

on *made* soil."[37] Furthermore, continuous control is necessary because the moral habits of one generation are not transformed into the instincts of the next.

If sympathy makes for helpfulness and the sense of injury makes for retaliation, their interaction leads to moral indignation, which in turn encourages the community to interfere and, in a gradual encroachment of society upon the individual, to transform wrongs into crimes, and to introduce and maintain social control.

> Like the hypothesis that storks bring babies, the theory that the moral instincts beget control has a distressing lack of finality. But how the mystery lights up when we reach the idea of *society,*—a something distinct from a bunch of persons! For we can regard this society as a living thing, actuated, like all the higher creatures, by the instinct of self-preservation. Social control, then, appears as one of the ways in which this living thing seeks to keep itself alive and well.[38]

Alive and well also, in Ross, is the organic analogy.

The control that society exercises is not always apparent. Sometimes society speaks to the individual in the language of sentiment rather than of interest. Sometimes control is adapted not to the real but to the supposed interests of society. Sometimes it outlives the conditions that brought it into being. And finally, its tenor changes from time to time. "The life of a given society reveals a bewildering series of metamorphoses in laws, moral standards, and personal ideals. And one might well hesitate to connect the changes in the legality or morality of slavery, insolvency, usury, heresy, or polygamy, with changes in the requisites of the social welfare."[39]

In his discussion of the direction of social control Ross makes an interesting point, namely, that public morality is never as high as private morality. The state, for example, expects its officers to perform on its behalf acts that it would not tolerate if they performed them on their own. The state requires the diplomat to lie, the spy to betray, and the soldier to kill. Similarly, all religions practice an ethical dualism, one code for themselves and another for the rest of the world.

CODES AND CONTROLS

Quite unexpectedly, and without introduction, Ross classifies the various codes and controls. First is the control of the crowd—aimless, arbitrary, and capricious, without respect for individual rights. Second, and superior

37. *Ibid.*, pp. 59–60.
38. *Ibid.*, p. 67.
39. *Ibid.*, p. 68.

to the crowd, is the moral code, which reflects and represents public opinion, a control guided by time and wisdom. The third of the norms (this is one of the few times that Ross uses this word) is custom. Customs possess a certain fitness because they have been hallowed by time, but, as companion to this virtue, they face the past rather than the future and often lose all semblance of rationality. Fourth is the religious code, the custodian of the obscure interests of society. Finally, there is the legal code, the code of the state, the least sentimental and most progressive of all. Ross recognizes that the moral code and the legal code are often at odds but spends little effort in analyzing their relationships.[40] The famous question of Tacitus—*Quid leges sine moribus*?—does not excite his curiosity.

SOCIAL CONTROL AND SOCIAL POWER

Social control is a function of society in its entirety, but nevertheless there are certain "radiant points" that can be discerned. Who, in society, manipulates the levers of social control? Sometimes a minority does this, but Ross does not approve on the ground that it implies a rupture of social consciousness. The subject leads him into a discussion of social power and to the following sentence: "Social power is concentrated or diffused in proportion as men do or do not feel themselves in need of guidance or protection."[41] Men transfer power to those in whom they feel confidence, and when they gain confidence in their own strength and wisdom, they withdraw the power from the class to which they had entrusted it and the monopoly of power ceases.

Ross associates power with prestige:

> The immediate cause of the location of power is prestige. The class that has the most prestige will have the most power. The prestige of *numbers* gives ascendency to the crowd. The prestige of *age* gives it to the elders. The prestige of *prowess* gives it to the war chief, or to the military caste. The prestige of sanctity gives it to the priestly caste. The prestige of *inspiration* gives it to the prophet. The prestige of *place* gives it to the official class. The prestige of *money* gives it to the capitalists. The prestige of *ideas* gives it to the élite. The prestige of *learning* gives it to the mandarins.[42]

Ross is almost certainly wrong in these contentions. Prestige and power are independent variables, as can be seen, for example, in that an honorific society, say Phi Beta Kappa, has prestige but no power; a criminal gang,

---

40. Ross's classification of the codes has some similarity to MacIver's. MacIver pays tribute to Ross in *Society*.

41. *Ibid.*, p. 78 (italics omitted).

42. *Ibid.*, pp. 78–79.

power but no prestige. Furthermore, the power of money and the power of ideas are quite different phenomena. The latter is influence rather than power.[43] But Ross is correct to note that social power, "which has hardly even yet drawn the attention of social science," tells us more of the inner constitution of society than does political power. The power of the priesthood was especially great from the sixth to the thirteenth centuries in Western Europe. The state, of course, is one of the "radiant points" of social control, as is also, in some societies, a mandarinate or an elite.[44] Finally, there is the genius, the man whom we have since learned to call the charismatic leader. Ross thinks it perfectly proper to follow the lead of superior men. To do otherwise is foolish and dangerous.

Ross comments on the individualism of American society and of the resistance of Americans to social control. "It is not nature," he says, "for men of a vigorous Northern breed to bend the neck." Writing in 1901, however, he predicts that the democratic tradition in this country will meet adverse conditions in the new century, that the moneyed man, the state, and the mandarinate will become increasingly powerful.[45]

THE INSTUMENTS OF SOCIAL CONTROL

The second, large, part of Ross's book is devoted to the means of social control, among which he discusses in turn such phenomena as public opinion, law, belief, education, custom, "social religion," and other related subjects. In the community's reaction to conduct that displeases it, Ross distinguishes public judgment, public sentiment, and public action, to which correspond the sanctions of opinion, intercourse, and violence, and which, taken together, constitute public opinion. The opinion that a man has of himself is very largely created by society. "Rarely can one regard his deed as fair when others find it foul, or count himself a hero when the world deems him a wretch."[46] For most, the blame and praise of the community are "the very lords of life." By the sanctions of intercourse Ross means the displeasure of one's fellows as exhibited in coldness or avoidance—"the cut direct, the open snub, the patent slight, the glancing

43. For an elaboration of these distinctions, see Robert Bierstedt, "An Analysis of Social Power," (1950), *Power and Progress: Essays on Sociological Theory* (New York: McGraw-Hill, 1974), pp. 220–241.

44. Among the former Ross mentions the mandarins of China, the pundits of India, the *Gelehrte* of Germany, the academicians of France, and the rabbis of Jewish congregations; among the latter, the Greek philosophers, the church fathers, the Schoolmen, the Humanists, and the Encyclopaedists. Again there is a failure to distinguish between influence and power.

45. By mandarinate Ross means those—then few as compared with a more recent period—who are college graduates.

46. *Social Control,* p. 90.

witticism." When the sanctions of intercourse become economic as well as social, the situation has become serious indeed. Ultimately, of course, we encounter the sanction of physical force, a sanction that in all civilized societies is entrusted to the law.[47] The gamut of rewards runs through a similar spectrum, from an approving glance to membership in exclusive societies.

Public opinion is less mechanical and thus less rigid than the law as a source of sanctions. Ross writes, in one of his colorful sentences, "The blade of the law playing up and down in its groove with iron precision is hardly so good a regulative instrument as the flexible lash of public censure."[48] If public opinion is less mechanical than the law so also it can enforce moral claims unrecognized in the law, can act in anticipation of an offense as the law cannot,[49] has the virtue of immediacy, and applies its sanctions economically. The virtues of public opinion in relation to the law are thus that the former has a wide gamut of sanctions and is flexible, penetrating, preventive, prompt, and inexpensive. Along with these virtues, however, public opinion has certain defects: It is primitive, vague in its requirements, indefinite as to kind and quantity of sanction, crude as to procedure, subject (in a stratified society) to divided jurisdictions, short in memory, and often impotent. It does not evolve as the law does. "Its frown is capricious, and its favor is fitful."[50] It is often intolerant and cruel. But it would be wrong to try to undermine its authority.

The law, of course, is the most specialized and highly developed instrument of social control. It has a double task—to act repressively against aggression and to deal compulsively with the failure to fulfill obligations. Whereas the sanctions of other norms include both rewards and punishments, the sanctions of the law are punishments alone. No one is rewarded for obeying the law. The treatment of law provides Ross with an opportunity to discourse on penology, with the conclusion that "a scientific penology will graduate punishments primarily according to the harmfulness of the offense to society, and secondarily, according to the attractiveness of the offense to the criminal."[51] It is good that the administration of the law be accompanied by ceremony—the grave demeanor, the archaic language, the sonorous oaths, the stiff formalities, the decorous manner—because ceremony confers dignity upon the process and prevents a

47. Physical sanctions outside the law include whipping, branding, riding out of town on a rail, tarring and feathering, and lynching.

48. *Ibid.*, p. 94.

49. "Its premonitory growl is more *preventive* than the silent menace of Justice." *Ibid.*, p. 95.

50. *Ibid.*, p. 99.

51. *Ibid.*, p. 110 (italics omitted).

person's life or liberty from being exposed to carelessness, cynicism, passion, or haste. Law owes much of its efficacy to the support of public opinion, and a breach between the law and public sentiment is avoided by the intentional failure to enforce unpopular laws. On balance, it is not crimes punished but crimes deterred that measure the worth of the law as an instrument of social control. However minor its role at a given moment, it "is still the cornerstone of the edifice of order."[52]

Both law and public opinion have defects as instruments of social control. They do not control the secret sectors of life, they are frequently paralyzed by the power of the offender, they reach only the outward deed, and they are both expensive.[53] They require a supplement, which Ross calls belief, by which he means "non-verifiable convictions respecting that which is beyond the field of human experience"—in short, supernatural sanctions. In Christianity, for example, the hope of heaven and the threat of hell play important roles in the formation and maintenance of social order. Nothing but belief can make excommunication punitive. It was the use of supernatural sanctions that enabled the church to succeed in the Roman Empire, whereas the pagan philosophies, using only moral suasion, failed. Because the threat of damnation was often too distant to serve effectively as a sanction, the institution of auricular confession was introduced, and the sanctions of penance became more immediate. In the long run, Ross observes, "the domination of a system of belief in the supernatural depends less on its plausibility than on the perfection with which its control meets the needs of the social organism."[54] Like other controls, belief has both advantages and disadvantages. Among the former Ross notes that it is cheap, that there is no concealment from its all-seeing eyes, and that in blending with law it increases the prestige of the latter. Among the disadvantages are that it gets in the way of newer and higher forms of control, that it perverts the social commandments,[55] that some of its recompenses,

52. *Ibid.*, p. 125.

53. Ross has forgotten that a few pages earlier he praised public opinion as "cheap."

54. *Ibid.*, p. 136.

55. As the whole scheme rests upon belief, this must be hedged about with the sharpest thorns. More than any wrong to fellow-man must the gods hate and punish doubt, unbelief, defiance of the priesthood, or neglect of churchly requirements. Not only does unbelief become the capital sin and faith the cardinal virtue, but even rack and stake will be used to drive out heresy. Such an inversion of ethical values shocks the natural moral judgment, and often lashes the best men of a society into revolt against an institution which ought to unite within itself all the impulses making for the perfection of character.

Ibid., p. 138. It is an interesting phenomenon that society regards "misbelief" as more serious than misbehavior. In our own society, for example, it is easier to commit adultery than it is to advocate it, and the sanctions are less severe. It is for this reason that Bertrand Russell once lost an appointment at the City College of New York. For a discussion see Robert Bierstedt, *The Social Order*, 4th ed. (New York: McGraw-Hill, 1974), pp. 168–169.

such as punishment in an afterlife, are not immediate, and that it is hard to manage. However useful supernatural sanctions may have been in the past, they seem now to be "a decaying species of control."

SUGGESTION AND CUSTOM

When Ross finishes his treatment of public opinion, law, and belief as three instruments of social control, he asks himself if the same social purpose may be achieved without the use of sanctions. He answers the question in the affirmative and avers that "there is, in fact, hardly any device of social control in which tradition, instruction, convention, example, or personal influence—in other words, suggestion—is not employed."[56] He is thus moved to discuss the role of suggestion in the way in which it shapes volition and conduct. The chapter in which he does this is psychological in content and makes use of such writers as James Mark Baldwin (*Handbook of Psychology*) and Boris Sidis (*The Psychology of Suggestion*). The sociological significance of suggestion is well expressed in the following paragraph:

> Everything we do reveals the pull on conduct exerted by social suggestion. Our foods and drinks, our dress and furniture, our amusements, our religious emotions, our investments, and even our matrimonial choices confess the sway of fashion and vogue. Whatever is common reaches us by way of example or advice or intimidation from a hundred directions. In our most private choices we are swerved from our orbit by the solar attraction—or repulsion—of the conventional. In public opinion there is something which is not praise or blame, and this residuum is mass suggestion. From this comes its power to reduce men to uniformity as a steam roller reduces bits of stone to smooth macadam.[57]

In this chapter, too, Ross makes a distinction between social influence, which operates in spheres where society is relatively indifferent, and social control, where individual and society are apt to be at odds. Two additional chapters deal with education and custom as forms of social suggestion.

The chapter on custom reveals the influence of Tarde, and indeed Ross uses the compound noun *custom-imitation.* He tells us that customs fall into two groups, in the first of which improvements proceed with little or no resistance, and in the second changes arouse opposition. In the first he lists language, costume, cuisine, games, and sports; in the second, politics, law, religious belief, ritual, ceremony, and moral codes. Aristotle, Bodin, Montaigne, Hooker, Bacon, and Burke all agree that in the case of law the

56. *Social Control,* p. 146.
57. *Ibid.,* pp. 148–149.

old is always better than the new. For purposes of control in general the superiority of the old is clear. Ross is thus able to lay it down as a law that "all institutions having to do with control change reluctantly, change slowly, change tardily, and change within sooner than without."[58]

Control by sanctions must be supplemented by control by belief, and this leads Ross to a consideration of what he calls social religion. Social religion is defined as "the conviction that there is a bond of ideal relationship between the members of a society and the feelings that arise in consequence of this conviction."[59] With the rise of social religion control becomes possible because of an inward disposition. To social religion Ross juxtaposes legal religion—God the father compared with God the lawgiver. "The struggle between 'justice' and 'mercy,' between hell-fire and love, marks the interference of these two great orders of socializing ideas."[60] The inner conviction that men are spiritually related is a powerful source of social control. In the course of social evolution the selection process rids society of men of violent temper and favors those who conform to social tendencies. As efficacious as social religion is, it degenerates when the ceremonial is substituted for the ethical, when worship takes precedence over right behavior. It should be remarked, perhaps, that the distinction Ross tries to maintain between legal religion and social religion is not altogether clear. Neither is the role social religion plays in social control. At the end of his chapter, for example, Ross expresses the hope that social religion will become "purer and nobler," no longer a "paid ally of the policeman" and no longer "a pillar of social order."

The role of culture—which Ross equates with literature, art, religion, codes, and moral disciplines—becomes apparent when he writes, "Social control is based not only on the ascendency of the many over the one, of the wise over the simple, of the rulers over the ruled, but yet more on the domination of the living by the dead."[61] But social control is not all "carpenter's work," the work of policemen, preachers, and Sunday-school teachers. The fact is that people themselves have a surprising knack of getting along together. In addition, society creates personal ideals for its members to admire. Society creates types—social types—with different virtues and obligations—the priest, the soldier, the lawyer, the clergyman, the engineer, the artist, the actor. In the priest, for example, we find, or expect to find, self-denial, chastity, and piety; in the soldier, fortitude, courage, and obedience. "Every party, labor union, guild, lodge, surveying corps, or

58. *Ibid.*, p. 192.
59. *Ibid.*, p. 199.
60. *Ibid.*, p. 205.
61. *Ibid.*, pp. 221–222.

athletic team will, in the course of time, develop for its special purposes appropriate types of character or observance, which exert on its members an invisible pressure subordinating them to the welfare or aims of the association."[62]

Ethical standards too are agents of social control. When ideals are internalized, a sense of self-respect on the one hand and of shame on the other operate as an automatic system of reward and punishment.[63] Ross, incidentally, believes that there are racial differences in the possession of such virtues as decency and integrity. He also believes that "control through ideals flourishes in the higher classes while yet the inferior orders are under the curb of custom and authority."[64] In any event, guidance by ideals is far superior to guidance by authority. Finally, in a moral mood, Ross discusses the "goodness" that is above all forms of social control and concludes his remarks on personal ideals with the following:

> Social order will have to rest on artifice till there is joined to natural altruism, as we find it developing in the family, a clearness of vision that sees in the upright discharge of the requirements of every social office and station the highest ministry to the welfare of our fellows.[65]

In Ross, as in Cooley and Sumner, it is not easy to distinguish the lectern from the pulpit.

CEREMONY, ART, AND CHARISMA

Ross does not seem to appreciate the significance of ceremony in social life. Indeed, he refers to "these tiresome and precise actions" as motivated by fear and indulged in for the purpose of propitiation. It is no more significant than fashion. He regards ceremony as a means of enforcing class distinctions and even refers to it as a "clumsy" kind of social control. Ceremony is at a disadvantage in a rational society and indeed, in the United States, the age of ceremony is nearly over. Like ceremony, art is a socializing influence, but it is not as powerful a support of the social order as religious beliefs and moral ideas. A chapter on personality, which might

62. *Ibid.*, p. 232.

63. "Compared with externally applied rewards and punishments they have the merit of dispensing with inquest and award by external authority, of being certain in operation, of regulating men when unobserved, of appraising motive as well as deed, and of shaping character as well as conduct." *Ibid.*, p. 234.

64. *Ibid.*, p. 236.

65. *Ibid.*, p. 246.

better have been entitled charismatic leadership, deals with the control exercised by such heroes as Giuseppe Garibaldi, Hernando Cortes, Sam Houston, the comte de Mirabeau, Napoleon Bonaparte, Joan of Arc, and Abraham Lincoln, to mention only a few whose exploits Ross praises. In "natural societies"—an expression that he does not explain—personal control is all the control there is. In any event, personality traits are evaluated differently in different periods of history. In this connection a striking paragraph appears:

> Society is always contending with the brittleness of its regulative instruments. The helmsmen of the state, the archons of religion, the shapers of moral disciplines, the framers of ideals, are painfully conscious of a certain impotence. Like the churchmen of the Dark Ages they find they cannot extend the truce of God over the whole of the week but must, for want of sufficient power, vacate a certain time to the devil of disorder. Hence society, through its guides, courts the aid of dominating persons, hoping to use their influence to strengthen its own.[66]

The military, government, and the church exemplify this phenomenon. Again, however, personal influence is destined to diminish as, especially in democracies, new mechanisms of control take over. Charismatic leadership is not the cornerstone of social order.

If Ross has undertaken to discuss, in these chapters, forms of control that are directed to feelings, he now wants to treat those that are directed to judgment, namely, enlightenment, illusion, and social evaluation. It is not easy to follow him in this section because his general frame of reference is so different from ours. The chapter on enlightenment, however, contains another remarkable passage, reveals Ross's conception of society:

> "Society" is, of course, a kind of fiction. There is nothing to it, after all, but people affecting one another in various ways. The thesis of this book is that from the interactions of individuals and generations there emerges a kind of collective mind evincing itself in living ideals, conventions, dogmas, institutions, and religious sentiments which are more or less happily adapted to the task of safeguarding the collective welfare from the ravages of egoism.[67]

Ross, no metaphysician, does not go into the nature of this "collective mind" and shows no awareness of the debate between Tarde and Durkheim on this issue. There are two references to Tarde in the book and one to Durkheim, all three of them minor.

66. *Ibid.*, pp. 287–288.

67. *Ibid.*, p. 293. There is also such a thing as a social mind (see pp. 341, 344) and a social conscience (see p. 347).

In much of the book social control means, for Ross, how to keep people virtuous and overcome their tendency to vice. Thus, "To show the coquette, the libertine, the gourmand, the cynic, the miser, the domestic tyrant, the sycophant, or the fakir as the psychological consummation of vanity, lubricity, gluttony, contempt of others, greed, self-will, flattery, or mendacity, is a well-tried and long-approved method of control."[68] Moral philosophy itself, in our secular century, is one of the forms of social control, but a far from perfect form.

Ross is as clear as Aristotle was when he affirms that society exhibits both superior and inferior individuals and that progress depends upon the former. In his chapter on social valuations, for example, he writes: "It is not society that kindles strange longings or invents new pleasure, but superior individuals. Society can only await these Prometheans and spread broadcast the fire they have stolen from the gods. If a people can provide no élite to discover the ideal goods, the higher tastes do not develop."[69] To the influence of the élite, however, must be added the force of tradition.

Among the agents and enforcers of social control are those, first, whose professional responsibility is involved in the process—rulers, priests, schoolmasters, magistrates, legislators, publicists, editors, educators, and those who are described as "social leaders" and "pillars of society." Second are those whom Ross calls "stablists," those who require order for their own purposes. In this category belong officials, property owners, traders, masters of industry, and businessmen in general. Finally, there is another élite, an ethical élite, which wants not only order but also the right kind of order.

Ross devotes a chapter to something called class control, defined as "the exercise of power by a parasitic class in its own interest."[70] It is usually a ruling class exploiting an inferior class by means of force, superstition, fraud, and pomp. Ross distinguishes class control from social control, although not clearly—except to say, "It is *what* men obey, rather than *why* they obey, that betrays the presence of class exploitation."[71] He decides that the military rule by brutality, the priesthood by superstition, the nobility by pride and pomp, and the rich by rapacity. Parasitic groups have a tendency to cooperate in their efforts to continue their exploitation of their unfortunate inferiors. Ross agrees with Spencer, Gumplowicz, and Ratzenhofer that the origin of the state is in conquest and exploitation: "Born in aggression and perfected in exploitation, the State, even now,

68. *Ibid.*, pp. 294–295.
69. *Ibid.*, p. 329. The Carthaginians and the Turks appear to have lacked these élites.
70. *Ibid.*, p. 376.
71. *Ibid.*, p. 379.

when it is more and more directed by the common will, is not easy to keep from slipping back into the rut it wore for itself during the centuries it was the engine of a parasitic class."[72] The classical example of exploitation by a parasitic class is the medieval papacy, which ruled by superstition.

That Ross is aware of change is apparent from the following:

> Never do we find the social pressure uniform through a long period. There are times when society holds the individual as in a vise, and times when he wriggles almost from under the social knee. There are epochs when the corporate will is ascendant, and epochs when the individual is more and more. In other words, social control fluctuates between strong and weak, between more and less.[73]

He accounts for these "vicissitudes," as he calls them, by changes in "the social need." Sometimes there is need for more control, sometimes less, and the supply of control adjusts itself to the demand for it. These changes are nearly all associated with changes in economic conditions. Other factors, however, are institutions that fail to work well over a period of time, the introduction of alien ethnic elements into a society, and, of course, such catastrophes as wars and mass migrations. In addition to changes in the social need, the amount of control changes with the rise and strife of social classes, with their conflicting economic interests. Sharp conflicts of interest, great inequality of means and possessions, and great inequality of opportunity all strain the social fabric. Countries with a dynamic economy, such as England, can usually survive such strains, whereas others, such as Italy and Spain, cannot do so without the help of repressive institutions. Ross hazards a prediction:

> It is likely, then, that when capitalistic production has everywhere put its full rending strain on social tissue, the static portions of the earth will become coercive, or socialistic, or both, while the dynamic lands alone will be able to remain at once individualistic, property-respecting, and free.[74]

Another cause of changes in social control is change in the culture and habits of a people—fresh knowledge, new ideas, foreign influences, novel experience. There are, however, no fixed cycles through which systems of control normally pass. "Actual societies, and with them their systems of control, have been so shattered, mutilated, and deformed by war, famine, depopulation, immigration, race degeneration, and class conflict, that no

72. *Ibid.*, p. 386.
73. *Ibid.*, p. 395.
74. *Ibid.*, p. 403.

laws can be framed for them that shall hold true of all cases and situations."[75] Thus, Ross ends his chapter on a note of agnosticism.

THE SUPPORTS OF ORDER

Toward the end of the book Ross gets around to classifying the supports of order into two major groups. Public opinion, suggestion, personal ideals, social religion, art, and social valuation are aimed not only at a social order but also at a moral order, and he calls them "ethical." Law, belief, ceremony, education, and illusion, on the other hand, have little to do with ethics and may therefore be called "political."[76] The ethical controls are preferred in some situations; the political, in others. Sanctions exhibit a gradation from current public opinion, through crystallized disapproval of society, through the opinion of generations, to the "frown of the Ruler of the Universe." Actions are first considered blameworthy, then unlawful, then shameful, and finally sinful. Controls also differ in their vitality. For some unknown reason Ross is of the opinion that etiquette, ceremony, and custom are fading away as instruments of control, to be replaced by moral instruction and public education. Art too will increasingly play a role, especially the art of Henrik Ibsen, a Leo Tolstoy, or a Victor Hugo.

Ross is conscious throughout of the opposition of order and freedom, control and liberty. He asks himself how far society should interfere with the individual, with the recognition that society is not a being but only people in their collective capacity. In posing this question he arrives at five "canons":

1. "Each increment of social interference should bring more benefit to persons as members of society than it entails inconvenience to persons as individuals."
2. "Social interference should not lightly excite against itself the passion for liberty."
3. "Social interference should respect the sentiments that are the support of natural order."
4. "Social interference should not be so paternal as to check the self-extinction of the morally ill-constituted."
5. "Social interference should not so limit the struggle for existence as to nullify the selective process."[77]

---

75. *Ibid.*, p. 410.

76. In its original sense, "pertaining to policy." *Ibid.*, p. 411.

77. These canons, and the author's discussion of them, may be found *ibid.*, chap. 31, pp. 417–427 (italics omitted).

All in all, he concludes, we need the most welfare that is consonant with the least abridgment of liberty.

In the final chapter Ross asks if there is reason to believe that less control will be needed in the future and answers in the negative. He draws a distinction between community and society similar to that of Tönnies,[78] notes that the sense of a common life that one finds in the parish, neighborhood, and village is suffering erosion, that community is being transformed into society, that in the community "the secret of order is not so much *control* as *concord*," and that "we are relying on artificial rather than natural supports to bear the increasing weight of our social order."[79]

It cannot be said that *Social Control* is a well-organized book. Its three major rubrics—The Grounds of Control, The Means of Control, and The System of Control—are much neater than the contents subsumed under them. The book is often repetitious; it is also frequently inconsistent. Ross says both that society is "a something distinct from a bunch of persons" and that it is just "people affecting one another in various ways." That the individual and society are quite distinct, however, is clear in his efforts to show how society tames and domesticates men and in his assertions that at times men attain an ascendancy over society and at other times are subdued by it. Not all control is social; some of it is moral and is attributable to an inner conscience. There is also a social conscience. For Ross the words *moral* and *social* are not synonymous. He fails to distinguish the instruments of social control from the agents of social control: Custom, social classes, law, judges, the police, the moral code, and crowds all exert control. His classifications are often confusing. His persistent and conspicuous racism requires no comment. Like Sumner, he is a Social Darwinist, sure that to dampen altogether the struggle for existence would result in racial degeneration.[80]

The book is nevertheless a milepost in the history of American sociology. If Ross wrote too rapidly and too often without adequate reflection, he also wrote with verve and style. His metaphors are colorful, his epigrams pungent. Whether he contributed anything of lasting importance to his subject, he at least perceived a sociological problem and was one of the first to do so. In *Social Control* he did indeed survey the foundations of the social order, that social order which is the central concern of sociological inquiry.

---

78. But he worked out the distinction before he became familiar with *Gemeinschaft und Gesellschaft*.

79. *Ibid.*, pp. 432, 435.

80. Indeed, Sumner might have written the following sentence: "The shortest way to make this world a heaven is to let those so inclined hurry hell-ward at their own pace." *Ibid.*, p. 423.

Foundations of Sociology

Ross published his second book, *Foundations of Sociology*, in 1905, while teaching at the University of Nebraska.[81] In his first chapter he tries to define the nature and scope of sociology and discusses some of the perennial problems this task requires—for example, the unit of inquiry, the question whether sociology is a general or a special social science, the relation of sociology to social psychology, and the relation of sociology to the other social sciences. He decides, for example, that the unit of inquiry is not the social aggregate or the social group, not social relations, not modes or forms of association (Simmel), not human achievement (Ward), but rather social phenomena themselves, which he defines as "all phenomena which we cannot explain without bringing in the action of one human being on another."[82] Social psychology he chooses to regard not as the top story of psychology but as the bottom story of sociology. Sociology is a general science of social phenomena, and some day it will include the others:

> So far as social life is one, there will be one master science of social life. If not to-day, then to-morrow, if not by this generation, then by the next, the necessity for sociology will be fully recognized. There is a vacant chair among the great sciences, and sooner or later that chair will be filled.[83]

Ross remarks that those investigators have fared best who looked beyond the boundaries of their own sciences and sought relationships between the forms of government, for example, and geographic facts, religion and family development, moral crises and changes in patterns of consumption. Sociology differs from ethics in that the latter is a normative science, whereas "sociology does not venture beyond the causes and laws of the phenomena it considers."[84] Politics also has some normative elements in it and on the whole is more of an art than a science. "If political science remains distinct, it will be because the breadth of the field calls for the specialist, and not because there are well-defined natural boundaries marking it off from sociology."[85] Economics is the greatest of the social sciences and, like linguistics, the most independent. Ross summarizes his views of the relationship of sociology to the other social sciences with the following figure:

---

81. Quotations in this section are taken from the fifth edition (New York: Macmillan, 1919). (Originally published, 1905).

82. *Foundations of Sociology*, p. 7.

83. *Ibid.*, p. 15.

84. *Ibid.*, p. 17.

85. *Ibid.*, p. 22.

The relation of the trunk of a tree to its branches is, I believe, a fit symbol of the relation of Sociology to the special social sciences. But the tree in question is a banyan tree. Each of the great branches from the main trunk throws down shoots which take root and give it independent support in human nature. In the case of a branch like politics these special stems are slight and decaying. In the case of a branch like economics the direct support they yield is more important than the connection with the main trunk. In every case an independent rootage in unsocialized desire is the fact that entitles a branch of social knowledge to be termed a science, and differentiates it from those branches which, having no source of life other than the main trunk, must be termed departments of special sociology.[86]

One wonders if Ross's contemporaries in political science and economics approved of his figure.

In another passage Ross has a more detailed account of the work of sociology. It is the science that

busies itself with imitation and custom and tradition and conventionality; that seeks the origin, meaning, and authority of the standards and ideals shaping individual action; that traces the connection between the constitution of a society and the opportunities and ambitions of its members; that inquires into the causes and the consequences of the spontaneous sentimental groupings of men; and that deals with the development of the social mind and the means and extent of its ascendency over the desires and valuations of individual minds.[87]

Ross regards Comte, Spencer, Lilienfeld, Schäffle, De Roberty, and Fouillée, as founders of this science but he subjects them all to various criticisms. He especially rejects any theory of unilinear evolution in institutions or societies.

From these writers and others Ross takes something called social laws. They have a rather quaint flavor today. Most of them are generalizations of one kind or another, and virtually none has any predictive utility. Lilienfeld, for example, in an echo of Haeckel's "ontogeny recapitulates phylogeny," expresses as a law that "the individual in his development from childhood passes through the culture epochs traversed by human society."[88] Ross does not think much of it: "The boy does not camp out because his ancestors did so in Caesar's time. Racial experiences of cave-dwelling, hunting and barter cannot get into the blood."[89] Another example is from de Greef: "Aggregates are variable in proportion to the heterogene-

86. *Ibid.*, pp. 27–28.

87. *Ibid.*, p. 40.

88. Quoted *ibid.*, p. 49. This notion later received some currency as "the culture epoch theory" in the literature of the John Dewey Society.

89. *Ibid.*, p. 49.

ity of their parts." About the attempt of Gumplowicz to find universal laws, applicable to all of the sciences,[90] Ross says: "We have tested the application to society of physical, biological and psychological laws and have seen that the method does not yield lasting results. All this work will have to be torn out and replaced by better masonry if the walls of sociology are to rise very far."[91] Ross recognizes the importance of finding sequences in the growth and development of social institutions, such as those in the family: for example, from promiscuity to polygamy to monogamy, but he doubts that these sequences are uniform or that they always represent evolution or progress. In short, "I cannot but conclude that the development of a particular order of institutions is, in a greater or less degree, *multilinear*, and that the endeavor to establish in each sphere of social life a single, typical sequence of changes is bound to fail."[92] Some what superior are the laws developed by Durkheim, Ward, Giddings, Tarde, Veblen, Bouglé, and Ross himself.[93] It will be the task of sociology to criticize and extend these laws and thus to have a stable body of scientific knowledge about society.

Although Ross has no respect for the philosophy of history, his discussion of the relationship between history and sociology is quite good. The two disciplines differ in that for the sociologist history repeats itself and for the historian it does not. Both propositions are true. The truth depends upon the level of abstraction—as we should say today—on which we approach the matter, upon whether we are interested in recurrent patterns or in singular events. Facts alone are of no interest to the sociologist. "Ere he can use them he must fade their brilliant tints to sober colors."[94] In such sober colors will be dressed numerous and minute occurrences which together add up not to epic and dramatic events, but to general statements, general notions, and, Ross hopes, general laws.

---

90. Gumplowicz has ten of these "laws," and it must be said that most of them are insipid. The second, third, and fourth, for example, are that phenomena run in sequences, that these sequences are law abiding, and that concrete objects have parts. *Ibid.*, p. 53.

91. *Ibid.*, p. 54.

92. *Ibid.*, p. 62.

93. Again, however, it must be said that few today would regard these as laws in any useful sense. Bouglé, for example: "Notions of human equality make their way in proportion as society becomes large, dense, mobile, complex, and unified." Giddings: "Impulsive social action tends to extend and intensify in a geometrical progression." And Ross, who announces a new law of his own: "Social order is stable in proportion as the power of each to resist exceeds his power to aggress, and his will to resist exceeds his will to aggress." These "laws" appear *ibid.*, pp. 65–67 (italics omitted). It is interesting to note the striving for some kind of mathematical expression; thus, the recurrence of "in proportion as" and Giddings's geometrical progression.

94. *Ibid.*, pp. 82–83.

When Ross returns to the subject of the unit of investigation in sociology he decides that the group is a good candidate for that position. Without making a point of it he classifies groups, in a sentence or two, as interest groups (guilds, corporations, and parties), likeness groups (classes, castes, and sects, "held together by consciousness of kind"), natural groups (family and neighborhood), and fortuitous groups (crowd and public). But sociology needs more than the group. Social facts appear not only in groups but also in relations. Institutions also require attention, but they are limiting if an institution is defined, as Ross does, as "a grouping or relation that is sanctioned or permitted by society."[95] Many things happen in society that are not so sanctioned.[96] In the end, Ross has five units of investigation—groups, relations, institutions, imperatives, and uniformities. These, in turn, are all *products* (italics in original) that precede and survive the individual, and from them we ascend to what Ross regards as the social process, a primordial fact since all of these products are a result of the actions and interactions of men. It is a mistake common to sociology, however, to emphasize one process at the expense of others—a mistake of which Spencer, Gumplowicz, Tarde, and Durkheim were all guilty.

Ross concludes his general discussion of the unit of investigation with a "Map of the Sociological Field,"[97] and with the following picturesque paragraph:

> The program of investigation herewith outlined is broad, but it is not too broad. Some will complain of omissions, but certainly no one will here discover anything that ought not to be considered by a science of society. Recently, social investigators have shown a slight tendency to narrowness. Each has been sure that the center of sociology lies just where his pickaxe turns up the richest ore. This is perhaps a good sign. It means that the promised land once surveyed afar from a mountain peak by Comte and Schäffle is now overrun with prospectors. It is well, however, for each of us occasionally to climb out of his gulch, inspect the nuggets his brethern are finding, and from some commanding point realize how vast are the dimensions of this new El Dorado.[98]

This cautionary note is not without merit today.

---

95. *Ibid.*, p. 88.

96. Prostitution, for example, is surely an institution.

97. *Ibid.*, p. 98. It is not necessary to reproduce this "Map" here because it exhibits little distinction as a taxonomy. The principal vertical rubrics are Preliminary, Social, and Reconstructive; the principal horizontal rubrics, Processes, Subjective Products, and Objective Products. The category Objective Products, for example, consists of Relations and Groupings. Listed under the latter are Fortuitous groups, Natural groups, Likeness groups, Interest groups (including Tribes [!]), Functional groups, Authorities, and Hierarchies.

98. *Ibid.*, p. 99.

THE MOB MIND

Although the transition is not clear, Ross begins his substantive discussion with a treatment of the mob mind—the characteristics of the mob, the theory of the mob, mob mind in city populations and in the public, the theory of the craze and the fad, and a recognition of the mob mind as a malady of our time. In this treatment Tarde's concept of imitation plays a prominent role. Ross defines a mob as "a crowd of people showing a unanimity due to mental contagion."[99] We see a mob mind forming in "an audience falling under the spell of an actor or an orator, a congregation developing the revival spirit, a crowd becoming riotous, or an army under the influence of panic."[100] It is not necessary, incidentally, that the members of a mob be a throng, that is, that they be at the same place at the same time. The mob mind is not a localized phenomenon.

In a succeeding discussion of the properties of groups, Ross suggests that the group is not necessarily a reflection of the characteristics of its members:

> The whole is not the algebraic sum of its parts. It is not a resultant of its units . . . but is a chemical combination possessing properties different from those of its elements. For this reason crowds are more alike than are their members. A mob of sages and a mob of hoodlums will think and behave in about the same way.[101]

The crowd is more emotional than the individuals who comprise it, and more dogmatic and intolerant. Although the crowd in general is the lowest form of human association, there are moments when it can inspire a revolutionary change for the good and help to create a higher and better form of social life. The fall of the Bastille is an example, as is the crowd phenomenon that led to the American Revolution. In any event, the crowd may exhibit certain forms of improvement, transforming itself first into a mass meeting, next a deliberative assembly, and then a representative body. A "public" is a dispersed crowd whose members respond to the same stimuli. One can belong to only one crowd at a time, but by subscribing to a number of newspapers, for example, one can become a member, so to speak, of several publics. A public may suffer some of the same vices and follies as a crowd, but in diminished measure.

Sects are marked by a too-exclusive intercourse among their members and the result is a certain tinge of fanaticism:

---

99. *Ibid.*, p. 103, italics omitted.
100. *Ibid.*, p. 105.
101. *Ibid.*, p. 119.

> Among union workers, for example, how mortal is the antipathy that springs up toward the "rat" or the "scab"! In priestly seminaries, with what hoofs and horns they picture the freethinkers! What bizarre notions of "*bourgeois* society" circulate in the taverns where anarchists touch glasses! What strange growths of belief or worship flourish in closed communities like the Shakers or the Doukhobors! What warped ideas of right and wrong become hallowed in codes of tribal or professional ethics! What absurd idolatries strike root in the Latin Quarter! What crazy cults in coteries of artists or writers![102]

Sects tend to set themselves off from the rest of society and even to form closed and secret assemblies. The sect, in fact, develops eccentricities that result from a too-exclusive and intimate association.

THE SOCIAL FORCES

In a discussion of the social forces Ross has a comment that is relevant to Lundberg's later efforts to reduce all social relations and interactions to transformations in a field of force and to similar efforts to strive for a more "scientific" language for the explanation of social phenomena. The comment is in fact criticism of similar attempts by Spencer to demonstrate that social evolution is a part of cosmic evolution and that social movements are simply social phenomena following the lines of least resistance. To these efforts Ross responds:

> After a human activity has been explained in terms of motive, why reëxplain it in terms of energy? If a principle such as *men go where they can most easily satisfy their wants* accounts for the currents of immigration, why try to account for them on the principle that *motion follows the line of least resistance*? If the rhythms we find in every field of human interest from dress to religion occur because "attention demands change in its object," why class them with rhythms due to "conflict of forces not in equilibrium?"[103]

Similarly, "The statement that a man's ambition to become an athlete or an orator is a mode of biotic energy tells me nothing."[104] Ross is clearly indisposed to accept any physical, geographical, or environmental explanation of the operation of social forces. They should be explained instead by human purpose and volition. The migrations of peoples and the routes of railroads, of course, have something to do with topography. The geographic factor must always be recognized: "Still, since the external facts are foreseen and taken into account in intelligent telic action, it is necessary

102. *Ibid.*, pp. 136–137.
103. *Ibid.*, p. 150.
104. *Ibid.*, p. 158.

to regard social phenomena as essentially psychic, and to look for their immediate causes in mind."[105] Here the influence of Ward is apparent. In another passage Ross anticipates Freud's theory of sublimation by remarking that the sexual instinct, when obstructed, "broadens into sympathy, philanthropy, poesy, the artistic impulses, and the longings of the religious mystic."[106]

For Ross, as for Ward, the social forces are psychic forces, and sociology is essentially a psychic science. "Its causes are to be sought in mental processes, its forces are psychic forces, and no ultimate non-psychic factors should be recognized until it is shown just how they are able to affect motive and choice."[107] As for the classification of the social forces, Ross compares Small, Ratzenhofer, Ward, and Stuckenberg—an exercise that need not be reproduced here. He makes no distinction between the "interests," for example, of Small and Ratzenhofer and his own natural and cultural "desires." It helps very little to be told that our natural desires can be classified as appetitive, hedonic, egotic, affective, and recreative and that our cultural desires can be classified as religious, ethical, aesthetic, and intellectual. We find the interesting observation, however, that the study of the natural desires belongs to anthropology, the cultural desires to sociology. In 1905 we are still in a stage in the development of the discipline when men try to classify basic springs of action, variously called—and by Ross also—forces, instincts, impulses, interests, desires, wishes, and wants. He offers an extended treatment of what he regards as the four principal means to the satisfaction of wants, namely, wealth, government, religion, and knowledge. As in this instance, he is given to curious juxtapositions, comparisons, and classifications. Again, for example, he writes, "Men always consider religion and government as infinitely more precious than discovery and invention."[108] It is not clear how the first pair here can be compared in any way with the second.

THE FACTORS OF SOCIAL CHANGE

Ross devotes a long chapter to the factors of social change. He accepts the distinction between social statics and social dynamics and then divides the factors into three groups: actively static, those that resist social change (religion, government, custom, law, and ceremony); passively static, those that are indifferent to social change (language, literature, art, industry,

105. *Ibid.*, p. 152.
106. *Ibid.*, p. 157.
107. *Ibid.*, p. 161.
108. *Ibid.*, p. 184.

education, and opinion); and dynamic (domestication, geographical discovery, exploration, migration, acclimatization, war, conquest, race-crossing, commerce, travel, invention, scientific discovery, "prophetism," and free thought). He distinguishes change from evolution, because the latter suggests an unfolding of something pre-formed,[109] and from progress, because change means any qualitative variation whereas progress implies amelioration. Furthermore, what is progress from the point of view of one sex, class, race, or group may be regress to others. Progress is therefore a subjective concept, and sociology should confine itself to the study of change.

As MacIver will do some decades later, Ross distinguishes between conditions and causes, regarding the latter as precipitants—for example, the igniting spark, the touch of the button, the turning of the lever. Of factors *a*, *b*, and *c*, however, any one of the three may be a cause and the other two, conditions. Furthermore, it is as important to look for the causes of social immobility as it is to look for the causes of social change. Most of the things that happen in society do not in fact change the status quo: "the round of love, marriage, and reproduction, so long as births and deaths balance; production, so far as it is balanced by consumption; exchange, so long as the argosies of commerce carry goods, but not ideas; education, so far as it passes on the traditional culture." And then, in a striking figure, "Society might be likened to a gyroscope, in that the greater its motion, the greater is its resistance to change of position."[110]

Among the principal extrasocial factors of social change Ross discusses in detail the growth of population, the accumulation of wealth, migration to a new environment, the innovating individual,[111] the contact and cross-fertilization of cultures, the interaction of societies, the conjugation of societies, and alteration in the environment. Each of these is treated with a wealth of historical examples, most of them from the history of the West. One wonders only why Ross should refer to them as "extra-social" or "sub-social" factors when these adjectives would seem to be appropriate for only the last of them. We receive a clue to the answer to this question in the final paragraph of the chapter, where he discusses those modifications that are brought about by the "social will," striving for an intelligently conceived

109. "It is unsafe to assume that the succession of social changes is predetermined, and that accidental, extraneous, and historic events and influences do not count." *Ibid.*, p. 185.

110. *Ibid.*, p. 200.

111. Ross rejects any "great man" theory of change, however, on the ground that all innovations are fusions of a series of small and sometimes unnoticed changes. Single individuals, however, are sometimes authors of change. Saint Benedict devised the "Rule" that helped to form the monasteries of the West and Hildebrand imposed sacerdotal celibacy upon the priesthood. There appears to be an inconsistency here.

goal. These latter, however, belong not to sociological theory but to practical sociology.

"RECENT TENDENCIES"

April 1902 Ross gave a series of lectures at Harvard on recent tendencies in sociology; these, for the most part, make up a chapter of *Foundations of Sociology*. Among the sociologists to whom he refers are Spencer, Le Bon, Tarde, Gumplowicz, Giddings, Simmel, Baldwin, Durkheim, Loria, Novicow, Vaccaro, Ratzenhofer, Lombroso, Brooks Adams, Patten, Demolins ("the brightest intellect of the Le Play school"), Veblen, Darwin, Galton, De Candolle, Kidd, Seeck, and Professor Thomas.[112] Among the "recent tendencies" he treats at some length the following (all italicized):

1. "To attribute the unity of the social group to socializing processes, in which individual ideas and aims are moulded by social contacts and relations."
2. "To look upon society as a theatre of struggle between classes, corporations, and parties for the advancement of their respective interests."[113]
3 "To account for certain groupings, oppositions, and interactions by original differences in persons."[114]
4. "To show how well-marked types are created by place, work, social environment and institutions."[115]

---

112. One assumes that the unidentified "Professor Thomas" is W. I. Thomas, but the assumption could be erroneous. He attributes to Thomas the curious notion that males expend energy whereas females store it up.

113. In his discussion of this tendency Ross has occasion to refer to what he calls a universal law, namely, that "the bonds of any group, be it great or small, tighten with danger and relax with security." *Ibid.*, p. 287, italicized in original. In another expression, " 'Iron sharpeneth iron,' and the clash with oppressors or foes hardens a folk and hushes the strife of factions." *Ibid.*

114. This somewhat obscure "tendency" has to do largely with different social types. Thus Patten found four: clingers, sensualists, stalwarts, and mugwumps. Giddings also had four: the forceful, the convivial, the austere, and the rationally conscientious.

115. In view of the strong strain of racism in Ross, one is surprised to come across the following in his discussion of this tendency:

> More and more the time-honored appeal to race is looked upon as the resource of ignorance or indolence. To the scholar the attributing of the mental and moral traits of a population to heredity is a confession of defeat, not to be thought of until he has wrung from every factor of life its last drop of explanation. 'Blood' is not a solvent of every problem in national psychology, and 'race' is no longer a juggler's hat from which to draw explanations for all manner of moral contrasts and peculiarities.

Ibid., pp. 309–310. In this discussion the influence of Demolins is both apparent and acknowledged.

5. "To recognize that institutions and policies work selectively upon a people, and may profoundly modify its destiny."[116]

When he gave these lectures at Harvard Ross had a sixth recent tendency, one having to do with economic determinism. He did not reproduce it in the book, however, because in the meantime Edwin R.A. Seligman had published *The Economic Interpretation of History* (1902), which Ross regarded as an "able presentation" of the subject. Ross's views on economic determinism appear here in a tribute to Giddings, whose work he compliments as a "first-class contribution":

> At a time when his brethren are precipitately striking their colors to the economic materialists, he sturdily flies the flag of intellectualism. Rightly, too; for there is a movement of the human intellect which has nothing to do with economic facts. The increase of knowledge and the alteration of economic conditions are independent causes of social change. Let intellectualism and economism be the Urim and Thummim of the sociologist. Both are needed, if our science is to move on an even keel.[117]

With respect to the changes of human societies in general, Ross first refers to the notion that societies, like human beings, pass through regular stages from birth to maturity to old age and death. Societies are not like organisms, however. They "do not lie under the sceptre of heredity," and so this analogy gradually came to be abandoned. With increasing appreciation of the role of social selection, the notion that societies too have their afternoons must be given renewed consideration. The career of any people is a parabola. Talent creates brilliant centers of energy and feeds the flame of civilization.

> But meanwhile certain searching primitive tests of manhood have been done away with, survival and reproduction have been turned askew by artificial arrangements, and motives have been unloosed which blunt the race-preserving instincts of the fittest. . . . When in time the eugenic capital is used up, we have a people no longer capable of matching the achievements of their sires. The very institutions that make a people great and happy may bring in at last a race decadence which presently announces itself in social decline.[118]

---

116. This section is devoted to social selection, which Ross distinguishes from natural selection:

> The social selections are by no means of a stripe with these natural selections. Nature eliminates the unfit; society eliminates the misfit. Nature rejects the defective; society preserves them, but burns the heretic and hangs the criminal. For the most part, though, the social selections do not eliminate anybody. They determine not who shall live, but who shall propagate the next generation. They select not survivors, but parents.

Ibid., p. 342.

117. *Ibid.*, p. 306.

118. *Ibid.*, p. 344.

So important is this process that a new Darwin may be expected to arrive, one who will do for social selection what the original one did for natural selection. The new Darwin will do it with a new quantitative sophistication and the use of mathematico-statistical logic.[119] In judging an institution we shall no longer ask whether it is ordained by God or strengthens the state, or promotes the increase of wealth, or conduces to human welfare. We shall ask instead the eugenic question, whether it improves the breed of human beings.

The final two chapters, one on the causes of race superiority and the other on the "value-rank" of the American people we can ignore without loss. Ross sees human society as a whole, as something divided into races. He is always conscious of Anglo-Saxon superiority and anxious to defend it against the assaults of lesser breeds without the law.[120] The book is not nearly as systematic as one would like "foundations" to be. Some of the chapters are reprints of essays written for other purposes. Despite a lively style—Ross is a good companion—his words, as we have seen, often tumble out in unaccountable juxtapositions. His random observations are imaginative and often ingenious, but he is seldom inclined to tie them together in manageable bundles of principles or propositions. We gain nevertheless a clear sense of what Ross conceives sociology to be.

Social Psychology

In 1908 two books appeared with the words *social psychology* in their titles. They were both pioneer efforts, efforts without predecessors. One of them was written, of course, by our sociologist, E. A. Ross, and the other, by the distinguished psychologist William McDougall.[121] They differ in intent and emphasis. Indeed, books on social psychology written since that early time by sociologists and psychologists have continued to differ in in-

119. There is an earlier comment on statistics: "The statistical method, which enables us to measure social phenomena exactly and to substitute quantitative truths for qualitative, constitutes an instrument of precision, which certainly is destined to be applied to sociological problems in ways yet undreamed of." *Ibid.*, p. 81.

120. "The superiority of a race cannot be preserved without *pride of blood* and an uncompromising attitude toward the lower races." *Ibid.*, p. 379.

121. E. A. Ross, *Social Psychology* (New York: Macmillan, 1908); McDougall, *An Introduction to Social Psychology* (New York: John W. Luce & Co. 1908). Subsequent references to Ross are to this first edition. His book, incidentally, is dedicated to Franklin Henry Giddings, "bold seeker and valiant proclaimer of truth," and a separate paragraph at the end of the Preface pays "heartfelt homage to the genius of Gabriel Tarde, . . . that profound and original thinker."

tent and emphasis, and this in itself is an interesting problem in the sociology of knowledge. Neither of the original books contains a mention of the author of the other, but that, of course, would have been unlikely, as they were published in the same year.[122] Ross's book looks like sociology, McDougall's like psychology.

McDougall, for example, is interested in the springs of human action—instincts, in short, which he defines as "certain innate specific tendencies of the mind that are common to all members of any one species."[123] Accordingly, much of the book is devoted to instincts, including the gregarious instinct, the repulsion instinct, the curiosity instinct, the reproductive instinct, the parental instinct, the pugnacity instinct, the flight instinct, the sexual instinct, and so on. Contrary to Comte and Durkheim, McDougall asserts that psychology lies at the base of all of the social sciences and expresses it as his thesis that

> human activities, both mental and bodily, are only to be explained or understood by tracing them back to a number of innate dispositions, tendencies to feel and act in certain more or less specific ways, in certain situations; tendencies which manifest themselves in each normal individual of the species independently of previous experience of such situations and which, like the similar innate tendencies of the animals, may properly be called instinctive.[124]

Instincts, incidentally, have three aspects: the cognitive, the affective, and the conative.

The concept of instinct, central to McDougall, does not appear in Ross's index and is no part of his social psychology. On the contrary, Ross is interested in such phenomena as suggestibility, the crowd, the mob mind, fashion, convention and conventionality, imitation, custom, conflict, compromise, public opinion, and something called "disequilibration." His definition of social psychology is as follows:

> Social psychology, as the writer conceives it, studies the psychic planes and currents that come into existence among men in consequence of their association. It seeks to understand and account for those uniformities in feeling, belief, or volition—and hence in action—which are due to the interaction of human beings, *i.e.*, to *social* causes.[125]

Uniformities for McDougall, thus, are due to instincts that are common to all normal members of a species; for Ross, to social causes. For Ross, no

---

122. Ross has two references to McDougall, however, in his *Principles of Sociology*.

123. *An Introduction to Social Psychology*, 8th ed. (New York: John W. Luce & Co., 1914), p. 22.

124. *Ibid.*, p. 385. To the eighth edition McDougall appends two supplementary chapters, one entitled "Theories of Action" and the other, "On the Sex Instinct."

125. *Social Psychology*, p. 1.

two persons have exactly the same hereditary endowment, and we therefore expect to find more dissimilarities among Ross and McDougall than we do in fact. The difference between social psychology and sociology is that the former omits the study of groups and structures. But social psychology precedes sociology in the proper order of study.

What Ross has to say about suggestibility and about the crowd, the mob, the public, the craze, and the fad is repetitious of what he said earlier in *Foundations of Sociology*, with perhaps a more extensive series of illustrations and quotations from other writers. Among the prophylactics against the mob mind he lists higher education; sound knowledge of body, mind, and society; familiarity with that which is classic; the influence of sane teachers; avoidance of the sensational newspaper; sports; country life; familism; ownership of property; participation in voluntary association; intellectual self-possession as an ideal; prideful morality; and vital religion. Fashion, which Ross defines as "a series of recurring changes in the choices of a group of people"[126] and attributes to the need for self-individualization, consists of two movements—imitation and differentiation. Ross believed that in his day the tyranny of fashion was diminishing because of the increasing number of people of independent judgment and good taste.

As if to justify his tribute to Tarde, much of Ross's book is devoted to the phenomenon of imitation. He is concerned to discuss what he calls "the radiant points of conventionality" and does so in a number of chapters. He avers that the lower classes imitate the upper and that power holders too are imitated. Similarly, the less successful imitate the more successful, the country imitates the city, and in democracies the minority imitates the majority. Ross, imitating Tarde, distinguishes between something he calls custom imitation and conventionality imitation. In conforming to custom we are imitating our ancestors; in conforming to convention we are imitating our contemporaries. Custom itself Ross defines as "any transmission of psychic elements from one generation to another."[127] Custom is transmission of a way of doing; tradition, the transmission of a way of thinking. Ross has a definite dislike of custom. Custom forces the living into bondage to the dead.[128] He expresses a similar dislike of a written constitution, including the Constitution of the United States, because, no matter how perfect it may be, it inevitably becomes an incubus upon the living. He does not see that the Bill of Rights, for example, serves as a shield to protect the people against the tyranny of temporary majorities.[129]

126. *Ibid.*, p. 94.

127. *Ibid.*, p. 196.

128. *Ibid.*, p. 215.

129. In view of Ross's later service as chairman of the board of the American Civil Liberties Union, it is surprising to discover that he favored censorship of sexually suggestive books, plays, and other materials. *Ibid.*, pp. 126, 145.

After discussing the circumstances under which it is not irrational to indulge in imitation, and treating also the various ways in which discussion and compromise can help to terminate conflicts, Ross turns in his final chapter to the manner in which the equilibrium of a society or a "social mind" is disturbed. One would ordinarily expect a society to achieve a state of equilibrium, when all conflict is resolved and all incongruities dissolved. This does not happen, however, for several reasons: the influence of a foreign culture, the shifting of the social foundations (*e.g.*, the increasing role of urban over rural life), and inventions and discoveries. In fact, a lasting equilibrium in the social mind is neither possible nor desirable. It is periods of disequilibrium that make possible the growth of individualism.

As can be seen from this brief description of the contents of the book, Ross is not writing social psychology in the contemporary sense of the word. Except for the chapter on suggestibility, his concerns are entirely sociological. Imitation—a phenomenon treated throughout—is for him not a psychological tendency but a social practice. His principal distinction is that between custom and conventionality, and of the two he greatly prefers the latter. Custom to him is not something that lubricates the gears of social interaction but rather an interference of the past with the present, and an obstacle to spontaneity. Ross is a forward-looking man, and custom spells backwardness to him. In this book he is interested not in the foundations of order, as he was in *Social Control*, but rather in the brakes that custom and tradition apply to social change.

Principles of Sociology

Ross published his systematic sociological theory at different times and under three different titles.[130] The first, on which he worked for seventeen years, is entitled *Principles of Sociology*. It appeared in 1920, with a revision in 1930 and a third edition in 1938. The second, *The Outlines of Sociology*, appeared in 1923, with a revised edition in 1933. It is the *Principles of Sociology* reduced in size by 30% and intended for classroom use. The third, entitled *New-Age Sociology*, appeared in 1940. It, too, is the *Principles of Sociology*, but with references to historic and contemporary non-Western societies omitted and with more emphasis upon American society and its problems. The details of the various revisions and editions need not detain us. For the most part, in what follows I shall be concerned with the *Principles of Sociology* itself, which is the largest of the three and contains Ross's most comprehensive statement.

130. All published by D. Appleton-Century, New York.

In the Preface to the first edition of this book, Ross writes:

> It [the book] contains *a system* of sociology, i.e., the parts are fitted to one another and taken together they are intended to cover the field; but I do not put it forward as *the system.* While it is that organization of knowledge about society which helps me the most, no doubt other equally valid systems are possible. True systems will, of course, not contradict one another, but they may differ in perspective. Sociologists equally sound may differ in perspective. Sociologists equally sound may differ as to which truths deserve the foreground and which should be relegated to the background. A system is a way of making some aspect of reality *intelligible,* and we differ as to how to present social reality so as to make it intelligible for the most people. In time sociology will discover, as the older sciences have done, the best perspective for exhibiting its results. Then the systems of sociologists will come into closer agreement.[131]

This Preface also contains the observation that although sociology follows the methods of science it has one "over-mastering purpose"—to better human relations. The third edition differs from the earlier ones in that it marks the abandonment of instinct psychology, uses materials from cultural anthropology, and recognizes the importance of the phenomenon treated in Sorokin's *Social Mobility.* It also emphasizes social processes rather than social structures and in this regard is faithful to the tradition of Park and Burgess who, in their *Introduction to the Science of Sociology* (1923), gave conceptual status to such processes as conflict, cooperation, accommodation, and assimilation.

An overview of the book's fifty-nine chapters reveals its division into eleven parts: (*a*) the social population, (*b*) primary social factors, (*c*) the genesis of society, (*d*) conflict and adaptation, (*e*) cooperation and organization, (*f*) class and caste, (*g*) society and the individual, (*h*) occupation and social function, (*i*) social progress and regress, (*j*) social products, and (*k*) projection into the future. The discussion of these contents will be swift and superficial, but I shall keep a sharp lookout for observations that are unusually striking or penetrating.

THE SOCIAL POPULATION

The book begins with an orthodox treatment of the population of the world, with special attention to the United States. Ross is aware of the pressure of increasing population but thinks that the increasing use of contraception may doom a population to extinction. He is afraid that the more

131. Reprinted in *Principles of Sociology,* 3d ed. (New York: D. Appleton-Century, 1938), pp. vii–viii. All subsequent references are to this edition of the book.

responsible elements in the population are reproducing at a slower rate than the less responsible, that new hygienic and medical measures are interfering with the processes of natural selection, and that those of the highest capability are having fewer children. War's selection, once positive, has become negative (the "culls" stay home and beget). Negative also is the social selection brought about by migration from the country to the city, occupational celibacy, social work (which interferes with natural selection), "mammonism" (those who aspire to riches do not want children), capitalistic individualism, the higher education of girls, and the emancipation of women. Practical eugenic measures would include the sterilization of mental defectives, a wider diffusion of birth control information, propagation of "sounder ideas of marriage," and encouragement of births among the superior. The final chapter in this first part deals with city and country, and here Ross indulges in the familiar comparisons.

PRIMARY SOCIAL FACTORS

The primary social factors for Ross are the geographic environment, human nature, and culture. After a mention of the coldward course of civilization, he discusses briefly the effect of climate on politics, on religion, on sex relations, and on government, but he arrives at no general conclusion. In the chapter on human nature he is concerned to show that "the original nature of man never drops out of the social drama."[132] As part of this original nature he mentions Sumner's hunger, love, vanity, and fear, and Thomas's four wishes. Culture he defines as "the total of acquired behavior patterns transmitted by imitation or instruction"[133] and shows that it is much more important than environment or human nature in determining the characteristics of a society. Now free for the most part of the racism that was rampant in his early writings, he is not yet prepared to say that all races are equal. He takes account of both cultural traits and cultural complexes, utilizes the distinction between material and nonmaterial culture,[134] and discusses both cultural diffusion and cultural lag.

THE GENESIS OF SOCIETY

Under this rubric Ross discusses association, communication, domination, and exploitation. Much of the discussion of association takes up the advantages of living in groups as compared with social isolation and

132. *Ibid.*, p. 89.

133. *Ibid.*, p. 103.

134. Except for him, unlike most writers, material culture consists of the knowledge and skill that lie back of implements and tools and not the implements and tools themselves.

solitude. Ross makes much of Cooley's looking-glass conception of the self, calling it "the mirrored self." In his treatment of communication he marvels at contemporary techniques and remarks on the decay of neighborhoods in both city and country that these techniques have brought about. Domination—a constant feature of social life—is exercised by parents over their offspring, the old over the young, husbands over wives, men over women, fighters over workers, the well situated over the ill situated, the strongest of allies over the rest, conquerors over the conquered, and the masters of the state over the subjects. It is necessary to exercise caution lest the clergy win ascendancy over everyone else.[135] Ross also warns against militarism, commercialism, and the ascendancy of a leisure class. As for exploitation, that is practically universal. Men exploit women, the rich exploit the poor, the leisured exploit the industrious, the intelligent exploit the ignorant, the organized exploit the unorganized, priests exploit the laity, conquerors exploit the conquered, and rulers exploit the ruled.

CONFLICT AND ADAPTATION

This part of the book (sixteen chapters) is devoted almost entirely to conflict: opposition in general, the "good side" of opposition, the "bad side" of opposition, personal competition, institutional competition, age conflict, sex conflict, race conflict, town–country conflict, class conflict, industrial conflict, religious or sectarian strife, conflict between the learned and the ignorant, and international conflict or war. A concluding chapter deals with social adaptation. What Ross has to say about these various kinds of conflict is perhaps less important than that he devotes so large and so central a part of his book to the phenomenon.

Conflict is not without utility for a society. Indeed, the more different kinds of conflict there are, the more tightly knit a society may become. Thus, conflict between Christian and Jew may be lessened if there is at the same time conflict between, say, managers and workers. In the latter conflict both Christian and Jewish managers will be pitted against both Christian and Jewish workers.

> So, paradoxical as it may sound, a society riven by a dozen oppositions along lines running in various directions may actually be in less danger of early break-up than one split along just one line. For each new cleavage narrows the

135. *Ibid.*, p. 154:

> In short, of all despotisms that of the priest is the least wicked but the most hopeless. No one can withstand whatever he sees fit to proclaim as God's will. Out of their mundane experience or common sense his flock can draw nothing to oppose to his obscurantism or fanaticism. His is the one despotism without check or limit.

> cross clefts; indeed, you might say that society is *sewed together* by its inner conflicts![136]

This is not necessarily to say that a society can tolerate an unlimited amount of conflict. On the contrary, all opposition except healthy rivalry, fair competition, and fruitful controversy is a waste of energy and an obstacle to cooperation. The two chief types of opposition, incidentally, are competition and conflict. Competition serves the "broad social function of assigning to each his place in the social system" when that function is not served by hereditary privilege.[137]

Ross omits from his discussion of conflict sectional conflict, nationality conflict, and party conflict on the ground that these are well treated by the political scientists. His discussion of sex conflict shows him to be a champion of the equality of the sexes, and the chapter on race conflict shows again that his racism has almost entirely disappeared.[138] His long treatment of class conflict deals largely with the conflict between capitalists and laborers. Because of constant improvement in the working conditions and the incomes of the laboring class, he does not expect class warfare to break out in the United States. Nor does he think that capitalism, despite numerous defects, will disappear. Among the processes that contribute to social adaptation and the lessening of conflict he treats in turn toleration, compromise, accomodation, assimilation, and amalgamation.

COOPERATION AND ORGANIZATION

The four chapters in this section deal, respectively, with cooperation, the organization of effort, the organization of will, and the organization of thought. Men cooperate with one another for many reasons, and the forms that cooperation takes vary from mutual aid to the division of labor. In discussing the organization of effort, Ross treats the rather obvious benefits of organization (the only way to get some things done), the "wastes" of organization (formalism and red tape), and the abuses of organization (nepotism, overspecialization). The chapter also includes some words of wisdom on how to run an organization.[139] By organization of will Ross means the process by which an organization receives its direction. The language is relatively unfamiliar here; for example, he writes that the "will

136. *Ibid.*, p. 201.

137. *Ibid.*, p. 216.

138. He would continue to bar immigrants with whom the natives will not freely mix. *Ibid.*, p. 341.

139. Compare Theodore Caplow, *Principles of Organization* (New York: Harcourt Brace & World, 1964): and *How to Run Any Organization* (New York: Holt, Rinehart, and Winston, 1976).

organization" of a group is determined by its stage of development, its composition, its purpose, and the nature of the matter to be dealt with. By the organization of thought he means the process by which ideas from different minds come together to form such a thing as Islamic theology, Roman law, or the science of astronomy. Thought is organized both unconsciously, as in the case of the development of language, and consciously, as in the Dialogues of Plato.

CLASS AND CASTE

This part of the book deals in six chapters with stratification, the rise of gross inequalities, gradation, segregation and subordination, equalization of opportunity, and the social circulation of individuals. In Ross's opinion stratification arises not because of the vertical social mobility of individuals but because of inheritance: "Social strata do not appear unless there is some kind of *inheritance*—of profession, of office, of authority, of property, of prestige, on the one hand; of lowly occupation, servitude, or disability, on the other."[140] Superiority was originally based on fighting capacity, and this inevitably meant a lower position for women. In some societies upper-class families were thought to be direct descendants of deities. For the most part, wealth is the foundation of a class structure. The state itself creates inequality: "The class-ruled state puts itself squarely behind social inequalities, but the democratic state resists the development of privilege and caste."[141] Frequently the fortunes that support class superiority have their origin in force, fraud, or corruption, but in these cases they may later be "deodorized" and legitimated, a process "whereby ill-gotten wealth is made to smell precisely like well-gotten wealth."[142] Martial, political, and priestly pursuits have always ranked high, with manual labor always at the other end of the scale. There is stratification even among the lower orders. Girls who work in mills will not admit girls who are domestic servants to their dances. There are, of course, gradations even in prison, where the forger has a higher status than the pickpocket. And then, as is well known, inherited wealth is superior to earned wealth because to the latter is attached the stigma of labor. Much of Ross's discussion of class is informed by a Veblen-like impatience with conspicuous consumption. His chapter on "The Social Circulation of Individuals" is indebted, with appropriate acknowledgement, to Sorokin's *Social Mobility*.

---

140. *Principles of Sociology*, p. 407.
141. *Ibid.*, p. 413.
142. *Ibid.*, p. 419.

SOCIETY AND THE INDIVIDUAL

The six chapters in this section deal with socialization, estrangement, social control, liberation, anticipation, and individualization. Socialization Ross defines as "the development of the we-feeling in associates and their growth in capacity and will to act together."[143] Among the conditions of socialization are a common background, a common speech, the primitive dance, common emotional experiences, eating together, the festival, group life, common possessions, and sport. A common enemy also generates the "we-feeling." The opposite of socialization is estrangement. In his discussion of this subject Ross draws on material from *The Polish Peasant in Europe and America,* by Thomas and Znaniecki. Almost as if by accident, Ross includes in his discussion of estrangement two otherwise unrelated paragraphs on social change:

> Do societies *have* to age and die? The idea of social old age and dissolution (Spengler) is nonsense. Every organism has a million generations behind it. Its life course has been fixed by heredity. It is like a watch that under even the best conditions can run only *so* long. A social aggregate, on the other hand, has not been rigidly pre-determined by its inheritance. It is a clock that can be rewound when it gives signs of running down. All the time, of course, societies are changing, strengthening their claim on the loyalties of their members, their grip on individual wills. Or else their inner bonds are loosening, the society is splitting, disintegrating.
>
> But "it's never too late to mend!" Society can be rejuvenated. That a society has endured a hundred years, half a thousand years, does not seal its fate. There is no cemetery for societies unless it be a military cemetery where are buried not the senile but those that stopped a bullet![144]

As before, in his 1901 book, Ross discusses the "radiant points" of social control, such as, for example, the elders and the learned. Unfortunately, repetition tarnishes the excellence of his expression. Again he prefers reason to the "slavish following of custom." He has an unusual assortment of the instruments of social control:

> Some of the instruments society employs bear upon the *will;* others, upon the *feelings;* still others, upon the *judgment.* In the first group are *social suggestion, custom and education,* which use direct means to give the will a certain

143. *Ibid.,* p. 471.

144. *Ibid.,* pp. 496–497. One does not quite know what to make of this. In any event, we can note that Ross has a fondness for exclamation points, especially after citations of facts that he considers preposterous. On advertising, for example: "A hundred thousand dollars will produce a certain perversion of public judgment to your ends, a million dollars will produce a much bigger perversion! [p. 398]." "How rarely we see a clean fight between truth and error! How often conflict is between systems of ideas equally arbitrary! [p. 497]."

bent, and *public opinion, law* and *religious belief,* which employ punishments and rewards. In the second group are *social religion, personal ideals, ceremony, art,* and *personality.* In the third group, *enlightenment, illusion* and *social valuation.*[145]

They all develop out of public opinion, but the religious and legal codes are "far more intelligent." The law, in fact, is "the cornerstone of the edifice of order."[146] The discussion ends with quotations concerning the control system in Lynds' *Middletown* (1929). By liberation, Ross means that societies and groups sometimes lose their grip on individuals, especially with the rise of critical thought. By the process of anticipation he means that we sometimes anticipate the effect that our institutions will have on us. And by individualization he means that sometimes there is too much regulation in human life—in the factory, the army, the government, the church, the university, and the welfare system. More freedom and humanity are needed.

OCCUPATION AND SOCIAL FUNCTION

Under this rubric Ross treats occupations, commercialization, and professionalization. Occupations should not be measured by the yardstick of Mammon; commercialization is a vice that is degrading the arts, recreation, and journalism. Most of the content of these chapters is devoted to denunciations of the business mentality in American society. Professionalization is a means of limiting certain callings to "men of honor" and of maintaining standards. The professional spirit is the antithesis of the commercial spirit. It places service over gain, as Parsons was to insist in his studies of the medical profession. We are a little more skeptical now.

SOCIAL REGRESS AND PROGRESS

The chapters in this section deal with ossification, decadence, deterioration of organs and structures, transformation, reshaping, and revolution. Ossification is similar to Ogburn's cultural lag; both procedures and institutions lose pliancy after a while and are retained when the need for them has disappeared. Thus, the long school vacation in the summer was designed for a time when children were needed to work on the farm. Ossification is caused by mental laziness, the control of society by the old, respect for the established, the authority of tradition, and veneration of precedent. The working man is most resistant to change; the intellectual, least. Ross

145. *Ibid.*
146. *Ibid.*, p. 508.

lists nine ways to prevent ossification, all of which suggest the flavor of his writing: Get the talented at the steering wheels; preserve the doer's freedom of initiative: keep a balance between clergy and other intellectuals; apply critical scholarship to the genesis and history of institutions; preserve inviolate the right of free inquiry; keep social institutions out of the grasp of religion; base right and wrong on human nature and the nature of society; let the learner study life as well as books, and test results by measurement.[147]

The decadence of a society has many causes. Among them Ross lists deterioration of the physical basis of society (adverse change of climate, deforestation and erosion, soil exhaustion); deterioration of the racial basis of society (race displacement, the cityward flow, selective emigration, extirpation of the superior); subjugation; internal causes (increasing heterogeneity, demoralization from shift of cultures,[148] unfavorable social surroundings, overgrowth of institutions so that natural leaders are intimidated, instincts set above reason, the rise of privilege and caste, and decadence in social culture).[149] Ross candidly admits that in his discussion of the internal causes "there is much fog." Disquieting trends in society, however, can be arrested: "It is the social scientist's job to discover and point out mal-functioning social organs,"[150] and, with an expression of simple faith, "If only those of good will among us can be brought to coöperate our major ailments can be remedied."[151]

The deterioration of organs and structures is caused by certain diseases, among them nepotism, corruption, red tape, indifferentism, formalism, obsolescence, absolutism, and perversion. Ross fails to see that his "causes" are the names of the diseases. The changes that simply happen in society he calls transformation; those that are willed he calls reshaping. Unfortunately, his discussion of the factors in social change is so eclectic that it fails to result in a theory. Nor are his factors on the same level; for example, the establishment of evolution as a social process and the discovery of means of contraception are both primary factors. Instead of searching for causes, he is too often content to list some of the changes that were occurring in the American society of his day. Much of his discussion is rhetorical and hortatory: "Must we be content with such betterments of society as come of

147. *Ibid.*, pp. 590–593 (italics omitted.) With respect to the last, Ross writes, "The nonmaterial culture lags behind the material culture largely because it has not lent itself to test and measurement." He does not say how this testing and measuring can be done.

148. "For when an immigrant has sloughed off his old-home culture before he has been mastered by the culture of his new home, he slumps morally." *Ibid.*, p. 601.

149. As in the glorification of war by fascist Italy.

150. *Ibid.*, p. 607.

151. *Ibid.*, p. 608.

themselves? Or may we put in a hand to bring about desired changes? Surely the latter!"[152] To laissez-faire he is opposed, not only in the economic realm but also in society in general, and Ross uses Ward to support this sentiment.[153] He is sure that an interventionist policy will shortly bring about the extirpation of prostitution and the sterilization of mental defectives. He is not above indulging in such jejune observations as that reforms must not misread human nature and that they must square with essential realities if they are to succeed. However respectable from the point of social policy, many of his propositions lack all sociological distinction. Indeed, for Ross social policy is indistinguishable from sociology.

In his chapter on revolution, influenced in part by the distinguished University of Chicago doctoral dissertation of Lyford P. Edwards,[154] Ross becomes even more vehement:

> Sociologists reject with contempt the theory, dear to beleaguered or refugee dominators, that revolutionary discontent is stirred up by the agitation of a few gifted but unscrupulous Utopians, soreheads, or power-seekers, whose inflammatory eloquence rouses people to revolt even when they are actually well-governed and have nothing serious to complain of. Bah! The bulk of men are not fools; they cannot be made discontented by vain imaginings nor can they be stampeded by seditious suggestions that clash with their upbringing, their settled habits and their intellectual leadership. Even sillier is the pretense that revolutions originate in sudden mysterious epidemics of mob madness![155]

The cause of revolution instead—the typical cause—is "the selfish blocking of greatly and generally desired social adjustments by the holders of power."[156] Once more we are disappointed, because Ross has given us a journalistic truism rather than a sociological proposition.

Ross does, however, contribute an insight. Revolution does not always happen when oppression is at its worst. Indeed, the American colonies were better off under George III than under his predecessors. What happens is sudden consciousness of what Stouffer was much later to label realtive deprivation. It was when the French bourgeoisie, despite gains in wealth and importance, became conscious of their relative insignificance in comparison with the nobility that they joined the revolt. Ross's personal observations in China, Mexico, and Russia of revolutions at various stages

---

152. *Ibid.*, p. 642.

153. He even uses the word *telesis*.

154. *The Natural History of Revolution* (Chicago: University of Chicago Press, 1927). A new edition of this book is included in the Heritage of Sociology series, edited by Morris Janowitz (Chicago: University of Chicago Press, 1970).

155. *Principles of Sociology*, p. 650.

156. *Ibid.*

gave him the impression that they all cost more than their leaders anticipated at the outset and that they all inspired excesses of one sort or another. On this point Sorokin would be in poignant agreement. Nevertheless, some good can come from revolution. Ross patriotically uses the American Revolution as an example.

SOCIAL PRODUCTS

Here we are introduced to culture planes, standards, groups, and institutions. It is difficult to know exactly what Ross means by "culture planes," but perhaps a quotation will help:

> Communicating men in time are likely to gravitate into common planes of belief or practice. In early ages only those of the same group, the same stock, or the same valley fell into these common planes. But culture gains radiant energy until such an element as the Arabic speech, the written characters of China, the religion of Islam, or the game of chess overcomes all rival culture elements in its neighborhood and draws myriads of people into one plane.[157]

The brief chapter on culture planes is in effect a discussion of cultural diffusion. In it Ross has occasion to praise Christian missionary activity in disseminating the "higher elements of a superior culture." His ethnocentrism prevents him from seeing that such activity might also be considered an immoral intrusion into another society's customs and beliefs.

By standards Ross means the behavior patterns that Sumner called the mores.[158] Standards are key products that express a society's individuality. "Tell me a people's behavior standards and I will sketch for you its social order."[159] Every group develops standards of its own; some are active standards and others are sleeping standards—the former in daily use, the latter, like taboos, thought about only when violated. Standards need not possess utility; indeed some are harmful. They are the product of collective experience.

The social processes Ross discusses throughout create groups, whose members are united by various bonds. These bonds include the blood bond, the place bond, the likeness bond, the common-experience bond, the fraternal bond, and the interest bond. As a classification of groups this is somewhat less than satisfactory, but Ross apparently has little interest in the subject.

157. *Ibid.*, pp. 662–663.

158. "I prefer this word to *mores* (suggested by Professor W. G. Sumner), because the latter is an alien unfamiliar word, and besides, its singular is unavailable." *Ibid.*, p. 667n.

159. *Ibid.*, p. 667.

Social institutions Ross defines as "sets of organized human relationships established or sanctioned by the common will."[160] They have seven elements: an underlying concept, a purpose,[161] permanence, a structure,[162] a code, authority, and personnel.[163] The examples Ross uses show that he has not decided whether institutions are customs or groups.[164] Thus, property and contract on the one hand and joint-stock companies and labor unions on the other are all institutions. A priesthood is a "quasi-institution," as is public worship. At Ross's stage of sociological inquiry it was apparently not important to distinguish between groups and institutions, although a regard for logic should have encouraged him to do so. The chapter, incidentally, includes quotations from both Cooley and MacIver.

Religion, once an institution, is coming to be a private matter, and education, once a private matter, is coming to be an institution. In this distinction one sees what Ross has in mind. An institution is a public, not a private, way of participating in an activity. If, as we have seen he is unfriendly to customs, he has a similar attitude toward institutions. He hopes that the day will come when enlightened individuals will no longer be "hampered" by them and will outgrow their need of them.

PROJECTION INTO THE FUTURE

Ross concludes his long book with two brief chapters under this rubric, the penultimate one entitled "Foreshadowing of the Next Culture," and the ultimate one, "Retrospects and Prospects." All we need say about them is that they show he is optimistic about the future of the human race.

Summary and Evaluation

We have, in effect, already summarized Ross's general sociological theory in the foregoing descriptions of the contents of his books. The importance of Ross rests not in the details of his theory but in his early comprehension of the nature of the field. If sociology at the beginning of the

160. *Ibid.*, p. 686.

161. Somewhat puzzling is Ross's assertion that "a group activity, *e.g.*, football, that gratifies participants in ways to which society does not object is still no institution, since it lacks a social purpose." *Ibid.*, p. 686.

162. Ross apparently has in mind apparatus, buildings, and equipment.

163. But personnel only if "operative." If "regulative"—such as, for example, betrothal, the family, rest days—they have no personnel.

164. "When an imposed activity or inhibition is so recurrent that it becomes a custom and this custom gains social approval and authority, it is an *institution*." *Ibid.*, p. 686.

century was an "empty chair" among the social sciences, it was a chair that he himself did much to fill. He was a "concerned citizen" long before the expression became current, and it was this concern that motivated his sociology. It does him no discredit to say that his passion for sociology was melioristic rather than scientific. Although he himself wrote that sociology should be more involved with causes than with cures, he lavishly indulged himself in prescriptions for a better society. He was sure that all right-thinking people, members, like himself, of a superior race, would come to the same conclusions about the future of society and the welfare of humanity. To this future, and this welfare, sociology would make a great contribution. "We part from those who insist that the development of society follows unchanging laws and from those who contend that man can mold society altogether to his liking. The truth is in between."[165]

Ross is one of the greatest of prose stylists in the history of sociology. On this subject Joyce Hertzler has said it all:

> His theoretical as well as his more popular writings are characterized by a brilliant and unique style and unrivalled powers of vivid and vigorous exposition. No sociologists, and few scientists generally, have been able to express themselves in such trenchant and gripping language. His pages are replete with similes, metaphors, epigrammatic statements, analogies, vivid imagery, clever and picturesque phrases, delightful bits of description, and fanciful anecdotes and representations. His sentences are crisp, spicy, and eye-catching; in them is verve and movement. He causes the reader to believe that he is not reading prosaic, dry-as-dust social theory, or a mere account of observations and interpretations of social problems at home or the commonplace and recurring in foreign countries, but rather that social science deals with living romance, and is social adventure and fascinating discovery.[166]

Like Cooley, Ross has his moral convictions but he expresses them with vigor rather than with piety. He is the Theodore Roosevelt, and not the Calvin Coolidge, of sociology.

On the positive side also is Ross's appreciation of the role of conflict in society. Indeed, he devotes more pages to this subject than to any other.

Some things must be said on the negative side. Ross fondly believed that he was creating a system of sociology. Actually, one finds little that is systematic in his writing. His enthusiasms interfere with his organization. As suggested earlier, the impression remains that he wrote too much too rapidly, and without adequate reflection. His ideas are clearly and colorfully expressed, but they are not always coherent. His classifications are illogical and his concepts often appear in curious juxtapositions.

165. *Principles of Sociology*, p. 707.
166. "Edward Alsworth Ross: Sociological Pioneer," pp. 608–609.

Finally, we find in Ross no sense of society as a phenomenon sui generis, a phenomenon with a structure of its own, with its own distinguishable components. There is no sense, in short, of a social order. He even—and quite unaccountably—looks forward to the time when customs and institutions will decline and disappear, thus depriving himself of two of the structural components of any society and, into the bargain, of society itself. Society dissolves into processes, as many as thirty eight in one place and forty one in another. If, as Bertrand Russell once suggested, reality can be viewed either as a pile of sand or as a bucket of molasses, it is clear that Ross is on the side of the molasses.

In sum, Ross had scope and altitude, but little depth, and no system at all. He wrote a book called *Principles of Sociology*—it was his major effort—but one looks in vain in it for principles. Recommendations are there in abundance, recommendations on all kinds of social policy. But his advocacy overwhelmed his sociology. One concludes that Ross may have missed his true vocation. He should have been the chief editorial writer for the *New York Times.* No one could have excelled him in that capacity.

CHAPTER 5

Florian Znaniecki

Science is reason challenging experience and forcing it into a rational order.

—*The Method of Sociology*, p. 233.

Florian Witold Znaniecki was born on January 15, 1882, near Swiatniki, in Poland. As one of three children of an estate manager, he received his earliest instruction at the hands of tutors, a private curriculum that included French, German, and Russian. At the gymnasium, or secondary school, he learned Greek and Latin, studied literature, and wrote poetry. In 1903, at the age of twenty one, he published a volume of verse entitled *Cheops: A Poem of Fantasy*, his first words to appear in print. At the University of Warsaw, where he began his undergraduate studies, he belonged to an underground group that was in rebellion against the Russian authorities; the students lectured to one another on forbidden subjects—namely, books written by Polish authors. When the students staged a protest against the administration, Znaniecki, chosen by his comrades to represent them, politely sent his card to the rector to announce his presence and was promptly expelled from the university. He thus never received a baccalaureate degree.[1]

Znaniecki thereupon began a period of romantic travel and study in Switzerland, France, and Italy. He attended the universities of Geneva, Zurich, and Paris, from the first of which he received an M.A. degree. Then he returned to Poland, where he received his Ph.D. degree from the University of Cracow in 1909. His *Wanderjahre* included a period in the French Foreign Legion, from which he was discharged with a shoulder wound, and also a period during which he served as editor of a French

1. My authority for this statement is Znaniecki's wife, Eileen Markley Znaniecki, who told it to me in his presence. Their daughter, however, and Lewis A. Coser both confer a Warsaw degree upon him. See Helena Znaniecki Lopata, "Florian Znaniecki: His Life," in Florian Znaniecki, *Social Relations and Social Roles: The Unfinished Systematic Sociology* (San Francisco: Chandler Publishing Co. 1965), p. xiii; and Lewis A. Coser, *Masters of Sociological Thought*, 2nd ed. (New York: Harcourt Brace Jovanovich, 1977), p. 538.

literary magazine. During these years his interests turned from poetry to philosophy; it was the latter field in which he took his doctorate and in which he won an early distinction both for his articles and for his Polish translation of Bergson's *L'Evolution Créatrice.*

For political reasons Znaniecki was ineligible for appointment to an academic post in his native country, then as at other times under the hegemony of Russia, and he accordingly accepted a position as director of the Emigrants' Protective Association. It was here that W. I. Thomas met him, in 1913, on one of his frequent trips to Europe. Thomas had begun to study the problems of immigrants to the United States, and particularly the Polish immigrants who were settling in large numbers in Chicago and Detroit. When Thomas learned that Znaniecki had no opportunity to pursue an academic career in Poland, he suggested that the young scholar go to the United States, which he did in 1914.[2] Thomas later arranged an appointment for him at the University of Chicago. Together they worked on their monumental *The Polish Peasant in Europe and America.* published in five volumes during the years 1918–1920 and in a new two-volume edition in 1927. In 1919 Znaniecki also published his own first book in the English language, *Cultural Reality,* intended as the first part of a general introduction to the philosophy of culture.

In 1920 Znaniecki returned to Poland, where he became professor of sociology (first professor of philosophy, but changed at his request) at the University of Poznan and where he founded the Polish Sociological Institute and the *Polish Sociological Review.* At Poznan he trained many students whose own works were later to add luster to the history of Polish sociology, and there he wrote his *Introduction to Sociology* (1922) and his massive *Sociology of Education* (1928–1930). His book, *The Laws of Social Psychology,* was published in English in 1925.

In 1932–1934 Znaniecki was back in the United States as visiting professor at Columbia University, where he supervised a number of dissertations in the Columbia Department of Sociology, then headed by Robert M. MacIver. In 1934 he published in English *The Method of Sociology;* and in 1936, back again in Poznan, his large volume, *Social Actions,* also in English. In the summer of 1939 he was once more in the United States,

2. There is some discrepancy in the record here. Morris Janowitz, in his Introduction to *W. I. Thomas: On Social Organization and Social Personality* (Chicago: University of Chicago Press, 1966), says that Thomas "neither invited him nor encouraged him to come" and "was completely unaware of his journey from Poland until he actually arrived penniless at Thomas' home [p. xxv]." Znaniecki, on the other hand, says, "During our conferences Thomas suggested that I should come to Chicago and help him translate and edit his material, perhaps collect some more material from the Poles in this country." "William I. Thomas as a Collaborator," *Sociology and Social Research* (March–April 1948): p. 765.

where he had been invited to deliver a series of lectures, again at Columbia University. At the end of summer, 1939, European clouds were heavy with the threat of war. MacIver tried to persuade Znaniecki to remain in this country, but Znaniecki insisted on returning. His ship, however, was intercepted by the Royal Navy and taken to a British port. On the day of the vessel's scheduled arrival in Gdynia the Nazi armies crossed the border of Poland to begin World War II. Znaniecki's name was on the list of Polish patriots and professors scheduled for execution.

Znaniecki then had no alternative but to return to the United States. He was offered an appointment as professor of sociology at the University of Illinois, and there he spent the last period of his active career with the exception of one postretirement year as visiting professor at Wayne State University. His wife and daughter, interned briefly in a concentration camp in Poland, managed to escape the country and join him in Urbana. A son by an earlier marriage, Juliusz Znaniecki, a poet and novelist, participated in the Warsaw uprising and was incarcerated at Dachau, from which he was released by Allied forces at the end of the war.

Znaniecki was married twice, the first time in 1906 to Emilia Szwejkowska, who died in 1915. In 1916 he married Eileen Markley, and this proved to be a most remarkable and successful marriage. The young Miss Markley, a graduate of Smith College, had taken her M.A. in history at Columbia University under James Harvey Robinson. She then experienced frustration in her efforts to matriculate at the Columbia Law School, because its doors were then closed to women. She accordingly went to the University of Chicago Law School, where she graduated with a distinguished record. It was in Chicago that she met the young Polish scholar, and after marriage she submerged her own career entirely in his. Except for several articles and chapters that she wrote on Polish sociology, she devoted all of her efforts to Florian's writing, beginning with *The Polish Peasant.* It is difficult to estimate the extent of her contribution to his career, but it was large indeed, and there should be nothing but the most profound recognition of her role as brilliant co-worker with her more famous husband. Only those who were close to both of them could understand and appreciate the significance of the role she played in his career. A daughter of this marriage, Helena Znaniecki Lopata, also became an important sociologist.

The years at Illinois were pleasant ones for Znaniecki. He occupied a large and comfortable house on a tree-shaded street in Champaign, a typical Midwestern street, and enjoyed the most congenial relationships with his colleagues in the department, which at that time included J. William Albig, Donald R. Taft, and E. T. Hiller. His daily regimen was seldom varied. From Catholic and aristocratic lineage, he was wholly unhampered by the Puritan ethic and accordingly spent his mornings in bed. By the time he rose at noon, however, he had added a number of pages to the corpus of his work. His afternoons were devoted to lectures, when classes were in session, his evenings to quiet reading or, as often as he could manage it, to bridge, a game in which he took great delight.

Znaniecki was a pure academician, one who was at home only in the realm of ideas. His colleagues at one time elected him rector of the University of Poznan, but administration was a duty he viewed with distaste and he escaped the responsibility as soon as he decently could. He served as president of the American Sociological Society in 1953–1954 and gave his presidential address on "Basic Problems of Contemporary Sociology."[3] In 1952 he published his last major work, *Cultural Sciences*, succeeded in the same year by a smaller work, *Modern Nationalities*. The first of these was dedicated "to the University of Illinois, in gratitude for ten free, happy, and productive years as a member of its faculty," and the second, to his students. His final years were devoted to writing a work he never finished, on systematic sociology, fragments of which were edited by his daughter and published posthumously in 1965 under the title *Social Relations and Social Roles*. He died at Urbana, Illinois, on March 23, 1958, at the age of seventy six.

During his last years Znaniecki spoke frequently of his desire to return to Poland. His friends dissuaded him from doing so, however, on the ground that a visit to that country might imply approval of the regime. He was always, of course, opposed to any restrictions on the freedom of inquiry—restrictions he had experienced in his student days—and he was particularly appalled by the fate of sociology in Poland after World War II. He was a scholar through and through, dedicated to the university, at home in its ambiance, zealous in it purpose, and happy in its service. He lived with grace and distinction "the social role of the man of knowledge."

Early Philosophical Writings

Znaniecki's reputation suffered from the fact that almost half of his books were written in Polish, a language inaccessible to most of his American and English readers. Like his countryman Joseph Conrad before him, however, he developed an enviable style in English. His small book, *The Social Role of the Man of Knowledge*, is a masterpiece of the literary

3. For a bibliography of Znaniecki's writings, compiled by Helena Znaniecki Lopata, see Znaniecki, *Social Relations and Social Roles*, pp. xx–xxviii.

art, a book that can be read today not only for its sociological sophistication but also for the aesthetic pleasure to be derived from its English prose. All of his English sentences, in all of his English books, are free of the jargon that sometimes disfigures sociological writing. All of them shine with lucidity and this, in an adopted tongue, is a high order of achievement. On his first voyage to the United States, in 1914, he practiced the new and unfamiliar language by writing an article, "The Principle of Relativity and Philosophical Absolutism." Accepted by *The Philosophical Review*, it was his first publication in English.

Znaniecki's first article published in Polish, in 1909, was a methodological critique of Lévy-Bruhl's *La morale et la science des moeurs*. The philosophical challenge to which he responded in his youth was an effort to develop a systematic theory of culture. In 1910 he published his first book, *The Problem of Values in Philosophy*, in which he formulated the hypothesis that all theories of culture require at their base a concept of values, which are the common data of human experience and which are not reducible to any combination either of natural objects or of subjective processes. They are unique and belong to a realm of their own, no part of the physical world and yet objectively accessible to inquiry. His second book, *Humanism and Knowledge*, published in 1912, belongs properly to the sociology of knowledge, although Znaniecki did not call it that. In it he developed the view that all knowledge, including scientific knowledge, is a product of the sociocultural or historico-cultural situation in which it arises. It is in these terms that he aspired to trace the evolution of civilization.

The problem of values was of prime concern to Znaniecki in these early philosophical writings. He wanted very much to build a bridge, undergirded with strong epistemological and ontological support, between this realm and the empirical world of the natural sciences in which values would ultimately be validated. He was interested similarly in the problem of creativity, a phenomenon that seemed to have no counterpart in the natural order of things. In *Cultural Reality*, his first book in English (1919), he addressed himself to these problems. He was concerned about the separation, and growing tension, between idealism and realism in philosophy, by the fact that philosophy itself had surrendered some of its historical issues, and by the failure, in his opinion, of both Bergsonian intuitionism and Deweyan pragmatism to offer satisfactory answers and constructive principles with which the problems of creativity and culture could be solved.

Znaniecki was puzzled especially by the fact that idealism, incomparably stronger from any fundamental logical point of view, had consistently given ground to realism, which proved itself able to solve a number of concrete problems. Idealism had thus become incapable of criticizing the internal organization and conclusions of the "realistic sciences" and had to derive only some small comfort by questioning their epistemological and metaphysical foundations. This abdication, however, does not serve the best interests of human culture, or of human knowledge; it violates indeed the highest standards of intellectual, moral, and aesthetic inquiry and reduces such inquiry to a mere by-product of a natural evolution. This is the framework in which Znaniecki pursued his thesis, often technical and often complicated, that culture constitutes a reality of its own and is no mere epiphenomenon of a natural universe. It is a reality that neither an unsuccessful idealism nor an illogical naturalism can explain. Among the many statements that express this view the following may be regarded as representative:

> If therefore modern thought intends to avoid the emptiness of idealism and the self-contradictions of naturalism, it must accept the culturalistic thesis. It must maintain against idealism the universal historical relativity of all forms of reason and standards of valuation as being within, not above, the evolving empirical world. It must maintain against naturalism that man is not a product of the evolution of nature, but that, on the contrary, nature, in a large measure at least, is the product of human culture, and if there is anything in nature which preceded man the way to find it leads through historical and social science, not through biology, geology, astronomy, or physics.[4]

This view, of course, contributes to Znaniecki's sense of the indispensability of social science.

Although little of *Cultural Reality* is directly relevant to sociology for the reason that its aims and purposes are primarily to guarantee an ontological status to the realm of culture, Znaniecki nevertheless touches upon sociology in his discussion of the kinds or "orders" of reality. These are four in number: the physical, the psychological, the sociological, and the ideal. With respect to the psychological order, Znaniecki approved of behaviorism insofar as it studied the natural processes of organisms in environment, but he pointed out that in doing so it became a part of biology and thus left the study of conscious data to other schools.[5] The basic problems of psychology are problems of situations and not of objects. It is the situation that gives us a ground for the explanation of personal experiences:

> A reality is supposed to assume similar aspects in similar situations; and if it has a certain aspect for the given individual at the given moment, it is because it is determined for his actual experience by some actual situation of which it is

4. *Cultural Reality* (Chicago: University of Chicago Press, 1919), pp. 21–22.
5. *Ibid.*, p. 274.

> a part. Therefore whenever similar situations are found, we expect similar experiences of given reality, and, on the contrary, in different situations we expect different aspects of this reality to appear.[6]

Furthermore, what we might be tempted to view as an objective, natural reality—whether thing, property, relation, or process—does not in its own identity afford the conditions of being experienced always and everywhere in the same way. Only when experienced in similar situations can such realities be compared. It is the situation that thus assumes significance. In fact, objects can have meanings only when we include the social dimension, and a dynamic psychology must therefore be a social psychology. Objects have meanings only when they are seen as elements of situations.

In his treatment of the sociological order of reality, Znaniecki endeavors to show that it is independent both of physical and of psychological reality. For him the social and the psychological are two separate "schemes." It is a self-contradiction to reduce the social to the psychological as it is indeed to reduce the psychological to the social.

> By conceiving society as a synthesis of psychological individuals we preclude the possibility of a rational solution of all particular problems which can be solved only with the help of common social schemes acting in and through individuals and yet existing independently of each of them. By conceiving the individual as synthesis of social schemes, we preclude the possibility of the solution of all those problems in which the continuity of personal life or the uniformity of experiences in all conscious individuals independent of the social groups to which they belong are the necessary resuppositions.[7]

It is not possible to divide the empirical world into two ontologically separate categories—the psychological and the social—they are rather two different ways of treating the same phenomenon.

When Znaniecki turns his attention to the conditions that are logically indispensable for the construction of an autonomous social science he states his fundamental proposition that social reality is formally constituted of schemes or rules, whether or not consciously formulated, "giving uniform and permanent definitions of personal situations."[8] If schemes or rules are the form, the matter is constituted of social values, which are products of the social order and which stand in an intermediate position between concrete historical reality on the one hand and the objects of natural reality on the other. These must necessarily be communicated, of course, and since

6. *Ibid.*, p. 276.
7. *Ibid.*, pp. 285–286.
8. *Ibid.*, p. 290.

there are limits to communication, the schemes themselves are limited to particular social groups.

Although we find in *Cultural Reality* echoes of ideas already expressed and anticipations of ideas to come, the book is basically an essay in ontology and methodology—the latter, of course, in the sense of the logic of inquiry—and it would satisfy only a minimum criterion of relevance to sociology. When Znaniecki went to Chicago he had had no instruction in sociology and for him the discipline was a "new experience." He had hoped to begin an academic career in America in philosophy, and it is testimony to the influence that Thomas benevolently exerted upon him during his period as research assistant that he rejected the old mistress and happily embraced the new. It was a decision he never regretted. But *Cultural Reality* belongs almost entirely to his philosophical phase. Only many years later, in *Cultural Sciences,* did he return again to the issues that had attracted the restless and roving mind of his youth.

The Polish Peasant in Europe and America

So much has been said and written about *The Polish Peasant,* in articles about both Thomas and Znaniecki, that it hardly seems necessary to expatiate upon it again. There is no doubt that it is a classic work in the history of American sociology. Even today, long after the Polish peasants who were the subjects of the book have been assimilated, it maintains its fascination and its significance for the insights it contains about the human person, his attitudes and values, his disorganization and reorganization, as he moves from one culture to another.

For a number of years prior to the meeting of Thomas and Znaniecki in Poland in 1913, Thomas had interested himself in the backgrounds, problems, and adjustments of immigrants then coming to the United States, especially those from central and eastern Europe—Poles, Russians, Rumanians, Czechs, Hungarians, and Jews. He had begun to collect materials about them, and especially about those in the peasant classes, for these made up the large majority of those who chose to emigrate. At some time Thomas decided that the exigencies of research would force him to limit his study to one of these groups, and it was the Poles that he selected, primarily because the Polish community in Chicago was a large one and one that seemed to exhibit special kinds of personal and social disorganization. In accordance with this design he visited Poland, talked with everyone he could find who knew anything about the emigrants—professors, newspaper editors, heads of agricultural bureaus, economists—and it was in pursuit of this trail that he was led to Znaniecki. By this time he had already collected a large amount of material, to which Znaniecki, as director of the Emigrants' Protective Association, was able to add a great deal more. It was the beginning of a long and unusually harmonious relationship, both intellectually and personally, with Znaniecki serving Thomas as research assistant, editing and translating Polish documents, helping to formulate the ideas that Thomas and he discussed in their conversations, and preparing drafts of various portions of the manuscript. The work was Thomas's in inception and plan, but it was Znaniecki who persuaded him to include an introductory note that would deal with the methodology of the enterprise. Thomas himself was not attracted to methodological or other theoretical issues, whereas these were the problems that lay at the center of Znaniecki's concerns. It was after Znaniecki wrote the Methodological note, in at least three drafts, that Thomas generously decided to add his name to the title page of the book.

Although the careers of the two authors diverged considerably after 1920 and although they were fairly far apart not only in intellectual emphasis but also in temperament, it may be said that their collaboration, precisely because of these differences, was an unusually successful one. It is doubtful indeed if either one of them alone could have brought *The Polish Peasant* to fruition in anything like the form in which we know it or could have made it the sociological classic it is generally conceded to be. Thomas's contribution was a psychological penetration, a comprehensive curiosity, and a rare wisdom; Znaniecki's, a philosophical sophistication, a historical eruditon, and a talent for systematization. Unfortunately, friends of each were sometimes tempted in later years to emphasize the contributions of one of them at the expense of the other. It was a game in which neither of the authors indulged. As one who knew both Thomas and Znaniecki well, I never heard either of them say anything that would in any degree denigrate the contribution of the other to their joint enterprise. Indeed, Znaniecki, in the article "William I. Thomas as a Collaborator," wrote:

> Never have I known, heard, or read about anybody with such a wide, sympathetic interest in the vast diversity of socio-cultural patterns and such a genius for understanding the uniqueness of every human personality. The famous statement of Terence: "I am a man and nothing human seems alien to me," expresses an ideal which few men have ever realized as fully as Thomas.[9]

Whatever Znaniecki's final view of the Note, and of *The Polish Peasant* in general, it is necessary to say that the book made major contributions to

9. Pp. 765–767.

the developing science of sociology. The first of these was the extensive use of personal documents as an instrument of research. Indeed, even before Thomas turned to this particular subject he had encouraged his students in Chicago to submit to him their autobiographies, including their sexual histories, all of which he regarded as important data for sociological purposes. The autobiography of a young Polish immigrant, Wladek, published originally as Volume 3 and then at the end of Volume 2 in the two-volume edition, is still perhaps the finest example of the use of an autobiographical resource. The credit for this, however, probably belongs to Władek himself as much as it does to Thomas and Znaniecki. It is an unusual document. Znaniecki continued to use personal documents in his research and at one time collected biographical material from his students at the University of Illinois, but the ensuing work, entitled "The Social Role of the University Student," was never published.

Of the theoretical contributions of *The Polish Peasant* it is necessary to say only that they were joint products—one the emphasis upon the famous four wishes, and two the emphasis upon attitudes—which provided a stimulus to attitude research in the history of American social psychology. Finally, there is, in the later volumes, the treatment of human personalities and their participation in social life, a participation that often issues, as in the case of the Polish peasant, in disorganization at first and then in reorganization.

In the Methodological Note itself a number of positions are advanced that represent the sociological thought of Thomas and Znaniecki at the time of writing it. First of all, science is regarded as a conscious and rational technique for controlling the physical world, and it is no less important that rational techniques be similarly applied to social reality. The rapid pace of social evolution requires it. For this purpose "common sense" does not suffice. In the first place, we do not "know" social reality simply because we have a certain "empirical acquaintance" with it; the acquaintance that each one of us has is always limited and cannot supply the required generalizations. In the second place, sociology, like the physical sciences, has to win a certain independence from practice. The reformer and the idealist have their roles to play, and important roles they are, but indignation and idealism have no place in sociological inquiry. Unfortunately, what is important in practice may not be important in theory. In the third place, sociology ought not to use current norms as a basis for inquiry because it is precisely in times of rapid social evolution and crisis that the norms themselves are changing. Nor is it desirable or even possible to separate any special set of social facts from the total context of a given society—except, of course, for purely analytical purposes. In the fourth place, theoretical work must not be bent to the service of immediate solutions to practical problems. Science must sooner or later pay its debt to society in the practical application of its results, but if utility is the ultimate criterion it must never be the immediate one.

The following section of the Note is addressed to the task of constructing some kind of synthesis in which both attitudes and values will assume their appropriate places and perform their necessary roles. This was clearly an effort—which Znaniecki later came to regard as an unsuccessful one—to bring Thomas's emphasis upon attitudes into some kind of a viable theoretical relationship with his own concept of values. In the course of the discussion sociology, unlike social psychology, with which it has a close affinity, is viewed as a special and not a general science of culture. The authors arrive at a basic methodological principle, in language that is wholly Durkheimian in flavor but not altogether Durkheimian in substance, when they say, "The cause of a value or of an attitude is never an attitude or a value alone, but always a combination of an attitude and a value."[10]

The authors reject the view that the sheer complexity of the social world precludes the search for laws or generalizations. The physical world is equally complex. Whether, despite the illustrations supplied, the method of *The Polish Peasant* has produced such social laws is a question that animated the critique of Herbert Blumer, a critique with which the authors largely agreed.[11] One of Blumer's observations was that the relationship between the method employed and the quality of the book may not be as close as was then commonly supposed. The distinction of *The Polish Peasant* may be attributable not to the method but rather to the talents of the authors—insight, imagination, intimate knowledge of their subject, and a superior sophistication.

Toward the end of the Note we have a discussion of the "four wishes" which, to Thomas's subsequent surprise, occupied so large a place in the histories of sociology. Here the wish for mastery is listed, although it was later to be replaced, by Thomas, by the wish for response, largely in order to include the sexual factor whose importance Thomas had come increasingly to recognize. The Note concludes with the modest affirmation that the book is devoted primarily to a study of the attitudes and values that obtain in a specific social group, namely, the migrating Polish peasants, with

10. William I. Thomas and Florian Znaniecki, *The Polish Peasant in Europe and America*, 2 vols. (New York: Alfred A. Knopf, 1927), vol. 1, p. 44 (italics omitted).

11. *Critiques of Research in the Social Sciences* Social (New York: Social Science Research Council, 1939), vol. 1.

the intent to show that both of these attributes are important factors in any effort to understand and define the situation. As a whole the Note is an eloquent and enduring contribution to the science of sociology.[12]

The Method of Sociology[13]

A claim can be made for the proposition that of all of Znaniecki's books in English, *The Method of Sociology* offers the most complete and satisfactory system, even though it is dedicated largely to issues of method rather than to issues of substance. It is concerned, that is, with the selection and determination of scientific data in general, with the principles of selection of cultural data, with the data of sociology, with a criticism of certain methodological tendencies of which Znaniecki disapproved, and finally with his own recommended method—the method of analytic induction. The book also offers almost all of the specific notions that informed Znaniecki's approach. When he wrote it he was conscious of the fact that sociology was passing through a critical period, that what had once been a synthetic science interested in "society" or "civilization"—a special kind of philosophy of history—was in process of becoming an analytic science directed to the investigation of detailed, particular, and specific kinds of empirical data. It was becoming not only distrustful of the sweeping generalization but in fact indifferent to it. This shift in the focus of the science seemed to Znaniecki to require a more thoroughgoing methodological sophistication than had previously been exhibited, and this was a prime factor in his decision to write this particular book. The time had come for sociology to indulge in "fundamental discussion concerning the general possibilities and conditions of its future development."[14]

Znaniecki gives in his preface a clear indication of three of the views that informed his sociological theory. The first of these is that sociology is a special and not a general social science; that it has its own special subject matter, its own "specific category of data" shared by no other science; and that, without being as formalistic as Simmel, for example, would have liked, it is nevertheless, and of methodological necessity, limited to the

12. All of the material in this chapter up to this point has been taken, with modifications, from the author's Introduction to Robert Bierstedt, ed., *Florian Znaniecki on Humanistic Sociology* (Chicago: University of Chicago Press, 1969), pp. 1–15. Copyright © 1969 by the University of Chicago. The first two paragraphs in the following section are also taken from this source.

13. (New York: Farrar & Rinehart, 1934).

14. *Method of Sociology*, p. vii.

treatment of a restricted but important range of facts. The second is that, in opposition to positivistic approaches to the study of society, Znaniecki decided to emphasize what he called "the primary and essential meaningfulness of social reality, to accept human values and activities as facts, just as human agents themselves accept them, but to study them objectively and with the application of the same formal principles as the physicist and the biologist apply to material nature." And finally, the third is that overzealous efforts to quantify social data often "sacrifice the substance of valuable knowledge and true discovery for the shadow of mathematical formulae devoid of significant content." At the same time, with respect to the last, Znaniecki recognized the importance of maintaining in his qualitative studies "the highest standard of logical exactness compatible with the nature of social data."[15] All three of these propositions, of course, attracted the citicisms of redoubtable polemicists like Sorokin and Lundberg.

SELECTION OF SCIENTIFIC DATA

Znaniecki begins his treatment by suggesting that knowledge, including sociological knowledge, was first collected for practical purposes—the need to solve a problem. In the many centuries of this existence man has accumulated a great deal of knowledge about social reality. Such knowledge, however, is relatively useless for theoretic purposes until it is organized into some kind of system. Each practical science—for example, bridge building—is served by several theoretic sciences—for example, physics, geology, economics—and each theoretic science—for example, chemistry—furnishes information to more than one practical science—for example, the dyeing industry, agriculture, pharmacology. Each theoretic science, however, possesses knowledge not yet utilized by any practical science and some that may never be so utilized. Utility can never be a criterion for the advancement of any theoretic science. In Znaniecki's own words:

> No theoretic science can, therefore, afford to have the selection of its object-matter prescribed to it by any practical considerations. It may, indeed, and often does undertake to study problems suggested by practical science, but these problems must lie within its field as circumscribed by theoretic criteria.[16]

The initial problem for sociology, therefore, is to find and define the theoretic standards by which to circumscribe the field, to find its own unique domain.

15. *Ibid.*
16. *Ibid.*, p. 7.

The facts of the universe, of course, are inexhaustible, and every science has to develop criteria in terms of which some of these facts will be filtered out and become part of a body of knowledge and others will be ignored. Furthermore, no phenomenon in the universe can be described in its entirety, not a wave on the surface of the water, not the fall of a leaf, not a mispronounced word. Once more we need standards, criteria of selection, some way of determining objectively and consistently what it is about these phenomena that we wish to know:

> Every successful and advanced science has not only its material limited by objective criteria of selection, but also the use which it means to make of this material determined by objective standards of relevancy and importance applied to the characters of its objects and the conditioning antecedents of its processes.[17]

It is these criteria that sociology now needs to find for itself.

First, however, Znaniecki develops the notion of the closed system. In order to find the criteria discussed in the preceding paragraph, it is necessary in all the sciences to make a fundamental assumption:

> It is the assumption that reality is constituted by innumerable and various *closed systems,* that is, systems each of which is composed of a number of elements more intimately inter-related with one another than with any objects which do not belong to the system, and each possessing a specific internal structure which isolates it in certain respects from external influences.[18]

It is always necessary to articulate the limits of such a system, to determine the elements it does and does not contain. It is this determination which in turn, relieves us from dealing with what would otherwise be "a bewildering mass of heterogeneous empirical data." Znaniecki has in mind here an empirical system—the solar system, for example—and not a purely logical system. The concept of the closed system also enables us to solve problems of functional dependence that the elements of the system have to one another and to explain changes in the system due to events external to it.

After a discussion of the distinction between idiographic and nomothetic sciences, a distinction Znaniecki finds relatively unsatisfactory,[19] he turns to the relationship between facts and theories in sociology. In the nine-

17. *Ibid.*, p. 11.

18. *Ibid.*, p. 12. Znaniecki attributes the notion of closed systems originally to a group of French methodologists writing in the *Révue de Metaphysique et de Morale* in the first decade of the century.

19. Because historical knowledge too must aspire to become scientifically valid. In both kinds of sciences we find a constant movement from concrete reality to abstract concepts and

teenth century sociologists were interested primarily in huge and abstract generalizations. Now they have gone to the other extreme and collect "enormous masses of undigested concrete observations." The proper course is clear to Znaniecki: "This course is *to determine exactly the general type (or types, if there be several) of those closed systems which it is the special right and duty of the sociologist to study.*"[20] Only in this way can sociology find the Aristotelian mean between fruitless speculation on the one hand and disjointed fact gathering on the other.

At the end of the chapter Znaniecki deplores Sorokin's failure—in *Contemporary Sociological Theories*—to circumscribe a special field for sociology. It should be remarked, however, that this was not a failure at all but an intentional refusal to do so.

SELECTION OF CULTURAL DATA

Znaniecki begins his discussion of this subject by distinguishing between natural and cultural systems. Here we need to attend to his own words because he introduces (although not for the first time) his famous concept of "the humanistic coefficient": "Natural systems are objectively given to the scientist as if they existed absolutely independently of the experience and activity of men."[21] There is then a discussion of natural systems. After which:

> Very different appear such indubitably cultural systems as those dealt with by students of language and literature, art, religion, science, economics, industrial technique and social organization. Generally speaking, every cultural system is found by the investigator to exist for certain conscious and active historical subjects, i.e. within the sphere of experience and activity of some particular people, individuals and collectivities, living in a certain part of the human world during a certain historical period. Consequently, for the scientist this cultural system is really and objectively as it was (or is) given to those historical subjects themselves when they were (or are) experiencing it and actively dealing with it. In a word, the data of the cultural student are always "somebody's," never "nobody's" data. This essential character of cultural data

---

back again. If history has been separated from the sciences, it is largely due to a misplaced respect for erudition.

> The resulting absorption in concrete data as such, apart from their significance for scientific generalization, encouraged by the old cult for erudition, has been perhaps the greatest check on scientific progress in sciences which draw their material chiefly from the past, just as the prevalence of practical over theoretic interests has hindered the advance of research bearing on the present.

Ibid., p. 26.

20. *Ibid.*, p. 29.
21. *Ibid.*, p. 35.

> we call the *humanistic coefficient*, because such data, as objects of the student's theoretic reflection, already belong to somebody else's active experience and are such as this active experience makes them.[22]

A language would not exist, for example, if people had never spoken it, nor would the Bank of England if people had not indulged in financial activities. It is noteworthy here—because it is a favorite point of Znaniecki—that science too is a cultural system. But most worthy of attention is the humanistic coefficient itself. It is the humanistic coefficient that distinguishes cultural systems from natural systems.

One detects the characters of cultural objects—a poem, a ceremony, a bank—in two ways: by interpreting what people who experienced them say about them and by observing people's outward behavior with respect to them. An additional distinction seems desirable, a distinction between "things," which are natural objects, and "values," which are cultural objects:

> A value differs from a thing in that it possesses both a given *content*, which distinguishes it as an empirical object from other objects, and a *meaning*, by which it suggests other objects—those with which it has been actively associated in the past; whereas a thing has no meaning, but only a content, and stands only for itself.[23]

It will not do, however, to confuse this distinction with that between the subjective and the objective. A value is as objective as a thing. It may also have positive or negative axiological significance. Thus, a poet may decide to use one word and decline to use another.[24]

Because it is human activity that creates cultural systems and human activity that holds their elements together, human activity becomes "the pivot of all research in the domain of culture."[25] It is an expression, however, to which he wants to give a greater precision. Before he does so he indulges in a negative disquisition on the naturalistic approach to the subject, the approach that regards activity as nothing but a biological process. Znaniecki's rejection of naturalism, however, does not mean that he would permit the intrusion of normative judgments in the realm of the cultural sciences, however important such judgments may be in other domains. "When theoretic investigation of activities is combined with their normative standardization, there is always the danger that the former will

22. *Ibid.*, pp. 36–37.

23. *Ibid.*, p. 41.

24. In discussing values in this sense Znaniecki invites attention to the extensive work he did on the subject in his early philosophical writings.

25. *Ibid.*, p. 44.

be subordinated to the latter with results detrimental to scientific validity."[26] The history of philosophy is a good example.

Now, on human activity itself, the practical man has the right slant. The only way really to know an activity is to indulge in it, to perform it. The way to understand what poetic activity is, for example, is to write a poem. "Actual performance is the *primary* source of empirical knowledge about activity."[27] If it be objected that an activity does not exist for an individual except when he is performing it, it may similarly be said that an object does not exist for him except when he is observing it. Znaniecki, however, is not interested in the general metaphysical question involved. Indeed, he dismisses metaphysical speculation and insists only that activities have an objective form and an objective function. By form he means what we are more likely today to call a pattern. Thus, there is a form or pattern in the construction of a cabinet, in the saying of a prayer, in the analysis of a Latin sentence. Teaching and learning would be impossible if these forms did not exist. It is these forms also that make possible the completion of an activity—the manufacture of an automobile, a scientific experiment—by someone who did not begin it. If we want to know the real meaning of any activity, the only possible approach is the humanistic one, the only one that takes us to the agent himself. "And there is no difficulty about it, for we are all agents and each of us can experience the activities of others by repetition, participation or reproduction"[28]—three processes that Znaniecki describes.

In the course of a discussion of activity, tendency, and attitude and the complex relations they have with one another, Znaniecki views an activity from the point of view of the actor as a tendency to construct a system of values. He employs the word *tendency* both because it implies a prospective determination—and intention—and because the determination may or may not be fulfilled. Again there are important differences between natural and cultural tendencies:

> Whereas natural tendencies are only manifested in so far as they are being realized, a cultural tendency can manifest itself empirically not only in the course of its realization as activity, but also at other times as an *attitude;* and it does this when it only defines the situation without solving it.[29]

About a cultural tendency two points may be made: First, it sometimes manifests itself as an activity and at other times merely as an attitude; se-

26. *Ibid.*, pp. 47–48.
27. *Ibid.*, p. 49.
28. *Ibid.*, p. 56.
29. *Ibid.*, pp. 59–60.

cond, a tendency manifesting itself as active sometimes succeeds and sometimes fails. In order to analyze tendencies we need not solve the problem of motivation. A tendency is simply there and can be taken as given. In concluding this matter, a discussion that has some puzzling features, Znaniecki arrives at two principles. The first of these, the principle of spontaneity, is that "a cultural tendency is always active unless hindered by an internal practical obstacle."[30] The second, the principle of achievement, is that "a tendency once active always achieves the construction of the system of values it started to construct and no other, unless deflected by perturbing factors."[31] He refers to these two principles as heuristic assumptions—heuristic in the sense that they are useful in empirical research but insusceptible of proof. Unfortunately, he does not offer illustrations of this empirical utility. The chapter concludes with a treatment of the duration and extension of cultural systems with emphasis upon the differences, in these respects, between natural and cultural systems.

THE DATA OF SOCIOLOGY

In its beginnings, as in Comte and Spencer, sociology was conceived of as a study of societies. Societies, in turn, were essentially natural closed systems consisting of biopsychological individuals. These closed systems were circumscribed by three principles, the first two of which were naturalistic, namely, the occupation of a specified territory and racial homogeneity, both susceptible to external observation.

> But the third principle made a breach in the consistency of the naturalistic standpoint through which an enormous mass of cultural data was introduced into this system. A collectivity of human beings of a certain racial stock (pure or mixed) inhabiting a certain territory constituted a "society" only if they belonged as members to a social group—horde, family, tribe, gens, village, city, state—or at least to a conglomeration of interconnected groups. Now, whatever might be said of "animal societies," human groups are cultural products; membership in a group, and even the mere existence of a social group, however rudimentary its organization, cannot be ascertained without the use of the humanistic coefficient. The gens, the tribe, the state, even the family and the horde have their being only in the experience and activity of their members, who have constructed them and now maintain them.[31]

Looked at naturalistically a society is a collection of individuals sharing certain geographical and racial features, but looked at culturally it is a

30. *Ibid.*, p. 65.
31. *Ibid.*, pp. 68–69, 91.

community sharing a common culture. Unfortunately this dual view of society failed to produce anything like a reliable generalization or law, or even a consistent classification of societies. The reason is that it contained a "striking fallacy":

> It identified two radically different and incommensurable concepts: "society" as a natural system of which the elements are individual animals of the species *Homo Sapiens,* and "society" as a combination of systems of which the elements are cultural values, like language, religion, technique, economic and political organizations, etc.[32] That a "logical discrepancy" of this magnitude did not attract the attention of even the best of the nineteenth-century thinkers is attributable to the monistic currents that characterized the philosophy of science of that time.

Now the naturalistic aspects of societies are more and more being assigned to such natural sciences as geography and physical anthropology. At the same time, sociology, by conceiving its mission to be the cultural study of entire communities, still undertakes a task that is far beyond its powers, indeed, beyond the powers of any one science:

> The conclusion is inevitable that the total cultural life of any human community is much too rich and chaotic, contains too many heterogeneous cultural systems influencing one another in the most various and incalculable ways and is too ceaselessly and unexpectedly changing, to make valid scientific synthesis ever possible—which obviously precludes any comparative science of cultural communities.[33]

Of course, there are relatively stable and limited systems, like cultural complexes for example, about which certain things can be said. But these are not coextensive with civilizations or total societies. They belong to ethnology, and ethnology itself is now historical rather than evolutionary.

> Historical ethnology has thus taken whatever wind there was out of the sails of sociology as a general theory of cultural communities—and it proved to be a weak breeze, merely allowing a careful sailing along the shore of historical facts, not a trade wind capable of driving the vessel of cultural science across the wide ocean of universal determinism.[34]

Znaniecki's argument throughout is that although cultural systems indubitably exert an influence upon one another, these influences cannot be the subject of a separate science. Investigation of these systems is the task

32. *Ibid.*, p. 93.
33. *Ibid.*, p. 97. This is the point of view that Sorokin so heavily criticizes.
34. *Ibid.*, p. 98.

of all of the social sciences, not of sociology alone. Efforts to revive the old synthetic conception of sociology will doubtless continue. But these efforts belong not to sociology but to the philosophy of history—an enterprise that Znaniecki does not intend to demean. "All we object to is having sociology, which aims to be a positive inductive science, exact and objective, so far misunderstand its possibilities and impossibilities as to undertake practically the same task."[35] That sociology might be a special kind of philosophy of history—a positivistic philosophy of history in the Comtean sense—is a view that Znaniecki vigorously rejected.

Durkheim and Tarde, however much they differed on other issues, both regarded sociology as a general theory of cultural data, and for Znaniecki this view of the matter is also wrong. Sociology has to be a special, not a general, social science. Nor, definitely, are the special sciences of culture subdivisions of sociology. They can all be studied, so to speak, without people:

> A language may be and often is studied without any other knowledge of the people who use it than that they do speak it and understand it. A factory can be described exclusively in terms of materials, machines, methods, products, with no mention of the social life of the men who run it except that these men furnish the active forces needed to do so. A physical theory can be fully understood even if nothing is known about the personal life of the scientist who created it, his social relationship with his original opponents, or the organization of the scientific societies or congresses where it was finally approved.[36]

A general theory of culture may conceivably be possible, but it will take centuries of effort, and in any event it would not be sociology.

For Znaniecki sociology is a special kind of discipline. To summarize, negatively, it is not a natural science; it is not social or political philosophy, or indeed any kind of normative discipline; it is not psychology or social psychology; it is not the purely formal discipline that Simmel would have liked; it is not a general theory of cultural data, as Durkheim and Tarde proposed (parts of *The Division of Labor* excepted); and above all it is not the philosophy of history as Barth envisaged it. Perhaps the outstanding significance of *The Method of Sociology* is that in this book Znaniecki gives his readers a sense of sociology as a distinctive discipline, a discipline with its own method and subject matter, and a discipline, needless to say, for which he had the highest aspirations.

35. *Ibid.*, p. 100. Znaniecki assigns much of the blame for this misunderstanding to Paul Barth, whose *Philosophie der Geschichte als Soziologie* appeared in 1914. This mistaken conception of sociology is also the weakest aspect of Sorokin's "otherwise very valuable work," *Contemporary Sociological Theories*. *Ibid.*, p. 95n.

36. *Ibid.*, p. 104.

If sociology is none of the kinds of inquiries just mentioned, it is important to say positively and precisely what it is in Znaniecki's conception. The answer is readily forthcoming. Sociology is a science of social systems. These systems in turn fall into four main subdivisions, which are, respectively, the theory of social actions, the theory of social relations, the theory of social persons, and the theory of social groups. The data of these subdivisions reveal as clearly as anything can that sociology is a special science and has its own special field of investigation; that social systems as such differ from other cultural systems, such as for example, technical, economic, religious, and linguistic systems; and that it is time for sociologists to abandon the superannuated claims of creating a "synthetic" or "fundamental" science of society or of culture. Sociology is a special and not a general social science, and on this point Znaniecki is adamant. Indeed, it is his principal thesis.

THE SOURCES OF SOCIOLOGICAL MATERIAL

Znaniecki begins his treatment of this subject with an interesting observation:

> Sociology, as we have already pointed out, is only beginning to learn how to make proper use of its material, which is being agglomerated at a tremendous rate. While many older sociologists on a slender foundation of fact built imposing speculative constructions, which crumbled down before they were finished, we are heaping up mountains of raw stuff and barely manage to raise on top of them small and unsightly shreds of timid theory. We dignify this procedure by ascribing it to scientific circumspection, whereas in most cases it is nothing but plain incapacity to do any better.[37]

Part of the problem is the unwillingness of sociologists to recognize and to appreciate the difference between two entirely different worlds—the world of nature and the world of culture. It is a mistake—and Znaniecki emphasizes this—to treat a phenomenon of this second world only as it is susceptible to study by the methods of the first world. In other words, attempts are still being made, and conscientious attempts too, to explain cultural phenomena in naturalistic terms. It is time unashamedly to treat sociological material as sociological whether or not we suffer condemnation as social philosophers for doing so.[38]

Znaniecki is now ready to discuss the four main sources of sociological

37. *Ibid.*, p. 154.

38. "I used to be indignant at being thus qualified until, on comparing notes, I found that the same reproaches had been addressed to men like Tönnies, Simmel, Vierkandt, Weber, Tarde, Durkheim, Small, Giddings, Ross, Park, MacIver. Now I am only proud to be in such company." *Ibid.*, p. 156n.

data: the personal experience of the sociologist, both original and vicarious; observation by the sociologist, both direct and indirect; the personal experience of other people; and observation by other people. To these four he adds a fifth, subsidiary, source, namely, generalizations made by other people with or without scientific purposes in mind. The emphasis upon personal experience, however, is clear, whether it is that of the sociologist or that of the subject he is studying. It is this emphasis which served as the methodological rationale for the utilization of personal documents in *The Polish Peasant* and elsewhere. Znaniecki never hesitated in his attacks on statistical methods and never ceased his insistence that only by the use of personal and even intimate sources, such as diaries, letters, and autobiographies, could the sociologist make full use of the humanistic coefficient which distinguishes the social from the physical sciences.

In one respect, however, Znaniecki, possibly in a moment of carelessness, goes too far. Although the expression "participant-observation" had not yet been invented, he nevertheless insists that just as we cannot experience a sentence without speaking it, a game of golf without playing it, and a geometrical theorem without proving it, so also we cannot know what friendship is without being a friend, what a marital relationship is without being married, and so on. He concludes therefore, "The only way actually to experience a social system at first-hand is to be active in its construction, for only thus are we directly aware of the tendencies involved in its structure and the actual significance of the values included in its composition."[39]

With these assertions, however, Znaniecki gave hostages to those who would deride the use of subjective data in sociology. It would follow that one could not understand such phenomena as the commission of a crime, the conducting of an orchestra, and the government of a monarchy without oneself being a criminal, a conductor, or a king. Fortunately, as he concedes in a subsequent paragraph, the range of anyone's own experience is fairly narrow and to have to remain within its boundaries would result in a limited discipline. He is still concerned to claim, however, even if the risks of error are greater, that the personal experiences of sociologists have the same objective validity as the "methodological observations" made by students of the physical universe. Incidentally, the use of the sociologist's own experience has nothing to do with the method known as "introspection" in psychology, and criticisms of the latter entirely miss the mark if applied to the former.[40] In any case, "Personal experience and observation are

39. *Ibid.*, p. 157.

40. In his treatment of the personal experience of the sociologist Znaniecki pays tribute to W. I. Thomas, "whose capacity for vicarious experience is probably unrivaled in modern

the ultimate bases of all knowledge, the final criteria of validity of all general concepts and laws."[41]

SOME METHODOLOGICAL TENDENCIES

In a chapter in which he criticizes certain methodological tendencies in sociology, Znaniecki makes several comments that merit attention. First is his insistence that sociology is an independent empirical science:

> The starting-point of all sociological research must be the firm and clear realization that sociology is an independent empirical science. This means that the only ultimate foundation of sociological theory is *empirical social data.* No sociological theory can be based on conclusions drawn from non-sociological theories, nor can any but social data serve to establish sociological truths.[42]

Thus, it helps not at all in sociology to use scientific truths developed in other sciences, whether psychology, biology, anthropology, or geography. Nor does it help to use other kinds of cultural data, whether economic, technical, religious, or whatever. Both theories and data must be social. Secondly, Znaniecki insists that although we cannot avoid using deduction at times, sociology must be a strictly inductive science. We measure new truths not by their logical agreement with old ones but solely by their agreement with empirical facts.

Induction, however, is of two kinds—enumrative and analytical. Of the two the former is by far the less powerful. It is the method by which the events of practical life led to the formulation of proverbs; for example, "Birds of a feather flock together." These formulations are generalizations based on experience and observation. Historians also use enumerative induction. For a time, when sociology began to emerge as a theoretic discipline in contrast to ethics and politics and as a nomothetic discipline in contrast to history, it also used enumerative induction as the only method available to it. The works of Spencer, Westermarck, and Sumner and Keller are classic examples of enumerative induction in its prestatistical phase. The advance from the enumerative induction of common sense to that of science consists merely in a greater degree of thoroughness and circumspection. An ordinary person will generalize from half a dozen instances; a Westermarck uses threescore.

There is an obvious limitation, however, to this kind of reasoning. How

---

sociology, [and who] has made a wider use than anybody before him of observable data and documents describing original experiences of other people." *Ibid.*, p. 172.

41. *Ibid.*, p. 195.

42. *Ibid.*, pp. 217–218.

many instances do we need to conclude not only that "some" S are P but also that "most" S are P? Here the statistical method enters, a method that enables us to know by counting exactly how many S are P. For vague words such as *some* or *most* we are able to find exact numbers or exact percentages and thus to increase the reliability and precision of our knowledge. In instances where complete enumeration is impossible we can use the law of probability to arrive at a conclusion that is at least a satisfactory approximation.

Notwithstanding immense improvements in enumerative induction, culminating in statistical method, however, its general character remains unchanged:

> This progress has been achieved primarily by improving the formal certainty of inductive judgments; secondarily, by increasing their *formal precision.* The question of their *material significance* for the advancement of knowledge was left out of consideration, and in the course of time this significance has come to be cheerfully sacrificed.[43]

And furthermore, "All the applications of social statistics for a hundred years have done nothing but *formally* prove or disprove already existing common-sense judgments of more or less shrewd politicians, businessmen, novelists, moralists, public-house or drawing-room philosophers."[44] Znaniecki's strictures on statistics are severe. The characters of any system, object, or process in the empirical world are always interdependent.

> The statistical method substitutes for this interdependence of all the characters of an empirical datum a multiplicity of arbitrary mental combinations of characters artificially isolated from their empirical context. By making the study of facts subservient in advance to its final purpose of a mathematical play with symbols, not only does it fail to stimulate progress in the analysis of these facts, but actually obstructs it.[45]

In statistics the prime mistake of medieval scholasticism is repeated, namely, juggling concepts (or, in this case, symbols) instead of investigating reality. Statistical method stands in direct contrast to the modern ideal of knowledge. Even further, "it stems the current of new ideas by making every idea unproductive."[46] "Science is reason challenging experience and forcing it into a rational order."[47] To this majestic enterprise statistics contributes nothing. In fact, and unlike such scientifically useless

43. *Ibid.*, p. 228.
44. *Ibid.*
45. *Ibid.*, p. 231.
46. *Ibid.*, p. 232.
47. *Ibid.*, p. 233.

activities as chess, it actually does harm. It encourages graduate students of sociology to substitute technique for thought.[48]

If enumerative induction and its issue—statistics—are inadequate, there is, fortunately, another kind of induction that Znaniecki calls analytic induction. It was used by Plato, Aristotle, Theophrastus, Galileo, and innumerable others since who have contributed to modern physics, chemistry, and biology, "not by agglomerating large masses of superficial observations, but by inducing laws from a deep analysis of experimentally isolated instances." In sociology Le Play and Durkheim both tried to use it but did so imperfectly and therefore with mixed results. W. I. Thomas was probably the first to use it extensively in sociological research but he did not give it a name. It means not the enumeration of many cases but rather the analytic study of particular cases, individual cases, using different instances of them for every generalization. If we have so far been unable to appreciate the method of analytic induction it is because we are too much devoted to definition on the one hand and to the deductive systematization and presentation of knowledge on the other. What Znaniecki promises to give us, then, is not a general theory of science of the kind that would satisfy a logician but rather an introduction to analytic sociology.

ANALYTIC INDUCTION IN SOCIOLOGY

The difference between enumerative induction and analytic induction might best be given in Znaniecki's own words:

> While in enumerative induction, as we have seen, a certain logical class is defined, and the problem is to find characters common to and distinctive of the particular objects belonging within this class which were not explicitly or implicitly included in the definition, in analytic induction certain particular objects are determined by intensive study, and the problem is to define the logical classes which they represent. No definition of the class precedes in analytic induction the selection of data to be studied as representatives of this class. The analysis of data is all done before any general formulations; and if well done, there is nothing more of importance to be learned about the class which these data represent by any subsequent investigation of more data of the same class.[49]

And again:

> While both forms of induction tend to reach general and abstract truths concerning particular and concrete data, enumerative induction abstracts by

48. Znaniecki wants to make it clear, however, that his strictures are directed only against statistics as a method of inductive generalization and have nothing to do with the legitimate use of statistics as an auxiliary technique in the measurement of measurable data.

49. *Ibid.*, p. 249.

> generalizing, whereas analytic induction generalizes by abstracting. The former looks in many cases for characters that are similar and abstracts them conceptually because of their generality, presuming that they must be essential to each particular case; the latter abstracts from the given concrete case characters that are essential to it and generalizes them, presuming that in so far as essential, they must be similar in many cases.[50]

It is for this reason that the method of analytic induction has sometimes been called the "type" method, or the method of typical cases.

These observations lead Znaniecki to say that abstraction and generalization are processes that lead to classification, and classification, in turn, is of supreme importance to science because it presents systematic knowledge of some area of reality. We should avoid the view that classifications serve merely an instrumental purpose or are a provisional survey of a field to be explored. On the contrary, every classification is already a theory about that aspect of reality with which it is concerned. It is the end result of a proper process of analytic induction which consists of the following steps:

> First, discover which characters in a given datum of a certain class are more, and which are less essential; secondly, abstract these characters, and assume hypothetically that the more essential are more general than the less essential, and must be found in a greater variety of classes; thirdly, test this hypothesis by investigating classes in which the former and those in which the latter characters are found; fourthly, establish a classification, i.e., organize all these classes into a scientific system based on the functions the respective characters play in determining them.[51]

Analytic induction needs principles of scientific abstraction other than comparison. Fortunately, such principles exist. They are the principle of structural dependence, which leads to static laws and to a genetic classification of social systems, and the principle of causality, which leads to dynamic laws and to a functional classification of social changes.[52] After an elaborate discussion of the principle of the structural dependence of the elements in a system, and of dominant and dependent elements, Znaniecki offers the following example of a static law: "If a social group contains an institution of ruling authority, it must contain a collective will."[53] Unfor-

50. *Ibid.*, pp. 250–251.

51. *Ibid.*, pp. 259–260. Here, however, one must exercise caution. It may not be the case that the more general characters are also the essential ones.

52. *Ibid.*, pp. 261–262 (italics omitted). It should be noted that throughout Znaniecki exhibits a distaste for the comparative method. See, for example, page 279.

53. *Ibid.*, p. 273.

tunately, this "law," like those found in the works of Giddings, does not shed much light. It may in fact be more of a tautology than a proposition asserting a relationship between two phenomena. By a collective will Znaniecki means a recognition on the part of the members of a group that- they can act as a whole and not merely as a sum of individuals.

Znaniecki offers no example of a dynamic law established by causal analysis. In his treatment of causation he refers to John Stuart Mill's justification for it in terms of the uniformity of nature. We can never know, in the case of the physical universe, whether this uniformity belongs to a real and objective world or whether it is an order produced by man himself in the construction of rational knowledge. In the case of the cultural universe no such doubt exists because in this case it is clear that the order has been produced by man. "Whatever the source of the apparent order which rational knowledge finds in nature, the order of culture proceeds from the same source as the order of rational knowledge, for rational knowledge itself is a part of culture."[54] Although, as mentioned, we have no example of a dynamic law, Znaniecki says that we have innumerable causal generalizations produced by common sense throughout the centuries and that searching for exceptions to them would be a fruitful task for sociologists to undertake.

Znaniecki concludes his book with a discussion of the legitimate uses of quantification. The humanistic coefficient is again the key to the answer. Obviously we use quantitatively variable terms all the time—more or less friendly, more or less valuable, more or less effective, higher and lower, larger or smaller, stronger or weaker, and so on. We can ask judges to grade these comparisons, as in the Bogardus scales of social distance, and such judges will usually agree more than they disagree. This procedure, however, if it can be called measurement at all, is ordinal measurement and not cardinal measurement; that is, it can answer the question where but not the question how much.[55] There is a further difficulty. Hostility, for example, is not simply a low degree of friendliness; it is a phenomenon of a different quality altogether. A small group, such as a family, is not merely small in relation to a large group, such as a political party, but a different kind of a group. There are large groups that are relatively small (the principality of Monaco) and small groups that are relatively large (a family with twelve children). "In short, quantitative variations as directly experienced in the social field are still essentially variations in degrees of irreducible qualities; and a degree which is quantitatively higher or lower

54. *Ibid.*, p. 304.

55. For an elaboration of this distinction, see Robert Bierstedt, *Power and Progress: Essays on Sociological Theory* (New York: McGraw-Hill, 1974), pp. 57–72.

than another is also qualitatively different.[56] Furthermore, we have no right to assume, for example, that the amount of space devoted to a certain event in a newspaper is an accurate measure of the importance of the event. It is the editor of the paper who establishes the correlation, not necessarily the importance of the event itself. Unfortunately, Znaniecki suggests no other possible index that would resolve this problem. He sees some possibilities for quantification, however, in the measurement of social forces, which he classifies as constructive, obstructive, and reconstructive.

Znaniecki supplies no general summary of his book. One nevertheless is found in the Preface, where he writes:

> The present book embodies the result of long and strenuous efforts to harmonize ideals with reality, to reconcile the standards of highest scientific perfection, derived partly from philosophy, partly from the methodologies of physical and biological sciences, with the need for preserving intact those characteristics which concrete social facts possess in our experience. It has been worked out in a continual conflict between the interests of exact analysis and strictly rational systematization on the one hand, and the interests of unprejudiced observation and empirical research with their inexhaustible variety of materials, on the other.[57]

It is this conflict above all that prompted Znaniecki to carve out a special area for sociological inquiry and to regard sociology as a special cultural science.

The Method of Sociology does not appear to have been extensively reviewed. In one journal Znaniecki is praised only for the annotated bibliographies he appends to his chapters. In another the reviewer is noncommittal. For some unknown reason there is no review in the *American Journal of Sociology*. The reviewer for the *American Sociological Review* was none other than Pitirim A. Sorokin. Sorokin, usually penurious with praise, calls the book a valuable contribution to sociology and one that merits careful study. He rather gently criticizes it, however, on two grounds. The first is that Znaniecki did not make sufficiently clear his concept of system and especially the concept of a closed system. The second is that although he was moving in the right direction, he did not move very far along the road. His methodological recommendations are still contaminated by the ideal of the physical sciences.[58] Many years later Lewis A. Coser confers his benediction on the book and says that it very much deserves contemporay reading.[59]

56. *Method of Sociology*, p. 310.
57. *Ibid.*, pp. vii–viii.
58. *American Sociological Review* 1 (October 1936): 817–819.
59. *Masters of Sociological Thought*, p. 526.

Social Actions[60]

Social Actions (1936), although it is over 700 pages long, requires less attention than its size and its chronological position in Znaniecki's career would seem to warrant. He writes in his preface that he worked on the book for fifteen years, rewriting parts of it no fewer than six times; indeed, internal evidence also suggests that much of it was written prior to *The Method of Sociology*, whose publication date is two years earlier. In any event, it is less well organized than the earlier books, less incisive in its view of sociology, and it offers the reader less sense of system. Its importance lies in its insights into the internal meaning of various types of actions and the manner in which investigation and analysis of such meanings can contribute to sociological theory.

The pivotal concept, of course, is actions. Znaniecki insisted that a systematic treatment of various types of social actions—indeed as many types as possible—was a necessary prerequisite for all sociological studies:

> Without knowing what the various ways are in which men tend to deal actively with other men and how those ways have evolved, we cannot understand their efforts to regulate normatively their mutual activities by customs, mores, and laws, or the social positions which they individually occupy and the functions they perform in their communities, or the organized groups which they create, maintain, and destroy.[61]

Znaniecki's primary task, therefore, as he conceived it, was the description, analysis, and classification of social actions. The major portion of the book, therefore, is devoted to analyses of various kinds of actions, including invitation, suggestion, incitement, persuasion, cooperative guidance, educational guidance, participative submission, purposive submission, imitation, primary opposition (*i.e.*, self-defense), coercion, repression (especially of criminal behavior), revolt, intercollective opposition, aggression, altruism, hostility, and compromise.

The emphasis continues to rest upon *social* actions. There is in addition a large category of nonsocial actions—for example, technical actions, linguistic actions, religious actions, economic actions, and so on—which, although often intimately related to social actions, nevertheless lie outside the purview of the sociologist. One might be tempted to say that all actions

60. (New York: Farrar & Rinehart, 1936). There is a new edition published by Russell & Russell, New York, 1967. All of the material in this section is taken, almost verbatim, from the author's Introduction to *Florian Znaniecki on Humanistic Sociology* by express permission of the University of Chicago Press. Copyright © 1969 by the University of Chicago.

61. *Social Actions*, p. ix.

indulged in by human beings are social because, except for those rare cases that are quite anomic, they all conform to norms of one kind or another, and that writing a book, painting a picture, and changing a tire are therefore social actions. One could say indeed that everything we do or even refrain from doing—above the level of sheer reflexive behavior—is social action. For Znaniecki, however, this view is unacceptable if sociology wants to have a domain of its own and thus take its place among the other sciences, each of which can justify on ontological grounds a separate and necessary field of inquiry. In his view social actions are those actions that deal with human beings, with human beings, furthermore, who are themselves experienced as conscious objects by the authors of the actions. The object of a social action is another individual (or a collectivity) who has a capacity to be influenced by the action. Otherwise the action, even though surrounded and constrained by norms, is not a social action. Social actions are thus actions directed solely to persons (or collectivities) and would seem, therefore, to be always interactions, although Znaniecki does not use this word until *Cultural Sciences*, a book that appeared some sixteen years later.

The autonomy of sociology in relation to psychology was a point of considerable importance to Znaniecki, and he always resisted any suggestion that his treatment of actions was in fact social psychology rather than sociology. His view of the matter is well expressed in the first chapter of *Social Actions*, which indicates clearly that he opposed any effort to deduce propositions about actions from psychology, whether the psychology is of the Freudian, behavioristic, or any other variety. He insists again that social actions have to be investigated and studied independently as independent empirical data without any relationship to psychological theory. One finds here, as in other places in Znaniecki's work, agreement with and no doubt also the influence of Durkheim. He would have rejected out of hand any reductionist tendencies in sociological theory.[62]

In the years 1928 and 1930 Znaniecki published in Polish the first and second volumes, respectively, of a book on the sociology of education. Much of it is summarized, although only briefly, in the chapter in *Social Actions* entitled "Educational Guidance" and in the essay that accompanies the references to this chapter. Sociology and education, although combined in the sociology of education, are in fact two different disciplines which should not be confused. Educators as such write on the history of education, on the learning process, on the school system, on the ends of educa-

62. In 1925, however, Znaniecki published *The Laws of Social Psychology* (Chicago: University of Chicago Press), in which he regarded social actions as the "object-matter" of social psychology.

tion, and so on. None of this is sociology. The sociology of education has a different task to perform, and that is to make an objective, theoretical study of the social facts involved in the educational process, the social action that goes on between the educator and what Znaniecki calls the "educand," the teacher on the one hand and the learner on the other. A general sociology will of course concern itself with more than actions—it includes also social relations, social persons, and social groups—and so also a sociology of education will some day attend to all four categories of theory. For the present, however, it is sufficient to begin with the first of these—the social actions of educators.

Educational guidance, as opposed to cooperative guidance, is concerned with the actions of some persons in teaching other persons what the latter do not yet know or know how to perform. In the first instance the mother teaches the child the various things he needs to know, and of course this is a process that occurs in all societies. The young are also taught in a primary way to cooperate with those who teach them originally—their parents—and in a secondary way with other adults. As the demands of adult society increase in scope and difficulty, however, the parents are no longer able, especially since they have a life of their own, to give all of the guidance required; consequently, an increasing part of the responsibility is assigned to people known as teachers or educators. The prototype of the educator is the old man of the tribe, full of the lore and the mysteries and eager to pass them on to the young. Hunters, warriors, priests, physicians, and rhetoricians often performed this function too, but in modern societies the role of educator is differentiated and requires special training for those who wish to play it. The chapter continues with discussions of patterns of educational guidance, education as a process in which the educand's social personality is formed, the guidance of the educand's "reflected self" (Znaniecki acknowledges his indebtedness to Cooley), the system of apprenticeship, the teaching of formal skills, the teaching of ideas, thinkers as educators, professional education, education as a means to a career, and the significance of authority and prestige in educational guidance.

Volume 1 of the larger work is concerned primarily with the social function of education; Volume 2, with the educational process as such. The latter begins, incidentally, with the humanistic coefficient, which played so prominent a part in everything that Znaniecki wrote. In both volumes he insists that education is a social process, once again with emphasis upon the adjective. In a long passage he also has occasion to discuss the sick role and, in conformity with contemporary medical sociology, to regard the sick individual as one of the most significant of all personality types, one that changes in different societies and in different periods of history. He also includes a chapter on the sociology of sport, a subject that, despite its importance in every modern society, has received little scientific attention. In this book too, Znaniecki used the expression "reference group" in almost the same sense in which Merton was later to give it conceptual significance.

One final issue invites a modicum of attention before we leave *Social Actions,* and that, once more, is Znaniecki's emphasis upon the dynamic quality of social relations. Znaniecki always regarded Comte's distinction between social statics and social dynamics as pernicious and he expressed his opposition to it with an earnest enthusiasm. The social world is a world becoming and not a world in being, and for this reason studies of social structure as such can lead only to distortion of social reality. Studies of this kind, in fact, are erroneous in basic premise because there is no such thing as a static action. Taking a cue from Heraclitus, Znaniecki insisted that all is action in society and that it is thus inconsistent and unwarranted to inquire into a social structure. One can no more talk about social structure than one can change a tire while the automobile is in motion. The opposing view, urged upon him without Eleatic malice by some of his associates, that society nevertheless exhibits patterns, constants, and regularities and that these too might be legitimate subjects for inquiry left him wholly unimpressed. In this connection too it is interesting to note that he seldom used such concepts as "community" or "society," usually maintaining that he did not know what they meant. As "static" concepts they violated his sense of the flux and changefulness of the human scene. He was a follower of Bergson rather than of Descartes.

The Social Role of the Man of Knowledge

As mentioned earlier, this book consists of four lectures that Znaniecki gave at Columbia University during the summer of 1939.[63] At the very beginning he is anxious to point out that sociology had shown imperialistic tendencies in its aspiration to be a general science of culture and that it would be far better if it were to cultivate its own special domain. "The sociology of knowledge" as an expression parallel with such others as "the sociology of religion" or "the sociology of art" usually means an attempt, beginning with Comte and including such writers as Durkheim, Scheler, and Mannheim, to trace the social conditions of knowledge. This usage, however, is one that Znaniecki deprecates. It suggests that knowledge itself is an appropriate subject for sociological investigation. The sociologist is in no position to test the validity of any system of knowledge except

63. (New York: Columbia University Press, 1940).

sociology, and to suggest the contrary is to put sociology in this curious positon of determining its own character as a science. For Znaniecki, therefore, the sociology of knowledge means something different; it means a study of those who are engaged in the acquisition, construction, development, transmission, and reproduction of knowledge. On this view of the matter the sociology of knowledge is not a discipline vainly trying to become another kind of epistemology but rather a discipline dedicated to its own *social* concerns.

The concept of role has been developed to facilitate this kind of study. A role may refer to a kind of activity that an individual performs—thus, priest, soldier, banker—or to an individual as a member of certain groups—thus, American, Methodist, grandfather, child. Individuals perform many roles throughout their lives, both successively and simultaneously, and the snythesis of these roles constitutes their social personalities. A role implies both a social person and a social circle, of larger or smaller size, and a common bond or complex of values. Thus, lawyers have clients; doctors, patients; kings, subjects; and so on. A person who performs a role for his circle is granted a certain social status, that is, rights and privileges that the circle enforces. In turn he is required to fulfill a social function. These four—social person, social circle, social status, and social function—Znaniecki regards as essential components found in all social roles.

The genesis of some role patterns is lost in an inaccessible past. Others can be studied in the course of their becoming and duration. Still others are explicitly formulated by legislation. Some are perpetuated by the mores, as for example, the roles of aristocrats, farmers, housewives, and servants.[64] The diffusion of these patterns from community to community and from society to society takes place in familiar ways, like the diffusion of other cultural items. This is the conceptual framework that Znaniecki will use to investigate the social role of the man of knowledge.

TECHNOLOGISTS AND SAGES

Znaniecki begins his second lecture with a question: "How can it be that scientists, men who indulge in cultivating knowledge instead of being efficiently active like everybody else, are not only tolerated by men of action but granted a social status and regarded as performing a desirable social function by the communities in which they live?"[65] Knowledge is needed in

64. Znaniecki doubtless should have used the word *folkways* here instead of *mores*.

65. *Social Role*, p. 23. Znaniecki frequently, and intentionally, uses the word *scientist* to mean everyone who is engaged in the process of contributing to knowledge.

every society, even comparatively simple societies. This knowledge is of two kinds: first, the specialized knowledge required for specific occupations, and second, the general knowledge that every adult individual needs as a member of the community. Znaniecki calls the first "technical knowledge." It is the kind of knowledge possessed by a hunter, a farmer, or a housewife as she goes about her cooking, sewing, spinning, weaving, pottery making, and so on.

The test of technical knowledge is a pragmatic one, whether or not it succeeds in accomplishing its purpose. When something goes wrong, however, advisers are needed, people who presumably know how to correct the situation. These advisers, whether of the priesthood or the laity, study techniques rather than use them, and thus technological knowledge arises. Two roles are then involved—the role of the technological leader, who defines the situation and makes plans, and the technological expert, who specializes in diagnosis. The technological leader, like an officer in an army, for example, coordinates the collective actions of others. He has to be a man of knowledge, of course, but his role as leader overshadows his role as scientist. Nevertheless, his success or failure is attributed to knowledge. This knowledge must be certain, it must be inductive, and it must be of the kind that makes prediction possible. It is the kind of knowledge that has produced human achievements in architecture, military and civil engineering, mining, and navigation.

If a task becomes too vast or too complex for the technological leader, however, he has to resort to the services of a technological expert, someone who has more knowledge than the technological leader but who will play no part in its practical application and make no decisions as to what is to be done. Thus, technological leaders such as kings, war lords, high priests, administrators, judges, legislators, and economic entrepreneurs have been using technological experts for centuries. It is not the task of the expert to initiate new knowledge, but he may often be expected to perfect that which already exists. He may be asked to invent alternative patterns of technical action in order to make it more effective. In any event, the problems are always set by the technological leader.[66]

The second kind of knowledge, as opposed to technical knowledge, is that which every member of a society is supposed to possess, although in unequal degree. It is "common sense knowledge." It is knowledge of language, for example, of religion, and of fundamental economic processes. It is possessed by everyone in society except idiots, children, and strangers. It is the support of the social order, although Znaniecki only

66. Znaniecki has a section here on the independent inventor, a role, he says, that was not recognized (except by inventors themselves) until the end of the nineteenth century.

hints at this function. It is the kind of knowledge about which we say "the exception proves the rule." Common sense knowledge, of course, is not a constant, and Znaniecki examines the ways in which it changes over the course of time. It changes largely by way of conflict between two groups of parties he calls, respectively, novationists and conservatives. Both parties turn to men of wisdom to rationalize and justify their positions, and thus the role of the sage arises. The sage must be a man of knowledge but he is interested in right and wrong rather than in truth or error. To him what is "right" must of course be "true" and what is "wrong" must of course be "false." Some sages, however, try to transcend the conflict of opposing parties and seek supreme standards of value—for example, Lao-tse, Socrates, and Marcus Aurelius. The knowledge of the sage is subjected to no practical test, as is the knowledge of the technologist, but depends almost entirely upon the number of people who accept it or reject it. (In this respect his knowledge is also different from the knowledge of the scientist, which has to confront theoretic and logical tests.) Despite the growth of scientific knowledge, Znaniecki expresses the opinion that the demand for sages in society is increasing. All kinds of people appear to satisfy this need—preachers, editorial writers, columnists in newspapers and magazines, radio commentators, and so on. Even scientists renowned for their contributions sometimes fail to resist the temptation to tell the world what is good for it. (Znaniecki invokes the name of Bertrand Russell in this respect) and sometimes men demand that the search for truth itself be subordinated to social ideals (for example, Robert S. Lynd in his *Knowledge for What?)*[67]

SCHOOLS AND SCHOLARS

Znaniecki has now answered, in part, his original question, namely, why society tolerates the man of knowledge. The answer is that knowledge is found to be useful by men of action. Unless the technologist or the sage became also a leader or ruler of men, however, his prestige among his contemporaries was never very high. "The knowledge that is needed as a condition of success in practical activity is always less highly esteemed socially than the success to which it is subservient."[68] Still, in all civilized societies

67. *Ibid.*, pp. 82–83:

> It seems thus, at first glance, as if the trend toward theoretic objectivity in the domain of cultural knowledge, until recently considered one of the most marked achievements of the nineteenth century, were condemned to disappear or to weaken; sages, individually or in schools, would then rule this domain as completely as they did formerly—a retrogression that would defeat entirely the very object of those who claim that the supreme function of scientific knowledge is its service to humanity.

68. *Ibid.*, p. 91.

there is respect for knowledge itself, in independence of any utility it might have. Schools that impart apparently useless knowledge have a higher prestige than vocational schools. Bearers of unpractical knowledge, such as Chinese mandarins, students of the Talmud, and members of the French Academy of Sciences, also have high prestige, and in Poland the official rank of a university professor is the same as that of a governor of a province. In all societies that have grown beyond the tribal stage, groups of men, usually priests, appear to communicate the sacred lore from the old to the young, and thus we have the origin of sacred schools. Sacred knowledge is indeed powerful because its very possession implies participation in the forces that rule the world. No practical tests are applied to it; to do so would be blasphemous because it has a divine origin. Nor does it have to satisfy a test of popular acceptance because if it is sacred it is also secret and given to individuals only gradually through a process of initiation. Thus the distinction arose between esoteric and exoteric knowledge—the former retained by the school and the latter shared with the laity. The true meaning of sacred books is a mystery to be solved only by the elect.

Znaniecki devotes a considerable amount of space to the role of religious scholars, as learners, as teachers, as commentators, and as interpreters of sacred texts. As sociologists we have no right to evaluate their work, but as philosophers we have to appreciate its importance in the history of culture. They may have done much to hinder the growth of what we respect as knowledge today, but on the other hand they did create a kind of knowledge that was not subservient to practical ends, to the satisfaction of material needs, or to the accomplishment of social goals. Gradually in the course of Western history the once-sacred knowledge became secularized; the universities, once dominated by religious scholars, were liberated from religious control, and the only remnant left of sacred scholarship was to be found in faculties of theology. Znaniecki does not imply, incidentally, that all knowledge was once sacred knowledge. He remarks that there were lay schools of medicine, of mathematics and astronomy, of philology, and of law even in antiquity, but these schools receive little of his attention.

When the scholars became secularized they began to exhibit different types. The first type is the discoverer of truth and here Znaniecki mentions a number of prominent examples in the history of Western science and philosophy. With them evolved a new standard of truth, the standard of rational evidence.

> Rationally evident knowledge, according to scholarly epistemology, is absolutely objective, not only superindividual but supersocial. Every thinking being who has become aware of a rationally evident truth is compelled by inner necessity to recognize it as absolutely valid, even if his traditional beliefs condemn it, his social prejudices make him wish it were false, his practical interests

> cause it to seem irrelevant, and his senses suggest to him conflicting representations.[69]

To the role of the discoverer of truth is added, second, the role of the systematizer, although these two roles may sometimes be combined in the same person. Systematization Znaniecki regards as an essential prerequisite for the scholar's teaching role. Those who write textbooks for use in university courses are systematizers. The third type is the role of the contributor. He is the one who finds mistakes and imperfections, observes more precisely the same or similar facts, compares different kinds of data, criticizes and improves methods of drawing conclusions, and provides more adequate interpretations of the facts. The contributor must do some of these things both as a test of scholarly ability and as a qualification for a teaching position. Thus, those who aspire to higher degrees must pass examinations indicating their control of some domain of knowledge and must in addition make some contribution to that domain.

In the world of knowledge there are, of course, rival doctrines, competing "schools," and conflicting theories. This situation gives rise to still another role, which Znaniecki labels "the fighter for truth." Although his function does not involve the construction of knowledge his role has been and continues to be an important one. Indeed, it is a role that discoverers, systematizers, and contributors often play in defending their own theories and attacking the theories of others. This role might more elegantly have been labeled the role of the polemicist or the role of the critic but, whatever the label, it has a certain amount of fascination for Znaniecki. Those who do not wish to join any particular "school" have created still another role—the role of the eclectic. The eclectic tries to find some truth in the doctrines of the competing schools and wishes to serve as an impartial judge or arbitrator. Closely related to the role of the eclectic is the role of the historian of knowledge, but this role receives only a brief mention.

More important is the role of the disseminator of knowledge. This role has two distinct types—the role of the popularizer and the role of the educator. The former, of course, disseminates knowledge to the general public; the latter, to students. In concluding his discussion of these roles Znaniecki pays eloquent tribute to the accomplishments of secular scholars.

THE EXPLORER AS CREATOR OF NEW KNOWLEDGE

When the man of knowledge, whether technologist, sage, or scholar, does more than his social circle expects him to do, then we have set the

69. *Ibid.*, p. 120.

stage for new and unanticipated developments. Some men of knowledge specialize in doing the unexpected, and these Znaniecki calls explorers. At first an isolated role, it came to be recognized and eventually found support in research institutions specifically organized for this purpose. The psychological processes that enable some thinkers to become explorers and to create new knowledge are as yet entirely unknown.

The first stage in scientific exploration is the search for facts, and thus we have the role of fact finder or, since this expression has a somewhat pejorative connotation, the role of discoverer of facts. Some facts, of course, are unwelcome, namely, those that threaten to refute a system of knowledge to which the discoverer is committed. The discovery of facts, however, can be a joyous and even thrilling experience. Sometimes the role has the character of a rebellion, a desire to discard the yoke of a traditional theory.

> The wide interest in new or forgotten astronomical, physical, chemical, and biological facts which during the fifteenth, sixteenth, and seventeenth centuries spread over Europe was largely a manifestation of intellectual revolt against all scholastic knowledge, irrespective of the differences between schools. Learned schools were aware of this and opposed the current of factual exploration as long as they could.[70]

The discoverers of facts, however, are not usually system builders, and so additional roles are needed in order for a science to develop.

We come therefore to the discoverer of problems, who explores empirical reality not with the intent of finding new facts but to discover new theoretic problems and who will then attempt to solve them with new theories. He is opposed to the dogmatism that social circles frequently impose upon technologists, sages, and members of sacred schools. The liberation of scientific thought from scholarly dogmatism is not easy to explain. Znaniecki attributes it to an historical trend in favor of intellectual freedom and to an increasing appreciation of creative individualism. The discoverer of problems knows that all science is inductive[71] and he can therefore also be called an inductive theorist. The function of inductive theorists, finally, "is to participate in the development of objective scientific thought by creating new systems of relative truths, founded upon less valid systems of their predecessors and serving as foundation for more valid systems of their successors."[72] By accepting this principle the inductive theorist can be aware of

70. *Ibid.*, p. 175.

71. "All science is inductive; deduction can serve only as an auxiliary method in raising problems for inductive research, never as the ruling method by which inductive solutions of those problems have to be validated." *Ibid.*, p. 185.

72. *Ibid.*, p. 190.

the dangers of dogmatism, of too firm a commitment to his own theories. There is, Znaniecki concludes, no such thing as absolute truth, either in the physical or the cultural sciences.

In brief summary, what Znaniecki has done in this small book is to give us a sociology of knowledge that is concerned not with the sociocultural conditions of knowledge, a sociological epistemology of the kind we find in Marx, Durkheim, and Mannheim, but rather with the roles that those who participate play in the accumulation, development, discovery, and dissemination of knowledge. His four principal roles, played always of course in conjunction with social circles, are the roles of technologists, sages, scholars, and explorers. Although all of these roles are important, only the explorers produce new knowledge. The new knowledge they produce, however, is always superseded because in the realm of knowledge there are no absolute or final truths.

In a long and favorable review of the book, Robert K. Merton suggests that it would have been strengthened if Znaniecki had used more documentation, provided more evidence, and applied more proficiently has own concepts of social circle, self, status, and function. But he concludes that the book is "a promise of things to come and a promise which is in part its own fulfillment."[73]

Cultural Sciences[74]

We have noted that as a young philosopher, Znaniecki was interested in the problem of values. He endeavored to find for them a place not in the realm of natural objects and not in the realm of subjective processes, but rather in a realm of their own, no part of the physical world and yet accessible to objective inquiry. Values, as the common data of human experience and as the necessary foundation of any theory of culture, are unique. They have an ontological status independent of the world of nature. This view Znaniecki continued to hold, but in *Cultural Sciences* his interest in culture is rather more sociological than ontological. Culture continues to be juxtaposed to nature, and it is the former, not the latter, that offers the larger opportunity for the unification of knowledge. Knowledge,

73. *American Sociological Review* 6 (February 1941): 111–115.

74. The full title is *Cultural Sciences: Their Origin and Development* (Urbana, Ill.: University of Illinois Press, 1952). The material in this section is taken from the writer's Introduction to a new edition of the book. (New Brunswick, N.J.: Transaction Books, 1980.) Used by permission of Transaction, Inc., from *Cultural Sciences*. Copyright © 1980 by Transaction, Inc.

including knowledge of the physical universe, is a cultural product. What Znaniecki has done is to reverse what some would consider to be the "natural" order of things. Culture is not a natural phenomenon, to be studied by methods appropriate to the natural sciences. Instead, our knowledge of nature—in astronomy, physics, chemistry, and biology—is a cultural product and is to be gained by methods appropriate to the cultural sciences. The word *science*, however, remains. Znaniecki regarded himself as a scientific investigator in the domain of culture, no less scientific than those who prowl with inquisitive minds in the domain of nature.

In the beginning of *Cultural Sciences* Znaniecki is fascinated by the problem of knowledge—not the problem of knowledge in the epistemological sense (how do we know?), but the problem posed by the existence of various kinds of knowledge. These various kinds he labels the pragmatic (how to do), the moral (including the aesthetic), the religious, the philosophic, and the scientific. The last of these is divided again into mathematics, natural sciences, the humanities, and the social sciences. He is puzzled by the relationships among these varieties of knowledge, the characteristics they have in common, and the respects in which they differ. Indeed, at the beginning he is interested not in the history of sociology, which he intended originally to write, not in the history of science (including social science), which he also aspired to do, but in the history of knowledge itself. How does it happen that certain kinds of questions come to be addressed to the universe, and how does it happen that answers to them are formulated? Why are some kinds of knowledge susceptible to tests of truth whereas others are not? Why are some controversial and others not? And what is the difference between what we call knowledge—even when controversial—and what we call, on the other hand, belief, prejudice, and illusion? What all kinds of knowledge have in common, Znaniecki decides, is their subject, which is order, in whatever universe is their domain, and when controversies persist they are attributable to different conceptions of order. In the last four centuries scientific knowledge has come to dominate the others. It has been able to do so because of its efficacy in resolving controversies, its avoidance of dogmatism, and its possession of a common method that makes cooperative endeavor possible. To this kind of inquiry the investigation of culture belongs.

Under the general concept of culture Znaniecki includes religion, language, literature, art, customs, mores, laws, social organization, technical production, economic exchange, philosophy, and science. Once again he insists that science itself is not a part of the natural order that scientists investigate. It belongs instead to the realm of culture.

Znaniecki's emphasis on the concept of order as fundamental to knowledge induces him to examine the subject in detail, and this is the task that occupies him in the early chapters of his book. It leads him into erudite paths of magic, religion, politics, technology, and metaphysics. Original constructions of order were primarily the result of deductive reasoning from universal premises a priori and this procedure, now largely overcome by the natural sciences, has retarded the development of the cultural sciences. One of the problems that early systematic thinkers had to face was the relationship between the natural order and what is now called the cultural order. In order to solve it they fashioned various metaphysical theories, including materialism, a philosophy as old as Democritus. Unfortunately, materialism, which seemed to work so well as a philosophy of the natural universe, foundered on certain intractable facts in the cultural universe—facts that are inexplicable in materialistic terms. One of these facts—one of the most important—is the creative experience of conscious human actors or agents. A materialistic metaphysics can explain neither individual nor social action because both escape the sequences of physical laws. Two phenomena in particular materialism has no way to explain—consciousness and creativity. Znaniecki's treatment of this subject is an elaborate refutation of materialism. But idealism, whose history he also traces, fares little better at his hands. Interested in ideas and ideals rather than in facts, idealism too has impeded the progress of the cultural sciences.

The answer to these problems is scientific thinking, which differs from both practical thinking and metaphysical thinking. It is characterized by methods that are peculiar to it, methods that combine empirical research and logical systematization. A science of culture can in fact render such metaphysical theories as materialism and idealism both redundant. These preliminaries concluded, Znaniecki's quest takes him into a discussion of theories of man, where he has to wrestle with such controversial issues as biological versus psychological determinants of culture, individuality versus collectivity, and determinism versus creativeness in the history of man and culture. Indeed, few problems of this kind escape his attention.

In Znaniecki's view not all the data of human experience, to the nature of which he devotes a discussion, are sensory. To think so would be to ignore such phenomena as memory, anticipation, and imagination. It would also ignore the fact that, in building our sciences, we are able to utilize not only our own conscious experience but also the conscious experience of others. To this latter process he applies his famous concept—the concept of "the humanistic coefficient." The order that the cultural scientist seeks is discernible in the actions of conscious human agents, and every datum has to be explored not only as it appears to the investigator, but also to the human individuals who experience it. It is this—the humanistic coefficient—that distinguishes the cultural sciences from the natural sciences. The natural scientist seeks an order of things that is independent of conscious human agents. He has no need of the humanistic coefficient. The cultural scientist, on the contrary, can apply the coefficient both to what conscious human agents think of natural objects—stars, mountains, plants, animals—and to such phenomena as myths, characters in novels, ethical ideals, and so on. The student of language, for example, wants to know what a word means to others; a student of religion what a ritual means to others; a student of philosophy what a concept means to others. This is not to say that cultural data are reducible to subjective psychological phenomena. Durkheim and his school have shown the impossibility of such a reduction.

One of the most impressive transitions in the history of thought, according to Znaniecki, occurred when cultural scientists—especially sociologists—turned their attention from cultural products as such to the human actions that resulted in their production. Indeed, for Znaniecki action is a central, ubiquitous, and all-but-universal category. Although he treated also such phenomena as social circles, social relations, and social roles, it is social actions that practically articulate the scope of sociology. The shift from entities to actions has been a significant factor in the development of all the cultural sciences. Thus, economics began to prosper when economists turned their attention from such phenomena as land, labor, capital, and money and to such actions as production, transportation, consumption, and exchange; linguistics, when students of language turned from such static entities as words to such actions as speaking and writing; religion, when students of that subject abandoned descriptions of mythical beings and turned to religious actions, both individual and collective. A similar transition is, or should be, in process in all of the cultural sciences.

Znaniecki's emphasis upon actions requires, and receives, an intensive examination of the subject. He prefers *action*, incidentally, to *act* because the latter is also used, with special connotations, in the theater and in law. Znaniecki's actions must be conscious; the agent must be aware of what he is doing and of what changes his actions are producing. Actions are always of limited duration, although their beginning is not always easy to determine. Some, such as drinking a glass of wine are relatively brief and elementary; others, such as building a house or weaving a rug, are more complex and may be interrupted without sacrificing their identity. Values are always involved in actions and it may be said, as Znaniecki does in italics, that "every human action is a limited, dynamic system of interdependent changing values." Complex actions are both organized systems of elementary actions and systems of values.

Znaniecki has some difficulty in deciding whether actions are teleological or determined; that is, to be explained by the ends the actor has in view or by the causes that propel him to act. He finds flaws in both theories. With respect to the first, he is unimpressed by Pareto's endeavor to deal with "nonlogical" or "nonrational" actions, an approach as old as Socrates and one that is scientifically defective because it requires a judgment by an observer as to the rationality of the actor. Many actions, for example those of animals, conform to a telic order but it may be doubted that they are guided by logic or reason. The deterministic theory is also defective. In the first place, the "explanation" of an action by instinct adds nothing whatever to what we already know about it from observation. In the second place, it is refuted by the simple but ineluctable fact that actions are creative, that purposes are dynamically formed and sometimes changed in the course of their performance. Both theories depend upon a priori postulates rather than upon an inductive study of actions themselves.

In Znaniecki's own theory the distinction between means and ends is denied. What appears as one is often the other and, as Wundt pointed out, the same means may be used for the attainment of different ends, and different means may be chosen for the attainment of the same end. But it is primarily in the progressive creation of new purposes and new values that Znaniecki casts his own theory of action—in the production, for example, in musical composition, poetry, and painting of values that did not exist before. The same, of course, is true of all innovations and inventions, in whatever field of human endeavor. Znaniecki is aware in this discussion that not all human actions are creative; some are imitative or habitual. These three—creative, imitative, and habitual—become his three principal types of actions. He chooses to emphasize the first of them because they illustrate most clearly the difference between conscious human action as a cultural phenomenon and organic behavior as a natural phenomenon. He concludes his treatment with a discussion of destructive actions, which appear to be different morally but not logically from the other three.

In a succeeding chapter Znaniecki deals with what he calls active tendencies, an expression he greatly prefers to such concepts as "wish," "desire," "volition," "urge," "instinct," and "motive." Even if some of these are helpful in the explanation of individual actions—or at least in their description—they cannot explain collective actions. One problem comes to be how the conscious action of one person can cause or change the conscious action of another. He concludes, not altogether satisfactorily, that one person cannot cause the action of another but can only change it. To understand this we have to use the humanistic coefficient and learn how the person whose values are being affected views the situation. For this purpose we need no psychological inquiry. As suggested earlier, Znaniecki always denied that his studies of actions had anything to do with psychology and was as insistent as Durkheim about the autonomy of sociology. Even his discussion of human attitudes, to which he devotes a chapter, has a flavor that is entirely sociological. Attitudes are definitions of situations by agents and can be understood only through the use of the humanistic coefficient. Furthermore, the study of attitudes is not a separate task; it is part of the study of actions.

One of Znaniecki's favorite contentions appears again in this book. It has to do with Comte's distinction between social statics and social dynamics. The distinction has been pervasive and from it have arisen two different areas of sociological inquiry—often, as Znaniecki notes, treated in separate books—social structure and social change. The distinction may be pervasive but, to Znaniecki, it is also pernicious. It is quite true, as he concedes, that it is impossible to investigate change until one knows what it is that is changing, but on the whole it is better to eliminate the distinction and consider all social phenomena in flux, to consider actions rather than entities of any kind. Znaniecki has a positive dislike, in short, for such concepts as social structure and social order. Ideas and actions are both changing phenomena, and for best results one should study them together.

Actions involve both values and norms and thus conform to what Znaniecki calls an axionormative order. They become integrated in the course of their performance into systems of action, and we can therefore talk about systems of religious action, systems of technical action, systems of economic action, and so on. If Znaniecki is interested in the organization of cultural systems, he is also interested in their disorganization; in consequence he devotes a chapter to the latter subject as well. One had not supposed, incidentally, that he had so firm a control of the literature of criminology as he exhibits here.

In the realm of culture there are categories of factual order entirely separate from the factual order of the physical universe. The cultural scientist, however, is able to construct four kinds of hypotheses—the taxonomic, the functional, the causal, and the genetic—all of which can be validated or invalidated by the methods of empirical science. The realm of inquiry has grown so large that cultural scientists, like natural scientists, have had to specialize. One way to do this is to concentrate on particular cultures during certain historical periods—to study, for example, ancient Egypt, Greece, Rome, medieval Europe, Italy, France, Germany, Japan, and so on. The other way is to carve out different realms of culture—for example, political science, law, economics, sociology, linguistics, musicology, and so on. Attempts to develop a general theory of culture, such as those of Vico, Condorcet, Herder, and Hegel, have not been successful. Znaniecki has high praise for Sorokin's effort but feels that he too failed because he paid insufficient attention to the humanistic coefficient and did not see that social systems—the state, the family, a political party, a university—are cultural systems in the same sense that language, science, religion, and the fine arts are. Unfortunately too, Sorokin used an idealistic metaphysics, one with theological implications. Durkheim and his followers did not try to develop a general theory of culture but fixed their attention instead on specific kinds of cultural phenomena.[75] In denying, in opposition to Tarde, any doctrine of psychological individualism, they also neglected any consideration of the individual as an innovator, imitator, leader, and follower. American sociological theories—Znaniecki mentions those of Ward, Small, Sumner, and Keller—are too comprehensive and inclusive. As inductive empirical research has proceeded, sociology has become a more limited and more successful discipline. It is best defined as the science of order among social actions. It is—and here again Znaniecki disagrees with Sorokin—a special, not a general, cultural science. It is a study of social actions as experienced by those who perform them, of social relations by those who participate in them.

Znaniecki's views are not entirely free of difficulties. It may be, for example, that his conception of social actions is too constricting. Religious ceremonies, collectively performed, for example, are not social actions. Neither are technical actions, such as building a road, creative actions, such as the playing of a symphony by an orchestra or economic actions, such as buying and selling. On the other hand, teaching and learning are social actions, and thus the sociology of education, which focuses upon them, is a legitimate part of sociology. All categories of cultural order, however, have common social foundations—the very existence of culture depends upon social actions by conscious human persons. Sociology is therefore the basic cultural science, playing the same role for the cultural sciences that physics does for the natural sciences. This claim, when baldly stated, sounds imperialistic. It has, however, the special meaning that Znaniecki attaches to it. In his own words, "Sociologists are gradually becoming aware that the importance of sociology for other cultural sciences *increases* in the very measure in which it *limits its task* to a comparative study of those social systems upon which the existence of every realm of culture depends."[76] His suspicion of general theories of culture remains, and he deplores that sociology was once identified with the philosophy of history.

Znaniecki devotes his final chapter to the practical applications of the cultural sciences, and especially sociology. He is not sanguine about the situation as he viewed it in the middle of the century. But he is optimistic

75. There is a contradiction here. In *The Method of Sociology*, Znaniecki says that both Durkheim and Tarde tried to develop a general theory of cultural phenomena (p. 101).

76. *Cultural Sciences*, p. 396.

about the future. Sooner or later all kinds of human problems will be entrusted to cultural scientists for their solution. He does not, it is true, envisage the world of Comte's construction, in which sociologists serve as legislators, but he believes that sociologists can become leaders in the creation of new cultural systems and can thus help to enrich and to diversify both the lives of individuals and the life of society.

Social Relations and Social Roles[77]

Znaniecki's last book is his unfinished systematic sociology, on which he was working at the time of his death. It was edited by his daughter, Helena Znaniecki Lopata, and published in the form in which he left it; that is, it contains no footnotes because he had not prepared them, and it contains undeleted references to issues that he intended to treat later on. It consists of nineteen chapters arranged in two parts titled by the editor "The Scope of Sociology" and "Social Relations." We shall run through it with some rapidity, partly because it repeats points of view expressed in Znaniecki's earlier works and partly because his prose, which served him so well in his earlier books, has become somewhat diffuse.

What Is Sociology?

Znaniecki's view of the nature of sociology—what it ought to be and do—remains unchanged. He notes that although there is wide disagreement on this question among sociologists themselves, there is also agreement on a number of points. First of all, everyone agrees that sociology belongs to the sciences and not to the arts, as these disciplines appear in university organization. Second, sociology is an inductive science, an investigation of the factual order of empirical data, and, unlike theology and metaphysics, productive of theories that are subject to empirical tests. Third, it is a generalizing science, and thus different from such descriptive disciplines as history and geography. Fourth, it is an objective, or theoretic, science, involved with categorical judgments about what is and not with normative judgments about what ought to be.

The disagreements concern the kinds of data that are involved and the methods that are employed, and in these respects sociology suffers a defect

---

77. (San Francisco: Chandler Publishing Co. 1965).

that does not afflict the natural sciences. Comte and Spencer, of course, conceived of sociology as a science of society, of total societies. This kind of study traces its origin to classical antiquity, but for the most part much of the emphasis until the eighteenth century was on political phenomena, and not such phenomena as religion, philosophy, science, technology, economics, literature, and art—in short, cultural phenomena. The principal task of sociology in this view is to develop a taxonomy or systematic classification of societies. Unfortunately, this task is complicated by so many differences that such a classification becomes impossible, unless one is satisfied with the simple distinction between primitive and civilized societies. The ambitions of Spencer have not been realized.

A second disagreement concerns the degree to which we can come to understand society by studying individuals. Although Spencer was skeptical of this possibility and Comte and Durkheim denied it, there are those who have thought that sociology must have a biological or psychological base. Sometimes this emphasis has become so radical, as in behaviorism, that those who advance it insist that only individuals exist and that groups and societies are only philosophical abstractions. This approach, in Znaniecki's opinion, is a failure because it cannot account for the common culture of a collectivity, for the diversity of cultures, for the growth of new cultures while the human organism remains essentially the same. It is impossible to explain a variable by a constant. On the other hand, sociologists may not neglect the study of individuals.

A third possibility would regard sociology as more limited than either of these two approaches and would regard it as concerned with phenomena observable in collectivities and not reducible to psychology or biology. This approach would create a specialty for sociology, namely, the study of social action and social interaction. Of course, social actions and social interactions have been studied for centuries. But what is new in sociology is the effort to make such studies conform to the canons of scientific investigation. Two especially important kinds of social action, for example, are cooperation and conflict. Of the two, Znaniecki regards cooperation as the more important and concludes his discussion with the suggestion that an organized group of cooperating agents constitutes a social system. He describes his procedure as follows:

> We may mention right here that we shall begin with a study of the systems of cooperative interaction between two individuals, popularly called *social relations* or *interpersonal relations;* investigate the integration of such relations into *social roles,* i.e., systems of cooperative interaction between a particular individual and several others; go on to the integration of the social roles performed by a number of individuals into organized *social groups;* and, finally,

consider the integration of many diverse social groups, not into one kind of society, but into several different kinds of societies.[78]

This, then, is Znaniecki's program, only part of which he was able to complete.

THE FIELDS OF SOCIOLOGICAL RESEARCH

Before he embarks upon this program, Znaniecki has a few words to say about where and how sociologists go about their research. He conceives of the locus of research as a spatial area or field, ranging from the small to the large. Thus, the various fields of sociological research include collective meeting places, communities (tribal or rural), cities, metropolitan regions, and finally the world itself.[79] As to the "ways" of research, Znaniecki discusses these in terms of the now familiar contrast between naturalistic and humanistic approaches. Even such apparently natural phenomena as immigration, emigration, fluctuations in births and deaths, ecological distributions, the satisfaction of biological needs, and the use of techniques can be understood only with the help of a humanistic frame of reference. By humanistic approach, of course, Znaniecki has in mind that whenever a sociologist observes a social phenomenon he is bound to take into consideration what the phenomenon means to the conscious agents who are involved.

SOCIAL RELATIONS IN COMMUNITIES

Communities exhibit a multiplicity and diversity of social actions, and these actions are therefore quite difficult to study even when the community is small. The number of social actions going on in any community in a given period of time may approach infinity, and the sociologist must select the actions he wishes to investigate from a much larger number. In this situation he does best to single out sequences of actions and reactions occurring between two identifiable individuals. These actions and reactions constitute a social relation, by which Znaniecki means "a system of functionally interdependent social actions performed by two interacting individuals."[80] Of course it is possible to extend the investigation to more than two people, as when, for example, one studies the relations that occur

78. *Ibid.*, pp. 19–20.

79. On one particular kind of group—the nationality group—Znaniecki wrote a small book: *Modern Nationalities* (Urbana, Ill.: University of Illinois Press, 1952).

80. *Social Relations*, p. 88

within a family. It will be observed that the individuals in these relations conform to certain standards of evaluation or norms of conduct and, to the extent that this is so the relations are culturally patterned. Some of these relations—kinship relations, for example—are obligatory but for the most part they are voluntary on both sides. In these relations one must also be aware of the possibility of conflict, which usually occurs when one or both of the individuals deviates from the norms involved; such deviation can result in the disorganization or even the dissolution of the relationship. Znaniecki mentions several types of conflict that can have these results. In discussing both cooperation and conflict he is leading up to the conclusion that a comparative study of social relations, when properly done, results in generalizations that can be scientifically tested.[81]

There are those who have criticized the view that social relations can be studied in and of themselves. They have done so on several grounds: that social relations depend upon psychological factors and should therefore be approached psychologically; that they depend upon environmental factors and that social control is therefore exercised by those outside the relationship; and that they are dependent upon total cultures and cannot be abstracted even for analytical purposes. Znaniecki has no trouble in disposing of these objections. In short, generalizations about social relations are possible without studying the psychology of the partners, without studying the whole social organization, and without studying the total culture of the community.

MOTHER-CHILD RELATIONS

Mother-child relations Znaniecki regards as extremely important and instructive because they shed light on social relations in general. There are various kinds of mothers—biological mothers, foster mothers, mothers by adoption, stepmothers, godmothers, and even divine mothers. Sometimes children are rejected by their biological mothers; infanticide may be permitted or even required in some societies. The process of acceptance of children by mothers is one that has many variations. But for the most part the child is accepted by the biological mother, and a long-lasting social bond is formed. Mothers have certain duties to perform with respect to their children, duties concerning the child's body (both before and after birth), making the child a conscious partner in the relationship, and educational guidance. In turn the child has certain duties with respect to the mother, including, Znaniecki says, trustful obedience and gratitude.

81. *Ibid.*, p. 97.

FRATERNAL RELATIONS

Znaniecki devotes a chapter to the relation of brotherhood, both involuntary, as in the case of biological siblings, and voluntary, as in the case of religious and secular fraternal associations. The reason fraternal relations are important is that they are often considered a model for all human relationships. The duties involved in fraternal relations are reciprocal and include the duty of sympathetic understanding, mutual aid by gifts, mutual aid by services, and collaboration, the last of which is a collective action.

MARITAL AND EROTIC RELATIONS

These two relations are different, although they may, of course, be engaged in by the same couple. The variety in marital relations in different cultures is great but what is common to all of them is that they are regulated by the community. In almost all societies men and women who reach sexual maturity are expected to marry—with the exception of those who are chosen for certain functions, usually religious, with which marriage would interfere, and with the exception too of those who may be considered mentally or physically inferior. Marital relations are also normally expected to be enduring, although that is obviously not the case in practice. The importance the community ascribes to the marital relationship cannot be explained by the need for sex or by the need for economic cooperation in a sexual division of labor, but can be explained only by the need for procreation, which guarantees the continuance of the community. Marital selection, like the marital relationship itself, is subject to much variation. Znaniecki briefly describes some of these variations and also the custom of the wedding. He also describes the mutual duties of husband and wife.

Erotic relations, unlike marital relations, are not intended to serve the perpetuation of the race but are entered into instead for the private satisfaction of the partners. Selection is based on mutual sexual attraction. Like marital relations, on the other hand, erotic relations are supposed to be exclusive and to last for a considerable period of time. (Znaniecki rules prostitution and fleeting liaisons out of his discussion on the ground that they are not truly erotic.) Erotic relations also entail mutual obligations, including but not limited to the giving of sensual pleasure. Finally, in Western Europe and the United States the ideal marital relation is coming to be that of a permanent erotic relation.

RELATIONS OF POLITE COMPANIONSHIP

In this chapter Znaniecki discusses the relations that people enter into for the sake of their common enjoyment—social intercouse that has no ulterior purpose and is indulged in for its own sake. The norms that govern these relations are the norms of etiquette. Znaniecki is interested in them because above the level of childhood they are universal in society and because they are explicitly integrated. He goes on to treat them in princely courts, among statesmen and visitors, among the nobility, and among others of the same social class.[82]

INTEGRATION OF SOCIAL RELATIONS

The relations Znaniecki has so far discussed are relations that for the most part are relatively uninfluenced by others—except that marital relations are often influenced by the parents of the partners. Now he wants to inquire into those relations where there are more than two partners, where a single individual has relations with a number of others, and the manner in which these relations are functionally integrated so as to avoid conflict. Here he uses the example of a dinner party in which host and hostess and all the guests are involved in a culturally patterned kind of companionate intercourse. He also considers the social relations that a father has with his descendants and the social relations that a child has with various adults. But what he means by integration does not become clear.

THE CONCEPT OF SOCIAL ROLE

Znaniecki begins this chapter with the following definition of a social system:

> In studying social relations, we found that, when the same individual is a partner in social relations with a number of others, these relations are usually integrated. Some social relations in which the individual participates have no connection whatsoever, while others even conflict. For a number of social relations to become integrated, there must be cooperation not only between the individual and each of his partners, but also cooperation among his partners. When such cooperation exists, and the social relations between him and certain of his partners are integrated, they constitute all together a social system.[83]

All of those who cooperate with an individual in these relations constitute his social circle. The members of the circle grant to the individual at the center certain rights which they then support with both positive and negative sanctions. Everyone, of course, is the center of a number of different social circles.

82. Simmel, E. T. Hiller, and David Riesman also treated this subject, and it is probable that in a finished draft Znaniecki would have included references to their work.

83. *Ibid.*, p. 199.

The possibility of an individual interacting with numerous others in different social relations is illuminated by the concept of social role, a concept that Znaniecki proceeds to elaborate with the help of the theatrical analogy. Actors play roles in the theater, and similarly individuals play roles on the stage of life. A role in society has four components—the person, his social circle, duties, and rights. Numerous and diverse roles are played outside of organized groups and in order to understand them it is necessary to investigate them throughout their duration. The concept of status as an abstract conceptual scheme defining rights, privileges, duties, and obligations is useful but it encourages the investigator to ignore the dynamic character and ever-changing diversity of roles.

PERSONS

Persons who play social roles are judged by their social circles in accordance with certain standards, including standards of sex and age, hereditary biological characteristics, artificial bodily traits (shaven heads, tatoos, clothing), and psychological characteristics. In discussing the last of these Znaniecki has occasion to mention the erroneous assumption that members of certain races or of higher social classes are somehow superior to others. Sometimes estimates of personal ability are based upon observation of previous performances. Seniority and achievement are always relevant to judgments of pesons and judgments of newcomers and strangers are always difficult.

SOCIAL CIRCLES

Some social circles are specialized—for example, those of physicians, professors, and shopkeepers—others are not—for example, the social circles of "polite society." Some are small, some are large, and some extend beyond the range of the community. There are inner circles and outer circles and sometimes circles within circles. Sometimes social circles depend upon the individuals at their center, but sometimes the circle exists before the arrival of a given individual, as in the case of parents awaiting the birth of a child. The social circle of a university student is similarly in place, so to speak, before he or she arrives. When a role is considered so important that a circle will always find someone to perform it, Znaniecki calls it an institutional role. Examples of institutional roles are member of the French Academy, a university president, and, of course, the president of the United States and the pope of the Roman Catholic church. Institutional roles supposedly do not permit innovations, but in practice they all do.

PERSONAL RIGHTS

In theology, philosophy, and law the concept of rights is cloudy and obscure. For sociological purposes it needs redefinition, which Znaniecki undertakes as follows:

> A personal right may be defined as whatever, in accordance with the norms accepted by a person's social circle, the participants in this circle are *obliged to do for him.* When we say obliged, we mean not only that it is a participant's duty to do what the norm requires and refrain from doing anything that would conflict with it, but that the fulfillment of this duty is subjected to definite sanctions of the circle.[84]

When his duties seem especially important, he is given prerogatives denied to others; and when his duties are minimal as compared to others he is said to have privileges. The question as to whether there are any universal rights Znaniecki answers in the affirmative. Everyone has the right to have his personal worth recognized by his social circle, although he may forfeit this right by persistent violation of the circle's norms. Znaniecki goes on to consider in detail a somewhat curious collection of rights, including rights to personal prestige, the right of inferiors to have their merit recognized by superiors, the right to personal esteem by equals, the right to physical safety, economic rights, the right to sympathetic understanding, the right to have authoritative judgments accepted, the right to obedience, and the right to perform new actions. In this chapter Znaniecki has a simple but useful definition of power: "We say that a social agent has power when he can compel people to do what they do not want to do or prevent them from doing what they want to do."[85]

PERSONAL FUNCTIONS

Personal rights are balanced by personal duties. Znaniecki discusses particular duties toward particular individuals, generalized duties within wide social circles, duties toward a person's social circle when it is an organized social group, duties of members of organized groups toward outsiders, and duties toward oneself. Social duties are usually fulfilled in culturally patterned actions. Personal functions are important because they provide the only possible means for classifying social roles.

SOCIAL ROLES

Znaniecki devotes the remainder of his book to roles in tribal communities, the social roles of kings, the functional differentiation of religious

84. *Ibid.*, pp. 241–242.
85. *Ibid.*, p. 266.

roles, the differentiation of the roles of warriors, and the evolution of political roles. He believes that roles in general can be understood only in terms of their historical evolution and differentiation. After political roles he intended to write on the evolution of aesthetic, technical, economic, intellectual, and educational roles and then on the evolution of the roles of women. But he did not live long enough to undertake these tasks. As intimated before, Znaniecki's sociology could never have been finished under even the best of circumstances—that is, the longest possible life—because he was always anticipating the work he wanted to do in the future.

Summary and Evaluation

Znaniecki's principal theses may be summarized in five propositions:

1. Sociology is a cultural and not a natural science, and culture is a reality in its own ontological right.
2. Sociology is a special and not general social science, concerned not with everything that happens in society, and not with society in general, but only with conscious agents as they interact with one another and thus create systems of social actions.
3. These systems, in turn, are the data of sociological knowledge.
4. Notwithstanding the differences between natural and social systems, investigation of the latter can be as objective, as precise, and as verifiable as investigation in the other sciences.
5. Sociology, although properly and necessrily limited in scope, is nevertheless the basic cultural science because all cutural products are created by men and women in interaction with one another.

Znaniecki's sociological theory has many merits. I should mention first of all, as I have before, his literary style. It has a grace and a lucidity that, among the sociologists treated in this book, can stand comparison with that of Ross and MacIver. Theodore Abel, in his obituary comment, said, "Excepting Herbert Spencer, there is hardly another sociologist who wrote with equal simplicity and clarity and who, in argument, was able to anticipate the reader's most penetrating questions."[86] This accomplishment is all the more remarkable because—and one tends to forget it—English was not his native language. One can mention, second, a trait that he himself did not rate highly—indeed for him it turns into a fault of the historians—and that is erudition. His writings ar full of allusions to the societies of antiquity, of the Middle Ages, and of succeeding centuries. He

86. "Florian Znaniecki, 1882–1958," *American Sociological Review* 23 (August 1958): 429.

is clearly at home in the history of philosophy, not to say the history of intellectual disciplines in general or, as he would call it, the history of knowledge, a history he once hoped to write.[87]

We should mention next Znaniecki's unusual talent for systematization. He believed that he could create a system of sociology with the use of four basic concepts which turn out to be six when one considers the entire corpus of his work, namely, social actions, social relations, social persons, social groups, social circles, and social roles. Of these six, social roles received the largest part of is attention and social groups the least. It should be said, however, that he intended to devote a future effort to the subject of groups. And it should be repeated that his study of the social role of the man of knowledge is the most comprehensive treatment of this role in the literature and in itself takes first rank as a contribution to sociology.

Finally, we may appreciate once more Znaniecki's steady insistence on the importance of sociology as an objective cultural science and his introduction of the concept of the humanistic coefficient. It is the humanistic coefficient that distinguishes the cultural from the physical sciences. And it is the humanistic coefficient that gives meaning and significance to sociological inquiry.[88]

There is also, of course, something to be said on the debit side of the ledger. Although it aroused some interest at the time Znaniecki proposed it,[89] the method of analytic induction has not endured. It is not today recognized as a method of sociological research. In fact, Znaniecki's presentation of it is not as clear as one would expect from a man of his methodological depth. If he means by it that individual cases are as important as populations and samples of populations his point has cogency. But if he intends to ignore the law of large numbers and to try to generalize from single instances he is almost certainly wrong. Indeed, his assault on statistical methods is uncharacteristically harsh.

A second difficulty with Znaniecki's general sociological theory is that his stress on social actions and on social roles leaves him without a sense of

87. Daniel W. Rossides, for example, refers to the "sustained conceptual sophistication" that he brought to *The Polish Peasant. The History and Nature of Sociological Theory* (Boston: Houghton Mifflin Co. 1978). p. 425n.

88. For another discussion of Znaniecki's virtues and accomplishments, see the thoughtful treatment by Lewis A. Coser, *Masters of Sociological Thought*, pp. 511–559 (the chapter deals with both Thomas and Znaniecki). Coser laments that Znaniecki has had little impact in the United States, in contrast to his role in Poland, and in truth the secondary literature on him is somewhat sparse.

89. See W. S. Robinson, "The Logical Structure of Analytic Induction," *American Sociological Review* 16 (December 1951): 812–818; and comments by Alfred R. Lindesmith, *ibid.* 17 (August 1952): 592–493, S. Kirson Weinberg, *ibid.*, p. 493, W. S. Robinson, *ibid.*, p. 494, and Robert C. Angell, *ibid.* 19 (August 1954): 476–477.

social structure, social organization, social order. There is no treatment of social organization at all, the organization either of groups or of society itself. It may be that men "produce" society with every social action and social interaction in which they are involved and that this "product" is always changing.[90] But this "product"—society—nevertheless has a form, a shape, a structure, and this structure can be studied in independence of individuals in interaction.[91] It is possible to study society without studying social actions, just as it is possible to study a language without studying speech. A society, like a language, has its norms, and these are what we would ordinarily refer to as its structure. Without this structure Znaniecki's actors would find themselves playing their roles without benefit of a script and having to improvise their lines as they went along.

On the other hand, it must immediately be said that this indictment is one that Zananiecki would welcome. He explicitly denounced the study of social structure as a sociological enterprise and dismissed with impatience the distinction that Comte or anyone else would draw between social statics and social dynamics. Unfortunately, however, this dismissal is unaccompanied by any kind of causal inquiry, and one looks in vain in Znaniecki for a theory of social change. He hoped that somehow his concept of system would obviate a search for causes and the infinite regression that such a search would involve.

Finally, perhaps the most serious criticism of Znaniecki's general theory is that in its sociological respects it is overly simple. The simplicity is best illustrated by his last book, his unfinished system. We have previously remarked that its style is somewhat diffuse. We now have to say, in addition, that its substance is slight. Znaniecki uses a thin skein of concepts—social relations and social roles—to tell us that husbands and wives are sometimes in conflict, that mother–child relations are usually the first in which individuals participate, and that one of the duties of a mother is to prepare the clothes in which her infant will be wrapped.[92] What Znaniecki has done in this last book is to impose a sociological vocabulary upon familiar facts.

It must quickly be said, however, that it is quite unfair to apply exacting standards to a book that a man writes in his old age. The thoughts tend to

90. This view has more recently been set forth by Anthony Giddens. See his *New Rules of Sociological Method* (London: Hutchinson, 1976). For a dissenting view, see the long review of this book by Robert Bierstedt, *Scottish Journal of Sociology* 1 (April 1977): 183–193.

91. See J. O. Hertzler who, in an otherwise highly favorable review of *Cultural Sciences*, says nevertheless that "we still have no working conception of social structure; and while social actions are dynamic we do not get a satisfying conception of societal operation." *American Sociological Review* 17 (October 1952): 628.

92. These propositons can be found, respectively, in *Social Relations*, pp. 92, 109, 118. Unfortunately, there are numerous similar examples.

stray and the pen to falter. But one is nevertheless constrained to say that Znaniecki's entire system exhibits this kind of simplicity. To say that sociology is the study of social actions, social relations, social persons, social groups, social circles, and social roles is all to the good. But too often—almost deliberately it seems, and despite his erudition—he empties these concepts of social and historical significance. Too often he deprives them of scientific and intellectual significance as well.

On balance, however, Znaniecki's virtues are considerable and indeed remarkable. If his rather special approach sometimes fails to challenge us, he nevertheless presented an original view of what he thought sociology should be and he transformed this view into a system of sociology. He was a contributor to knowledge, one who inquired into the deep meanings of social roles, especially the social role of the man of knowledge, and one who thus won for himself, in his own terminology, the label of "explorer" in the history of social thought.

CHAPTER 6

Robert Morrison MacIver

Custom is always at work turning example into precedent and precedent into institution.

—*The Web of Government*, p. 34.

Robert M. MacIver was born on April 17, 1882, in Stornoway, Scotland. It is the principal town and port on the Isle of Lewis, in the Outer Hebrides, separated from the mainland by the rough waters of the Minch. His father, a descendant of a line of crofters and fishermen, was a successful merchant of Harris tweeds, the best-known product of the Isles of Lewis and Harris. He grew up in the dour atmosphere of Scottish Presbyterianism, a gloomy, restrictive religion that he learned to resist and finally to resent, one that in his youth required daily rituals of domestic prayer both before and after meals and forbade all play and "promiscuous" reading on the Sabbath. Besides the Bible and devotional works, however, the MacIver home contained the books of the Brontës, Scott, Dickens, Thackeray, Ruskin, Tennyson, Browning, and other Victorian writers. He was educated at the Nicholson Institute, a local school whose headmaster punished unruly pupils by stuffing snuff up their nostrils. A succeeding headmaster, however, opened MacIver's eyes to the delights of English literature and, as he says, changed the climate of his life.[1] He was also taught the orthodox subjects of Latin, Greek, and "Euclid," together with some French and science.

Having placed high in the bursary competition, which assured the best students of Scotland an education in one of the four universities—Aberdeen, St. Andrews, Glasgow, or Edinburgh—MacIver chose the last of these and went off to the city known variously as "the Athens of the North" and as "Auld Reekie." He was sixteen years of age and it marked his

1. *As a Tale That Is Told: The Autobiography of R. M. MacIver* (Chicago: University of Chicago Press, 1968), p. 20:

> The difference between good teaching and poor teaching is like that between a clear-shining lamp and a smoky, flickering flame. I had the best of reasons for appreciating the difference. The new dispensation changed the climate of my life. Ever since, I have recognized that teaching is a high art, the most essential, the most socially significant of all the arts, and the prime utility of civilization.

transition from the Outer Hebrides to the outer world—the world of the university, the theater, and the museum. Edinburgh, however, was a disappointment, the first year "humdrum" and laborious, the second even worse. Although there were men of eminence on the faculty—George Saintsbury in English, Andrew Seth Pringle-Pattison in logic, and James Seth in moral philosophy—for the most part the professors were dreary and uninspiring, almost wholly uninterested in their students and seldom in any personal contact with them. Seldom did they even read the papers of their students; this task was left to their assistants. There were no seminars, no tutors, no advisers—only lectures and examinations. MacIver's standing in Greek, for example, was at the top of his class, and yet he never had an interview with his professor. The last year at Edinburgh, however, was a happier one. At the same time, he did not particularly relish the thought of a lifetime devoted to the history and literature of Greece and Rome and he began to wish that he could explore the new fields of the social sciences, to which Edinburgh was not then hospitable. In any event, he graduated with first-class honors in classics and proceeded to Oriel College, Oxford, on a substantial scholarship.

At Oxford more than half the students were the sons of privilege; the remainder, like MacIver, were there to study. The former, "commoners," took the "pass" course; the latter, "scholars," took one of the "honors" programs. MacIver's program was in the ancient curriculum of *Literae Humaniores*, known as "Greats," in which he took a double first. There were two examinations, one entirely in classics and the other, with a few more options, in philosophy. Although Plato and Aristotle, of course, were standard fare, no one seemed interested in the concerns of *The Republic* or the *Politics*, that is, government, economics, and sociology. The latter subjects, however, increasingly attracted the young scholar's attention, and it was in the British Museum that he encountered and read the works of such modern writers as Simmel, Durkheim, and Lévy-Bruhl. Apart from the provosts of Oriel, MacIver mentions by name only his tutor, W. D. Ross, a Scot who was a distinguished Aristotelian scholar. But the Oxford years were serene. For recreation there was golf, tennis, and punting; there were frequent trips to London, and a brief European tour, punctuated by periodic visits to his native island. With the American sequence reversed, MacIver received his B.A. degree from Oxford in 1907, four years after he received his M. A. from Edinburgh. Later, in 1915, he took his Ph.D. at Edinburgh.

Although MacIver entertained an early ambition to be a "writer"—presumably of novels, perhaps of plays[2]—he was by this time committed to

2. MacIver did in fact write a novel and several plays. These, however, were not successful. He also wrote one poem each year—a New Year's greeting to his wife.

an academic career. His first appointment, in 1907, was as lecturer on political science at Aberdeen. The social sciences were no more in evidence there than they were at Edinburgh and Oxford. There was a little economics, a little political science (the history of political philosophy from Machiavelli to Hegel), and no sociology. MacIver, however, persuaded his superior to permit the introduction of a course in sociology, and from 1911 to 1915 he was lecturer in political science and sociology.

As a lecturer, without vote in faculty, MacIver served at Aberdeen under the authority of the professor of moral philosophy, J. B. Baillie, the translator of Hegel's *Phenomenology of Mind.* The relationship between them was a warm one. MacIver often played golf and chess with Baillie and was often a guest at the latter's estate on the Deeside. One morning, however, when MacIver arrived at the office they shared, Baillie did not return his greeting or favor him with so much as a glance. In response to entreaty as to how he had offended, there was again only silence. MacIver soon learned, although not from Baillie, the source of the trouble. He had published an article highly critical of Bosanquet's *The Philosophical Theory of the State* and Baillie, a Hegelian like Bosanquet, had interpreted it as an attack upon himself. MacIver had no such intention, and indeed there is no mention of Baillie in the article.[3] But the damage was done. The situation at Aberdeen was now so awkward that MacIver had to seek another appointment. By this time he had published a number of articles, and the manuscript of his book *Community* had won a prize offered by the Carnegie Trust for the Universities of Scotland.[4] When the University of Toronto offered him an appointment as associate professor of political science, therefore, he was glad to accept.

In Aberdeen MacIver met Ethel Marion Peterkin, herself a native of the city and a graduate of the university. After a year in Paris, studying French literature at the Sorbonne, she had returned to take additional work in moral philosophy. An outstanding student, she came under the tutelage of MacIver and the tutorial relationship ripened into a marital one. They had three children—two boys and a girl. The family lived in Aberdeen, Toronto, New York City, and finally in Palisades, New York, and had summer homes first in the Lake Muskoka district of Ontario and later at Chilmark, Massachusetts, on Martha's Vineyard.

3. Bosanquet's own response to MacIver was altogether cordial, and they engaged in a friendly exchange of views. This correspondence is reprinted in MacIver, *Politics and Society*, ed. David Spitz (New York: Atherton Press, 1969), pp. 238–247, with an additional letter to MacIver on the same subject from the Oxford political philosopher R. F. Alfred Hoernlé. The article itself, originally entitled "A Criticism of the Neo-Hegelian Identification of 'Society' and 'State,'" also appears in *Politics and Society* under the title "Society and State," p. 325–337.

4. The articles appeared in such journals as *Sociological Review*, *Philosophical Review*, *Political Quarterly*, and *International Journal of Ethics*.

The outward life of a scholar, so many of whose lonely hours are committed to study, is apt to be uneventful. Certainly this may be said of MacIver during the twelve years he spent at Toronto. They were productive years but quiet ones. He did serve as vice chairman of the War Labor Board of the Dominion of Canada from 1917 to 1918, a task that resulted in the book *Labor in the Changing World.*[5] Other than that, he served as professor and then, for five years, as head of the department of political science. For a time he also administered the school of social work. But at no time at Toronto did he have an opportunity to teach a course in sociology.

Despite the years spent in Canada, MacIver developed no sense of permanent attachment to that country and regarded its effort to create a distinctive culture as a somewhat precarious endeavor. He became attuned to the Canadian wilderness, however, about which he writes:

> In that flat, unpeopled northland of rocks and pines, of streams and marshes and lakes and islands, I gained a sense of intimacy with nature I never had known before. Echoes of it still reverberate in my memory—the wavering, lonely call of the loon, the white stripe of the skunk threading through the trees in the evening, unmoved and fearless as we passed, the savor of the shallow lily pond where we hunted for bull frogs, the ledge below the little waterfall where we camped at night, the sough of the fresh breeze at dawn, the sudden storm of a late afternoon, the fire round which we sat under the wakening stars and listened to the whispering scrabbles in the undergrowths, the insistent, raucous note of the nightly whippoorwill.[6]

It was in Canada too that he developed an expert interest in mushrooms, which was to serve him as a hobby during the rest of his life.[7]

In 1927 MacIver became an immigrant again, this time to the United States, where he accepted appointment as head of the department of economics and sociology at Barnard College, Columbia University. He welcomed it as an opportunity to strengthen his endeavors as a sociologist. Two years later he was awarded the Francis Lieber Chair of political philosophy and sociology at Columbia, a post he retained until his retirement in 1950. Administration of the department of sociology proved to be a much more difficult task than the chairmanship he had held at Toronto. After the departure of Giddings the department had fallen into a state of decay, with its repute far less than that of the department at the University of Chicago. At one point an effort was made to abolish it, a move that

5. (New York: E. P. Dutton, 1919).

6. *As a Tale That Is Told,* p. 92.

7. His research in this field and his extensive correspondence with professional mycologists induced his close associates to believe that he had written a book on this subject. No such manuscript, however, was found among his papers.

MacIver, with the help of John Dewey, successfully resisted. The Depression years of the 1930s were not conducive to departmental development and MacIver encountered difficult and often insoluble problems. With the help of his own high reputation, however, to say nothing of that of the university, he was able to recruit for the staff such men as Robert S. Lynd, Paul F. Lazarsfeld, Robert K. Merton, and, as a visitor for a period, Florian Znaniecki. Whether or not he occupied the chair of the department—a rotating chore—he became a leading figure on a distinguished faculty and one of its most respected members.

MacIver's attitude toward sociology, however, was always an ambivalent one. On this matter he writes:

> Sociology has always been for me a kind of beloved mistress with whom I seemed unable to get on really comfortable terms. I regarded, and still regard it, as a great and challenging subject. I fought lonely battles to get it accepted in Scotland and in Canada. Yet I was never happy with my accomplishment in that field. My own books in sociology did not give me anything like the degree of satisfaction I got from my books in political science, *The Modern State*, *The Web of Government*, and *Power Transformed*. The popular texts of the time I regarded as diffuse, lacking definition, sprawling over into genetics and anthropology and ethics, whereas I wanted to offer a systematic account of the structure of society.[8]

As indicated above MacIver held his Columbia post until 1950, at which time he was given emeritus status. He had, however, an unusual postretirement career. He continued to be active as director of several research projects—one an evaluation of the work of the various and often competing Jewish agencies in the country, another on academic freedom, and still another on the United Nations. Among the board memberships he held in New York City, including the New York School of Social Work, the Russell Sage Foundation, and the American Civil Liberties Union, was the board of the New School for Social Research. As chairman of a committee appointed to select a new president for the school, he and his colleagues had suffered several disappointments. To his surprise, his associates on the board suggested that he assume the presidency. He was then eighty one years old and had no administrative ambitions. Indeed, he had often declined consideration for presidential appointments. He was so devoted to the educational enterprise that the New School represented, however, that he accepted the assignment. Accordingly he served with great success first as president and then, honorifically, as chancellor. He retired finally in 1966 at the age of eighty-four. During the years following his retirement

8. *Ibid.*, p. 109.

from Columbia he also wrote nine more books, including three of philosophical reflections—*The Pursuit of Happiness, Life: Its Dimensions and Its Bounds,* and *The Challenge of the Passing Years.*[9] He died on June 15, 1970, of the complications of old age.

MacIver often described himself as a "scribbler." Indeed, he piled sentence upon sentence every day of his adult existence, until the result was an impressive row of books. Like Bertrand Russell, and unlike lesser mortals, he never needed to revise.[10] Except for the change of a word or two or the interlineation of a more felicitous expression, his first draft was his last. No one outside the family ever caught him at work. Afternoons frequently found him playing chess at the Faculty Club on Morningside Drive, and evenings, at the bridge table. But every day without exception he wrote his two pages of manuscript. He was thus a steady worker rather than a hard one, a trait in which he took some pride. Even as a student he invariably—and as a matter of principle—spent the day before an important examination on the golf course rather than in his rooms. His memory was phenomenal. He could recite reams of Byron, Shelley, Keats, Browning, and Shakespeare. In his personal relationships he was cautious and reserved, almost shy. Few addressed him by his first name—it was a practice he did not encourage—and a nickname was unthinkable.

MacIver was elected president of the Eastern Sociological Society in 1934 and of the American Sociological Society in 1940. Among additional honors was the Woodrow Wilson Prize of the American Political Science Association for his book *The Web of Government.* Indeed, he was the most "decorated" sociologist of his generation. Columbia, Harvard, Yale, Princeton, the Jewish Theological Seminary of America,[11] the New School for Social Research, Toronto, Edinburgh, and Aberdeen all gave him honorary degrees—the last, in exception to a rule, in absentia. He was especially pleased by the Doctorate of Letters he received at the Harvard Tercentenary in 1936, where he was cited for introducing order and system into our knowledge of the nature of society.

---

9. A bibliography of MacIver's works may be found in *Politics and Society* pp. 533–539. It contains twenty-one books, three reports, twenty-five books edited by MacIver, and ninety-seven articles.

10. Bertrand Russell remarks in his autobiography that he once tried to revise an article he had written and the revision was so far inferior to the original that he never tried it again.

11. With Louis Finkelstein, then chancellor of the seminary, Harlow Shapley, the Harvard astronomer, Lyman Bryson of Columbia, Charles S. Johnson, president of Fisk University, Richard McKeon, professor of Greek and philosophy at the University of Chicago, and others, MacIver was a founder of the Conference on Science, Philosophy, and Religion and of the Institute for Religious and Social Studies, for which he edited a long series of books and planned and chaired for many years a winter lecture program.

Community

Inasmuch as the most mature expression of MacIver's system of sociology appears in *Society*, it will be permissible, even desirable, to slight somewhat his earlier works. *Community*, to the manuscript of which reference has already been made, appeared in 1917. Of two quotations on its title page, one from Fouillée reads, "Nous assistons aujourdhui à l'avènement de la sociologie, qui est le commencement d'une ère nouvelle dans la philosophie même." It was to this "commencement" that MacIver aspired to contribute. The subtitle of the book is "A Sociological Study," and, continuing, "Being an attempt to set out the nature and fundamental laws of social life." The concept of community for MacIver is a universal, not a particular, and his concerns therefore have nothing to do with ethnography. Community means the common life, the life that transcends all special interests, whether they be economic, political, educational, religious, or whatever. Although still very much in an inchoate state, there can be a science of this subject, and that science is sociology. He repudiates altogether the view he says he held earlier that the special sciences, such as economics and politics, for example, exhaust the meaning of the social. Community itself is a real, a vital phenomenon.

At the outset, indeed in his Preface, MacIver declares his disaffection for much that at this time had characterized this kind of inquiry: "Many a vain and specious formula has been set forward in the name of sociology, many a hollow generalisation has been declared an eternal social law, and too frequently the invention of terms has taken the place of the discovery of principles."[12] He also takes a methodological stance to which he will consistently adhere, namely, that the methods of the physical sciences do not suffice for the social sciences. The passage is also important enough to quote:

> The author is firmly convinced that social science will never advance except by freeing itself from subjection to the methods and formulae of both physical and biological science. As it has a subject-matter of its own, so it has a method of its own. Social relations can never be adequately stated in quantitative terms or understood as expressions of quantitative laws. Certain writers have declared that unless we can formulate the laws of society with the same exactitude with which we formulate the laws of physics, our subject is no science. It is unprofitable to quarrel over names. If men care to reserve the title of science to those subjects which admit of quantitative statement, they may be permitted

12. *Community* and ed. (London: Macmillan & Co, 1920), p. viii. (Originally published, 1917.) Although there are no citations, MacIver is referring to theories of community that would single out struggle, adaptation, environment, race, economic interest, or population as explanatory principles.

> the reservation. But many kinds of *knowledge*, and among them those most worth knowing, will then remain outside the sciences.[13]

This view, however, is not to be interpreted as an opposition to statistical information. Statistical data are important even though they do not rise to the level of social facts.

Early on, MacIver, always careful to define his terms and conscious of the confused condition of the sociological vocabulary, begins to make some of the distinctions—between community and association, for example—to which we shall attend in the sequel. He insists, as he did in his argument with Bosanquet, that community and state are not identical—a mistake made not only by the Greeks but again, and more seriously, by the Hegelians. The state, despite its importance, is only one of the associations that arise in the community and, like other associations, it has a limited purpose. It is an agency of the community; it is not, and cannot be, an all-inclusive entity, one that encompasses all the rest. This is a recurrent theme in MacIver and one that establishes the base of his support of democracy. There are certain rights with which the state may not interfere, even when it has the capacity to do so, and this it is MacIver's intention to emphasize. It achieves the status of an axiom in his political philosophy, and it is firmly lodged in the nature of society itself.

Another issue that detains our attention, and one that MacIver made a strenuous effort to solve, concerns the kind of "reality" that society—or in this case, community—might be said to possess. Is society real, or may we attribute reality only to individuals? The question is as old as Plato and Aristotle and is one that became a predominant theme, under a somewhat different guise, in medieval philosophy. It was introduced into medieval thought by Boethius's translation of Porphyry's *Introduction to the Categories of Aristotle.* Porphyry wanted to know whether genera and species exist or whether they are names only.[14] The question, however, came to be one concerning the reality of universals: are they generic phenomena or only generic names? In order to illustrate the problem, we may ask the simple question, What is the singular of the word *men*? An incautious answer would be that the obvious answer is *man.* The incautious answer would be wrong. The singular of *men* is not *man* but *a man. Man* is a universal; it means mankind. *Men,* on the other hand, is the plural of a

13. *Ibid.*, p. ix.

14. "For the present I shall not discuss the question whether genera and species really exist or are bare notions only; and if they exist whether they are corporeal things, or incorporeal and rather separated or whether they exist in things, perceived by the senses and in relation to them." Quoted in A. I. Aaron, *The Theory of Universals* (London and New York: Oxford University Press [Clarendon], 1952). Aaron's book is a comprehensive treatment of the problem, not only in medieval philosophy but also in the British empirical tradition.

particular. It now behooves us to ask whether the universal is real, or whether only particulars are real.[15] Three medieval answers were offered. The first, that universals exist *ante rem* ('before the thing') and are therefore real, was supported by Saint Anselm and William of Champeaux, the latter of whom insisted that man, therefore, is something more than an individual. This view came to be known as realism. The second, that universals exist *post rem* and are therefore only names, was supported by Roscellinus (condemned as heretical by the Council of Soissons in 1121) and, later, by William of Occam, who was excommunicated for his pains. In this view only particulars are real, and this position came to be known as nominalism. A third view, supported by Abélard, held that the universal is neither before nor after the thing, but is in the thing (*in re*); that is, that as a thing the universal exists only in the individual and outside the individual it exists only as a concept. This view was called conceptualism, and this too was condemned by the church.

The problem had considerable medieval importance, not only theoretical but also practical. Does the one, holy, universal Roman Catholic church exist, or is the church only an aggregation of particular Christian communities and of Christian believers? Does God exist, as a universal, or can we attribute existence only to the Father, the Son, and the Holy Ghost, as particulars? It can be seen that the latter position was fraught with dangers to the medieval church—it would substitute a polytheism for a monotheism.

The question has contemporary relevance as well. On the architrave of Langdell Hall, of the Harvard Law School, for example, appears "Non sub homine, sed sub Deo et lege." The question is, is there something—The Law—which exists, or do we have only laws, that is, acts of legislatures and decisions of courts.[16] As another example, the Fourteenth Amendment to the Constitution of the United States says that no state may "deprive any person of life, liberty, or property, without due process of law; nor deny to any person within its jurisdiction the equal protection of the laws." It would be difficult to exaggerate the difficulties encountered in trying to interpret these clauses. Does the "person" referred to include corporations, and do they also therefore deserve these protections? So far, the Supreme Court has answered in the affirmative—a corporation is a legal person—but this interpretation has been questioned on occasion, notably by the late Justice Hugo L. Black. The Court, however, is hardly qualified to resolve the metaphysical problem.[17]

15. Goethe had the problem in mind when he asked, Does Europe exist?

16. Or, more extreme, is the law only what the judges say it is?

17. MacIver has a relevant comment in this connection: "What endless debate the writers on jurisprudence would have been saved could they only have found for an associational unity some other term than that of legal *person*!" *Community*, p. 92.

The problem is no less persistent in sociological theory. Here it takes the following forms, among others: Is the group real, or only the individuals who compose it? Is the group more than the sum of its parts? Is there a group mind? A crowd mind?[18] And finally, if social facts are defined as external to the individual, can they also be real? Those who accept the view that groups are real have received the medieval appellation of sociological realists, and those who accept the opposing view that groups are only aggregations of individuals, that of sociological nominalists.

The last question—whether social facts are real—invokes the shade of Durkheim, and indeed it was he who aggravated the problem in sociology. It was he who affirmed that social facts are both external and real. And it was he who used such expressions as the group soul (*âme*), group mind, the mentality of groups, collective thought, collective effervescences, the collective conscience (or consciousness), and collective representations. These are the expressions, together with the metaphysics that supports them, that aroused the vigorous opposition of Gabriel Tarde in their great debates.[19]

It is in this context that MacIver addresses himself to the nature of community. First, he dismisses as false the ancient organic analogy, the notion that community either is or is like an organism. This analogy, he says, took "whimsical" form in the writings of Nicolas of Cusa (d. 1464), who found that the offices of the state were limbs of the great organism, the laws were the nerves, decrees were the brains, the fatherland was the skeleton, and its members were the flesh.[20] He has no trouble disposing of this notion. He argues, with Spencer, that an organism has single center, whereas the community has many. "A community does not act in unity like an organism, or reproduce like an organism, or die like an organism. The central difference renders the whole analogy vain."[21]

18. See, for example, Gustave Le Bon, *The Crowd* (1895), which is subtitled "A Study of the Popular Mind," and Robert K. Mertons's perceptive Introduction to the Compass edition thereof (New York: Viking Press, 1960).

19. Tarde accused Durkheim of "scholasticism" and asked, Are we going to return to the realism of the Middle Ages? For their exchanges, see Steven Lukes, *Emile Durkheim: His Life and Work* (New York: Harper & Row, 1972), pp. 302–313. Roscoe Hinkle suggests that it was Durkheim's realism that offended American sociologists and explains his dilatory reception on this side of the Atlantic. See Hinkle, "Durkheim in American Sociology," ed. Kurt Wolff, *Emile Durkheim, 1858–1917* (Columbus, Ohio: Ohio State University Press, 1960), pp. 267–295.

20. *Community*, pp. 72ff. Among organicists of the nineteenth century belong the names of Bluntschli, Lilienfeld, Schäffle, Worms, and Fouillée, although the last of these tempered the analogy in his late writings. Spencer, of course, also used the organic analogy, but he also pointed out the respects in which society is not an organism.

21. *Community*, p. 73.

Secondly, MacIver disposes of the contention that community is a group mind or soul. We do not pursue his argument but only state his conclusion: "There is no more a great 'collective' mind beyond the individual minds in society than there is a great 'collective' tree beyond all the individual trees in nature."[22] On the other hand, we can speak of a society or a forest as a unity, and here his view seems to be congruent with the conceptualism of Abélard.

Finally, MacIver speaks directly to Durkheim and to the notion that community is somehow greater than the sum of its parts. In response to some of his critics, Durkheim reaffirmed, in his Preface to the second edition of the *Rules of Sociological Method*, that when elements combine they produce new phenomena that do not initially reside in them. Life, for example, cannot be found in the atoms of hydrogen, oxygen, carbon, and nitrogen that compose it; the hardness of bronze cannot be found in the malleable copper, tin, and lead that are its constituent parts; and the fluidity of water cannot be found in the gases of hydrogen and oxygen that compose it.[23] Similarly, the synthesis that is society yields new phenomena that do not reside in the members who compose it. These phenomena reside in society itself and cannot be found in the individual consciousness.

MacIver enters the contest on a note of despair: "Shall we ever learn to study society directly in itself, and not in the distorting mirror of analogy?" And continuing:

> The "whole question" as asked by M. Durkheim is mere confusion. In the case of chemical composition we are first given the elements uncompounded. They enter into combination, passing through a process of modification, and a new unity results. Here not only is there no analogy whatever to social process, but it is not even true that we have found a whole which, in the required sense, is "greater than the sum of its parts." For all that M. Durkheim and those who use similar expressions mean is that the character and properties of the whole resulting from the chemical process are different from the character and properties of any of the several constituents *as they existed before entering into the combination*. But the constituents so understood are in no sense *parts* of the resulting unity, the copper and tin and lead are not parts of the bronze. It is a still greater confusion to say that community is greater than "the resultant of its parts." It should be obvious that there is no analogy between the chemical process, or any other process which gives resultants properly so called, and the social process. We can find one only if we fall back on some obsolete "social contract" doctrine of society which discovers men existing in some void out of society and brings them in. If individuals never exist out of society, where

22. *Ibid.*, pp. 81–82.

23. *The Rules of Sociological Method*, ed. George E. G. Catlin and trans. Sarah A. Solovay and John H. Mueller (Chicago: University of Chicago Press, 1938), pp. xlvii–xlix.

shall we find the non-social lead and copper and tin which make the social bronze?[24]

And concluding:

> There is no "sum of individuals," no "sum of the parts" of a community. The social relationships of every individual are not outside him, they are revelations of his personality. How can you sum things if part of their being consists in their relationships to one another? To talk of a "sum of individuals" is to think first of individuals as abstract, relationless, desocialisable beings. Understand individuals as concrete beings whose relations to one another constitute factors of their personality, and you realise that these *are* society, these and these alone—and the metaphysical confusion which leads you to look for something beyond this, something beyond these unsummable social individuals, passes away.[25]

MacIver thus concludes his argument, all of which supports his initial assertion that "there are no individuals who are not social individuals, and society is nothing more than individuals associated and organised."[26]

There is much more of interest in this early book, much indeed that is relevant to MacIver's theory of society. But these matters receive more careful and systematic attention in *Society*, and we can therefore turn without serious loss to the second of his sociological works. Before doing so, however, I will mention that the English reviewers in general, and some of the American reviewers, hailed the book as a masterful achievement, as a work of unmistakable originality, as one of "great interest and profit" (Lord Bryce), and as marking an epoch in English sociology (George Unwin). Robert E. Park, however, damned it as "thin, vague, insubstantial, and jejune."[27] It must be admitted that it is a youthful book and somewhat "over-written." But it contains an initial presentation of the views that were to sustain MacIver's sociological theory in the future.

---

24. *Community* pp. 89–90. Ernest Wallwork tries to rescue Durkheim from his difficulty by assigning to his view the label of "relational realism." It is doubtful, however, that Durkheim would have recognized himself under this label. See Wallwork, *Durkheim: Morality and Milieu* (Cambridge, Mass.: Harvard University Press, 1972), p. 18.

25. *Community*, pp. 90–91.

26. *Ibid.*, p. 70 (italics omitted).

27. Quoted from *As a Tale That Is Told*, p. 87. MacIver was especially annoyed by this last word. Actually (so fragile is memory), Park did not use the word. His adjectives were "vague, thin, plausible, and innocuous." The review is almost entirely negative. See *American Journal of Sociology* (January 1918): 542–544.

The Elements of Social Science

The small book (only 177 pages) bearing this title appeared in 1921. The ninth edition appeared in 1949, and it was frequently reprinted. It is not well known in the United States, although copies were still displayed in the section on current sociology in the bookstore of the London School of Economics as late as 1967. In it MacIver begins by telling us what society means:

> Wherever there is life there is society. For life can arise and continue only in its own presence, in the society of like beings. In the lower stages of development the society whence new life arises is incredibly brief and slight, a mere moment of conjunction or proximity, but in the higher stages life is always obviously social. It is born and nurtured in society, it finds its degree of fulfilment, its character, its limitation, in society. Society is more than our environment: it is our nature. It is within us as well as around us. Aristotle revealed this truth long ago when he defined man as a "social animal." All animals are in their degree social, but the highest is of necessity the most social.[28]

The force of this introductory paragraph, of course, is that there is a phenomenon known as society, that it is a universal, and that it merits inquiry in its own name and for its own sake. If this seems obvious to us today, it was not so, especially in the United Kingdom, when MacIver wrote. Indeed, he goes on to justify in more explicit terms the need to inquire, not only into such particular phenomena as the state, the law, and the economy but also into the more comprehensive phenomenon of society.

In the course of his discussion of "the elements" MacIver has occasion to treat the nature of society, the stages of society, society and environment, interests and associations, the structure of society, and the evolution of society. He begins to clarify and refine the concepts that will serve him in his later, and larger, *Society*—such concepts as community, association, and institution. "Society" itself is an abstract and universal concept, including "every kind and degree of relationship entered into by men," and meaning "the whole system of social relationships." He repeats his strictures on measurement, directed against those who believe that measurement is synonymous with science:

> We are apt to think we know what time is because we can measure it, but no sooner do we reflect upon it than the illusion goes.
>
> So it appears that the range of the measurable is not the range of the

28. *The Elements of Social Science*, 9th ed. (London: Methuen & Co. 1949), p. 1.

knowable. There are things we can measure, like time, but yet our minds do not grasp their meaning. There are things we cannot measure, like happiness or pain, and yet their meaning is perfectly clear to us. . . . It is only quantity we can measure, but it is only quality we can experience.[29]

Finally, only confusion can result from efforts to assign to the quest for sociological principles the sphere and method of the other sciences. These methodological views persist in MacIver's work and later become the platform of a protracted controversy with Lundberg.

As in the case of *Community,* it is unnecessary to pursue the argument and analysis of *The Elements* in detail. It is interesting to note, however, that both of these books contain the seeds that will effloresce in the more elaborate and more systematic *Society.*

Society

Society, MacIver's central contribution to sociological theory, appeared in three editions, the last with the collaboration of a former student, Charles H. Page, himself a sociologist of distinction.[30] It would not be profitable to compare the three editions, and in what follows, accordingly, I shall refer only to the last and, somewhat unfairly, shall use only the name of the senior author.

MacIver introduces the book with "A Word about Sociology Itself," in which he distinguishes the discipline from anthropology, economics, history, psychology, and social psychology and insists, as he did in *Community,* that the difference is one of focus of interest. Sociology alone of these disciplines focuses upon social relationships themselves, society itself. There is, of course, an economic aspect to the life of man, a legal aspect, an aesthetic aspect, a religious aspect, and so on, but "blending into them all is the social aspect." It is not altogether clear whether he considers the social as a category parallel to the economic and political, for example, in which case sociology is a special science, or a category that encompasses these others, in which case it is a general science.[31] But the weight of his emphasis suggests that it is the former he has in mind and that, like Tönnies, Simmel, and Znaniecki, and unlike Sorokin, he declines to consider sociology as a

29. *Ibid.*, pp. 14–15.

30. *Society: Its Structure and Changes* (New York: Ray Long & Richard Smith, 1932); *Society: A Textbook of Sociology* (New York: Farrar & Rinehart, 1937) and *Society: An Introductory Analysis* Rinehart and Co., 1949).

31. Compare Sorokin's paradigm and position, *Society, Culture, and Personality* (New York: Harper & Brothers, 1947), pp. 7–8.

generic inquiry or as an inquiry into "everything that happens" in society. Sociology deals with whatever relates man to man, and society is "the marvelously intricate and ever-changing pattern of the totality of these relationships.[32]

MacIver's initial task in writing about society is to honor the Aristotelian injunction to define his terms. In view of the looseness of ordinary speech it is an important task, a task that will doubtless never be finished. But MacIver made notable contributions to it and these contributions therefore merit some examination. We have offered an introductory definition of society. MacIver expatiates: "Society is a system of usages and procedures, of authority and mutual aid, of many groupings and divisions, of controls of human behavior and of liberties. This ever-changing, complex system we call society. It is the web of social relationships."[33] He notes that these relationships, like all social phenomena, are intangible and that they have a "psychic" dimension in that mutual awareness is essential. Without this mutual awareness there is no such thing as a social relationship, and no society. "Society exists only where social beings 'behave' toward one another in ways determined by their recognition of one another. Any relations so determined we may broadly name 'social.' "[34] These relationships also have a wide range. They may be hostile or friendly. But they all involve a sense of community:

> If there were no sense of community, if there were no co-operative undertakings by man, there would be no social systems, no society or societies—there would be practically nothing for sociologists to study. Hence the relationships which are central to sociology are those which involve both mutual recognition and the sense of something held or shared in common.[35]

Social relationships are not confined to man. There are insect and animal societies as well, and social relationships between different species (as between a man and his dog), but these MacIver does not intend to study.

Again like Aristotle, MacIver treats the roles of likeness and difference in social relationships and asserts that both are significant. In a favorable reference to his predecessor at Columbia, Giddings, he uses the convenient concept of "consciousness of kind." But difference is subordinate to likeness: "The division of labor in society is co-operation before it is division. For it is because people have *like* wants that they associate in the performance of unlike functions." Finally, he insists that Aristotle was never

32. *Society: An Introductory Analysis,* p. v.
33. *Ibid.*, p. 5.
34. *Ibid.*, p. 6.
35. *Ibid.*, p. 6.

more correct than when he said that man is a social animal.[36] Indeed, as we shall see, it is this assertion that serves MacIver as the base for his theory of the origin of government.

The second of MacIver's primary concepts is that of community.[37] The word *community* may connote a settlement, a village, a city, a tribe, a nation, or indeed the world. But two criteria require satisfaction, the first of which is a common territory and the second a common sentiment.[38] There are borderline cases—a convent, a prison, an ethnic group—but for the most part, when these criteria are satisfied, the test of community is that all of one's social relationships may be contained within it. Later on he devotes an entire chapter to this subject and especially considers the nation as a type of community.[39] The concept that contrasts most clearly with that of community is the concept of association. An association is a group organized for the pursuit of an interest, or group of interests, that the members have in common. It is not a community but an organized group within a community. It is appropriate to ask for what purpose it exists; the same question makes no sense when directed to the community. In the borderline cases an association may also be a community, at least temporarily, and so also in the case of a trading post or a company town.

Two other social groupings present difficulties in terms of these definitions, and MacIver immediately directs his attention to them. The first is the family. Here he decides that since husband and wife are contracting parties, with definite ends in view, the family is clearly an association. For the child, however, at least in the earlier years, it is a community. The state is also an association, an especially wide-ranging and important kind of association, but still one association among many. It is an agency of the community. Unfortunately, the same proper noun is used for both state and community. Thus, when we say that Sweden signed a treaty with Norway, we are talking about the state or, more correctly, the government, an association. When we say that Sweden imports all of her coal, we are talking about the community. Examples of associations are a trade union, a political party, a club, a church.

By the term *group* MacIver means "any collection of social beings who

36. *Ibid.*, p. 8. Aristotle went on to say that only a beast or a god is fit to live alone. To which the irreverent Nietzsche added, in the nineteenth century, "or a combination of both; that is, a philosopher." Actually, the expression is *zoon politikon*, but in Aristotle there is no distinction between the city-state and society.

37. Incidentally, Znaniecki frowned upon the use of both concepts, society and community. He always insisted, somewhat impishly, that he did not know what they meant.

38. On the first of these criteria, he apparently changed his mind. In *Community*, p. 73, he had written that community is a matter of degree, with no set bounds.

39. *Society*, chap. 12, pp. 296–304.

enter into distinctive social relationships with one another."[40] It is important to recognize that reciprocity is required, as are awareness and interaction. Not all sociologists accept this usage, although perhaps a majority does. It creates some difficulties, as we shall see.[41] In any event, an association is an organized group. Since social classes and crowds, for example, are not organized, they are not associations.

Neither, for MacIver, is an institution an association. On the contrary, he constructs a sharp distinction between them. If an association is an organized group, an institution is an established procedure. There are rules and regulations in associations, which govern their operations and define the relations of the members to one another; these are what he calls institutions. Every association has its own characteristic institutions; thus, the church has its sacraments and rituals, the family has marriage and the ceremonies of the home, the university has a lecture and examination system, and so on.[42] The distinction becomes quite clear when MacIver says that we can belong to an association but not to an institution. It is not so clear in ordinary speech. Thus, we often speak of a hospital or a university as an institution. Here, for sociological purposes, we have to attend to what we are talking about. If we are thinking of the hospital as an established procedure for healing and care of the sick, then it is an institution; if we are thinking instead of an organized group of administrators, doctors, and nurses, then it is an association. And similarly for the university. If we are thinking about it as a means or procedure for teaching, research, and learning, it is an institution; if, on the other hand, we are thinking of it as an organized group of administrators, teachers, and students, then it is an association.

Institutions arise not only in associations but also in the community. As examples of communal institutions, MacIver uses movie-going and dating. He refers to Sumner's distinction between crescive and enacted institutions, with the hint of a suggestion that communal institutions are crescive, and associational institutions, enacted. He immediately rejects the suggestion, however, on the ground that no institution can be said to have a definite beginning, and thus all are crescive. There is some ambiguity here, however, because on the succeeding page he refers to the "enacted instruments of associations" as institutions. It is one of the few ambiguities in MacIver's nomenclature. Institutions, finally, may be studied historically, comparatively, or functionally, the last of which concerns the interrela-

40. *Ibid.*, p. 14.

41. For further discussion of this point see Chapters 9, 10, this volume.

42. *Ibid.*, See p. 18, for a chart illustrating the relationships between associations, institutions, and interests.

tions they have with others. Thus, marital institutions are related to legal, kinship, property, and religious institutions.

The last of MacIver's basic concepts are customs, folkways, and mores. Customs are simply usages, modes of behavior, accepted procedures, accredited ways of acting. The difference between customs and institutions is one of degree. The latter implies a more definite recognition. Courtship practices are customs; marriage, an institution. The concept of institution stresses an impersonal factor in social relations; custom more often a personal one. We are more concerned about threats to our institutions, however, than we are to changing customs. We speak of "undermining" hallowed institutions, but seldom, if ever, of undermining customs.

Folkways and mores together seem to be synonymous with customs. In general MacIver follows, quotes, and approves of Sumner's definitions. With respect to the difference between the folkways and the mores, he suggests that when we view the folkways not merely as norms of behavior but as regulators of behavior, then they are mores. On the other hand, the folkways also regulate behavior, and so he surrenders the difference. Indeed, he goes further and warns us against distinguishing between folkways and mores. The latter are the former in their capacity as instruments of social control. MacIver rejects Sumner's distinction between the folkways and mores—that the latter but not the former are conducive to societal welfare—and suggests only that there are degrees of compulsion and of conformity. He treats briefly the variety of the mores, their origins in chance rather than contrivance, and their conservatism. Finally, the mores have three functions: they determine much of individual behavior, they identify the individual with the group, and they are the guardians of group solidarity.

I have treated MacIver's definitions at some length because of their importance as contributions to the nomenclature of sociological theory. For the most part they are lucid, and straightforward. The distinctions between community, association, and institution are especially sharp and useful. Sorokin's criticism of MacIver's concepts as "unnecessary duplications of the same thing" is without merit, especially because he introduces distinctions of his own that, by comparison, are almost wholly devoid of precision.[43] If a few minor ambiguities remain, these have been clarified and the concepts refined by later writers. When we consider the time in which MacIver constructed his definitions—a time of much conceptual confusion and a total absence of a standardized terminology—his achievement seems meritorious indeed.

The task of definition completed, MacIver turns to more substantive

43. Sorokin, *Society, Culture, and Personality*, p. 86.

concerns. Like Ratzenhofer and Small before him, he takes as his starting point the concept of interests and develops a distinction between interests and attitudes, the former being subjective, the latter, their objects. Thus, friend and enemy are interests; love and fear are attitudes.[44] He even essays a classification of attitudes based upon such rubrics (in columns) as "dissociative," "restrictive," and "associative," and (in rows) attitudes implying inferiority, superiority, and neutrality. It is a curious exercise and plays no part in his subsequent discussion. He treats briefly, and with some skepticism, the possibility of measuring attitudes in any mathematical sense—thus joining a controversy that roiled the intellectual waters in the 1930s—and suggests certain limitations in the practice of polling public opinion. Statistical techniques such as these, however superficially useful, can never provide *understanding*, a word he italicizes but does not elevate to the status of a method, as the Neo-Kantians and Max Weber did.[45]

At this point, however, MacIver is more interested in a distinction between the like and the common, and this is one that he frequently employs.[46] Like interests are those we have distributively, each to himself; common interests are those we have collectively, the interests we share without possibility of division or distribution. Thus, students have like interests in grades, credits, courses, and degrees at their university; they have a common interest in its prestige.[47] Attitudes are never common, but interests frequently are. And it is when men identify themselves with a social group and become attached to it that they have a sense of having

44. Although the words are different the distinction is similar to that drawn by Thomas and Znaniecki between attitudes and values in the Methodological Note to *The Polish Peasant in Europe and America.*

45. On *Verstehen*, see the important paper by Theodore Abel, "The Operation Called Verstehen," *American Journal of Sociology* 54 (November 1948): 211–218. See also Marcello Truzzi, ed, *Verstehen: Subjective Understanding in the Social Sciences* (Reading, Mass.: Addison-Wesley, 1974), in which Abel's paper is reprinted, and Truzzi's extensive bibliography on the subject, pp. 165–173. One may speculate that the German word *Verstehen* carries more weight than the English *understanding* and doubt that in English it would ever have attained the stature of a method. But see n. 1 in Abel's article.

46. It appears first in *Community*, p. 103. The same distinction, between distributive and corporate interests, is also found in E. T. Hiller, *Social Relations and Structures* (New York: Harper & Brothers, 1947), p. 253.

47. In a later section, on associations and interests, MacIver redefines the distinction:

> We shall speak of *like* interest when two or more persons severally or distributively pursue a like object or value, each for himself; we shall speak of *common* interest when two or more persons seek a goal or objective which is one and indivisible for them all, which unites them with one another in a quest that cannot be resolved merely into an aggregate of individual quests. Like interests are individualized; common interests are necessarily shared.

Society, p. 440. Both kinds of interests are served by associations. He will later also distinguish between like-interest crowds and common-interest crowds.

something in common, that they in fact "belong." Inclusion, however, means, also and inevitably, exclusion, and so we have the "we" and the "they," the in-group and out-group of Sumner. One of the problems of our time is the inability of the nations to rise above their separate concerns and realize their common interest in a more inclusive community.

Every systematic thinker in sociology must at some time come to grips with the geographical and biological factors that have something to do with the structure of society and that influence the cultural variations within it. This obligation MacIver does not neglect. His treatment is a balanced one, one that appreciates the significance of both heredity and environment and one that does not overestimate the role of either. He distinguishes between what he calls the outer environment, including the material culture of a society, and the inner environment, synonymous with the social heritage. The "social heritage" is a concept that MacIver prefers to "culture," although the latter term has now become standard in the literature.[48] He reserves the word *culture* for a later distinction that he will make between culture and civilization. We need not pursue his treatment of the social heritage except to say that it depends to some extent upon an earlier treatment of Graham Wallas[49] and follows a fairly orthodox but important course.

MacIver comes into his own, as it were, when he turns to the social structure itself and delineates in detail what he calls "the sustaining forces of code and custom." Here he is interested in social cohesion and social control, in codes and sanctions, in the folkways and mores. His general label for these latter phenomena is the *social codes*, a term also used on occasion by Sumner but one now more or less discarded for the more prevalent use of *norm*, a word that MacIver also uses in a definition:

> The folkways and mores represent the *norms* or *modes* of procedure in a society or in a group—they present to us the most frequent or most accepted or most standardized ways of doing this or that. They are also, as we have seen, regulative, exerting pressure upon individual and group to conform to the norms.[50]

The codes themselves are sustained by sanctions, sanctions of reward and penalty, and especially the latter. MacIver finds four principal kinds of social codes: associational, communal, moral, and legal. Although he was an ingenious taxonomist, this classification leaves something to be desired. In the first place, it exhibits no clear *fundamentum divisionis*. In the second

48. There is still disagreement, however, over whether to include material elements in its denotation.

49. *Our Social Heritage* (New Haven, Conn.: Yale University Press, 1921).

50. *Society*, pp. 138–139.

place, the adjectives *associational* and *communal* exhaust a universe of discourse—all codes are one or the other. The moral code, to which MacIver gives independent status, is obviously a communal code, and the legal code is just as obviously an associational code in accordance with his own treatment of the state as one of the associations of society.

In the third place, he finds an ambiguity in "the moral code," which it does not in fact possess:

> Sometimes it means those rules of conduct which are held by the group or community to be right and proper and which they impose on deviating members by various degrees of the same sanctions which are the guardians of custom in general. In this sense morals are simply those customs the violation of which is regarded in the community as definitely wrong—in a word, they are the *mores.* But in the stricter sense the moral code is that body of rules which the individual "conscience" upholds as constituting right or good conduct. Here there appears, sometimes in harmony with, and sometimes in opposition to, the social sanction, an inner and personal sanction, the feeling of guilt entailed by violation.[51]

Although he admits that "for most of our daily occasions mores are nearly synonymous with morals," MacIver forfeits one of the great insights of Sumner[52] and one of the great contributions that sociology has made to moral philosophy. The mores are not "nearly synonymous" with morals; they are identical with morals—unless one wants to posit some extrasocial source of morality and some extrasocial source of guilt. What this source might be, however, is a question on which MacIver is silent. It is clearly the case, as he indicates, that an individual may feel a moral obligation contrary to the prescriptions of the group, but in these cases he is conforming to the moral obligations prescribed by some other group—perhaps an earlier group in history. A physician's conscience may prescribe the destruction of a monstrously deformed infant (the illustration MacIver uses in this connection), in violation of both the communal and the legal code. But the conscience itself can have no other source than society. MacIver's own concept of the multigroup society should have deflected this error, especially if "multigroup" is construed in a diachronic and not merely a synchronic sense. Again, the notion that morals may vary from individual to individual whereas the mores characterize the group or the community, which MacIver also entertains, is one that cannot be sustained.

MacIver justifies his separation of the legal code from the others. The legal code is the one code—apart from such exceptions as may be found in the family, the play group, the college fraternity, and the criminal

51. *Ibid.*, p. 141.

52. Sumner's own usage, however, as we have seen lacks consistency.

gang—that possesses the ultimate sanction of physical force. Outside the legal code the use of force is illegitimate, but this proposition is almost entirely tautological. One of the exceptions warrants an additional comment. That a parent may use physical force to restrain a child from touching a hot stove or running into the path of an automobile would be denied by no one. The legal code sanctions such an act and the moral code requires it.[53]

In a succeeding section MacIver gives appropriate recognition to the fact that neither hope of reward nor fear of punishment suffices to explain individual conformity to the codes. Other processes are also at work, including especially indoctrination and habituation. These are processes that help to perpetuate the mores.

MacIver is most incisive when he distinguishes between authority and leadership—a necessary distinction and one often confounded. Authority is impersonal, leadership personal. Authority requires an office, leadership does not. The policeman, the judge, and the monarch represent authority, but all three may be devoid of leadership qualities. Finally, MacIver gives his approval to Weber's concept of charismatic authority, although it is significant that he refers to it as charismatic leadership, which in fact, and contrary to Weber, it is. MacIver regards both authority and leadership as sources of social power, but here he is almost certainly mistaken. Authority is one of the resultants of power, not its source, and leadership is not a power phenomenon at all.[54]

The importance MacIver ascribes to ritual and ceremony may be indicated by his definitions:

> By ritual we mean a formal *rhythmic procedure* controlling a succession of acts directed to the *same end* and *repeated* without variation on the appropriate occasions. Ritual is distinguished from mere habit or routine in that it is accompanied by a peculiar sense of rightness and inevitability. To deviate from it in any way, no matter what the circumstances, is felt to be wrong or undesirable, not on utiliatrian grounds, but because deviation breaks the rhythm, disturbing the emotional response, the solemn and often "mystical" rapport between the person and the occasion.[55]

Ritual may have either a personal or a group character, the former when it assumes an emotional or compulsive character and becomes a habit. And again, "Ritual invests an occasion with importance or solemnity and thus combats the process by which often-repeated acts become tedious and com-

53. MacIver offers an expanded chart of codes and sanctions, *ibid.*, p. 143.

54. See Robert Bierstedt, "The Problem of Authority," in the MacIver Festschrift, *Freedom and Control in Modern Society*, ed. Morroe Berger, Theodore Abel, and Charles H. Page (New York: D. Van Nostrand Co. 1954), reprinted in Bierstedt, *Power and Progress: Essays on Sociological Theory* (New York: McGraw-Hill, 1974).

55. *Society*, p. 150.

monplace."[56] Ceremony is a more inclusive concept than ritual. It means "*any* established procedure of a formal and dignified nature designed to make and impress the importance of an event or occasion."[57] Ceremony lacks the rhythmic and repetitive character of ritual, but both introduce cohesion into the cohort of men, and both support the social order. Finally, MacIver emphasizes the importance of symbols, including, for example, the totem and the flag, in marking and reinforcing the unity of the group: "Indoctrination and habituation could not take place, leadership and authority would be at a loss, ritual and ceremony would be rendered meaningless, were it not that social man has the ability to create and to use *symbols.*"[58]

Brief excerpts cannot convey the lucidity of MacIver's analysis. He is at his best perhaps in discussing the role of force, or coercion, in society. As to definition:

> Whenever men act, or refrain from acting, in a manner different from that which they themselves have chosen or would choose in a given situation, *because others deliberately limit the range of their choice* either directly, through present control over it, or indirectly, through the threat of consequences, they may be said to be under *coercion.*[59]

There are as many forms of coercion as there are forms of social power, but the ultimate form is physical force or, as Bertrand Russell called it, "naked power."[60] Like Russell, MacIver regards force as essential in society. Without its final sanction the social order itself would be insecure. An entire paragraph requires quotation:

> Physical force cannot, as the anarchists claim, be abolished altogether from the social system. For there must always exist some socialized force to restrain the antisocial manifestations of force itself, whether exerted by individuals or by organized groups. It is necessary to restrain within limits the self-interest, the greed, the lawlessness, the intolerance ever ready to assert its will over others. It is necessary for the maintenance of any system of rights and obligations in a complex society. No rule is secure if the heedless or the unscrupulous or the dissident can transgress it with impunity. It is necessary to settle the disputes that arise eternally among men and that, were there no appeal to a force-invested authority, would issue in the violence of individuals or groups

56. *Ibid.*

57. *Ibid.*, p. 151. One may offer the slight remonstrance that ceremony need not be dignified. Many ceremonies have the contrary character. MacIver has forgotten the ceremony of the rector's address (it is the sole function of this official) at Edinburgh University, which the students ceremonialize by throwing vegetables and fruit onto the rostrum.

58. *Ibid.*, p. 153.

59. *Ibid.*, p. 155.

60. In *Power* (London: George Allen & Unwin, 1938), pp. 84–107.

> against one another. It is necessary also to curb the encroachments of stronger organizations over weaker ones, or of organizations, such as the economic, over those who are otherwise at the mercy of the powers they wield. There are fundamental forms of order and of security which can be maintained only under laws all must obey. The real service of force is as a safeguard of this order.[61]

Force, when rightly used, is the servant of liberty. It is the *ultima ratio* of society.[62]

In the following chapter, entitled "The Major Social Codes," MacIver again discusses the varieties of social codes and again offers a classification. We now have five major types: religious codes, moral codes, legal codes, the codes of custom, and the codes of fashion. He is interested, he says, in contrasting religion and morals, custom and law, and custom and fashion. His reason for distinguishing between the religious code and the moral code is that the former is supported by a "suprasocial" sanction. Again I take issue with him. No one would deny that there is a difference between religion and morality, between what is "sinful" and what is wrong, between an action that presumably offends divine beings and one that offends human beings. But to suggest that there is such a thing as a "suprasocial" or a supernatural sanction is unnecessary, not to say erroneous. Eternal damnation as a sanction for the commission of sins is a fear that can only be socially instilled and can have no source outside society. Sanctions ranging from penance to excommunication are applied by people, acting under authority granted them by an association to which they belong, and are thus social in exactly the same sense that other sanctions are. The belief that one may be punished directly by deities or by demons, however firmly held, could not, to be sure, arise without religion, but religion is a social phenomenon.[63]

The distinction between the code of custom and the legal code, on the other hand, is an apposite one. The former is supported by the community, the latter by the state. Both are social codes, but the latter is also associational because the state is an association and the community is not.[64] Law is

---

61. *Society*, p. 156.

62. MacIver also notes that however essential force may be, it is nevertheless a limited and inefficient device. It is the negation of cooperation, the denial of sociality. Traffic lights at heavily traveled intersections are more effective than machine guns would be. Force is most successful when it is least obtrusive. For a more recent treatment, see William J. Goode, "The Place of Force in Human Society," *American Sociological Review* (October 1972): 507–519.

63. As Lecky observed, in a quite different context, Christianity is an admirable auxiliary to the police force. W. E. H. Lecky, *History of the Rise and Influence of the Spirit of Rationalism in Europe*, 2 vols., rev. ed. (1865), vol. 1, p. 167.

64. We need not argue here whether there is such a thing as primitive law. Books have been written on the subject. But it is an extension of the concept of law that MacIver is not inclined to accept. The matter is wholly semantic and presents no substantive issue.

enacted, custom is not. Here again Sumner's word *crescive* is useful. There are often conflicts between law and custom, and between religion and the mores, but these are large areas of inquiry into which—beyond acknowledging them—we need not enter here. Fashion MacIver well defines as "the socially approved sequence of variation on a customary theme."[65] He distinguishes fashion from custom on the ground that the former is the more changeful and superficial and the latter, more traditional and enduring. Fashion satisfies two contrary needs—the need for novelty and the need for conformity. Convention and etiquette, separately defined, are both regarded as aspects of custom.[66] On the distinction between custom and habit he is clear and perceptive. They reinforce each other, but the former is social and the latter individual.

Although it may be, at base, a philosophical rather than a sociological problem, no sociologist can avoid the question of the relationship between the individual and society. MacIver refers to it often. He treats it in some detail in a chapter entitled "Social Codes and the Individual Life." The necessary sociological emphasis upon the existence and operation of the social codes may leave the impression that the individual is merely a creature of the codes, merely a product of society.[67] No one escapes the pressure of dominant groups, the pressure of authority, the pressure of institutions.[68] But there are conflicts between the codes and between the in-

---

65. *Society*, p. 181.

66. *Ibid.*, p. 183.

67. On this subject, see the now classic article by Dennis H. Wrong, "The Oversocialized Conception of Man in Modern Sociology," *American Sociological Review* 26 (April 1961): 183–193.

68. Durkheim also had some pertinent observations:

> The coercive power that we attribute to it is so far from being the whole of the social fact that it can present the opposite character equally well. Institutions may impose themselves upon us, but we cling to them; they compel us, and we love them; they constrain us, and we find our welfare in our adherence to them and in this very constraint.

And again:

> Because beliefs and social practices thus come to us from without, it does not follow that we receive them passively or without modification. In reflecting on collective institutions and assimilating them for ourselves, we individualize them and impart to them more or less personal characteristics. Similarly, in reflecting on the physical world, each of us colors it after his own fashion, and different individuals adapt themselves differently in the same physical environment. It is for this reason that each one of us creates, in a measure, his own morality, religion, and mode of life. There is no conformity to social convention that does not comprise an entire range of individual shades. It is nonetheless true that this field of variations is a limited one. It verges on nonexistence or is very restricted in that circle of religious and moral affairs where deviation easily becomes crime. It is wider in all that concerns economic life. But, sooner or later, even in the latter instance, one encounters the limit that cannot be crossed.

Preface to the second edition, in *The Rules of Sociological Method*, ed. George E. G. Catlin, 8th ed. (Glencoe, Ill.: Free Press of Glencoe, 1962), nn., pp. liv, lvi.

dividual and the codes, and in these conflicts the individual makes choices, uses his own judgment, and finds his moral liberty. There are eloquent passages here, many of which encourage quotation. There is space for only one:

> *In so far as* the social order reflects the common interests of men, which must be shared in order to be realized, the individual is both free within, and sustained in his individuality by, society. In this situation, he is able to say "we" instead of merely "I," and thereby to liberate important elements of his socially dependent personality. For he finds *himself* also in that which he shares with others, in identifying himself with a common cause, in the exercise of his individuality through devotion to his family or community or nation or political party or business or trade-union or cultural group. In this devotion he loses his isolation and finds his individuality. Were it otherwise the group could not evoke as it does man's greater loyalties and enthusiams and aspirations.
>
> The deeper loyalty, therefore, is not that which slavishly follows the social code—"my country, right or wrong"—but that which responds to it in the spirit and the obligation of the common cause for which it, however imperfectly, stands. The individual who slavishly follows the code of nation or class or religion or other group is unconscious of or unfitted for a greater social obligation. Within him society has, paradoxically, no deep roots. He is bound to the code by the superficial and uncreative bonds of imitation and compliance: he reflects but does not express society.[69]

A central theoretical concern in sociology, of course, is the nature and types of groups, and to this subject MacIver makes a distinctive, although imperfect, contribution. First, he reminds us that social relationships—some degree of reciprocity and mutual awareness—are necessary criteria of a group and that people of the same age or income or intelligence when considered together are better thought of as statistical aggregates. He then refers to previous efforts to systematize the classification of groups by Simmel, von Wiese and Becker, Sanderson, and Logan Wilson and utilizes the now orthodox concepts of Cooley, Sumner, and Giddings—the primary group, in-group and out-group, and consciousness of kind. Omitting what is orthodox in his long discussion, I shall treat only his own classification. It is entitled "Schematic View of Major Types of Groups in the Social Structure," and it contains three major categories, with illustrations, as follows:

I. Inclusive territorial unities
   Generic type: community
   Specific types: tribe, nation, region, city, village, neighborhood
II. Interest-conscious unities without definite organization
   Generic type (a): social class

69. *Society*, p. 208.

Specific types: caste, elite, competitive class, corporate class
Generic type (b): ethnic and "racial" groups
Specific types: color groups, immigrant groups, nationality groups
Generic type (c): crowd
Specific types: like-interest crowd, common-interest crowd

III. Interest-conscious unities with definite organization
Generic type (a): primary group
Specific types: family, play group, clique, club
Generic type (b): large association
Specific types: state, church, economic corporation, labor union, etc.[70]

The classification of groups is not an easy exercise, as those who have attempted it will readily testify. This is one of the reasons, perhaps, why there is no standard classification in the literature. We have had no Linnaeus and no Mendeleev, and, consequently, no satisfactory list of social genera and species, no periodic table of social elements. Our classifications are as primitive as the pre-Socratic classification of the physical elements into earth, air, fire, and water. This is surprising in view of the fact that if there is one concept that is primordial and central in sociology it is the concept of the group. This situation, in fact, is one of the serious deficiencies in sociological theory.

MacIver's effort to repair the deficiency, although far superior to Sorokin's, is nevertheless a disappointment. With the admission that nothing is easier than criticism, let us look at some of the questionable features of his classification. In order to be acceptable a classification must satisfy three logical criteria: It must have a single *fundamentum divisionis* (i.e., a single basis of classification must be used throughout); its categories must be mutually exclusive and clearly so (i.e., there must be one and only one place into which every item fits); and it must be inclusive of its subject (i.e., it must have a place for every kind of the items it arranges). Unfortunately, MacIver's classification satisfies none of these criteria. In the first place, there is no single *fundamentum divisionis.* Here we are given two—territorial unities and interest-conscious unities. We are offered territorial unities versus (presumably) nonterritorial unities, interest-conscious unities versus (presumably) non-interest-conscious unities, generic and specific types with and without definite organization, and large associations versus (presumably) small associations. In the second place, the classification advertises its lack of inclusivity by the appearance of the "etc." at the end. In the third place, the second rule is violated in a number

70. *Ibid.*, p. 215.

of instances, of which we shall attend to only a few. Nationality groups appear as interest-conscious unities, although tribes, nations, regions, cities, villages, and neighborhoods do not in this respect. One wonders how a nation differs from a nationality group. Economic corporations assuredly have definite organization, but apparently a corporate class does not. Assignment of the primary group to the category of unities with definite organization is almost certainly a mistake. Similarly, cliques need not be organized; nor do factions. There is no place for committees—a ubiquitous form of association in complex societies—and none for small associations, such as a small business or a local conservation society. We need not multiply examples. Finally, although MacIver insists upon reciprocity, there is no clear sense in which the members of "color groups," social classes, and corporations always interact with one another to form a group. We may conclude these observations on MacIver's classification of groups with the comment that, for whatever reason, his work on this subject does not conform to his own high taxonomic standards.

The subject of groups concludes MacIver's treatment of the components of the social structure. In the remaining chapters of this part of *Society*, he discusses particular groups, including the family; the community; city, country, and region; social class and caste; ethnic and racial groups; herd, crowd, and mass communication; associations and interests; three kinds of "great associations"—the political, the economic, and the cultural—and a final phenomenon called functional systems, in which he makes a distinction between culture and civilization.[71] On all of these subjects he has wise and penetrating observations, of which there is space to note only a few.

The chapter on class and caste in the 1949 edition of *Society* is considerably more comprehensive and detailed than the one in the 1937 edition, and one may suppose that many of the additions were contributed by Charles H. Page.[72] In both places, however, MacIver denies that class can be defined by any purely objective criterion, even the economic. "Economic division does not unite people and separate them from others

71. In this distinction he follows Alfred Weber (*Kulturgeschichte als Kultursoziologie*) in regarding those things we want for themselves—a picture, a poem, a cathedral—as belonging to the cultural order and the technological equipment required to create them as belonging to the civilization order. Thus, a novel is a part of culture; the typewriter on which it is written, a part of civilization. It was doubtless MacIver's desire to retain this connotation for the concept of culture that induced him to use "the social heritage" for the more inclusive connotation. The distinction appears also in *The Modern State* and in *Social Causation*. It aroused Sorokins's ire in *Social and Cultural Dynamics*, 4 vols. (New York: American Book Co., 1937–1941), vol. 4, chap. 4.

72. Page wrote his doctoral dissertation, 1940, at Columbia under MacIver's supervision. See his admirable new Introduction to *Class and American Sociology: From Ward to Ross*, rev. ed. (New York: Schocken Books, 1969).

unless they *feel* their unity or separation."[73] Class is thus a social phenomenon, not an economic one, and may be defined quite simply as "any portion of a community marked off from the rest by social status." And continuing, "A *system* or *structure* of social classes involves, first, a hierarchy of status groups, second, the recognition of the superior–inferior stratification, and, finally, some degree of permanency of the structure."[74] Status distinctions can be found in almost every society and even in its various parts. Thus, there are class distinctions in the slums and in penitentiaries, as well as in societies at large. When class status is fixed at birth and remains almost wholly stable, then we have the phenomenon of caste.

In both editions MacIver refers, without agreement, to the treatments of the subject by Weber and Marx. In both editions too he introduces an important distinction between "corporate class consciousness" on the one hand and "competitive class feeling" on the other. The two are not only different but also, in fact, antagonistic. The first unites an entire group; the second determines the interactions of individuals without involving recognition of group membership. In a society with high social mobility, competitive class feeling will far outweigh corporate class consciousness and indeed reduce the latter to insignificance. Insofar as the United States is concerned, Veblen's emphasis upon emulation, competition, display, and conspicuous consumption seems to MacIver to be much more appropriate than Marx's emphasis upon class consciousness. It is this distinction that renders Marxian theory inadequate as a treatment of social class in general and especially in societies such as that of the United States. The sentiment of equality, which has always informed the American ideology; the Puritan ethic, which sanctifies work as such; and high occupational mobility all tend to heighten competitive class feeling and to discourage the formation of a corporate class consciousness. Furthermore, Marxian theory takes quite inadequate account of the middle class, which is so prominent a phenomenon in the United States.[75] In sum, class as a phenomenon of corporate consciousness in which individuals are engaged in a common struggle is one thing; class as a spur to individual competition is quite another.

In his discussion of crowds and other unorganized and temporary groups, MacIver utilizes his earlier distinction between the like and the common. Thus, there are like-interest crowds (people assembled to watch a fire or the aftermath of an accident) and common-interest crowds (those who gather to participate in a national celebration, such as a Fourth of July

73. *Society*, p. 349.

74. *Ibid.*, pp. 348–349.

75. MacIver's disagreement with Weber is slight. Although Weber talked about status groups, his conception of class was essentially economic.

parade), and both of these again may be focused (a panic crowd, a lynching mob) or unfocused (a street aggregation, a victory celebration). In a like-interest crowd the presence of others interferes with the participation of each; in a common-interest crowd the participants sense their solidarity and everyone works together in support of an interest, a goal, or a cause. In neither case, however, should we attribute to a crowd—despite the loss of individuality it sometimes exhibits—anything like a group mind. As we have seen, the concept of a group mind is a literary device that calls attention to increased interstimulation and a heightened suggestibility but is otherwise devoid of meaning.

In the final chapters of the section on social structure, MacIver treats associations and interests and presents a classification of the former in terms of the latter.[76] Associations satisfy both like and common interests but any classification is afflicted by four complications: The professed interest is not always the determinant interest;[77] the professed interest is modified by variant conditions; the main interest is sometimes difficult to determine;[78] and some important interests (e.g., interest in acquiring prestige or distinction) do not necessarily create specific associations.

MacIver goes on to discuss three kinds of "great associations"—the political, the economic, and the cultural.[79] It is not necessary to follow this discussion in detail. Once more, however, in his treatment of political associations, he insists that the state is an agency of the community but that it is a limited agency, one among many. Some functions are peculiar to the state because only the state can perform them (e.g., the maintenance of the legal order). For the performance of others the state is well adapted (e.g., conservation of resources); for still others it is ill adapted (e.g., the arbitration of scientific endeavor and of religious controversies); and, finally, there are functions that the state is incapable of performing (e.g., the governance of taste, opinion, or morality). He realizes, of course, that controversies of great and historic moment reside precisely in these issues. His own views, however, are consistent with those to which he gave expression during his entire career as a political philosopher. They are something more. They represent a defense of democracy on sociological grounds; that is, if the state is incapable of performing certain kinds of functions, then it is futile to make the effort. Totalitarian states, which seek to govern every avenue of life, are therefore bound to fail.

In the last part of *Society* MacIver turns his attention to the problem of

76. *Ibid.*,p. 447.

77. Compare Merton's distinction between manifest and latent functions.

78. Is the main interest of a denominational college religious or educational?

79. Religious associations, social clubs, and learned societies are examples of the cultural.

social change. He presents no grandiose theory, after the fashion of a Spengler or a Sorokin, but rather presents a mild version of evolutionary theory. Once again we attend to some of his distinctions. Beginning with the neutral word of *change* itself, he tells us that process is change plus continuity, evolution is process plus direction, and progress is evolution toward a desirable goal. Thus, the distinctions between change, process, evolution, and progress become clear. The last is wholly subjective and can only mean an ever-more-complete realization of the values we cherish. As to evolutionary theory, that Herbert Spencer indulged in some insupportable generalizations should not induce us to depreciate the principle itself. Just as there are cyclical rhythms in the processes of society, so also are there evolutionary ones. Differentiation, for example, is an evolutionary process, and there is no question that it occurs. Wherever in society we discern an increasing specialization—not necessarily novelty and not necessarily increasing complexity—then we see the evolutionary principle at work. It manifests itself in such social processes an an increasing division of labor, an increase in the number and variety of associations and institutions, and in a greater diversity and refinement of the instruments of communication.

Succeeding chapters deal with biological (including demographic), technological (including economic), and cultural factors in social change. MacIver rejects altogether the Marxist claim of economic determinism on the ground that it is a gross oversimplification, if, indeed, it is not a gross error. He finally rejects any deterministic theory of social change: "Certainly human nature is always responsive to environment, but *how* it responds may depend on its own creative character as well as on the environment it in part creates."[80] A deterministic explanation of social change underestimates the complexity of the relationship between life and environment and between man and his social heritage. The human mind, and not only the environment, is a factor to be reckoned with in the vast and incessant processes of social change.

> The dogma that human nature does not change (from within) would make it an anomaly in the cosmos. If the configurations of the earth are changeful, if the skies themselves are so changeful that we can discern their inconstancy through the abysmal depths of space, if every living thing bears the signs of its own different past, if man's body has evolved from something anthropoid and beyond that from shapes of dim age-buried creatures—how can one share the assurance that his mind, so restless and energetic, so uniquely purposeful, remains miraculously the same, or is so lacking in character, in the quality of development, that is forever merely reflects a changing environment? If no two

80. *Ibid.*, p. 572.

offspring of the same family are quite alike, if in truth men display remarkable diversities of disposition, why should the race be immutable or reveal no trend of change within itself? If man follows forever his unresting purposes, visioned before they are realized in space and time, why should not these too prepare a path of change and how can they be dismissed as the only inefficacious realities in the whole scheme of things?[81]

The questions are rhetorical, but they clearly point to MacIver's disinclination to accept any deterministic doctrine. Unfortunately, he does not systematically expand upon his appreciation of the role of mind in the social process.

MacIver's reluctance to attribute causal efficacy to any external factor, whether the environmental, technological, or economic, does not extend to the cultural factor, which indeed exerts an influence. The apparatus of civilization is indifferent to the uses to which it is put. Culture steers the course. Thus, MacIver utilizes his distinction between civilization and culture as follows:

The civilizational means may be represented by a ship which can set sail to various ports. The port we sail to remains a cultural choice. Without the ship we could not sail at all; according to the character of the ship we sail fast or slow, take longer or shorter voyages; our lives are also accommodated to the conditions on shipboard and our experiences vary accordingly. But the direction in which we travel is not predestined by the design of the ship.[82]

Goal or purpose is thus set by culture; civilization is the means of its attainment.

In reading MacIver's discussion of cultural factors in social change, it is necessary to remember that he is using the word *culture* in his own (and Alfred Weber's) special sense, and not in the sense in which it is used in sociology and anthropology today. It is akin to what other writers call values or ideas or ideologies. Thus, it is a category to which religious doctrines belong, and so too beliefs about the role of sex in human life, the ideas of prophets and creative minds in producing cultural styles, and economic ideologies. With respect to the last of these, MacIver notices the ultimate self-contradiction in the Marxist theory of social change. It is not changing modes of production that can explain the Russian revolution and the subsequent history of the Soviet Union, but it is rather the Marxist philosophy itself. The important factor is not economic but ideological or, as MacIver would have it, cultural.[83] Culture, in short, is both a direct

81. *Ibid.*, p. 572.

82. *Ibid.*, p. 581.

83. The entire paragraph reads as follows:

Curiously enough, the determinist school has provided the supreme illustration of the influence of cultural attitudes on society. It is not possible to explain the Soviet Revolution along the lines of

source of social change and, in its impact upon the technological order, an indirect one.

Weber's thesis on the Protestant ethic would seem to be a superior example of MacIver's own contentions concerning the role of culture. He is nevertheless somewhat sparing in his praise of it and finally regards it as less than conclusive. One difficulty is that the relationship Weber tried to establish is more complex than Weber supposed. Another is that we can find other instances of the rise of capitalism, as in late-nineteenth-century Japan, where Protestantism was absent. MacIver will concede only that cultural values create social systems and that every change in valuation is reflected in institutional change.

Although he takes great pains to dissociate himself from any simplistic theory of evolution—the notion, for example, that there is a linear sequence of development in which the institutions of simpler societies pass by similar processes into the institutions of advanced societies—MacIver nevertheless commits himself to an evolutionary theory that sees the emergence of more specific forms of social institutions from the less specific.[84] The general line of evolution may be seen in the movement from communal custom to differentiated association. The formation of institutions around nuclei of interests usually precedes—often by a long interval—the formation of associations. In communal customs, political, economic, familial, religious, and cultural usages are fused. They come to be differentiated first into communal institutions and then into the differentiated associations of the state, the corporation, the family, the church, the school, and so on. In the increasing diversity of communal life lies hidden the germ of a new associational order, the order that characterizes complex societies.

In a discussion of progress, MacIver advances the view that progress must not be confused with evolution, that it can have no universally accepted reference, and that it is indeed a subjective concept. Is progress then one of those "alien, intrusive concepts" that prevent us from seeing society as it is? This question, to which a negative answer is implied, leads to a consideration of the degree to which social science is or ought to be value

---

> Marx's "materialistic interpretation of history." That revolution was not inspired by the necessity to adjust the culture of Russia to the existing economic situation or to that of the other capitalistic countries. It was the social philosophy of Marxism, wrought into a dynamic evangelism and finding its opportunity in the suffering and disillusionment of a catastrophic war, which gained control of the economic and political order, and by persistent cultural propaganda, aided by the terrorism of the Revolution, transformed it over a vast feudalized territory.

Ibid., p. 581.

84. As early as 1931, in the first edition of *Society*, MacIver recognized that it was already fashionable to minimize the significance of evolutionary theory. See page 423 of that edition.

free. MacIver's conclusion is straightforward: "The only clear and indubitable sense in which sociology can be value-free is that in dealing with value-facts the sociologist should never suffer his own valuations to intrude into or affect his presentations of the valuations which are registered in the facts themselves."[85] Social science can nevertheless enter the area of value judgments in two ways: it can test the adequacy of evidence in support of value judgments, and it can test the validity of value conclusions insofar as they are supported by premises containing statements of fact. Finally, with respect to progress, itself a value judgment, we can deny its reality, but we cannot dispense with it as a concept. "To live is to act, and to act is to choose, and to choose is to evaluate."[86] Progress is a historical fact to be reckoned with in the study of social change. It may be a myth, but it is a vital one. It may not be susceptible to scientific scrutiny, but it is an ineradicable part of the creative strivings of life.

Social Causation

Some have contended that *Social Causation* (1942) is MacIver's most successful book. Others have expressed a contrary opinion. Some have been especially dubious about a sociologist's effort to vindicate a principle, namely, the principle of causality, which 2000 years of philosophical analysis had been unable to do. Aristotle, of course, was the author of the original classification of causes—formal, final, material, and efficient—and if the first two of these had received a medieval emphasis, it was the last two that informed the scientific inquiries of the more modern age. But no one had been able to answer the skeptical Scot, who maintained that we experience only succession, not causation, that we have a sensation of succession and a succession of sensations, but no sensation of causation. The difficulty—not to say impossibility—of refuting Hume had induced some twentieth-century thinkers to surrender the principle altogether and to opt instead for a principle of probability. But all inquiry, except that which has only description or taxonomy as its goal, depends upon the validity of the category of causation. Without it inquiry fails. Without it "the world of nature dissolves into pure confusion and the world of history into pure caprice."[87] Without it knowledge itself becomes fortuitous, and scientific

85. *Society*, p. 617 (italics omitted).
86. *Ibid.*, p. 619.
87. Robert Bierstedt, *The Social Order*, 4th ed. (New York: McGraw-Hill, 1974), p. 530.

knowledge, impossible. As Lucretius said many centuries ago, *Felix qui potuit causas rerum cognoscere.*[88] But causal knowledge does more than contribute to happiness; it is the sine qua non of scientific inquiry.

This is the majestic theme to which MacIver turns his attention in *Social Causation.* He wants not only to vindicate the principle but also to ask whether causation in the social sciences differs from causation in the physical sciences, a question to which, in accordance with his methodological predilections, he wants to give an affirmative answer.[89] MacIver advises that the reader untrained in philosophical analysis should omit the first two of his chapters and attend to the rest, where he deals with *social* causation. We may nevertheless take a brief look at his efforts to allay the skepticism of Hume on this difficult and tantalizing problem.

In the first place, Hume himself certainly intended his observations on causality to have some *effect,* and if that is the case he must have imputed to them some causal efficacy. In the second place, we all know the difference between succession on the one hand and causation on the other.[90] We do not ordinarily confuse temporal sequences with causal chains. Night follows day and day follows night, but no one claims that one is the cause of the other. In the third place, the application of the category is universal. "Whenever we set about any task we assume causation. Whenever we use an active verb we postulate a cause, and whenever we use a passive one we postulate an effect."[91] Continuity and process both imply causation. We cannot conceive of change without causation, and in fact there is no escape from the web of cause and effect. Finally, there is the sense we have—that even a child has—that we can *make something happen.* On these arguments, although developed of course in more depth and detail, MacIver is content to rest his case.

At the beginning of his treatment MacIver tells us that the question *Why?* has a number of different "modes" and presents them in a schematic diagram (Figure 6.1). In presenting this diagram he assures us that the

88. This, incidentally, is the motto of the London School of Economics and Political Science. See also Francis Bacon, *Vere scire est per causas scire.*

89. For other treatments of this subject by sociologists, see Florian Znaniecki, *Cultural Sciences* (Urbana, Ill.: University of Illinois Press, 1952), and Pitirim A. Sorokin, *Socio-Cultural Causality, Time, Space* (Durham, N.C.: Duke University Press, 1943).

90. Hume's problem, of course, was how do we know this if sensation is the source of all knowledge. MacIver's answer is that we do not immediately perceive *any* relationship. This answer, however, is almost certainly suspect. Some relationships—proximity and similarity, for example—are clearly perceptible. Hume is saying that succession is perceptible whereas causation is not.

91. *Social Causation* (Boston, Ginn and Co. 1942), p. 6.

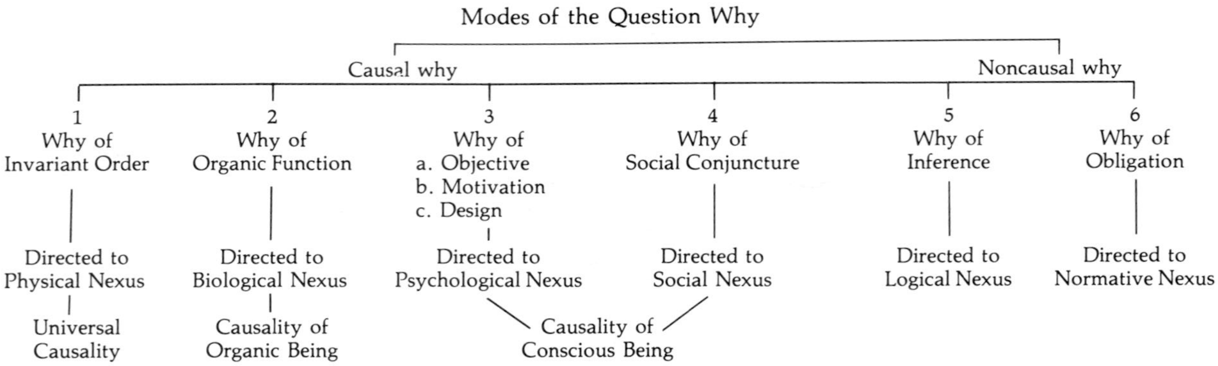

Figure 6.1. MacIver's schematic diagram of the modes of the question *why*. [Reproduced from *Social Causation*, p. 24.]

psychological nexus and the social nexus have to do with conscious beings and that the causality of conscious beings will be his main concern. The "why?" of inference is directed to a logical rather than a causal nexus, especially in deduction, and here we have a reason rather than a cause. Similarly the "why?" of obligation is directed to a normative nexus. Both of the latter two are noncausal, except that, in a way that is not clearly explained, the "ought" of the latter can be transformed into objective and motive, whereupon it enters the realm of causality as a teleological determinant of action.

MacIver is dissatisfied with the kinds of causal analysis that he finds in the literature of social science, not only in sociology but also in psychology, economics, political science, and education. In the great majority of instances causal imputations are too facile and receive only a fragile support.[92] The social sciences, of course, present peculiar difficulties. The phenomena to be explained not only are complex and imperfectly demarcated but also often represent combinations of both physical and teleological causation. The social sciences, in the "plight" in which they find themselves, often take refuge in substitues for causal explanations, all of which are evasions of the issue. Sometimes a refuge is sought in correlations. Correlations, however, have no causal significance; we seek them, when we do, because we first suspect a causal relation. Sometimes a refuge is sought in the discovery of periodicities, but these, however enlightening, are descriptions rather than causal explanations and sometimes, as in Spengler, represent a "dogmatic neglect" of causality. Sometimes a refuge is sought in a quest for origins—and MacIver finds examples in Spencer, Freud, Kautsky, Oppenheimer, Durkheim, Lévy-Bruhl, and Hubert and Mauss all of which are unsatisfactory. And sometimes a refuge is sought in a "key cause," for example, in the geographic theories of Buckle and Huntington, the racial theories of de Gobineau, the economic theories of Marx,[93] and in the "challenges" of Toynbee.

Speaking more positively, MacIver finds a "refuge" for himself in Mill's canon of difference. "Any effective causal inquiry should be addressed to a

92. This is especially the case with respect to treatments of the causes of crime. See *Ibid.*, pp. 80–95. For MacIver's own treatment of the causes of juvenile delinquency, see *The Prevention and Control of Delinquency* (New York: Atherton Press, 1966), especially pp. 41–92.

93. *Ibid.*, p. 117:

> In all the voluminous writings of Karl Marx there is nowhere any attempt to test the doctrine of the "materialistic interpretation of history." Constantly we are bidden to view events and situations in the light of the doctrine. We are told, for example, that "the ideas of freedom of thought and of religion express only the dominance of free competition within the spere of knowledge." The analogy is ingenious, if left as such. The "only" turns it into a dogma.

specific difference between comparable situations."[94] We may seek the "why" of events, of processes, or of trends, the last of which is a variant of the second. There is also the "why" of statistical facts, and in illustration MacIver utilizes Durkheim on suicide, to which he pays high tribute. When we seek the "why" of "responsive attitudes," however, we are on more tenuous ground. A look at studies of marital adjustment discloses some of the difficulties, among which is the use of elusive concepts such as, for example, "happiness," or "adjustment" itself.[95] When concepts are as elusive as these we should surrender our efforts to construct linear scales and resort to case studies instead.

MacIver entertains a certain skepticism about singling out specific causes of large-scale phenomena—such as attributing World War I to the assassination at Sarajevo—and labeling them precipitants. Precipitants may vary in significance, they are part of an enormously complex system of interdependent factors, and "It is only as a temporary heuristic expedient that we can select any item as 'cause' and speak of the rest as 'conditions.' "[96] Nevertheless,

> We have seen that it is the perception of difference that prompts our causal enquiries. We do not usually raise the question why so long as things pursue what we regard as their normal or typical course. It is the exception, the deviation, the interference, the abnormality, that stimulates our curiosity and seems to call for explanation. And we often attribute to some one "cause" all the happenings that characterize the new or unanticipated or altered situation. Somewhat more strictly, we mean by "precipitant" any specific factor or condition regarded as diverting the pre-established direction of affairs, as disrupting a pre-existing equilibrium, or as releasing hitherto suppressed or latent tendencies or forces. The presumption is that a system is operating in a manner congenial to its self-perpetuation, until something intervenes; that a system is relatively closed, until something breaks it open. The "something" is then a precipitant.[97]

And this is one of the ways that help us to understand the problems of continuity and change.

---

94. *Ibid.*, p. 123. See John Stuart Mill, *A System of Logic* (London; Longmans, Green and Co., 1843), bk. 3, chap. 8. The four canons, which Mill himself called methods of experimental inquiry, are agreement, difference, concomitant variation, and residues. Durkheim, it may be recalled, expressed a preference for the canon of concomitant variation but often, in fact, used the method of residues.

95. MacIver includes a note on the operationalism of George A. Lundberg and, the originator of the theory, Percy W. Bridgman. I confront the issue in my discussion of Lundberg, Chapter 8.

96. *Social Causation*, pp. 171–172.

97. *Ibid.*, pp. 172–173. MacIver devotes an entire chapter to "Cause as Precipitant," in the course of which he freely uses the concepts of equilibrium and inertia.

In the same chapter MacIver discusses, with appreciation, Weber's "ideal type." The ideal type helps us to grasp a social situation or historical epoch as something coherent and permits us to escape the profusion of detail. Of course, this procedure entails the risk that we shall underestimate the tendencies to change that already obtain in a situation—a risk that Weber did not always avoid. In any case, it is difficult to regard as a precipitant something that moves as slowly as does a change in attitudes. (Unfortunately, MacIver's mention of Weber is too brief to be serviceable as a contribution to the controversy that Weber's thesis aroused.) Sometimes precipitants are purely chance factors—as in accidents—and sometimes there are "anti-precipitants" that counter the precipitants. It is not Weber but rather Tolstoy's famous discussion of the outbreak of the 1812 war between Napoleon and Alexander I to which MacIver's skepticism is directed. Tolstoy had contended, in brief, "In historical events great men—so called—are but the labels that serve to give a name to an event, and like labels, they have the least possible connection with the events themselves." To which MacIver responds that "the fact that numerous other conditions are equally *necessary* for the result affords no ground for the denial of the distinctive role of the precipitant," which in this case was what Napoleon did and what Alexander did.[98] The problem is complicated by causal chains, where crucial events occur in series, each one dependent upon its predecessor.

MacIver is curiously ambivalent about treating incentives or motives as causes. On the one hand, he is suspicious of all efforts that pretend to find basic needs or drives in the human organism or person, including Sumner's hunger, love, vanity, and fear; the four wishes of Thomas; the residues of Pareto; all instinct theories; the sexual emphasis of Freud; and the economic motivations of Marx. On the other hand, as will be remembered, he begins his own architectonic of social structure with interests, and he clearly wants to preserve the causal efficacy of subjective factors. He recognizes that the imputation of motives is a hazardous enterprise because it is difficult to "get at" motives, motives ascribed by individuals to their own conduct are frequently nothing but rationalizations, and some motives are entirely unconscious, unconscious even to the extent that individuals resist their own awareness of them.[99] These argument's however, should not induce us to desist altogether from our quest for motives. We have to draw whatever inferences we can from whatever evidence is available and recognize that the knowledge resulting therefrom is undependable. Inasmuch as the art of controlling and manipulating motives is now far ad-

98. *Ibid.*, pp. 182–183.
99. "We have, so to say, strong motives for ignoring our motives." *Ibid.*, p. 209.

vanced—as in advertising, for example—"shall science, the truth seeker, abjure that knowledge altogether?"[100] The implied answer to that question, however, leaves at least one reader less than satistied.

MacIver is more insightful when he includes responsibility—as in legal liability—among the causes that operate in the social sphere. There is no such phenomenon in the physical universe, and the subject itself thus supports his basic thesis that social causation differs from physical causation. We are, after all, the "author" of our acts and the "engineer" of their consequences. We can be held to legal account both for acts of commission and for acts of omission. Both have consequences, and therefore both are causes. Failure to report a crime, for example, or failure to observe a contract, may both proceed from some "animus," and the animus thus becomes a cause. That anticipation of consequences characterizes a "willed act" gives to such acts a distinctive status in the realm of causation.[101] The introduction of the will, however, leads to a somewhat unsatisfactory disquisition on the metaphysical riddle concerning the freedom of the will, a riddle MacIver attempts to solve by suggesting that the proper contrast is not that between free will and determinism but is that between freedom and constraint on the one hand and determinism and indeterminism on the other.[102] MacIver suggests in addition that the choice between alternatives is free, although it is not the choice of what the alternatives shall be. Both the political issue and the metaphysical problem are too imposing to pursue in this place. In a way it is unfortunate that MacIver permitted himself to be drawn into these thickets. Causation, in fact, implies determinism. If a cause does not determine it can hardly be a cause—but we must ourselves avoid the temptation to which he succumbed. His conclusion, somewhat weak, is that causal considerations are relevant only to preliminary imputation of criminal conduct and should have little or nothing to do with the legal processes that result in indictment, conviction, and punishment. The latter problems belong to the legislator and the judge, not to the

100. *Ibid.*, p. 217.

101. *Will* is defined as "the decisive capacity of the conscious being to act along certain lines; *intention* as the direction of the will." *Ibid.*, p. 229. Concepts such as "will" and "intention," however, only whet our curiosity. The first is an ancient term in mental philosophy, now entirely discarded by psychology, and the second involves the philosophy of law, a subject to which there are only a few footnote citations. Unfortunately, MacIver accords to neither of these concepts the kind of attention that they seem to require. He is content to say that "the conscious agent, as initiating and directing action, or in other words as willing, may be considered a causal factor in a quite distinctive sense." *Ibid.*, pp. 231–232.

102. For a discussion of this problem couched in terms of political philosophy, see MacIver's essay "The Meaning of Liberty and Its Perversions," ed. Ruth Nanda Anshen, *Freedom: Its Meaning* (New York: Harcourt, Brace & Co., 1940), pp. 278–287.

criminologist and the sociologist.[103] One wishes, in conclusion to this point, that MacIver had exploited to a greater degree his insight that legal liability is a unique kind of social causation.

We are thus reduced to an imaginative reconstruction of what a social situation would have been had one or more of its components been missing, or what it would have been had another factor been present. MacIver, however, should not have used the word *reduced*, as if the procedure were a last and unwelcome resort. Indeed, he sees this kind of reconstruction as an advantage that is denied to causal inquiry in the physical sciences. He sharpens the difference as follows:

> The chain of physical causation does not need mind except for its discovery. The chain of social causation needs mind for its existence. What importance we attach to this difference depends on our respective philosophies. But the difference remains, whatever these philosophies may be. There is that which characterizes all reality and there is that which is revealed only in some areas of it. There are therefore principles and methods common to all science, including the principle of causal investigation we have just been discussing, and there are principles and methods relevant only to distinctive aspects, simply because they have proved applicable to the investigation of these aspects. There is no point in seeking to apply to social systems the causal formula of classical mechanics, to the effect that if you know the state of a system at any instant you can calculate mathematically, in terms of a system of coordinates, the state of that system at any other time. We simply cannot use such a formula. It fits into another frame of reference. On the other hand we have the advantage that some of the factors operative in social causation are *understandable* as *causes*, are validated as causal by our own experience. This provides us a frame of reference that the physical sciences cannot use. We must therefore cultivate our own garden. We must use the advantages we possess and not merely regret the advantages we lack.[104]

Thus, although it is difficult and often impossible to find valid causal relationships in the social sphere, the fact that the sphere is social and contains

103. On this question Alan A. Stone, who is both professor of psychiatry at the Harvard Medical School and professor of law at the Harvard Law School, has an interesting observation. He suggests that law and psychiatry are inherently incompatible disciplines.

> Essentially we are talking about two separate systems of belief—one in the social sciences and one in the law—built on mutually contradictory assumptions. Law rests its case on theories of moral causation and the concept of volition. Man in the eyes of the law is rational and he makes conscious choices. This notion of free will, however, is antithetical to the theories of contemporary social sciences—economics, sociology, behaviorism, or psychoanalysis. Their assumptions are essentially deterministic. Efforts to bridge the gap between these two belief systems—with the notion of intent, for example—are futile.

As quoted in *Harvard Today* 18 (Fall 1974): 3.

104. *Social Causation*, pp. 263-264.

the category of mind offers us a kind of compensation that is absent in the sphere of physical science. This, in essence, is the thesis of MacIver's book.

The imaginative reconstruction that enables us to pursue the quest for causes in the social sphere receives from MacIver a new name—"the dynamic assessment." An example of it is easily found. It is involved in all decision. The businessman who decides to take a trip weighs all the conditions, the effects of alternatives, the possibility of unforseen contingencies—in short, he *assesses* the situation. It is his dynamic assessment. A definition is more difficult. "A dynamic assessment weighs alternatives not yet actualized, sets what would be the consequences if this course were taken over against what would be the consequences if that course were not taken. It is in this regard a causal judgment."[105] It is dynamic in the respect that the situation assessed in making a decision may not persist through the action itself, and it may therefore require reassessment. The assessment is constantly changing, or must be ready to do so. Its virtue is that it brings together into a single order all of the factors, including the external factors, that determine conscious behavior.[106] It does more; it introduces coherence and consistency into our understanding of the cultural, the technological, and the social order, all three of which belong to the order of conscious being. Considerations such a these "show once more how unavailing is the simply quantitative approach that seeks to attach particular weights to the several 'factors,' attributing to each so much push or pull in a total push or pull." It is only in the dynamic assessment that the factors can be weighed.[107]

In his conclusion MacIver restates and reemphasizes his basic contention that causation in the social sciences is different from causation in the physical sciences. The social sciences do not, of course, abrogate the universal reign of law in the physical world. They rather add a new nexus, the sociopsychological nexus, which supervenes. They add a realm of conscious experience, which is also the realm of society. As to the method of causal inquiry, once again it is a process that begins by noticing a difference

105. *Ibid.*, p. 293.

106. MacIver sees some similarity between his dynamic assessment and W. I. Thomas's "definition of the situation." For the latter concept, see Thomas, *The Unadjusted Girl* (Boston: Little, Brown & Co., 1923), p. 42:

> Preliminary to any self-determined act of behavior there is always a stage of examination and deliberation which we may call *the definition of the situation*. And actually not only concrete acts are dependent on the definition of the situation, but gradually a whole life-policy and the personality of the individual himself follow from a series of such definitions.

107. *Social Causation*, p. 332. The dynamic assessment is not only an individual phenomenon. Taken together, the assessments of many individuals, arrived at sometimes alone and sometimes in groups, affect the social process and eventuate in social change.

between two comparable situations and then by seeking the factor or factors that explain the difference. "Observe in passing," says MacIver, "that the difference between one social situation and another is never the mere presence or absence of a single factor, never even the more or the less of one particular factor. It is the situation *as assessed* that is dynamic for social change."[108] Causal inquiry in the social sciences is a process of progressive delimitation, a process of successive discriminations, the progressive revision of a hypothesis. The discovery of the causes of social phenomena, in fact, is always progressive, always approximate, and always incomplete. In our causal quests let us use all the evidence we can find, all our skill and all our imagination. But let us remember that if certainty is our goal, it is a goal we shall never reach. Although our endeavors may always bring us nearer, the goal of causal knowledge is never attained.

Sorokin's review of *Social Causation* is full of his characteristic bombast.[109] Although he praises MacIver for emphasizing the importance of the subject and for insisting that causation in the social sciences is something different from causation in the physical sciences, his judgments of MacIver's performance are wholly negative. First, *ad hominem*, MacIver lacks the philosophical training to undertake inquiries that require a rigorous logic, and he has had no experience with empirical investigation. He says that causality is undefinable and then proceeds to define it. He both rejects and accepts a theory of specific causal factors. He repudiates the role of technology and then appreciates it in his examples. His use of concepts is careless, his distinctions sterile. He emphasizes the canon of difference to the neglect of the canon of agreement. His suggestion that the narration and description of antecedent events can explain such a phenomenon as the French Revolution would make causal inquiry unnecessary.[110] His explanations are either incorrect or tautological, and in any case vitiate everything he has said. His effort, therefore, falls far short of his objective, and his results are worthless. Sorokin's misinterpretations, almost willful, of some of MacIver's propositions are easy to expose. One of his points, however, has a degree of cogency. As noticed by other critics as well, MacIver's explanation of the increase of the divorce rate in the United States has the flavor of tautology. After an examination of this

108. *Ibid.*, p. 377.

109. *Harvard Law Review* 56 (1943): 1023–1027.

110. *Ibid.*, p. 1026:

> If we are to believe MacIver, there is no need to worry about the causes of any historical event or process. We have thousands of descriptions and narratives. Therefore, all problems of their causation are already solved. We need only to take any text in history or biography to have all the causes in our hands. Happy MacIver and happy social sciences! They have already solved all their causal problems!

phenomenon, he writes that "divorce is more prevalent in those areas where the continuity of the family through several generations has less significance in the scheme of cultural values than formerly or than elsewhere."[111] Does this, Sorokin demands, mean any more than that when family bonds are strong they are strong and when they are weak they are weak?

Other reviews of *Social Causation* are more favorable. Page, for example, regards it as MacIver's most mature theoretical work, one that finds a golden mean between those who find social causation identical with physical causation and those who would deny altogether the applicability of causation to social phenomena.[112] Furfey calls it the best treatment of causality from the standpoint of sociology in existence and particularly appreciates it as a defense against those who believe that causation is only "an episode in the history of thought."[113] Catton, assigns to MacIver the status of the Kepler of sociology, half way between animism and naturalism.[114] Harry Estill Moore praises MacIver for a "temperate, well reasoned, logical statement of the problem" and finds MacIver's position to be an answer to the "rampant mathematics" of Dodd and Lundberg on the one hand and the "cloisteral mysticism" of Sorokin on the other.[115]

On the other side again, Calhoun finds fault with MacIver's tendency to confuse common sense with scientific evidence and asks why subjective factors should be privileged.[116] Frank H. Knight's long essay-review is almost entirely negative. The "dynamic assessment" means little more, if anything, than the rational evaluation of objectives, and the book as a whole is confused, obscure, and unintelligible.[117]

Among the most thoughtful reviews is that of Ernest Nagel.[118] Nagel compliments MacIver for his suggestive distinctions, for his wise if elementary observations on the scientific method, and for propositions that are provocative "even when they fail to carry conviction." On the other hand, he rejects MacIver's contention that mathematics, however useful in sym-

111. *Social Causation*, p. 338 (italics omitted).

112. In the section on MacIver by Page in Nicholas S. Timasheff, *Sociological Theory: Its Nature and Growth*, 3rd ed. (New York: Random House, 1967), pp. 250–255.

113. *The Scope and Method of Sociology* (New York: Harper & Brothers, 1953), pp. 69–70.

114. *From Animistic to Naturalistic Sociology* (New York: McGraw-Hill, 1966), pp. 98–115.

115. *Social Forces* 21 (December 1942): 246–247.

116. *American Sociological Review* 7 (October 1942): 714–719. "The cause of science is not served by repeated appeals to 'general assent' [p. 719]."

117. *American Journal of Sociology* 49 (July 1943): 46–55. See also MacIver's rejoinder, *ibid.*, pp. 56–58.

118. *The Journal of Philosophy* 39 (September 1942): 552–556. This review is reprinted in Nagel, *Logic Without Metaphysics* (Glencoe, Ill.: Free Press, 1956), pp. 369–375.

bolizing variations in a timeless order, lacks the capacity to represent the dynamic order. About this MacIver is in fact mistaken. "If a lean cowherd may drive fat cattle, why is it impossible for the non-dymanic to 'represent' the dynamic?"[119] MacIver's observations on the origin of the idea of cause are "unsupported and essentially unclear." The experience of making something happen is not the same as the scientific task of connecting conditions with consequences. MacIver's explanation of the increase in the divorce rate (as Sorokin also noted) is in fact tautological and raises the very question it seeks to answer. Finally, "if causal efficacy is attributed to the subjective elements which Mr. MacIver prizes so highly, the method for ascertaining whether those factors are causally operative does not differ in principle from the causal methods employed in the natural sciences." Imaginative projections, however suggestive, do not themselves qualify as causal knowledge. And "Mr. MacIver has not offered convincing grounds for his contention that the logic of social inquiry is essentially different from the method of natural science."[120]

Our own conclusion is a negative one for a number of reasons, among them the fact that MacIver's own conclusion is negative. The argument meanders. It returns again and again to the starting point and never reaches the finish line. Answers to causal questions are always contingent, always precarious. They are insecure, incomplete, and at best approximate. The goal of causal knowledge is never attained. Our inquiries converge upon a point at which they never arrive. These words are all MacIver's, and they reflect what might be called a causal pessimism, not to say a causal agnosticism.[121]

It is not necessary to examine the philosophical problem here except to state my own conviction that MacIver has not been able to put Hume's causal skepticism to rest. His effort to validate the category by our sense of "making something happen" is both primitive and anthropomorphic. Indeed, it contradicts his own assertion that we never directly experience any relation, including the causal. The "dynamic assessment" is itself ambiguous. Is it something the actor does when he decides upon a course of action (as MacIver's examples indicate), or is it something that the observer

119. *Ibid.*, p. 553. MacIver is also mistaken, according to Nagel, about the exclusively quantitative character of mathematical relations.

120. *Ibid.*, p. 556.

121. In 1964 MacIver wrote a new introduction for the Harper Torchbook edition of *Social Causation*. Its last sentence tells us again that causal inquiry in the social sciences is always incomplete and, at best, progressive. It is interesting to note that Comte himself surrendered the search for causes and decided to search only for "invariable relations of succession and resemblance." *The Positive Philosophy of Auguste Comte*, freely translated and condensed by Harriet Martineau, 3 vols. (London: George Bell and Sons, 1896), vol. 1, p. 2.

does when he tries to explain the action and to find the causal conjunctures it represents? On this essential point MacIver is—uncharacteristically—unclear. Is the "dynamic assessment" anything more than an admonition to do the best we can under difficult circumstances? The questions are more than rhetorical. They imply that the answers to them are in the negative. Is causation in sociology something different from causation in physics? Here one can concede that such phenomena as obligation, legal liability, and responsibility are social phenomena that cannot be found in the physical universe. But MacIver fails to exploit the insight. He denies, in fact, that responsibility can be regarded as a kind or degree of causality and thus forfeits what could have been a significant support to his central thesis. We can only conclude, as others have, that MacIver has made a brave assault upon an intractable problem. But the intractability remains, and the assault is ultimately an unsuccessful one.

Society and the State

Inasmuch as we are here concerned with sociological theory, it is unnecessary to deal in extensive detail with MacIver's books on political theory. A few points nevertheless merit attention.

The Modern State (1926) is appositely titled. In it MacIver first asks what it is,[122] and then traces its evolutionary development from city-state to "country-state," discusses its powers and functions, its forms and institutions, and concludes with theories and interpretations of the state. Throughout he is pleased to place his heaviest emphasis upon the theme that runs through both his sociological and his political theory, namely, that the state is an association, like other associations in most respects, unlike them in some (e.g., the legitimate use of force), but always a limited association. It is custom that reveals the limits, customs that "grow everywhere in the soil of society," customs that arise spontaneously, customs that the state has the power neither to create nor destroy. Even the power of the autocrat "depends so intimately on the support of custom that he must be its guardian and servant in order to rule."[123] "The things that are not Caesar's" belong to other associations, and to the community itself. The state is not, therefore, an all-powerful, all-encompassing unity but is

122. "The state is an association which, acting through law as promulgated by a government endowed to this end with coercive power, maintains within a community territorially demarcated the universal external conditions of social order." *The Modern State* (London and New York: Oxford University Press, 1926), p. 22.

123. *Ibid.*, p. 160.

rather an organ of community. Along the way MacIver has occasion to discourse on such subjects as sovereignty, force,[124] state and family, state and class, the movement from absolutism to democracy, two major forms of the state (the dynastic and the democratic), governmental powers, and the party system. He develops here also one of his favorite distinctions, that between culture and civilization. He reminds us that the sociologist, inquiring into any part of the social scheme, whether the state or anything else, confronts a peculiar difficulty—"the difficulty of reconciling an objective or scientific understanding of its character with the necessary appreciation of its ethical value." The former is necessary in order to give validity to values; the latter, to give meaning to the social structure. Finally, on the relationship of law and custom:

> There are many customs which are observed at least as faithfully as political laws. Now customs are sustained by the community as such, not as a rule by the aid of any organization. Law, on the other hand, is sustained by the state. But ultimately they rest alike on the same basis, for the state itself is sustained by the community. Ultimately they are both expressions of the social sense, the sense of solidarity, the sense of common interest. In this subjective fact we find the root of the unity of society, not in the state, which is only a form through which that unity is expressed.[125]

It is thus the community, not the state, that ultimately governs.

These themes engaged MacIver again in *The Web of Government*, which he wrote at the height of his powers and which is perhaps his most eloquent book.[126] Some of it is dated now—the treatment of the totalitarian states at the time of World War II—but the defense of democracy is cogent still, and cogent also is his analysis of the sociological phenomena of power and authority. He begins by distinguishing two types of human contrivances—myths and techniques. Myths are the "value-impregnated beliefs and notions that men hold, that they live by or live for."[127] Myths hold a

124. Again, force is the *ultima ratio*, but MacIver's treatment of it is not as incisive as it is in *Society*.

125. *Ibid.*, p. 481.

126. (New York: Macmillan, 1947).

127. *Ibid.*, p. 5:

> When we speak here of myth we imply nothing concerning the grounds of belief, so far as belief claims to interpret reality. We use the word in an entirely neutral sense. Whether its content be revelation or superstition, insight or prejudice, is not here in question. We need a term that abjures all reference to truth and falsity. We include equally under the term "myth" the most penetrating philosophies of life, the most profound intimations of religion, the most subtle renditions of experience, along with the most grotesque imaginations of the most benighted savage. We include all human approaches and attitudes, all the modes in which men face or formulate the business of living. Whatever valuational responses men give to the circumstances and trials of their lot, whatever conceptions guide their behavior, spur their ambitions, or render existence tolerable—all alike fall within our ample category of myth.

society together and sustain all its activities. There is no science of government in the sense of a systematic body of knowledge that can guide the statesman, as the science of physics guides the engineer or physiology the physician, because government too is sustained by myths, themselves constantly changing. We should think of government, therefore, as an art rather than as a science.

The origin of government can be found neither in force, as Marx and the Social Darwinists thought,[128] nor in contract, as Hobbes and Rousseau thought. Its breeding ground is found instead in the family, already a government in miniature. The codes that regulate sex expression, the relations between the family members, the inheritance of property, and the division of labor already adumbrate the government that will come to be. Government is not therefore something that supervenes in society, or is an accessory to it, but it is part of its very nature. It is necessary to return to the insight of Aristotle and insist that man is a political animal.[129]

Government rests, then, upon the myth of authority. "The man who commands may be no wiser, no abler, may be in no sense better than the average of his fellows; sometimes, by any intrinsic standard, he is inferior to them. Here is the magic of government."[130] MacIver accordingly turns his attention to authority and the manner in which it is supported by lore and ceremony and institution. He discusses the transformation of the myth of authority from the simple society to what he calls the multigroup society, the latter of which is also the multimyth society. The multigroup society can sustain itself only under a form of government that can accommodate conflicting myths—and that form, as he later elaborates in detail, is democracy.

The sociological significance of MacIver's stately treatise on government can be seen again in his reiteration of the fact that there is an order—a social order—that lies beyond the realm of government. And here we find one of the most eloquent paragraphs in the entire corpus of MacIver's work:

> The authority of government does not create the order over which it presides and does not sustain that order solely by its own fiat or its accredited power. There is authority beyond the authority of government. There is a greater consensus without which the fundamental order of the community would fall

128. "The notion that force is the creator of government is one of those part-truths that beget total errors." *Ibid.*, p. 15.

129. It is in this chapter that MacIver pens a most remarkable sentence: "Custom is always at work turning example into precedent and precedent into institution." *Ibid.*, p. 34. Here, as the present writer has said, is an entire system of sociology.

130. *Ibid.*, p. 13.

> apart. This consensus plays a different role under different forms of government. Sometimes it has nothing to do with the processes that make or unmake the princes or potentates who rule the people. Sometimes it has no mode of expression, should the ruler get out of hand and violate the fundamental order he is presumed to protect, save the rare violence of revolution. Sometimes it is alert and sensitive to all that government does and sets its seal of approval or disapproval on the policies that government pursues. But always, whether mainly acquiescent or creatively active, it is the ultimate ground on which the unity and the order of the state repose.[131]

No one can treat the problem of authority without inquiring at the same time into the nature of power, and this MacIver does in a chapter entitled "The Pyramid of Power." Power is not authority and power is not status but it is closely related to both. "By social power we mean the capacity in any relationship to command the service or the compliance of others."[132] "By authority we mean the established *right,* within any social order, to determine policies, to pronounce judgments on relevant issues, and to settle controversies, or, more broadly, to act as leader or guide to other men."[133] With respect to authority, the accent is on right, not power. The two important sources of power are property and status, but cultural activity also plays a role. The power of government is formally supreme in that it carries the right of coercion. But it is always subject to opposing power, including especially economic power. The Marxist emphasis on the dominant role of economic power, however, is an exaggeration.[134] No single form of power is absolute. The king goes to Canossa, but the pope is exiled to Avignon. "The state dissolves the economic corporation, but the economic corporation finds a way to control the state. Government at one time forbids labor to organize, and at another time organized labor dictates to government. The church is subservient to the money interests—and the money changers are whipped out of the temple."[135] It is important to note

---

131. *Ibid.*, p. 85.
132. *Ibid.*, p. 82.
133. *Ibid.*, p. 83.
134. *Ibid.*, p. 92:

> The economic strength of any group or class is no longer, as it tended to be under feudal conditions, the measure of its political strength. The relative ease with which powerful economic interests have been defeated in the political arena, the many encroachments of government, by taxation and regulation, on the prerogatives of wealth, the progress of "social legislation" all along the line, and the manner in which various governments, without any proletarian revolution, have taken over such important sectors of capitalistic enterprise as railroads and public utilities, demonstrate the inadequacy of the Marxian thesis to comprehend the complex relationship between economic and political power.

On this theme, see also MacIver *Democracy and the Economic Challenge* (New York: Alfred A. Knopf, 1952).

135. *Web of Government*, p. 93.

that the power of government is different from the power that gains access to it. The clash of opposing interests requires that the power of government be supreme, but again it is important to recognize that this power is only one of several kinds. Furthermore, it is a power that in a democracy is a carefully limited one. Finally, the power structure of a society is always pyramidal. The pyramid may take slightly different shapes, as when oligarchy is contrasted with democracy, but the basic form remains.

Power is accompanied by status and property, and the latter two phenomena thus receive a share of MacIver's attention. He conceives of status in the ordinal sense and associates it with the notion of hierarchy. Social class is then "a status-defined stratification of the community."[136] It is a hierarchy determined by prestige and is not to be identified with any other differences between men, including that between capitalists and workers. Differential status may not always "breed" class—it does not in the simplest of societies, but it does in the more complex, and all the great states of historical societies have been controlled by a ruling class. Here the exaggerations of Marx and Engels contain an important truth. Even in the democratic state some relationship remains between government and class. It is the party system of democracy that prevents the relationship from being a total one. The Russian revolution did not—could not—abolish social class; it merely substituted one class for another. Government may be in the hands of a ruling class, but the social structure itself is not created by that class; it is bent and shaped by forces beyond its control. Although economic factors are often present in the struggle of group with group and of class with class, they seldom suffice to explain the struggle. Nor does class struggle suffice to explain the processes of social change.[137]

Once more, in this book, MacIver gives eloquent expression to his own central "myth":

> Everywhere men weave a web of relationships with their fellows, as they buy and sell, as they worship, as they rejoice and mourn. This greater web of relationships is society, and a community is a delimited area of society. Within this web of community are generated many controls that are not governmental controls, many associations that are not political associations, many usages and standards of behavior that are in no sense the creation of the state. In the community develops the law behind law, the multi-sanctioned law that existed before governments began and that the law of government can never supersede. Without the prior laws of the community all the laws of the state

136. *Ibid.*, p. 115.

137. "It is one of the great paradoxes of history that the revolution vaticinated by Marx, the revolution that was to overthrow capitalism in favor of a proletarian collectivism, should have been inaugurated in Russia, where there was no swelling proletariat and very little capitalism." *Ibid.*, p. 257.

> would be empty formulas. Custom, the first "king of men," still rules. The *mores* still prescribe. Manners and modes still flourish. The laws made by governments cannot rescind them, cannot long defy them or deeply invade them.[138]

It is democracy, and democracy alone, that gives constitutional sanction to this universal principle.

A few years before his death, while serving as president of the New School for Social Research, MacIver returned to the subject of power. He had entered the ninth decade of his life but the habit of writing every day was one that he had not broken. Accordingly, he published his *Power Transformed* in 1964.[139] The reviews were almost universally favorable. At the same time, it must be admitted that his prose is less supple, his arguments more diffuse, his distinctions less clear, and his organization less tight and controlled. The first part of the book is both a personal and political history of two world wars and the precarious peace between. The second part is a renewed analysis of the role of power in society. Once more, power is "the capacity to contol, regulate, or direct the behavior of persons or things."[140] Among its sources are knowledge, personality (including the quality of leadership and the strength of will), possessions, organization, and, interestingly, the impressiveness of power itself. Authority is defined as "the possession of legitimate power, associated with the fulfillment of function."[141] There is, however, insufficient distinction between authority as power and authority as competence. And an example of diffuseness appears in a discourse on the relationship between power and the creative mind.

MacIver is concerned to emphasize the ubiquity of power. It resides in everything in nature, from the tender blade of grass to the shattering earthquake. It resides everywhere in society because all men seek power, the philosopher in his study no less than the general in the field. (Here, however, he is confusing influence with power.) Among the social types who exercise power are the professional soldier, the adventurer (including the speculator, the explorer, the mountain climber, and the big-game hunter), the entrepreneur, the professional, and the artist.[142] The chapter closes with a paean to the human spirit.

The concluding sections of the book, which illuminate its title, tell the story of the transformations of power in the world at large through such

138. *Ibid.*, p. 193.
139. (New York: Macmillan).
140. *Ibid.*, p. 77.
141. *Ibid.*, p. 82.
142. The analytical virtue of treating all of these as power phenomena is far from clear.

stages as the establishment of the supertribal community, the rise of the democratic principle, the liberation of mankind from slavery, and the dissolution of the colonial empires. The book trails off without a conclusion. If central thesis be sought, however, the words of the subtitle can serve: "The Age-Slow Deliverance of the Folk and Now the Potential Deliverance of the Nations from the Rule of Force."

Miscellaneous Writings

In 1948, in a book entitled *The More Perfect Union,*[143] MacIver turned his attention to a social problem in the United States, namely, the reduction of intergroup tension and discrimination. Although the book presents a program for action, it is not devoid of theoretical relevance. In a chapter entitled "Balances and Circles," for example, he examines the principle of circular causation as it operates in society and explains the nontautological fact that prejudice is one of the causes of prejudice and discrimination of discrimination. Relying to some extent upon Myrdal's treatment of the same phenomenon in *An American Dilemma,* he introduces the notion of "the self-fulfilling postulate," which Merton, in an article published the same year, calls "the self-fulfilling prophecy."[144] It is the now familiar phenomenon by which a rumor, itself false, that a bank is on the brink of insolvency can cause the insolvency in fact. MacIver links it to a similar phenomenon on the individual level, where fear of failure, in taking an examination, for example, can be one of the causes of failure. The latter phenomenon he calls "the self-fulfilling anticipation." Merton's label came to be the accepted one, and indeed his analysis is the more comprehensive of the two.

A second contribution appears in a chapter entitled "The Distorting Mirrors," where MacIver distinguishes between two kinds of prejudice. One acquires the first simply through indoctrination and habituation, by being a member of a group that owns and expresses the prejudice. Prejudices of this kind are absorbed in the same way that one absorbs the norms and ideologies of the groups of which he is a member. The second kind has its source in the life history of the individual himself, in some traumatic experience, for example, some tension or frustration that hones the edge of

143. (New York: Macmillan); facsimile ed. (New York: Hafner, 1971).

144. Merton's article of that title appeared first in *The Antioch Review,* 8 (Sumner, 1948). It is reprinted in both the 1949 and 1957 editions of *Social Theory and Social Structure* (Glencoe, Ill.: Free Press of Glencoe) and carries a footnote reference to MacIver's treatment.

hostility. The first of these represents the normal conformity of individual to group; the second, on the contrary, is a deviation from the norms of the group. The difference is relative rather than absolute, and both may be manifest in the same person. The book as a whole is a program of "social engineering" rather than a theoretical contribution as such. But it has its own appropriate place in MacIver's bibliography.

It remains to mention the numerous additional studies that MacIver wrote, even during the waning years of his career. One is devoted to the subject of academic freedom, another to the United Nations, a third to juvenile delinquency, and still others to political and philosophical themes.[145] The last of these are directed not to technical problems in the discipline, the kind he had attacked in *Social Causation*, but rather to poetic musings on the meaning of life and time and happiness. Reading them is an enriching experience. Finally, there is the David Spitz collection of some forty selected essays (of a total of nearly 100) that MacIver wrote over a period of sixty years, published under the title of *Politics and Society*.[146] At the conclusion of his Introduction Spitz writes as follows:

> I have said enough perhaps to indicate the rewards that await the reader of these essays. I hope I have said enough, too, to support my conviction that MacIver's eminent achievements, in both method and vision, stamp him as the most distinguished of our social and political theorists. Whether history will share this judgment it is not now of course possible to say. But that MacIver

145. *Academic Freedom in Our Time* (New York: Columbia University Press, 1955); *The Nations and the United Nations* (New York: Manhattan Publishing Co. 1959); *The Prevention and Control of Juvenile Delinquency* (New York: Atherton Press, 1966). Other miscellaneous works include *Leviathan and the People* (Baton Rouge, La.: Louisiana State University Press, 1939); *Towards an Abiding Peace* (New York: Macmillan, 1943); *The Ramparts We Guard* (New York: Macmillan, 1952); *Democracy and the Economic Challenge* (New York: Alfred A. Knopf, 1952); *The Pursuit of Happiness* (New York: Simon and Schuster, 1955); *Life: Its Dimensions and Its Bounds* (New York: Harper & Brothers, 1960); *The Challenge of the Passing Years* (New York: Simon and Schuster, 1962); and, mentioned earlier, the autobiography, *As a Tale That Is Told*. Also mentioned earlier is the indispensable collection of MacIver's essays collected by David Spitz, *Politics and Society*. Attention is invited also to books and articles about MacIver, appended to Spitz's Bibliography, and especially to Spitz's Introduction, *ibid.*, pp. ix–xx. See also Spitz, "Robert M. MacIver's Contributions to Political Theory," ed. Morroe Berger, Theodore Abel, and Charles H. Page *Freedom and Control in Modern Society* (New York: D. Van Nostrand, 1954); Harry Alpert, "Robert M. MacIver's Contributions to Sociological Theory," *ibid.*; Harry Alpert, ed., *Robert M. MacIver: Teacher and Sociologist* (Northampton, Mass.: Metcalf Printing and Publishing Co., 1953); Alpert's article on MacIver in the *International Encyclopedia of the Social Sciences*, ed. David L. Sills, 18 vols. (New York: Macmillan and the Free Press, 1968); and Leon Bramson, ed., *Robert M. MacIver on Community, Society, and Power* (Chicago: University of Chicago Press, 1970).

146. Bibliographical details are in preceding footnote.

has resolutely stood in the mainstream of social and political theory, that he has remained true to the noblest traditions of his calling, that he has significantly extended the frontiers of our knowledge—these are beyond contestation.

Summary and Evaluation

Summaries, necessarily brief, do little justice to a man's work, especially when that work has the range of MacIver's. There is scarcely a subject or a problem in sociology and political philosophy that did not attract his attention. His major contribution to sociological theory, of course, consists in his systematic treatment of the structural components of society, and especially his masterful discussion of the social codes. There is order beyond the order of government—the social order itself—whose locus is the community, and it is this that justifies—indeed requires—an autonomous discipline of sociology. *Society,* in which he examines this order, is thus a major contribution to the literature and one that easily sustains comparison with other systems in the sociological tradition. Indeed, MacIver is more *systematic* than most, if by that adjective we mean, this time, not the order that society itself exhibits but the order that he introduced into our knowledge of society. More than that, he introduced it in a prose that is lucid, stately, and often eloquent.

I have judged his treatment of social causation as somewhat less than satisfactory. It fails to justify MacIver's own contention that causation in society is different from causation in nature and that a different kind of causal knowledge ensues. If his analysis, sometimes simplistic, is finally inconclusive, we nevertheless pay him tribute for a major effort to solve this most complex and vexing problem. He asks more questions than he is able to answer, but there is a probing intensity in the asking of them.

As a political philosopher, MacIver's name appears on a distinguished roster. He insists, with a constant emphasis, that government is no mere legal phenomenon, no mere political phenomenon, but primarily and in a larger sense a social phenomenon. Government is no fictitious affair residing in the formal structure of the law or in the vague superstition of sovereignty. Government springs from the community and owes its source and practice to the society of men. And here, more than incidentally, lies the strength of democracy. Democracy recognizes that government is a limited institution, contrived for limited purposes, and democracy alone gives constitutional sanction to the distinction between the community and the state. The state is the servant, not the master, of the community.

In his writing on sociology and political philosophy MacIver did not hesitate to wear the mantle of the moral philosopher and thus belongs to an old and honorable—even Scottish—tradition. He never forgot the importance of defining the relationship between the individual and society. He believed that "the individual is never wholly absorbed in his society, wholly responsive to it, wholly accounted for by it." He gladly taught that "it is in individuals that all social values are realized" and that "we cannot, except by a flight into mysticism, attribute to this whole, society, any fulfillment except the continuing fulfillment of its members." He had no patience with a code so conservative, so rigid, or so authoritarian that it menaces "the autonomy of judgment which is the prime condition of an enlightened adult morality." He denounced the dogmatist who, "secure in his own faith, would refuse other men the right to theirs." And he was an enemy forever of the "immoral intolerance which only the exclusive visionary possession of an unreasoned faith can inspire."[147]

We may say finally that in intellectual poise, sociological sophistication, and moral solicitude, Robert MacIver has no peer in the history of the discipline.

147. The words in quotation marks in this paragraph are MacIvers own.

CHAPTER 7

Pitirim A. Sorokin

Sociology appeared with criticism, has grown with criticism, and lives with criticism. If we care to promote sociology as a science, a critical attitude must be displayed by all sociologists as regards any sociological theory, without any exception whatsoever.

—*Contemporary Sociological Theories,* p. xxiii

Pitirim Alexandrovich Sorokin was born on January 21, 1889, in the far north of Russia. His mother, of the Komi people and region, died when he was three years old. His father, who had migrated to the region from the ancient city of Veliki Ustyug, was an itinerant icon maker who succumbed to alcoholism when the boy was eleven years old. A year earlier, Pitirim and a brother, four years older, left him to make their way on their own, roaming from one village to another cleaning and gilding icons, whitewashing church interiors, cleaning and painting roofs and steeples. The little family life the boys had time to enjoy was offered by an uncle and aunt who served, at intervals, as surrogate parents. The region was one of vast forests and swift rivers, of clear lakes and fresh meadows, about which Sorokin is rhapsodic in his autobiography,[1] and the principal occupations of the peasants were hunting, fishing, trapping, and lumbering. Each village normally had, in addition, its priest, teacher, doctor, storekeeper, and policeman, although, with respect to the last, thefts were so few that the houses had no locks on their doors. The peasants normally spoke two languages—their native Komi (related to Ugro-Finnish) as the first, and Russian as the second.

Sorokin did not remember when or where he learned to read and write. His nomadic life, both before and after his father's death, prevented a regular attendance at village schools, and he had no memory of graduating from an elementary school. He did, however, remember the first prize he

1. There are two autobiographies: *Leaves from a Russian Diary* (New York: E. P. Dutton, 1924,) and enlarged ed. (Boston: Beacon Press, 1950); *A Long Journey* (New Haven, Conn.: College and University Press, 1963).

won for scholastic excellence. It was a scrap of paper in which a piece of candy had once been wrapped. He was so proud of it that he tacked it to a wall of his uncle's house, alongside the icons, and he tells us that it meant more to him than any of the honors he later received. He was not, however, denied the company of books. The Komi people had a relatively high degree of literacy, third only to the Russian Germans and the Russian Jews, and in the villages whose churches he painted and whose icons he restored he found the classics of Russian literature—Pushkin, Gogol, Turgenev, Tolstoy, Dostoevski—and Mark Twain and Charles Dickens as well. At one of the villages, named Gam, where he and his brother were working, Sorokin attended the entrance examination, an important village ceremony, for those who aspired to become pupils in the advanced grade school. When he discovered how easily he could answer the questions he volunteered to become a participant and thereupon won a scholarship, which gave him five rubles ($2.50) for each of the three years he then spent at the school. It was enough to pay his room and board for the nine months of the academic year. His early education was enriched by the priests and deacons whom he met in the course of his work and who took an interest in him. The Komi people were Russian Orthodox in faith, and it was a faith he apparently never surrendered. At an early age he served as a teacher and preacher at village religious meetings and acquired, as he disseminated, the moral values of the Christian religion. When asked, in later years, about his political and religious convictions, he always replied that he was conservative Christian anarchist.

Sorokin's next school, which he entered at the age of fourteen in 1903, was the Khrenovo Teachers' Seminary, in the province of Kostroma. The seminary was a teachers' training school administered by the synod of the Russian Orthodox church. His two years there introduced him to a wider world and culture than he had experienced before. They also led him to question some of his earlier beliefs. He became a zealous opponent of the czar and the leader of the Social Revolutionary Party in the province, speaking often at meetings of students, workers, and peasants. For this activity he was rewarded by his first arrest and imprisonment. The year was 1906, and he was a month less than eighteen years old. He was automatically expelled from his school, where he was nevertheless regarded as a hero. After his release from prison he went underground as "Comrade Ivan," and became a full-time "missionary" and propagandist for the revolution, always in danger of arrest and sometimes of his life.

After many months of this kind of activity Sorokin decided to go to Saint Petersburg and resume his education. There, befriended by a professor of Komi origin, he attended a night school in order to prepare himself for the university. He passed the required examinations in 1909 and in the same year entered the Psycho-Neurological Institute at Saint

Petersburg, an institute whose faculty was graced by two distinguished sociologists, M. M. Kovalevsky and E. V. De Roberty. Attendance at lectures was voluntary, and Sorokin turned this freedom to personal advantage, deciding to attend only those lectures in which the professor had something original and important to say that was not yet published. There, and later at the University of Saint Petersburg, he came to know, in addition to Kovalevsky and De Roberty, such scholars and scientists as V. M. Bekhtereff, Leon Petrajitzky (whose *General Theory of Law and Morality* proved to be a lasting influence), M. I. Rostovtzeff, M. I. Tugan-Baranovsky, Ivan P. Pavlov, N. O. Lossky, and N. Rosin. He appears to have made an impression upon all of them and in his first year of graduate work received an appointment as a lecturer in sociology at the institute. His transfer from the institute to the university was occasioned by the fact that students at the latter, but not at the former, were exempt from the draft. "Regarding compulsory military draft as the worst form of coercive servitude imposed upon a free person by the Czarist regim, and military service as training in the art of mass-murder, I neither had any desire to be drafted nor regarded a positive response to the draft as a moral duty."[2] This attitude was shared by his professors, who arranged for him a fairly comfortable scholarship.

Sorokin began to publish at the age of twenty one, when the first of a series of papers on the Komi people appeared in print. During his undergraduate years he also published papers in anthropology, sociology, law, and philosophy, and in his junior year (1913) his first substantial volume appeared, *Crime and Punishment, Service and Reward.* During his undergraduate years also he undertook intensive studies in philosophy, psychology, ethics, history, and, especially, sociology and law. During these years too he became acquainted with the work of Comte, Spencer, Durkheim, Tarde, Simmel, Weber, and Pareto. Gradually his own views took shape; these were the orthodox positivistic views growing out of the sociologies of Comte and Spencer, together with a high regard for empirical methods and research. These were views that, as we shall see, he was destined not to retain. Upon his graduation in 1914 he was offered a stipend to remain at the university and prepare for his higher degrees. He chose criminal law, penology, and constitutional law as his principal areas of endeavor.

During his student years at Saint Petersburg he intensified his political activities—writing articles, organizing "cells," speaking at revolutionary meetings, and in general becoming, as he calls himself, a "subversive." He and his associates were arrested so often that they came to regard the police as more of a nuisance than a threat, and indeed the police themselves were

2. *Long Journey,* p. 72.

often sympathetic to their anticzarist activities. His last arrest under the regime occurred in 1913, on a charge of writing a pamphlet critical of the government, and again he was treated decently in prison, with intellectual colleagues and books as his companions. He was not able to say the same of his later imprisonments by the Communists.

Intending to use as his dissertation for the master's degree—a degree whose requirements were more stringent than those for the American or German Ph.D.—the volume on *Crime and Punishment*, mentioned earlier, he successfully passed his oral examination after two years of study, rather than the normal four and became a "magistrant of criminal law" in 1916. For the degree of "magister of criminal law," however, he had to defend his dissertation in public, and this event, scheduled for March 1917, became a casualty of the revolution, when almost all university activity ceased. When the universities were revived and their degree-granting privileges restored, Sorokin was awarded his doctorate in sociology. His dissertation for the degree was his two-volume *Sistema Soziologii* (*System of Sociology*), which he had managed to write, and subversely to publish, in 1920.[3] He successfully defended it on April 22, 1922, before a large gathering of faculty, students, journalists, outside scholars, and interested members of the public. The audience greeted the verdict with an ovation, and the event became the subject of an editorial entitled "The Dispute of Professor Sorokin" in the *Ekonomist*. Sociology, incidentally, had been introduced into the curriculum under the Kerensky regime in 1917 and was expanded into a separate department in the years 1919–1922, with Sorokin as its elected chairman.

Sorokin's harrowing experiences during the revolution of 1917 and its aftermath are told in such detail in both of his autobiographies that we need merely allude to them here. By 1917, when he was twenty eight, he was well acquainted with the leading political, intellectual, literary, and scientific figures of the day, and his own name had become prominent. He was a high-ranking member of the Kerensky government, serving Kerensky as his secretary, a member too of the Council of the Russian Republic, the Constituent Assembly, and the Russian Peasant Soviet. He was also one of the editors of the two Social Revolutionary Party newspapers *Delo Naroda* and *Volia Naroda*. When the Communists overthrew the Kerensky regime, all of the moderates were suspect. Many were summarily shot. Sorokin was arrested on January 2, 1918, on the trumped-up charge of having tried

3. It was printed in secret with a forged seal of approval by the Communist censorship apparatus. When it was discovered, the government ordered all copies confiscated and destroyed. During the years 1918–1920 he also wrote two texts, one on law and the other on sociology.

to assassinate Lenin. Release after fifty-seven days did not relieve him of the status of a fugitive, and for two months he hid in the forests, moving by stealth from village to village, subsisting on berries and mushrooms and such foodstuffs as generous peasants were able to provide. His friends arranged a place of hiding for him but knowing that capture was only a matter of time, he made the desperate decision to give himself up. Once more he found himself enduring the misery, the starvation, the cold, and the filth of a Communist prison. Every day some of the prisoners were taken out and shot—sometimes five, sometimes seven, the number varied—and no one knew when his turn would come.

For Sorokin, however, the miracle happened. Lenin decided that the country could not afford to lose its intellectuals and personally ordered his release. The terror continued, however, and finally the regime decided to banish the surviving scholars who would not conform. In this way Sorokin and his wife, Elena, whom he had married in 1917, went into exile.

After a brief stay in Berlin, Sorokin received an invitation from Thomas Garrigues Masaryk, sociologist, and president of Czechoslovakia, to come to Prague and teach at the Charles University. After a pleasant year in that baroque city, surrounded by other Russian émigré scholars, Sorokin received invitations from Edward Cary Hayes and Edward A. Ross to lecture, respectively, at the Universities of Illinois and Wisconsin. Accordingly, he embarked for the New World and arrived in New York in October 1923. He had left earlier than necessary in order to practice the English language and was able, by invitation of Henry Noble MacCracken, then president of Vassar, to spend six weeks there before going on to the Midwest. In the next few months lecture invitations were numerous, and Sorokin earned enough to send for his wife to join him in the United States. After a summer session (1924) at the University of Minnesota he was offered an appointment there for the following year, in the department headed by F. Stuart Chapin. He remained at Minnesota for six years, which proved to be the most productive years of his life. Indeed, he produced so much that his friend E. A. Ross, in a letter of January 26, 1928, cautioned him that overwork might undermine his health. In these six years he published *Leaves from a Russian Diary* (1924), *The Sociology of Revolution* (1925), *Social Mobility* (1927), *Contemporary Sociological Theories* (1928), *Principles of Rural-Urban Sociology*, with Carle C. Zimmerman (1929), and the first of a three-volume work, *A Systematic Source Book in Rural Sociology*, with Zimmerman and Carl J. Galpin (1930)—all these in a language he did not speak until 1923. Sorokin is especially grateful to his early American audiences for tolerating his English. It was always a broken English, even after he had lived in this country for four decades. Later on he would either apologize for his "Harvard accent" or confess, with an engaging grin, that he had forgotten his Russian and never learned English. In any event, the years at Minnesota were happy and fruitful ones. Mrs. Sorokin took her Ph.D in botany, but because the nepotism rule at the university made her ineligible for an appointment there, she became professor of botany at Hamline University in Saint Paul.

In October 1929 Sorokin received an invitation to accept a new chair of sociology at Harvard, beginning the following year, with the privilege of placing it in the department of his choice. In reply he suggested that it would be even better if Harvard were to establish a department of sociology, a suggestion to which the administration agreed. Harvard, like Oxford and Cambridge, had been a laggard in the development of sociology. The economist Thomas Nixon Carver had taught courses in the discipline, and there was a Department of Social Ethics whose members touched on social problems. But the establishment of a chair in 1930 was late indeed, compared to Yale, Chicago, Columbia, the midwestern universities, and, interestingly enough, the women's colleges in the East.[4] Harvard's acceptance of an autonomous department was qualified by two requirements: that all of its members be recruited from the Harvard faculty and that it absorb the Department of Social Ethics. Sorokin himself maintained that, because of the difficulty of the subject, it should be only a graduate department, but on this point he was outvoted. In any event, a committee, of which Sorokin was chairman, ironed out the difficulties, and the new Department of Sociology came into being in the fall of 1931.

Sorokin retained the chairmanship until 1944 and attracted to the university an unusually large number of students who themselves became distinguished sociologists. Several became university presidents. His administration, however, was a turbulent one, and personal relations with his colleagues were often difficult. A man of great, and sometimes winsome, charm, he could nevertheless churn the emotions of those with whom he disagreed. For most American sociologists he had nothing but contempt and indeed subjected them, in his lectures, to frequent and savage criticism, criticism from which his own students enjoyed no exemption:

> Sorokin's attitude toward the work of his students was similarly one of an almost ritual hostility. After tea in the afternoon—a pleasant custom—the seminar would convene, with Sorokin in the chair. During the first hour one of the students would present a paper. During the second hour Sorokin, in full panoply, would tear it apart, paragraph by paragraph—almost, as it then

4. "President Lowell told me that Harvard had already decided to establish a chair of sociology some twenty-five years before. They had not done so until then because there was no sociologist worthy to fill the chair. Now, in their opinion, such a sociologist had appeared, and they had promptly made the decision." *Long Journey*, p. 238.

> seemed, syllable by syllable—until at the end of the period, vituperation unexhausted, he would conclude, "And so you see, gentlemen, this paper, it is worth nothing!" We were hardy souls in those days, and most of us wore our scar tissue with pride.[5]

The Memorial Minute adopted by the Faculty of Arts and Sciences at Harvard on December 3, 1968, contains the following words:

> On balance, the testimony of his many students and colleagues is that Sorokin's influence was predominantly creative and positively stimulating. It was not, however, an influence of steady, consistent leadership—he was never mainly an "organization" man. His frequent warm and supportive relations with students and colleagues were often, unpredictably, broken by spells of impassioned antagonism and intemperate criticism. He was, as one of his former students and teaching assistants put it, an "incomparable showman" as a lecturer, but this showmanship sometimes included a major ingredient of picturesque invective, made all the more picturesque by a strong Russian accent which more than forty years in this country did not change much.[6]

Companion to Sorokin's critical excesses was an ego as large as the vault of heaven—an ego almost inoffensive because it was so startling. We shall see many examples of it in his writing. For the moment two illustrations will suffice. Once at a reception a Radcliffe student approached him and asked, in all innocence, what he thought about the future of civilization. "Well," he promptly began, "I be quite frank with you," as if that future had been confided to him alone. In the Introduction to Volume 4 of his *Social and Cultural Dynamics,* he wrote, "History so far is proceeding along in accordance with the schedule laid down in my *Dynamics.*" This remarkable statement drew from Robert M. MacIver, who reviewed the book for the *American Sociological Review,* the wry comment: "Happy Mr. Sorokin. Thrice happy Mr. Sorokin. He knows the secret of history."[7]

A man of slight build, Sorokin nevertheless had enormous stamina and enjoyed hard physical labor. He was also a gardener of distinction, growing azalea, rhododendron, lilac, rose, and wisteria at his suburban home in Winchester, winning prizes for his azalea. He had an exemplary family life. He and Elena had two sons, both educated at Harvard, one of whom became a physicist and the other a physician. Their closest friends were the Koussevitzkys—Serge, the distinguished conductor of the Boston Sym-

5. Robert Bierstedt, *Power and Progress: Essays on Sociological Theory* (New York: McGraw-Hill, 1974), pp. 2–3.

6. Prepared by a committee consisting of Robert F. Bales, George C. Homans, Florence Kluckhohn Taylor, Robert W. White, and Talcott Parsons, Chairman.

7. Vol. 6 (December 1941): 904–907, quote on p. 904.

phony Orchestra—and the Rostovtzeffs—Michael, the great historian of Rome.

Sorokin was a man of incredible courage and impeccable honesty. Steeled in the hardships of the Russian revolution, he had no trouble, during the McCarthy period, with federal investigators who came to his Harvard office and inquired into the loyalty of students who were under consideration for government appointments. He always replied that none of them could possibly be as subversive as he. He once remarked that having seen the inside of czarist prisons and Communist prisons, he hoped that before he died he would see the inside of an American prison. It was an ambition he failed to achieve.

After his retirement from the chairmanship in 1944, Sorokin devoted attention and extensive labor to his books and to a new project, the Harvard Research Center in Creative Altruism. Subsidized by the philanthropist Eli Lilly, the center was established in 1949. Deploring the tendency of other sociologists to study such pathological phenomena as war, crime, narcotics addiction, and mental disorder, Sorokin and his associates turned to such subjects as love, altruism, friendship, heroism, saintliness, and genius. The result was a number of articles and books, most of the latter written or edited by Sorokin; but few of them had the impact he desired.

Sorokin retired from Harvard on December 31, 1959, with the title of professor emeritus. He devoted the remaining years of his life to "spoiling more pieces of white paper" (as he referred to his writing), to lecturing by invitation at numerous colleges and universities, and to attending national and international scientific meetings. He received a shock when a paper of his on Herbert Spencer, delivered at the annual meeting of the American Sociological Association in New York in August 1960, was rejected by the *American Sociological Review.*[8] Because of his intense and incessant criticism of American sociology and sociologists, he had regularly been passed over for nomination to the presidency of the American Sociological Association. In 1965, however, a group of his former students, aware that the dereliction reflected more on the association than on Sorokin, succeeded in nominating him by petition, the first such nomination in its history. He was easily elected and delivered his presidential address in Chicago on September 1, 1965.[9] He died on February 10, 1968.

The Memorial Minute referred to earlier concludes with the following:

> Pitirim Sorokin was a complex and in some ways a paradoxical man. Carry-

8. An account of this episode appears in *Long Journey,* pp. 303–304.
9. "Sociology of Yesterday, Today, and Tomorrow," *American Sociological Review* 30 (December 1965): 833–843.

ing with him the tragic burdens of a life spent largely in exile, he felt deeply the conflicts of the time in which he lived and gave them notable expression. His influence on social science and beyond, through both his writing and his teaching, has been immense.

To this we may add a postcript, in words he often used, *"Feci quod potui faciant meliora potentes"* ("I did what I could; let those more capable do better").

Social Mobility

By the time Sorokin published *Social Mobility,*[10] he had already published, as we have seen, a number of books in Russian and *Leaves from a Russian Diary* and *The Sociology of Revolution* in English. In the last named he found nothing constructive in the Russian revolution and regarded revolutions in general as perversions of behavior. It was a personal book, almost the autobiography over again with a few statistics added to the mix.

Social Mobility, on the contrary, is an impersonal and serious study, one entirely in harmony with the orthodox positivism that at that time characterized his methodological position. He treated both horizontal and vertical mobility, the former occurring when people change their place of residence or occupation, the latter when they ascend or descend on the scale of social class. Sorokin noted that both individuals and groups could be subjects of these processes; that is, there can be individual "infiltration" and "collective ascent or descent." Societies arrange themselves on a continuum with respect to mobility, but there is none in which mobility is completely free or, on the other hand, completely restricted. Certain occupations are favorable for mobility and can be used as escalators—for example, the army (especially in time of war), the church, the school, and the state bureaucracy. Others, such as farming and factory labor, are not conducive to ascent. The circulation and distribution of individuals are not matters of chance, but may be attributed to three factors: differential birth and death rates in different classes, dissimilarity of parents and children, due to differences in character and ability, and other social changes, such as the alternations of war and peace. On the whole, Sorokin concluded that a mobile society possesses certain advantages over an immobile one and that it leads more easily to prosperity and progress.

10. (New York: Harper & Brothers, 1927).

We include only this brief mention of *Social Mobility* here but regard it as an important item in Sorokin's bibliography and one that continues to merit attention.[11]

Contemporary Sociological Theories

Sorokin finished *Contemporary Sociological Theories* in 1927, and it was published in 1928.[12] Translated into many languages, it immediately gave him an international reputation and is certainly—and deservedly—responsible for his invitation to move to Harvard. It also almost certainly accounts for the number of superior graduate students who were attracted to Harvard to study with him in the 1930s. Although the word *contemporary*, meaning a period of some sixty or seventy years, appears in its title, Sorokin's use of ancient sources such as the Sacred Books of the East and the Chinese and Greek philosophers of antiquity gave the book a scope hitherto unknown in the literature of sociology. His control of languages, at least for research purposes, attested to the power of his scholarship, as did also the numerous and detailed footnotes scattered through his 761 pages.[13] How he managed to produce it only one year after *Social Mobility* remains a mystery, especially because he had no assistance except that which the librarians at the University of Minnesota supplied in the course of their normal duties. The book is a *tour de force.*

He wrote it, Sorokin says, for several reasons. In the first place, there was no book in the field that did the job he wanted done, and consequently no text suitable for the use of his graduate students. In the second place, the literature has become so voluminous that few can comprehend it all—a situation that results in what he called the "Columbus complex"—scholars toiling arduously to find land that had been discovered long ago. In the third place, there are now so many theories that it is necessary to separate the valid ones from the invalid. Except for these reasons there is no excuse for a man to be writing a book about other books [!].

As incidental and additional points, Sorokin tells us that despite his effort to be impartial some subjectivism has doubtless "slipped" into his selection and treatment of the material. Those who have read the book can

11. Sorokin returned to the subject in *Society, Culture, and Personality*, published twenty years later. See especially chaps. 24–28.

12. (New York: Harper & Brothers).

13. Someone has determined that it contains more than 5000 references, although counting them would seem to be an unrewarding exercise.

only smile at the understatement. Although the selections are fair, Sorokin is the most prejudiced of writers. He cultivates his prejudices with care and expresses them with enthusiasm, not to say vehemence and vituperation. He proposes to deal not with speculative and "philosophical" theories but for the most part with factual and inductive studies. Here Sorokin is still in his positivistic stage; the great tergiversation has not yet occurred. He proposes to omit also all theories that prescribe what ought to be in society. They are outside the realm of science. Finally, he will indulge in relentless criticism, a criticism that implies no disrespect for the authors criticized—indeed, the contrary; they are worth criticizing. Criticism is the essence of science—"It appeared with criticism, has grown with criticism, and lives with criticism. If we care to promote sociology as a science, a critical attitude must be displayed by all sociologists as regards any sociological theory, without any exception whatsoever."[14] Some of his students, to their subsequent dismay, took this advice too literally in criticizing Sorokin's own theories.

No synopsis of the book can possibly provide an idea of the richness of its content. One of its major contributions, however, is Sorokin's classification of the various schools of sociological theory. It should be noted that these "schools" are for the most part single-factor interpretations of the structure of society and of social change. They are various ways of interpreting society, not, as is so often the case, various ways of interpreting sociology. They have nothing to do with such approaches to sociological inquiry as functionalism, exchange theory, symbolic interactionism, and others. The first chapter, for example, deals with the mechanistic school, those who have regarded society as some kind of a machine, exhibiting the operation of both centripetal (associative) and centrifugal (dissociative) forces. Among these writers Sorokin includes the pre-Socratic Greek philosophers and especially the so-called social physicists of the seventeenth century (Hobbes, Spinoza, Descartes, Leibniz, and, a little later, Berkeley). Saint-Simon, Fourier, Comte, and Quételet also appear on Sorokin's mechanistic roster. His principal attention, however, is devoted to social energetics and includes such names as H. C. Carey, Voronoff, Haret, Lotka, Barcelo, Solvay, Ostwald, Bechtereff, Carver, and Winiarsky—names that do not ordinarily appear in the histories of sociology. In any event, Sorokin dismisses them all as writers who have contributed nothing to the understanding of social phenomena. The concepts of physical force and physical energy, such as the conception of society as an astronomical system, are little more than absurd. To one writer in this

14. *Contemporary Sociological Theories*, p. xxiii

school he gives favorable, but critical, treatment, and that is Pareto.[15] He regards Pareto's ideas as "sound and promising," but defective nevertheless. On a positive note,

> Pareto's studies show that, properly taken, the social physics of the seventeenth century is not a mere dream of a bold human mind, but may be developed into a real scientific sociology which will probably not be able to disentangle all the 'mysteries' of human behavior and human history, but may clarify, to some degree, the more important of them.[16]

The second chapter is devoted to Frédéric Le Play and his school —Demolins, de Tourville, de Rousiers, Pinot, and others. Here Sorokin's verdict is largely favorable, and indeed he regards the *Nomenclature*, which we would today regard as a schedule, as "really a great contribution to the method of social science."[17] Of greater interest is the fact that he devotes more than twice the space to Le Play and his disciples than he does in later chapters to Durkheim and Weber combined. In any event, it was Le Play, conservative to the core, who regarded Thomas Jefferson as a disastrous influence upon American society. To his credit is that he generated his own data, in his investigation of the budgets of working-class families in Europe, and was one of the earliest of sociologists to do so. One does not assign him similar credit for his notion that the whole of sociology was contained in the Ten Commandments.

In a long (ninety-five pages) chapter on the geographical school, Sorokin considers the influence of geographical factors upon the distribution of population, on clothing, on food and drink, on economic life and organization, on race, on health, on human energy and efficiency, on mental efficiency, on suicide, on insanity, on crime, on birth, death, and marriage rates, on religion, art, and literature, on social and political organization, and on genius and the evolution of civilizations. He is willing to concede that geographical factors influence some social phenomena more than others—notably those that concern such primary needs as food, clothing, and shelter—but he is devastating in his criticism of geographers like Ellsworth P. Huntington, who try to use these factors as keys to explain the rise and fall of civilizations.

The next school to come under consideration is the "bioorganismic," and here Sorokin criticizes all those who have used the organic analogy in their treatment of society, and especially Lilienfeld, Schäffle, Worms, and

15. "Pareto's treatise is the product of an original and outstanding scientific mind." *Ibid.*, p. 39.

16. *Ibid.*, p. 62.

17. *Ibid.*, p. 73.

Novicow. In the chapter on the "anthropo-racial, selectionist, and hereditarist school," he does the same for those who would use heredity or race as explanations of behavior—de Gobineau, Galton, Pearson, Ammon, and Lapouge, among many others. Here he accepts the "evidence" of studies, profuse in the 1920s, that the white race is superior to the black in intelligence and in the production of genius.[18] In a reference to E. B. Reuter he denies that "the various races and peoples of the world are essentially equal in mental ability and capacity for civilization."[19] On the other hand, he recognizes that any claim for superiority is a purely subjective judgment and notices that differences between the upper and lower classes of the same race are greater than differences between the races. He is inclined to ascribe more importance to heredity than his successors in sociology and regards the theories of the school as important and valuable when not exaggerated. In a chapter on the struggle for existence and the sociology of war, he concludes, again:

> In spite of its many defects, taken as a whole, the [biological] school has represented one of the most powerful currents of sociological thought; has thrown light on many social phenomena; has given a series of valuable correlations; and has shown many deep factors which lie under the picturesque surface of the social ocean. For these reasons it must be recognized as one of the most important sociological schools. Whether we like it or not, it will exist. The greater and more accurate are the findings of biology, the more accurate are going to be the biological interpretations of social phenomena, and the more powerful influence they are likely to exert on sociological thought in the future.[20]

Sorokin did not return to the subject again. Indeed, he later regarded geography and biology as consisting of "pre-sociological information."

Sorokin uses the same critical technique with respect to the demographic school and arrives at the same general kind of conclusion, namely, its theories are useful when not mistaken or "one-sided." By the "sociologistic" school, next on his list, he means those theories that emphasize the importance of social interaction, which regard society as a reality sui generis and which deny that sociology can be served by psychological explanations. Among the members of this school—in addition to Buddha, Confucius,[21] Plato, and Aristotle—he lists, among many others, Comte, De Roberty,

18. *Ibid.*, p. 297.

19. *Ibid.*, p. 302, n. 170.

20. *Ibid.*, p. 355.

21. "Confucianism contains all the essentials of the modern sociologistic theories, especially of the contemporary theory of *mores* developed by W. G. Sumner, and the 'family-sociology' developed by Le Play's school and Ch. H. Cooley." *Ibid.*, p. 436.

Espinas, Izoulet, Draghicesco, Cooley, Durkheim, and Gumplowicz. Sorokin does not care for the "fictitious entity," independent of individuals, which he regards as Durkheim's conception of society, but he appreciates Durkheim's work on suicide. On balance, however, Durkheim's sociology is fallaciously one-sided and "monopolistic."[22]

To the sociologistic school Sorokin adds a "formal school" consisting of Tönnies, Stammler, Simmel, von Wiese, Vierkandt, Litt, Bouglé, Park, and Burgess.[23] The claims of this school, especially that it is new, that there is a supportable distinction between the form and content of social phenomena and that therefore sociology is an autonomous science of social relationships as such are invalid. "I do not know any 'formal' work which has produced anything above an average scholastic value."[24] And, "The very attempt of formal sociology to build 'an independent sociology' is rather fallacious."[25] The school has, however, contributed something in systematizing human relations and social processes, and in this respect Sorokin pays unexpected tribute to Ross, Cooley, Giddings, Hayes, Park and Burgess, and Bogardus. But, "If we had followed literally the pretensions of the formal school, the result would have been a transformation of sociology into a purely scholastic and dead science, a kind of almost useless catalogue of human relations."[26]

A special branch of the sociologistic school is the economic, and in a chapter devoted to it Sorokin treats Marx and Engels with contempt. Indeed, his treatment is more of a demolition project than a discussion. The economic interpretation of society and of social change is as old as the history of social thought, and Marx and Engels did little but add dogmatism to it. The theory of the class struggle is entirely fallacious. "All in all, Marx and Engels have rather hindered the progress of social science than facilitated it. . . . Only a metaphysician could now be busy with the Marx-Engels conceptions."[27] The remainder of the long chapter is devoted to inductive studies of correlations between economic factors and various other social phenomena.

In the chapter on the psychological school, Freud fares no better than Marx did in the preceding chapter. Having been a student of Pavlov, Sorokin is relatively kind to him (a "real" behaviorist), but not to Watson.

22. *Ibid.*, pp. 479, 480.

23. Another criticism of Durkheim: "One cannot help thinking that Durkheim intentionally gave to his social types names which were opposite to those given by Tönnies." *Ibid.*, p. 491. The criticism of Simmel is severe. *Ibid.*, p. 502, n. 26.

24. *Ibid.*, p. 505.

25. *Ibid.*, p. 506.

26. *Ibid.*, p. 513.

27. *Ibid.*, p. 546.

Sorokin does not hesitate to locate his own studies of inanition in the behavioristic school.[28] Sorokin attends also to those sociologists who emphasize the roles of desires, conations, pain, pleasure, interests, wishes, wants, volitions, and attitudes in social life. Although he has a few kind words for Tarde, Ward,[29] and Ross, the "attitude" of Park and Burgess is "a logical monster," and his general view of those who use concepts such as these is negative:

> Like a prestidigitator, the authors betimes put into a manbag a series of wishes and desires, and after that, with a serious expression, they take out of the bag one or several of the desires and wishes, according to the circumstances, and convincingly add: "This agency is responsible for the actions or events studied." The procedure is certainly easy, but one may seriously doubt as to whether or not it has any cognitive value.[30]

Finally, psychological theories, whether "introspectivist" or behaviorist, have their limitations as explanations of social phenomena. At the end of the chapter Sorokin anticipates his own future position by criticizing mechanistic and quantitative approaches and defending the importance of introspection and the *Verstehende* sociologies of Weber, Spranger, and Jaspers.

The next chapter deals with the role of beliefs, magic, myths, superstitions, ideologies, and religion as factors in social change and attends briefly to the theories of de Coulanges, Ellwood, Durkheim, Le Bon, Frazer, Bouglé, Ross, Sorel, Kidd, and Weber. Sorokin gives high marks to Weber but in general finds his theses questionable. Sumner's theory of the folkways and mores is tautological. To say that they determine behavior is

---

28. Sorokin's *Influence of Inanition on Human Behavior, Social Organization, and Social Life* was destroyed by the Soviet government in 1922 while it was being printed. Mrs. Sorokin found the proofs of this book after his death, and it was published in 1975 by the University Presses of Florida, Gainesville, under the title *Hunger as a Factor in Human Affairs*, translated and with a prologue by Elena P. Sorokin and edited and with an introduction by T. Lynn Smith.

29. Sorokin has an interesting observation on Ward:

> Take further L. Ward's hypothesis of the *replacement of the blind character of natural evolution by a conative and teleological progress in the course of time.* As far as this theory, and a similar theory of Professor L. T. Hobhouse, claim that in the course of time man's behavior becomes more and more rationalistic and the social processes tend to be more and more controlled by the conscientious [conscious?] volitions of human beings, the theory is far from being proved. It appeals to us and appears convincing, and yet, when carefully tested, it must be recognized as being at least questionable. Modern man in some respects is certainly more rationalistic than primitive man; but in other respects we are likely to be a prey of blind forces in a greater degree than the peoples of the past and ancient societies.

Contemporary Sociological Theories, p. 655.

30. *Ibid.*, p. 647.

to say no more than that behavior determines behavior. Petrajitzky's theory of law as a psychosocial factor suffers from a similar flaw. Finally, in the last substantive chapter, we have studies of the role of the family, neighborhood, occupation, rural-urban environment, personality types, leadership and intelligence, and, along with this miscellaneous grouping of factors, studies of the fluctuations, rhythms, and cycles of social processes, studies of the migration, diffusion, and mobility of cultural objects and individuals, and studies of "sudden, cataclysmic, revolutionary, and catastrophic changes."

Sorokin's conclusion is entitled "Retrospect and Prospect." At the time of writing, sociology seemed to resemble a half-wild forest rather than a carefully cultivated garden. Some planning is doubtless desirable, but it should not be overdone, because the complex nature of social phenomena requires a variety of approaches. The field contains both sterile flowers and weeds. The sterile flowers are those works that tell us what sociology should be. The weeds are those works whose authors indulge in moral pronouncements, telling us what ought to be instead of what is. Among other weeds are

> an insufficient study of the facts in time and space; a mania for generalizing a certain conclusion far beyond the factual basis on which it is built; an ignorance of the theories and studies made by others and in preceding times; a failure to make from a certain hypothesis all the important conclusions and to verify them as to whether they are corroborated in space and time; [and] a failure to test an invented hypothesis seriously.[31]

On the other hand, sociology can also exhibit many "potentially strong trees, fine plants and beautiful flowers."

Sorokin also essays a definition of sociology:

> It seems to be a study, first, of the relationship and correlations between various classes of social phenomena, (correlations between economic and religious; family and moral; juridical and economic, mobility and political phenomena and so on); second, that between the social and the non-social (geographic, biological, etc.,) phenomena; third, the study of the general characteristics common to all classes of social phenomena.[32]

Sorokin is especially insistent upon this last point: "Sociology has been, is, and either will be a science of the general characteristics of all classes of social phenomena, with the relationships and correlations between them;

31. *Ibid.*, p. 759.
32. *Ibid.*, pp. 760–761.

or there will be no sociology."[33] For Sorokin sociology is a general, not a special, social science, and in this view he was consistent.

Society, Culture, and Personality

Society, Culture, and Personality contains all of Sorokin's systematic sociology, both his theory of the social structure and his theory of social change.[34] The theory of social change, of course, was developed in *Social and Cultural Dynamics.*[35] The theory of social structure was developed first in 1920, in the two-volume *Sistema Soziologii,* which Sorokin defended as his doctoral dissertation in 1922. The "theory," or system, in 1947 is in all important respects the same, as he tells us himself. Although he almost never reread his books, he had to reread *Sistema* in order to prepare his later volumes:

> As a result of these rereadings I find that, despite several defects, the volumes gave what appears to me the first logically systematic and empirically detailed theory of social structures: "The Structure of the Elementary Social Systems," developed in Volume I, and "The Structure of the Complex (Multibonded) Social Systems," expounded in Volume II.
>
> If in these later works I virtually reiterated in concise form the theory developed in my *Sistema Soziologii,* the reason for such repetition was that I found my early theory more logically consistent, more empirically valid, and more scientifically adequate than any other theory of the social structure in the world literature of sociology and social sciences.[36]

One does not quite know how to interpret the expression "in concise form" in this quotation. *Society, Culture, and Personality,* for example, consists of no fewer than forty-eight chapters in 723 double-column pages. It is, in fact, too large for a respectable synopsis, and we shall ignore portions of it that have largely lost their relevance for contemporary sociology.

In his Preface Sorokin suggests that so much fact finding has been going on in sociology that the greatest need now is to assimilate the facts and to organize them in some kind of a logical order; in short, to rebuild the framework of sociology as a systematic science. This is what he proposes to do. Accordingly, at the beginning of the text itself he discusses the nature of sociology as a science. It belongs to the superorganic, just as biology

33. *Ibid.*, p. 761.
34. (New York: Harper & Brothers, 1947).
35. 4 vols. (New York: American Book Co. 1937–1941).
36. *Long Journey,* p. 96.

belongs to the organic, and physics to the inorganic. The superorganic is synonymous with the realm of mind in all its manifestations and is the exclusive product of human interaction. Without it we would be feral people, no different from animals. Sorokin makes the usual distinction between generalizing sciences and individualizing sciences and assigns sociology, of course, to the former and history to the latter. He insists, as we have seen, that sociology is a general, not a special, social science and constructs a useful paradigm to illustrate the point (the letters refer to elements or factors or variables):

Economic: *a, b, c, n, m, f*
Political: *a, b, c, h, d, j*
Religious: *a, b, c, g, i, q*
and so on.[37]

Thus, sociology differs from such special social sciences as economics, political science, the study of religion, and so on. It studies the *a*'s, *b*'s, and *c*'s that are common to all of them and in addition studies the relationships between the uncommon elements—for example, the relationship between crime and the business cycle. Neither of these tasks is performed by any other science, and thus sociology has its own domain. Social man also differs from economic man, political man, religious man, and so on. "*Homo socius* of sociology is viewed as a generic and manifold *homo*, simultaneously and inseparably economic, political, religious, ethical and artistic, partly rational and utilitarian, partly nonrational and even irrational, with all these aspects incessantly influencing one another."[38] Similarly, sociology is concerned with the relationships among all social phenomena—artistic, political, religious, or anything else. For Sorokin there is no special category of "the social." The social is the sum and manifold of all the others. It is necessary to view society as a whole, and this is the task of sociology.

Despite the clarity and emphasis of these propositions, Sorokin is moved to assert that sociology is also a special science:

> Though sociology is a generalizing science dealing with the sociocultural universe as a whole, this does not mean that it is an encyclopedic survey of all the social sciences or that it is a vague philosophical synthesis. The study of the common and current properties, relationships, and uniformities of sociocultural phenomena involves as much specialization as does a study of the unique or segmentary traits and relationships. *In spite of its generalizing nature sociology remains a strictly special science.*[39]

37. *Society, Culture, and Personality*, p. 7b.
38. *Ibid.*, p. 8a.
39. *Ibid.*, p. 14b.

Here, perhaps imperialistically, Sorokin compares the task of sociology with that of the president or treasurer of a company, officials who are specialized in their ability to oversee the enterprise as a whole. In any event, sociology depends upon the other disciplines and in turn exerts an influence upon them. In summary—and here is his definition—"Sociology is a generalizing science of sociocultural phenomena viewed in their generic forms, types, and manifold interconnections."[40] Internally, sociology deals with both the structure and the dynamics of sociocultural phenomena, and indeed, unlike Znaniecki, Sorokin regards Comte's distinction between statics and dynamics as the most fruitful division of the discipline. Finally:

> This delineation of sociology is logically more adequate and better corresponds to what sociology has actually been than other definitions, such as the science "of culture." "of society," "of human relations," "of social interaction," "of forms of social relationships," and the like. These definitions are far too loose. They do not point out the specific characteristics of sociology or differentiate it from other social sciences. On the other hand, the sound part of these definitions is well incorporated into the above delineation.[41]

His last comment on this point is the important one that many who are not sociologists have written on sociology and, conversely, sociologists have written on other subjects than sociology.[42]

After a chapter on the development of sociology in the Orient, Greece, Rome, medieval Europe, and Arabia, in Europe from the Renaissance to modern times, and recent and contemporary sociology, Sorokin plunges into his task of building his structure. Most sociologists—at least systematic sociologists—have some trouble finding an appropriate *point de départ* or *point d'appui*. What is the initial, or the basic, unit of sociological inquiry? Is it the individual, the *socius*, the dyad, the plurel, the group, the norm, the institution, the interest, the act, the role, the family, the tribal society, or what? Different sociologist have made different choices, and the initial choice, of course, determines the vectors of the system. For Sorokin the basic concept or, as he calls it, the most generic social phenomenon, is meaningful human interaction. All three words are important. Without the attribute of *meaning* no social phenomenon, properly speaking, appears. When a man kills another with a gun we have no interest in the trajectory of the bullet or the medical cause of death. We want to know instead

---

40. *Ibid.*, p. 16a. Incidentally, we learn on this page that Confucius, John Locke, and Voltaire were sociologists. This, of course, is in accord with Sorokin's comprehensive view of the discipline. Anyone, in any age, who said anything at all about society or social relationships belongs on his roster.

41. *Ibid.*, p. 17a.

42. His illustrations, however, are unfortunate. It is a little disingenuous to call Le Play and Spencer engineers and Comte a mathematician.

whether the act was first degree murder, manslaughter, killing in self-defense, or an act of heroism, as in war. *Human* is self-explanatory; Sorokin is not writing animal sociology. And *interaction* implies mutuality, recognition, influence. Unless one person influences another in some way, there is no social phenomenon as such. The influence must be tangible, observable, and noticeable. Thus, no purely statistical group can qualify.[43]

The next step is to outline the components of the generic social phenomenon, or meaningful human interaction. They are three: the human beings themselves, subjects of interaction; meanings, values, and norms; and "overt actions and material phenomena as vehicles or conductors through which immaterial meanings, values, and norms are objectified and socialized."[44] The flaws in this schema are immediately apparent. In the first place, Sorokin has an inveterate attachment to triads and classifies phenomena in three categories even when he has two, or four. Here, for example, he has four—individuals, norms, actions, and material phenomena. It is not clear how actions and material phenomena can belong together in a single category, both subsumed under the general rubric of meaningful human interaction. Material phenomena assuredly have significance for action but they are not themselves action or interaction. Second, the arrangement of meanings, values, and norms in the same category is a dubious procedure. The three words are far from synonymous. There is no attempt, here or elsewhere, to define *meaning* or *value* and no appreciation of the fact that these concepts are among the most complex in the entire vocabulary of philosophy. But let us watch Sorokin as he elaborates on his components.

With respect to the subjects of interaction, which may be either individuals or groups, both the number and qualities of the interacting individuals are important. The number of individuals may be two, or three, or four, or more. The relationship, moreover, may be one–one, one–many, or many–many. The sheer number of individuals involved in social interaction is significant, as writers such as Simmel have emphasized. With respect to the qualities of the interacting individuals Sorokin mentions only two, or, rather, one pair—homogeneity and heterogeneity. That is, the interaction may be between members of the same or different race, nationality, age, sex, and so on. But now he discusses under this first rubric a subject he

43. In his classification of groups Sorokin forgets this condition and includes such phenomena as "semi-nominal" and purely nominal plurels.

44. *Ibid.*, pp. 41b–42a. In a typical aside, Sorokin informs us that this three-componential scheme appears also in a somewhat vague and undeveloped way in the writings of W. I. Thomas, Malinowski, Linton, Kluckhohn, M. Mead, and Radcliffe-Brown (p. 42a, n. 6).

has assigned to his third, namely, the character of the actions. Again the classification is odd. Actions may be catalytic, active, passive, or tolerant. They may also be effective and ineffective, durable and short-lived, and purposive and nonpurposive. Few would regard this as an adequate classification of actions. It gives Sorokin an opportunity, however, to criticize all those, including Parsons, who, to him, appear to regard all social actions as purposive, as involving the conscious application of means to ends—a position that, he argues with the help of Petrajitsky and Pavlov, is entirely fallacious:

> In the light of this conclusion the inadequacy of the schema "means and end," even in application to conscious actions and social relationships, is evident. Since the basic assumption is false, the results of this pseudo-teleological analysis of social phenomena have been either negligible or (more often) misleading. Only with reference to purposeful phenomena is the schema applicable and helpful, and they constitute merely a small fraction of sociocultural phenomena.[45]

One gathers from observations such as this, which appear in profusion, that Sorokin is more interested in attacking Parsons than he is in seriously advancing the view that nonpurposive actions are more important than the reverse, especially in a discipline in which the "meaningful" looms so large.

In any event, the meaning of a sociocultural phenomenon is independent of its physical or biological manifestation. Thus, the Christian Credo has the same meaning whether it is spoken, written on paper, engraved in stone, recorded on a phonograph, or broadcast on the radio. The converse is also true. Cloth of the same color and texture may serve as a diaper, a turban, or a flag of surrender. The same may be said of biological manifestations. Love may be expressed by a kiss, a caress, an endearing word, a gift, and in sexual intercourse. On the other hand, sexual intercourse, physiologically the same, can have such different meanings as seduction, rape, adultery, prostitution, and the lawful communion of married partners. From these obvious but important observations Sorokin draws the erroneous inference that therefore all naturalistic and behavioristic theories are fallacious:

> The preceding analysis clearly shows the absurdity of the so-called naturalistic and behavioristic study of sociocultural phenomena. If it were consistently carried out, it would be necessary to classify all sociocultural phenomena as identical or different solely on the basis of their biophysical properties, in which case there would be no political, economic, religious, scientific, aesthetic, or juridical classes of phenomena, since each of these classes is

45. *Ibid.*, p. 47a.

> composed of the most hererogeneous objects, persons, actions, events, and processes.[46]

For this reason, none of those who have enthusiastically espoused the naturalistic and behavioristic position—such as Pareto, Lundberg, and Dodd in sociology and Chapple and Coon in anthropology—have been able to carry out their own programs.

Sorokin's discussion of his third component of the generic social phenomenon—namely, the material culture—is a curious one. He treats it in terms of the vehicles or conductors of interaction and proceeds to classify these vehicles as sound conductors (speech, music, and noise), light and color conductors (street lights and pictures), pantomimic conductors (gestures and expressive movements), thermal conductors, mechanical conductors, chemical conductors, electrical and radio conductors, and material-object conductors. In this last category he lists such examples as a dollar bill, a lock of hair, a wedding ring, a family heirloom, a scepter, a cross, a national flag, a trophy cup, the keys of a city, Notre Dame cathedral, the White House, and the Lincoln Memorial. "In a large proportion of meaningful interactions the parties use a chain of different conductors joined to one another with human beings as the linking agents. The whole mechanism of transmission may be compared to a complex system of cogwheels, one of which sets in motion the next, and so on, until the whole system is completed."[47] No one, of course, belittles the importance of material culture; no one, on the other hand, has adopted Sorokin's treatment of it in terms of vehicles and conductors.

Despite some idiosyncratic language, he does, however, score important points when he discusses the retroactive influence of vehicles and the "fetishization of vehicles." It is clear that the very existence of roads, bridges, and buildings has something to do with our behavior and that clothing, especially uniforms, can seriously affect our modes of thought and probably also our personality:

> Political prisoners experience a decisive change in mentality upon donning prisoners' garb. Officers stripped of the symbols of their rank—a sword, stars, or other insignia—and donning civilian clothing, undergo a mental change which is sometimes permanent. On the other hand, if an ordinary citizen is invested with the insignia of pomp and power, he may be transformed into a self-confident, proud, and arrogant personality.[48]

Similarly, what Sorokin calls sound symbols—titles of nobility and of ad-

46. *Ibid.*, p. 50a.
47. *Ibid.*, p. 57b.
48. *Ibid.*, p. 60b.

dress, such as "Your Honor," "Sir," "Doctor," "Colonel"—have the same effect. By "fetishization of vehicles" he means the tendency, apparent in all societies, primitive and civilized, to confuse the symbol with what it symbolizes. A national flag, for example, physically only a colored cloth attached to a stick, becomes a fetish, an idol, a sacred object, more important to some than the ideals for which it stands. Patriotic societies thus require that a worn flag be buried with respect and not used as a dust cloth or cleaning rag. Words are also fetishized and take on a mystical power of their own, and the names of the deities are often forbidden to be spoken or written in full. On this subject Sorokin is quite insightful.

This part of the book concludes with the declaration that personality, society, and culture are an inseparable trinity and that no one can make sense out of any of the three without considering the other two. Sorokin takes issue with writers such as Znaniecki and von Wiese who would limit sociology to the study of the social. A study of the social without the cultural would be a meaningless enterprise and in fact could not be carried out. "Society" and "culture" are concepts that cannot be sharply separated from each other. "The only possible differentiation is that the term 'social' denotes concentration on the totality of interacting human beings and their relationships, whereas 'cultural' signifies concentration on meanings, values, and norms and their material vehicles."[49] Sorokin himself exhibits a strong preference for the compound adjective *sociocultural*.

These preliminaries concluded, Sorokin turns his attention to the structure of the social universe, beginning with a chapter entitled "Organized Systems of Interaction: Groups or Institutions." The juxtaposition is surprising. Indeed, Sorokin says in so many words, "The terms 'organized group' and 'institution' as used here are identical."[50] But surely there is a difference between these two, a difference that it is essential to maintain. Business is an institution. Is it also an organized group? A ship's company is an organized group. Is it also an institution? The distinction would seem to be clear. In any event, the chapter deals neither with groups nor with institutions, but with norms, and the emphasis he gives to them is altogether appropriate:

> Every day we have to perform thousands of actions in interaction with hundreds of different persons, under the most diverse constellations of conditions. If for a moment we imagine that none of us had any law-norm which would clearly indicate what should be our actions when we enter a store to get something, when we converse with the members of our family, when we go into the office or place of our work, meet our neighbors, call a doctor or

49. *Ibid.*, p. 65b.
50. *Ibid.*, p. 77b.

> plumber, superiors and inferiors, attend a public meeting, enter a church or theater, and so on; if indeed we had no law-norms pointing out how to act in each of these and thousands of other situations, we should meet each moment of our lives with the greatest difficulty, never knowing what to do in each case. We should be lost in a jungle without map or orientation.[51]

This is "pure" sociology. Like Sumner, MacIver, and many others, Sorokin is insisting that without norms the individual would be helpless in social situations and that the burden of decision would be intolerable. More than than, without norms organized groups would be impossible. He is clearly correct.

His treatment of the subject, however, is another matter. Inconsistencies are rampant. It is unnecessary to notice more than a few. His use of the compound noun *law-norms,* apparently following Petrajitsky, is a redundancy. It accomplishes nothing that the word *norms* itself cannot accomplish, and it is inconsistent in that he distinguishes law-norms from statutes and "official law."[52] It is quite true that norms serve as guides to conduct, but when he tells us in addition that they are our chief motivating force he is making the same point for which he criticized Sumner previously in *Contemporary Sociological Theories.* He tells us that it is fallacious to define law-norms as obligatory rules of conduct backed by force and on the other hand that "compulsory enforcement" of the law-norms is inevitable.[53] The inconsistencies increase as the discussion proceeds and are especially prominent in his classification:

1. Law norms
   a. Official
   b. Unofficial
2. Other norms
   a. Moral norms
   b. Technical norms
   c. Norms of etiquette, fashion
   d. Norms of religion, mores, folkways, customs

We notice first that although Sorokin has previously distinguished laws from law-norms, laws reappear in the discussion as "official" law-norms. When he writes that "law is a real power that establishes, crystallizes, and overthrows all social institutions, from the family up to the State-Leviathan and even superstate organizations,"[54] we must assume that he is talking about law-norms because that is what the brief paragraph is about. Now

51. *Ibid.*, p. 76b.
52. *Ibid.*, p. 77b.
53. *Ibid.*, pp. 72a, 78b.
54. *Ibid.*, p. 77.

we are induced to wonder how "official" law-norms could be instruments for overthrowing the state. We notice second that moral norms and mores both appear in the list. Are they the same, or different? Sorokin does not tell us. We notice third that etiquette and fashion merit a place of their own, as phenomena distinct from folkways and customs. We notice fourth that folkways and customs are separately mentioned and wonder if they are the same or not. And finally, are the norms of religion aspects of the mores of a society or are they the law-norms of organized groups, namely, religious associations? Again we are left in the dark. Sorokin either writes so rapidly that he does not perceive these inconsistencies or does not take consistency to be a virtue.

In blithe unawareness of his own taxonomic deficiencies, Sorokin goes on to devote a long section to criticism of the definitions of others—Sumner, Thomas and Znaniecki, Blumer, MacIver, Parsons, Malinowski, Warner and Lunt, and Mills. These definitions are first quoted and then denounced as inadequate, fallacious, superficial, and vague. "For this reason all the subsequent operations and elaborate structures built upon them comprise an indeterminate structure built upon vague, foggy, and unknown foundations."[55] MacIver's folkways, mores, and institutions, for example, are only "unnecessary triplication of the same thing. The specifications are vague and consequently the whole theory becomes fallacious."[56] Sumner's "blunders" are inevitable because he has dumped together in one "grocery basket" all kinds of different norms without distinguishing between them.[57] And finally, "Such definitions of institutions as those of T. Parsons are about as defective as all the quoted ones. Everything in this cumbersome pile of words is unclear." The remedy for all of these defects, of course, is to adopt Sorokin's definitions.[58]

We are next treated to a discussion of "other characteristics of organized groups or institutions." Here Sorokin writes that once the law-norms, both official and unofficial, are given, all relationships and forms of conduct can be divided into three classes: lawful, moral or recommended, and prohibited or unlawful. Since moral norms are merely recommended and not obligatory, their details are left to the will and wisdom of individuals.[59] Law-norms, on the contrary, are precisely specified, especially those that define unlawful or prohibited conduct. The same section contains a brief

55. *Ibid.*, p. 86a.

56. *Ibid.*, p. 86b.

57. *Ibid.*, p. 87a.

58. *Ibid.*, p. 87a. Sorokin's carelessness reaches its own kind of absurdity when he tells us that when the norms are adequately defined, they are easily definable. (p. 87b).

59. Both parts of this proposition raise serious questions, and it is doubtful if any other sociologist would agree with them.

discussion of status, which Sorokin defines as "the totality of the rights and duties each individual has in a group," and makes the excellent point that each individual has as many different statuses as there are groups of which he is a member.[60] It is these statuses that account for the differentiation and stratification of the members of a group. The chapter concludes with an enumeration of "unorganized and little organized groups," including "as if organized groups," public, crowd and mob, and seminominal plurels, the last of which includes men of genius and racial and sexual groups, which are also "as if" organized. None of these is awarded more than a paragraph of discussion. The chapter as a whole is an almost unmanageable melange of careless inconsistencies and insightful observations.

A chapter on solidary, antagonistic, and mixed systems of interaction, together with familistic, mixed (contractural), and compulsory types of interaction, requires little attention. Much of it is devoted to severe and sometimes savage criticism of such writers as von Wiese, Park and Burgess, Ross, Le Play, Lavrov, Kropotkin, Cooley, Tönnies, Scheler, Durkheim, and MacIver, all of whose conceptions are defective. Tönnies's *Gemeinschaft* and *Gesellschaft* are vague, incomplete, and primitive. Durkheim's mechanical and organic solidarity are no better. And MacIver's distinction between community and association is not only barren but is "one of the best examples of these fallacious theories."[61] In fact, each of MacIver's concepts is poorly defined, all overlap, and "the whole classification exemplifies an elaborate effort to create a multitude of superfluous pseudo-definitions."[62] The remedy, again, is to adopt Sorokin's "theory":

> The preceding critical survey should suffice to show that the classification of the solidary, antagonistic, and mixed relationships offered by this work embodies all the valid and significant traits of other classifications and at the same time is free from most of their defects. It is more complete than other classifications. . . . Finally, in its psychological motivation my analysis is more adequate and precise than that of other conceptions.[63]

Precise it is not. As a creator of consistent distinctions Sorokin can hardly compare with most of those he criticizes and especially with MacIver.

Sorokin's explanation of the factors involved in solidarity and antagonism is less than satisfactory. Here he suggests that the necessary conditions for solidarity are adherence to the golden rule and the concordance of the law and moral norms of each group with those of all the others. This

60. *Ibid.*, pp. 89a, 89b.
61. For Sorokin any concept, definition, or classification appears to be a theory.
62. *Ibid.*, p. 117b, n. 48.
63. *Ibid.*, pp. 118a–118b.

concordance, in turn, is determined by the social and cultural milieu of the groups. Sorokin himself seems dissatisfied with this "explanation." The problem should be pushed further in this chain of causes, he says, but that is a task for a special monograph.[64] The only positive proposition to emerge from the discussion is his recognition of the solidary effect of uniting against a common enemy, but this, of course, is an old and respectable sociological principle. He concludes with a melancholy description of the "contemporary hurricane of sharpest antagonisms raging over the whole of humanity."[65]

Sorokin's treatment of the organized group is the next subject to engage our attention. First of all, he regards such a group as a unity and finds it desirable, therefore, to classify unities. They are of six different kinds: spatially contiguous and perceptionally similar; spatially contiguous and mechanically cohesive; indirect causal-functional; direct causal-functional; meaningful; and meaningful-causal-functional.[66] It is one thing to insist that an organized group is a unity, but the utility of classifying unities is not clear. Sorokin uses the exercise as an excuse to criticize those who would see meaningful unity only in "teleological groups with a common purpose of the members" and those "pseudo-empiricists" such as Lundberg, who, he says, would deny the meaningful unity of organized groups.[67] In any event, Sorokin proceeds to indicate the main properties of an organized group. It is a curious list, including reality,[68] individuality, general

64. *Ibid.*, p. 125, n. 4.

65. *Ibid.*, pp. 130a–131b.

66. This classification differs from the less congested one offered in *Social and Cultural Dynamics*, vol. 1, p. 10, where there are only four: spatial or mechanical adjacency, association by an external factor, functional or causal integration, and internal or logico-meaningful unity. In this book he was principally concerned with advancing something called the logico-meaningful method to be used in discovering logico-meaningful unities. For a criticism of this *petitio principii*, see Robert Bierstedt, "The Logico-Meaningful Method of P. A. Sorokin," *American Sociological Review* (December 1937): 813–823. He was also concerned with distinguishing between causal-functional methods, as used in the physical sciences, and his logico-meaningful method, which he recommended for sociology.

67. *Society, Culture, and Personality*, p. 148, n. 6:

> Lundberg's case is humorous in its self-contradiction; on the one hand he ardently desires to describe everything in terms of a mere physicochemical science; on the other hand he incessantly breaks this desire by an uncritical use of the most "meaningful" terms—family, school, YMCA, church, arts—stressing irrelevant characteristics of a group like its geographical contiguity, etc., and omitting the true charjcteristics of the real groups. He and his like seem to be unaware that the family, university, business firm, church, and state are first of all and most of all meaningful unities, which cannot be found among the strictly causal relationships and unities of the biophysical world.

68. Durkheim is not exempt from Sorokin's criticism on this point. Sorokin accuses Durkheim of entertaining the notion that groups are external to their individual members and exist irrespective of them. This notion can nowhere be found in Durkheim.

and differential interdependence and conductivity, spatial compatibility,[69] continuity, "change in togetherness," self-directing, susceptible to external forces, selectivity, and limited variability. These properties, he says, belong to all organized groups and exhaust their generic characteristics.[70]

The problem of the classification of groups is one of the most troublesome in sociology. There is no standard classification, and every systematic sociologist is therefore tempted to offer his own. Sorokin is no exception. If we were to rank these classifications in the order of merit, however, Sorokin's would win a place at the bottom of the list. His procedure is typical. First, he criticizes the classifications of other sociologists, pronouncing them all defective, and then he produces his own. It is reproduced here in order to justify the judgment just made:

Summary Classification of Groups

I. Unorganized and semiorganized groups
  1. Externally united, "as if" organized
  2. Public
  3. Crowd, mob
  4. Seminominal plurel
  5. Purely nominal plurel

II. Important organized groups
  A. Unibonded groups
    1. Biosocial groupings
      a. Race
      b. Sex
      c. Age groups
    2. Sociocultural groupings
      a. Kinship
      b. Territorial
      c. Language
      d. State
      e. Occupational
      f. Economic
      g. Religious
      h. Political
      i. Ideological and educational groups
      j. Nominal groups of the elite

69. By this property Sorokin means that two or more groups can occupy the same space. Thus, there are thousands of groups in New York City. Similarly, the state of Massachusetts and the United States of America coexist in the same territory.

70. *Ibid.*, p. 158b.

B. Multibonded groups
   1. The family
   2. Clans
   3. Tribes
   4. Nations
   5. Castes
   6. Feudal estates
   7. Classes
C. Structural varieties
   1. Large or small in size
   2. Well-organized or semiorganized
   3. Centralized or decentralized
   4. With monarchical, aristocratic, oligarchic, democratic, republican, tyrannical, and other forms of government
   5. Stratified in various ways
   6. Long-lived and short-lived
   7. Solidary, antagonistic, mixed
   8. Integrated, unintegrated, mixed culture
   9. Rich and poor in the components of meanings and vehicles; in the quality of members
   10. With mutual intergroup relationships
       a. Solidary (as subgroup to group, or as co-ordinated groups)
       b. Antagonistic
       c. Neutral
       d. Unrelated
       e. Stratified

The defects in this classification are so glaring that one can hardly suppress a grimace. It violates all the canons of taxonomy, to which Sorokin himself gives expression.[71] I shall list only a few of them:

1. The major rubrics "unorganized and semi-organized groups" and "important organized groups" are not a dichotomy but a continuum.
2. The second rubric contains the word *important* with no criteria of importance specified.
3. There is therefore no place in the classification for "unimportant" organized groups, such as, for example, a temporary *ad hoc* committee.
4. The three subrubrics under Important organized groups—Unibonded groups, Multibonded groups, and Structural varieties—are a

71. *Ibid.*, pp. 159–168. Classification of groups reproduced from p. 178.

gross violation of a *fundamentum divisionis* because "structural varieties," of course, is not a kind of a group at all.

5. Nominal groups of the elite appear under organized groups, whereas *nominal* and *organized* would appear to be a contradiction in terms.
6. Kinship groups are uninbonded, whereas the family and clans are multibonded.
7. Classes (II, B, 7) are presented to us as *organized* groups.

If one were as critical as Sorokin himself it would easily be possible to find more defects than these.

The classification of groups concludes Sorokin's treatment of the structure of the social universe. He turns next, in a section of its own, to a detailed discussion of many of these groups, under the title of "social differentiation and stratification." It is a discussion we need not follow except to notice certain points of interest.[72] Needless to say, he exhibits throughout his bibliographical virtuosity.

In his treatment of territorial and neighborhood groups Sorokin observes that under conditions of high mobility the importance of locality groups has declined. The locality group has become more unibonded and less multibonded, and thus those sociologists who continue to emphasize community as a territorial group are making a "notable mistake." This does not imply, however, that these groups now have no importance. Sorokin's view of the state is fairly traditional. He observes that in totalitarian systems the state becomes more and more multibonded and less unibonded. He has a full appreciation of the importance of nationalism and of patriotic sentiment, even among those who strive to overthrow a particular government. The extent of social differentiation in contemporary societies suggests that no single group, including the state, can serve all the needs of human beings without depriving them of their freedom and autonomy. Political parties, which can be found in uncrystallized form even in preliterate populations, demand such loyalty that persons of independent and creative minds avoid joining them. The result is that their leaders for the most part are mediocrities and hypocrites. Even in modern democracies the individual is a negligible unit. As for religious groups, they influence and modify other groups, and there is no reason to suppose that they will disappear. All of the foregoing, according to Sorokin, are unibonded groups.

The following section is devoted to multibonded groups. Here Sorokin

72. It would be a tiresome exercise to mention the many inconsistencies that mar these pages. One, however, occurs almost immediately. Having classified age, race, and sex groups under the rubric of "important organized groups," he says, only two pages later, that if the members do not interact with one another they remain nominal plurels. *Ibid.*, p. 182a.

hopes to build a "chemistry of groups," indicating the affinities that some unibonded groups have with others in the formation of more complex groupings. He regards this "sociological chemistry" as an important task for the future. At the moment we are limited to such generalizations as the following:

> A political party bond easily compounds with state, language, territorial, occupational and religious bonds, as well as with sex, age, race, and kinship bonds.
>
> The state group bond frequently coalesces with religious, territorial, language, racial, and political-party bonds.
>
> The occupational group bond readily enters into a union with sex, age, kinship, territorial, political-party, and race bonds. It combines less readily with religious, state, and language group bonds.[73]

It is difficult to know what to do with observations like these. Upon examination the suspicion grows that they are either trite or false. It is trite, for example, to assert that there is an easy linkage between state bonds and political party bonds. And it is false—or at least questionable—to say that occupational bonds do not combine well with religious or language bonds. In New York City the sanitation workers have tended to be Italian, the police, Irish, and the teachers, Jewish. In any event, Sorokin devotes many pages of proposition to his "bonds," some of them suggestive but most of them lacking empirical support.

Although Sorokin pretends a dislike for the concept of social class,[74] he wants to study a group that has exerted a powerful influence and yet is different from the family, tribe, or nation. There is such a group, and its "formula" is as follows:

> It is (1) legally open, but actually semiclosed; (2) "normal"; (3) solidary; (4) antagonistic to certain other groups (social classes) of the same general nature, X; (5) partly organized but mainly quasi-organized; (6) partly aware of its own unity and existence and partly not; (7) characteristic of the western society of the eighteenth, nineteenth, and twentieth centuries; (8) a multibonded group bound together by two unibonded ties, occupational and economic (both taken in their broad sense), and by one bond of social stratification in the sense of the totality of its essential rights and duties as contrasted with the essentially different rights and duties of other groups (social classes) of the same general nature, X.[75]

73. *Ibid.*, pp. 241a–241b.

74. "Whether we designate the group in question as a social class or by some other term is unimportant. We may call it X, if we prefer." *Ibid.*, p. 271a.

75. *Ibid.*, p. 271a.

Although Sorokin devotes many pages to criticizing the definitions of others, his own "formula" can hardly sustain examination. We shall pass it by with only the comment that it has not been utilized by the many writers on this subject who have succeeded Sorokin.[76] He concludes his general treatment of this subject, which includes an entire chapter on the stratification of all kinds of groups, with the observation that he has put "an end to the anarchic and crude state of the current structural analysis and classification of social groups and strata."[77]

In the final chapter in this section Sorokin tells us how to analyze the group structure of an entire population. After criticizing the efforts of others, notably Spencer and Durkheim, to do this, he essays a "constructive" analysis of his own. The main types are urban and rural agglomerations and agglomerations with or without a dominant group. Such dominant groups would be the family (as in traditional Chinese society), the tribe, the caste, the social order, the social class, the state, or the religious group. These are the types that sociologists should use. At any moment of history we have a complex constellation of groups and strata, some solidary and some antagonistic, in constantly changing juxtaposition with one another. All efforts to attribute the historical process to the domination of only one group are bound to fail.

Finally, the ancient problem of the relation of the individual to society is fallaciously posed. There is no society as such, but only this complex of unibonded and multibonded groups:

> Whatever case of so-called antinomy between the individual and society we take, we find it is not a conflict of the individual and the "whole society" but rather a conflict of individuals with individuals or of a group with a group. Instead of the fictitious unilinear relationship: individual and society, we have a multilinear relationship of individuals to individuals, factions to factions, groups to groups. All the dramatic effusions on the "tyranny of society over the individual" and on the "despotism of the individual over the society"belong to the realm of poetry rather than to social science. The whole problem is a pseudo-problem.[78]

Thus easily does Sorokin dispose of one of the most profound problems of social philosophy.

Although Sorokin devotes several hundred pages to the structure of the

76. In the last two or three centuries Sorokin discerns four major classes: the industrial-labor or proletarian class, the peasant-farmer class, the dwindling class of large landowners, and the capitalist class, "now being transformed into the managerial class." *Ibid.*, pp. 273a–273b.

77. *Ibid.*, p. 295.

78. *Ibid.*, p. 308b.

cultural—as opposed to the social—aspects of the superorganic universe, we need not follow him through his discourse. He intends to include also the personality aspects of this universe—largely, one supposes, to justify his title—but in fact his interest in this subject lags. Briefly summarized, there are three (always three!) kinds of cultural systems—ideological, behavioral, and material. These systems in turn may be integrated, unintegrated, or contradictory. There are systems within systems, from the smallest system to the "supersystem." Thus, to take an example from the realm of the ideological, the proposition that the sum of the angles of a triangle is equal to two right angles is a system, albeit a small one. It is a subsystem of a larger system, the system of geometry. Geometry, in turn, is a subsystem of mathematics, itself a subsystem of science. Finally, science itself may be a subsystem of a supersystem of truth—a "colossal supersystem"—that embraces a comprehensive conception of "reality." This same exercise in Chinese boxes may be performed for philosophy, religion, ethics, law, the fine arts, and language. Sometimes these systems exhibit integration, sometimes contradiction. Sometimes indeed we find not a system but only a congeries, a set of wholly unrelated items, such as (one of his favorite examples) the material culture of Harvard Square.[79] This insight Sorokin claims as an advance over those philosophers of history, like Spengler and Toynbee, who have treated all cultures as if they were integrated.

Sorokin has now laid a conceptual foundation for his treatment of social and cultural dynamics. The "vastest known supersystems" express major premises about the nature of reality, truth, and value. They are—again—three in number: the sensate, the ideational, and—a mixed form—the idealistic. Let us look at Sorokin's definitions:

> Some ideological cultures answer that the true reality and true value is sensory, that beyond the reality and value perceived by our sense organs there is no other reality and no value. Having answered it in this way, such ideological cultures build upon this answer their vastest supersystem in which most of their scientific, philosophical, ethical, and other systems articulate exactly this major premise. Such ideological supersystems can be called sensate.
>
> Other highly integrated ideological cultures answer the problem by stating that the true reality and true value is the supersensory, super-rational God ("Tao," "World Soul," "Brahman," etc.), the sensory reality and value being either a mere illusion, or the least important, least real, sometimes even negative, reality and value. The vastest ideological supersystem built upon this premise can be called ideational.
>
> Still other highly integrated cultures assume that the true reality and value is partly sensory, partly rational, partly supersensory and super-rational infinite

79. *Ibid.*, pp. 334b–335a.

> manifold. The ideological supersystem erected upon this major premise can be called idealistic.[80]

Taoist China, Greece before the fifth century B.C., Brahamistic and Buddhistic India, Christian medieval Europe, and such preliterate tribes as the Zuni and the Hopi Indians are ideational supersystems in their ideological culture. Greece and Rome from the fourth century B.C. to the third century A.D., the Western world after the fifteenth century, China at some periods of its history and in some regions, and such preliterate tribes as the Dobuan are sensate. Finally, Confucianist China, ancient Egypt in some periods and regions, ancient Greece in the fifth century B.C., Europe in the thirteenth and fourteenth centuries, and "several other groups and persons" are idealistic.[81]

Sorokin uses the same six kinds of unities for cultural systems that he has previously outlined for organized social groups. Needless to say, he criticizes all other theories of cultural integration found in the literature, Most of them, in comparison with his own, "represent in fact a hash of the crudest metaphysics, mixed with the shreds of biologism, behaviorism, Freudianism, all sprinkled by a poorly understood relationship of means and end, interpreted now as a causal sequence, now as a purposive relationship, now as the relationship of the antecedent and the consequent, now as a mere spatial or time adjacency."[82]

Although, as I have remarked, Sorokin pays less attention to personality than to the other two parts of his trinity—society and culture—he nevertheless develops a theory of its sociocultural origin and structure. Much of it is orthodox and contains little that Cooley would not have approved. Again we are regaled by excited criticism of the theories of others, especially Freud's, which Sorokin regards as a "degrading fairy tale."[83] His own theory, quite simply, is that the individual has as many selves or egos as there are groups of which he is a member. If these groups have compatible norms the individual will have an integrated personality; if the norms are incompatible then we have the Dr. Jekyll and Mr. Hyde syndrome. In any case, one exhibits different personalities to the world in accordance with the role one happens to be playing at a given moment of the day, whether in the family, at work, in church, or in social interaction with friends. The

80. *Ibid.*, p. 320a (italics omitted).

81. The individual, too, can exhibit various degrees in the integration of his personality. In one of the writer's favorite Sorokinian sentences, he says, "A human being is neither perfectly logical and rational, nor entirely nonlogical, illogical, nonrational and irrational. He is partly both." *Ibid.*, p. 325b.

82. *Ibid.*, p. 339b–340a.

83. *Ibid.*, p. 347b.

increase of social differentiation since the Middle Ages has resulted in a pluralism of selves and has led to inevitable conflict and often to mental and physical deterioration. The multiplicity of statuses or positions that the contemporary person is forced to occupy in a complex society contributes to the same result.

War and Revolution

Throughout his career Sorokin devoted a great deal of attention to the phenomena of war and revolution. As we have seen, he wrote a book on the sociology of revolution and mounted a major quantitative assault on the sociology of war in *Social and Cultural Dynamics* (vol. 3). In the latter place he derived conclusions from a study of some 967 wars in the histories of Greece, Rome, Austria, Germany, England, France, the Netherlands, Spain, Italy, Russia, Poland, and Lithuania from 500 B.C. to 1925 A.D. Using as indexes the percentage of casualties in proportion to total population and the percentage of casualties in proportion to total army enrollment, he discovered that the twentieth century—with only one-quarter of it in his figures—is the bloodiest of centuries. He arrived at other conclusions, among them, that in the history of states and nations war occurs on the average every two or three years; that there are no marked differences between nations in their propensity for waging wars; that democracies and republics have no better record for peace than autocracies and and monarchies; that there is no apparent periodicity in the incidence of war; that although the duration of wars exhibits a large variation, the modal duration is from two-and-one-half to four-and-one-half years; that wars attain their maximum incidence in transition periods from sensate to ideational culture, and vice versa; that war, total in preliterate groups, became a matter of engaging only a small part of a population as professional soldiers, and then, more recently, became total again; and that there is no evidence to support the claim that history discloses a trend toward either the increase or decrease of wars.[84]

Sorokin's explanation of the causes of wars and revolutions—as contrasted with his quantitative efforts and empirical findings—is unfortunately simplistic. He once read a paper in which he asserted that the cause of war was the disintegration of social relationships, without apparently realizing that his "cause" is part of the definition of war. His explanation in

84. Sorokin's treatment of this subject receives appropriate recognition in Quincy Wright's monumental volume, *A Study of War*, 2 ed. (Chicago: University of Chicago Press, 1965).

Society, Culture, and Personality is little better. After criticizing alternative theories, especially theories of multiple causation, as "pitiable," he tells us that the cause of both internal and international peace is conformity to the golden rule and, more specifically, that:

> In a given universe of societies or within a particular society the probability of peace varies directly with the integration of the systems of the basic values and their mutual compatibility. When their integration and harmoniousness decline, especially suddenly and sharply, the chances for international or civil war increase.[85]

Conversely, war occurs when societies or parts of societies with contradictory value systems come into contact. Murder, incidentally, is "individual war," and the same explanation serves. There can be no lasting peace in a decaying sensate society, such as our own, and any effort to achieve it through such "patchwork" devices as the United Nations or a world government are doomed to failure. The only possible remedy is a return to an ideational culture.

The Mortality of Groups

Sorokin has an interesting treatment of the life span, mortality, and "resurrection" of groups. Like an individual, groups are mortal; they die when one or all of their components are lost or when the "meaningful-causal belt" that unites them disappears. He attends, with statistics, to the life spans of economic organizations, local "cultural" organizations (parent-teacher associations and the like), the family, universities and colleges, cities, states, religious groups, and some multibonded groups. His explanation is again unsatisfactory:

> As to the problem of why social organizations do not last forever and sooner or later cease to exist, the answer is almost the same as that for the question: why biological organisms die. Style the cause as "destiny," as "immanent," as "law of life and death," or as something else, the names do not matter. What matters is that the duration of social organizations seems to be finite: "what has a beginning in this empirical world has an end." "That is that," and all the numerous words can hardly add much to this.[86]

Sorokin does offer reasons why some social organizations have greater

85. Pp. 507b–508a (italics omitted).
86. *Ibid.*, p. 532a.

durability than others. Duration is negatively correlated with rapidity of formation, positively with size, and positively with richness of meanings, values, and norms. Similarly, some groups are "resurrected." Sorokin supplies such examples as Poland, Bohemia, and Egypt.

Social and Cultural Dynamics

I am now ready to describe Sorokin's theory of social and cultural dynamics, his most distinctive—and controversial—contribution. With the help of assistants who combed with him the crevices of history over a period of 2500 years, he produced three volumes of his *Social and Cultural Dynamics* in 1937 and added a fourth in 1941.[87] With prodigious effort he surveyed all of the compartments of culture—philosophy, art (including painting, sculpture, music, and architecture), psychology, ethics, law, and religion—in order to discover some pattern, some trend, some meaning in the vast processes of social change. The result is nothing less than a comprehensive theory—a philosophy of history. It is a major assault upon the ark where Clio closely guards her secrets, an assault comparable in vigor, industry, and magnitude to those of Spengler and Toynbee.[88]

Let us look again at Sorokin's Chinese boxes (the expression is not his). The smallest boxes are single items of culture, whether ideological, behavioral, or material. Examples would be the proposition that $2 + 2 = 4$ for the first, the norm of filial piety for the second, and a spark plug for the third. These are parts of larger wholes, making up systems such as arithmetic, ethics, and the internal combustion engine. These in turn build up into larger systems—patterns, configurations, complexes—until we arrive finally at what Sorokin calls "the vastest known supersystems." These are the sensate, the ideational, and a "mixed" system that he calls the idealistic. In his examination of the course of history, especially Western history, he finds, as we have seen, periods in which one or the other of these "mentalities" has been dominant. He recognizes, as we have also seen, that not all periods are "pure." Sensate remnants may remain in

87. This timing made it possible for him to answer in the fourth volume those who had criticized the theory as presented in the first three.

88. Sorokin had a high respect for Toynbee especially, and characterized his *Study of History* as a "real masterpiece of historical and macrosociological knowledge." Sorokin, *Sociological Theories of Today* (New York: Harper & Row., 1966), p. 197. Toynbee, in turn, has written gently critical essays of Sorokin. See, for example, "Sorokin's Philosophy of History," ed. Philip J. Allen *Pitirim A. Sorokin in Review* (Durham, N.C.: Duke University Press, 1963), pp. 67–94.

ideational periods, and vice versa. Furthermore, not all cultures are integrated. There are systems on the one hand and mere congeries on the other.[89] The assumption that all cultures are integrated and the failure to note that some are not systems but only congeries are the principal mistakes of other philosophers of history and especially Spengler and Toynbee.[90] Let us look at Sorokin's definitions again:

> The vastest known supersystems that have actually been embodied in various cultures are the sensate, idealistic, and ideational supersystems. They are based upon the most comprehensive and general of all the ontological principles, namely, *the one defining the ultimate nature of reality and value.* Ontologically there are no more all-embracing concepts than the three following definitions of the ultimate nature of reality and value: (a) True reality and true value are sensory—the major premise of the sensate supersystems. (b) True reality and value consist in a supersensory, superrational God, Brahman, Atman, Tao, or its equivalent—the major premise of the ideational supersystem. (c) True reality and value are an infinite manifold, partly supersensory and superrational, partly rational and partly sensory—the premise of the idealistic supersystem.[91]

Each of these supersystems has its own characteristic form of art, philosophy, ethics, and so on.

The contrasts are clearest perhaps in the fields of the fine arts and philosophy. In the discussion that follows I shall ignore the idealistic, to which Sorokin himself pays less attention, and concentrate on the sensate and the ideational.

Ideational art deals with the supersensory kingdom of God:

> Its "heroes" are God and other deities, angels, saints and sinners, and the soul, as well as the mysteries of creation, incarnation, redemption, crucifixion,

---

89. *Society, Culture, and Personality*, p. 589b:

> It should be reiterated that even the vastest supersystems known—the ideational, sensate, and idealistic—do not integrate 100 percent of all the systems, congeries, the phenomena of a given total culture, but only the major portion of its major systems. Less comprehensive supersystems integrate a still smaller percentage of the cultural phenomena.

90. *Ibid.*, p. 591, n. 5:

> (1) They assume that the total culture of each of their cultures is integrated into its major system; I claim that only the major part of each of these cultures is integrated into one system or supersystem; (2) the major premises of their systems of each culture are outlined very vaguely, often left without any defninition; (3) they tried to discover the specific major system of each of their cultures, Mexican, or American, Chinese or Hindu, and so on. My supersystems are the most general types of supersystems given in various cultures, of which their major systems are but species.

91. *Ibid.*, p. 590b.

> salvation, and other transcendental events. It is religious through and through. It pays little attention to the persons, objects, and events of the sensory empirical world. Its objective is not to amuse, entertain, or give pleasure, but to bring the believer into a closer union with God. It is a part of religion, and functions as religious service. It is a communion of the human soul with itself and with God. As such it is sacred in its content and form. As such it does not admit any sensualism, eroticism, satire, comedy, caricature, farce, or anything extraneous to its nature. Its emotional tone is pious, ethereal, and ascetic.[92]

Sensate art, of course, is the reverse:

> Sensate art lives and moves entirely in the empirical world of the senses. Farmers, workers, housewives, girls [!], stenographers, teachers, and other human beings are its personages. At its over-ripe stage, prostitutes, criminals, street urchins, the insane, hypocrites, rogues, and other subsocial types are its favorite "heroes." Its aim is to afford a refined sensual enjoyment: relaxation, excitation of tired nerves, amusement, pleasure, entertainment. For this reason it must be sensational, passionate, pathetic, sensual, and incessantly new. It is marked by voluptuous nudity and concupiscence. It is divorced from religion, morals, and other values, and styles itself "art for art's sake." Since it must amuse and entertain, it makes wide use of caricature, satire, comedy, farce, debunking, ridiculing, and similar means.[93]

One can only wonder at Sorokin's choice of farmers, workers, housewives, girls, stenographers, and teachers as sensate types.

In any event, ideational art has characterized the cultures of the Hopi and Zuni Indians, "the Negro tribes of Africa,"[94] certain Australian tribes (not specified), Taoist China, Tibet, Brahmanic India, ancient Egypt, Greece from the ninth to the sixth centuries B.C., and early and medieval Christianity. Sensate art can be found in Paleolithic man, in "many a primitive tribe, such as the Bushmen of Africa, many an Indian and Scythian tribe, Assyria, Egypt in the later stages of the Old Kingdom, in the Creto-Mycenaean culture, in the Graeco-Roman culture from the third century B.C. to the fourth century A.D., and in Western Europe in the last five centuries." These, Sorokin insists, are not subjective judgments; they are conclusions derived from a study of more than 100,000 pictures and sculptures. Sorokin supplies hundreds of graphs and charts illustrating the rise and fall of these two cultures (or supersystems), one even indicating fluctuations in nudity in art over a period of 2500 years.

It is easy to fill in the details, so easy indeed that the reader can now do it for himself. Ideational painting and sculpture depict the saints and other religious figures; sensate painting and sculpture dwell on the nude human

92. *Ibid.*, p. 593a–593b.
93. *Ibid.*, p. 594a.
94. Sorokin does not specify which tribes.

body. Ideational music is the Gregorian chant and the plainsong; sensate music, the cacophonies of jazz. Cathedrals, churches, monasteries, and abbeys display the essence of the ideational in architecture; town halls, railroad stations, and skyscrapers, the essence of the sensate. Ideational literature deals with divine love and the lives of the saints; sensate literature, with profane love and the lives of ordinary people. Sensate art is not devoid of achievement. It is now, however, in its decadent stage:

> Housewives, farmers and laborers, business-men and salesmen, stenographers, politicians, doctors, lawyers, and ministers, and especially detectives, criminals, gangsters, and "double-crossers," the cruel, the disloyal, hypocrites, prostitutes and mistresses, the sexually abnormal, the insane, clowns, street urchins, or adventurers—such are the "heroes" of contemporary art in all its principal fields. God, saints, and real heroes are, as a rule, conspicuous by their absence. Even when—as an exception, a contemporary novel, biography, or historical work chooses a noble or heroic theme (such as George Washington, Byron [!], or some saint), it proceeds, in accordance with the prevailing psychoanalytical method, thoroughly to "debunk" its hero.
>
> Contemporary art is primarily a museum of social and cultural pathology. It centers in the police morgue, the criminal's hide-out, and the sex organs, operating mainly on the level of social sewers.[95]

Sensate art, however, may now have reached its limit, and there is reason to anticipate the dawn of a new ideational era.

The story of philosophy, which Sorokin calls "systems of truth," is the same. Ideational truth is the truth of faith; sensate truth, the truth of the senses. The ideational system of truth is exemplified by such doctrines as idealism, indeterminism, fideism, quietism, pietism, absolutism, mysticism, supernaturalism, (medieval) realism, asceticism, and monasticism. The sensate, on the other hand, is exhibited in materialism, determinism, empiricism, positivism, skepticism, pragmatism, operationalism, instrumentalism, (medieval) nominalism, relativism, and utilitarianism. Tertullian's *Credo quia absurdum est* catches the essence of ideational truth; John Locke's *Nihil in intellectu quod non prius fuerit in sensu,* the essence of sensate. Truth itself is a function of the supersystem; that is, what is true in a sensate culture may be false in an ideational, and vice versa. Indeed, the entire "mentality" of a society—what is true and what is false, what is knowledge and what is ignorance—is determined by its dominant system of truth.[96] Furthermore, in a sensate culture something happens also to sociology and psychology:

95. *Ibid.*, p. 604a.

96. *Ibid.*, pp. 616a, 616b. Sorokin is uncomfortably aware that in thus subscribing to relativism, his own sociological theory becomes sensate. He makes numerous efforts to solve the problem, but it cannot be said that any of them succeeds. For a discussion, see Robert K. Merton, "The Sociology of Knowledge" in *Social Theory and Social Structure,* rev. ed. (Glencoe, Ill.: Free Press of Glencoe, 1957), pp. 475–476, 481.

> The social and psychological sciences begin to imitate the natural sciences, attempting to treat man in the same way as physics and chemistry treat inorganic phenomena. In the field of the social sciences all mental and cultural phenomena come to be treated behavioristically, physiologically, "reflexologically," "encrocrinologically," and psychoanalytically. Society becomes economically minded, and the "economic interpretation of history" begins to hold undisputed sway. A quasi-pornographic conception of human culture acquires a wide vogue in biographies, history, anthropology, sociology, and psychology. Anything spiritual, supersensory, or idealistic is ridiculed, being replaced by the most degrading and debasing interpretations. All this is closely analogous to the negative, warped, subsocial, and psychopathic propensities exhibited by the fine arts during the decadent phase of sensate culture.[97]

Man himself becomes nothing more than an animal organism, a reflex mechanism, "a psychoanalytical 'bag' filled with physiological libido."[98] Indeed, in a sensate culture religion itself degenerates into a political creed, a gospel of social reform, and the church becomes a lecture hall rather than a place of worship.

This dreary litany continues when we turn our attention to ethics and law. The ideational ethic abjures us, "Lay not up for yourselves treasures upon earth, where moth and rust doth corrupt. But lay up for yourselves treasures in heaven, where neither moth nor rust doth corrupt." The sensate, on the contrary, says *Carpe diem* and "eat, drink, and be merry, for tomorrow we die." Similarly, in ideational law crime and sin are synonymous; in sensate law heresy, apostasy, and sacrilege cease to be crimes. Sensate law is "a mere instrument for the subjugation and exploitation of one group by another."[99] In our overripe sensate culture ethical and juridical norms have "lost their moral prestige and have been degraded and demoted to the status of a device used by clever hypocrites to fool the exploited simpletons.[100] Our moral conscience has disappeared, and thus we cannot be surprised by the increase in our century of crimes, revolutions, and wars.

The Pattern of History

What then is the pattern of history? What is the direction of social change? Frank Manuel has written that we have only two choices, two im-

97. *Society, Culture, and Personality*, p. 613b.

98. *Ibid.*, p. 613a.

99. *Ibid.*, p. 626b. This is one of the contentions of "critical" or Marxist criminology. See, for example, Richard Quinney, *Critique of Legal Order: Crime Control in Capitalist Society* (Boston: Little, Brown & Co. 1974).

100. *Society, Culture, and Personality*, p. 628b.

ages of history. It is either a Jacob's ladder or an Ixion's wheel.[101] Sorokin says that the linear theory prevails in sensate cultures and the cyclical in ideational. Neither image, however, satisfies him. No process is "limitlessly linear" nor "eternally cyclical."[102] His sociology will transcend these images and utilize instead a rhythmic theory—rhythms that may be periodic or nonperiodic, of long or short duration. To his supersystems he now adds "superrhythms" and declares that his predictions of an increasingly decadent and destructive sensate culture in our own time "have turned out to be incomparably more accurate than the host of predictions by narrow specialists in economics and sociology, politics and business, by statesmen, educators, and the public."[103] The tempo of the ideational culture tends to be slow, of the sensate, more rapid. It becomes irregular in the transition periods between the two. What we have then is not linear progression or cyclical repetition but rather a trendless fluctuation from the sensate to the ideational and back again, moving always through the mixed or idealistic form.

We need finally to inquire into the cause of these vast rhythms. What is the urge, the nisus, the stimulus, the push that moves these processes in trendless flux? We wait now with bated breath for Sorokin's answer. It arrives in Volume 4 of *Social and Cultural Dynamics* and is restated near the end of *Society, Culture, and Personality.* And it is one of the great anticlimaxes in the history of sociological theory. After all these words, all these pages, all these volumes, Sorokin tells us that sociocultural systems change because it is their nature to change! "The cause of the changes in a social system is inherent in the system itself."[104] Just as an acorn grows always and inevitably into an oak tree and not into a plum tree, so sociocultural systems change from what they are to what they must become. Change is an inherent property of all functioning systems. Of course, external factors—geographical, biological, and even sociocultural—may exert an effect, may accelerate or retard, modify or distort. But they cannot fundamentally change what a system is or will become. All systems are autonomous and self-directing. The ultimate cause of change is immanent causation. Each supersystem, whether sensate or ideational, carries within it the seeds of change that will ineluctably move it, sooner or later, in the direction of its opposite.

Why cannot a sensate culture become ever more sensate, an ideational ever more ideational? The answer is this: because of the principle of limits.

101. *Shapes of Philosophical History* (Stanford, Calif.: Stanford University Press, 1965).
102. *Society, Culture, and Personality,* p. 680b.
103. *Ibid.,* p. 689b.
104. *Ibid.,* p. 696b.

A system can move only so far in one direction because it reaches a limit, an impermeable boundary, after which it must reverse itself and begin to move in the opposite direction. Sorokin illustrates his principle with the help of a piano. Strike a key on a piano, and the result will be a sound. Strike it harder, and the result is a still louder sound. But there comes a time when, with increasing force, the result is not a louder sound but a broken piano! Such is the principle of limits, which operates not only with pianos but also with the vastest known sociocultural supersystems. They change because it is their nature to change, and they reverse themselves because, in accordance with the principle of limits, there is no alternative.

From this theory Sorokin derives a ray of hope. Despondent as he is about living in a now overripe stage of a sensate culture, we are nevertheless witnessing its last gasp, and sooner rather than later a new idealistic and possibly ideational supersystem will appear, "destined to continue the creative role of the superorganic on this planet."[105] "Let us hope," he says in his peroration, "that the great passage to a new and integrated society will be made without additional tragedy or apocalyptic catastrophe."[106]

Criticism

Social and Cultural Dynamics was one of the publishing events of the 1937 season. It was prominently reviewed in the leading literary journals, magazines, and newspapers. It received front-page attention in the *New York Times Book Review*, where Arthur Livingston, the distinguished translator of Pareto, inexplicably paid tribute to Sorokin's clear, simple, and beautiful style, appreciated Sorokin's assurance that the next ideational age would be "magnificent," and called him "Pareto for the pious." He expressed his distress, however, at Sorokin's fondness for past ideational ages, which he regarded as "shabby, low-grade affairs."[107] Sidney Hook, in the *Nation*, found Sorokin's statistical paraphernalia "so much lattice work for weasel interpretations," his construction vulnerable on almost every point, his theory of immanent causation meaningless and tautological, his descriptions faulty and sometimes absurd, and his work as a whole altogether without wisdom.[108] Lewis Mumford, in the *New Republic*, ac-

105. *Ibid.*, p. 706b.

106. *Ibid.*, p. 723b.

107. *New York Times Book Review* (June 20, 1937): 1, 17. Much of the review is devoted to Pareto rather than to Sorokin.

108. "History in Swing Rhythm," *Nation*, July 10, 1937, pp. 48–49. Hook also reviewed *Society, Culture, and Personality* in the *New York Times Book Review* (August 17, 1947): 4,

cused him of "unbridled prejudice." "blind vanity," and "puerility" and taxed him with a total lack of emotional poise. Sorokin's statistical demonstrations are "extremely subjective and extremely superficial," and the same fallicies occur over and over again in every chapter. "Loathing what he calls 'sensate culture,' he proclaims himself an insensate reactionary who seeks an ideologues's revenge for his own unfortunate state of mind."[109] The most unkind cut of all, however, came from the *New Yorker,* where Clifton Fadiman, in his year-end list of book "awards," called Sorokin's *maximum opus* "Emptiest Barrel Making Most Noise."[110]

Four of Sorokin's Harvard colleagues reviewed the first three volumes of *Social and Cultural Dynamics,* all quite negatively. Abbott Payson Usher, of the Department of Economics, regarded Sorokin's sensate, ideational, and idealistic cultures as ideal types and said they revealed the fundamental weakness of the procedure:

> This vast treatise [vol. 2], which purports to be an abstract analysis of sociological forms existing only in "social space" becomes in fact a singularly arbitrary and dogmatic interpretation of history which even forecasts a specific development in the future. The method of ideal types has invariably led to precisely such a confusion between the construction of categories of reference, and the interpretation of historical events. . . .
>
> The temptation to treat categories of reference as organic social entities is well-nigh irresistible, and once this mistake is made, further elaboration of the study makes the errors more and more serious.[111]

Usher agreed that Sorokin's tables and graphs fail to exhibit any trends, but this is the inevitable result of the method employed, a method that tears historical phenomena out of their historical contexts. D. W. Prall, of the Department of Philosophy, writing on Volume 1, suggested that a layman might "confuse Sensate mentality with empirically verifiable good sense,

---

22. There he referred to "the fancied rhythms of historical waves," indicted Sorokin for equating causation with destiny, accused him of sheer tautology, remarked, "To say that a man dies because it is his nature to die doesn't get us very far in the study of senescence," characterized his judgments as so violent that they become denunciations rather than descriptions, and invited attention to Sorokin's tendency to indulge in "reckless generalizations." Favorable only is his response to Sorokin's notion that one has as many egos or selves as there are groups of which he is a member. But even here, Sorokin fails to account for the unity of personality and for the fact that one may be in revolt against some of his groups.

Similarly, Robert M. MacIver, reviewing *The Reconstruction of Humanity* (1948), referred to Sorokin's prophetic declamations and vehement italics and concluded that his prescriptions amounted to little more than a plea that man cease to be sensate and try to become ideational. *Ibid.,* April 18, 1948, pp. 21–22.

109. "Insensate Ideologue," *New Republic* (July 14, 1937): 283–284.

110. (December 25, 1937): 53.

111. "Sorokin and the Dangerous Science," *Harvard Guardian* 2 (November 1937): 6.

and Ideational mentality with the fanatically superstitious, the dogmatically religious, or the irrationally ascetic," remarked that the writing is inexcusably prolix and prejudiced, and called it all a naive elaboration of the obvious. A blind man can hardly serve as a guide to the fluctuations of art through the centuries:

> It would be absurd to accept even Professor Sorokin's terms. For he has read his own scheme of values into his account of civilization by using terms heavy with moral connotation as the basis of his analysis. His definitions sound like tremendous oaths to frighten us into agreement. But the fallacy of reading into your definitions such feeling as requires oaths for its expression and then deducing your condemnation of modern art as a scientific conclusion is a little too obvious. The logical circularity is clear. And it appears to have been made possible by a blithe ignorance of the nature and the strength of the prejudices that express themselves in the original defining terms.[112]

William Yandell Elliott, of the Department of Government, writing on Volume 3, complimented Sorokin on his bold endeavor and found him far superior to Pareto (then in vogue at Harvard). "But, even the most elementary knowledge of the dangers of statistical methods would lead one to view with scepticism, if not with horror, the proof of his pudding contained in such statistics of revolution and war as are produced in the third volume."[113] He concluded therefore that Sorokin's study of wars and revolutions is without significance. Crane Brinton, of the Department of History, attended to all three volumes in an article in the *Southern Review*. His title, and that of Sorokin's response to it, indicates the vitriolic character of the exchange.[114]

Reviews in the sociological journals were similarly unsympathetic. The *American Sociological Review* devoted a lead article to a critique of Sorokin's logico-meaningful method and three long reviews to the first three volumes, the first by the director of an art museum, the second by a philosopher, and the third by a sociologist. The article, written by the author (then a student of Sorokin), was addressed to three principal points: First, Sorokin was guilty of *petitio principii* in arguing that one had to use his logico-meaningful method in order to discover logico-meaningful integration. Second, the propriety of applying the logical canons of identity and contradiction to cultural traits, rather than to what we say about them (i.e., terms and propositions), was not clear. Third, Sorokin's principle of "immanent self-regulation and self-direction" of a culture was entirely

112. *Ibid.*, p. 12.

113. *Ibid.*, p. 15.

114. Brinton, "Socio-Astrology," *Southern Review* (Autumn 1937): 243–266; Sorokin, "Histrionics," *ibid.* (Winter 1938): 564.

useless as an explanation of social and cultural change. The critic concluded, in short, that the logico-meaningful method was not logical, not meaningful, and not indeed a method.[115] M. R. Rogers, then of the City Art Museum of Saint Louis, sprinkles his review of Volume 1 with genuine tributes to Sorokin's "wide culture, extraordinary erudition and imaginative grasp." He complains, however, of "many statements which if not actually contrary to fact seem most certainly to contort the truth to fit the simple outlines of his scheme," notices (as who could not) Sorokin's personal biases, and objects to the prolixity of the writing. John Herman Randall, Jr., of the Department of Philosophy, Columbia University, sees no merit in Volume 2: "Indeed, it is much easier to take his whole elaborate work as a parody of American social science, and it does vastly more credit to his intelligence, than to treat it seriously as a contribution to the theory of history." Hans Speier, then of the New School for Social Research, writes a gentler and more complex review of Volume 3. He agrees with Sorokin's view that history discloses neither a cyclical nor a progressive development. With respect to some of Sorokin's concepts, however, he writes as follows:

> The distinction between different historical periods of predominantly familistic, contractual and compulsory relations respectively depends on the validity of the concepts. I do not think that it is fruitful to apply these concepts to historical reality, even if they are consistent formulations. The result will always be the extinction of historic individuation, i.e., of the concrete meaning of historical configurations. The truth that might be gained this way can better be obtained philosophically.

Speier concludes with the hope that Volume 4 will resolve some of the unanswered questions.[116]

It is unnecessary to add to this list of negative responses. Needless to say, Sorokin's work attracted admiration as well as criticism—some of it extravagant. Carle C. Zimmerman, whose own career was closely associated with Sorokin's, both at Minnesota and at Harvard, gave the first Sorokin Lecture at the University of Saskatchewan in 1968, published under the title *Sorokin, The World's Greatest Sociologist.* This little book was expanded in part and published again in 1973 under the title *Sociological Theories of Pitirim A. Sorokin.*[117] In a Foreword to the latter book the editor quotes

115. Robert Bierstedt, "The Logico-Meaningful Method of P. A. Sorokin," *American Sociological Review* 2 (December 1937): 813–823. See also Sorokin's "Rejoinder," pages 823–825. Both the article and the rejoinder are reprinted in Bierstedt, *Power and Progress,* pp. 12–30.

116. All three of these reviews appear in the issue cited in n. 115.

117. Edited by T. K. N. Unnithan (Bombay: Thacker & Co. 1973).

Leopold von Wiese, "In comparison with Sorokin's great work, the works of August Comte, Herbert Spencer, Vilfredo Pareto, and Oswald Spengler appear to be arbitrary and fanciful," and Florian Znaniecki, "It is certainly superior to all the philosophies of culture developed by his predecessors, including Hegel, Comte, Spencer, Pareto, Arnold Toynbee and others." The English historian F. R. Cowell has written two books on Sorokin, both complimentary in the extreme.[118] Indeed, to him Sorokin is one of the greatest figures in the history of thought and his *Dynamics* is a watershed of sociology:

> The fertilizing streams that flow from it will swell to irrigate many arid zones of the sociological world, and indeed in the world of history, education, aesthetics, law, government and elsewhere. The findings contained in *Social and Cultural Dynamics* have this power because they bring within one conspectus the whole vast world of human values.[119]

This is only one of many observations in a similar vein. Indeed, Cowell compares Sorokin favorably with Bacon, Descartes, Leibniz, Newton, Kant, and Darwin.[120]

Summary and Evaluation

Sorokin is easy to criticize. It would be uncharitable to find fault with his literary style, or lack of it, because he wrote in a language over which he had no mastery and little control. On the other hand, his publishers' editors should have removed the solecisms, the tautologies, and the numerous inconsistencies that disfigure his work. There is probably nothing they could have done about his excessive verbiage. Sorokin surely did not require half a million words to present his system of sociology in *Society, Culture, and Personality*, even though it contains the substance of his other works. The bombast and the fustian to which Sorokin was addicted amuses for a while but then begins to pall. His assaults on the theories of others, in prose both

118. *Values in Human Society: The Contributions of Pitirim A. Sorokin* (Boston: Porter Sargent Pub. 1970), and *History, Civilization, and Culture: An Introduction to the Historical and Social Philosophy of Pitirim A. Sorokin* (Boston: Beacon Press, 1952). The latter book, slightly revised, appears as Chapter 5 of the former.

119. *Values in Human Society*, p. 275.

120. See also *Pitirim A. Sorokin in Review*, ed. Philip J. Allen (Durham, N.C.: Duke University Press, 1963), and *Sociological Theory, Values, and Sociocultural Change: Essays in Honor of Pitirim A. Sorokin*, ed. Edward A Tiryakian (Glencoe, Ill.: Free Press of Glencoe, 1963).

purple and pugnacious, is often sullied by misinterpretations of what they had to say. His taxonomies are constructed without the slightest appreciation of the canons of classification. All this we have to accept.

The substantive criticisms are more serious. The truth is that in the four volumes of *Social and Cultural Dynamics* he gave us no theory of social and cultural dynamics. We have a description—one of trendless flux—but no cause. As I have said, the notion, advanced quite seriously, that cultures change because it is their nature to change is one of the greatest anticlimaxes in the history of sociology. Sorokin's doctrine of "immanent causation" can only—to borrow again—be a fig leaf we use to conceal the nudity of our ignorance. One must not judge too harshly his failure to provide a theory of social change, but one is emptied of all sentiment by his pretension that he has done so.

Secondly, his sensate and ideational cultures are the children of his prejudices. We realize, early in our reading, that the ideational is everything he admires and the sensate everything he detests. Indeed, there are paeans of praise for the art, the religion, the literature, the music, the philosophy, and even the mysticism of the early Middle Ages. His most violent adjectives are hurled at anything that has the taint of the sensate. He is willing—but only infrequently—to agree that sensate cultures produce their own achievements. Science and invention, for example, are sensate accomplishments. But when these concessions are made the diatribes begin again. The word "sensate" is an epithet, not a judgment.

In consequence, and thirdly, Sorokin's comparisons lack all sobriety and are ultimately illicit. It is easy to take what is best in an ideational era and contrast it with what is worst in a sensate. It would be as easy to do the reverse—to emphasize the poverty, the ignorance, the superstition, and the misery of the Middle Ages and contrast it with the material comfort, the technology, the medicine and science of the twentieth century. Sorokin has every right to his historical nostalgia. But nostalgia is no substitute for sociology.

The critical skepticism expressed in these summary remarks raises a last and serious question. If Sorokin's general theory has these defects, how do I justify the inclusion of his work in this book? What is now, and what is likely to be, Sorokin's place in the history of sociological theory? On these questions one can write with confidence. Despite the defects to which I have invited attention, Sorokin's place is secure. He gave to sociology a scope and significance that, except in Ward, was nowhere approached by his predecessors. For him sociology is no mean and petty discipline, occupied with problems "left over" by such other disciplines as economics, political science, and jurisprudence, but is a strong and vital inquiry into the processes of society and of history. Sorokin's treatment of the structure of society, however marred by inconsistency, is at least a system, and a system, one might say, produced on a grand scale. Many of his insights are spectacular. One always knows that one is in the presence of a man who knows what sociology is. His theory of social and cultural dynamics may be entirely fanciful, but at least he had the courage to address himself to this vast problem, and along the way to show how sociology could deal not only with social interaction in a narrow sense but also with the integration of art, literature, music, architecture, science, philosophy, law, and government in one comprehensive synthesis. Whatever one may think of his answers, there is no doubt that he always asked the right questions. Sorokin gave size to sociology.

CHAPTER 8

George A. Lundberg

Even if I should admit that social scientists are today merely chipping flint in the Stone Age of their science, I do not see that we have any choice but to follow the rough road that other sciences have traveled.

—*Can Science Save Us?* p. 24

George Andrew Lundberg was born in Fairdale, North Dakota, on October 2, 1895, the son of Swedish immigrants. He grew up on his father's farm, in that remote prairie country, and received his elementary education in a one-room country school, so typical of the region in that time and place. The population of his community was Scandinavian, German, and Russian, and, as he says, he never saw a black, a Jew, or an Oriental until he went to college. Life on the farm consisted of hard labor for the children as soon as they were old enough to do their share and although there was plenty to eat, there was no money for such luxuries as magazines and books. Indeed, the only reading matter available seems to have been the Sears Roebuck and Montgomery Ward annual catalogues.[1]

Lundberg did not attend high school. The nearest one was too far away, and, in any event, his presence was required on the farm. Instead and, as it turned out, to his advantage, he enrolled in a college preparatory course offered by a correspondence school in Chicago and received a diploma from that source. After several years of teaching in country schools he managed to save enough to enter the University of North Dakota, from which he received a degree in education in 1920. His undergraduate career was interrupted by the World War I, and he accordingly spent fifteen months in the army, achieving by the end of that period the exalted rank of corporal. Most of the time he spent keeping records of the boxcars in the railroad yards of Paris. Again he was fortunate in that he was able, during demobilization, to spend three months in London, and to attend lectures by Hobhouse and Westermarck at the London School of Economics.

Back from the war, and armed with a bachelor's degree in education,

1. At some point he ran across *Les Misérables*, possibly purchased from one of the mail-order catalogues. The book made a profound impression upon him, and he read it over and over again.

Lundberg began what he presumed to be his career, namely, high school teaching and administration. In 1920 he was offered the superintendency of schools in a small town in North Dakota. Rumors reached the board, however, of his activities on behalf of the Non-Partisan League, and his appointment was abruptly cancelled. Lundberg demanded a hearing, which was granted, and the story of that episode may be told in his own words:

> There were no facts in dispute, or at least both sides disdained to resort to them. All felt that High Principle was really the issue. The Board made no allegations regarding my membership or activity on my part on behalf of the League, and I offered no apologies for my political and economic views. Neither party appealed to any laws, regulations, or rules governing the dismissal of teachers in North Dakota at this time. The whole proceeding was carried on in an air of moral grandeur that was awe-inspiring.
>
> The meeting was opened by the president of the Board of Education, whom I shall call Mr. Blank from here on. Mr. Blank was also president of the First National Bank in the parlor of which we met. I shall give only the verdict and its justification. In his role of judge, prosecutor, and Pontifex Maximus, Mr. Blank intoned as follows: "I don't think it would be proper," he said, "for this Board to ask whether you are a Methodist or a Presbyterian; but we do think that we have a right to ask, 'Are you a Christian?' In the same way, it would never occur to this Board to ask whether you are a Republican or a Democrat. But we do think we have a right to ask you, 'Are you a Socialist?' "[2]

Lundberg's case was hopeless from the beginning. He managed to find another appointment, however, as professor of psychology, education, and sociology—with the additional title of director of the Teacher Training Department—at a small church-related college in Nebraska.

By attending three summer sessions Lundberg was able to earn his M.A. degree in 1922 at the University of Wisconsin. His zeal for social reform induced him to take it in sociology, where he accordingly came under the influence of such teachers as E. A. Ross and John L. Gillin, and read the books of McDougall, Veblen, Bernard, and Cooley. Three years later, in 1925, he received his Ph.D. degree from the University of Minnesota, under the tutelage of F. Stuart Chapin, L. L. Bernard, and M. C. Elmer, with a dissertation on the history of poor-relief legislation in that state. A postdoctoral summer session at Columbia University completed his formal education.

Lundberg's first university appointment, which he held from 1925 to 1926, was an assistant professorship at the University of Washington, in Seattle. In 1927 he became associate professor of sociology at the Univer-

2. Otto N. Larsen, "Lundberg's Encounters with Sociology and Vice Versa," in *The Behavioral Sciences: Essays in Honor of George A. Lundberg,* ed. Alfred de Grazia *et al.* (Great Barrington, Mass.: Behavioral Research Council, 1968), p. 5.

sity of Pittsburgh, a post he held until 1930. In the latter year he was appointed director of the Bureau of Social Research of the Pittsburgh Federation of Social Agencies. In 1931 he moved to Columbia on a visiting appointment in order to undertake the research that resulted in his book on leisure.[3] After a year as research supervisor for the Federal Emergency Relief Administration, in Washington, he joined the young and lively faculty of Bennington College, where he was something of a "star." He concluded his career again at the University of Washington, where he became Walker Ames Professor of Sociology in 1945 and served from 1945 to 1953 also as chairman of the department. Relatively late in life (1956) he married Sylvia Kjeldstad. He died in 1966, under anaesthesia, while undergoing an operation.

In 1926 Lundberg published four articles, one in *School and Society*,[4] two in *Social Forces*, and one in the *Journal of the American Statistical Association*. These were only the first of a stream of articles, some eighty in all, that Lundberg published during his professional career, most of the more important and controversial ones in the *American Sociological Review* and the *American Journal of Sociology*. Indeed, almost all of his ideas were presented to the public first in the form of journal articles. In 1929 he, Read Bain, and Nels Anderson edited and published a book entitled *Trends in American Sociology*.[5] The contributors, including the editors, were the "young Turks" of the time, anxious to obliterate the taint of social reform and moral uplift that characterized sociology and to transform the discipline into an objective and value-free science. Meanwhile, Lundberg, who taught the courses Social Surveys, Social Statistics, and Social Exhibits, produced a textbook on the methods of social research, building on the earlier work of L. L. Bernard, F. Stuart Chapin, M. C. Elmer, and R. E. Chaddock.[6] In this book, relatively noncontroversial, he emphasized the importance of quantitative techniques. His most important book, *Foundations of Sociology*, appeared in 1939, and I shall attend to it in the sequel. Later on he wrote several articles for *Harper's*

3. *Leisure: A Suburban Study*, with Mirra Komarovsky and Alice McInerny (New York: Columbia University Press, 1934).

4. This first one, entitled "Sex Differences on Social Questions," *School and Society*, May 8, 1926, pp. 595–600, was the result of a questionnaire survey administered to sociology students at the University of Minnesota. Two of the questions were "Is it right to kiss a man or woman you do not expect to marry? (*Yes* or *No*)," and "Was the Bible verbally inspired by God? (*Yes* or *No*)." An issue arose as to whether it was proper for a professor to invade the privacy of a captive audience and what effect such questionnaires would have on the reputation of the university. Despite objections, the president encouraged him to continue his research.

5. (New York: Harper & Brothers).

6. *Social Research* (New York: Longmans, Green & Co., 1929); 2d ed., 1942.

Magazine that were expanded and published in a small book entitled *Can Science Save Us?*[7] Lundberg's answer to his own question, of course, was a resounding affirmative. Not only can science save us but it also is the only device that can. The book is pure propaganda in favor of the application of scientific method to the solution of social and political problems. During the remainder of his career, Lundberg continued to publish polemical papers, not only on sociological theory as such but also on international relations, foreign policy, education, and race relations.

Lundberg's prominence brought him the customary rewards of his profession. He was at various times president of the American Sociological Society, the Eastern Sociological Society, the Pacific Sociological Society, and the Sociological Research Association. He was a fellow of the American Association for the Advancement of Science and a member of the Institute of Mathematical Statistics, the American Statistical Association, the Population Association of America, the Psychometric Society, and the Econometric Society, among others. He was invited to lecture at numerous American universities and also at several universities in Norway and Sweden. The University of Minnesota conferred on him its Distinguished Service Medal in 1951, and the University of North Dakota, an honorary LL.D. in 1958.

With the possible exception of Sorokin, Lundberg was the most redoubtable polemicist of his generation of sociologists. Although a man of liberal and even radical political persuasions in his youth, a member of all the respectable associations, such as the Non-Partisan League and the American Civil Liberties Union, and a signer of all petitions in protest against one injustice or another, he nevertheless took an impish delight in breaking the icons of his liberal friends. "Science," an addiction that was absolute for Lundberg, would not permit a soft or sentimental approach to the social and political issues of the day. In an address to the American Council for Judaism, in New York City on April 27, 1957, he accused the major Jewish organizations (the Council excepted) of fostering the kind of prejudice they sought to combat, deplored the fact that they exercised a political influence out of all proportion to their numbers, regarded as "coercive intrusions" their efforts to support a foreign nation (Israel) while enjoying United States citizenship, and denounced their efforts to secure privileges and immunities (such as the censorship of books and movies) denied to other groups. It was Jewish ethnocentrism to which he was opposed—an ethnocentrism as dangerous as that of any other group and the principal cause of anti-Semitism.

Lundberg did not hesitate to apply his "scientific" conclusions to other

7. (New York: Longmans, Green & Co., 1947); rev. ed., 1961.

minorities as well. About Myrdal's *An American Dilemma,* for example, he wrote,

> I find no evidence in these two volumes, or anywhere else, that the "dilemma," which unquestionably is a dilemma to the author and to a large group of intellectuals and other admirable people of more than average literacy, is in any observable degree a dilemma for the great masses of American citizens, white and colored, who are thoroughly habituated to the existing caste or class system.[8]

On the minorities problem in general, he came to conclusions of which the following statement may be regarded as typical:

> It is wholly absurd to contemplate a social order in which there are no restrictions on the activities of minorities, and indeed on all other sub-groups of a society. For the same reason, all the loose talk about abolishing discrimination is entirely fatuous. The basic structure of society consists of a complicated system of discriminatory behaviors on the part of all individuals. The most that can or should be done about this by the community is to objectify, formalize, codify, and institutionalize, as far as possible, whatever rules governing discrimination a community decides to support. Here again, science becomes invaluable in making available to people a reliable account of the probable costs and consequences of different types of discrimination.[9]

Lundberg complained, of course, when the charge of prejudice was directed against him and contended, in defense, that all cultural groups should be open to criticism without the imputation that the critic was somehow a sinister character.

Lundberg attracted criticism similarly for joining Harry Elmer Barnes and others in expressing "neo-revisionist" opinions about American participation in World War II. He believed that the Japanese attack on Pearl Harbor was intentionally provoked by President Roosevelt and that given the same provocation, even the Grand Duchy of Luxembourg would have declared war on the United States. In his presidential address to the American Sociological Society, in 1943, he warned against a "hard and vindictive" peace settlement that would do violence to everything sociologists apparently knew about the basic conditions of community life. For expressing opinions such as these, and for his blunt views on the undesirability of Jewish agitators, his address—possibly for the only time in the history of the society—was greeted with vocal disapproval by members of the au-

8. "Science, Scientists, and Values," *Social Forces* 30 (May 1952): 374, n. 3.

9. "Applying the Scientific Method to Social Phenomena," *Sociology and Social Research,* September-October 1949, p. 5.

dience.[10] Most of the address turned on the necessity of discarding "moralistic-legalistic" approaches to the solution of social problems and the substitution therefore of scientific method. It was his favorite theme and one he repeated again and again. Although declaring his own preference for democracy, he liked to insist that science had historically prospered in all kinds of political regimes, including totalitarian ones. He had nothing but contempt for ministers who maintained in their sermons during the war that God was on the side of the democracies. "That," he said, "is a remarkable claim in view of the social organization of Heaven!"

All in all, Lundberg luxuriated in his iconoclasm and relished his polemical writing, which, as he once wrote to Howard Odum, he regarded as the "legitimate amusement" of an academic career. Most of his disputes, however, were engagements with other sociologists—MacIver, Znaniecki, Blumer, Furfey, even his old friend Read Bain—and all others whom he suspected of being traducers of the scientific method.

Foundations of Sociology

As we have noted, *Foundations of Sociology* appeared in 1939.[11] It was prepared as the first of a two-volume work, with the second volume to be written by Stuart C. Dodd. Dodd, then on the faculty of the American University in Beirut, had been performing experiments in rural hygiene, with control and experimental groups, and these attracted Lundberg's attention as impressive examples of what sociological research should be. Accordingly, the two of them engaged in a voluminous correspondence beginning in 1934, and they spent a summer together in the Lebanon mountains planning what they hoped would be a momentous turning point in the history of sociology. Lundberg, in his book, would lay down the methodological foundations on which the new sociology was to be built, and Dodd, in his, would build the building, that is, construct a quantitative systematic science of sociology. Unfortunately, the joint plan had to be abandoned. The difficulties of wartime communication between the Middle East and the New York publisher, and the complications involved in settng Dodd's formulations in type, delayed the publication of the second volume until 1942, when it appeared under the title *Dimensions of Society*. The two thus appeared as independent books, bearing their own titles.[12]

10. "Sociologists and the Peace," *American Sociological Review* 9 (February 1944): 1–13.
11. (New York: Macmillan).
12. Lundberg writes,

> A word should be said regarding the relationship of the two volumes. The position adopted in the present work undoubtedly contemplates a development *in the general direction and of the general*

In any event, Lundberg had come to the conclusion that nowhere in the literature was there an adequate or explicit statement of the postulates of social science, nowhere an explanation of the processes by which generalizations were derived. One would have thought, incidentally, that these postulates and processes had been thoroughly treated in textbooks of logic—especially the superior text of Morris R. Cohen and Ernest Nagel, which appeared while Lundberg was engaged in his own writing.[13] Unfortunately Lundberg, untrained in philosophy in general and logic in particular, was innocent of this literature—an innocence that led him into errors of an elementary kind. In any event, it was his task, as he conceived it, to utilize the power and rigor of positivistic methods—the methods of the natural sciences—in sociological inquiry and thus to place the discipline of sociology upon a firm and sound foundation. Once more a man is moved by the dream of Auguste Comte.

The first four chapters contain the substance of Lundberg's methodological views. Much of their content consists of repetition and paraphrase of earlier papers.[14] Lundberg begins with the observation that science is a "human adjustment technic" and is therefore an integral part of sociology itself. All inquiry has its origin in tension or imbalance in the organism, a tension that interferes with adjustment and disturbs an organic equilibrium, which is then restored when the answers are supplied. This process is quite familiar with respect to our knowledge of the natural universe. Earthquakes, storms, and floods are all explained in the framework of natural science, and therefore, however much devastation they may cause, they induce little intellectual strain or tension. The situation is different in the social world. Wars, revolutions, and crimes, because their causes are imperfectly understood, are all given emotional rather than scientific treatment, and no progress is therefore made in their resolution. These latter social phenomena (Lundberg prefers the adjective *societal*) are

---

type exhibited in Professor Dodd's volume. The latter in turn undoubtedly proceeds upon the postulates and according to the general reasoning maintained in the present volume. The position here advanced, however, is also compatible with an indefinite number of other possible specific systems of classification and notation. The validity of the approach and the central theses of the present volume are not contingent, therefore, on the ultimate usefulness of the *particular* system so ingeniously expounded in Dodd's work. At the same time the latter affords, as will be seen from my numerous references to it, elaboration and illustration of general theoretical principles with which the present volume is chiefly concerned.

Ibid., pp. ix–x.

13. *An Introduction to Logic and Scientific Method* (New York; Harcourt Brace, 1934).

14. Including "Is Sociology Too Scientific? *Sociologus* 9 (September 1933): 298–322 (with a reply by MacIver); "Quantitative Methods in Social Psychology," *American Sociological Review* 1 (February 1936): 38–54; "The Thoughtways of Contemporary Sociology, 1" *ibid.* (October 1936): 703–723; "The Concept of Law in the Social Sciences," *Philosophy of Science* 5 (April 1938): 189-203; and "Contemporary Positivism in Sociology," *American Sociological Review* 4 (February 1939): 42–55.

just as "natural" as the former, and our efforts to understand them should therefore be placed in exactly the same framework. *Natural* and *physical* are merely words in terms of which we describe a type of adjustment:

> Unfortunately, it is at present very generally assumed that these terms represent not merely a type of adjustment technic on our part, but that such terms as "physical" and "natural" are inherent characterizations of *some* phenomena in the universe but not of others. The other type or types of data are variously and vaguely designated as "social," "cultural," "mental," and "spiritual." These terms, instead of being regarded as describing those situations to which we make at present a relatively subjective and emotional type of adjustment, are likewise *attributed to data as inherent characteristics.* The result of this semantic confusion has been a most mischievous separation of fields of knowledge into the "natural" and "physical" on the one hand as against the "social" and "cultural" (mental, non-material, spiritual) on the other. As a consequence, it has been assumed that the methods of studying the former field are not applicable to the latter. The generally admitted lag in the progress of the "social" as contrasted with the "physical" sciences has been a further result.[15]

The history of science bears witness that phenomena once thought to be "mental" or "spiritual" have steadily and successfully been brought into the purview of the "physical" and "natural," and this despite resistance at every step of the way. Some there are who are still resistant to bringing the "social" into this purview.

One would like to omit from description Lundberg's statement of his own postulates, which he regards as the postulates of science. They are a rather odd list, however, and in fairness to him it is desirable to quote them:

> 1. All data or experience with which man can become concerned consist of *the responses of the organisms-in-environment.* This includes the postulate of an external world and variations both in it and the responders to it.
> 2. Symbols, usually verbal, are invented to represent these responses.
> 3. These symbols are the immediate data of all communicable knowledge and therefore of all science.
> 4. All propositions or postulates regarding the more ultimate "realities" must always consist of inference, generalizations, or abstractions from these symbols and the responses which they represent.
> 5. These extrapolations are in turn represented symbolically, and we respond to them as we respond to other phenomena which evoke behavior.[16]

These postulates are a veritable rat's nest of epistemological and metaphysical problems. One is tempted to echo Sorokin on Parsons and say, "Everything in this cumbersome pile of words is unclear." I shall only

15. *Foundations of Sociology*, pp. 7–8.
16. *Ibid.*, p. 9.

note—and query—the notion that the data of all knowledge and of all science are symbolic representations of responses. What has happened to the "natural" world that it is the province and privilege of science to investigate? In fact, these and most of Lundberg's subsequent propositions belong to an idealistic metaphysics—a philosophy he would normally deplore—and he has neither a natural world nor a God to guarantee the status of the symbols he invents.[17]

Lundberg is willing to concede that "as a metaphysical necessity we grant *that which* in the universe outside of the responding mechanism precipitates the response," but he insists that "all assertions about the *ultimate* 'reality,' 'nature,' 'essence,' or 'being' of 'things,' or 'objects' are therefore unverifiable hypotheses, and hence outside the sphere of science."[18] But if "nature" and "objects" are members of this category, what has happened to the "nature" that is the "object" of natural science? We should not, of course, require Lundberg to solve the problems of philosophy in a treatise on sociology (after all, Kant too had his noumenon, his *Ding-an-sich*), but, as I have said, an idealistic metaphysics permeates his doctrine and has serious consequences for the objectivity and verifiability of his sociological knowledge.

Lundberg is convinced that sociologists are merely "chipping flint in the Stone Age of their discipline." One of the problems is an antique, not to say archaic, vocabulary. Just as chemistry had to abandon the word *phlogiston* as the explanation of combustion after the discovery of oxygen, so sociologists will have to abandon such words as *will, feeling, ends, motives, values,* and others appropriate to the category of *mind*. "These are the phlogiston of the social sciences."[19] Of course, the older generation, accustomed to these words, will feel that something has been "left out" of

---

17. One is reminded of the doggerel that Ronald Knox wrote to describe the philosophy of George Berkeley:

> *There was a young man who said, "God*
> *Must think it exceedingly odd*
> *If he finds that this tree*
> *Continues to be*
> *When there's no one about in the Quad."*

To which there is the following anonymous response:

> *"Dear Sir: Your astonishment's odd:*
> *I am always about in the Quad.*
> *And that's why the tree*
> *Will continue to be,*
> *Since observed by* Yours faithfully,
> *God."*

18. *Ibid.*, pp. 9, 10.
19. *Ibid.*, p. 11.

the explanation if these words are not employed. They would be right. But the something "left out" is only a word. "I have no doubt that a considerable part of the present content of the social sciences will turn out to be pure phlogiston."[20] The remedy is operational definitions, a subject upon which Lundberg will discourse at length as his argument proceeds. The notion that we cannot explain social phenomena without words tainted with emotional and subjective meanings is illustrated by the tendency, for example, to regard familiar words as essential components of situations.[21] And here he arrives at his famous—or notorious—argument with MacIver. First he quotes MacIver:

> There is an essential difference, from the standpoint of causation, between a paper flying before the wind and a man flying from a pursuing crowd. The paper knows no fear and the wind no hate, but without fear and hate the man would not fly nor the crowd pursue. If we try to reduce fear to its bodily concomitants we merely substitute the concomitants for the reality experienced as fear. We denude the world of meanings for the sake of a theory itself a false meaning which deprives us of all the rest.[22]

Then he continues,

> Note the essential nature of the words *hate* and *fear* in this analysis. Even their translation into terms of their behavior-referents is alleged to "denude the world of meanings." Now if anyone wishes to interpret the flying of a paper before the wind in terms of hate and fear, as has doubtless frequently been done in ages past, I know of no way of refuting the analysis for it is determined by the terms, the framework, and the meanings adopted. *These categories* are not given in the phenomenon. Neither are the categories I should use in scientific description so given. In fact, I have no objection to the words "fear" and "hate" if they are defined in terms of physico-chemical, biolinguistic, or sociological behavior subject to objective verification. I have no doubt, either, that descriptions in these terms would vary widely in different cases of flying objects. For this reason, I do not declare MacIver's analysis of the man and the crowd as *false*. I merely point out that possibly I could analyze the situation in a frame of reference not involving the words "fear" or "hate" but in operationally defined terms of such character that all qualified observers would independently make the same analysis and predict the behavior under the given circumstances.[23]

---

20. *Ibid.*, pp. 11–12.

21. One nevertheless finds within the space of a few pages such expressions as *sympathy* (*ibid.*, p. 296), *understanding* (p. 297), *group-consciousness* (p. 302), a *group's self-consciousness* (p. 302), and *sensitivity* (p. 303).

22. Quoted *ibid.*, p. 12, from MacIver, *Society: A Textbook of Sociology* (New York: Farrar & Rinehart, 1937), pp. 476–477.

23. *Foundations of Sociology*, pp. 12–13.

The law of parsimony, says Lundberg, requires that all instances of flying objects be brought into the same frame of reference. Thus the man and the crowd and the paper and the wind will be interpreted "as the behavior of an object of *specified characteristics* reacting to a stimulus of *specified characteristics* within a specified field of force."[24] Thus *fear* and *hate* also become the phlogiston of sociology. One only wishes that Lundberg had supplied the specifications to which he refers.

The position that Lundberg has adopted does not, he insists, require that sociologists leave out of their considerations any phenomena whatever. Physicists have no trouble studying echoes and shadows, and similarly sociologists can study all of the phenomena denoted by words such as *mental* or *conscious*, and *values*, *meanings*, *ideals* and *ideas*. So long as they are responses to observed behavior they can be investigated by the methods of science. In any case, meaning is a type of classification, categories are generalized language habits, and utility is the test of all thought systems. The important point is that the Neo-Kantian distinction between the *Naturwissenschaften* and the *Kulturwissenschaften* is indefensible, as is similarly the distinction between an *erklärende* and a *verstehende* method. "Understanding" is the goal of all of the sciences and the method of none. Finally, Lundberg stresses the nonethical nature of science and distinguishes between a social problem (*e.g.*, the prevention of crime) and a sociological problem (*e.g.*, the relationship between the incidence of crime and population density). Not all problems are scientific. It is not incumbent upon a sociologist to solve social problems any more than it is incumbent upon a priest to explain the cellular structure of the Holy Ghost. They are two different tasks, conceived and executed in different systems of thought.[25]

---

24. *Ibid.*, p. 14.

25. *Ibid.*, p. 31. Lundberg attends to the relationship between man and society only in a footnote, and I shall follow his example:

> Fine literary phrases such as "the whole is more than the sum of its parts," derive their impressiveness chiefly from their obscurity. The problem when objectively examined is quite simple. Consider the much quoted illustration of hydrogen and oxygen considered separately and in the compound H_2O. Is the latter "more than the sum of" the former? The question has no sensible operational meaning. All that needs to be pointed out is that hydrogen and oxygen act upon *different sense organs* (or act differently upon the same sense organs) when combined into H_2O than when uncombined. That they should give us a *different* sensation in combination than in separation is, therefore, no mystery requiring weird philosophical conjuring about the whole-part relationship. One is neither more nor less than the other. They produce different sensations, each of which is equally "real," "whole," and otherwise a legitimate phenomenon for study. This is perhaps generally recognized with respect to such phenomena as are used in the above illustration. But when the same problem rises as between "man" and "society" it sometimes gives rise to protracted futile discussion.

Ibid., p. 43, at end of n. 23. Lundberg was apparently unaware of the debates between Durkheim and Tarde on this issue.

If the language of sociology is in a primitive state, as Lundberg believes it is, it is necessary to indicate how it can be improved, which is what he proceeds to do in his second chapter. The problem is not unique to sociology. It is an inadequate symbol system, for example, that accounts for Zeno's paradox, the notion that although Achilles runs ten times as fast, he can never overtake the tortoise, who has been given a 100-yard head start. Using modern methods and symbols "unknown to the Greeks," we discover that "Achilles definitely overtakes the tortoise at the end of 111.11 seconds."[26] It is difficult to understand how Lundberg, a statistician, could have committed such a "howler."[27] His "solution" is not 111.11 seconds but 111.111111111111 + seconds. The decimal repeats itself to infinity, and thus there is no finite time at which Achilles catches up with the tortoise—which is just what Zeno had been saying!

Much of the trouble with sociological terminology is that it is dominated by Aristotelian laws of thought, laws that have handicapped thinking for centuries and that the physical sciences have abandoned. Aristotelian logic encourages the construction of dichotomies that are then taken to be inherent in the universe:

> Illustrations of the prominent but mischievous role which these dichotomies have played in the history of human thought are too well-known to require more than mention. For example: (1) the induction–deduction controversy is, in the light of modern psychology, simply obsolete. (2) The heredity–environment controversy is another case in point. (3) Further illustrations are found in many of the arguments regarding structure *versus* function, organization *versus* process, form *versus* activity, etc. What is overlooked is that a structure is merely a persistent function while a function is merely a series of changing structures. (4) The arguments about case studies *versus* statistical method, likewise disappear upon the reflection that all statistics necessarily consist of cases and that therefore there can be no antithesis or mutual exclusiveness between the two methods. The scientific import of the most thorough genetic or case or configuration analysis, on the other hand, lies in the demonstrability of its generality. The attempt to contrast quantitative technics with theory is

26. *Ibid.*, p. 46.

27. Lundberg uses and accepts the "algebraic solution" provided by Stuart Chase in *The Tyranny of Words* (New York: Harcourt Brace, 1938), pp. 153–154:

> With the same assumptions [the tortoise runs a yard per second, Achilles, ten times as fast], let us translate the problem into simple algebra. Let r be the rate of the tortoise. Then Achilles' rate will be $10r$. Let x be the time in seconds taken by the tortoise before they meet. We know that the distance traveled by the tortoise equals the distance traveled by Achilles. The distance a body travels is its rate of travel multiplied by the time traveled. Using this formula:
>
> Tortoise's distance $= r \times x$
> Achilles' distance $= 10r \times (x - 100)$
> or $rx = 10rx - 1000r$
> or $9x = 1000$
> Therefore $x = 111.11$ seconds.

likewise fallacious, because quantitative approaches may be as theoretical as any others.[28]

Lundberg is thus posing as an avenging angel, a destroyer of dichotomies—which induced Clifford Kirkpatrick wryly to observe that "differences between phenomena noted by others are not really differences because of similarities noted by Lundberg."[29]

Lundberg's remedy for our semantic confusions and terminological troubles is the adoption of operational definitions. In fact, "the only way of defining anything is in terms of the operations involved."[30] The theory of operationalism was propounded by the Harvard physicist, Percy W. Bridgman, in two books, *The Logic of Modern Physics* (1927) and *The Nature of Physical Theory* (1936), and in a series of papers in which he explained, defended, and sometimes modified his point of view. It was praised by John Dewey as one of the outstanding intellectual achievements of the twentieth century, and it generated a lively controversy in the journals of physics, psychology, sociology, and the philosophy of science. Lundberg accepted it with a cry of delight. It would solve all the conceptual problems of sociology and would resolve all disputes concerning the meaning of words. We need not determine how far or in what respects his interpretation of the theory may have strayed from Bridgman's formulations. We need only attend to his use of it and in order to avoid misunderstanding, I quote the following passage:

> Perhaps the best known illustration of futile quarreling over the meaning of words instead of arbitrarily agreeing on them (which is how they got their meaning in the first place) is the voluminous controversy over intelligence testing or more specifically whether what the tests tested really was intelligence. Indeed, it was regarded as a *reductio ad absurdum* some years ago to accuse the testers of defining intelligence as *that which* the tests tested—a theoretically entirely defensible definition. Logically, and particularly in the logic of natural science, this is perhaps the best definition that can be given. No platitude is more common in sociology than the remark that in order to measure, we must first define, describe, or "know" what we are measuring. The statement usually passes as a self-evident fact which needs no examination. That measurement *is* a way of defining, describing, and "knowing" seems to have been overlooked. If one confuses words with the things they signify and regards the process of definition as a mysterious intuitive revelation, instead of an ordered and selective way of responding to a situation, the idea of measur-

28. *Foundations of Sociology*, p. 49.

29. Review of *Foundations of Sociology*, *American Sociological Review* 5 (June 1940): 438. Furthermore, one does not quite know what Lundberg means by the "induction-deduction controversy" or what, if anything, it has to do with psychology. He is convinced, however, that the phenomenon of thought is the province of psychology, not logic, and that logic is concerned only with consistency. *Foundations of Sociology*, p. 50.

30. *Foundations of Sociology*, p. 58.

> ing anything without first defining it (in words supposed to possess some final essence), seems the height of absurdity. In the meantime, however, it happens that physical scientists have proceeded in just this manner. Since Einstein, at least, they have blatantly declared that space *is* that which is measured with a ruler; time *is* that which is measured by a clock; force *is* that which makes pointers move across dials, etc. For a couple of thousand years before Einstein, physicists too, were of the impression that they must first "define" these "entities" before measuring them. Let the history of science bear witness to the barrenness of the quest, and to the enslavement of intelligence for some two thousand years by the persistence of this thought-pattern. Today the *definition* of force and its *measurement* turn out to be the same *operation.* Contrast the liberation and the forward strides of physics through the acceptance of the latter doctrine, namely, that things ARE *that which* evokes a certain type of human response, represented by measurement symbols.[31]

And again:

> As science advances we find less and less interest in such questions, for example, as "what" electricity *is.* Except for certain types of philosophers, children, and other more or less semantically deranged persons (from the scientific point of view), most people find it sufficient to define what electricity is in terms of what it does. It IS *that which* under certain circumstances kills people, makes trains go, flashes in the clouds, illuminates lamps, makes the hand of the voltmeter move to a certian score, etc., etc. As social science advances we shall doubtless also find this type of answer adequate for the question as to what socio-economic status *is.* We shall be content to say that it IS *that which* under certain circumstances makes people beg on streets, cringe before the local banker, behave arrogantly to the janitor, *that* status which is associated with certain kinds of houses, food, clothing, education, occupation; more specifically, we shall probably say that a person will be accorded status, i.e., people will behave toward him *according to their estimate of the probability that he will achieve* the maximum goals of socio-economic striving. That is what we have meant by the term in prequantitative days; it is likely to continue to be what we mean by it under a quantitative terminology except that we shall state it in terms of a number of units on a scale. Each person will then know exactly what others who use the term mean.

This, then, is Lundberg's theory of operationalism.

Excursus on Operationalism

Operationalism is a theory that has certain surface attractions. It is clearly the case that the vocabulary of sociology is not standardized, that its concepts have different meanings in different and sometimes even the

31. *Ibid.*, pp. 59–60, 62.

same contexts, and that even such ubiquitous words as *status* and *role*, for example, exhibit ambiguity in use. What could be more sensible and effective than connecting our concepts to the operations employed in investigating their referents? Why bother with the meaning of intelligence, when we can define it as that which the intelligence tests test; with the meaning of attitude, when we can define it as that which is measured by a Thurstone scale; with the meaning of socioeconomic status, when we can define it as that which is measured by the Chapin scale? It is surely a matter of practical wisdom that we introduce as much clarity and precision as possible into the language we use. The admonition to define our terms, of course, is much older than the twentieth century. It is an Aristotelian admonition. Unfortunately, the theory of operationalism does not advance us very far in the desired direction. It is riddled with difficulties, inconsistencies, and circularities.

First, curiously enough, the word *operation* itself is unclear, both in Bridgman and in Lundberg. At the outset Bridgman intended to limit operations to those activities that are carried on in the laboratory, that is, actual physical operations. When it was pointed out to him, however, that it would be difficult to find a laboratory operation that could give meaning to such a concept as the square root of minus one, he modified the theory to include mental operations, verbal operations, and "paper-and-pencil" operations and in the end defined an operation as any "directed activity." The theory thus lost its distinguishing characteristic and came to mean anything a speaker or writer wanted it to mean. In Lundberg a different kind of confusion obtains. When he defines intelligence as that which the intelligence tests test, he has in mind an operation that the investigator performs. When he defines electricity as that which makes trains go, he has in mind an operation that the object itself performs. Unfortunately, as Ernest Nagel has pointed out (in a personal communication to the writer), such a definition of electricity is sterile from the point of view of electromagnetic theory. Moreover, it is also the operational definition of diesel oil.

Second, the theory leads to palpable absurdities. Aristotle once asked whether the road from Athens to Piraeus was the same road as the road from Piraeus to Athens. Operationally they would have to be different roads because we traverse them in opposite directions. The conceptual difficulties encountered in crossing the road at any point are infinite.

Also, suppose we want to test the intelligence of Johnny Jones, age twelve. Not knowing what intelligence is until we test it, we have no way of knowing what test to use. Suppose, however, that someone has given us the most recent test devised for use by the United States Army and also the old Stanford University revision of the original Binet–Simon test. If we use them both and Johnny scores an IQ of 112 on the former and 128 on the latter, we should have to conclude, on operational grounds, that this fortunate lad has two intelligences. Two operations are involved. Conversely, those whose intelligence is not tested have no intelligence. Bridgman candidly accepted this consequence of his theory, insisting that length measured by a surveyor's instrument and length measured by a yardstick were two different concepts and should therefore be differently labeled as $length_1$ and $length_2$. Lundberg argues that if we have several tests of socioeconomic status, for example, "none of them can be declared either right or wrong as among themselves or as against the Chapin scale. All of them are right according to their own criteria and wrong according to others."[32] One wonders why it would not be desirable—operationally—to define socioeconomic status as that which is measured by Lundberg, and then no other sociologist would ever have to bother with it.

As another absurdity, consider that no one knows how hard the wind can blow. At its height it blows the anemometer away. There is thus no operation in terms of which we can measure maximum wind velocity, and we would have to conclude, on operational grounds, that the concept of maximum wind velocity has no meaning.[33]

Third, Lundberg is unclear whether his operationalism is a theory of meaning or a theory of existence, and his capitalization of *ARE* when he tells us that "things *ARE that which* evokes a certain type of human response" is no help.[34] Are we to suppose that we can confer existence upon something—such as intelligence or socioeconomic status—by giving it an operational definition? One can easily define in this way hippogryphs, unicorns, leprechauns, fairies, and other creatures of whose existence there is some question. We can also define God as that which people worship—surely as defensible as defining electricity as that which makes trains go—but it is doubtful if the definition would satisfy either the theologian or the man who prays. Finally, nothing would be easier than to define "phlogiston" as that which makes fire burn, and thus to ruin—operationally—Lundberg's favorite example of antiquated concepts. The theory is thus simplistic in the extreme. Lundberg's world is a veritable garden of "that whiches," all of them hiding behind the shrubbery of his operations.

Fourth, the theory of operationalism results in an infinite multiplication of concepts and thus violates the law of parsimony. No two operations are identical—not even the measurement of a table top by the same individual with the same yardstick twice—and thus we would have as many concepts as there are operations to be performed. We say this with no desire to involve the Heraclitean flux in the simple problems of practical measurement

32. *Ibid.*, p. 63.

33. The point is made by Charles E. Whitmore, "The Analogy of the Record," *Journal of Philosophy* 37 (1940): 716–717.

34. *Foundations of Sociology*, p. 60.

but only to exhibit the consequence of an insistence that all operations be unique.[35]

Fifth, Lundberg's theory erases the distinction between the reliability and the validity of a test. Reliability refers to the degree to which a test produces consistent results upon repeated application. Validity refers to the degree to which a test tests what it purports to test. It is obvious that on operational grounds all tests are valid because whatever they test is given by the test itself. As MacIver sagaciously observes, "All tests are equally good for testing 'that which they test.' "[36] One would therefore never have an incentive to revise a test (Lundberg refers to the third revision of the Chapin scale) because the first version would, by operational definition, be as good as any subsequent revision.

Sixth, as a corollary, the theory supplies no criterion in terms of which one can select one test rather than another. Lundberg once applied the Chapin scale to the residents of a small Vermont village and then asked the village banker and a village janitor to rate the residents according to their estimates of socioeconomic status.[37] He was gratified to discover that the three ratings—the Chapin scale, the banker's, and the janitor's—exhibited a high degree of agreement. His gratification, however, was inconsistent with his theory. It rests on the assumption that there was a single phenomenon in the village that could be tested in three different ways, not that there were three phenomena because three different operations were employed.

Seventh, the theory erases the distinction between nominal and real definitions. It will be helpful in understanding this distinction if we look in for a moment on Adam and Eve in the Garden of Eden. The first pair had a need to name the things that they were the first to be privileged to see, and how this was accomplished is explained in Eve's diary, as translated from the original by a latter-day descendant named Mark Twain:

> During the last day or two I have taken all the work of naming things off his [Adam's] hands, and this has been a great relief to him, for he has no gift in

35. Harry Alpert, for example, notes that Lundberg's "that which" procedure would result in conceptual anarchy. "George Lundberg's Social Philosophy: A Continuing Dialogue," in *The Behavioral Sciences: Essays in Honor of George A. Lundberg,* pp. 54–55. See also the perceptive "Comments on Lundberg's Sociological Theories," by Franz Adler, *ibid.*, pp. 34–47.

36. *Social Causation* (Boston: Ginn & Co. 1942), p. 157, n. 24. And continuing:

> Of course, if the testers were to come out and say, "We are not measuring intelligence but only that which we measure," nobody would object and nobody would care. Every different test would measure a different *that which,* and there would be as many objects of research as there were variant researchers, and the more they differed the less they could possibly disagree, and everything would become perfectly "objective" and perfectly meaningless.

37. "The Measurement of Socio-Economic Status," *American Sociological Review* 5 (1940): 29–38.

> that line and is evidently very grateful. He can't think of a rational name to save him, but I do not let him see that I am aware of his defect. Whenever a new creature comes along I name it before he has time to expose himself by an awkward silence. In this way I have saved him many embarrassments. I have no defect like his. The minute I set eyes on an animal I know what it is. I don't have to reflect a moment; the right name comes out instantly, just as if it were an inspiration, as no doubt it is, for I am sure it wasn't in me half a minute before. I seem to know just by the shape of the creature and the way it acts what animal it is.[38]

So long as Eve is only inventing names for the animals—names not yet in existence—we have no problem with her. When she says, however, that the name she chooses is the "right" name and that she knows by the shape of the creature what it is, then we do have a problem—a problem that can be solved only by the distinction between nominal and real definitions.[39]

A nominal definition is a resolution or a stipulation to use a certain word in a certain way. Thus, Eve may decide to call a new animal a "dodo." It is a stipulation, not a proposition. Since it is not a proposition, it has no truth claims and cannot be used in inference. A real definition, on the other hand, is a proposition asserting the conventional intension of a word. If Adam asks Eve what a dodo is and she replies that a dodo is a native European wildcat of the species *Felis sylvestris*, she is expressing a proposition.[40] Since it is a proposition, it has truth claims and may be used in inference. Eve is indeed conveying information with her real definition. It is important to realize that she may call her animal anything she wants, so long as the word is a new one. If the word *dodo*, however, is already in her vocabulary signifying something stupid, silly, or foolish and if the animal appears to be intelligent, she would be careless or capricious to do so. And if the animal is in fact intelligent, she would then be wrong to call it a dodo.[41] A real definition asserts, in short, that two expressions, *each of which has an independent meaning*, are equivalent to each other. In a nominal definition only the *definiens* (the defining phrase) has an indepen-

38. "Eve's Diary," in *The Family Mark Twain* (New York: Harper & Brothers, 1935), pp. 1117–1118.

39. Socrates, Hermogenes, and Cratylus also confront the problem in the Dialogue of Plato that bears the name of Cratylus. The solution of Socrates is unsuccessful.

40. "Eve's Diary," p. 1118:

> When the dodo came along he thought it was a wildcat—I saw it in his eye. But I saved him. And I was careful not to do it in a way that could hurt his pride. I just spoke up in a quite natural way of pleased surprise, and not as if I was dreaming of conveying information, and said, "Well, I do declare, if there isn't the dodo!"

41. In deference to Mark Twain I have permitted Eve to call a bird an animal. Actually, of course, the dodo is a large heavy, flightless bird (*Didus ineptus*) that, now extinct, once flourished on the island Mauretius.

dent meaning, and we decide arbitrarily to set our *definiendum* (the word being defined) as equivalent to it. Real definitions convey information and contribute to knowledge. Nominal definitions do not.[42]

When Lundberg tells us that intelligence is what the intelligence tests test, he is saying, "Let the word *intelligence* mean what the intelligence tests test." It is a stipulation, a plea for agreement, and since it is not a proposition, it cannot be false. No one is asserting anything. The word *intelligence* has no meaning, as he himself insists, except the meaning that he assigns to it. Indeed, he urges us arbitrarily to agree on the meanings of words because that is how they got their meaning in the first place. But twice—inadvertently and unconsciously—he refutes himself. The first time is when he writes, "Correlation is not merely the name of a certain statistical operation invented by Karl Pearson. It is, as the dictionary says, 'the act of bringing under relations of union, correspondence or interaction; also, the conceiving of two or more things as related.' "[43] In other words, *correlation* has a conventional intension apart from a statistical operation. The second time is when he disagrees with Eubank's attempt to substitute the word *category* for the word *class*. Lundberg wants the term *class* to conform to its usage in science and logic generally because it is a "pre-empted usage."[44] His "pre-empted usage" is precisely what we have called the conventional intension of a concept. He fails to notice that such concepts as "electricity," "steam," "intelligence," "attitude," and "socio-economic status" also have "pre-empted usages," that is, connotations independent of his operational definitions. It is thus appropriate to ask whether the measuring instrument in fact reaches or grasps this "pre-empted usage."

Nominal definitions, in short, because they are stipulations, have no truth claims, and they cannot contribute to knowledge. When we define man as a rational animal (a real definition), we are saying that what we mean by *man* is the same as what we mean by *a rational animal.* The proposition is true, and we have an item of knowledge. The stipulation that intelligence is what the intelligence tests test is neither true nor false. Thus, it is apparent, as I have said, that Lundberg has erased the distinction between nominal and real definitions and that his operational definitions, being nominal, do not contribute to knowledge. One is inclined to doubt that

42. Nominal definitions nevertheless have their uses. They are the only way of introducing a new word into a language, or a new concept into a scientific vocabulary, and they help us to economize time, space, and energy by using a shorter expression—usually a single word—for a longer one. Without them the dodo would not have a name.

43. *Foundations of Sociology*, p. 52.

44. *Ibid.*, p. 368, n. 4.

this is a conclusion that he would be happy to accept. But it is an ineluctable consequence of his operational reasoning.[45]

Eighth, and finally, the theory erases—deliberately and dogmatically in Lundberg's case—the distinction between cardinal and ordinal measurement, that is, the kinds of comparisons that can be made with cardinal numbers and those that can be made only with ordinal numbers. It is unnecessary to go very far into the logic of measurement in order to expose Lundberg's error. Since, for him, weight is that which is measured by a scale and radicalism, for example, is also that which is measured by a scale, there is no logical difference between the two measures. Indeed, the notion that there are two kinds of measurement is a pernicious and false assumption, a carry-over from a primitive folklore. All measurement is of the same kind, and the failure to recognize this, he says, has retarded the development of the social sciences.

Lundberg's error appears in the following passage:

> If, by the procedure described [the Thurstone technique], one person scores 5 and another 10, one may be called "twice" as radical as the other with precisely the same logic which declares that one stone is twice as heavy as another. The latter statement means that we have abstracted weight-quality out of a total complex of some kind and represented the abstraction by symbols of some kind, in this case, units-on-a-scale. In terms of this *scale*, one stone is twice as heavy as another and in no other "inherent," "fundamental" sense. In either case, it is a meaningful statement only to people who accept the symbolic operation involved. Note that in the above illustration, I have first defined radicalism in terms of the scores-on-a-scale, just as weight must be so defined in terms of its scale. It is unnecessary to argue whether what is tested is "really" an attitude, because attitude is defined as *that behavior* evoked by this test. It is likewise futile to argue whether a certain behavior considered in a test is "really" radical. For the constructors of the test and the scale agree to *call* it radical. It is therefore, also unnecessary to argue whether the statement that one individual is twice as radical as another is "comparable," "similar," and as logically defensible as the statement that one stone is twice as heavy as another because in terms of the units of the two scales (both of which assume an arbitrary, rational origin) one is obviously twice the other in both cases. Controversy over such matters illustrates the hopeless current confusion of linguistic and logical constructs with metaphysical postulates of existences, essences, beings, etc.[46]

The problem here is Lundberg's denial of the distinction between cardinal

45. For an expanded treatment of this subject, see Robert Bierstedt, "Nominal and Real Definitions in Sociological Theory," in *Power and Progress: Essays in Sociological Theory* (New York: McGraw-Hill, 1974), pp. 156–187. See also Ralph Eaton, *General Logic* (New York: Charles Scribner's Sons, 1931), pp. 294–305; and Cohen and Nagel, *Logic and Scientific Method*, pp. 224–241.

46. *Foundations of Sociology*, p. 72.

and ordinal measurement or, more precisely, the fundamental measurement, in cardinal numbers, of extensive properties and the classification, arrangement, and comparison, in ordinal numbers, of intensive properties.

The trouble is that cardinal and ordinal numbers look alike. In practice they are the same symbols, but the two number systems have different characteristics. Ordinal numbers indicate place of position in an array; the numbers are quite arbitrary except with respect to order, and they are subject to no arithmetical manipulation. Cardinal numbers, on the contrary, express the results of counting, answer the question How many?, represent interchangeable units, and are subject to arithmetical manipulation. Properties measured by ordinal numbers are called intensive, those by cardinal numbers, extensive. Lundberg denies the distinction in the following words:

> The basic issue involved in this position is the philosophical dichotomy between intensive and extensive qualities. It may be said at the outset that if one chooses to postulate such a dichotomy as inherent in phenomena, the reasoning leading to the conclusion here under attack regarding the immeasureability, or different logical nature of measurement, in the case of certain phenomena doubtless follows. But I reject this postulate.[47]

Unfortunately for his case, the difference is not a postulate but a fact.

The fact that length, for example, is an extensive property and temperature, for example, an intensive one can be shown by a simple illustration. Let us agree to say that a piece of rope 100 feet long is twice as long as one 50 feet long and that, *in terms of our scalar units,* a metal bar at a temperature of 100° F is twice as hot as one at 50° F. There is, however, an essential difference between these two assertions. The difference is that in the second case it is necessary to include the italicized phrase and in the first case it is not. Despite an equivalent grammatical form, the two assertions do not mean the same thing. When we assert the first, we mean that the first piece of rope is twice as long as the second—that its length is twice that of the second. When we assert the second, we can mean only that the scalar number of the first temperature is twice that of the second. The latter assertion is, in addition, clouded with confusion. It is wholly erroneous to say that one metal bar is twice as hot as another. It is incorrect, although meaningful, to say that the temperature is twice as great. It is logically defensible to say only that the scalar number is twice as great.

Let us now perform a simple exercise. Change the temperature readings into the centigrade scale, and the new readings will be 37.77+° for the 100° F and 10° for the 50° F. Similarly, in the case of the rope transform

47. *Ibid.*, p. 85, n. 49.

the lengths from the English scale to the metric scale, and the 100 feet becomes 30.48 meters and the 50 feet becomes 15.24 meters. After this transformation the first temperature is no longer twice the second; the length of the first piece of rope, however, is still twice that of the second. This is the case in spite of the fact that, as Lundberg himself insists, "the units of the metric system have nothing in common with units of the English measure."[48] The relationships are clearly seen as follows:

Scale	Ratio	Scale	Ratio
Length			
100 ft	2	30.48 m	2
50 ft	1	15.24 m	1
Temperature			
100° F	2	37.77+ ° C	3.77+
50° F	1	10.00° C	1.00

This exercise demonstrates that one piece of rope can be twice as long as another piece of rope in terms of any scale whatever, or in terms of no scale. One metal bar, on the other hand, can be twice as hot as another only in terms of a particular scale, and even then, as I have said, it is improper to use the expression twice as hot. It is the scalar number that is twice as great, not the temperature. In the case of the rope, both the scalar numbers and the length are twice as great. This is indeed a remarkable fact. It is a fact that obtains in independence of the scales that happen to be used. All scales will give equal ratios for lengths. No two scales will give equal ratios for temperatures. This demonstration proves that there is a difference between the measurement of length and the measurement of temperature. The difference is a fact and not a postulate.[49]

It is clear, therefore, that anyone who is tempted to define weight as that which is measured by a scale and radicalism as that which is also measured by a scale and to say that therefore both operations permit the judgment that something is twice as much as another has fallen into error. The fault is vital and stems directly from the theory of operationalism itself. In the theory operations are absolute in their determination both of the quality measured and the quality defined. The two operations merge, in fact, into

48. *Ibid.*, p. 87, n. 58.

49. The preceding three paragraphs, slightly altered, appear also in Bierstedt, *Power and Progress*, pp. 66–68. For the logic of measurement in general, see Cohen and Nagel, *Logic and Scientific Method*, pp. 289–301. For a penetrating application to measurement in sociology, see Robert K. Merton, "Fact and Factitiousness in Ethnic Opinionnaires," *American Sociological Review* 5 (February 1940): 13–28.

one. Since the operation itself is the sole criterion, no inquiry may be made concerning the appropriateness of the operation in measuring the quality. Operationally, any measure is *ipso facto* appropriate. The operationalist does not ask whether this or the other quality is extensive or intensive. Indeed, he cannot, because the theory renders the question redundant. The only alternative—a straw grasped by Lundberg, and inconsistently grasped—is to attribute the difference to a lag in the technology of measurement and to assert that when mensurational techniques advance, more and more qualities will be brought into the extensive category. Unfortunately for the theory, the logic of measurement does not depend upon history.

All measurement, in short, is an act of comparison. Some comparisons are quantitative and can be made with cardinal numbers. Others are qualitative and can be made with ordinal numbers. Great ingenuity has been expended in creating instruments for the second kind of comparison, and they are more refined now than in the days when Thurstone measured attitudes and Chapin socioeconomic status. But the difference remains, and it is basic. Lundberg has boxed himself into an untenable position. In order to compare two things, it is necessary to have two things. He has only one—the one that is given to him by his operation. The independent character of the other he denies. The following observations by C. I. Lewis go to the heart of the matter:

> The size of Caesar's toga is relative to the yardstick. But if we say, "The number of square yards in the toga is determined by the yardstick," the statement is over-simple. Given the toga, its size in yards is determined by the yardstick; given the yardstick, the number of yards in the toga is determined by the toga itself. If the toga had not a determinate sizableness independent of the yardstick, or if the yardstick had no size independent of the toga, then there would be no such fact as the number of yards in the toga; the relation would be utterly indeterminate. This independent character of the toga, or of the yardstick, is what we should be likely to call its "absolute" size. This can only be described in terms of *some* measure, though the description will vary according to what this measure is. The size of the toga in yards is relative to the yardstick, but it is nevertheless an independent property of the toga, a true report of which is given by its correct measurement in yards. Thus what is relative is also independent; if it had no "absolute" character, it would have no character in relative terms.[50]

This brilliant passage is a one-paragraph refutation of operationalism.[51]

---

50. *Mind and the World Order* (New York: Scribners, 1929), pp. 168–169.

51. For an extended treatment, see "The Operationalism of George A. Lundberg," in Bierstedt, *Power and Progress*, pp. 41–72. Lundberg returned to these issues in a later paper, "Operational Definitions in Social Sciences," *American Journal of Sociology* 47 (March 1942): 727–743, but unfortunately committed there the same errors. That paper is an effort to refute a paper by Herbert Blumer, "The Problem of the Concept in Social Psychology," *ibid.* 45 (March 1940): 707–719.

From Methodology to Sociology

After Lundberg presents his methodological point of view he is ready to turn to other problems, the first of which is the classification of the sciences and the place of sociology with respect to the others. After indulging in his familiar assertion that all classifications are arbitrary, he nevertheless expresses reservations about the Comtean hierarchy. "A more tenable and useful view is to regard the sciences as having developed simultaneously and through interaction with each other, rather than serially in a one-way dependence."[52] As for sociology in particular, he is quite willing to agree with Sorokin's conception of the field and indeed quotes Sorokin at length. The system he intends to construct must be judged in terms of four criteria—comprehensiveness, parsimony, objectivity, and verifiability. If he is accused of imitating the methods of the natural sciences, he will reply that the alternatives are to imitate the methods of theology, metaphysics, or astrology, and his preference for science therefore needs neither explanation nor defense. Unfortunately, the "annual grist" of sociological researches that Lundberg has examined over the years, however much the studies have contributed to the "harmless employment" of their authors, has done little or nothing to advance the science of sociology. The sociology may be there, but the "science" is lacking. This is the situation that Lundberg proposes to remedy.

Lundberg will use not only the methods of the natural sciences but also many of its concepts. Thus, behavior for him means "movement within a field of force in time," and "field" becomes synonymous with W. I. Thomas's "situation."[53] Social phenomena, even those (such as Catholicism and Communism, for example) that lack definite geographical boundaries, are to be treated in spatial terms and represented in systems of graphs, charts, coordinates, gradients, potentials and, finally, in equations. Lundberg is especially partial to such symbolic representations as those introduced by Dodd. Thus, for example:

$$\frac{PD}{V} = E$$

in which P = number of people desiring a specific value; D = their average intensity of desire for it; V = the available quantity of that value; and E = societal tension.[54] Formulations such as these are to be regarded as hypotheses for investigation, and their great merit is that they are

52. *Foundations of Sociology*, p. 94.
53. Note that this is not an operational definition.
54. *Ibid.*, p. 111.

rigorously defined. This is the way sociologists will have to proceed if they want a cumulative science.[55]

Lundberg describes his own procedure:

> Having chosen to regard interhuman behavior in its most generalized form as a system of energy operating within a field of force, we next postulate that similarities and differences of characteristics, behavior, intensity of interaction, attractions, and repulsions—imbalances of whatever sort—within this total system determine the direction and the vigor of the flow of this energy. The vigor and direction of the flow of this energy in turn determine the configurations, the structure, the sequences, and the correlations in the behavior of human groups. The similarities and the differences or imbalances which determine the flow of societal energy may be of any kind—social-spatial (status), temporal (e.g., age), sexual, economic, esthetic, temperamental, developmental, ideational, or any other. Specific behavior of any kind is then regarded as the resultant of all these similarities and differences, attractions and repulsions, as they operate in the delimited field of force (the situation) within which any or all of the factors or components may influence any or all of the others. The central task of sociology is to formulate predictable sequences (principles) of behavior within situations so standardized and defined as to allow the use of these principles in *any* situation whose significant deviations from the standardized situation can be measured.[56]

Unfortunately, we are not told how to measure the "vigor and flow" of this energy in a field of force, nor what instruments and units to use. When questions like these arise, Lundberg is content to refer the reader to Professor Dodd. The time has come to systematize the entire field of general sociology in quantitative symbols, and this is the task whose undertaking is promised in Dodd's *Dimensions of Society*.[57]

Having been told that behavior is a system of energy operating within a field of force, we are told also that it is a mechanism and that sociology ac-

---

55. Lundberg's language, incidentally, is didactic, frequently hortatory, and almost always polemical.

56. *Ibid.*, p. 115.

57. Lundberg, incidentally, is frequently on the defensive about his use of physical concepts in sociology:

> It may be pointed out in passing that most of the objections to the use of the terminology of other sciences in sociology is simply a reflection of the unfamiliarity of sociologists as to the meaning of these terms even in the sciences where they are admitted to be useful. The delusion is still widespread in sociology that such terms as, for example, atom, electrons, or quanta, energy, force, etc., are small pieces of rock or explosives, or matter of some kind instead of merely words representing convenient observation units of *any* subject matter. In short, if the word atom in the English language means merely an elementary unit of observation, it is as proper for us to use it in sociology as in chemistry. . . . Indeed, it is not only proper to adopt such terms, but necessary for intelligible communication with other scientists.

Ibid., p. 125. On the other hand, Lundberg is not a reductionist; see pp. 128–129.

cordingly has to move from vitalism to mechanism. It also has to dispense with determinism and accept the notion of statistical probability. Unfortunately, "the application of the logic of quantum physics to human will and choice is as yet in its infancy,"[58] but there is no doubt that it is an infant that will grow and thrive. If mechanism is the appropriate word to describe the behavior of an individual, it is no less appropriately applied to a group.[59] Unfortunately, the social sciences are still handicapped by the vocabulary of "journalists, theologians, and other evangelists."[60] Since all words are only convenient labels for our responses, and since we respond to groups as we do to individuals, the former are every bit as real as the latter, and there is no such thing as a group fallacy. Both individual and group are linguistic conventions. In this connection Lundberg offers a definition of "reality." It is a "feeling of familiarity which allows curiosity, doubt, and other tensions to come to rest."[61] Lundberg has no more objection to the concept of a group mind than he does to an individual mind, because both concepts are obsolete. In any event, folkways are collective habits, uniformities in the behavior of a group, and customs are relatively persistent folkways. Traditions are group memories, and the mores are those behavior patterns in which conformity is induced by coercion. "Institutions are the most stable, uniform, formal, and general of the group behavior patterns."[62] All of these words, however, are somewhat vague and require replacement by the precise formulations of Professor Dodd.

Throughout his book, as I have noticed, Lundberg is partial to the concepts of physics and chemistry and does not hesitate to use them in his sociological discourse. Thus, societal groups are electron–proton configurations,[63] and such concepts as motion, energy, and force are applicable to all behavior. Energy is "but a name for *amounts of changes in relationships*, and force is the rate of such changes in time."[64] One does not

58. *Ibid.*, p. 161.
59. *Ibid.*, p. 163:

> We shall in this book use the word mechanism to describe that necessary and sufficient set of relations or circumstances by means of which any behavior whatsoever takes place, whether it be the jump of an electric spark, the thoughts of a human being (including his telepathic and clairvoyant powers, if any), the milling of a mob, or the vote of a deliberative assembly.

60. *Ibid.*, p. 164.
61. *Ibid.*, p. 166.
62. *Ibid.*, p. 182.
63. *Ibid.*, p. 204.
64. *Ibid.*, p. 205:

> In the social sciences (and even in physics) these terms have been widely misused as the *cause* of the observed behavior. From this insidious linguistic fallacy of imputing a *causal* property to words which merely indicate a *relationship* of societal significance vast confusion has arisen in the social sciences especially. As a result, a large part of the literature of sociology has been given over to the elaboration of long lists of "interests," "desires," "wishes," "satisfactions," "drives," and "in-

know what kind of meaning to ascribe to these curious propositions or to the notion, in the accompanying footnote, that interests, drives, and instincts are relationships rather than causes. Lundberg has a section on the transformation of energy and demands recognition of the point that it is basic to all activity, and to all science, social as well as physical, but again leaves us without an example of its sociological application. Generosity of interpretation would induce one to believe that Lundberg is indulging in metaphor when he writes about electron–proton configurations, the transformation of energy, equilibrium, and force. Unfortunately, that is not the case. He is in dead earnest. This is the language of science; it must therefore be the language of sociology.

Lundberg has no difficulty with the problem of heredity versus environment in the explanation of behavior. It is a pseudoproblem. It will never be solved. It will be abandoned because it is as senseless as asking which leg of a three-legged stool is most important. In any case, "there is no such thing as 'the original nature of man' (i.e., it is an unprofitable postulate). We shall learn to get along without it in science pretty much as we learned to get along without the concept of God."[65] It appears also that we have to get rid of the primitive notion of causation:

> We have stressed the necessity of regarding all behavior as *interaction*—the resultant of multiple influences within a closed system or field of force. In this connection, we stressed the purely analytical, correlative, and verbal character of such constructs as organism-environment and stimulus-response. The full implications of the concept of interaction displace the primitive notion of causation to which there is still a great deal of adherence in the social sciences. This adherence with its attendant handicaps will necessarily continue until sociologists develop or become more generally familiar with the symbolic technics of mathematics in terms of which perhaps alone the more complicated forms of interaction can be represented. Although sociologists have in recent years especially given much attention to the vast influence of technological development upon societal behavior, they do not so frequently recognize the import of this fact as applied to their own science. In no department of societal affairs has technology wrought greater transformations than in science. The long delayed technological revolution in the social sciences is not likely to be less sweeping in its effects than it has been in other departments of societal activity. When that revolution comes some of the suggestions of this volume and of Dodd's *Dimensions of Society* will perhaps appear as very modest aspirations.[66]

stincts" as *causes* of observed behavior. The congeniality of this mode of thought in sociology is probably to be attributed to the training of early sociologists in theology rather than in science and consequently the adoption of thoughtways from the former rather than the latter.

65. *Ibid.*, p. 226.
66. *Ibid.*, p. 234.

Lundberg does not seem to notice that he has twice used the word *influence* in this passage, that technology has "wrought" transformations, and that technological revolutions have "effects."

Similarly, association and dissociation in society are attraction–repulsion patterns in a field of force. Status is the position of a societal movement at a given moment. "We describe the movement we call sociation as association or dissociation according to the direction of the movement toward or away from any status-point we choose to select," and " 'Toward' and 'away from' are of course purely linguistic conventions in terms of which we agree to designate behaviors in opposite directions from any chosen point."[67] Association and dissociation are therefore different degrees of the same process. What we need then are instruments to measure the degrees, and when we have them it is only a formality to assign cardinal numbers [!] to different points on the scale.[68] Cooperation, competition, and conflict may be regarded as gradations of an underlying process that Lundberg calls communication.[69] Similarly, social status and social distance are entirely relative and depend upon the scales that we devise to measure them. In the future such scales will be as familiar to us as yardsticks are now.[70] Similarly also, the difference between primary and secondary groups rests solely in degrees and all we need are scales to measure the degrees and the capacity to think in terms of continuous rather than discrete variables.[71]

Lundberg is at times uncomfortably conscious that he is not himself doing the job that needs to be done. Indeed, the construction of scales for social processes "must be the work of many men through many centuries. But as a knowledge of the nature of our foundations and blue-prints of the contemplated structure are a necessary preliminary to systematic and economical building, we have no apology for the present rudimentary

67. *Ibid.*, p. 263.

68. *Ibid.*, p. 266.

69. Lundberg appears frequently to be paralyzed by his operational position, and whenever he addresses himself to a new concept or phenomenon he stops to warn the reader that he is not talking about "what really is." For example:

> The caution must be constantly repeated, because the objections to such a procedure as that advocated above reduce ultimately almost always to the refrain that opposition, accommodation, cooperation, etc., defined as suggested above, unfortunately *are not* opposition, accommodation, cooperation, etc. Of course they are not. Words *never are* what they *stand for.* Words are *symbols.* Social scientists have already spent too much time hunting for things in nature to correspond to words in their vocabulary. That vocabulary was invented for the most part by primitive and superstitious men. To be sure, the words in that vocabulary may be used to state *hypotheses.* But as in the case of all hypotheses, we must feel free to abandon them when they do not serve as profitable nuclei around which to correlate experience.

Ibid., p. 278.

70. *Ibid.*, p. 316.

71. *Ibid.*, p. 317.

undertaking although we know that the blue-prints must change as the structure grows."[72] But clearly words such as *behavior* and *communication* will replace such "mentalistic" words as *instincts, wishes, desires, interests, purposes, motives, experience,* and *expression.*[73]

Our redoubtable operationalist is unable to supply operational definitions for all of his concepts. When he discusses, in the final part of his book, the principal sectors of society, we find such words as *plurel, class, aggregation,* and *group.* Thus *plurel* designates "any plurality, collectivity, aggregation, class, or group of *homo sapiens*" [sic]; *class* designates "*any* assortment of people according to specified similarities and differences of the constituent members or their situation"; *aggregation* designates any plurel whose members are in geographic proximity; and *group* designates any plurel in which observable interaction is present.[74] The most elementary unit of sociology, however, is none of these but is rather the person, the individual "with his societal conditionings."[75] One proceeds from the person, the monad, to the dyad, the triad, and so on. In any case, the sole basis of classification should be the degree of interaction. For example, "We may, then, agree to designate as a community any plurel which has a given minimum degree of geographic homogeneity *and* a given minimum degree and kinds of interaction."[76] (As so often in his discourse, one wishes that he had specified the "given minimum degree.") We find also a nonoperational definition of "mechanism." It is "any arrangement or relation of parts or conditions which results in a given observable event."[77] We are not told how a relation can result in an event—unless it is a *causal* relation, an adjective Lundberg avoids.

It is not necessary to pursue all of Lundberg's definitions and to comment on them in detail. His definition of "institution," however, seems unexceptionable. This refers to "*some types* of group behavior patterns," namely, those that are relatively stable and formal, as contrasted with folkways, fashions, and customs, which are unstable and informal.[78] The difference again is one of degree, which we need scales to measure. He also makes an appropriate distinction between manifest and latent behavior patterns—although it is not clear how observable behavior could ever be la-

72. *Ibid.*, p. 280.

73. Lundberg, incidentally, has no use for psychoanalysis, whose therapeutic value he compares with that of the Catholic confessional, Christian Science, and the Grotto at Lourdes. Only when psychoanalysts abandon their present vocabulary and begin to keep records that are susceptible to statistical analysis will their science advance. *Ibid.*, p. 284. n. 30.

74. *Ibid.*, pp. 340–341.

75. *Ibid.*, p. 347.

76. *Ibid.*, p. 361.

77. *Ibid.*, p. 375.

78. *Ibid.*, p. 376.

tent.[79] Lundberg goes on to discuss a number of institutions—familial, sexual, and kinship patterns; economic patterns; political patterns; and religious and recreational patterns—not to summarize what we know about them but only to illustrate how numerous preconceptions have handicapped their scientific study.

It is interesting—sometimes almost amusing—to see how easily Lundberg solves problems that seem complex to other sociologists. Marxism, for example, suffers from the same terminological faults as psychoanalysis, but less pardonably so.[80] The economic interpretation of history is as arbitrary as any other:

> From the point of view we have adopted, such assumptions of inherent priority of *any* component of a societal situation has been shown to be incompatible with the scientific orientation. Scientists take any variable or component as an "independent" variable and observe the fluctuation of others around it. They choose their independent variable on the basis of its convenience and relevance to the particular problem they have in mind and do not deceive themselves that this selection is dictated by an inherent "independence" or other characteristic in the "nature" of one factor as contrasted with others. Accordingly, such wearisome and futile questions as to the "truth" of "the economic interpretation of history" become obsolete in the scientific orientation, however appealing it may be as a viewpoint or an article of faith to those highly conditioned to see economic factors as independent variables. The "economic interpretation" of history has from the scientific point of view precisely the same validity as any other interpretation supported by an equal amount of relevant data. That is, the economic pattern of behavior of any group may be *taken* as an independent variable with reference to which the variations in all other behavior may be studied. The same may be said of any other pattern. Convenience and the results achieved by each approach will constitute its sole justification in any case.[81]

Thus, the economic interpretation of history is solely a matter of convenience and has nothing to do with cogency.

Lundberg's iconoclasm, to which I have earlier referred, is apparent again in his discussion of the relativity of economic standards:

> This line of reasoning, namely, the recognition that conformity to a certain minimum of group standards is necessary to the *biological* survival of man, is

79. Even here the physicalistic language persists: "The scientific problem with respect to all these patterns, therefore, is the problem of formulating the laws of societal gravity or the description of how societal energy develops and distributes itself in space (both geographic and social) and time (astronomic or social)." It is a problem of "energy flow," both past and present. *Ibid.*, p. 380. "Societal energy" and "societal gravity" are nowhere defined, operationally or otherwise.

80. *Ibid.*, p. 284, n. 30.

81. *Ibid.*, p. 387.

> not seriously questioned as it applies to the lower economic levels. Its applicability also to the higher levels is not so generally recognized on account of certain preconceptions and prejudices which are common against the upper income classes. The millionaire who shot himself because the market collapse in 1929 reduced his fortune to a mere quarter of a million dollars may be regarded as having died from the lack of a "minimum of subsistence" just as truly as the unemployed and destitute man who likewise disposed of himself. The same would be true if the latter had starved to death outright. The essential point is that in their *respective situations* both organisms were *unable* to survive—the evidence for this conclusion being that they *did not* survive.[82]

It is customary for sociologists to devote at least some of their attention to the problem of social change, and Lundberg is no exception. Unfortunately, he offers no theory but only definitions. Thus, "change is merely a continuous view of the successive positions which the components of a field of force occupy at successive intervals."[83] The problem again is one of transformation of energy. All attempts to describe historical change as linear, spiral, or cyclical are barren because the data are deficient and because rigorous scientific methods have not been applied to them. In any case sociologists should adopt a more modest view, undertake not to explain the course of social change in general but rather to discover trends, fluctuations, and cycles in particular kinds of behavior. Cycles and trends do not inhere in the data in any event but are merely our ways of responding to them. The concept of cultural lag too often refers to a disparity between what things are and what a writer or speaker thinks they should be. Scientifically, lag means only a lack of synchronization between two or more variables. "The whole protracted and wearisome discussion in sociology about the meaning of 'normal,' 'adjustment,' 'pathological,' 'balance,' 'equilibrium,' 'lag,' etc., is purely and simply an attempt to introduce and reconcile the meaning of these terms as employed in a theological framework with the completely different framework and meaning of the terms in science."[84] Similarly, the long and sterile controversy over the role of invention in social change is vitiated by an erroneous, antiquated, and unscientific notion of causation. We can select any variable at will and measure changes of others with respect to it, given of course the appropriate instruments, which it is now the business of sociology to devise. Finally, there is no incompatibility between social action and social

82. *Ibid.*, p. 391. Here one is reminded, in pure outline, of Stouffer's theory of relative deprivation and of Merton's theory of reference groups. One is also reminded of the observation of Anatole France that "the law in its majesty prohibits the rich as well as the poor from sleeping under bridges."

83. *Ibid.*, p. 504.

84. *Ibid.*, p. 523.

science. The development of social science—the task to which Lundberg has devoted his labor—is itself a form of social action.

Dimensions of Society

Inasmuch as Lundberg is inclined to refer to Professor Dodd all queries that the reader may entertain about the application of his theories, it becomes appropriate to examine Dodd's volume, *Dimensions of Society.*[85] Stuart Carter Dodd was born in 1900 and educated in psychology and economics at Princeton University and the London School of Economics. He taught at the American University in Beirut, Lebanon, for an extended period, and it was during this time, as we have seen, that the friendship of Lundberg and Dodd grew and prospered. In 1946 he joined Lundberg as professor of sociology at the University of Washington, and Seattle became the *fons et origo* of the new sociological doctrine. Indeed, their graduate students appositely referred to *Foundations of Sociology* as the Old Testament and *Dimensions of Society* as the New Testament.

Dimensions of Society is a work of remarkable ingenuity and of Herculean effort. It contains little methodological discussion. Indeed, Dodd accepts the methodological principles outlined by Lundberg, especially the theory of operationalism. The book will present the first genuinely operational system of sociology.[86] It begins with a proposition that generates the entire system—"People's characteristics and environments change." This proposition, Dodd tells us, can be more rigorously stated in the form of an equation:

$$S = T\colon I\colon L\colon P$$

In words, "Any quantitatively recorded societal situation can be expressed as a combination of 4 indices, namely: of time [T], space [L], a human population [P], and indicators [I] of their characteristics." Each of these

85. (New York: Macmillan, 1942).

86. A year after the publication of *Dimensions of Society* Dodd accepted the challenge of his critics to define operational definitions operationally. The following variants appear: "A definition is operational to the extent that the definer (*a*) communicates the actions to be done as means of identifying or generating the *definiendum*, and (*b*) finds high reliability for it"; "An operational definition is thus any statement, whether as brief as a sentence or as long as a book, which reliably tells what to do, first, second, third, and with what ingredients, in order to test for the presence of, or to produce, that which is defined." "Operational Definitions Operationally Defined," *American Journal of Sociology* 48 (1943): 482–489. A favorite example of both Lundberg and Dodd is a cake, the best definition of which is its recipe.

symbols is, or may be, modified by scripts, as many as possible being actual numbers.[87] The operators (:) are eight in number: for adding (+), subtracting (−), multiplying (×), dividing (÷), aggregating (:), cross-classifying (::), correlating (•), and identifying ('). In short, "The S-theory is a system of hypotheses which assert that combinations of these basic concepts will describe and classify every tabulation, graph, map, formula, prose paragraph, or other set of quantitative data in any of the social sciences."[88] The book contains some 300 equations, all expressing some social situation. Thus, the system can be used to symbolize all kinds of social phenomena from the tonnage of wheat shipped from the United States to Europe in a given decade to the fertility of women in different districts in large cities. Two examples will suffice:

1. A table of annuity rates showing the variables age at last birthday, cost of $100 annuity per annum payable yearly, and amount of annuity that $1000 will purchase for both males and females is symbolized as follows:

$$S_{29} = ' \, {}_{t}T^{+1} : P_{p} : {}_{u}T^{-1} : \%I$$

In words: S_{29} (the situation) records ${}_{t}T$ (forty-one ages), $^{+1}$(beginning at ten), P_p (for each sex), for each of which there corresponds ${}_{u}T^{-1}$ (three periods of premium payment) with corresponding I (premiums) $\%I$ (in a relative number of dollars).

2. A drawing indicating the proportion of automobiles to population in 1922, showing California (1:5) with the highest ratio and Mississippi (1:27) with the lowest, is symbolized as follows:

$$S_5 = (PI^{-1})_p$$

In words: S_5 (the situation) records P (the number of persons), I^{-1} (per automobile) in each of I_p (two states).

Dodd trained his students in the use of this symbolism and was pleased to note the high degree of reliability with which they used the symbols to describe the same situations.

In a later paper Dodd asked himself what uses his S-system might have and made the following claims for it, the first three of which resulted from later developments not included in the book itself:

87. The postsuperscript is the exponent; the postsubscript denotes a series of classes, the presubscript, of class intervals, and the presuperscript, of cases.

88. The material in quotation marks above is taken from the frontispiece, "Summary of Formulae of S-Theory," *Dimensions of Society*.

> The new methodological S-system seems to the author to have five chief uses: A) for calculating sociological unknowns, both quantitave and qualitative; B) for proving sociological theorems and corollaries; C) for checking the formulation of sociological problems; D) for operationally defining reliable concepts; E) for systematizing fields of science.[89]

Let us have a look at the system.

The first curiosity is the notion that the proposition "People's characteristics and environments change" can be more rigorously expressed as $S = T : I : L : P$, or that "any quantitatively recorded societal situation can be expressed as a combination of 4 indices." There are three quite different verbs competing for attention: first, *to change*, second (the "=" in the formula), *to equal*, and third, *can be expressed*. Surely, these verbs do not mean the same thing, and one has reason, therefore, to doubt Dodd's skill as a "rigorous translator." If the equality sign is so loosely translated, what are we to say about the semicolons or, more frequently, the colons in $T : I : L$: P? Inasmuch as eight operations are possible, how do we know which ones are involved in a given example? Is the basic formula, in fact, an equation? In what sense is a social situation equal to time added to (?), multiplied by (?), correlated with (?) space, numbers of people, and their characteristics?

Dodd seems uncomfortably aware of a problem here and accordingly makes a distinction between what he calls descriptive equations and calculative equations:

> In a descriptive equation one member is observed and defines the other member which is set equal to it. Thus here, the left-hand member, S, is not directly observed independently of the right-hand member. In a calculative equation both members may be independently observable. If a term is unknown in the calculative equation, it can be solved for. As many unknowns can be solved for as there are independent simultaneous calculative equations. But in a descriptive equation the term defined is the unknown, and a second unknown in the same equation, taken alone, cannot be solved for. Defining concepts by descriptive equations based on objectively observable quantities is the first step, however, in manipulating them and discovering and testing relationships among the concepts.[90]

He is willing to concede, and does so several times, that his equations and formulas are descriptive rather than calculative. But one is induced to wonder why, even after a term has been operationally defined, it continues to be unknown. What has happened to the utility of the system?

The "I" (indicators of people's characteristics) also attracts suspicion.

89. "Of What Use Is Dimensional Sociology?" *Social Forces* 22 (1943): 169.
90. *Dimensions of Society*, p. 59.

Time, space, and numbers of persons—all quantities—surely play their part in sociological investigation. But most of this investigation deals with the characteristics of people and their relations to one another. Dodd does, it is true, try to resolve this question by quantifying as one the presence of a characteristic and as zero its absence. But the procedure is as curious as its premise. As Ethel Shanas pointed out in her critique of *Dimensions of Society,* the $T : I : L : P$ formula is like dividing everything in the universe into (*a*) men; (*b*) trees; and (*c*) everything else.[91] In this case the "everything else," the indicators of people's characteristics, constitutes almost the whole of sociological inquiry. Similarly, Donald Calhoun notes, in his review, "Once the indicators in the residual category are enumerated and quantified adequately, there are not four variables, but forty, or four thousand."[92]

Let us examine Dodd's own claims for his sytem. First, he says, it helps us to calculate for sociological unknowns, "both quantitative and qualitative." But if the equations are only descriptive, the possibility disappears, as he concedes:

> In its *form,* the S-formulae are (a) descriptive more than calculative. They describe the form of the social situations analyzed and usually do not enable the calculation of unknown variables in the situation. The S-formulae serve (b) to classify societal phenomena more than to reveal their functioning.[93]

In the later paper to which I have referred, Dodd makes an unconvincing effort to show how his system can be used for calculating unknowns. He refers to an item on an intelligence test, namely, "A Pueblo woman baking bread is to a white housewife ironing as a Pueblo boy dancing is to *X*." Four picture choices are presented for selection, and the correct answer is a white boy playing baseball. Dodd translates this procedure into his own notation. It does not occur to him that if the analogy is correct, the notation is superfluous; if it is incorrect, the notation will not reveal the error. His claim that since the publication of the book certain "syntactic rules have been developed for the new symbols, permitting calculative deductions," and that his system "goes beyond current mathematics and logistic," is thus seen to be without foundation.

Similar considerations apply to the second claim, that the S-system can be used to prove sociological theorems and corollaries. Dodd comes to this conclusion by showing that his system is susceptible to exact translation in-

91. "A Critique of Dodd's *Dimensions of Society,*" *American Journal of Sociology* 48 (September 1942): 214–230.

92. *Social Forces* 20 (May 1942): 498–504, quote on p. 503.

93. *Dimensions of Society,* p. 843.

to the symbols of modern logic. His mistake proceeds from the unexamined assumption that symbolic logic can prove sociological theorems and corollaries. Any symbol system can express or state theorems or propositions, no matter what their content. Proof is quite another matter.

The third claim, that the S-system can be used to check sociological formulations, remains largely undeveloped.[94]

The fourth claim, that the system can be used for defining concepts operationally, can be readily conceded. All of Dodd's definitions are operational definitions. Indeed, it is presumably for this reason that Lundberg constantly refers to *Dimensions of Society* as a work that satisfies his recommendations of what definitions in sociology should be.

The fifth and last claim, that the S-system can be used to systematize fields of science, requires only a brief word. Dodd takes pride that he can translate into his system the signs of symbolic logic, statistical correlations, chemical formulae, mathematical operations, cultural indexes, and the categories of Aristotle and Kant. He is quite correct; he can. But all of these things can also be translated into Gregg shorthand. And indeed, the process is precisely the same.

The editor of the *American Sociological Review,* doubtless impressed by the size, and scope, and possible importance of *Dimensions of Society,* offered it for review both to a mathematician, E. T. Bell, and to a sociological theorist, Talcott Parsons.[95] Bell wondered why it had been given to a mathematician because, as he wrote, except for the chapter on correlation, there is no mathmatics in the book:

> No matter how ingeniously contrived, or how readily apprehended the symbols may be, there is no mathematics about them until processes for combining the symbols, according to standardized rules devised once for all, have been prescribed. If the symbolism is not to be utterly barren, the rules must be such that, when applied to given combinations of symbols, new and *interpretable* combinations, not immediately obvious, result; in short, the symbolism must be inherently creative.

Parsons, possibly also impressed by the magnitude of the enterprise, pointed to the absence of reference to any other theorists in the sociological tradition and hoped that not everyone would climb on Dodd's bandwagon.

94. "This checking means determining whether the two sides of an equation have the same dimensionality, i.e. have the same sectors and exponents. This is the major use of dimensional analysis in physics, but its use in sociology is as yet largely unexplored." "Of What Use Is Dimensional Sociology," p. 172.

95. The reviews appear in vol. 7 (June 1942): 707–714. For a criticism of these reviews, and a staunch defense of Dodd, see Read Bain's communication to the editor, *ibid.*, 8 (April 1943): 214–216.

He also perceptively noted that "Professor Dodd does not really develop a theoretical system at all, even in its beginnings, but only what may be called a 'language,' and that the book is in large part a work of translation."

The basic flaw in Dodd's *Dimensions of Society* is nakedly apparent. All of his definitions are nominal definitions. There is not a single real definition in the book. There is only one sociological proposition, namely, that people and their characteristics change. Nominal definitions, as we have seen, are stipulations; they cannot be used as premises in inference, and accordingly they do not contribute to knowledge. The test of a real definition is its truth. The test of a nominal definition is its utility. The sole remaining question is whether Dodd's nominal definitions help to save time, space, energy, and attention. And here, unfortunately, the response is again in the negative. It is a difficult system to teach and a difficult one to learn. His formulae are difficult to type and difficult to print.[96] It has not replaced the English language (with all its defects) in sociological discourse. No one uses it. In any case, it is forever impossible to get more out of a nominal definition than is put into it by fiat in the first place. Whatever utility it may have as a nomenclature, the S-system is sterile. It cannot inseminate the data it embraces. Like the mule, an amiable beast, it has no pride of ancestry, no hope of progeny.

Summary and Conclusion

The preceding criticism of both Lundberg and Dodd has been rather more severe than the writer would like. It takes no account of the many distinguished pieces of research that Dodd conducted both before and after his work on *Dimensions of Society*, especially in the fields of public opinion polling and in message diffusion. His efforts, in a profusion of separately published papers, to capture social phenomena with Cartesian coordinates, to find and exhibit curvilinear relationships, are remarkable for their ingenuity, and there is no doubt that he has not received the recognition he deserves. The zeal and creativity with which he attempted to apply

96. Donald Calhoun noted in his review that there is no practical advantage to be gained by using Dodd's symbols.

> Even with the legend at hand, no actual statistical analysis can be performed, without going back to the old fashioned tabulation of the data. The question then arises as to what is the use of transforming precise statistical formulae and equations into this rather clumsy notation, insufficient to convey all the content information even when a long legend is attached.

Social Forces 20 (May 1942): 502.

mathematical methods to the study of social phenomena can only stimulate admiration. *Dimensions of Society* is a work of misguided genius. If it was a failure, it was at least a prodigious one and indeed an instructive one. If Dodd's research studies exhibit the limitations of mathematics as an instrument of sociological inquiry, his *Dimensions of Society* illustrates the danger of inattention to that most basic discipline of human thought, the discipline of logic.

Lundberg himself did little research after the publication of *Foundations of Sociology*. He continued, however, to publish polemical papers, striking down all those whom he considered traducers of the scientific method, all those who entertained the slightest doubt that science was the wave of the future, the panacea for the solution not only of all sociological problems but of all social problems as well.[97] He remained a missionary, eager to bring the enlightment of science to minds still mired in what he called the legalistic-moralistic orientation of theology.

His chapter on sociological laws is almost entirely of this character. He offers no laws but only criticisms of those who doubt that they can be discovered. He tells us, for example, "that by certain methods, through certain inventable operations, the subjective becomes objective, the nonhomogeneous becomes homogeneous, the 'complex' becomes 'simple,' and the nonmeasurable becomes measurable."[98] Unfortunately, he fails to supply the "certain methods" or invent the "certain operations." As Clifford Kirkpatrick wrote, "Lundberg might be regarded as the John the Baptist of sociological positivism who cries the gospel of quantification, baptizes with operational definitions, and heralds the coming of S. C. Dodd as a methodological Messiah bearing the perfected doctrine.[99] The sociology of the future will be that foreshadowed not only by Dodd but also by the work of Stouffer on intervening opportunities and of Murdock on the

97. The titles of some of these papers are informative: "What Are Sociological Problems?" *American Sociological Review* (June 1941): 357–369; "The Growth of Scientific Method," *American Journal of Sociology* 50 (May 1945): 502–513; "Sociology Versus Dialectical Immaterialism," *ibid.* 53 (September 1947): 85–95; "Alleged Obstacles to Social Science, *The Scientific Monthly* 70 (May 1950): 299–305; "Can Science Validate Ethics?" American Association of University Professors, *Bulletin* 36 (Summer 1950): 262–275; "The Natural Science Trend in Sociology," *American Journal of Sociology* 61 (November 1955): 191–202; "Quantitative Methods in Sociology: 1920–1960," *Social Forces* 39 (October 1960): 19–24; and "The Place of Supra-Empirical Statements in Sociology," *Sociological Inquiry* 31 (1961): 117–127.

98. *Foundations of Sociology*, p. 149.

99. Review of *Foundations of Sociology*, *American Sociological Review* 5 (June 1940): 438–440, quote on p. 438.

Human Area Relations File at Yale.[100] Stouffer's law especially, as stated in a mathematical equation, is a veritable model of what that future will be.[101]

Lundberg's own system of sociology is rudimentary. When he finishes his methodological exhortations and turns to social phenomena themselves, he is content to quote long passages from other writers, especially Cooley, Mead, and Chapin, and to announce that he is in full agreement with their views. With respect to this part of the book, Sorokin was surprised at "the remarkable traditionalism" of the author who, instead of being a revolutionary, showed himself to be "a good Rotarian in sociology."[102] In any case, demography is that part of sociology which is the most developed because it is the most quantitative. When the same quantitative methods are applied to the rest of sociology, the millenium will have arrived.

It appears that almost all of the judgments in this chapter are critical and negative. Lundberg's logic is naive, his grammar uncertain, his inconsistencies obtrusive, his points repetitious, his prose hortatory, and his science simplistic. *Foundations of Sociology* is all program and no performance. Lundberg and Dodd are not the Copernicus and the Newton of the social sciences, as they so earnestly and industriously aspired to be. Lundberg was handicapped by an innocence of epistemology; Dodd, by inattention to an elementary logical distinction between nominal and real definitions. Few today read *Foundations of Sociology* and *Dimensions of Society*, few salute their authors. Why, then, do I include them in this history of American sociological theory? The question requires an answer.

The answer is that Lundberg, although not single-handedly, won a famous victory. During the years of his active career he was the leading protagonist of the use of scientific method in sociology, of the purification, by operational means, of the concepts of sociology, and of the notion that society, as a natural phenomenon, is susceptible to inquiry by the methods of the natural sciences. Many others contributed as well, including in earlier years Franklin Henry Giddings, William Fielding Ogburn, and

100. Samuel A. Stouffer, "Intervening Opportunities: A Theory Relating Mobility and Distance," *ibid.* 5 (December 1940): 845–867; George Peter Murdock, "The Cross-Cultural Survey," *ibid.* 5 (June 1940): 361–370.

101. "The number of persons going a given distance is directly proportional to the number of opportunities at that distance and inversely proportional to the number of intervening opportunities." "Intervening Opportunities," p. 846. This law to Lundberg is as exact as Newton's law of gravitation and as important a discovery. Neither Stouffer nor Lundberg seems to have noticed that it tells us little more than that people travel only as far as they have to in order to get what they want.

102. Sorokin's harsh review of *Foundations of Sociology* appears in the *American Journal of Sociology* 45 (March 1940): 795–798. Lundberg wrote and circulated, but did not publish, a reply to it.

F. Stuart Chapin and in later ones Paul F. Lazarsfeld and Samuel A. Stouffer. The view of sociology entertained by Robert K. Merton, especially with respect to his "theories of the middle range," although entirely uninfluenced by Lundberg and exhibited with much more sophistication, is nevertheless in a good congruence with that of Lundberg. He too wants a cumulative sociology, a sociology that, like a coral reef, shows accumulations of verified empirical generalizations that will ultimately be related to one another and constitute a body of knowledge about society. The course of American sociology from roughly 1930 to 1980 and later conforms to Lundberg's designs. The pages of the professional journals are filled with the kind of quantitative studies that he demanded. In the years since the publication of *Foundations of Sociology* scientific method in sociological research has become more precise and the statistical techniques more versatile.

But a problem remains. The problem is that the significance of sociological research, at the moment of writing these pages, varies inversely with the precision of the methods employed.

CHAPTER 9

Talcott Parsons

The central fact—a fact beyond all question—is that in certain aspects and to certain degrees, under certain conditions, human action is rational. That is, men adapt themselves to the conditions in which they are placed and adapt means to their ends in such a way as to approach the most efficient manner of achieving these ends. And the relations of these means and conditions to the achievement of their ends are "known" to be intrinsically verifiable by the methods of empirical science.

—*The Structure of Social Action*, p. 19

Talcott Parsons was born in Colorado Springs, Colorado, on December 13, 1902, the son of a Congregational minister who later became president of Marietta College, in Ohio. For his secondary education he was sent to Horace Mann School in New York City, an experimental school operated by Teachers College, Columbia University. After graduating in 1920 he went to Amherst College, long before Amherst introduced instruction in sociology. A career in medicine attracted him at first, and accordingly he studied a great deal of undergraduate biology and spent a summer working in a laboratory at the famous Oceanographic Institution at Woods Hole, Massachusetts.[1] Although he later wrote a great deal on the medical profession, Parsons was not destined to become a physician. At Amherst he came under the beneficent influence of two of its most distinguished faculty members, Walton Hamilton and Clarence Ayres, the former going on to become a professor of law at Yale University and the latter, a professor of economics at the University of Texas. Both of these men admired the work

1. These and other biographical details can be found in Talcott Parsons, "A Short Account of My Intellectual Development," *Alpha Kappa Deltan* 29 (Winter 1959): 3–12. This issue of the journal is devoted entirely to the work of Parsons, and it contains a bibliography of Parsons's writings to 1958. For a later bibliography, see Harold Bershady, *Ideology and Social Knowledge* (New York: John Wiley, 1973). The most complete biographical account, however, is Talcott Parsons, "On Building Social System Theory: A Personal History," *Daedalus*, 99 (Winter 1970): 826–881, reprinted in Talcott Parsons, *Social Systems and the Evolution of Action Theory* (New York: Free Press, 1977), pp. 22–76.

of Veblen, and both bent their student's mind in the direction of the social sciences. Ayres offered a course entitled "The Moral Order" in the philosophy department, and inasmuch as the works of William Graham Sumner, Charles Horton Cooley, and Emile Durkheim were on the reading list, it served Parsons as an introduction to sociology.

From Amherst Parsons went to the London School of Economics, where he spent the academic year 1924–1925 and attended the lectures of Leonard Trelawny Hobhouse, Morris Ginsberg, and Bronislaw Malinowski, only the last of whom seems to have made an impression upon him. From London he went to Heidelberg on a scholarship, and that proved to be a fateful experience. Although Max Weber had died in 1920, he was still the dominant influence at Heidelberg, and he came to be the dominant influence also in Parsons's intellectual development. Everyone at the university was familiar with the work of Weber, and the young student's imagination was fired by his first reading of *The Protestant Ethic and the Spirit of Capitalism*, which Weber had written in 1904–1905. Parsons himself translated this famous essay into English and published it in 1930,[2] and it is Parsons—especially with the publication of *The Structure of Social Action* in 1937—who began the process that moved Weber's name into a position of prominence in sociological circles in the United States. Parsons wrote his dissertation on the concept of capitalism in the work of Marx, Sombart, and Weber, and received his Heidelberg Dr. Phil. in 1927.

When Parsons returned to the United States he taught for a year in the economics department at Amherst, where he completed his dissertation. The following year, 1927, he moved to the economics department at Harvard, where he fell under the influence of Joseph Schumpeter, from whom he gained a sense of the meaning of a system of theory, and Frank William Taussig, who emphasized for him the importance of Alfred Marshall, whose work marked the culmination of classical economic theory. From Alfred North Whitehead, the philosopher, he learned more about the nature of systems and from Whitehead also the "fallacy of misplaced concreteness," with which he was later to belabor his opponents, the positivists in sociology. It was about this time also that he began to read the work of Pareto.

In the early 1930s Pareto was something of a cult in the Boston area. Among the group who gathered to study him and later to write books and articles about him were Bernard de Voto, then editor of *Harper's*

2. It was the second of Weber's works to be translated into English, the first being Frank Knight's translation of the *General Economic History* in 1927. Parsons later edited and translated, with A. M. Henderson, Part 1 of Weber's *Wirtschaft und Gesellschaft*, *Max Weber: The Theory of Social and Economic Organization* (London and New York: Oxford University Press, 1947).

Magazine, Charles P. Curtis, a lawyer, and such academics as L. J. Henderson, the biochemist, Clyde Kluckhohn, the anthropologist, and sociologists George C. Homans and Parsons.[3] In this group Henderson was the dominant influence, and Parson expresses great appreciation to him, for both professional and personal reasons, in his autobiographical essay. Another "role-model" was Durkheim. Parsons had encountered the name of Durkheim in the Ayres course mentioned earlier and also in Malinowski's lectures at the London School of Economics (the latter's evaluation of Durkheim was negative), but he did not begin to read him seriously until his second or third year at Harvard.[4] It was only much later that Freud came into his ken in a major way.[5] Parsons undertook a didactic analysis, and then the influence of Freud began to loom large indeed, only to wane again in the later stages of his career.

Except for a postretirement year at the University of Pennsylvania, another at Rutgers University, and visiting appointments at Chicago, Columbia, and Cambridge, Parsons spent his entire career at Harvard. Advancement was slow at first. Indeed, he spent nine years in the rank of instructor, four of them in economics and five in sociology. Sorokin, his chairman in sociology, was unsympathetic to his work and was not eager to promote him or even, on at least one occasion, to support his reappointment. In one unpleasant episode, later on, Sorokin accused Parsons of plagiarism. Nevertheless, Parsons enjoyed considerable support in the power structure of the university and was promoted to assistant professor in 1936, associate professor in 1939, and full professor in 1944. He served as chairman of the department from 1944 to 1946 and in the latter year became chairman of the newly constituted Department of Social Relations, a department that included sociology, cultural anthropology, and social

3. For an extravagant piece on Pareto, see Bernard De Voto, "Sentiment and the Social Order," *Harper's* (October 1933): 569–581. See also Homans and Curtis, *An Introduction to Pareto* (New York: Alfred A. Knopf, 1934); and Henderson, *Pareto's General Sociology* (Cambridge, Mass.: Harvard University Press, 1935). Parsons wrote the article on Pareto in the *Encyclopedia of the Social Sciences,* 15 vols. (New York: Macmillan, 1933), vol. 11, and also on Pareto as sociologist in its successor, *The International Encyclopedia of the Social Sciences,* ed. David L. Sills, 18 vols (New York: Macmillan and Free Press, 1968), vol. 11.

4. "Introduction," *Social Systems,* pp. 18–19:

> In the light of my later experiences, centering on Weber in Germany and independently especially on Durkheim, I decided that *for me* as a sociological theorist the latter two models were the primary ones I would follow. In a sense, this review, written forty years after the experience, documents my "declaration of independence" from the utilitarian tradition more generally, from Hobhouse and Ginsberg in particular. The wisdom of this declaration of independence may be left to "historical" judgment.

5. Parsons uses the adjective *Freudian* twice in *Structure of Social Action.* Otherwise there are no references. See John Finley Scott, "The Changing Foundations of the Parsonian Action Scheme," *American Sociological Review* 28 (October 1963): 716–735.

and clinical psychology. He retained the departmental chair until 1956. He retired in 1973, having served forty-six years on the Harvard faculty. On the occasion of his retirement 150 former students, ranging in age from twenty three to sixty three, and in place from Germany to California, came to Cambridge to honor him.[6]

Other honors as well came to Parsons in the course of his long career. He served as president of the Eastern Sociological Society in 1941–1942 and of the American Sociological Society in 1949–1950. He was a corresponding member of the British Academy, an honorary fellow of the London School of Economics, and a member of the American Association for the Advancement of Science, the American Philosophical Society, and the American Academy of Arts and Letters, the last of which he also served as president. He held honorary degrees from Amherst, Cologne, Chicago, Boston, and the Hebrew University, Jerusalem. In 1927 he married Helen B. Walker, the daughter of an American physician whom he met at the London School of Economics, and they had three children. His retirement years brought no respite to his pen. Indeed, he published in 1977, his seventy-fifth year, not one but two books—a seventh and eighth collection of his essays. He died on May 8, 1979, in Munich, where he had gone to deliver a series of lectures.

The Great Language Barrier

In the Preface to *Structure of Social Action,*published shortly before his thirty-fifth birthday, Parsons conscientiously thanks those to whom he owes his greatest debts. Among them is his father, who went over the manuscript in "an attempt to improve its English style" and who gave it whatever readability it possesses. There is an unfortunate irony in this tribute. For the truth is that Parsons has no English style. His sentences are thickets of the densest underbrush through which his reader has to hack and claw his way. Consider the following, written not specifically for sociologists but for a general intellectual audience, the readers of *Daedalus*:

> Since the role of empirical cognitive knowledge was so central to the original formulation of the rationality problem, this concern with the value aspect of empirical cognition, both in the grounds of the cognitive validity of the knowledge mobilized in the instrumental aspects of rational action and in the cognitive problems of the justification of commitment of instrumental poten-

6. See the account in the *New York Times* (June 14, 1973).

tialities among goals, in a sense brings consideration of the problem of rationality full circle in that the considerations involved in the grounding of value-choices, including their more or less religious bases, are seen to be of the same order as those involved in the grounding of the validity of empirical knowledge.[7]

Although there are, of course, lapses into clarity, this is all too typical an example of his prose. Some of the descriptions that have been applied to it are "ponderous," "cumbersome," "labored," "involuted," "tortuous," "obscure," and "opaque." Tom Bottomore remarks that what was falsely said of Condorcet may truly be said of Parsons, namely, that he "writes with opium on a page of lead."[8]

What can be said about his sentences can be said about his words as well. Parsons has a regrettable tendency to combine nouns in hyphenated arrays. Thus, in addition to "value-choices" in the preceding quotation from Parsons, we find system-pattern, value-element, value-attitude, object-relationship, need-disposition, role-expectation, system-level, orientation-modality, goal-states, object-system, action-interests, orientation-selection, expression-discipline, boundary-processes, gratification-significance, problem-foci, status-focus, reinforcement-extinction, value-acquisition, esteem-symbolism, pattern-complexes, system-processes, and system-integrative, to name only a few. We encounter also such miserable specimens as "latent pattern maintenance phases" and an "institutionalized ascriptive-qualitative pattern-complex," and we are informed that the size of a society is "an integrative exigency." Sometimes we find three of these hyphenated sets in a single heading: "The Pattern-Alternatives of Value-Orientation as Definitions of Relational Role-Expectation Patterns."[9] We even find an oxymoron, "symmetrical asymmetry"—a far cry from Shakespeare's cruel kindness and sweet sorrow.

Expressions such as those mentioned run through the entire Parsonian corpus, from his earliest writing to his last. They are responsible in part—because of Parsons's eminence in the profession—for the view of too many members of the literate public that the entire tribe of sociologists is guilty of indulgence in an unintelligible and therefore despicable jargon. They do not note the graceful prose of a Robert MacIver or a Robert Nisbet. In any event, Parsons's stylistic eccentricities have at least two serious consequences. The first is that they "force him to devote an inor-

7. "On Building Social System Theory," p. 873, reprinted in *Social Systems and the Evolution of Action Theory* (New York: Free Press, 1977), p. 74.

8. In a review of four of Parsons's books, entitled "Out of This World," *New York Review of Books* (November 6, 1969): 34–39, quote on p. 36.

9. *The Social System* (Glencoe, Ill.: Free Press, 1951), p. 58.

dinate amount of time and attention to the explanation of his own vocabulary, in the course of which the problem frequently disappears. The second is that many of the issues then discussed have their source in the vocabulary itself and have no independent locus."[10] And finally, Edward C. Devereux, Jr., author of what is by all odds the most lucid exposition of Parsons's writing through 1959—an exposition that is also sympathetic—found it necessary to refer to "the Parsonian theoretical forest," "vast and tangled, a veritable jungle of fine distinctions and intertwining classifications."[11]

Parsons is well aware of his stylistic reputation and responds to it in the following way, with the help of two double negatives:

> I am not at all prepared to discount entirely the view that there are peculiar and unnecessary obscurities in my writings. At the same time I can claim to be somewhat sophisticated in the sociology of knowledge and hence in the interpretation of resistances to certain types of intellectual innovation. In this role I cannot entirely dismiss the possibility that some of the complaints may be manifestations of such resistances. In any case, it is not possible for an author to be fully objective about the reception of his work; any more ultimate judgment will have to be left to the outcome of the process of natural selection through professional criticism by which scientific reputations ultimately come to be stabilized.[12]

His defense in brief, mustered in other places as well, is that he is dealing with matters so complex that they cannot be treated in simpler language and that all intellectual innovation encounters a similar resistance. The suspicion lingers, however, that obscurity of language is companion to obscurity of thought and that, as Jonathan Swift observed, when the waters are clear you can see to the bottom. In any event, Parsons's language will surely detract from the "scientific reputation" that his work might otherwise have enjoyed. The time may come when a new generation of sociologists will decline the burden of reading it.

Two other mannerisms may briefly be mentioned. The first of these leads to great difficulties in exposition. It concerns what Devereux calls Parsons's "exasperating tendency to insist that each and every point in his entire system is fundamental."[13] Another favorite word is *crucial.* The trouble is that when an author insists that all of his points are fundamental or crucial,

---

10. Robert Bierstedt, "Review of *Essays in Sociological Theory* rev. ed.," *American Sociological Review* 20 (February 1955): 124–125.

11. "Parsons' Sociological Theory," ed. Max Black, *The Social Theories of Talcott Parsons,* (Englewood Cliffs, N.J.: Prentice-Hall, 1961), pp. 1–63.

12. "The Point of View of the Author," *ibid.*, pp. 320–321.

13. "Parsons' Sociological Theory," p. 2.

the reader begins to suspect either that few of them are or that the author is unwilling to make the appropriate discriminations. The second mannerism is a puzzling one. In person and in personal relationships Parsons was the most modest of men. Unassuming, uncritical of others, reluctant to mention himself in conversation, much less to talk about his accomplishments, he becomes the opposite in his writing. In writing he claims for himself many "major breakthroughs" in the development not only of his own theory but also of sociological theory itself. In fact, he equates his own theory with sociological theory. He claims, for example, that the "genuine systematization" that he achieved in *Structure of Social Action* was "well in advance of previous attempts" and that even more advances have since been achieved, advances in "clarity of definition, analytical refinement, and better theoretical integration."[14] Observations such as this are frequent in Parsons's works. He has a tendency, in short, to usurp the function of the critic, to trace the phases of his own intellectual development, and to praise his own theoretical achievements. He writes indeed as if he were his own principal disciple.

A final consequence of Parsons's famous—or infamous—style is that any exposition of his sociological theory is necessarily ensnared in it. The expositor may often have to use Parsonian language to explain Parsonian concepts and thus to join him on the sinner's bench.

The Place of Ultimate Values in Sociological Theory

When the young Parsons returned to this country from Heidelberg he "found behaviorism so rampant that anyone who believed in the scientific validity of the interpretation of subjective states of mind was often held to be fatuously naive."[15] Apparently, at the tender age of twenty four he had already adopted the position he was to maintain and defend during his entire career, namely, that the realm of the subjective is susceptible to scientific study and interpretation. To explain how this can be the case, to indulge in such study, to construct a theory of the subjective for sociological

14. "Point of View of the Author," p. 321.

15. "On Building Social System Theory," p. 830. In the sentence immediately following he writes: "Also rampant was what I called 'empiricism' namely the idea that scientific knowledge was a total reflection of the 'reality out there' and even selection was alleged to be illegitimate." One is at a loss to know who, among American philosophers and sociologists, subscribed to this idea of empiricism. Parsons himself, as we shall see, became quite fond of the adjective *empirical,* freely applied it to his own work, and insisted that *Structure of Social Action* was an empirical study.

use—these became the goals of his life work. He is George A. Lundberg in reverse; everything that Lundberg stood for in sociology was anathema to Parsons—and vice versa. They were not antagonists, however, because they took no account of each other. Although there is a negative footnote reference to Parsons in Lundberg, they might otherwise have lived on separate planets.

Parsons's first important theoretical statement is not *Structure of Social Action* but rather a paper he published two years earlier, in 1935, entitled "The Place of Ultimate Values in Sociological Theory."[16] The article contains, in essence and germ, almost all of the ideas he was later to espouse. The first paragraph is especially illuminating:

> The positivistic reaction against philosophy has, in its effect on the social sciences, manifested a strong tendency to obscure the fact that man is essentially an active, creative, evaluating creature. Any attempt to explain his behavior in terms of ends, purposes, ideals, has been under suspicion as a form of "teleology" which was thought to be imcompatible with the methodological requirements of positive science. One must, on the contrary, explain in terms of "causes" and "conditions " not of ends.[17]

This paragraph is illuminating because at once, and directly it establishes Parsons's position. It should be said, however, that he never argues the philosophical issue involved. On the contrary, he simply assumes, in this essay and in his subsequent work, the superiority of something he calls "idealism" to positivism.[18] Positivism has tried to "objectify" the study of human behavior, to regard behavior as a physical phenomenon, to study it with the methods of the physical sciences, and to ignore or at the very least to obscure the subjective aspects of action. Of course, he says,

> The results of analysis of human behavior from the objective point of view (that is, that of an outside observer) and the subjective (that of the person thought of as acting himself) should correspond, but that fact is no reason why the two points of view should not be kept clearly distinct. Only on this basis is there any hope of arriving at a satisfactory solution of their relations to each other.[19]

What Parsons fails to appreciate is that by separating the subjective from the objective so clearly and distinctly, and assuming a relationship between them, he has involved himself in an uncomfortable dualism that he makes

16. *International Journal of Ethics* 45 (April 1935): 282–316.

17. *Ibid.*, p. 282.

18. He associates Weber, Simmel, and Tönnies with idealism and Pareto and Durkheim—at least in their original orientations—with positivism.

19. *Ibid.*, p. 283.

no effort to overcome. He now has a mind on the one hand and a body on the other without Descartes's pineal gland to serve as a link between them. It is all very well to see two separate points of view—the subjective and the objective—but the writer who does so then has to assume the responsibility of exhibiting the relationship between them. This Parsons does not do. All he says is that ends and values, for example, are subjective categories that must not be "squeezed out" of consideration by positivistic analysis. That there are problems of severe philosophical import—both epistemological and ontological—in this dualism does not seem to occur to him. He has no answer for a critic who might contend that dualism itself is ultimately an indefensible metaphysical position.

The means–end schema, of course, is a voluntaristic schema. It is also rationalistic, since it involves the rational application of means to ends, the rational choice between alternative means to achieve an end. The conception of rational choice is "essential to the whole voluntaristic conception of action put forward here."[20] The process is not an automatic one but comes about through "the exercise of will." Furthermore, "the subjective point of view is that of the *ego*, not of the body, or even the 'mind.' "[21] Now the difficulties have multiplied. One had thought that "the will," for example, had disappeared with the demise of faculty psychology. But here it is, in Parsons's means–end schema. And here is something else—an ego—which is neither mind nor body. If we wonder what it is, we shall find no clue in Parsons's paper.

Parsons announces it as a *fact*, italicized, "that man stands in significant relations to aspects of reality other than those revealed by science."[22] Among these other aspects is the realm of value, which he defines as "the creative element in action in general, that element which is causally independent of the positivistic factors of heredity and environment."[23] He very early became convinced that positivism, "the tendency to imitate the physical sciences and to make physical science the measuring-rod of all things," is inadequate, that "these positivistic theories somehow, by a kind of logical jugglery rather than by empirical proof, were squeezing what I have here called the 'value'-elements out of their interpretation of social life."[24] The paper ends with a brief discussion of the differences between science and philosophy and produces a striking contradiction. After saying that there are aspects of reality that are not revealed by science, and to

20. "Place of Ultimate Values," p. 294.
21. *Ibid.*, p. 289.
22. *Ibid.*, p. 290.
23. *Ibid.*, p. 306, n. 19.
24. *Ibid.*, p. 313.

which we had thought his paper was devoted, he observes that "the task of sociology, as of the other social sciences, I consider to be strictly scientific—the attainment of systematic theoretical understanding of empirical fact," and concludes with the asseveration, "I stand squarely on the platform of science."[25]

The Structure of Social Action

My treatment of Parsons in this chapter is necessarily selective. He wrote an unusually large number of books and articles, and it would be unwise to try to consider them all. There is little doubt, however, that *Structure of Social Action* is his most influential book, the book that made his reputation, and we shall therefore give it a major share of our attention.[26] Indeed, none of the many books that followed had quite the impact of this one, written when its author was in his early thirties.

The subtitle of the book refers to it as "A Study in Social Theory with Special Reference to a Group of Recent European Writers." It is quite literally, as Parsons emphasizes in his Preface, a study in social theory, not theories. That is, it is not a secondary study of the theories of four European writers—Marshall, Pareto, Durkheim, and Weber—but is rather an effort to abstract from their work a single theoretical scheme. This scheme will henceforth serve not as one sociological theory, among others, but as sociological theory itself, not only for now but for all time. Parsons's book will be an "empirical" demonstration that the first three of these writers, stemming from a positivistic tradition, and the fourth, stemming from an idealistic tradition, all converged on the same scheme—the voluntaristic theory of action. This convergence is remarkable because, so far as the last three writers are concerned, the differences between them are conspicuous. Pareto was Catholic, Italian, and upper class; Weber, Protestant, German, and middle class; and Durkheim, Jewish, French, and lower class.[27] It is even more remarkable—although Parsons does not make this point—because each of the three largely ignored the work of the other two.[28] If there is a convergence in their sociological theory, it must come about not

25. *Ibid.*, pp. 314, 316.

26. (New York: McGraw-Hill, 1937). A second edition, in paperback, was published in two volumes by Free Press, New York, in 1968.

27. The religious identification here is only a background factor. All three, to use Weber's expression again, were "religiously unmusical."

28. As a point of startling fact, none of the three, with three minor exceptions, ever mentions the names of the other two. On the mutual "ignoring" of Durkheim and Weber, see Edward A. Tiryakian, "A Problem for the Sociology of Knowledge," *European Journal of*

by conscious agreement among the three of them, and not as a recognition or acknowledgment of similar endeavors, but rather as an artifact of Parsons's anfractuous dialectic.

At the outset Parsons wonders why the positivistic and utilitarian tradition, typified notably by Herbert Spencer, is dead, or at least was so pronounced by Crane Brinton and now by Parsons himself.[29] Scientific theory has evolved beyond Spencer. In contrast to Merton's view of the history of sociological theroy, Parsons believes that these newer evolutionary developments are not reflections of social changes in general but are immanent changes within the realm of social theory itself, together with changing knowledge of empirical fact. Theory is not only a dependent variable—dependent upon the accumulation of facts—in the history of science but an independent variable as well. The point is that new discoveries or changes in fact have to have consequences for an integrated series of propositions, logically related to one another, and if they do not, they have nothing to do with the evolution of a science. On this subject Parsons is quite clear:

> The *scientific* importance of a change in knowledge of fact consists precisely in its having consequences for a system of theory with which scientists in that field are concerned. Conversely, even the most trivial observation from any other point of view—a very small deviation of the observed from the calculated position of a star, for instance—may be not only important but of revolutionary importance, if its logical consequences for the structure of theory are far-reaching. It is probably safe to say that all the changes of factual knowledge which have led to the relativity theory, resulting in a very great theoretical development, are completely trivial from any point of view except their relevance to the structure of a theoretical system. They have not, for instance, affected in any way the practice of engineering or navigation.[30]

Sociology 7 (1966): 330–336. So far as the writer knows, there is no mention of Pareto in any of the books of Durkheim and Weber, and the latter two names are missing from the Index of Pareto's four-volume (in English) *The Mind and Society*. The minor exceptions are a reference to Durkheim's work on totemism in a part of Weber's *General Economic History* that Frank Knight neglected to translate (I am indebted to my former student, Steven Seidman, for this information); a two-sentence review of an 1899 article of Pareto by Durkheim in *L'Année Sociologique*, 3: 163; and a brief review by Pareto of Durkheim's *Le Suicide* in *Zeitschrift für Sozialwissenschaft* 1 (1898): 78–80.

29. "Who now reads Spencer? It is difficult for us to realize how great a stir he made in the world. . . . He was the intimate confidant of a strange and rather unsatisfactory God, whom he called the principle of Evolution. His God has betrayed him. We have evolved beyond Spencer." Crane Brinton, *English Political Thought in the Nineteenth Century* (Cambridge, Mass.: Harvard University Press, 1949), pp. 226–227 (originally published, 1933). *Structure of Social Action* begins with this quotation. Parsons agrees. Interestingly enough, he resurrects Spencer in two books written much later in his career, books to which I shall attend in the sequel.

30. *Structure of Social Action*, pp. 7–8.

And again: "Theory not only formulates what we know but also tells us what we want to know, that is, the questions to which an answer is needed."[31] There is furthermore something about theory that requires it to become logically closed. By logically closed Parsons means that any proposition in the system can be derived from or can find expression in another proposition in the system. This does not mean that all of them can be derived from a single proposition. If that were the case, that single proposition would suffice, and all the others would be redundant. The kind of system Parsons has in mind is that represented, for example, by a set of simultaneous equations in algebra, and it is obviously his hope that something of the same kind can be constructed for sociology—indeed that this kind of theory can be abstracted from the work of his four social scientists.

Let us attend to Parsons's own words as he describes the nature of his enterprise:

> In one of its main aspects the present study may be regarded as an attempt to verify empirically this view of the nature of science and its development in the social field. It takes the form of the thesis that intimately associated with the revolution in empirical interpretations of society sketched above there has in fact occurred an equally radical change in the structure of theoretical systems. The hypothesis may be put forward, to be tested by the subsequent investigation, that this development has been in large part a matter of the reciprocal interaction of new factual insights and knowledge on the one hand with changes in the theoretical system on the other. Neither is the "cause" of the other. Both are in a state of close mutual interdependence.
>
> This verification is here attempted in monographic form. The central focus of attention is in the process of development of one coherent theoretical system, that to be denoted as the *voluntaristic theory of action*, and the definition of the general concepts of which this theory is composed.[32]

---

31. *Ibid.*, p. 9.

32. *Ibid.*, p. 11. One does not quite know what to do with expressions such as "empirical interpretations." Insofar as they are "sketched above," the following passage is relevant:

> A basic revolution in empirical interpretations of some of the most important social problems has been going on. Linear evolutionism has been slipping and cyclical theories have been appearing on the horizon. Various kinds of individualism have been under increasingly heavy fire. In their place have been appearing socialistic, collectivistic, organic theories of all sorts. The role of reason and the status of scientific knowledge as an element of action have been attacked again and again. We have been overwhelmed by a flood of anti-intellectualistic theories of human nature and behavior, again of many different varieties. A revolution of such magnitude in the prevailing empirical interpretations of human society is hardly to be found occurring within the short space of a generation, unless one goes back to about the sixteenth century.

Ibid., p. 5. One can only wish that Parsons had supplied specific examples of these "revolutions." On another page (p. 51) he claims, somewhat to the contrary, that action theory is as old as social thought itself and that by the nineteenth century it dominated Western thought.

The significant point, in Parsons's view, is that this voluntaristic theory of action emerged from two quite different—indeed contrary—traditions: the tradition of positivistic utilitarianism on the one hand and the tradition of "idealism" on the other. Of the first, Spencer is the exemplar, of the second, Weber.

One of Parsons's early statements about positivistic utilitarianism—or utilitarian positivism—gives at least one reader some trouble:

> The utilitarian branch of positivistic thought has, by virtue of the structure of its theoretical system, been focused upon a given range of definite empirical insights and related theoretical problems. The central fact—a fact beyond all question—is that in certain aspects and to certain degrees, under certain conditions, human action is rational. That is, men adapt themselves to the conditions in which they are placed and adapt means to their ends in such a way as to approach the most efficient manner of achieving these ends. And the relations of these means and conditions to the achievement of their ends are "known" to be intrinsically verifiable by the methods of empirical science.[33]

The trouble with this passage is not only its apodictic character—"a fact beyond all question," " 'known' to be intrinsically verifiable"—but also what the author means by his assertion that human action is rational. By "rational" in this passage he appears to mean capable of making the right rather than the wrong choice of means in order to attain an end. In this case the opposite of rational would be *irrational.*[34] In other passages, where he insists that rational choice is essential to the voluntaristic theory of action, he appears to mean capable of choosing, whether the choice is right or wrong. In this case the opposite of rational choice would be determined choice, or determinism.[35] This ambiguity is a constant in *Structure of Social Action.*

The introductory chapter contains brief descriptions of the nature and plan of the work, disquisitions on such matters as residual categories, the relationship between theory, methodology, and philosophy, and types of concepts, and concludes with a brief "Note on the Concept 'Fact.' " Two additional matters attract attention. The first is another description of the purpose of the book:

---

33. *Ibid.*, p. 19.

34. See also *ibid.*, p. 58.

35. For example: "It is, indeed, no wonder that utilitarianism shows such a strong tendency to slide off into some form of positivistic determinism, for once rational choice is eliminated in this fashion there is nothing left to determine action but biological and psychological drives." "The Place of Ultimate Values," p. 294. Parsons also speaks of "the rational unity of cognitive experience" and remarks, "Rational knowledge is a single organic whole." *Structure of Social Action*, p. 22; see also p. 64 n., where two additional distinctions are made, and p. 133 n., where he equates rationality with efficiency.

> The empirical subject matter with which this study is concerned is that of human action in society. A few of the main characteristics peculiar to this subject matter which raise methodological problems may be noted. It is a fact, however it may be interpretated, that men assign subjective motives to their actions. If asked why they do a given thing, they will reply with a reference to a "motive," It is a fact that they manifest the subjective feelings, ideas, motives, associated with their actions by means of linguistic symbols as well as in other ways. It is, finally, a fact that both in action and in science when certain classes of concrete phenomena are encountered, such as black ink marks on sheets of paper, they are interpreted as "symbols" having "meanings."
>
> These facts and others like them are those which raise the central methodological problems peculiar to the sciences concerned with human action. There is a "subjective aspect" of human action. It is manifested by linguistic symbols to which meaning is attached. This subjective aspect involves the reasons we ourselves assign for acting as we do. No science concerned with human action can, if it would penetrate beyond a superficial level, evade the methodological problems of the relevance of facts of this order to the scientific explanation of the other facts of human action. This study will be intensively concerned with them.[36]

The study of human actions may indeed raise the "methodological problems" to which Parsons refers. These assertions, again apodictic, constitute a substantive premise and not only a methodological one. Without "facts" of this subjective kind—without subjectivity, in short—there would be no voluntaristic theory of action. The problem that Parsons fails to confront is the problem of transforming facts of this subjective kind into objective knowledge. It may be that he would regard his entire enterprise as an effort in this direction. But, if so, many if not most of the steps are missing. How Parsons or any one else can construct a science of the subjective, in short, is far from clear, especially when objectivity is one of the canons of science.[37]

The second matter concerns a brief sentence that provides another clue to the character of the Parsonian enterprise. He regards social action as only one of four schemata that could be used, the other three, also derived from Znaniecki, being social relationships, social groups, and social personality, and then goes on to say that any one of them may involve subschemata. And then the clue: "Supply and demand is to be considered as a subschema of action."[38] At this point in his career Parsons was im-

36. *Structure of Social Action*, p. 26.

37. For an elaboration of this point, see Robert Bierstedt, "The Means-End Schema in Sociological Theory" (1938), in *Power and Progress: Essays on Sociological Theory* (New York: McGraw-Hill, 1974), pp. 31–40.

38. *Structure of Social Action*, p. 30. Later on he will define economics in terms of the means-end schema as "the science which studies the processes of rational acquisition of scarce means to the actor's ends by production and economic exchange, and of their rational allocation as between alternative uses." *Ibid.*, p. 266.

pressed by the elegance, the rigor, and the systematic character of classical economic theory, especially as it reached a peak in the work of Alfred Marshall.[39] His ambition then was to construct a sociological theory equally elegant, rigorous, and systematic that would embrace and include economic theroy. Economic actions are also social actions and the latter is obviously the more inclusive category. What Parsons aspired to do, in short, was to develop a theory of the relationship of means and ends that would do for action in general—that is, for social action—what the relationship of supply and demand does for action in particular—that is, economic action. Certainly no one can fault the ambition. The question is whether he can extract such a theory from the work of Marshall, Pareto, Durkheim, and Weber.

The Means-End Schema

The scheme is simple enough. It begins with a unit act. A unit act implies (*a*) an actor; (*b*) an end;[40] (*c*) a situation, which in turn contains two elements: means, over which the actor has control, and conditions,[41] over which he does not; and (*d*) a normative orientation. The last of these requires a brief explanation:

> Within the area of control of the actor, the means employed cannot, in general, be conceived either as chosen at random or as dependent exclusively on the conditions of action, but must in some sense be subject to the influence of an independent, determinate selective factor, a knowledge of which is necessary to the understanding of the concrete course of action. What is essential to the concept of action is that there should be a normative orientation, not that this should be of any particular type.[42]

The schema thus has seven concepts: an act, an actor, an end, a situation, means, conditions, and norms, of which two, means and conditions, are subsumed under situation. Nothing would seem to be simpler than this. But the pages that follow are devoted to an almost endless elaboration; complications set in; and finally the reader is mired in such distinctions as the one between a concrete end—"the total anticipated future state of affairs, so far as it is relevant to the action frame of reference"—and an analytical

39. See also *ibid.*, p. 173.

40. An end is defined as "a future state of affairs toward which the process of action is oriented." *Ibid.*, p. 44. In a footnote Parsons says, "In this sense and this only, the schema of action is inherently teleological."

41. "Conditions" appears to be a residual category (in this schema).

42. *Ibid.*, pp. 44–45.

end—"the *difference* between the anticipated future state of affairs and that which it could have been predicted would ensue from the initial situation *without the agency of the actor having intervened.*"[43]

The schema has implications as well as complications. First of all, the category of time is basic; the category of space disappears.[44] Second, in any action there exists the possibility of error; the actor may choose inappropriate means for the attainment of his end. Third, the schema is subjective. And fourth, in using the schema it is not necessary or desirable to break the elements mentioned into smaller elements because for the purposes of the theory the smallest conceivable element is the unit act. It is the third of these implications that is most troublesome. Because of the possibility of misinterpretation that lurks in paraphrase, we need once again to turn directly to Parsons's words:

> Third, the frame of reference of the schema is subjective in a particular sense. That is, it deals with phenomena, with things and events *as they appear from the point of view of the actor* whose action is being analyzed and considered. Of course the phenomena of the "external world" play a major part in the influencing of action. But in so far as they can be utilized by this particular theoretical scheme, they must be reducible to terms which are subjective in this particular sense. This fact is of cardinal importance in understanding some of the peculiaritities of the theoretical structure under consideration here.[45]

And again: "While the social scientist is not concerned with studying the content of his own mind, he is very much concerned with that of the minds of the persons whose action he studies."[46] How a social scientist can enter the minds of other persons is a process that Parsons never explains. He might reply that he need only ask the actor. But, as the present writer has noted,

> The human penchant for *post factum* rationalization of the ends and means of action should give ample warning of the practical impossibility of explaining a given unit act in terms of the means which the actor says he has employed for the attainment of ends he says he had in "mind." What the actor says about his action is no better and is almost always less reliable than what the observer could have learned simply by watching the action.[47]

---

43. *Ibid.*, pp. 48, 49. "Correspondingly, in an analytical sense, means will not refer to concrete things which are 'used' in the course of action, but only to those elements and aspects of them which are capable of, and in so far as they are capable of, control by the actor in the pursuit of his end" (p. 49).

44. "That is to say, *relations in space* are not as such relevant to systems of action analytically considered." *Ibid.*, p. 45, n. 1.

45. *Ibid.*, p. 46.

46. *Ibid.*

47. Bierstedt, "The Means–End Schema," pp. 39–40.

It is fair enough for Parsons to say that by the word *objective* he means from the point of view of the observer, and by *subjective*, from the point of view of the actor. It is a reasonable distinction. But now a more serious problem arises. Consider:

> A still further consequence follows from the "subjectivity" of the categories of the theory of action. When a biologist or a behavioristic psychologist studies a human being it is as an organism, a spatially distinguishable separate unit in the world. The unit of reference which we are considering as the actor is not this organism but an "ego" or "self." The principal importance of this consideration is that the body of the actor forms, for him, just as much part of the situation of action as does the "external environment." Among the conditions to which his action is subject are those relating to his own body, while among the most important of the means at his disposal are the "powers" of his own body and, of course, his "mind." The analytical distinction between actor and situation quite definitely cannot be identified with the distinction in the biological sciences between organism and environment.[48]

An organism, as Parsons says, is a spatially distinguishable unit in the world; an actor is not. There would seem to be an insuperable difficulty in dealing with an ego or self or actor who is not an organism and not an individual, who is not in space, and whose mind has powers that Parsons neglects to describe or delineate. In fact, we are left entirely in the dark with respect to the ontological status of Parsons's actor. One does not ordinarily expect a sociologist to assume the tasks of a philosophical anthropologist or a psychologist, but a sociologist who makes so radical a separation between an actor and an organism would seem to have some obligation to do so. It is interesting to note that many years later Parsons came to appreciate the importance of relating his theory of action to the organic world.[49]

It is also interesting to note that after an elaborate construction of the means–end schema there is no effort to utilize it in any analysis of actions in which individuals—or selves—engage. There are only four concrete references to it in *Structure of Social Action*, one concerning a student writing a term paper for a course (pp. 48–49), one to a housewife boiling a potato (p. 65 n), one to the manufacture of an automobile (p. 23), and one to driving a car from Boston to New York (p. 257). Otherwise, the schema lies useless and unattended. Indeed, it disappears completely from his subsequent theory.

48. *Structure of Social Action*, pp. 46–47; see also p. 252, where he writes, "The subjective point of view is that of the ego not of the concrete biosocial individual."

49. See the "General Introduction" to *Social Systems and the Evolution of Action Theory*, pp. 4–8.

After constructing the means–end schema, Parsons devotes a chapter to the historical development of what he calls "individualistic positivism in the theory of action," a chapter that includes comments on Hobbes, Locke, Malthus, and Marx and additional comments on Darwinism, utilitarianism, and evolutionism. He is now ready to demonstrate the emergence of the voluntaristic theory of action from the positivistic tradition and the convergence of the work of Marshall, Pareto, Durkheim, and Weber on what is to Parsons's mind a single conceptual scheme.

Emergence and Convergence

A careful reading of Parsons's chapter on Marshall unfortunately fails to disclose anything resembling a means–end schema. Parsons discusses Marshall on wants and activities, on utility theory, on the factors of production, on cost, on free enterprise, on laissez-faire, on maximum satisfaction, on social evolution, on something called "the natural order," on economic motives, and on the scope of economic theory. But we find no actor, no author of unit acts choosing means and bound by conditions trying to achieve other than a random end in accordance with a normative orientation. If there is a new antipositivistic element in Marshall's thought, it has, to use Parsons's own words, "escaped detection in spite of the intensive preoccupation of more than a generation of economists with Marshall's works."[50] Apparently only Parsons has detected it. In any event, he soon lost interest in Marshall, and I shall therefore pass over this chapter with no more than the brief observation made in this paragraph.

The subsequent treatment of Pareto, Durkheim, and Weber, which occupies 519 pages, obviously cannot be pursued in detail. Such a pursuit would be a secondary study of a secondary study and would involve interpretations of the work of these three authors. It must nevertheless be said that Parsons's interpretations are open to serious question. These questions are particularly troublesome in the cases of Pareto and Durkheim.

That Pareto objected to the positivism of Comte and Spencer is true. He regarded their positions, as he regarded the positions of most of his predecessors, as dogmatic and metaphysical. But that he himself repudiated the methodology of the physical sciences, as Parsons says,[51] is contrary to fact. Indeed, Pareto wrote that he wanted to construct a system of sociology on the model of physics, chemistry, and celestial astronomy.[52] He emphasized what he called the "logico-experimental method" as the

50. *Structure of Social Action*, p. 176.

51. *Ibid.*, p. 181.

52. *The Mind and Society*, ed Arthur Livingston (New York: Harcourt, Brace & Co., 1935), sec. 20.

essence of science and required of hypotheses that they be "uniformly subject to verification by experience."[53] He conceded that perhaps a small amount of information about external facts could be derived from knowledge of the processes of the mind and from language, "but that small amount is small indeed, and once a science is at all advanced, more errors than truths are obtained in that fashion."[54] And he objected to a dictionary definition of the concept "good" in terms of the concept "end," because "one thing unknown and lying outside the experimental field ('the good') is defined by another thing even more unknown and likewise lying outside the experimental field ('the end').[55] Pareto's view that no theory can explain a concrete phenomenon in all its detail is insufficient ground for claiming, as Parsons does, that he "explicitly rejects" the empiricism of Marshall.[56] Nowhere in the four volumes of Pareto's *The Mind and Society* is this explicit rejection to be found. There is only one brief reference to Marshall, and it concerns Marshall's acceptance of wheat prices as an economic indicator.[57] That Pareto includes "meanings" in the realm of experimental facts or observable phenomena Parsons only infers, with the concession that "he nowhere makes the inclusion explicit."[58] It is true that Pareto discusses means and ends in two brief passages,[59] in distinguishing between logical and nonlogical actions. But these concepts play so small a part in his general theory that there is no index entry for "means," and the references to "ends" concern for the most part the antiquity of the maxim that the end justifies the means. There is a distinction between voluntary and involuntary crimes,[60] but nothing about voluntarism, or a voluntaristic theory of action.

Sorokin, in *Contemporary Sociological Theories*, has a long chapter on the mechanistic school in which he regards Pareto as the most prominent member and indeed "originator of this school in contemporary sociology."[61] Parsons, on his part, finds it odd that Sorokin "treated Pareto,

53. *Ibid.*, sec. 59.
54. *Ibid.*, sec. 108.
55. *Ibid.*, sec. 478.
56. *Structure of Social Action*, p. 183.
57. *Mind and Society*, sec. 2282.
58. *Structure of Social Action*, p. 183.
59. *Mind and Society*, sec. 150, 151.
60. *Ibid.*, sec. 1235, 1253–1256.
61. *Contemporary Sociological Theories* (New York: Harper & Brothers, 1928), p. 39. Indeed, he writes,

> Pareto's studies show that, properly taken, the social physics of the seventeenth century is not a mere dream of a bold human mind, but may be developed into a real scientific sociology which will probably not be able to disentangle all the "mysteries" of human behavior and human history, but may clarify, to some degree, the more important of them.

Ibid., p. 62.

Durkheim, and Weber as belonging to entirely different schools, and did not once mention a relation between any pair of them."[62] Max Handman regarded Pareto as a behaviorist: "In a sense Pareto is a most thoroughgoing behaviorist. He deals with nothing but the outside manifestations of individuals. What goes on within the individual's consciousness does not concern him, although he would not deny the right of a psychologist to study such phenomena."[63] This interpretation Parsons, of course, emphatically rejects.[64]

In the face of Pareto's own remonstrances in favor of his logico-experimental method it is unlikely that he would recognize his own theory in Parsons's interpretation of it. Indeed, there are long passages in Parsons's three chapters on Pareto that have nothing to do with him but consist instead of Parsons's development of his own theory. He goes so far as to confess, at the end of his general conclusions on Pareto, that Pareto's theory was incomplete and that it had "proved possible to add to it in certain directions for the particular purposes of this study."[65] One can only regard these "additions" as pure invention.

Parsons's treatment of Durkheim is equally wayward. Durkheim, of course, wrote on many subjects, but not, so far as his numerous expositors, exegeticists, biographers, and critics are concerned, on the voluntaristic theory of action. In fact, there are at least two explicit rejections of a means–end schema. In *The Rules of Scoiological Method* Durkheim writes, "If society is only a system of means instituted by men to attain certain ends, these ends can only be individual,"[66] society could be explained only in terms of the individual, and sociological laws would only be corollaries of the more general laws of psychology. Needless to say, it is Durkheim's principal purpose in *Rules of Sociological Method* to oppose this view. In *Suicide* Durkheim writes plainly that "an act cannot be defined by the end sought by the actor, for an identical system of behavior may be adjustable to too many different ends without altering its nature."[67] Durkheim's

---

62. *Social Systems and the Evolution of Action Theory*, p. 26, n. 9.

63. "The Sociological Methods of Vilfredo Pareto," in *Methods in Social Science*, ed. Stuart A. Rice (Chicago: University of Chicago Press, 1931), pp. 139–153, quote on p. 148.

64. *Structure of Social Action*, p. 212 n.

65. *Ibid.*, p. 300.

66. *The Rules of Sociological Method*, ed. George E. G. Catlin (Glencoe, Ill.: Free Press, 1950), p. 97.

67. *Suicide*, ed George Simpson (Glencoe, Ill.: Free Press, 1951), p. 43. Whitney Pope observes that "Parsons's attempt to distinguish between regulation and integration [in *Suicide*] is based on such an array of pervasive misrepresentations that it may be unhesitatingly rejected." *Durkheim's Suicide: A Classic Analyzed* (Chicago: University of Chicago Press, 1976), p. 41.

sociological concerns, in fact, bear no resemblance to Parsons's. The notion that he broke out of his original and dark positivistic forest and emerged into the sunlight of voluntarism is one of the most dubious of Parsons's theses. That he was deeply interested in the theme of moral integration does not justify Parsons's characterization of him as a voluntarist. The plain fact of the matter is that Durkheim was not interested in "action" at all. Even in *Suicide* he was interested not in the act but in its incidence. Parsons himself has to concede that "instead of generalizing the means–end schema for systems of action he thought of the individual acting in a social environment and went on to analyze the elements of this environment. . . . On the whole relatively little of Durkheim's attention was centered on the intrinsic means–end schema as such."[68] One can only ask, in all seriousness, whether any of it was.

In Weber, on the other hand, there is no doubt that there is a means–end schema, a subjective point of view, and a category called action. Indeed, he defined sociology itself as "a science which attempts the interpretative understanding of social action in order thereby to arrive at a causal explanation of its course and effects."[69] Nevertheless, Parsons devotes two long chapters to Weber's sociology of religion and one to his methodology—140 pages in all—before he gets around to Weber on social action. And then he has to concede, as he did in the case of Durkheim, that "unlike Pareto, Weber did not set out to build up a generalized theoretical system in the social field. Indeed, there is little evidence that he had any clear conception either of the possibility of doing so or of its usefulness if it could be done."[70] Again, "Weber's methodological position was such as seriously to obscure the status of a generalized theoretical system."[71] Nevertheless, Parsons contends that his conception of the role of the economic element and his treatment of the means–end schema was the same as that of Pareto, and in his discussion of religious ideas, institutions, ritual, and value attitudes Parsons finds a point-for-point correspondence with Durkheim's treatment of the same phenomena. Therefore, "it is legitimate to maintain that in these fundamental respects the convergence has not merely been suggested or made to seem likely but has been *demonstrated* as a matter of empirical fact. It can only be doubted on the ground that the work of the three men has here been radically misinterpreted, and that is a question of fact."[72] Un-

68. *Structure of Social Action*, p. 710.

69. *Ibid.*, p. 641 (Parsons's translation).

70. *Ibid.*, p. 686.

71. *Ibid.*, p. 714.

72. *Ibid.*, p. 714; for a summary of the argument for convergence, see the long footnote to p. 723.

fortunately, these doubts have continued to grow in the years since the publication of the book.

Parsons's penultimate chapter deals with so-called empirically verified conclusions. Indeed, that is its title. He insists that his enterprise has been an empirical one and that he has written an empirical monograph. The facts that he has observed are theories, of course, but they are nonetheless facts susceptible to "empirical observation."[73] Parsons has a striking fondness for the adjective *empirical* and uses it more often perhaps than any other.[74] It is not clear why he should be so intent on this, and so insistent. In no other respect does he try to associate himself with any empirical tradition. Indeed, the contrary is the case.

In any event, Parsons's "empirically verified conclusions" are five in number. The first of these is "That in the works of the four principal writers here treated there has appeared the outline of what *in all essentials*, is the *same* system of generalized social theory, the structural aspect of what has been called the voluntaristic theory of action."[75] The only differences that can be discerned in these writers are different labels for the same phenomena, different distances to which the analysis was carried, and differences in "mode of statement." I shall pause for a note on the last of these. Parsons writes that "the moral element appeared for Pareto first as ultimate ends, one element of the residues; for Durkheim as institutional norms."[76] This kind of "agreement" or "convergence" is typical of Parsons. That there is a similarity between the ultimate ends of Pareto and the institutional norms of Durkheim can be doubted on more grounds than one.

---

73. *Ibid.*, p. 697. One wonders what other kind of observation there is. It is obvious that theories are read. That they are observed, as humming birds and begonias are observed, is quite another matter. Parsons, however, contradicts himself in the following, the final, chapter, where he says that "scientific theory is not itself an empirical entity; it is an ideal representation of empirical phenomena or aspects of them" (p. 754).

74. He sometimes uses it also in odd juxtapositions. For example, empirical interpretations (*ibid.*, p. 3), empirical insights (pp. 19, 306), empirical subject-matter (p. 26), empirical significance (p. 38), empirical relevance (pp. 52, note), empirical justification (p. 84), empirical opinion (p. 176), empirical views (p. 178), empirical frequency (p. 204), empirical ends (p. 256), empirical generalizations (p. 268), empirical consequences (p. 274), empirical level (p. 285, n. 4), empirical theories (pp. 288, 292), empirical prominence (p. 297), empirical argument (p. 324), empirical importance (p. 338n), empirical criticisms (p. 362), empirical proof (p. 533), empirical verification (p. 697), empirical observation (p. 697), empirical monograph (p. 698), empirical centers of attention (p. 720), empirical validity (p. 725 n), empirical implications (p. 728), empirical scholar (p. 759), empirical adequacy (p. 760 n), and even, yes, empirical reason (p. 259) and empirical experience (pp. 24, 69). This list is far from exhaustive. "Empirical insights," for example, appears with what, following Parsons, I am tempted to call empirical frequency!

75. *Ibid.*, pp. 719–720.

76. *Ibid.*, p. 720.

To make matters worse, a search of the four volumes of *The Mind and Society* fails to disclose in Pareto a single instance of the expression "ultimate ends."

The second "empirically verified conclusion" is "That this generalized system of theoretical categories common to the writers here treated is, taken as a total system, a *new* development of theory and is not simply taken over from the traditions on which they built."[77] Parsons has here forgotten that he told us at the beginning of his book that the means-end schema is as old as the history of human thought.

The third conclusion is "That the development of this theoretical system has in each case stood in the closest relation to the principal empirical generalizations which the writer in question formulated."[78] In discussing this conclusion Parsons says that none of the writers he has treated can be finally placed in either a positivistic or idealistic position and that the more one probes into their theories the more central to them becomes the voluntaristic theory of action.

The fourth conclusion is "That one major factor in the emergence of the voluntaristic theory of action lies in correct observation of the empirical facts of social life, especially corrections of and additions to the observations made by proponents of the theories against which these writers stood in polemical opposition."[79] In his elaboration of this conclusion Parsons once again seizes the opportunity to emphasize the remarkable convergence of his four writers in a single system of theory, the more remarkable because of the different points of view they entertained at the start of their separate enterprises. That this convergence might, as mentioned before, be an artifact of Parsons's own dialectic is a possibility that he recognizes—and dismisses—in the following words:

> It is, of course, conceivable that the convergence does not exist at all, but that its appearance in this study is the result of an accumulation of errors of interpretation by the present author. It is also conceivable, though very improbable, that it is the result of an accumulation of random errors on the part of the various theorists themselves. If either of these possibilities is to be considered, it might be instructive to calculate the probabilities that this might occur, considering the number of different elements and their combinations to be taken into account.[80]

These possibilities dismissed, Parsons reiterates his confidence in the convergence as a demonstrated fact and makes the additional—and wholly un-

77. *Ibid.*, p. 720.
78. *Ibid.*, p. 720.
79. *Ibid.*, p. 721.
80. *Ibid.*, p. 722.

warranted—claim that it shows that the concepts of the voluntaristic theory of action are therefore sound concepts and that the theory can serve as the basis for future theoretical work in sociology.

The fifth, and final, conclusion requires no additional comment: "That the four above conclusions, taken together, constitute the hoped-for empirical verification, for this particular case, of the theory of the development of scientific theory stated in the first chapter."[81]

The final chapter of the book contains Parsons's "tentative methodological conclusions." After some epistemological reflections he advances a position he labels "analytical realism," discusses again the action frame of reference, drops the adjective *voluntaristic* because action theories are necessarily voluntaristic, laments Weber's failure to develop a generalized theory, exhibits an awareness of the difficulties involved in his concepts of actor, ego, and self, offers the advice that good common sense "often yields better results than bad theoretical analysis."[82] and supplies a definition of sociology as "the science which attempts to develop an analytical theory of social action systems in so far as these systems can be understood in terms of the property of common-value integrations."[83]

So ends *Structure of Social Action.* One must pay tribute to the author's diligence and his industry. For reasons intimated in the preceding discussion, however, it is impossible to accept his thesis. It raises too many questions. The first concerns the accuracy of Parsons's interpretations of Pareto, Durkheim, and Weber. Skepticism on this score has been continuous. The present writer criticized Parsons's interpretation of Pareto only a few months after the book's publication.[84] Louis Wirth, in his long review, wrote that Parsons's procedure "occasionally involves drawing inferences from and imputing meanings to the texts which are difficult to sustain as intended by the writers" and says that Parsons "takes advantage of his position . . . to go beyond the confines of the writings of the men with whom he deals, and to read into their words implications of which they may not have been aware or with which perhaps they would not wholly

81. *Ibid.*, p. 725.

82. This is what the present writer calls the fallacy of illicit comparison. Flagrant examples of it occur in the following two sentences: "There is no doubt that an ordered empiricism is superior to an unbridled rationalism. But so also is a disciplined rationalism superior to a planless empiricism." Bierstedt, "A Critique of Empiricism in Sociology" (1949), in *Power and Progress*, pp. 148–149.

83. *Structure of Social Action*, p. 768. The chapter also contains a paradox. In discussing the relationship of scientific concepts to something called "reality," Parsons writes, "In particular, it has been necessary to criticize, in terms of their unfortunate empirical implications, a group of views which have been brought together under the term empiricism [p. 728]." It is interesting that a writer who is so fond of the adjective should be so distrustful of the noun.

84. *Saturday Review of Literature*, March 12, 1938, pp. 18–19.

agree."[85] More recent criticism has been quite severe, especially that of Pope, Cohen, and Hazelrigg. To take only two examples, these authors write of Durkheim that he "did not view individual subjective states as positable antecedent conditions of social phenomena" and "did not subscribe to the basic tenet of the voluntaristic theory of action that social phenomena are to be dealt with *'as they appear from the point of view of the actor,'* " as Parsons contends; and of Weber:

> In contrast to Parsons' claim that Weber's rational action is normative because it entails the selection of means to ends, Weber specifically denied that selection of means to ends is necessarily normative. Indeed, Weber deliberately *contrasted zweck-rational* action with action that is oriented toward norms. Weber's entire passage seems to have been written to preclude precisely the kind of misrepresentation offered by Parsons.[86]

In another article Pope writes, "Every fiber of Durkheim's theoretical being would cry out in protest against Parsons' attempt to portray him as an action theorist, voluntaristic or otherwise."[87]

When commentators refer to Pareto as a behaviorist or attribute to Durkheim a behavioristic objectivism, Parsons simply disagrees on the ground that such interpretations are contrary to the central structure of their thought. When Pareto and Durkheim themselves write sentences that are embarrassing to Parsons's interpretations his answer is the same.[88]

The notion that Pareto and Durkheim ever used subjective categories, ever looked at the world or society from the point of view of an actor who is not a body and who is not in space, ever used or praised a means-end schema, ever adopted a voluntaristic theory of action, or ever in fact addressed themselves to a problem called the structure of action is wholly unacceptable. Despite ardor and labor, Parsons's "empirical demonstra-

85. *American Sociological Review* (June 1939): 400.

86. Pope, Cohen, and Hazelrigg, "Reply to Parsons," *ibid.* 42 (October 1977): 809–811. See also, by the same authors and in the same journal, "De-Parsonizing Weber: A Critique of Parsons' Interpretation of Weber's Sociology," 40 (April 1975): 229–41; and "On the Divergence of Weber and Durkheim: A Critique of Parsons' Convergence Thesis," 40 (August 1975): 417–427; and Pope, "Classic on Classic: Parsons' Interpretation of Durkheim," 38 (August 1973): 399–415. See also Talcott Parsons, "On 'De-Parsonizing Weber,' " 40 (October 1975): 666–670; "Comment on 'Parsons' Interpretation of Durkheim' and on 'Moral freedom through Understanding in Durkheim,' " 40 (February 1975): 106–111; and "Reply to Cohen, Hazelrigg and Pope," 41 (April 1976): 361–365. Relevant also in Parsons, "Comment on: 'Current Folklore in the Criticisms of Parsonian Action Theory,' " *Sociological Inquiry* 44 (1974): 55–58.

87. "Parsons on Durkheim, Revisited," *American Sociological Review* 40 (February 1975): 114.

88. See, for example, *Structure of Social Action*, pp. 212, n. 1, 349, n. 1.

tion" cannot be sustained in these two cases. With respect to Weber, Parsons is consistently unhappy with Weber's failure to construct a generalized system of theory, voluntaristic or otherwise, and by Weber's negative view of such an enterprise.

A second question concerns the ontological status of this strange Parsonian creation, the actor—a point we have adumbrated above. We are told that this actor is an ego or self, and we are forbidden to view him as a body or even as a mind. Inasmuch as a mind is required, however, to choose one of a number of alternative means to achieve an end of action, it would seem that Parsons is derelict in his philosophical responsibilities. At the very least as mentioned earlier, he should have told us more about the nature of this actor. As for the voluntaristic theory of action, one had thought that the will, as a psychological concept, had died a natural and not unwelcome death with the demise of faculty psychology at the end of the nineteenth century.[89]

A third question, also mentioned earlier, concerns the ability of an observer, the sociologist in this instance, to get into the minds of actors and discover what is going on there as decisions are being made and means chosen. Parsons insists that this process is necessary but provides no method by which it can be accomplished. E. C. Tolman, the psychologist whose work Parsons repeatedly praised and who was invited to Harvard to work with Parsons and others on a project that resulted in a book,[90] once wrote as follows:

> All that can ever be actually observed in fellow human beings and in lower organisms is behavior. Another organism's private mind, if he have any, can never be got at. And even the supposed ease and obviousness of "looking within" and observing one's own mental processes, directly and at first hand, have proved, when subjected to laboratory control, in large part chimerical: the dictates of "introspection" have proved over and over again to be artifacts of the particular laboratory in which they were obtained.[91]

Indeed, the realm of the subjective—action seen or sought to be seen from the point of view of the actor—contains hazards and pitfalls—the Baconian

89. In a fascinating article John Finley Scott ably argues that voluntarism disappeared altogether from Parsons's work after World War II and was replaced by something he calls "programmatic behaviorism." "The Changing Foundations of the Parsonian Action Scheme," *American Sociological Review* 28 (October 1963): 716–735. The replacement thesis may be questioned, but it is clear that Parsons lost all interest in his means–end schema after the publication of *Structure of Social Action*.

90. See p. 416.

91. Quoted in Scott, "Changing Foundations of Parsonian Action Scheme," p. 719, n. 12. It is from Tolman's *Purposive Behavior in Animals and Men* (New York: Century, 1932).

idols for example—that only objective inquiry can surmount. The subjective lacks all verifiability. That is why objectivity, or striving therefore, is so prized a part of the scientific enterprise.

A last question concerns the "convergence" that Parsons claims to have discerned and demonstrated in the sociological theory of Pareto, Durkheim, and Weber. The claim, as I have intimated, cannot be supported by an examination of their work. Pope, Cohen, and Hazelrigg reject it out of hand. Similarly, Anthony Giddens writes, "The Parsonian account of the unacknowledged 'convergence' of ideas in the thought of Durkheim and Weber (and others whose writings are discussed in the book) has little plausibility."[92] And Reinhard Bendix says without qualification that "Weber's purpose was diametrically opposed to that of Durkheim" and that the work of the two scholars "manifests an almost complete divergence of method and substance."[93]

Even more to the point, perhaps, is that the three writers themselves were unaware of the "convergence." As we have seen, none of the three discussed or, with three trivial exceptions, even mentioned the other two. Is it likely that three scholars, all contemporaries,[94] all able to read the languages in which the other two wrote, two of them editors of social science journals,[95] all interested in the methodology of the social sciences, would have failed to recognize that their work represented a major "breakthrough" in sociological theory and that it all converged in something called a voluntaristic theory of action? The question answers itself.

Parsons nevertheless continued to insist, in 1976, "Now, some thirty-eight years after the publication of *The Structure of Social Action*, I 'still' adhere to the thesis of convergence, not in the sense of diminishing confidence, but, on the contrary, of enhanced confidence, with the benefit of wider and more extensive theoretical insight since that time."[96] Let us, in conclusion of this point, give Parsons the benefit of any doubt that may remain. Let us stipulate that he is right, that the theories of Pareto, Durkheim, and Weber all converged in a voluntaristic theory of action. Do

92. "Classical Theory and the Origins of Modern Sociology," *American Journal of Sociology* 81 (January 1976): 723. And continuing, "The Durkheimian version of sociological method would have been abhorrent to Weber" (p. 724).

93. "Two Sociological Traditions," in *Scholarship and Partisanship: Essays on Max Weber*, ed. Reinhard Bendix and Guenther Roth (Berkeley, Calif: University of California Press, 1971), pp. 282–298.

94. Durkheim died in 1917, Weber in 1920, and Pareto in 1923.

95. Weber subscribed to Durkheim's *L'Année Sociologique* and had a complete set of it in his library.

96. "Reply to Cohen, Hazelrigg and Pope," p. 364.

we need to agree, in addition, that this—to Parsons—remarkable fact guarantees the validity of the theory? The answer again is in the negative. That thousands of Jesuit theologians agree with the philosophy of Saint Thomas Aquinas or that thousands of disciples agree with the economic and social doctrines of Karl Marx hardly suffices to support the "truth" of these philosophies and doctrines. To think so is to ignore Francis Bacon's idol of the theater—the notion that the merit of a theory is somehow measured by the eminence of those who adhere to it, or their number.

The Theory Grows

In 1946 the Department of Sociology as such disappeared at Harvard and was succeeded by a new Department of Social Relations. It included not only sociology but also social and cultural anthropology and social and clinical psychology. The people associated with this department, among them Gordon W. Allport, Clyde Kluckhohn, Henry A. Murray, Robert R. Sears, Richard C. Sheldon, Samuel A. Stouffer, and, especially, Talcott Parsons, motivated partly by the new administrative arrangement, were anxious to build theoretical foundations for the social sciences, foundations strong enough to bear the weight of all three of the disciplines involved. To this end they invited the psychologist Edward C. Tolman from California and the sociologist Edward A. Shils from Chicago to join their collaborative endeavor. The result was a book published in 1951 entitled *Toward a General Theory of Action* and edited by Parsons and Shils.[97] It contains contributions by all of the men mentioned above.[98] The longest section, amounting to almost half of the book, was written by the two editors, with the assistance of James Olds, and is entitled "Values, Motives, and Systems of Action." Parsons believed that he and Shils accomplished "a real breakthrough" in these four chapters, on a level not shared by the others, and that they carried out the implications of their reasoning to a more distant point. They worked so closely together that Parsons says it is impossible to disentangle their separate contributions. Because of this fact I shall give the book little attention here.

It may be said nevertheless that these chapters are heavily Parsonian in

97. (Cambridge, Mass.: Harvard University Press); Harper Torchbook edition appeared in 1962. Reasons for omitting economics and political science are offered on pp. 28–29.

98. Tolman's contribution is almost entirely behavioristic, and in it he equates action with behavior. Stouffer's contribution, written with Jackson Toby, appeared in the same year in the *American Journal of Sociology* and has nothing to do with a general theory of action.

intent and emphasis. The first deals generally and in detail with the action schema; the second, with personality as a system of action; the third, with systems of value-orientation; and the fourth, with the social system. The "pattern-variable" schema, which ties these systems together in a "strategically crucial" way, is developed in elaborate detail.[99] A brief concluding chapter summarizes the discussion, and in it the authors somewhat immodestly claim that what they have brought forth in these pages represents "an important advance toward the construction of a unified theory of social science."[100] Furthermore, "It perhaps may be said to put together more elements, in a more systematic way, than any other attempt yet made on this level of abstraction." On the other hand, the authors concede that their effort is a tentative one, that it may present serious difficulties to critics, and that others may prefer different conceptual schemes. Nevertheless,

> The whole course of development of work in the social sciences to which this monograph has sought to give a more systematic theoretical formulation is such that it is scarcely conceivable that such a large measure of conceptual ordering which connects with so much empirical knowledge should be completely "off the rails." It seems therefore that however great the modifications which will have to be introduced by empirical application and theoretical refinement and reformulation, the permanently valid precipitate will prove to be substantial.[101]

The authors do not seem to have noticed that they have not exhibited any of the empirical knowledge to which they claim their conceptual scheme "connects."

The Social System

The Social System is surely one of the oddest books published since the invention of movable type.[102] Part of it is intelligible. It contains sentences such as this: "The whole nature of the theory of action in general, and hence of the theory of social systems, as here developed, is such that precisely with respect to variability of structure, patterns of value-

99. The pattern-variables will be treated later in the chapter.

100. This expression is quite indicative of the nature of the Parsonian enterprise as a whole. It is indeed more of a theory of social science than a theory of society.

101. All the quotations in this paragraph are from *General Theory of Action*, pp. 238–239.

102. (Glencoe, Ill.: Free Press, 1951).

orientation as the focus of institutionalization, *must* play a crucial role."[103] Even if one regards the last comma as a typographical error, it is difficult to make sense of it. One sentence in it became a space filler in *The New Yorker.*[104] *The Social System* also contains a large number of complex tables and classifications, with few of the latter exhibiting any clear *fundamentum divisionis.* It is essentially an expansion, by Parsons alone, of the four long chapters entitled "Values, Motives, and Systems of Action," by Parsons and Shils, to which reference has just been made. Indeed, the last of these chapters is entitled "The Social System."

It is not easy, however, to describe the contents of the book. Parsons tells us that it is not a system of theory but rather a theory of systems. We are thus induced to characterize it not as a work of sociological theory but rather as a contribution to metasociology, that is, a work directed not to the nature of society but to the nature of sociology or, better yet, to the language one might use in the analysis of social systems. Parsons says that he intends to fulfill Pareto's effort to "delineate the social system as a system." It is perhaps advisable to allow him to describe his enterprise in his own words:

> The present volume is an attempt to bring together, in systematic and generalized form, the main outlines of a conceptual scheme for the analysis of the structure and processes of social systems. In the nature of the case, within the frame of reference of action, such a conceptual scheme must focus on the delineation of the system of institutionalized roles and the motivational processes organized about them. Because of this focus and the very elementary treatment of processes of economic exchange and of the organization of political power, the book should be regarded as a statement of general sociological theory, since this is here interpreted to be that part of the theory of the social system which is centered on the phenomena of the institutionalization of patterns of value-orientation in roles.[105]

We have, in short, an obsession with system, with the construction of a systematic conceptual scheme to be used in the analysis of social systems. The repetition of the word *system,* in title and content, is serious and intentional.[106]

Parsons's social system is, of course, built on the foundation of the

103. *Ibid.,* p. 152.

104. "The fact that all human populations are classifiable by sex into two and only two categories (with negligible exceptions) forms a crucial focus of orientation to human individuals." *Ibid.,* p. 89. To which the magazine appended the comment: "If you're trying to pick an argument, you've come to the wrong fellow." *The New Yorker* (February 5, 1972): p. 82.

105. *The Social System,* p. vii.

106. Parsons owes his sensitivity to the importance of system, as he acknowledges, to both Pareto and L. J. Henderson.

voluntaristic theory of action earlier outlined in *Structure of Social Action*. It is defined as follows:

> Reduced to the simplest possible terms, then, a social system consists in a plurality of individual actors interacting with each other in a situation which has at least a physical or environmental aspect, actors who are motivated in terms of a tendency to the "optimization of gratification" and whose relation to their situations, including each other, is defined and mediated in terms of a system of culturally structured and shared symbols.[107]

A social system, as thus defined, is only one aspect of a completely concrete system of social action. The other two, analytically independent but closely related, are personality systems and cultural systems. Although analytically independent, transformations between them are possible, and the action frame of reference is common to all three. The reader is warned against considering any one of these systems as somehow more basic than the other two.[108] In any event, a society is then defined as a social system "which meets all the essential functional prerequisites of long term persistence from within its own resources."[109] Any social system that does not qualify as a society under this definition is called a partial social system. Modern medical practice, for example, is a partial social system, as are also the economy, the polity, and a household. Whether Parsons would call the Commonwealth of Virginia or the city of New York a partial social system or a society is not clear.

Some of Parsons's concepts, and definitions of them, merit favorable attention. One can applaud, for example, his distinction between status and role—the former being the positional aspect of an individual as he is located in social space, the latter the "processual" aspect, what he does with the position he occupies.[110] Parsons is only incorrect when he says, briefly and unnecessarily, "There are no roles without corresponding statuses and vice versa."[111] A status without a role, for example, would be a temporarily

107. *Ibid.*, pp. 5–6.

108. *Ibid.*, p. 18:

> The fundamental building stones of the theory of social systems, like those of personality and culture theory, are common to *all* the sciences of action. This is true *not of some of them but of all of them.* But the ways in which these conceptual materials are to be built into theoretical structures is not the same in the cases of the three major foci of action theory. Psychology, as the science of personality, is thus not the "foundation" of the theory of social systems, but *one* main branch of the great tree of action theory of which the theory of social systems is another. The common foundation is not the theory of the individual as the unit of society, but of action as the "stuff" out of which both personality systems and social systems are built up.

109. *Ibid.*, p. 19.

110. *Ibid.*, p. 25.

111. *Ibid.*, p. 39 n.

unfilled position in the table of organization of an association. On the other hand, one can play a number of roles—clown, nurse, teacher, for example—without occupying the corresponding statuses, which are to be found in the circus, the hospital, and the school.[112] Nevertheless, the distinction between status and role is clear, and this is to the good inasmuch as it is often blurred in the literature. "Role-expectation" and "role-pattern" are less clear. "An *institution* will be said to be a complex of institutionalized role integrates, or status-relationships, which is of strategic structural significance in the social system in question."[113] Although it is logically impermissible to include the word *institutionalized* in the *definiens* of the word *institution*, one nevertheless has a sense of what Parsons has in mind.[114] Full institutionalization is for him the polar opposite of anomy. A collectivity, as contrasted with an institution, is "a system of concretely interactive specific roles." Here, however, we encounter a difficulty. One would have thought that a collectivity is a group of people, not a group of roles, and apparently Parsons inconsistently thinks so too because he also refers to a particular family as a collectivity.[115] Parsons admits that his discussion of modes and types of action-orientation, culture patterns, and institutions is "rather complex," and accordingly he comes to the assistance of the reader by supplying a long and complicated outline. It is there, for example, that we learn that the modes of motivational orientation of action are three in number—cognitive, cathectic, and evaluative.[116] Shortly thereafter we meet the "pattern variables" which play so prominent a part in his theory.

The Pattern Variables

One would like to be lucid in discussing concepts of such importance to Parsons. Unfortunately, the task is difficult, and Parsons himself is of little help. No one knows how many pattern variables there are or exactly what they are. One would normally except the author from a generalization such as this, but not even he is sure of their number and he sometimes contradicts himself about their character. As he says, "The pattern-variable scheme underwent over the years rather complex vicissitudes."[117] If we

112. For an elaboration of this point, see Robert Bierstedt, *The Social Order*, 4th ed. (New York: McGraw-Hill, 1974), pp. 255–258.

113. *The Social System*, p. 39.

114. On institutions, see Bierstedt, *Social Order*, pp. 328–334.

115. *The Social System*, p. 40.

116. *Ibid.*, p. 57.

117. "On Building Social System Theory: A Personal History," *Social Systems and the Evolution of Action Theory*, p. 42.

begin by asking how many pattern variables there are, we can answer four, five, or six, and all three answers will be correct at different periods of his career. In his lectures in the mid-1930s there were four, two of which later disappeared as others were introduced. In his chapters with Shils and in *The Social System* there are five. In a later essay he came to the conclusion that a sixth was needed, one that he declined firmly to label but hinted that it might be called "external-internal" or "instrumental consummatory."[118] It is difficult to take seriously his contention that his pattern variables exhaust the possibilities both because of his own uncertainty as to their number and because he has both subtracted from and added to the list as his scheme developed. Since they occur in sets of two whose terms appear to be contraries, one can also ask whether we have a dichotomy or a continuum. Parsons insists that the two terms in his sets of variables are dichotomies but in response to criticism that at least one set represents a continuum, says, with a fine disregard of the law of contradiction, that a mutual exclusiveness is not incompatible with continuity of variation.[119]

The origin of the scheme seems fairly clear. "The pattern variables first emerged as a conceptual scheme for classifying types of roles in social systems, starting with the distinction between professional and business roles."[120] Later on "the scheme was substantially revised and its relevance extended from role-analysis in the social system to the analysis of all types of systems of action."[121] But they are not only a conceptual scheme; they are also a series of dilemmas. It appears that every actor in every situation confronts a series of dilemmas, one horn of which the actor must grasp (or choose) in order for the situation to have meaning for him. In Parsons's own words, "The pattern-variable scheme defines a set of five dichotomies. Any course of action by any actor involves (according to theory) a pattern of choices with respect to these five sets of alternatives."[122] And again, "A *pattern variable* is a dichotomy, one side of which must be chosen by an actor before the meaning of a situation is determinate for him, and thus before he can act with respect to that situation."[123] It is immediately after this second definition that he tells us that there are only five pattern variables, that they derive directly from the frame of reference of the theory of action, and that in the sense that they are all thus derived,

118. "Some Comments on the State of the General Theory of Action," *American Sociological Review* 18 (December 1953): 618–631; see especially pp. 624b and 626b, n. 13.

119. *Ibid.*, p. 624a.

120. "Pattern Variables Revisited: A Response to Robert Dubin," *ibid.*, p. 25 (August 1960): 467.

121. *Ibid.*

122. Parsons and Shils, *General Theory of Action*, p. 48.

123. *Ibid.*, p. 77.

they constitute a system. They are (*a*) affectivity–affective neutrality; (*b*) self-orientation–collectivity-orientation; (*c*) universalism–particularism; (*d*) ascription–achievement; (*e*) specificity–diffuseness. These represent, respectively, (*a*) the gratification–discipline dilemma; (*b*) the private-versus-collective-interest dilemma; (*c*) the choice between types of value-orientation standards; (*d*) the choice between "modalities" of the social object; and (*e*) the definition of scope of interest in the object.[124]

Just when we have fixed our minds on the fact that the pattern variables are dilemmas of choice that every "actor" confronts, we discover that they are much more. They are also "characteristics of value standards," a scheme for the formulation of value standards, "categories for the description of value-orientations," "crucial components in the definition of role expectations," tools for the classification of need-dispositions and role-expectations, characterizations of differences of empirical structure of personalities or social social systems, inherent patterns of cultural value-orientation, "alternative directions in which the orientation of action can go," a way of "making explicit and formulating in a technical and orderly way the basic frame of reference in terms of which" certain properties of action "make sense," "categories for the orderly description and comparative analysis of the 'structure' of systems of action as systems," not only categories of social structure but also categories of systems of action in general, modes of organization of symbolic meanings, a conceptual scheme for classifying the components of an action system, "the *properties* of actor's orientations and objects' modalities", rubrics of classification, and components of the structure of social systems. We are asked to believe, in short, that the pattern variables, at one and the same time, are concepts, choices, dilemmas, categories, properties, components, and directions.

The situation deteriorates. We are also asked to believe that a pattern variable in its cultural aspect is a normative pattern, in its personality aspect, a "need-disposition," and in its social system aspect, a "role-expectation." This is what Max Black refers to as the "systematic ambiguity" in Parsons's theory.[125] To make matters still worse, the pattern variables "enter the action frame of reference at four different levels": (*a*) the concrete level of actors' choices "which every actor makes before he can act"; (*b*) the personality level as habits of choice; (*c*) the collectivity level as aspects of role definition; and (*d*) the cultural level as aspects of value stan-

124. The listing is the same in *General Theory of Action*, p. 77, and in *The Social System*, p. 67, except that the two terms of *d* are reversed in the two places.

125. "Some Questions about Parsons' Theories," *Social Theories of Talcott Parsons*, pp. 268–288, quotes on pp. 281 and 284.

dards.[126] One hopes that all of this is "perfectly clear." Actually, all that is clear about it is that Parsons is much less interested in his pattern variables as dilemmas of choice for individual actors than he is in them as basic components of his conceptual scheme.

Having listed his five pattern variables, Parsons's mind leaps to possible relationships between them. Thus, the first three "derive from the problems of primacy among the modes of orientation"; the last two, "from the indeterminacies in the object situation." Later on he rearranges them and renames the fourth. The list then appears as follows: (*a*) specificity–diffuseness; (*b*) affectivity–affective neutrality; (*c*) universalism–particularism; (*d*) quality–performance; (*e*) self-orientation–collectivity-orientation. With this arrangement the first two form a pair, the second two another pair, and, because the scheme is one of "symmetrical asymmetry," the fifth is unpaired. In addition, the first two sets refer to orientations, the actor's relationship to the objects in his situation; the second two, to modalities, the meaning of the object for the actor. "The orientation set of pattern variables 'views' the relationship of actor to situation from the side of the actor or actors; the modality set views it from the side of the situation as consisting of objects."[127] Again, the fifth set does not quite fit this level of analysis.

Parsons believes that he can use his pattern-variable scheme to describe all kinds of social relationships. Business relationships and family relationships, for example, are polar opposites, differing in each set of variables. Thus, business relationships are characterized by affective neutrality, specificity, universalism, performance, and self-orientation. Family relationships are characterized by affectivity, diffuseness, particularism, quality, and collectivity orientation. The doctor–patient relationship is like a customer–clerk relationship except that it is collectivity-oriented rather than self-oriented.[128] The social worker–client relationship is like that of Parsons's doctor–patient relationship except that it is diffuse rather than

126. *General Theory of Action*, p. 78. The pattern variables in *The Social System* are used also to characterize four types of social structure, depending upon whether they conform to the universalistic–achievement pattern (the United States), the universalistic–ascription pattern (Germany), the particularistic–achievement pattern (China), or the particularistic–ascriptive pattern (Spanish-American societies).

127. "Pattern Variables Revisited," p. 468.

128. This, at least, is Parsons's opinion. One may doubt, however, that many patients would be happy if their surgeons were thinking about some collectivity while they are on the operating table. Most, it seems reasonable to believe, would be much happier if the doctor were taking a self-oriented pride in his own surgical skills. "After all," writes Parsons, "the surgeon is trained to operate, he feels active, useful, effective when he is operating." *The Social System* p. 466.

specific. In this way Parsons believes that he has a more refined instrument for characterizing, describing, and classifying relationships than such a dichotomy as the *Gemeinschaft–Gesellschaft* of Tönnies, which gave Parsons's scheme its initial impetus.

Parson's pattern-variable scheme has encountered severe criticism, especially by the distinguished philosopher Max Black.[129] First of all, Black says that if the word *choice* is taken in "a narrow and emphatic sense," it is patently false to say that a person contemplating an action has to make five choices of the pattern-variable kind before he can act. To elaborate upon Black, a bridge game, for example, would be impossible if each player had to make these choices before making a bid or playing a card. Furthermore, when Parsons says that the choices may be explicit or implicit, he almost surrenders his scheme. An implicit choice is a contradiction in terms.

Black's second criticism concerns Parsons's language. The words are "barbarous neologisms." Parsons also has different connotations for the same term; thus, *affectivity* means now "impulse," now "gratification," now "permissiveness." His third criticism concerns Parsons's logic. The scheme lacks an intelligible principle of organization, a *fundamentum divisionis.* A fourth criticism, to which I have already referred, is that Parsons insists that his variables are dichotomies rather than continua and then contradicts himself. A fifth criticism is that, contrary to Parsons's insistence, the pattern variables are not required by his general theory. A sixth is the suggestion that Parsons could have expanded his list: "For it is easy to think of any number of other ways of classifying the selected attitude of the 'actor' to his objects." Black offers some examples. Other examples would be personal–impersonal and interested–disinterested, the second of which Parsons used in his first formulations and then discarded. As Philip Selznick also writes, "Where does Parsons get the particular pattern variables he chooses to stress when, on abstract grounds, so many others might be chosen?"[130]

To these criticisms many others could be added. Two in particular merit mention. The first is that despite the complexity of the scheme, it is in fact not a noticeably sharp instrument of discrimination. Clearly, business relationships and family relationships are different in character. The former are

129. "Some Questions about Parsons' Theories," pp. 283–288. The book in which this essay appears consists of nine expository or critical essays on Parsons's work, resulting from an intensive study of it by 10 faculty members of Cornell University during the academic year 1957–1958 in meetings and in seminars. See also Parsons's reply, "The Point of View of the Author," pp. 311–363. See also the reviews of this book by Philip Selznick, *American Sociological Review* 26 (December 1961): 932–935, by Bennett Berger, *Commentary* 40 (1962): 507–513, and by Lewis Feuer, *Journal of Philosophy* 59 (March 29, 1962): 182–193.

130. *American Sociological Review* 26 (December 1961): 935.

impersonal; the latter, personal. But if we concede that the doctor-patient relationship is characterized by affective neutrality, specificity, universalism, performance, and collectivity-orientation, so also are such relations as teacher-student, minister-parishioner, coach-player, forman-worker, tax collector-taxpayer, conductor-orchestra member, captain-crew, and vice president-secretary, to mention only a few. Some of these are arguable but so, as I have mentioned, is Parsons's characterization of the doctor-patient relationship. Parsons himself says that in all cases where authority is involved we have a collectivity-orientation.[131]

A final criticism is that the scheme is burdened with unnecessary variables. All we need to say is that some social relations are status relations—tax collector-taxpayer, for example—and others are personal relations—parent-child, for example. Here also we have a continuum and not a dichotomy. Some status relations, continued over a period of time, take on personal characteristics. One can get to know one's doctor and lawyer as persons and friends and not only as healer of ailments and drafter of wills.[132] Although Parsons clearly would not agree, it is possible to argue that his pattern variables represent a pervasive violation of the law of parsimony.

The Place of Sociological Theory

At the end of *The Social System* Parsons discusses the place of sociological theory among the analytical sciences of action. He tells us again, with emphasis, that the book is meant not to offer a theory of any concrete phenomenon but rather to construct a systematic theory, a logically articulated conceptual scheme. The book is an essay *in* systematic theory but is not itself a system *of* theory. It is here that he says, in an interesting juxtaposition of the words, that "it is a theory of systems rather than a system of theory," and "the concept of a theory of systems is the most strategic tool for working toward the attainment of a system of theory."[133] Indeed, he stoutly maintains that in the present state of our knowledge a general system of theory cannot be formulated. He has previously said, with perhaps an equal emphasis, that we do not have a

131. Incidentally, Parsons treats very few of these relationships in his work. They are too concrete to quality for his attention.

132. On the subject of statuses as components of the structure of society, see Bierstedt, *The Social Order*, pp. 250–279. For an older treatment, see E. T. Hiller, *Social Relations and Structures* (New York: Harper & Brothers, 1947), pp. 330–648.

133. *The Social System*, p. 537.

general theory of the processes of social change and may, in fact, never have one.[134]

What Parsons wants to do in this concluding chapter, however, is to suggest that the theory of social systems is an integral part of a larger conceptual scheme, the theory of action in general. The other two parts, or subsystems, of action theory are the theory of personality and the theory of culture. All three subsystems, of course, are interdependent.[135] Acknowledgment of this interdependence makes possible a level of clarification not hitherto reached.[136] At the same time that one acknowledges the interdependence of theories of culture, personality, and social systems, however, one must insist upon their independence. The theory of social systems cannot be "reduced" to a theory of personality, nor on the other hand is it encompassed by a theory of culture. The first of these faults Parsons sees exemplified in the work of Floyd H. Allport, in which social systems are viewed as resultants of interacting personalities, a view that "ignores the organization of action about the exigencies of social systems as systems."[137] The second he sees in the work of Ruth Benedict, with her emphasis upon "patterns of culture" and the implication that a social system constitutes one of these patterns. For the first time both interdependence and independence are clearly recognized, and this Parsons thinks of as an advance over even the deepest insights of Durkheim and Freud:[138]

> This fundamental relationship between need-dispositions of the personality, role-expectations of the social system and internalized-institutionalized value-patterns of the culture, is the fundamental nodal point of the *organization* of systems of action. It is the point at which both the interdependence and the independence from each other of personality, social system and culture focus.[139]

---

134. *Ibid.*, p. 534.

135. Much later a fourth subsystem enters the system: "Finally, it has also become clear that what is usually called 'the personality system' is by no means the only major theoretical reference for consideration of the 'individual.' I have tended to deal with a fourth primary subsystem of what I would call the general system of action under the heading of the 'behavioral organism.' " Still later, at the suggestion of two of his students, Victor Lidz and Charles Lidz, he decided to leave the behavioral organism in the environment after all and introduce into the action system a fourth subsystem now called "the behavioral system," a system that deals with cognitive functions, patterns, and capacities. See "The Present Status of 'Structural-Functional' Theory in Sociology," in *Social Systems and the Evolution of Action Theory*, p. 106, n. 17. This paper appeared first in Lewis A. Coser, ed., *The Idea of Social Structure*, (New York: Harcourt Brace Jovanovich, 1975), pp. 67–83.

136. "By this is meant a clarification going well beyond what is now current in even the best literature of the subject." *The Social System*, p. 537.

137. *Ibid.*, p. 539.

138. The large influence of Freud on Parsons's thought did not become evident until after the publication of *The Social System*. See especially the essays in Parsons, *Social Structure and Personality* (Glencoe, Ill.: Free Press, 1964).

139. *Ibid.*, p. 540.

It is this insight that makes possible the level of analytical refinement that the theory of the social system exhibits.[140]

System-Problems

In the middle years of the century Parsons's theory expanded rapidly. Indeed, there is some reason for thinking that *The Social System* became obsolete on the day of its publication. This judgment, however, would not be fair to him inasmuch as the basic scheme, including the pattern variables, served as the essential trunk from which branches continued to proliferate. One of the most imporant of these branches, finally a competitor for the position of trunk itself, was something variously called system-problems, system-dimensions, essential functional imperatives of any system of action, functional subsystems of action, and functional problems of systems. It began with work in the summer of 1952, in collaboration with Edward A. Shils and Robert Freed Bales, and resulted in the publication in the following year of *Working Papers in the Theory of Action*, with all three as authors.[141]

What happened may be explained by Parsons in his own words:

> The crucial outcome, in light of subsequent development, was the emergence of what we now call the "four-function paradigm." Its genesis lay in a convergence between the system comprising the four elementary pattern variables and a classification that Bales had set forth in his *Interaction Process Analysis*.[142] We concluded that systems of action generally could be exhaustively analyzed in terms of processes and structures referable to the solution—simultaneously or in sequence—of the four functional problems that we called "adaptation," "system (not unit) goal-attainment," "integration," and "pattern-maintenance and latent tension-management." Though there were many defects in our formulations at that time, this basic classification has remained with me for the more than fifteen years since it first emerged and has constituted a primary reference point of all my theoretical work.[143]

140. In the concluding chapter of *The Social System* Parsons somewhat equivocally changes one of the postulates he advanced in *Structure of Social Action*. He says that the subjective point of view—the study of action from the point of view of the actor—"is not essential to the frame of reference of action in its most elementary form" but that it becomes essential again when culture, or shared symbolic patterns, becomes involved. *The Social System*, p. 543.

141. (New York: Free Press, 1953).

142. (Cambridge, Mass: Addison-Wesley, 1950).

143. "On Building Social System Theory: A Personal History," in *Social Systems and the Evaluation of Action Theory*, p. 43.

It is this scheme, called the "A, G, I, L" scheme, that he has endlessly elaborated in his subsequent writing. It is also the source of innumerable fourfold tables that go to seed in the Technical Appendix to *The American University*.[144]

Although it would be unprofitable to pursue Parsons's work with his four-function paradigm, a few observations may be in order. Inasmuch as the statement of the "A, G, I, L" system is rather brief in the preceding quotation, it may be useful to look at the slightly more explanatory version in the following paragraph:

> The four basic functional problems of systems of action we have formulated are (1) "adaptation," i.e., to objects in the situation outside the system, (2) "goal-attainment," i.e., establishment of "consummatory" relations to situational objects—by "instrumental" processes, (3) "integrative," the maintenance of a state of internal "harmony" or absence of "conflict" among the units of the system and (4) "latent pattern-maintenance and tension-management," the maintenance *both* of the structure of the internalized-institutionalized normative or cultural patterns, *and* motivation to conformity with their requirements.[145]

Parsons insists that his four functional problems of systems constitute an irreducible and unexpandable list.[146] It is difficult to know why he regards this as necessary or desirable. Note that the fourth functional problem contains two expressions, "latent pattern-maintenance" and "tension-management." Either these two expressions are synonymous, in which case one of them is redundant, or they are not, in which case he himself has added a fifth to his list.

---

144. Parsons and Gerald Platt, *The American University* (Cambridge, Mass.: Harvard University Press, 1973). In addition to this, and *Working Papers*, mentioned earlier, see Talcott Parsons, "Some Comments on the General Theory of Action," *American Sociological Review* 18 (December 1953): 618–631; Parsons, Robert Freed Bales, James Olds, Morris Zelditch, and Philip Slater, *Family, Socialization, and Interaction Process* (New York: Free Press, 1955); Parsons and Neil J. Smelser, *Economy and Society: A Study in the Integration of Economic and Social Theory* (Glencoe, Ill.: Free Press, 1956); Parsons, "Pattern Variables Revisited," pp. 467–483; Parsons, "An Outline of the Social System," in Parsons, Edward Shils, Kaspar D. Naegele, and Jesse R. Pitts, *Theories of Society*, 2 vols. (Glencoe, Ill.: Free Press, 1961), pp. 30–79; Parsons, "The Point of View of the Author," in *Social Theories of Talcott Parsons*, ed. Black, pp. 311–363; and Parsons, "Some Problems of General Theory in Sociology," in *Theoretical Sociology: Perspectives and Developments*, ed. John C. McKinney and Edward A. Tiryakian (Englewood Cliffs, N.J.: Prentice-Hall, 1970), pp. 26–68, reprinted in Parsons, *Social Systems*, pp. 229–269.

145. "Some Comments on the General State of the Theory of Action," pp. 624–625.

146. "It seems clear that this is an irreducible list, judged by the needs of the frame of reference of action. It has worked sufficiently well, so that I think it is legitimate to place the burden of proof on him who would reduce it farther or expand it." *Ibid.*, p. 625.

It is also difficult to know in exactly what sense, as he claims, the pattern variables and the functional problems "converge," or in what sense the latter are "grounded" in the former. There is no doubt that Parsons is able to find many relationships between them, as illustrated for example in the following table, which appears under the caption "System Problems and Pattern Variables":[147]

System-problem	Attitudinal aspect	Object-categorization aspect
Adaptation	Specificity	Universalism
Goal-attainment	Affectivity	Performance (achievement)
System-integration	Diffuseness	Particularism
Pattern-maintenance and tension-management	Affective neutrality	Quality (ascription)

This table, whatever it may mean, can only begin to suggest the permutations and combinations of concepts with which Parsons's mind delights to play.

A final observation concerns the effort Parsons has made to relate his fourfold system-problems to the institutions of society. It appears that the economy is concerned primarily with the system-problem of adaptation, as are also to some extent education and defense. The polity, on the other hand, is concerned with goal-attainment. The church, with the help of other institutions, appears to serve the integrative function. And the family or, as Parsons sometimes says, the household, engages in the functions of pattern-maintenance and tension-management. About this effort to relate his system-problems to institutions, one need only say, with Devereux that the fit is far from perfect.[148]

Societies in Evolutionary Perspective

Although far from weary of metasociological speculation—indeed, this kind of speculation is both endemic and persistent—Parsons turned to a

147. *Ibid.*

148. Edward C. Devereux, Jr., "Parsons' Sociological Theory," in *Social Theories of Talcott Parsons*, ed. Black, p. 61.

study of actual historical societies in two small books published five years apart.[149] As the title of the first of them indicates, the perspective is both comparative and evolutionary. That it should be evolutionary is the occasion of some surprise in view of the dismissal of Spencer at the beginning of *Structure of Social Action.* Parsons contends, however, that his view of evolution is much more sophisticated than Spencer's in that it makes allowance for multiple and variable origins of societal types. But the evolutionary emphasis is clear and candid, and Parsons furthermore indicates an interest in finding as many linkages as possible between biological evolution and societal evolution. Such evolutionary concepts as variation, selection, adaptation, differentiation, and integration are central to his concerns, and sociocultural evolution, like organic evolution, is conceived of as a movement from the simple to the complex.

His task, as Parsons sees it, consists of four "interdependent yet in certain respects independent" parts: (*a*) to lay out his general conceptual scheme, the theory of social systems which, he is not diffident about claiming, underlies all sociological analysis; (*b*) to treat total societies as one type of social system (others, for example, are local communities, schools, business firms, and kinship units); (*c*) to analyze the evolutionary developments themselves, both in total societies and in their parts; and (*d*) to consider problems of variation as distinct from problems of stage and sequence.

The first of these tasks, a renewed visit to the general theory of action, is undertaken both in a long chapter in the first of these volumes and again in the second. It is not necessary to pursue it here, despite emendations and extensions that Parsons may regard as "crucial." It will suffice to say that social systems constitute one subsystem of the action system in general and that to the three earlier subsystems—social systems, cultural systems, and personality systems—he now adds a fourth—his behavioral organism. As is noticeable throughout his work, he finds it congenial to treat concepts and categories in clusters of four rather than three, and indeed almost all of his classifications exhibit a fourfold character. It is a practice to which

149. *Societies: Evolutionary and Comparative Perspectives* (Englewood Cliffs, N.J.: Prentice-Hall, 1966); and *The System of Modern Societies* (Englewood Cliffs, N.J.: Prentice Hall, 1971). These will be republished in one volume, Jackson Toby, ed., as *The Evolution of Societies.* See also "Evolutionary Universals in Society," *American Sociological Review* 29 (June 1964): 339–357, reprinted in Parsons, *Sociological Theory and Modern Society* (New York: Free Press, 1967); and "Comparative Studies and Evolutionary Change," in *Comparative Methods in Sociology: Essays on Trends and Applications,* ed. Ivan Vallier (Berkeley, Calif.: University of California Press, 1971), reprinted in Parsons, *Social Systems and the Evolution of Action Theory,* pp. 279–320. The Introduction to Part 3 of the latter book is also relevant.

Lewis Feuer refers as Parsons's "quadromania."[150] In any event, when one focuses upon the social system the other three subsystems become part of its environment. The variables formerly known as system-problems are now seen as the four primary functions of all action systems and they play a prominent role in Parsons's analysis of historical and modern societies. Also, in terms of the theory, the social system serves the function of integration; the cultural system, that of pattern-maintenance; the personality system, that of goal-attainment; and the behavioral organism, that of adaptation.

We have here in addition a treatment of the concept of society, which Parsons defines as "a type of social system, in any universe of social systems, which attains the highest level of self-sufficiency as a system in relation to its environments."[151] Finally, we are introduced to a new concept, "the societal community," which is the integrative subsystem of a society, whose function it is "to articulate a *system* of norms with a collective organization that has unity and cohesiveness,"[152] and which defines the obligation of loyalty. Parsons proceeds to discuss the relationship of his societal community to pattern-maintenance, to the polity, the economy, the legal system, market systems and bureaucratic organization, and associational organization. He concludes his preliminary treatment in *System of Modern Societies* with a brief mention of *four* (Parsons's italics) processes of structural change which, as they interact, "constitute 'progressive' evolution to higher system levels."[153] These are differentiation, adaptive upgrading, inclusion, and value generalization. We are also informed that there are four structural components of societies—values, norms, collectivities, and roles. Values have to do with pattern-maintenance; norms, with the integrative function; collectivities, with goal-attainment; and roles, with the adaptive function.[154]

Parsons sees evolution itself as a process of increasing adaptive capacity of societies to their environments. He distinguishes three broad stages—the primitive, the intermediate, and the modern—with recognition that any such division into stages or levels is bound to be arbitrary. The intermediate differs from the primitive by the criterion of literacy; the modern, from the intermediate by the criterion of law. Each of the three stages has subdivisions or sublevels. Thus, we have primitive societies (Par-

150. Review of *Social Theories of Talcott Parsons*, Black, ed., *Journal of Philosophy* 59 (March 29, 1962): 184.

151. *Societies*, p. 9; See also *System of Modern Societies*, p. 8.

152. *System of Modern Societies*, p. 12.

153. *Ibid.*, p. 26.

154. *Ibid.*, pp. 18–20.

sons uses aboriginal Australia as an example) and "advanced" primitive (some of the African kingdoms). The intermediate stage is divided into the archaic (the Indian subcontinent, China, Southeast Asia, the New World societies of the Aztecs, Mayans, and Incas, ancient Egypt, and the Mesopotamian empires) and the advanced, or historic, intermediate (China and India again, at different periods, the Islamic empires, and the Roman Empire). In addition, there are two "seed-bed" societies, Israel and Greece, which constitute a new type and not merely a new subdivision. These two societies are seen as highly significant for their cultural contributions to social evolution. They are also, however, "dead-end societies." By a process of negative selection they were eliminated in the sense that they did not become a part of the continuous process of evolutionary development, and no close approximation of these two societies exists in the modern world. The kingdoms of David and Solomon disappeared, as did the Greek city-states.[155]

System of Modern Societies is devoted, after another sketch of Parsons's theoretical orientation, to the modern type of society. It advances the thesis that this type emerged from the base of Western Christendom and that its single "evolutionary arena" is the West. If the Western system of societies succeeded when others have failed it is because it has exhibited a greater adaptive capacity. No comparable development occurred elsewhere in the world except through Western colonization and, in the case of Japan, Western influence. Emphasis is also given to the United States as "the new lead society," the "leader of the modern system."[156]

Parsons is uncomfortably aware that a certain ethnocentrism, not to say temporocentrism,[157] may color these propositions. He tries to build a defense against this indictment, however, on three grounds: Adaptive capacity may not be the highest human value; a "post-modern" phase may emerge with different characteristics; and the processes of cultural inclusion or diffusion may introduce into the system of modern society ingredients that have their origin elsewhere. Any current talk of postmodern society, however, is premature. Current trends into the next century will probably exhibit evolutionary completion of the type of modern society that now ex-

155. The expression "dead-end" is reminiscent of Arnold Toynbee's highly controversial characterization of Israel as a "fossil." See the critical essays in *Toynbee and History*, ed. M. F. Ashley Montagu (Boston: Porter Sargent, 1956), and especially "The Professor and the Fossil," pp. 316–319, by Frederick E. Robin, and "The Toynbee Heresy," pp. 320–337, by Abba Eban.

156. This is not "in the usual political sense but through structural innovations central to the main course of modern societal development." *System of Modern Societies*, p. 122.

157. Temporocentrism is the temporal analogue of ethnocentrism. See Bierstedt, "The Limitations of Anthropological Methods in Sociology" (1948), in *Power and Progress*, p. 127.

ists. With this prediction Parsons concludes his study of human societies in evolutionary perspective.

It is difficult to know what to say about it. A number of observations, however, would appear to have some relevance. In the first place, Parsons's theoretical apparatus overwhelms his evolutionary account of the transitions from primitive through intermediate to modern societies. It is true that he devotes only one chapter in each book to his conceptual scheme, but throughout he is more interested in the scheme than he is in the course of history. Here, and everywhere in his writings, the need to revise, elaborate, and vindicate his theory takes precedence over any subject matter to which it is applied.[158] Thus, we come to know little more about the evolution of modern societies from primitive societies than we did before.

A second observation concerns the evolutionary theory itself. Parsons is perfectly well aware that sociocultural evolution is not linear and even insists upon the point, distinguishing his conceptions from earlier ones, presumably those of Spencer and the Social Darwinists:

> Socio-cultural evolution, like organic evolution, has proceeded by variation and differentiation from simple to progressively more complex forms. Contrary to some early conceptions in the field, however, it has not proceeded in a single neatly definable line, but at every level has included a rather wide variety of different forms and types.[159]

But one can destroy a thesis by too much qualification, and this Parsons has a tendency to do. Furthermore, he fails to demonstrate linkages between the aboriginal Australians, for example, and any more "advanced" primitive society, or linkages between any African society and Mesopotamia, for example, and, as we have seen, chooses to regard Israel and ancient Greece as social systems that did not survive. If ancient Israel and ancient Greece are "dead-end" societies because neither survived as social systems, neither did the Roman Empire survive as a social system nor, for that matter, did the Holy Roman Empire. It is true, as Parsons says, that Roman law survived as a cultural system, but so also did Judaic religion and Greek philosophy. With respect to the claim that evolution proceeds from the simple to the complex, one can concede that the transition from medieval fief to modern nation seems like this kind of a change. But it would seem more appropriate, on the other hand, to describe the transition

158. There are exceptions; for example, Parsons's brilliant article on Christianity in the *International Encyclopedia of the Social Sciences,* which is entirely free of his ordinary conceptual language.

159. *Societies,* p. 2.

from Roman Empire to medieval fief as a change from the complex to the simple. As Alice might say, "How arbitrary everything is!"

The following passage raises still more questions: "It is reasonable to suppose that the evolutionary path from the earliest human societies to the present ones involved major jumps in adaptive capacity. Our thesis is that the emergence of the modern system of societies, through a complex process lasting several centuries, constituted such a jump."[160] The first question here is how "major jumps" are consistent with evolutionary theory, which, by definition, means slow and gradual change, in effect, continuous variation. Parsons tries to have it both ways by calling a "major jump" something that, he tells us in the same sentence, lasted several centuries. The second question is more serious. Parsons, like Spencer, whose evolutionary theory he regards as inferior, fails to offer an explanation of the evolutionary process. What is the urge, the push, the nisus, the cause? What is it that moves this great engine of evolution? We are told only that societies evolve and survive because of their "adaptive capacity." Here, unfortunately, we are reluctantly but irresistibly reminded of Molière's bourgeois gentleman, who explained that opium puts people to sleep because of its dormitive property. Furthermore, the proposition fails to explain why numerous societies are consigned to "niches," where they survive for long periods of time but do not "evolve."[161] According to the theory, these societies do not evolve because they have an adaptive capacity inferior to those that do evolve. But is it not equally reasonable to argue that they do not evolve precisely because they are so well adapted to their environments that there is no need or stimulus to change?

We may summarize the questionable aspects of Parsons's evolutionary theory as follows:

1. His interest in his conceptual scheme overwhelms his interest in the evolutionary progression of human societies.
2. His qualifications are so numerous that they call into question his central evolutionary thesis.
3. If the social organization of "dead-end" societies such as Israel and Greece did not carry through into a more advanced level, neither did the social organization of the Roman Empire.
4. Parsons asks us to believe that a complex process lasting several centuries constituted a "major jump" in adaptive capacity.
5. "Adaptive capacity" does not suffice as an explanation of so vast and complex a historical process. Parsons's engine of evolution lacks an ignition key.

---

160. *System of Modern Societies*, p. 3.

161. *Societies*, p. 110.

Conclusion

Even in this long chapter I have been unable to attend to many facets of Parsons's work. He has published, in addition to his many thematic books, six or seven volumes of essays, depending upon the way they are counted.[162] These essays cover a wide—indeed an incredibly wide—range of topics, from Christianity (mentioned earlier) to psychoanalysis. I have been unable especially to do justice to his work on the sociology of medicine (especially the doctor–patient relationship), on the economy and society, on personality, on the family, on education, and on such subjects as influence, power, and force. The best and most systematic treatment of the essays may be found in a small book by Guy Rocher.[163] Rocher, a sympathetic expositor and critic, nevertheless finds it necessary to remark that Parsons's writing "style" had done him a disservice in that it is "lourd et maladroit."[164]

Critics of Parsons have been severe and often harsh. Among them we can consider only two or three. One of the most penetrating is the philosopher Max Black, whose commentary on the pattern variables we have already discussed. On the Parsonian enterprise in general, he commends Parsons for his reach, for his imagination,[165] for his industry and ingenuity, and for his stimulating and pioneering labors. But his criticisms overwhelm his compliments. The first of these criticisms, offered by many other commentators as well, is that Parsons's system is essentially static, that although the basic concept is that of action, we see in fact little if any action but only orientation to action. The actor never acts, never moves, never approaches or attains the ends he seeks. Lewis Feuer, in agreement, says, "Action in the Parsonian system has a tendency to be translated into inaction."[166] And William Foote Whyte, also in agreement, writes, "In the

162. There is overlap in the first and second collections. See Parsons's explanation in "General Introduction," to *Social Systems and the Evolution of Action Theory,* p. 1.

163. *Talcott Parsons et la sociologie américaine* (Paris: Presses Universitaires de France, 1972).

164. *Ibid.*, p. 171. Among other books on Parsons in French and German, see Alois Gunter Brandenburg, *Systemzwant und Autonomie: Gesellschaft und Personalichkeit in der soziologischen Theorie von Talcott Parsons* (Düsseldorf: Bertelsmann Universitätsverlag, 1971); François Chazel, *La théorie analytique de la société dans l'oeuvre de Talcott Parsons,* (Paris: Mouton & Co. 1974); Heinrich Kunze, *Soziologische Theorie und Psychoanalyse: Freuds Begriff der Verdrängung und seine Rezeption durch Parsons* (Munich: W. Goldmann, 1972); and Helmut Notle, *Psychoanalyse und Soziologie: Die Systemtheorien Sigmund Freuds und Talcott Parsons'* (Bern: Hans Huber, 1970).

165. "Science needs men of imagination, willing to incur the risks of speculative construction." *Social Theories of Talcott Parsons,* ed. Black, p. 274.

166. Review of *Social Theories of Talcott Parsons,* p. 155.

world of Talcott Parsons, actors are constantly orienting themselves to situations and very rarely, if ever acting. The show is constantly in rehearsal, but the curtain never goes up."[167] Similarly, Parsons has emphasized throughout the corpus of his work statics rather than dynamics, systems in equilibrium rather than systems in conflict. As I have intimated, this is a criticism that has been emphasized by almost all of the commentators.[168]

Black and others have also noticed the conspicuous absence of causal propositions in Parsons's work. His pattern variables, his system-problems, and all of his quadrilateral figures and tables are classifications only and have nothing to do with causal inquiry. If, as Lucretius observed, happiness consists in seeking the causes of things, Parsons has not achieved that beneficent state. As Black remarks, "I would be surprised if genuinely causal laws could be shown to hold between 'orientations,' 'goals,' and the like."[169] The only significant approach to causal inquiry appears in the two small books on societies in comparative and evolutionary perspective, and there, as we have seen, the causal inferences are precarious indeed. For the most part, causal inquiry, like social change in general, simply fails to attract Parsons's attention. When it does, he throws up his hands and says that such knowledge cannot be achieved in our lifetime.

We have already remarked on the "systematic ambiguity" that Black finds in Parsons's concepts. This problem is related to another, namely, the source of these concepts. About this Black writes, "On the whole, it seems to me, the component concepts of Parsons' scheme are laymen's concepts in the thin disguise of a technical-sounding terminology."[170] And continuing:

> The following might be the result of trying to express Parsons' postulates in plain English:

---

167. "Parsonian Theory Applied to Organizations," in *Social Theories of Talcott Parsons*, ed. Black, p. 255.

168. See especially Ralf Dahrendorf, "Struktur und Funktion: Talcott Parsons und die Entwicklung der soziologischen Theorie," *Kölner Zeitschrift für Soziologie und Sozialpsychologie, vol. 12, no. 4 (1955);* and "Out of Utopia: Toward a Reorientation of Sociological Analysis," *American Journal of Sociology* 64 (September 1958): 115–127, reprinted in Dahrendorf, *Essays in the Theory of Society* (Palo Alto, Calif.: Stanford University Press, 1968), pp. 107–128. In the latter article he writes as follows: "Parsons' statement in *The Social System* that this 'work constitutes a step toward the development of a generalized theoretical system' is erroneous in every respect I can think of and, in particular, insofar as it implies that all sociological problems can be approached with the equilibrium model of society" (pp. 125–126). Dahrendorf prefers a conflict model. For an American effort to satisfy his preference, see Randall Collins, *Conflict Sociology: Toward an Explanatory Science* (New York: Academic Press, 1975).

169. *Social Theories of Talcott Parsons*, p. 278.

170. *Ibid.*, p. 279.

1. "Whenever you do anything, you're trying to get something done."
2. "What you do depends upon what you want, how you look at things, and the position you find yourself in."
3. "You can't do anything without thinking and having feelings at the same time."
4. "Human life is one long set of choices."
5. "Choosing means taking what seems best for you or what others say is the right thing."
6. "When you deal with other people, you always have to take account of what they expect you to do."
7. "There's a lasting pattern to the way people behave."
8. "Families, business firms, and other groups of persons often behave surprisingly like persons."[171]

These sentences, Black suggests, contain nearly all of the content of the Parsonian principles.[172] In his summary, Black writes,

> I am forced to conclude that Parsons' principles are not founded in empirical generalizations, in any plausible sense of "empirical generalizations." He has provided us with a web of concepts, whose correspondence with the concepts which laymen use for thinking about social relations and human action is barely disguised by a new terminology.[173]

Parsons was given, of course, an opportunity to respond to the criticisms of Black and his colleagues at Cornell in a long chapter that concludes Black's book. Unfortunately, Parsons does not genuinely confront more than two or three of these criticisms. Instead, he seizes the opportunity to develop further his own theory, especially that of the pattern-variables. When he does confront a criticism, he translates it into his own conceptual scheme, where, with the wave of a magic wand, it disappears. In response to the criticism of Whyte, for example, that there is no action in the action schema, he says that Whyte is looking for action on the wrong level. The physical behavior of organisms is no part of his concern. That would be another subsystem of action. In response to the criticism that the concept of equilibrium plays too prominent a part in his general theory, he writes:

> In my opinion this concept is an inherently essential part of the logic of science, of importance proportionate to the level of theoretical generality aimed at. The denial of its legitimacy in the conceptual armory of social science is at the least, in my perhaps not very humble opinion, symptomatic of the denial that social science itself is legitimate, or realistically possible. On this

171. *Ibid.*

172. C. Wright Mills similarly "translated" some of Parsons's paragraphs. See *The Sociological Imagination* (New York: Oxford University Press, 1959), chap. 2.

173. *Social Theoris of Talcott Parsons*, p. 283.

> point I have thus remained completely unimpressed by the barrage of persistent criticism.[174]

No one, of course, has denied the legitimacy of the concept. The problem is one of excessive emphasis to the neglect of concepts of far greater significance in studying the motions and commotions of human societies. In any event, it cannot be said that Parsons comes to terms with his Cornell critics.

A considerable portion of Alvin W. Gouldner's *The Coming Crisis of Western Sociology* is devoted to Talcott Parsons.[175] Unfortunately, much of it is political polemic. Gouldner's treatment, in fact, crosses the line that separates criticism from blame. He seems to regard as morally reprehensible Parsons's unconcern with the depression decade of the 1930s and his indulgence instead in detached, technical, and "self-engrossed" theory construction in sociology. The success of Parsons and the influence of his work Gouldner attributes primarily to the prestige of Harvard University and the ability of its social science faculty, "protected by a corporate university structure to define and pursue problems in terms of a relatively autonomous *technical* tradition, rather than in terms more responsive to publicly salient concerns."[176] This, of course, has been the function of universities since their founding in the Middle Ages. Although there is methodological and substantive criticism in Gouldner as well, most of his discussion is in this political vein.[177]

In a long essay on Parsons, Tom Bottomore raises a number of issues, many of them treated by other critics as well.[178] His first objection—that *Structure of Social Action* is deficient as an interpretation of a phase of European intellectual history—is answered, of course (as he himself

---

174. *Ibid.*, p. 338.

175. (New York: Basic Books, 1970). Part 2, pp. 167–338, is entitled "The World of Talcott Parsons."

176. *Ibid.*, p. 171. Parsons is

> singularly insensitive to the sheer suffering of the desperately afflicted. Nowhere is the word "poverty" mentioned in *The Structure of Social Action*, although it is written in the midst of a national experience with breadlines, unemployment, and hunger. Instead, Parsons' response is concerned to avoid institutional discontinuities and to maintain traditional loyalties; that is, he is concerned with discouraging radical social change. It is not so much the suffering of individuals as the resultant threat to the established culture, to which Parsons is responding. It is in this way a conservative response to a social crisis.

Ibid., p. 196.

177. Gouldner does object to the "promiscuous" proliferation of concepts in Parsons. "New distinctions are mated to produce new conceptual offspring, and they, in turn, are bred incestuously either with their parents or with one another to produce still another generation of concepts." *Ibid.*, p. 206.

178. "Out of This World," *New York Review of Books*, November 6, 1969, pp. 34–39.

recognizes), by the fact that the book was never intended to be such an interpretation. Thus, the omission of Marx and Freud (especially) can hardly be regarded as a flaw, however great their importance in other contexts.[179] Bottomore argues next that Parsons has offered no thoroughgoing *philosophical* analysis of his basic concept, the concept of action. This is indubitably the case. It may be remarked, on the other hand, that every system of thought contains at least one primitive and undefined term. Without it discourse could not begin.[180]

Like other critics, Bottomore notes the abstract level on which Parsons's theory proceeds—so abstract indeed that it poses no fundamental questions about American or any other society.[181] Again, order and stability are Parsons's concerns, and he pays no attention to strain, conflict, and change. Indeed, Parsons seems insensitive to the social and political issues of his society. The result is a kind of intellectual isolation from the currents of the time, a body of work that has simply made no entry into contemporary social and political thought. One reason for this is Parsons's language. "A deeper reason perhaps is that Parsons's work generally fails to arouse any intellectual excitement or sense of discovery, and this failure is certainly connected with the fact that much of what he actually says about social life, when expressed in ordinary language, proves to be commonplace."[182]

For Bottomore the source of many of the defects in Parsons's work is not his political conservatism—indeed, politically he is a liberal—but rather is his curious notion of the nature of sociological theory. In the first place, his theory is limited to the construction of conceptual schemes. Nowhere does he strive for empirical generalizations of the sort that led Marx to try to explain the French Revolution, Weber to explain the rise of capitalism, or

179. Parsons has published at least two extended treatments of Marx: "Social Classes and Class Conflict in the Light of Recent Sociological Theory" (1949), chap. 15 in *Essays in Sociological Theory*, rev. ed. (Glencoe, Ill.: Free Press, 1954), pp. 323–335; and "Some Comments on the Sociology of Karl Marx," chap. 4 in *Sociological Theory and Modern Society* (New York: Free Press, 1967), pp. 102–135. The total absence of American names in *The Social System*—"writers whose work has given us our conceptual tools"—is the subject of a caustic complaint by Ellsworth Faris. *American Sociological Review* 18 (February 1953): 103–106.

180. For the same reason, every definition is ultimately circular. A logical fact, however, need not be a logical deficiency if the circle, as Herbert Feigl once expressed it, is not too small.

181. Parsons's abstractions have worried almost everyone. Sorokin, for example, refers to Parsons's work as an "orgy" of abstractions. *Sociological Theories of Today* (New York: Harper & Row, 1966), p. 433n. Sorokin's treatment of Parsons in this book is consistently hostile. Similarly, William Foote Whyte has written of the absence of data to accompany Parsons's concepts. In *Social Theories of Talcott Parsons*, ed. Black, pp. 255–262. And the present writer has remarked on the absence of empirical referents. "The Means-End Schema," pp. 31–40.

182. "Out of This World," p. 36.

Durkheim to explain the variable incidence of suicide. In these cases a problem is perceived and an explanation sought. "In Parsons' work it is just this focus of attention which is lacking from the outset, since in his original interpretation of the classical sociologists he disregards the question of the validity of their explanations in order to concentrate upon the nature of the concepts which they employ."[183] It is precisely the absence of a problem that is so noticeable in Parsons.[184] In the second place, Parsons has not thought it necessary to include in his conception of theory any discussion of the logic or methodology of sociological inquiry. Those sociologists with the greatest eminence have wondered about the possibilities and limits of sociological knowledge and about the nature of causal propositions in social thought. In Parsons we find no such curiosity. At the very least he should have examined the logical foundations of his own theory.

At the end of his essay Bottomore returns to Parsons's isolation from the social, political, and intellectual currents of his time and concludes with the question "How is it possible to discover a vital interest and concern, a clear direction, in thought which is so willfully irrelevant?"[185]

The roster of Parsons's critics is quite long, and it would be profitless to examine it in detail. Although the critics are clearly in the majority, it is erroneous to assume that he has no followers. Among those whose work has been built upon Parsonian foundations one would include especially Marion J. Levy, Jr., and Harry M. Johnson.[186] He has been the subject of a number of books, not only in English but also, as we have seen, in other languages.[187] At least two books have been written in his honor, one in two

183. *Ibid.*, p. 37.

184. Dahrendorf makes the same point. How can sociologists, of all people, lose touch with the riddles of experience? How can they have lost their "problem-consciousness"? "Out of Utopia," p. 124. Similarly, Robert Nisbet writes, "It is a truth we should never tire of repeating that no genuinely good or seminal work in the history of sociology was written or conceived as a means of advancing theory—grand or small. Each has been written in response to a single, compelling intellectual problem or challenge provided by the immediate intellectual environment." *Sociology as an Art Form* (New York: Oxford University Press, 1976), p. 20. For Nisbet's criticism of Parsons on societies in evolution, see pp. 96–98. Nisbet claims that Parsons has given us not change but only the illusion of change.

185. "Out of This World," p. 39.

186. Marion J. Levy, Jr., *The Structure of Society* (Princeton, N.J.: Princeton, University Press, 1952); and Harry M. Johnson, *Sociology: A Systematic Introduction* (New York: Harcourt Brace, 1960).

187. In addition *Social Theories of Talcott Parsons*, see Herman Turk and Richard L. Simpson, eds., *Institutions and Social Exchange: The Sociologies of Talcott Parsons and George C. Homans* (Indianapolis, Ind.: Bobbs-Merrill, 1971); William Mitchell, *Sociological Analysis and Politics: The Theories of Talcott Parsons* (Englewood Cliffs, N.J.: Prentice-Hall, 1967);

volumes.[188] No one disputes the rare distinction that Talcott Parsons has achieved, a distinction that the present writer too is glad to celebrate.

I belong, however, as is clearly apparent, to the ranks of Parsons's critics. His work contains a fatal flaw. It conveys no sense of the intellectual problems posed by the nature of society, as does the work, for example, of the great names in the history of social thought, beginning with Plato and Aristotle and continuing through Comte and Spencer, and on to our own day. It gives us no sense of society, as we find it, for example, in the work of MacIver and Sorokin. Instead, we constantly confront something called a social system, which is a logical construction of the sociologist's mind rather than a phenomenon of an actual world. When Parsons announces a "breakthrough" or an "advance" in sociological theory—something he does all too often—it means not that he has discovered something new about society or social relationships or even social action. It means only that he has noticed a symmetry or parallelism among the concepts in his own conceptual scheme. Sometimes, alternatively, it means that he has conjured up a new concept—or, more likely, four new concepts—that will disclose hitherto undetected relationships between concepts already members of his system. In no case do these discoveries produce new knowledge. After he has constructed his general theory of action we know no more about social actions than we did before. Indeed, Lester Frank Ward and Florian Znaniecki both told us more about social actions than Parsons has.

The Parsonian enterprise is for the most part a sad picture of misdirected industry. A child noticed that the emperor was naked. In the case of Parsons there is plenty of clothing—but no emperor. To change the figure, in Parsons we have a structure that is all scaffolding and no building. To change the figure again, we meet in Parsons a master at chess, a suzerain of the 64 squares, whose game, like that of other chess masters, bears no conceivable relationship to the society in which it is played. When we read Parsons we are reminded of Hippolyte Taine, who said of his contem-

and Harold J. Bershady, *Ideology and Social Knowledge* (Oxford: Basil Blackwell, 1973). Parsons's review of the Bershady book is reprinted in Parsons, *Social Systems and the Evolution of Action Theory*, together with Bershady's response to Parsons. See also Thomas Burger, "Talcott Parsons, the Problem of Order in Society, and the Program of an Analytical Sociology," *American Journal of Sociology* 83 (September 1977): 320–334, together with Parsons's "Comment on Burger's Critique," immediately following, pp. 335–339, and the extensive bibliography, pp. 332–334.

188. Jan J. Loubser, Rainer C. Baum, Andrew Effrat, and Victor Meyer Lidz, eds., *Explorations in General Theory in Social Science: Essays in Honor of Talcott Parsons* (New York: Free Press, 1976).

porary Maine de Biran: "His bad style has made him a great man. If he had not been obscure we should not have believed him profound."

We are reminded finally of Immanuel Kant. In the *Critique of Pure Reason* he teaches, among others, two fundamental lessons. One of them Parsons always knew—that percepts without concepts are blind. The other he never learned—that concepts without percepts are empty.

CHAPTER 10

Robert K. Merton

It would seem reasonable to suppose that sociology will advance in the degree that its major concern is with developing theories of the middle range and will be frustrated if attention centers on theory in the large.

—*Social Theory and Social Structure*, p. 9

Robert K. Merton was born on July 5, 1910, in the slums of South Philadelphia to parents of Eastern European origin. He remembers the slum as a lively, noisy, and interesting place, and as a child he participated with zest in the gang warfare—largely ceremonial, he says—that was a constant feature of the city streets. At the age of eight he had already discovered the public library and had begun to devour its delights. At the age of twelve he was introduced to delights of a different kind, namely, the art of conjuring, at which he became so proficient that he was able to earn from $5 to $10 a performance at various school and neighborhood groups.[1] In 1927 he went to Temple University on a scholarship and almost immediately distinguished himself by the caliber of his academic work. Two of his teachers there were James Dunham, the philosopher, and George E. Simpson, the sociologist, and it was the latter's discipline, of course, to which he made his career commitment.

In 1931, at the age of twenty one, Merton won a fellowship that took him to Harvard and graduate work in sociology. The department had been founded by Sorokin only a year before, and Merton became a member of the first group of students to whom instruction was offered. Among important influences there, in addition to Sorokin, were L. J. Henderson, the biochemist, George Sarton, the historian of science, and the young Talcott Parsons, then an assistant professor. Merton began to publish early in such journals as *Social Forces*, the *American Journal of Sociology*, the *American Sociological Review*, the *Quarterly Journal of Economics*, *Sociology and Social Research*, *Isis*, and the *Scientific Monthly*. He began to write his doctoral dissertation in 1933 and completed it two years later. It was first

1. These and other biographical details are from a "Profile" of Merton written by Morton M. Hunt that appeared in the *New Yorker* (January 28, 1961).

published in *Osiris* in 1938 as *Science, Technology and Society in Seventeenth-Century England.*

In 1934 Merton became an instructor and tutor at Harvard. In the same year he married Suzanne Carhart, a social worker who had also been a student at Temple. After five years in the Harvard post he was appointed first associate professor and then professor at Tulane University, where he also served as chairman of the department. Two years later, in 1941, he accepted appointment as assistant professor of sociology at Columbia University, where he spent the remainder of his teaching career.

In 1963 Merton was appointed Franklin Henry Giddings Professor of Sociology and was later given Columbia's highest rank, that of University Professor, a rank shared by such men as I. I. Rabi, the physicist, Jacques Barzun, the historian, Meyer Schapiro, the art historian, and Ernest Nagel, the philosopher. Reversing the usual sequence, he served as president of the American Sociological Association in 1956–1957 and president of the Eastern Sociological Society in 1968–1969. He holds honorary degrees from Temple, Emory, Loyola (Chicago), Kalamazoo, Western Reserve, Chicago, Tulane, Colgate, Yale, Leyden, Wales, and Harvard.

Archilochus reputedly said that the fox knows many things, but the hedgehog knows one big thing.[2] To the extent that this is indeed the case, we should have to refer to Merton as a fox.[3] The range of his interests has been unusually wide. A glance at his bibliography indicates that he has written on science, housing, mass persuasion, the interview, business administration, the student-physician, the freedom to read, social problems, Durkheim, Le Bon, Arabian intellectual development, invention, military technique, civilization, population, time, the sociology of knowledge, bureaucracy, personality, crime, the family, questionnaires and scales, radio and film propaganda, discrimination, mass communication, public opinion polling, influence, research policy, epidemiology, friendship, medical schools, professions, the corporation, quantification, genius, nursing, anomy, leadership, and aging.[4] If sociology were defined as that which sociologists do, one would have to conclude that in Merton's case

2. Isaiah Berlin elaborates on this theme in his small book, *The Hedgehog and the Fox, An Essay on Tolstoy's View of History* (New York: Simon & Schuster, 1953).

3. It would delight Merton—fascinated as he is by similar and independent occurrences—to know that these lines were written before the writer read Lewis Coser's use of the figure in his tribute to Merton in Coser, ed., *The Idea of Social Structure, Papers in Honor of Robert K. Merton* (New York: Harcourt Brace Jovanovich, 1975).

4. For a comprehensive bibliography to 1975 see Mary Wilson Miles, "The Writings of Robert K. Merton: A Bibliography," *ibid.*, pp. 497–516. Appended is a respectably long bibliography of commentaries on Merton's work.

sociology is a rummage sale rather than a discipline. At the same time, although he is altogether and enviably proficient in sociological theory, he has never produced a systematic theory or a system of sociology. This would seem to be a rather curious omission in one who has written so much at so high a level of competence. It is especially odd in view of the fact that both of his mentors at Harvard—Sorokin and Parsons—produced systematic sociological theory. Indeed, if I may anticipate my critical conclusion, this is the most puzzling and significant question we can ask about Merton's place in the history of sociology. There is, in short, no book about society.

The Sociology of Science

Our concentration in this chapter will be on Merton's sociological theory, and I shall make no effort, therefore, to describe or to view critically what he has written on the many other subjects, mentioned earlier. One of these, however, merits special mention, and that is the sociology of science. To ask what Merton has contributed to this area of inquiry is almost to ask the wrong question. The sociology of science is a sea over which he exercises an admiral's suzerainty. It was he who explored it, surveyed it, and drew its charts. Historians of science we have had, and philosophers of science too, but not—until Merton—sociologists of science. Sociologists had readily turned their attention to the institutions of society—government, religion, business, education, even recreation—but none had inquired into the institution of science. Sociologists had studied thieves, hoboes, and prostitutes but had exhibited little interest in scientists. It was this deficiency, under the special influence of Sarton and Sorokin, that Merton set out to repair.

It began with his youthful doctoral dissertation, *Science, Technology and Society in Seventeenth-Century England.*[5] In a graceful preface to the 1970 edition he writes:

> The inquiry began as he was rummaging about in seventeenth-century England, trying to make some sense of the remarkable efflorescence of science at that time and place, being directed in the search by a general sociological orientation. The orientation was simple enough: various institutions in the society are variously interdependent so that what happens in the economic or

5. Harper Torchbook edition (New York: Harper & Row, 1970). Quotations are from this edition.

> religious realm is apt to have some perceptible connections with some of what happens in the realm of science, and conversely. In the course of reading the letters, diaries, memoirs and papers of seventeenth-century men of science, the author slowly noted the frequent religious commitments of scientists in this time, and even more, what seemed to be their Puritan orientation. Only then, and almost as though he had not been put through his paces during the course of graduate study, was he belatedly put in mind of that intellectual tradition, established by Max Weber, Troeltsch, Tawney and others, which centered on the interaction between the Protestant ethic and the emergence of modern capitalism. Swiftly making amends for this temporary amnesia, the author turned to a line-by-line reading of Weber's work to see whether he had anything at all to say about the relation of Puritanism to science and technology. Of course, he had.[6]

In the Preface Merton also expresses surprise that most of the commentators on his book attend only to the relationship between Puritanism and science and ignore three other subjects—recruitment to various occupational fields and shifts of interest among the sciences; economic and military influences on the spectrum of scientific investigation; and population, social interaction, and science. In sheer quantity, as he shows, he devoted more pages and a higher percentage of content to the second of these than to the Puritan thesis. Furthermore, he confesses that he himself is "more partial" to the part of the book dealing with the influence of economic and military factors on the growth of science. He therefore finds the responses of the commentators odd.

As Merton must realize, his brief quantitative comparison has little to do with the case. The reason that his thesis on the relationship between Puritanism and science attracted almost all of the attention is precisely because it is so closely related to the great work of Weber on the relationship between Puritanism and capitalism. Is it possible that Martin Luther and John Calvin had something to do with the development of science in the seventeenth century, as they had with the development of capitalism in the eighteenth and nineteenth? Such a thesis would reverse the conventional conclusions about the relationship between religion and science, as characterized by the title of Andrew Dickson White's classic work, *The History of the Warfare of Science with Theology in Christendom.* If the conflict was obvious on the surface—after all, Galileo had been summoned to the bar of the dreaded Inquisition once in 1616 and five times in 1633 for daring to believe, and to publish, that the earth moved around the sun—it

6. *Ibid.*, p. xvii. What Weber had said was that one of the future tasks in his line of inquiry would be to trace the influence of ascetic rationalism upon scientific empiricism and technology. "Once identified," Merton concludes, "Weber's recommendation became a mandate."

is nevertheless the case, if Merton's thesis is correct, that there was something about the Protestant ethic that served as an encouragement to the growth of science. Although clearly unconscious of it, Richard Baxter, in writing his *Christian Directory*, was contributing to the mood and temper that would result in science. As Merton says,

> It is evident that the formal organization of values constituted by Puritanism led to the largely unwitting furtherance of modern science. The Puritan complex of a scarcely disguised utilitarianism; of intramundane interests; methodical, unremittent action; thoroughgoing empiricism; of the right and even the duty of *libre examen*; of anti-traditionalism—all this was congenial to the same values in science. The happy marriage of these two movements was based on an intrinsic compatibility and even in the nineteenth century, their divorce was not yet final.[7]

Like Weber before him, Merton does not rest with mere assertions of "intrinsic compatibility" or "elective affinity." He introduces evidence to show that Protestant academies in France emphasized scientific instruction to a far greater extent than the Catholic ones, that even in a Catholic country like France Protestants made more than their share of contributions to science, and that Huguenot exiles from France included a large number of scientists. Similarly, Pietists in Germany encouraged the introduction of scientific subjects into the universities in that country. In Prussia—although here Merton moves to the nineteenth century—more Protestants than Catholics are found in schools that emphasize scientific training. In short, available statistics show a preponderance of Protestants among scientists. It is unnecessary to repeat here either Merton's evidence or more of his argument than is necessary to exhibit his procedure. He is profoundly impressed, for example, by the fact that in Havelock Ellis's list of outstanding British scientists, twenty one were from Protestant Scotland and only one from Catholic Ireland.[8] In fact, it is the quantitative character of the book that attracted attention and applause and won for Merton the label of quantitative historian.

The second thesis that Merton advanced concerned the influence of economic and military factors upon scientific development. Here he turns the equation around, so to speak, and considers the utility of science for developing technologies in mining, transportation, navigation, reforestation, and the manufacture of the weapons of war. In short, science also

7. *Ibid.*, p. 136.

8. If one considers notable actors, the proportions are reversed: Ireland produced many, Scotland almost none. *Ibid.*, p. 132. The land of John Knox was not hospitable to the theatrical profession.

prospered because of its utility for the practical affairs of life.[9] In his concluding chapter Merton has a look at a number of miscellaneous factors that have had something to do with scientific advance, including population density, social interaction, the cultural context, utilitarianism, and the belief in progress.

Now Merton is not so "fatuous" (his word) as to suppose, much less to claim, that the Protestant Reformation was somehow necessary to the advancement of science in England or anywhere else in the seventeenth century, or that without that Reformation modern science would have been impossible. Furthermore, he is perfectly well aware of the many contributions to science and especially to medicine made in the same century by men who lived and worked in the Catholic cities of Italy. All he wants to claim is that, *as it happened* (his italics), Puritanism provided not exclusive, not indispensable, but major support for science in that particular period of history. As he says in the final sentence of the book itself, a sentence that continued to give him satisfaction in 1970, "On the basis of the foregoing study, it may not be too much to conclude that the cultural soil of seventeenth century England was peculiarly fertile for the growth and spread of science."

The book has had its critics. Merton lists their papers in his 1970 bibliography and deals harshly with one of them, Lewis S. Feuer,[10] in his Preface. In any event, it is not to be supposed that Merton's doctoral dissertation exhausts his contributions to the sociology of science. In succeeding decades he published more than twenty papers on the subject, papers collected and published by Norman W. Storer.[11] Of the Storer book, Joseph Ben-David, himself a sociologist of science, comments, "This collection of papers is, and is likely to remain for a long time, one of the most important books in sociology. . . . They are one of the few examples of sociology as science; of a series of discoveries based on meticulous research which have

---

9. For a summary of the "utilities" of science, see *ibid.*, the 1970 Preface, pp. xx–xxi.

10. *The Scientific Intellectual* (New York: Basic Books, 1963). See also Randall Collins, who writes,

> The "Merton thesis" on Puritanism has almost no supporters among historians and historical sociologists of science; there were far too many Catholic scientists in the seventeenth century (an overwhelming number, outside of England), and in England itself it turns out that most of the Royal Society members, and its most eminent figures, were not real Puritans at all, but latitudinarians and backsliders.

Review of *The Idea of Social Structure: Papers in Honor of Robert K. Merton*, ed. Lewis A. Coser, in *Contemporary Sociology* (March 1977): 151.

11. Robert K. Merton, *The Sociology of Science*, ed. Norman W. Storer (Chicago: University of Chicago Press, 1973).

generated new research, and which stood up to the test of re-examination over a prolonged period of time."[12]

Sociological Theory

If Merton has not himself given us a theory of society, or of the social order, he has nevertheless written a great deal on sociological theory. These writings consist of separate papers, published at various times, and then brought together in collections, which are then themselves revised and enlarged. Thus we have *Social Theory and Social Structure,* first published in 1949, with a revised and enlarged edition in 1957 and another enlarged edition in 1968. The introduction to this book was expanded into two chapters and appears with the three originally grouped together under the rubric "Sociological Theory" in a book entitled *On Theoretical Sociology: Five Essays Old and New,* to which we shall now attend.[13]

In the first of these chapters, entitled "On the History and Systematics of Sociological Theory," Merton makes a sharp distinction between the history of sociological theory on the one hand and the systematic substance of current sociological theory on the other. Confusion of these two separate but related enterprises, he says, is "artless," and indeed he indulges in some pejorative remarks about the former. The kind of history to which he objects is that represented by this very book, namely, an exposition and criticism of past theories, "spiced with short biographies of major theorists." This kind of history he calls "parochial" and "almost Pickwickian," and indeed an anomaly in a period when the historians of science themselves are beginning to use sociological methods in their research. "The rationale for the history of science,"he writes, "is to achieve an understanding of how things came to develop as they did in a certain science or in a complex of sciences, not merely to put synopses of scientific theory in chronological order."[14] He demands something he calls "authentic histories" of sociological theory:

> These would have the ingredients and formal characteristics of the better histories of other sciences. They would take up such matters as the complex filiation of sociological ideas, the ways in which they developed, the connec-

12. *New York Times Book Review,* November 11, 1973, p. 34. For a different view of Merton as a sociologist of science, see Collin's review of *Idea of Social Structure,* pp. 151–152.
13. (New York: Free Press, 1967).
14. *Ibid.,* p. 3.

> tions of theory with the changing social origins and subsequent social statuses of its exponents, the interaction of theory with the changing social organization of sociology, the diffusion of theory from centers of sociological thought and its modification on the course of diffusion, and the ways in which it was influenced by changes in the environing culture and social structure.[15]

What Merton wants, in short, is a sociological history of sociological theory.

One of the troubles with the traditional history of theory in sociology is that it deals only with theories as they appear in print—the actual products, as it were—and takes no account of the road the theorist traveled in arriving at his conclusions. Traditional histories take no account of "intuitive leaps, false starts, mistakes, loose ends, and happy accidents that actually cluttered up the inquiry."[16] Merton introduces apt quotations from Bacon and Leibniz to support his position. Let us have not only the materials of the history of science but the raw materials as well. Only then can we understand how a science develops. In fact, he views with approval Lester Frank Ward's six-volume *Glimpses of the Cosmos* as exemplifying the kind of material we need to have in order to do justice to the history of sociological theory. In the Foreword that he wrote to Lewis A. Coser's *Masters of Sociological Thought* he compliments the author for producing exactly the kind of history of sociological theory that he recommends, and especially for bringing that history into some kind of relationship with the social, economic, and political conditions under which it appeared.

Merton clearly has a point in these observations. It would be an important point if the history of sociological theory resembled the construction of a building, with each workman contributing so many bricks and building on top of the bricks earlier contributed by others and with the whole elegant in design, a work of art and artifice, a pleasure to behold. Unfortunately, sociological theory as we know it today is not the kind of logically ordered structure that Merton has in mind. Instead, it is a series of essays, of views of the nature of society presented by men as different as Sumner and Cooley or Sorokin and Parsons. Sociology is not unfortunately a single edifice, as it would be if it were the kind of science that Lundberg, for example, and Merton wish it to be. It is rather a number of structures as different as the architectural styles of Sanford White, Frank Lloyd Wright, Walter Gropius, and I. M. Pei. The history of sociological theory resembles the history of philosophy much more than it does the history of any of the sciences.

---

15. *Ibid.*, p. 2.
16. *Ibid.*, p. 4.

What Merton is asking for is no less than the application of all the resources of the sociology of knowledge—itself an inexact science—to the history of sociological theory. It is almost certainly an unattainable goal. Who could trace the changes in the "environing culture and social structure" that have influenced the course of sociological theory? The effort to do so, as in Lewis A. Coser's otherwise splendid book,[17] results in the hauling in of information—such as the date (1835) when the Krupps installed their first steam engine, the number of people (50,000) in the British Civil Service in 1880, and the fact that the annual production of pig iron in the United States increased by a factor of sixteen from the end of the 1860s to the end of the century—that only the wispy skeins of fantasy could relate to sociological theory. It is much more likely in fact that the sociological theories of Spencer and Sumner set the tone of English and American industrial society during the decades mentioned than the other way around.

It is doubtless true, as the philosopher Whitehead used to say, that there is no unrelated thing in the universe. Everything can ultimately be related to everything else, and by a process of free association one can find some connection, for example, between a hockey stick and the transcendental unity of apperception of Immanuel Kant. But this is not to say that it is a meritorious enterprise to find relationships as tenuous as these. Furthermore, Merton's recommendations beg the entire question posed by the sociology of knowledge. Suppose, on the contrary, that the realm of ideas is an autonomous realm, that the history of ideas—including sociological theories—is determined not by environing conditions but only by antecedent ideas—as Kant, for example, was awakened from his dogmatic slumbers by David Hume. Suppositions that environing conditions have everything to do with ideas and that they have nothing to do with them are both extreme. The truth doubtless lies between. But if one had to answer all of Merton's questions, including the social status of the theorist, in order to write what he calls an "authentic history" of sociological theory, it is doubtful if the history of sociological theory could be written at all. His reach exceeds the grasp of anyone—even that of Lewis Coser. Finally, although Ward's *Glimpses of the Cosmos* is choice intellectual entertainment, it is little more than that. It neither adds to nor detracts from our appreciation and understanding of Ward's sociological theory. We should be relieved that other sociological theorists did not follow his six-volume example.

There is another matter in these pages to which one may take exception.

17. *Masters of Sociological Thought*, 2nd ed. (New York: Harcourt Brace Jovanovich, 1977).

In the Introduction to *Social Theory and Social Structure,* but not repeated in the two-chapter expansion of that Introduction in *On Theoretical Sociology,* Merton takes a position on the relationship between theory and research that does not win universal assent. Here, in contrast to his supposition discussed earlier, he recognizes that sociological theory is not cumulative:

> The clearly visible fact is that the early history of sociology—as represented, for example, in the speculations of a Comte or a Spencer, a Hobhouse or a Ratzenhofer—is very far from cumulative. The conceptions of each seldom build upon the work of those who have gone before. They are typically laid out as alternative and competing conceptions rather than consolidated and extended into a cumulative product. Consequently, little of what these early forerunners wrote remains pertinent to sociology today. Their works testify to the large merits of talented men, but they do not often provide guidelines to the current analysis of sociological problems.[18]

The noncumulative character of sociological theory, which Merton concedes in this passage, is not consonant with the kind of sociological history of sociological theory that he demands in the other passage.

Here, however, we have another issue in mind. Why should the theories of the talented men mentioned by Merton "provide guidelines to the current analysis of sociological problems?" Surely it was not their intention to do so. Again, and earlier on the same page, Merton allows us to learn what our predecessors have said about society as an adjunct to our training but insists that "it is no substitute for training in the actual use of theory in research." Here Merton appears to be denigrating any theory that is not useful in research.[19] Surely it is an odd notion that theory somehow has to justify itself by being useful for research. The notion that sociological theory is "an analytical tool," an instrument that helps to carry on research, is surely an erroneous or at least a wayward one. Of what use is Kant's *Critique of Pure Reason* or Locke's *Essay Concerning Human Knowledge* in research? Similarly, why should one expect Ward's *Dynamic Sociology,* Sumner's *Folkways,* or, for that matter, Merton's *Science,*

18. *Social Theory and Social Structure,* rev. ed. (New York: Free Press of Glencoe, 1957), Introduction, p. 5; see also pp. 23, 26–29.

19. Similarly Parsons, writing on the sociological theories of the past, says, "Generally speaking, as total systems they have not proved usable by the contemporary research social scientists, and those smaller elements of them which are useful have for the most part become incorporated into more recent work in more usable form than the original." "The Position of Sociological Theory," *American Sociological Review* 13 (April 1948): 157, n. 3. For elaborations of my disagreement with both Merton and Parsons on this issue, see Robert Bierstedt, *Power and Progress: Essays in Sociological Theory* (New York: McGraw-Hill, 1974), pp. 146–147, 161–162.

Technology and Society in Seventeenth-Century England to be useful in research? Why this emphasis upon utility—a criterion that Merton himself cautioned against in his youthful dissertation[20]—and especially such a narrow utility—utility in research, not utility for the advantage of mankind?

Merton will have much more to say about the relationship between theory and research in sociology. For the moment, therefore, let me suggest only that it is research that should be useful to theory, that theory is the end product of our endeavors and not the starting point, that theories of society such as those produced by our predecessors are an end in themselves and require no utilitarian justification, that the function of research is to accumulate evidence that will support or refute our theories, and that theory is the goal for which the game is played. Knowledge in the form of theory is the end of inquiry, in both senses of the word *end*, and it is a good in itself.

In the essay under consideration, Merton goes on to explore continuities and discontinuities in sociological theory and observes, "The historian of ideas runs the risk either of claiming to find a continuity of thought where it did not in fact exist or of failing to identify continuity where it did exist."[21] He then indulges in one of his favorite exercises—a treatment of independent multiple inventions, of rediscoveries of old ideas, of anticipations of new ones, and of adumbrations, all characteristic of the history of thought.[22] Here Merton elaborates in fascinating detail one of his favorite apothegms, namely, the observation of Whitehead that "everything of importance has been said before by somebody who did not discover it."[23] He finds Shakespeare anticipating Freud, Epictetus anticipating W. I. Thomas,

20. See *Science, Technology and Society*, pp. 228–232. After quoting Bacon, Hobbes, Locke, and Shaftesbury in statements praising such knowledge and only such knowledge as is useful, Merton goes on to write:

> But a crude utilitarianism is not an unfailing cultural basis for the espousal of science. In its extreme form, the norm of utility, narrowly interpreted, imposes a limitation on science, since it then finds science desirable only insofar as it is directly profitable. The intellectual myopia involved in this point of view precludes any attention to basic studies which do not promise immediate fruits.

Ibid., pp. 230–231. This passage is qualified, of course, by such adjectives as *crude* and *extreme*, but the intent is clear.

21. *On Theoretical Sociology*, p. 8.

22. Discoveries and rediscoveries refer to substantial identity between ideas, anticipations to resemblances rather than identities, and adumbrations to mere foreshadowing of later ideas. *Ibid.*, p. 13.

23. He might also have quoted in this connection Whitehead's observation that the entire history of Western philosophy is but a series of footnotes to Plato. To which his younger colleague at Harvard, Raphael Demos, an authority on Plato, retorted, "Plato should have written the footnotes himself!"

Sumner anticipating Walter Lippmann, an example of the "Hawthorne effect" in John Stuart Mill, and a seventeenth-century example of the self-fulfilling prophecy in Pierre Gassendi. Examples such as these, he says, are easy to find, but he warns that "they easily degenerate into an antiquarianism that does not advance the *history* of sociological theory at all but merely duplicates that battle between advocates of the Ancients and the Moderns which used up so much intellectual energy in the seventeenth and eighteenth centuries."[24] Somewhere along the line Merton might have quoted the author of the Book of Ecclesiastes, who wrote that there is nothing new under the sun.

The notion of cumulation in the advancement of knowledge continues to occupy Merton in a section where he compares the physical sciences, the social sciences, and the humanities in this respect. The social sciences, of course, inhabit the middle position, not so cumulative as the physical sciences but more so than the humanities. When he reflects upon the study of classic works of sociology, identified by name as those of Comte, Marx, Spencer, Durkheim, Weber, Simmel, Pareto, Sumner, Cooley, and Veblen,[25] he again appeals to the criterion of utility: "The study of classical writings can be either deplorably useless or wonderfully useful. It all depends on the form that study takes. For a vast difference separates the anemic practices of mere commentary or banalization from the active practice of following up and developing the theoretical leads of significant predecessors."[26] Again, why is it not enough to say that the classic writings are thrilling, exciting, enriching, intellectually rewarding? Why do they also have to be useful? The answer is that Merton, for all of his superior sophistication and erudition, has basically the same view of sociology as Lundberg. Both see sociology as a science that *develops*, that develops moreover by both factual and theoretical increments until it constitutes a coherent body of knowledge.

After a discussion of the tension that obtains between erudition and originality in the history of science, Merton moves to the functions—or uses, if you will—of classical theory in sociology. They are five in number. First, knowledge of the classics prevents rediscoveries of what has previously been said or known. Second, and related to the first, one can sometimes find in the classics ideas that one has in mind but has not perhaps clearly formulated. Third, one may find something that casts doubt upon an idea or proposition that one is currently entertaining. Fourth, the classics provide a model for intellectual work and help to form

24. *Ibid.*, p. 19.
25. *Ibid.*, p. 29.
26. *Ibid.*, p. 30.

standards of taste and judgment.[27] Fifth, and finally, the classics are worth rereading because they offer a different harvest when read at different ages. Only in this last do we find a suggestion, however faint, that the classics are worth reading for themselves.

On "Sociological Theories of the Middle Range"

The second of the five essays in Merton's small book carries the title "Sociological Theories of the Middle Range." It is a relatively long elaboration of a few pages in the Introduction to *Social Theory and Social Structure.* Merton will later on delve into the many meanings of the word *theory* but here he is concerned to say, "Throughout this book, the term *sociological theory* refers to logically interconnected sets of propositions from which empirical uniformities can be derived."[28] It is a definition that presents certain difficulties. In the first place, the nature of the logical interconnectedness is not indicated. Is it the kind of relationship that propositions in a syllogism or a sorites have to one another? Presumably not. In the second place, Merton does not tell us what these propositions are about. Are they about society, about behavior, about social relationships in general? He deserves immediate exoneration on this count, however, on the ground that he does not here intend to discuss the subject matter of sociology. In the third place, theory is again conceived of as a utility rather than as a product; it is useful in the process of deriving empirical uniformities. And in the fourth place, it is not clear that empirical uniformities are derived. They may be perceived, they may be discovered, but the sense in which they are derived from a set of propositions is not clear.

In any event, Merton wants to discuss theories of the middle range. They are "theories that lie between the minor but necessary working hypotheses that evolve in abundance during day-to-day research and the all-inclusive systematic efforts to develop a unified theory that will explain all the observed uniformities of social behavior, social organization and social change."[29] They are used primarily to guide empirical inquiry. Examples of middle range theories are the theory of reference groups, the theory of relative deprivation, and Merton's own theory of the role-set. In each case, according to Merton, the theory generates theoretical problems—problems

27. Surely, in dissent, one would not recommend that anyone today imitate the disorganization of Sumner or of Weber.

28. *Ibid.*, p. 39.

29. *Ibid.*, p. 39.

that could not have been perceived without it. These theories are quite different from those all-embracing total systems of sociological theory. The quest for the latter "has the same exhilarating challenge and the same small promise as those all-encompassing philosophical systems which have fallen into a deserved disuse."[30] Once more the criterion of utility comes to the fore. And here Merton comes perilously close to suggesting that the history of philosophy deserves to be forgotten.[31] So far as sociology is concerned, he is impatient with those who believe that we can have "*the* general sociological theory" now. This is a "premature and apocalyptic belief. We are not ready.[32] The fathers of sociology—Merton here mentions Comte, Spencer, Gumplowicz, Ward, and Giddings—followed the example of the philosophers, each fashioning his own system. The trouble is that these systems compete with one another and, instead of having one general and genuine sociological theory, we have a multiplicity of theories. Merton does not conceal his distaste for this kind of endeavor. It leads to the "balkanization" of sociology.[33]

We need therefore the Aristotelian mean, theories of the middle range. Middle range theories now hold the largest promise, provided that we do not forget more pervasive concerns with consolidating them some day into theories of a higher level of generality. Merton goes on to suggest that his call for theories of the middle range has not been greeted by universal assent. Indeed, responses have been polarized. Those engaged in "theoretically oriented empirical research" have tended to agree. This is the sort of thing they have been doing anyway. Those engaged in humanistic concerns involving the history of social thought or those now trying to create systematic theory have tended to disagree. Merton rallies to his cause an impressive array of figures in the history of thought, including Plato, Bacon, and Mill, and such sociologists as Hankins, Ginsberg, Mannheim, and Sorokin, all of whom had favorable things to say about theories of the middle range. Among those who, he says, reject theories of the middle range and who would banish them from social science, he includes Dahrendorf and the present writer. Dahrendorf can speak for himself, but the notion that I would "reject" or "banish" any theory—small, medium, or

30. *Ibid.*, p. 45.

31. A few pages later he returns to the theme: "To concentrate entirely on a master conceptual scheme for deriving all subsidiary theories is to risk producing twentieth-century sociological equivalents of the large philosophical systems of the past, with all their varied suggestiveness, their architectonic splendor, and their scientific sterility."*Ibid.*, p. 51.

32. *Ibid.*, p. 45.

33. The name of Parsons is not mentioned in this discussion, but it is appropriate to note that these ideas originally grew out of a commentary on a paper by Parsons, "The Position of Sociological Theory," *American Sociological Review* 13 (April 1948): 156–164.

large—is a "polarized" interpretation of what I had said.[34] In calling for a larger vision one does not necessarily reject the lesser. As to whether Durkheim's *Suicide* or Weber's *Protestant Ethic* more clearly typifies theories of the middle range, I am willing to concede Merton's point that both of them do. It is probably unnecessary to argue with Merton as to which is the superior contribution. It seems to me, however, that Durkheim's study, exemplary as it is, is focused on a rather small and not very serious social problem, whereas Weber's is an important support of the ideological interpretation of social change.

The essay on middle range theory concludes with a summary and retrospect, a plea for codification of sociological theory, a quizzical view of literary style in sociological writing, and a treatment of the function of paradigms in the development of science.

"MANIFEST AND LATENT FUNCTIONS"

The essay that bears this title may well be Merton's most famous. Parsons, who shares with Merton the label of "arch-functionalist," regards it as a seminal paper and says, "In that essay and in other writings, he clearly made a major contribution to the understanding and clarification of the theoretical methodology of what he, I think quite appropriately, called 'functional analysis'—what it was about, what its assumptions were, what some of its potentialities were, and the like."[35] Neither Parsons nor Merton, however, likes the words *structural-functionalism;* both prefer *functional analysis.*

The essay begins with a semantic exercise, in which Merton shows that the word *function* is burdened with different connotations and that the same connotation is expressed by a variety of words, including *use, utility, purpose, motive, intention, aim, consequence.* The result is a lack of rigor, a situation that can be rectified only by appropriate codification. The prevailing postulates in functional theory are three, which may be ex-

34. See Merton on "The process of polarization," *On Theoretical Sociology,* pp. 53–56. I include here the passage to which Merton objects:

> We have even invited to forego those larger problems of human society that occupied our ancestors in the history of social thought and to seek instead what T. H. Marshall called, in his inaugral lecture at the University of London, "stepping stones in the middle distance," and other sociologists since "theories of the middle range." But what an anemic ambition this is! Shall we strive for half a victory? Where are the visions that enticed us into the world of learning in the first place? I had always thought that sociologists too knew how to dream and that they believed with Browning that a man's reach should exceed his grasp.

"Sociology and Humane Learning" (1960), in *Power and Progress,* pp. 309–321.

35. "The Present Status of 'Structural-Functional' Theory in Sociology," *Idea of Social Structure,* p. 67.

plained in Merton's own words: "Substantially, these postulates hold first, that standardized social activities or cultural items are functional for the *entire* social or cultural system; second, that *all* such social and cultural items fulfill sociological functions; and third, that these items are consequently *indispensable.*"[36] With respect to the first of these, Merton faults Kingsley Davis and Wilbert E. Moore for overestimating the integrative function of religion in society and ignoring the divisive effects that religion has clearly had in the actual history of human societies. This error he attributes to the practice of carrying over, without modification, theories and conceptions derived from the study of nonliterate societies into the study of literate societies.[37] In discussing the second of the postulates, the anthropologist Clyde Kluckhohn becomes the victim of his gentle criticism. In discussing the third postulate, Merton suggests that the notion of functional indispensability be avoided in view of the number of functional alternatives that can be discerned in societies.

Merton next addresses himself to the indictment that functional analysis contains an implicit ideological commitment. He has little trouble with this charge because it has been criticized by some as conservative and by others as radical. He is concerned to emphasize that functional analysis is widely prevalent in the other sciences, especially in the biological sciences. The situation is not so clear in sociology, where we find a variety of conceptions of what functional analysis is and how it should be pursued. In order to remedy this situation, Merton sets out a long and complicated paradigm, including concepts and queries, and containing eleven rubrics or headings: (*a*) the item(s) to which functions are imputed; (*b*) concepts of subjective dispositions (motives, purposes); (*c*) concepts of objective consequences (functions, dysfunctions);[38] (*d*) concepts of the unit subserved by the function; (*e*) concepts of functional requirements (needs, prerequisites); (*f*) concepts of the mechanisms through which functions are fulfilled; concepts of functional alternatives (functional equivalents or substitutes); (*g*) concepts of structural context (or structural constraint); (*h*) concepts of dynamics and change; (*i*) problems of validation of functional analysis; and (*j*) problems of the ideological implications of functional analysis.[39] The paradigm

36. *On Theoretical Sociology*, p. 79.

37. "It is at least conceivable that a theoretic orientation derived from research on nonliterate societies has served to obsure otherwise conspicuous data on the functional role of religion in multi-religion societies." *Ibid.*, p. 83. On this subject in general, see also Bierstedt, "The Limitations of Anthropological Methods in Sociology," *Power and Progress*, pp. 116–131.

38. This includes manifest and latent functions.

39. For the entire paradigm, see *On Theoretical Sociology* pp. 104–108.

has three purposes (one is tempted to say "functions"): (*a*) "to supply a provisional codified guide for adequate and fruitful functional analysis"; (*b*) "to lead directly to the postulates and (often tacit) assumptions underlying functional analysis"; and (*c*) "to sensitize the sociologist not only to the narrowly scientific implications of various types of functional analysis, but also to their political and sometimes ideological implications."[40]

A large part of the essay is devoted to a discussion of manifest and latent functions. Merton is concerned that sociologists often confuse conscious motivations and the objective consequences of behavior. In order to ward off this confusion, Merton says, he is going to indulge in a practice that is not always commendable, namely, introducing new terms into the vocabulary of sociology—the terms *manifest* and *latent*. Indeed, he not only introduces the terms *manifest* and *latent* functions but also "christens" the distinction between them:

> Since the occasion for making the distinction arises with great frequency, and since the purpose of a conceptual scheme is to direct observations toward salient elements of a situation and to prevent the inadvertent oversight of these elements, it would seem justifiable to designate this distinction by an appropriate set of terms. This is the rationale for the distinction between manifest functions and latent functions; the first referring to those objective consequences for a specified unit (person, subgroup, social or cultural system) which contribute to its adjustment or adaptation and were so intended; the second referring to unintended and unrecognized consequences of the same order.[41]

Merton notes that almost every contributor to the history of social thought has been aware of the distinction and concludes his essay with the modest observation that it "has done little more than indicate some of the principal problems and potentialities of this mode of sociological interpretation."[42]

"THE BEARING OF SOCIOLOGICAL THEORY ON EMPIRICAL RESEARCH"

At the beginning of this essay Merton invites attention to two opposing emphases in sociology—one that seeks generalizations on a grand scale,

40. *Ibid.*, p. 109. This last purpose would seem to be inconsistent with Merton's previous contention that functional analysis has no inherent ideological commitment. His explanation is as follows: "It has been emphasized in a preceding section that functional analysis has no intrinsic commitment to an ideological position. This does not gainsay the fact that *particular* functional analyses and *particular* hypotheses advanced by functionalists may have an identifiable ideological role."

41. *Ibid.*, p. 117.

42. *Ibid.*, p. 136. See the closely related, earlier essay (1936) "The Unanticipated Consequences of Purposive Social Action," reprinted in *Sociological Ambivalence and Other Essays* (New York: Free Press, 1976), pp. 145–155.

and another that does detailed research. Those who prefer the first know that what they do is significant but not whether it is true. Those who prefer the second know that what they demonstrate is true but have doubts about its significance. These emphases, however, need not be opposed: "Generalizations can be tempered, if not with mercy, at least with disciplined observation; close, detailed observations need not be rendered trivial by avoidance of their theoretical pertinence and implication."[43] The relationship between theory and research nevertheless requires examination, and this is what Merton proposes to do.

Merton finds it desirable first to suggest that the word *theory* in sociology has many different meanings and distinguishes six of them: (*a*) methodology, (*b*) general sociological orientations, (*c*) analysis of sociological concepts, (*d*) *post factum* sociological interpretations, (*e*) empirical generalizations in sociology, and (*f*) sociological theory. To these he might have added working hypotheses, about which he has a brief and sensible word earlier in the book.[44] And to which he doubtless should added metasociological theory—that is, theory whose subject is sociology rather than society—because all of the essays in this book and indeed almost all of Merton's theoretical writing belong to this category. In any event, all of these types are self-explanatory except the last, sociological theory, where Merton unaccountably uses the same expression for a part that he does for the whole. By "sociological theory" he means scientific laws, statements "of invariance derivable from a theory," and these, of course, are conspicuous by their absence in sociology: "Despite the many volumes dealing with the history of sociological theory and despite the plethora of empirical investigations, sociologists (including the writer) may discuss the logical criteria of sociological laws without citing a single instance which fully satisfies these criteria."[45] Merton's assertion that a sociological theory is a statement of invariance derivable from a theory is uncharacteristically unclear, and his use of Durkheim's theory of suicide as an example is uncharacteristically unhelpful. He nevertheless offers some wise observations on his six types of sociological theory, and the essay is still worth rereading. It concludes with the usual call for a clearer connection between theory and research in sociology.

"THE BEARING OF EMPIRICAL RESEARCH ON SOCIOLOGICAL THEORY"

In this, the last essay in the book, the words *theory* and *research* are reversed, and now we are invited to examine the relationship of the second

43. *Ibid.*, p. 139.
44. *Ibid.*, p. 39.
45. *Ibid.*, p. 150.

to the first. Research is much more than the testing and verifying of hypotheses. It plays an active role: "It performs at least four major functions which help shape the development of theory. It *initiates*, it *reformulates*, it *deflects* and it *clarifies* theory,"[46] With respect to the first of these, Merton has occasion to discourse on *serendipity*, a word that gives him inordinate pleasure, and a pattern that appears with some frequency in the history of science. Again, the four functions that research performs for theory are self-explanatory, but in the brief essay Merton offers some apposite illustrations of their operation in sociology. In both of these last essays he is devoted to bringing theory and research more closely together in a field where a conspicuous gap obtains between them.

"SOCIAL STRUCTURE AND ANOMIE"

"Social Structure and Anomie," published first in 1938, is Merton's most reprinted article. His bibliography lists no fewer than twenty-eight reprintings, not counting the times he reprinted it himself in three editions of *Social Theory and Social Structure.* He was twenty-seven years old when he first published it, two years after receiving his Ph.D. degree, and it brought him immediately to the attention of the sociological fraternity in the United States. The analysis used in the paper is frankly labeled functional, and it is original to the degree that not only conformity but also deviance is considered to be a product of social structure. Instead of setting the individual in opposition to a social structure that constrains him in either a Durkheimean or Freudian sense, Merton wants to show that structure is an active factor, that it produces motivations that cannot be predicted from a knowledge of native impulses or drives. It is not wayward personalities but ordinary social structures that motivate behavior that is then labeled deviant. In addition, some deviations from an old structure are almost certainly part of the process of creating a new one. In Merton's own words:

> To speak of "legitimate power" or authority is often to use an elliptical and misleading phrase. Power may be legitimized for *some* without being legitimized for *all* groups in a society. It may, therefore, be misleading to describe non-conformity with *particular* social institutions merely as deviant behavior; it may represent the beginning of a new alternative pattern, with its own distinctive claims to moral validity.[47]

It is in this respect that Merton believes he is extending "the theory of functional analysis" from the study of social structure, where it involves ques-

46. *Ibid.*, p. 157.
47. *Social Theory and Social Structure*, p. 122.

tions of order and maintenance, to the study of social change. This is a response to critics who have insisted that functional analysis in sociology is essentially static, that it takes no account of social conflict and social change.

Merton's primary aim in this essay "is to discover how some *social structures exert a definite pressure upon certain* persons in the society to engage in non-conforming rather than conforming conduct."[48] In order to do this he first distinguishes between cultural goals in a society and the institutional norms that arise to regulate the pursuit of them. The relationship is not a constant one, and indeed social control appears in a variety of forms, among which are prescription, preference, permission, and proscription. Although all societies have norms that govern conduct, they differ in the degree to which these norms are integrated with the hierarchy of values or cultural goals that appear in them. When integration is poor, deviant behavior can be expected. In Merton's own words, "It is, indeed, my central hypothesis that aberrant behavior may be regarded sociologically as a symptom of dissociation between culturally prescribed aspirations and socially structured avenues for realizing these aspirations."[49]

There is a difference between technically effective means of achieving goals and culturally legitimate means of achieving them. When the two coincide the society tends to be stable. When they draw apart or when technical efficiency is emphasized over cultural legitimacy, then the society becomes unstable and approaches a state of anomy, or normlessness.[50] Merton uses competitive sports as an illustration of this sort of thing. The intensity of the competition and the insistence upon winning induces the competitors to use illegitimate means in order to achieve their goal:

48. *Ibid.*, p. 132.

49. *Ibid.*, p. 134.

50. Merton unfortunately uses the French form of this word—*anomie*—and other writers also do so. Indeed, he accuses MacIver of "resurrecting the sixteenth-century and long obsolete spelling of the word." *Ibid.*, p. 161. Actually, *anomy* needed no resurrection. It has appeared continuously in English dictionaries, including Samuel Johnson's dictionary of 1755. There is no more warrant for using the French *anomie* in an English sentence than there is for using the French *anarchie* in preference to *anarchy*. For a brief discussion of the word, its history and meanings, see Robert Bierstedt, "Anomy (Anomie)," *A Dictionary of the Social Sciences*, ed. Julius Gould and William L. Kolb (Glencoe, Ill.: Free Press, 1964).

Merton wonders in a footnote (p. 135) why the word has lately come into frequent use. The obvious answer is the increasing attention paid to Durkheim in American sociology, beginning in the 1930s, when English translations of his work began to appear and when Parsons gave him a prominent place in *The Structure of Social Action*. Indeed, one of Merton's earliest articles (1934) was a long review of *The Division of Labor*, "the first magnum opus of this hegemonic protagonist [!] of the sociologistic school." *American Journal of Sociology* 40 (November 1934): 319–328.

> The star of the opposing football team is surreptitiously slugged; the wrestler incapacitates his opponent through ingenious but illicit techniques; university alumni covertly subsidize "students" whose talents are confined to the athletic field. The emphasis on the goal has so attenuated the satisfactions deriving from sheer participation in the competitive activity that only a successful outcome provides gratification.[51]

It is the cult of success that is responsible for the attenuation.

In contemporary American culture this cult is especially noticeable—someone has referred to success as "the bitch goddess" of the society. Indeed, Merton goes so far as to say that this culture "appears to approximate the polar type in which great emphasis upon certain success-goals occurs without equivalent emphasis upon institutional means." And of course it is monetary success that is praised the most. What are the consequences then for those individuals who are constrained to accept the goal but who are denied the resources to achieve it? This question Merton answers by means of his famous "Typology of Modes of Individual Adaptation," as follows:

Modes of adaptation	Culture goals	Institutionalized means
Conformity	+	+
Innovation	+	−
Ritualism	−	+
Retreatism	−	−
Rebellion	±	±

These categories refer to behavior, not personality, and the same person may use different modes of adaptation in different circumstances.

Conformity is the most widely diffused and the most common type of adaptation; otherwise, the society would be unstable. Innovation occurs when an individual accepts the goals but rejects the norms governing the means of achieving them. It is a familiar phenomenon in business, where it is frequently difficult to distinguish between legal and illegal activities, between legitimate competition and sharp practices. It is also the adaptation of the criminal. If there is more crime in the lower socioeconomic classes than in the higher, it is because of a class structure that limits opportunities in these classes at the same time that the social structure in general continues to stress the importance of monetary success. "It is only when a system of cultural values extols, virtually above all else, certain *common*

51. *Social Theory and Social Structure*, p. 135.

success-goals *for the population at large* while the social structure rigorously restricts or completely closes access to approved modes of reaching these goals *for a considerable part of the same population,* that deviant behavior ensues on a large scale."[52] This seems to explain the relationship between poverty and crime in our society, although not necessarily in others. Ritualism occurs when an individual, so to speak, drops out of the "rat race" that monetary success requires but continues to go through the motions required by the norms of the society. Here we find the frightened employee, the zealous bureaucrat, the occupant of the teller's cage in the bank. Merton suggests that it is the lower middle class that exhibits a relatively high incidence of ritualism—although the suggestion lacks empirical support. Retreatism involves rejection of both goals and norms, and the people who fit into this category are "the true aliens"—psychotics, pariahs, outcasts, vagrants, vagabonds, tramps, drunkards, and drug addicts. the prototype for this is the character created by Charlie Chaplin. Finally, in rebellion we find persons who reject both the goals and the norms of the old structure and accept—indeed, actively work for—the goals and norms of the new.

The social structure here examined thus contains within it a strain toward anomy. It may not operate evenly in all sectors of society, and there are indeed other than monetary indexes of success. But the strain remains. A concluding section deals briefly with the role of the family in inculcating in children the cultural standards and sometimes unrealistic goals of the society. But it is the imperfect coordination of goals and means that leads to anomy.

In a subsequent paper entitled "Continuities in the Theory of Social Structure and Anomie," Merton indulges in a long discussion of those who have written on the subject, some of them in direct response to his earlier paper. I shall single out only a few points to mention here. First, Merton notes that some writers, MacIver and Riesman among them, have used a rather more psychological than sociological conception of anomy. Thus, in MacIver's treatment it means not the absence or weakening of norms in the social structure but rather the state of mind of an individual who has lost his own standards and whose sense of social cohesion has disappeared. Still another distinction has been made, between simple and acute anomy, in which the former refers to a confusion or conflict of value systems in a society and the latter means the disintegration of value systems. Merton restates his own position in the following words, words that have more than the usual importance because he makes a significant distinction be-

52. *Ibid.*, p. 146.

tween cultural structure and social structure, something that sociologists have not always found it easy to do (I have noticed that Sorokin usually prefers the compound adjective *sociocultural*.):

> Cultural structure may be defined as that organized set of normative values governing behavior which is common to members of a designated society or group. And by social structure is meant that organized set of social relationships in which members of the society or group are variously implicated. Anomie is then conceived as a breakdown in the cultural structure, occurring particularly when there is an acute disjunction between the cultural norms and goals and the socially structured capacities of members of the group to act in accord with them. In this conception, cultural values may help to produce behavior which is at odds with the mandates of the values themselves.[53]

Cultural structure, in short, is an organized set of values; social structure, an organized set of relationships.

In the second place, Merton returns to the success theme in American culture. What is so distinctive about a society holding out aspirations that many of its members cannot hope to realize? Is this not true of all societies of any size? After all, as Weber noted, the pursuit of gain, the desire to have as much money as possible, is common to all sorts and conditions of men. Merton's answer to this is that American culture is distinctive in that it holds out the hope of economic affluence to all of its members, not just to some of them. "The moral mandate to achieve success thus exerts pressure to succeed, by fair means if possible and by foul means if necessary."[54] If studies show that a higher proportion of those in higher social classes than in lower social classes adhere to a success motive, we should not infer that more of them will fail or turn to deviant paths. It is the absolute numbers that are important, not the relative numbers, and there are simply more people in the lower classes than in the higher. As Merton says, in a passage that deserves more than the footnote location that he gives it,

> Important as it is in its own right, the *relative* proportions of those in various social strata and groups exhibiting particular attitudes, talents, wealth or any behavior-pattern should not be allowed to obscure, as they often do in sociological studies, the equally important fact of the *absolute numbers* manifesting these items in different strata and groups. From the standpoint of effects upon the society, it is often the absolute numbers and not the relative proportions that matter.[55]

53. *Ibid.*, p. 162.
54. *Ibid.*, p. 169.
55. *Ibid.*, p. 175, n. 28.

In the third place, in a renewed discussion of innovation, Merton makes the important point that not all deviant behavior is dysfunctional for a society. Indeed, a society in which every one of its members consistently followed the pattern of conformity would be a static society, one that would never change. Finally, one must not assume that deviant behavior, even dysfunctional deviant behavior, is unethical. On moral grounds it is entirely conceivable that a lone individual may be right and the norms of his society wrong. Merton does not seem to be aware, however, of the problem that this last conclusion raises. The individual who with great courage stands against the norms of his own society is in fact conforming to the ethical norms of another society in another time or place. If this is not the case, a distinction between morals and the mores is required and so also is an appeal to some kind of a natural law or divine law that transcends the ability of sociologists to discern.

What is to be said about Merton's treatment of anomy as an instigation to deviant behavior? Let us first dispose of those who argue that functional analysis in general is a static kind of performance, that it is partial to stability rather than change, that it underplays the role of conflict in human societies, and that it assumes an order that may not exist in any actual society. One of these relates directly to Merton's typology:

> It is as though individuals in society are playing a gigantic fruit machine, but the machine is rigged and only some players are consistently rewarded. The deprived ones then either resort to using foreign coins or magnets to increase their chances of winning (innovation) or play on mindlessly (ritualism), give up the game (retreatism) or propose a new game altogether (rebellion). But in the analysis nobody appeared to ask who put the machine there in the first place and who takes the profits. Criticism of the game is confined to changing the pay-out sequences so that the deprived can get a better deal . . . . What at first sight looks like a major critique of society ends up by taking the existing society for granted.[56]

This criticism, clever as it is, misses the mark. Merton is not engaged in a "critique of society," major or minor. All he is trying to do is to suggest that structural factors have something to do with deviance, that deviance is not a phenomenon that can be explained by motivational factors alone. Whatever may be said about deviance as a psychological phenomenon, it is a sociological phenomenon as well. If this conclusion is correct, it would apply to any society, not just "the existing society." Furthermore, Merton is quite aware of the processes of social change. Two of his five categories—innovation and rebellion—concern change, and there is, in ad-

56. Laurie Taylor, *Deviance and Society* (London: Michael Joseph, 1971), p. 148.

dition, a final section of the second paper on changing social structure. Finally, Merton is a sociologist, not a moralist. The "function" of functional analysts is not to criticize society but only to understand it.

Criticism of the theory as an explanation of criminal behavior might best perhaps be left to the criminologists. In this respect, however, it is worth mentioning again that Merton is modest in his claims. He is not trying to explain all kinds of deviance; indeed, crime and juvenile delinquency are labels for a wide range of behavior, and it is too much to expect that a single theory can explain it all. Furthermore, not all deviance is criminal. Illness and genius may both be viewed as deviance, although neither violates the norms of a society. In short, the theory, although elaborated at too great length and in words that are consequently often repetitious, is highly suggestive and continues to merit thoughtful attention. Let us give to Merton himself the last word on this subject:

> It should also be said again, since it is so easily forgotten, that to center this theory upon the cultural and structural sources of deviant behavior is *not* to imply that such behavior is the characteristic, let alone the exclusive, response to the pressures we have been examining. This is an analysis of varying *rates and types* of deviant behavior, not an empirical generalization to the effect that *all* those subject to these pressures respond by deviation. The theory only holds that those located in places in the social structure which are particularly exposed to such stresses are more likely than others to exhibit deviant behavior. Yet, as a result of countervailing social mechanisms, most even of these stressful positions do not *typically* induce deviation; conformity tends to remain the model response.[57]

But why some and not others? And which some and which others? These questions Merton's theory cannot answer. Nor can it explain the incidence of deviance in societies in which no stress or emphasis is placed upon monetary success. Finally, Merton's strain toward anomy is contrary to Sumner's strain toward consistency. Since these are contrary positions, both could be wrong, and one must be.

Bureaucracy

The two papers on bureaucracy which appear in *Social Theory and Social Structure* are entitled "Bureaucratic Structure and Personality" and "Role of the Intellectual in Public Bureaucracy." The first begins with

57. *Social Theory and Social Structure*, p. 183.

descriptions of bureaucracy, Merton's own and that of Max Weber, both of which assert the primacy of status relationships over personal relationships in those social organizations (associations) in which technical efficiency is deemed to be important. Modern bureaucracies exhibit the degree to which the worker is controlled by the instruments and equipment of production, something that must be acknowledged not as an item of Marxist ideology but simply as a matter of fact. The physicist does not own his cyclotron or the astronomer his telescope. As a separate point, bureaucracy, whether private or public, almost always involves secrets, that is, skill, knowledge, and techniques that are hidden from competitors and from the public. If bureaucracy has characteristics that conduce to efficiency it also has certain dysfunctions and the very word *bureaucrat* has become an epithet. One of the troubles is that bureaucratic procedures lead to what Veblen called a "trained incapacity," an ability to conform so closely to the rules that one is blinded to the larger purposes of the association. To put it simply, one can be strangled in red tape and the rules can become more important than the goals. The rules that promote efficiency in general often produce inefficiency in specific instances. The rules may even become more symbolic than utilitarian.

The second of the two papers is concerned with intellectuals, the study of whom Merton regards as quite as important as the study of beggars and thieves. He defines intellectuals as those who "devote themselves to cultivating and formulating knowledge."[58] He is especially concerned with social scientists and indicates that in a number of respects their role in public bureaucracies is different from that of physical scientists. There is more indeterminacy in sociological knowledge, for example, than in the knowledge of the electrical engineer. This indeterminacy cannot help but affect the relationship between the social scientist and the client and makes it difficult for the latter to evaluate the qualifications of the former, which in turn requires policymakers to use still other experts in the evaluation process. In addition, policymakers themselves have some knowledge in the areas in which the social scientist is an expert—or at least they think they have—and this too can affect the relationship. And finally, since the recommendations of the social scientist have value implications, he is peculiarly vulnerable to clients who have different values.

In a following section Merton looks at the alienation of intellectuals from the business world and at the preference some of them have for government rather than the university as the locus of a career. The preference is based largely upon a desire to be closer to the decision-making processes of the

58. *Ibid.*, p. 209.

society. They are interested in social policy and want to exert some influence upon it. They are contrasted with technicians, those who want no part of policy and no responsibility for it. Although the intellectual and the technician are two different types, the pressures of bureaucratic life bring them closer together and may even eliminate the distinction between them. Throughout the discussion, Merton assumes that the policymaker or client is not an intellectual and that the function of the intellectual is to offer advice as to alternative lines of action or decision. The unattached intellectual is one whose perspectives are free from bureaucratic constraint but on the other hand, having no access to policymakers, he or she is apt to have little influence. Merton does not seem to consider that an unattached intellectual—a John Maynard Keynes, for example—might by his writing alone exercise more influence upon a government than even a cabinet minister does. He concludes in fact that "if the intellectual is to play an effective role in putting his knowledge to work, it is increasingly necessary that he become a part of a bureaucratic power-structure."[59] And it was Keynes himself who remarked that those who think they are creating policy are usually following the theories of some long-dead "academic scribbler." Merton, however, is doubtless correct where lower levels of both bureaucrats and intellectuals are concerned.

Where the bureaucrat defines the scope of a research problem, the work of the intellectual has a propensity for shoring up the status quo, for preserving institutional arrangements, and is thus a conservative factor in society. Something else happens to intellectuals in a bureaucracy; they take on some of the coloration of their clients in becoming less theoretical and more practical. The intellectual whose values differ from those of the client has three alternatives:

> (1) He can accommodate his own social values and special knowledge to the values of the policy-makers. (2) He can seek to alter the prevailing policies of the executives in the bureaucratic apparatus. (3) He can respond in terms of a schizoid dissociation between his own values and those of the bureaucracy, by regarding his function as purely technical and without value-implications.[60]

Merton supposes that the third alternative is the most frequently chosen and that bureaucratic life thus transforms the intellectual into a technician. Clearly the policymaker, especially one from the business world, and the intellectual have difficulty tolerating each other; the clash of interests and values is too great. The intellectual who enters the bureaucracy must thus

59. *Ibid.*, p. 217.
60. *Ibid.*, p. 219.

anticipate many frustrations, some of which arise from this conflict of values and others from the nature of bureaucratic organization itself.

Reference Group Theory

Reference group theory, now associated with Merton's name, is treated in two long papers, the first of which, written in collaboration with Alice S. Rossi, deals with the theory itself and the second with continuities in the theory.[61] The first is directed almost entirely to *The American Soldier*, a two-volume work prepared by a research team under the direction of Samuel A. Stouffer, under the auspices of the Information and Education Division of the War Department in World War II, and published in 1949.[62] Merton and Rossi intend to consolidate, on a higher and more general level of abstraction, the research and theory presented—the latter sometimes inadvertently—in these volumes.[63] One of the concepts that came to receive prominence is the concept of "relative deprivation," and to this concept Merton and Rossi give extended discussion because it relates to what they want to call reference group behavior. It appears that people in the army were happy or unhappy with their situations depending upon the situations of persons or groups with whom they compared themselves. Those who might objectively be better off nevertheless often felt themselves to be deprived in relation to some other group to whom they made reference. Thus relative deprivation and reference group both come into being as sociological concepts. Reference groups are of three kinds: those with whom the men are in actual association, those with whom they share the same status or social category, and those who have a different status or social category. An example of the first would be the man who compares himself with friends and acquaintances; of the second, a captain who compares himself with other captains; and of the third, enlisted men comparing themselves to officers. It will be seen that the men sometimes compare themselves with groups of which they are members and sometimes with groups of which they are not. Thus, both membership and nonmembership groups are involved. As the authors say, "Reference groups are, in principle, almost innumerable: any of the groups of which one is a member, and

61. The two essays are chaps. 8 and 9 in *Social Theory and Social Structure*.

62. The two volumes are entitled, respectively, *Adjustment during army Life* and *Combat and Its Aftermath*. (Princeton, N. J.: Princeton University Press, 1949.)

63. For another, and quite different, evaluation, see Nathan Glazer, " 'The American Soldier' as Science," *Commentary* 8 (1949): 487–496.

these are, of course, legion, can become points of reference for shaping one's attitudes, evaluatings and behavior."[64] That people orient their attitudes and behavior toward the other members of the groups to which they do not belong becomes the important focus of inquiry in reference group theory.

In the course of their discussion, Merton and Rossi raise a question that throws some doubt upon Merton's earlier thesis on anomy. In that theory, as outlined earlier, monetary success is demanded of everyone in the society but the institutional means for achieving it are denied to most, with crime and delinquency as consequences. The two relevant sentences follow:

> The sociological factors which lead men to consider their own, relatively low, social position as legitimate, as well as those which lead them to construe their position as a result of defective and possibly unjustified social arrangements clearly comprise a problem area of paramount theoretical and political importance. When are relatively slim life-chances taken by men as a normal and expectable state of affairs which they attribute to their own personal inadequacies and when are they regarded as the results of an arbitrary social system of mobility, in which rewards are not proportioned to ability?[65]

The degree to which people regard their own lack of monetary success as "legitimate," the degree to which they blame themselves rather than society, is the degree that casts doubt on Merton's theory of social structure and anomy.

In various places throughout their discussion the authors seem to be defensive about the propositions to which they give expression. They are defensive because the propositions often seem commonplace. The following note, which refers to indexes and observations needed to provide continuity in the theory of value-assimilation, is an example:

> The reader might be tempted to say that most of the following have been recognized as probably significant variables from the earliest days of modern sociology. But here, as at many points in this paper, it must be said that there is a great difference—in fact, all the difference—between impressionistic and sporadic references to such variables, and *systematic* incorporation of these variables into research. Only through the latter procedure will theory and research both advance.[66]

The point of their paper would seem to be that such studies as *The American Soldier* exemplify the kind of "*systematic* incorporation" to which they refer and furthermore that such commentaries as their own

64. *Social Theory and Social Structure*, p. 233.
65. *Ibid.*, p. 240.
66. *Ibid.*, p. 258, n. 34.

make additional gains in this systematic process. They could of course be right. But so many of their observations are problematic (locating and identifying problems) or programmatic (suggestions for future research) that a reader who is not a sociologist could easily conclude that little has been said and that that little is obvious. A reader who is not a sociologist might also wonder why the fact that people compare themselves with others can be elevated into something called reference group theory. The reader might be even more puzzled by the almost endless elaboration of this idea without being told with *what* others people compare themselves—a problem surely answerable by empirical research.

One of the findings of *The American Soldier* that attracts the attention of Merton and Rossi is that soldiers who conformed to the norms of the army were more likely to be promoted than those who did not. This finding, hardly surprising on the surface, puzzled them because they perceived two sets of norms—one the official army set and the other the norms of their associates—and these two sets often seemed at odds. "In the language of reference group theory, therefore, attitudes of conformity to the official mores can be described as a positive orientation to the norms of a nonmembership group that is taken as a frame of reference. Such conformity to norms of an out-group is thus equivalent to what is ordinarily called nonconformity, that is, nonconformity to the norms of the in-group."[67] The authors realize, of course, that the boundaries between in-groups and out-groups are often unclear and often shifting, that what is in one reference an out-group may be in a succeeding one an in-group. Thus, an in-group may be as small as a marital pair and as large as the inhabitants of the planet Earth.[68] Now it is perfectly reasonable to suppose that soldiers who want to be promoted would conform to the norms of the army, and indeed that persons who want to be promoted in any kind of organized enterprise would conform to its norms. But Merton and Rossi persist in making a problem out of this simple fact. They see in it two additional problems—one the consequences of conforming to the norms of a group other than one's own and the other the factors that encourage or discourage such behavior. The first of these produces a new concept, the concept of "anticipatory socialization," which means that individuals begin to conform to the norms of the groups to which they want to belong in preference to the norms of the groups to which they actually belong. Anticipatory socialization operates, of course, only in situations where vertical social mobility is

67. *Ibid.*, p. 264.

68. For a discussion of this phenomenon, see Robert Bierstedt, *The Social Order*, 4th ed. (New York: McGraw-Hill 1974), pp. 298–303.

possible. But this is the case in all of the career patterns of life—medical student into doctor, graduate student into professor, lawyer into law firm partner, recruit into member of the team, clerk into supervisor, farmhand into farmer—and one wonders again why such a point is made of it.

The situation in the military raises a significant problem that does not occur to the authors. It is this: Soldiers may pretend to conform to the norms of the organization—the army—in order to win promotion but do so with mental reservations that induce them to believe that they continue to conform to the norms of those who are not promoted. The entire argument somehow misses the point that proficiency in performance of duty may be more important in promotion than such a phenomenon as anticipatory socialization. It also overemphasizes the disparity between the norms of one's own group and the norms of the group one aspires to join. Thus, in an office it may be that the majority are striving to succeed, to move up the ladder, to qualify for a higher salary, and for these there may be no disparity in the norms at all. Note, for example, the following observations by the executive secretary to a corporation president, who likes her job:

> I enjoy one thing more than anything else on this job. That's the association I have with the other executives, not only my boss. There's a tremendous difference in the way they treat me than what I've known before. They treat me more as . . . on the executive level. They consult me on things, and I enjoy this. It stimulates me. . . .
>
> I know myself well enough to know that I've always enjoyed men more than women. Usually I can judge them very quickly when I meet a woman. I can't judge men that quickly. I seek out the few women I think I will enjoy. The others, I get along with all right, but I feel no basic interest. I don't really enjoy having lunch with them and so on.
>
> You can tell just from conversation what they talk about. It's quite easy. It's also very easy to tell which girls are going to last around the office and which ones aren't. Interest in their work. Many of them aren't, they just don't dig in. They're more interested in chatting in the washroom. I don't know if that's a change from other years. There's always been some who are really not especially career-minded, but they have to give a little bit and try a little harder. The others get by on as little as possible.[69]

Merton and Rossi argue further that although anticipatory socialization may be functional for the individual, it can be dysfunctional for the group. The reason this may be the case is that conformity to the norms of the group one wants to join means defection from the norms of the group of which one is actually a member. Here again the authors may be exaggerating the differences in the norms of the two groups. They do recognize

69. Studs Terkel, *Working* (New York: Pantheon Books, 1972), pp. 55–56.

that conformity offers rewards to individuals and helps to sustain the structure of authority in the group and in larger social systems. It is worth considering too that the army under study was for most of its members an involuntary association. Whether the norms of different levels in the hierarchy of a voluntary association would present the same kinds of differences is a question that, like many others, the research was not designed to answer. In any event, it is easy to agree that sociologists have probably spent more time studying group cohesion than they have group alienation. And clearly, as the authors say, "one group's renegade may be another group's convert."[70]

Finally, the process of moving from one group to another, where possible, has a momentum of its own. As the individual expresses or exhibits anticipatory socialization, he incurs the hostility of his in-group, which stimulates him to increasing conformity to the out-group, and finally the former out-group becomes the in-group. We can only fault the authors for failing to recognize the many situations in society where anticipatory socialization is quite legitimate and where it is supported and even encouraged by an in-group, most of whose members may be engaged in precisely the same process. Thus, elementary school pupils anticipate the time when they will be high school students; high school students, when they will be college students; medical students, when they will be doctors; and so on. There is nothing mysterious about these anticipations. Aspiration does not necessarily arouse the hostility of one's associates, even in the army.

At the end of the paper Merton and Rossi give credit to Herbert Hyman for coining the term *reference group* and refer not only to him and to Muzafer Sherif and Theodore Newcomb, but also to such earlier writers as W.E.B. DuBois, E. Franklin Frazier, Sumner, William James, Cooley, and Mead. Reference group behavior is indeed an expansive and comprehensive concept:

> An Army private bucking for promotion may only in a narrow and theoretically superficial sense be regarded as engaging in behavior different from that of an immigrant assimilating the values of a native group, or of a lower-middle-class individual conforming to his conception of upper-middle-class patterns of behavior, or of a boy in a slum area orienting himself to the values of a settlement house worker rather than the values of the street corner gang, or of a Bennington student abandoning the conservative beliefs of her parents to adopt the more liberal ideas of her college associates, or of a lower-class Catholic departing from the pattern of his in-group by casting a Republican vote, or of an eighteenth century French aristocrat aligning himself with a revolutionary group of the time.[71]

70. *Social Theory and Social Structure*, p. 269.
71. *Ibid.*, p. 278.

The great merit of reference group theory is that it can fold all of these examples together and put them in the same envelope. In this way sociological theory grows, "cumulates," and matures.

Six years after Merton and Rossi wrote their paper, Merton continued his inquiry by writing "Continuities in the Theory of Reference Groups and Social Structure," which runs to 106 pages in *Social Theory and Social Structure.* One of the ways in which sociological theory advances , according to Merton, is in increasing clarification of the concepts it employs. Although some critics have claimed that there is nothing new in reference group theory, Merton insists on the contrary that it contains some *distinctive* ideas and italicizes the adjective. It appears that there are two kinds of reference groups, the normative type, "which sets and maintains standards for the individual," and the comparison type, "which provides a frame of comparison relative to which the individual evaluates himself and others."[72] Merton explicitly denies that there is a third type—groups to which persons aspire to belong—but his reasoning here is not clear. Nor is it clear when he says that the two types are "only analytically distinct," since they can both perform the two functions just mentioned.

Merton's next concern is to clarify the concepts of group and group membership. It may be, in fact, that the concept of reference group is a misnomer (Merton's word) because it is applied not only to groups but also to individuals and social categories. It is therefore necessary to examine critically and closely the concept of "group" in sociology. As his first criterion shows, he conforms to the custom of most sociologists in utilizing the notion of interaction. Thus,

> The *sociological* concept of a group refers to a number of people who interact with one another in accord with established patterns. This is sometimes phrased as a number of people having established and characteristic social relations. The two statements are, however, equivalent, since "social relations" are themselves patterned forms of social interaction, enduring sufficiently to become identifiable parts of a social structure.[73]

Note that in discussing "established and characteristic social relations" Merton is ruling out of his concept such groups as the inhabitants of the United States of America, the middle class, readers of the *New York Times,* those who voted in a presidential election, those who have been elected to the Hall of Fame, and those who huddle silently in a doorway to escape a sudden shower. The privilege of doing this is not in question. The problem, however, is that then one has to find some other word than *group* for the clusters of people just mentioned.

---

72. *Ibid.,* p. 283.
73. *Ibid.,* p. 285.

Two additional criteria are introduced. The first of these is that the interacting persons regard and define themselves as members of a group and the second that others so regard them.[74] There are, then, three criteria for a group—"enduring and morally established forms of social interaction, self-definition as a member, and the same definition by others."[75] One does not quite know what to do with the word *morally*, and our author supplies no explanation.

Merton recognizes that the boundaries of a group are not always easy to draw or, for that matter, to maintain. Furthermore, group membership and nonmembership are not as definite as they may seem to be. There are both nominal and peripheral members of groups. There are subgroups, and possibly subgroups of subgroups.

Although specific examples are lacking in this discussion, a single mention of the army suggests that Merton is talking about organized rather than unorganized groups. Whether he would wish to equate unorganized with informal groups and organized with formal is a question that the text fails to answer. In any event, groups are not to be conceived of as static entities. Both group membership and group structures are dynamic phenomena. Redefinitions constantly occur, by both group members and nonmembers.[76]

From these considerations Merton turns to the concept of nonmembership, a concept that fascinates him even more than the concept of membership. He moves immediately to Simmel's concept of "completeness." "The concept of completeness refers to a group property measured by the proportion of *potential members*—those who satisfy the requirements for membership as established by the group—who are *actual members.* Trade unions, professional associations, alumni groups are only the most conspicuous kinds of examples of organizations with varying degrees of completeness."[77] These examples again suggest that Merton is thinking here of *organized* groups and not unorganized ones. Only organized groups have *requirements* for membership, and all of them do. Unorganized groups

74. At this point in his discussion Merton, without warning and without definition, has a sentence distinguishing between formal and informal groups. But there is no elaboration, and he simply assumes that his readers will know what he is talking about.

75. *Ibid.*, p. 286.

76. As an example of this last, Merton quotes the following observation by Albert Einstein in an address at the Sorbonne: "If my theory of relativity is proven successful, Germany will claim me as a German and France will declare that I am a citizen of the world. Should my theory prove untrue, France will say I am a German and Germany will declare that I am a Jew." *Ibid.*, p. 288, n. 12.

77. *Ibid.*, p. 288.

have criteria in terms of which membership may be determined, but not requirements that people themselves must satisfy.

Nonmembers of a group may be either eligible or ineligible for membership, and those in the former category may aspire to belong, may be indifferent to belonging, or may be antagonistic to the idea of belonging. There are also, of course, indifferent, ineligible nonmembers, and for these the group is not a reference group. Next, there are open and closed groups, but Merton's one example—elites—is of an unorganized group. He might have noted in this connection that all organized groups are closed. All of them have tests of membership even when, as in the case of a political party, they are easy to satisfy. Attention is next invited to the time perspective of group members; that is, members may become nonmembers over the course of time, and vice versa. In one of his assertions, however, Merton is almost certainly wrong:

> It may not be too much to suggest that the vernacular registers this tendency of the group to respond with marked affect toward those who abandon membership in it. Witness the extensive array of affectively toned terms designating ex-members: renegade, apostate, turncoat, heretic, traitor, secessionist, deserter and the like; it is difficult to find neutrally-toned vernacular denoting the same fact.[78]

On the contrary, the innocent words *former member* and *exmember* do quite well, and there need be nothing pejorative about them, nothing to arouse the hostility of those who remain members. One may "abandon" a national association simply by failing to pay one's dues, and this is a common enough phenomenon. One may stop being a member of the American Sociological Association, for example, without being considered a traitor or a turncoat. All horizontal mobility in a society involves leaving one group and becoming part of another. And one becomes an exmember of a university by the simple process of graduating from it, something considered to be a praiseworthy act, and even an achievement.

Merton takes exception to the notion attributed to Sumner that in-groups invariably exhibit hostility to out-groups on the ground that in-groups may also exhibit a positive orientation to out-groups. He is right; in-group cohesion does not necessarily produce out-group hostility. But Merton does not consider the obverse of this sentence, that out-group hostility does produce in-group cohesion. Sumner's principle is too important to surrender, and it need only be more carefully stated. Thus, "any threat, imaginary or real,

78. *Ibid.*, p. 296.

from an out-group tends to intensify the cohesion and the solidarity of the in-group."[79] In this form the proposition is almost certainly correct. Indeed, it is one of the few "laws" that sociology has.

I have already noted Merton's definition of a group. When he returns to the subject he treats groups, collectivities, and social categories. In order to be a group the criterion of social interaction must be satisfied. When social interaction is absent, then we may have collectivities, "people who have a sense of solidarity by virtue of sharing common values and who have acquired an attendant sense of moral obligation to fulfill role-expectations. All groups are, of course collectivities, but those collectivities which lack the criterion of interaction among members are not groups."[80] And finally, social categories are "aggregates of social statuses, the occupants of which are not in social interaction."[81] All of this, if not entirely clear, is at least defensible. Any sociologist has the privilege of using the word *group* in any way he chooses and then has only the moral and logical obligation to use it consistently in the chosen sense.

To say that Merton's terminology is defensible, however, is not to say that it is wise. It is unwise for two reasons. In the first place, no sociologist who had adopted so limited a connotation for the word *group* has been able to be consistent. All of them invariably forget their own definition and begin to talk, for example, about those with a similar socioeconomic status as a group whether or nor there is social interaction among them. In the second place, the word *group* is too useful to be given so small and narrow a connotation. If one wanted to talk about certain purely statistical groupings of mankind, he would be precluded from calling them groups. *Categories* is not an adequate substitute. Merton himself illustrates the significance of both of these reasons. After making his distinctions between groups, collectivities, and social categories, he immediately confuses the matter by writing, unaccountably, that reference groups can be any one of the three: "Upon examination, then, the concept of reference 'group' can be seen to include, in undifferentiated fashion, social formations of quite different kinds: membership and non-membership groups, collectivities, and social categories."[82] That the word *group* appears in quotation marks illustrates the second. He has to use the word here because there is no other word available. Furthermore, and substantively, how nonmembership

79. Bierstedt, *The Social Order*, p. 302. Here it is explicitly recognized that out-groups are not always hostile. See also the discussion in Lewis Coser, *The Functions of Social Conflict* (New York: Free Press of Glencoe, 1956), especially pp. 87–95.

80. *Social Theory and Social Structure*, p. 299.

81. *Ibid.*

82. *Ibid.*, p. 300.

groups can deserve the label without demonstrating that nonmembers satisfy the criterion of interaction—that is, that nonmembers of groups interact with one another—is altogether unclear. Finally, the typology is not exhaustive. There is no name for the kind of group in which there may be interaction but not common sharing of a body of norms or a sense of solidarity. An example would be the passengers in a limousine traveling from an international airport to a city, especially a foreign city. Another example would be a street crowd gathered to witness a fire or the aftermath of an accident.

Merton invites the attention of his reader to the fact that there are both positive and negative reference groups. As examples, the Greeks rejected the infectious theory of disease because it was held by "barbarians," and Americans frequently reject notions, otherwise meritorious, because they are held by Russians. The point is well taken. But here Merton is violating his own admonition that the word *group* is stretched too far, made only two pages earlier: "The term *group* has often been stretched to the breaking point, and not only in reference group theory, by being used to designate large numbers of people among the greatest part of whom there is no social interaction, although they do share a body of social norms. This loose usage is found in such expressions as 'nationality group' to designate the total population of a nation."[83] These should be called collectivities rather than groups. Merton's Greeks and barbarians, Americans and Russians, should therefore be called, on his own recommnedation, negative reference collectivities. As intimated earlier, this is one of the things that can easily happen when one adopts too restricted a connotation for a concept.[84]

Merton next addresses himself to the fact that there are both reference groups and reference individuals. The reference individual is similar to a role model, except that a role model is more restrictive. In a reference individual usually more than one role is involved. Although, as we have seen, Merton is fascinated by nonmembership groups, he warns that in fact people are probably more influenced by the groups of which they are members. He is then ready to turn to the problem of group classification, with appropriate recognition that taxonomy, although not of course the whole of sociological theory, is nevertheless an indispensable part of it. He cannot permit himself to believe, however, that a classification of groups might be good to have for its own sake, as the culmination and product of an intellectual process, as an exercise in logic that provides both logical and

83. *Ibid.*, p. 299.

84. There is a well-known principle in logic—of which this is an illustration—that the intension of a term varies, if at all, inversely with its extension.

aesthetic satisfaction. It must rather be useful, either in the development of sociological theory or sociological research.[85]

In any event, Merton proceeds to list and to discuss briefly the following properties of groups:

1. Clarity or vagueness of social definitions of membership in the group[86]
2. Degree of engagement of members in the group
3. Actual duration of membership in the group
4. Expected duration of membership in the group
5. Actual duration of the group
6. Expected duration of the group
7. Absolute size of a group, or of component parts of a group
8. Relative size of a group, or of component parts of a group
9. Open or closed character of a group
10. "Completeness": ratio of actual to potential members
11. Degree of social differentiation
12. Shape and height of stratification
13. Types and degrees of social cohesion
14. The potential of fission or unity of a group
15. Extent of social interaction within the group
16. Character of the social relations obtaining in the group[87]
17. Degree of expected conformity to norms of group: toleration of deviant behavior and institutionalized departures from the strict definitions of group-norms[88]

---

85. Thus, reference is made to Sorokin's classification "which awaits further systematic use in current research." *Ibid.*, p. 310.

86. It is not clear in what sense this can be a property of a group itself.

87. "This property has traditionally been adopted as the major one distinguishing various types of groups, as can be seen from such established classifications as primary and secondary groups, in-group and out-group, *Gemeinschaft* and *Gesellschaft*, formal and informal groups, etc.," to which Merton adds the pattern-variables of Parsons. *Ibid.*, p. 317. There appears to be something wrong with Merton's taxonomy here, which the "etc." does nothing to correct. On the one hand there are too many different kinds of phenomena grouped together under the rubric of "character of the social relations," and on the other some or most of the other rubrics also deal with "character of the social relations."

88. This one is also a bit of a puzzle. Merton suggests that there is more "patterned leeway" to deviate from the norms of some groups (e.g., creativity groups, research groups) than of others (e.g., bureaucracies). But if the "leeway" is "patterned," it has become part of the norms of the group. It could be argued further that no group permits much deviation from its norms, even though the conduct itself may look different to the outsider. The member of an institute or center for advanced studies in an American university probably conforms to the norms of his group just as much as the Prussian bureaucrat does to his. It is difficult, in short, to make much sense out of such expressions as "patterned leeway" and "institutionalized evasion of in-

18. The system of normative controls
19. Degree of visibility or observability within the group[89]
20. Ecological structure of the group
21. Autonomy or dependence of the group
22. Degree of stability of the group
23. Degree of stability of the structural context of the group
24. Modes of maintaining stability of the group, and of the structured context
25. Relative social standing of groups
26. Relative power of groups

At this point the listing of "properties" comes to an end—arbitrarily, as Merton recognizes. The list could be longer or shorter. In order for such "classifications" to be useful, standardized measures of the properties need to be developed.

What can be said about this exercise in group analysis? First, the classification of groups is an important problem in sociological theory and one that seems far from satisfactorily solved. Notice the strenuous efforts that both MacIver and Sorokin, for example, devoted to it. Second, Merton approaches it with a large number of insights and indulges throughout his discussion in observations that are often penetrating and sometimes profound. On the other hand, the word *properties* is misused and has no consistent connotations; sometimes the part is taken for the whole and sometimes the whole for the part (the sin of synecdoche); the different numbered rubrics vary widely in their degree of generality and level of abstraction; there is no organization or logical progression in the list; it exhibits no recognizable *fundamentum divisionis;* it contains unexplained and undefined distinctions; and it omits altogether one of the most important of all of the properties of groups, that is, whether it is an organized or an unorganized group. The properties of organized groups are quite different from those of unorganized groups and this fact is given no recognition.

stitutional rules." If the evasion is institutionalized it has become a new norm. On Merton's behalf, however, his complete paragraph should be read, and attention is especially invited to its final sentence: "It may be conjectured that an appreciable amount of tolerated deviation from norms is functionally required for the stability of complex social structures." *Ibid.*, p. 318. In these situations again, however, the tolerance has itself become a norm.

89. Here Merton is referring to the visibility of norms and role-performances. It is not clear in what sense norms can be "seen." They are not physical objects. Simmel's word, to which Merton refers, is *übersehbar*, which Kurt Wolff translated as "surveyable," and this would seem to be preferable, on both physical and metaphysical grounds, to "visible" or "observable."

That the discussion is programmatic and propaedeutic Merton admits, but throughout, as mentioned earlier, the emphasis is upon utility rather than logical rigor. Despite its defects, however, this section of a very long paper is probably its most important.[90] It is in this essay that Merton introduces his concept of role-set:

> Without engaging in heavier deliberation than the subject deserves, we must note that a particular social status involves, not a single associated role, but an array of associated roles. This is a basic characteristic of social structure. This fact of structure can be registered by a distinctive term, *role-set,* by which I mean *that complement of role relationships which persons have by virtue of occupying a particular social status.* As one example: the single status of medical student entails not only the role of a student in relation to his teachers, but also an array of other roles relating the occupant of that status to other students, nurses, physicians, social workers, medical technicians, etc.[91]

The proposition that these are in fact multiple roles (simply because interaction with people of different statuses are involved) is one that can be questioned. The law of parsimony suggests here that Ralph Linton's formulation, to which Merton refers, may be superior to Merton's and that the concept of role-set is redundant. The issue here depends entirely upon the definition of *role* that one adopts. That a medical student interacts in one way with a medical school professor and another with a nurse is not in question. That is what their statuses require. Both of them, however, interact with him as a medical student.

Merton confesses that this chapter runs to an "unconscionable length," and one is tempted into a gratuitous agreement with him. I have already indicated difficulties with certain points and differences at others, and no summary criticism is required. I should, however, like to suggest that the adjective in "reference group" is itself redundant for the purpose of sociological analysis—although it may not be so for psychological analysis. That is, Merton is talking about groups, their classification, their properties, their structure, and it really does not matter for these purposes whether someone uses them as references or not. Indeed, this is a psychological consideration and has little or nothing to do with the structure of the group. It is helpful to be reminded that people conform not only to the norms of the groups of which they are members but also sometimes to the norms of groups of which they are not. Here, as in a few other places in his work, Merton is genuinely writing sociological theory, that is, ad-

90. For another, more concise treatment of groups and their properties, see Bierstedt, *The Social Order,* pp. 280–309.

91. *Social Theory and Social Structure,* p. 369.

dressing himself to an analysis of groups—a substantive sociological subject. One can only wish that he had done it with more brevity and, if one cannot ask for wit, at least with a greater degree of internal organization. It is not a system of sociology, but it is part of what every such system should contain. Merton himself calls it an interim report.

"PATTERNS OF INFLUENCE: LOCAL AND COSMOPOLITAN INFLUENTIALS"

Discussion of this essay can be brief. It is a study in 1943 of those who wield influence in "Rovere," a town of some 11,000 persons on the Eastern Seaboard. In the town eighty-six informants mentioned 379 persons who had exerted some influence upon them, fifty seven of whom were mentioned four or more times, and thirty of these were subsequently interviewed. The first categories into which these influential persons were arranged proved to be "sterile," and new ones had to be found. Because the first part of the work was "unproductive," Merton recommends, in a footnote, that sociologists doing qualitative research should recount not only their conclusions but also the steps, both right and wrong, that they took in arriving at them. It is fervently to be hoped that no one will follow this advice. There is enough tedium in the literature as it is.

The categories finally adopted were "local" and "cosmopolitan." Merton says that he adopted these terms from Carle C. Zimmerman, who used them as translations of the *Gemeinschaft* and *Gesellschaft* of Ferdinand Tönnies.[92] Apparently Merton made the suggestion to Zimmerman in the first place. If so, one can speculate that Oswald Spengler's emphasis upon the importance of this distinction had made a permanent, although unremembered, impression on his mind. Spengler wrote that with the rise of the world-city "there were no longer noblesse and bourgeoisie, freemen and slaves, Hellenes and Barbarians, believers and unbelievers, *but only cosmopolitans and provincials.* All other contrasts pale before this one, which dominates all events, all habits of life, all views of the world."[93]

To return to Merton's study, he and his associates found that fourteen of the "influentials" they interviewed could rather reliably be classified as cosmopolitan and sixteen as local. He concedes that a larger sample might disclose an intermediate type that could not clearly be placed in either of these two categories. The difference in basic orientation is related to other differences: "(1) in the structures of social relations in which each type is

92. Actually, what Tönnies meant by these terms is far from exhausted by the words *local* and *cosmopolitan*.

93. Spengler, *The Decline of the West*, trans. Charles Francis Atkinson, 2 vols. (New York: Alfred A. Knopf, 1939), vol. 2, p. 99.

implicated; (2) in the roads they have traveled to their positions in the influence-structure; (3) in the utilization of their present status for the exercise of interpersonal influence; and (4) in their communications behavior."[94] Much of the remainder of the chapter elaborates the implications of these four kinds of differences. There is a footnote that would have warmed the heart of Lester Frank Ward.[95] An error may nevertheless lurk here. The notion that the total amount of influence exercised in a community by the majority of the people who individually exercise little assumes that influence, like purchasing power, is a property that conforms to the laws of addition in arithmetic. Unless Merton can identify a *quantum of influence* (his expression), a discrete unit that can be added to others, his conclusion is an impermissible inference. That Merton is aware of problems involved in the measurement of influence is clear from the Addendum to this chapter.[96] But he offers no solution. In fact, he appears to be arguing here that the noninfluentials in a community, because of their greater numbers, are more influential than the influentials—a unique conclusion indeed.

"THE SELF-FULFILLING PROPHECY"

This essay, published originally in the *Antioch Review* (1948) is one of Merton's most seminal. The expression has entered the language and is used by persons who have never heard of Merton. The notion itself, as he is quick to point out, appears in such disparate writers as Bossuet, Mandeville, Marx, and Freud. In sociology Sumner, "the erudite, dogmatic and occasionally sound Yale professor . . . . who lives on as the Karl Marx of the middle classes,"[97] was well aware of it. It receives its clearest

94. *Social Theory and Social Structure*, pp. 394–395.

95. It appears that a disproportionate number of "influentials" in Rovere are in top social strata. Merton cautions, however, "Despite this concentration, it appears likely that more personal decisions in a community may be the result of advice by the many people ranking low in the influence-structure than by the few ranked at the top." The footnote:

> The empirical force of this consideration is like that found in studies of the social distribution of genius or talent (or, for that matter, of the distribution of purchasing power). It has been repeatedly found that the upper social and educational strata have a relatively higher proportion of "geniuses" or "talents." But since the numbers in these strata are small, the great bulk of geniuses or talents actually come from lower social strata. From the standpoint of the society, of course, it is the *absolute number* and not the *proportion* coming from any given social stratum which matters.

Ibid., p. 411 and n. 16.

96. There is no indication of the year in which the Addendum was written. See also "Fact and Factitiousness in Ethnic Opinionnaires," *American Sociological Review* 5 (February 1940): 13–28, where he properly criticizes L. L. Thurstone for ignoring the difference between cardinal and ordinal measurement.

97. *Social Theory and Social Structure*, p. 421.

sociological expression perhaps in "the Thomas theorem"—the observation by W. I. Thomas that "if men define situations as real, they are real in their consequences." And, as we have seen, MacIver used the less euphonious expression "the self-fulfilling postulate" in a book also published in 1948.[98] Merton alludes to, but does not discuss, a counterpart of the self-fulfilling prophecy, something he calls the "suicidal prophecy," a prophecy "which so alters human behavior from what would have been its course had the prophecy not been made, that it *fails* to be borne out. The prophecy destroys itself."[99] The present writer has called this "the self-falsifying prophecy," because "suicidal" seems too strong to be apposite. It is best illustrated perhaps by the following, by Robert W. Friedrichs:

> Jonah, we are told, prophesied the destruction of Nineveh due to its multiple transgressions; but the Ninevites are reported to have heeded the import of the prophecy and sought Yahweh's forgiveness through a return to his ways. And since the glory of the biblical God lay not in his justice but in his grace, they were indeed saved. In the process, Jonah's prophecy of their destruction was of course falsified; hence a demoralized and indignant Jonah, for his claim to omniscience had clearly been denied.[100]

Merton's definition of the self-fulfilling prophecy and its operation is as follows: "The self-fulfilling prophecy is, in the beginning, a *false* definition of the situation evoking a new behavior which makes the originally false conception come *true*. The specious validity of the self-fulfilling prophecy perpetuates a reign of error. For the prophet will cite the actual course of events as proof that he was right from the beginning." This is a phenomenon that occurs only in the social world and is unknown in the natural. "Predictions of the return of Halley's comet do not influence its orbit."[101] Thus, the character—indeed the truth—of sociological knowledge is called into question.[102]

Merton, however, is in this place interested not in the character of

98. *The More Perfect Union* (New York: Macmillan, 1948).

99. *Social Theory and Social Structure*, p. 423, n. 423. See also Merton, "The Unanticipated Consequences of Purposive Social Action," where he uses the label "self-defeating prediction"; reprinted in *Sociological Ambivalence and Other Essays*, pp. 145–155.

100. "Dialectical Sociology: Toward a Resolution of the Current 'Crisis' in Western Sociology," *British Journal of Sociology* 23 (September 1972): 263–274.

101. *Ibid.*, p. 423.

102. See the discussion in Bierstedt, *The Social Order*, pp. 23–25. See also the observation by Robert M. MacIver: "Most other kinds of philosophy do not affect the nature of the things they profess to explain, however foolish or however wise the philosophy may be, but this kind [political philosophy and sociology] makes and remakes the system that controls our lives." *The Web of Government* (New York: Macmillan, 1947), p. 404.

sociological knowledge but rather in the role of the self-fulfilling prophecy in explaining race prejudice and discrimination in the United States.[103] In the discussion he also makes effective use of the in-group–out-group distinction and the "moral alchemy" that turns in-group virtues into out-group vices. Although race prejudice and discrimination have greatly diminished in the United States since the time, almost thirty years ago, when Merton wrote the article, it is still worth reading for the insights it contains.[104]

Conclusion

We shall forgo a summary of Merton's writings and attend only to an evaluation. Indeed, a summary of the many subjects to which he has applied his nimble mind would be all but impossible. The entire chapter is a flawed effort in this direction. The first merit badge to be pinned on him is precisely this almost incredible range of interests, his moving with the speed and grace of a humming bird from one blossom to the next, never still but always seemingly in flight. How can a man do so many things so well? It is an appropriate question, for throughout his work we find an altogether superior level of competence. The scholarship is there, the erudition, the footnotes. The footnotes themselves, if brought together in one place, would make a fascinating volume.[105] Before leaving Merton, the reader should have a look at *On the Shoulders of Giants,* which Merton published in 1965.[106] In tracing the incidence of this particular expression through several centuries of Western history, the book is at once a work of massive scholarship and a spoof of the kind of scholarship it represents. Ideas are toys for Merton, colored balls to be conjured out of nowhere, thrown in the air, and caught again with a magicians's flair and finesse.

Among his substantive contributions, let me emphasize once more his outstanding work in the sociology of science, a field in which he has no peer. His *Science, Technology and Society in Seventeenth-Century England*

103. This, of course, was also the subject of MacIver's book, *The More Perfect Union.*

104. The two essays on the sociology of knowledge included in *Social Theory and Social Structure* will not be discussed in this volume. They conform in all respect to the standards of excellence expected of Merton, but they are largely critical, the first of Durkheim, Granet, and Sorokin, and the second of Mannheim.

105. On Merton's footnotes see Lewis A. Coser, "Merton's Uses of the European Sociological Tradition," *Idea of Social Structure,* pp. 89–90.

106. (New York: Free Press).

takes a rank second only to Weber's *The Protestant Ethic and the Spirit of Capitalism.* And if its rank is second, it is not because of inferior scholarship but because it advances two theses rather than one: that scientific development in seventeenth-century England was stimulated and encouraged by the Puritan ethic on the one hand and that it was stimulated and encouraged by material and technological necessities on the other. The two theses are not in harmony. The first points to an ideological interpretation of social change; the second, to a technological interpretation. Had Merton been tempted to employ "the theoretic bias,"[107] he would have had such companions as Buckle, de Gobineau, Marx, Durkheim, Weber, and Freud, with whose names we associate single-factor theories of social change. In Merton we have a double-factor theory. His two somewhat contrary theses deprive his book of thrust.

Merton's theoretical merit lies in the power of his analyses of particular social phenomena and in the concepts and expressions he has utilized to illuminate them. The most important of these expressions are theories of the middle range, paradigms, unanticipated consequences of purposive social action, sociological ambivalence,[108] the self-fulfilling prophecy, reference group, anticipatory socialization, the role-set, manifest and latent functions, and functional analysis itself. Some of these are more useful than others, some may raise unnecessary problems, but all are extraordinarily suggestive. All go to the heart of some methodological or sociological problem. They are part of the coin of sociological exchange.

On the critical side we have to say that Merton has the defects of his virtues. The extensive range of his interests has blurred what might otherwise have been a clear and consistent focus. As mentioned earlier in this chapter, he has given us no systematic work, no theory of the social order, no system of sociology. The omission, however, was deliberate. In an autobiographical essay he writes,

> Almost from the beginning of my independent work . . . . I was resolved to follow my intellectual interests as they developed, rather than to hold fast to a predetermined plan. That is to say, I chose to adopt the practice of a self-selected master-at-a-distance, Emile Durkheim, rather than the practice of my

107. On the theoretic bias, see Bierstedt, "Sociology and Humane Learning," *Power and Progress*, pp. 319–320. It involves the deliberate use of exaggeration, the pushing of a single factor as far as it is possible to go in the explanation of a social phenomenon, with the expectation that the exaggeration will be corrected by future critics.

108. See the essays collected in *Sociological Ambivalence and Other Essays.* Interestingly enough, *ambivalence* is the word that Sorokin uses to criticize Merton's sociological theories. *Sociological Theories of Today* (New York: Harper & Row, 1966), p. 447.

> master-at-close-range, George Sarton. Durkheim had repeatedly changed the subjects which he investigated. Starting with studies of the division of labor, he examined suicide, religion, moral education and socialism, all the while evolving a theoretical orientation that, to his mind, could be most effectively developed by attending to these varied aspects of man's life in society.[109]

This is the pattern he decided to emulate.

His decision, deliberate as it was, is nevertheless to be regretted. For all of his insistence on the independent reality of society, and therefore the autonomy of sociology, Durkheim wrote little about the structure of society—parts of *The Division of Labor* excepted—and the relationship of its component parts to one another. The corpus of his work does not add up to a systematic sociology. There is nothing like MacIver's *Society* or Sorokin's *Society, Culture, and Personality.* Nor, with Durkheim as a "role model," do we find a general theory of society in Merton. To look at society itself, to see it steadily and to see it whole—this Merton decided not to do.

In fact, he has hurled pejorative adjectives at such an enterprise—adjectives like *grandiose* and *premature.* The systems of the past lack all utility. They testify to the merits of talented men, but they cannot be used in contemporary research. They give us no guidelines. Here we can only wonder at the blind spot in Merton's vision. Was Plato premature? Or Aristotle, Saint Augustine, Machiavelli, Bodin, Hobbes, Montesquieu, Rousseau, Condorcet, Comte, Spencer, and a host of others? It was never the intention of the masters of social thought to provide guidelines for research. They were trying instead to say something about the nature of human society. If "research" could help them, well and good—Aristotle, after all, collected the constitutions of 158 city-states—but previous theories were more relevant to their concerns. Let us in fact admire those who, because of their superior observation of the society in which they lived, their knowledge of history, and their intimate familiarity with the thought of their predecessors, could generate theory *without* doing research. In any event, theory was not an instrument to be judged by its utility in research but the goal of their endeavors, an enterprise with its own intrinsic merit.

Merton, on the contrary, as we have said, has a Lundbergian view of sociology. The science of Merton and Lundberg walks on two legs, like a man. One of the legs is called theory, and the other, research. Only when research accumulates can we have a body of knowledge worthy of being called sociology. The trouble with this view is that it has failed to happen. The history of sociology shows no such accumulation. If Merton had

---

109. Quoted in Coser, "Merton's Uses of the European Sociological Tradition," p. 89.

forgotten about the criterion of utility and applied his extraordinary talents to the creation of a system of sociology, his place in our pantheon would be more exalted, and more secure.

There is, however, a final word for Merton, and that word is *quality*. He does not commit the remarkable mistakes of writers like Sorokin and Lundberg, mistakes to which attention has been drawn in other chapters of this book. He is a serious and thoughtful scholar, a superb sociologist, and one who has illuminated every subject to which he has directed his attention.

Epilogue

We may, in a comparatively brief epilogue, look at our sociologists as a group and indulge in some random observations about them.

The Sociological Label

In the first place, they were all sociologists, but not all of them all of the time. Sumner began his career as an Episcopalian rector; Ward for most of his career was a botanist and paleontologist; Znaniecki turned to sociology from philosophy; Ross and Parsons received their first academic appointments in economics; and MacIver was both political philosopher and sociologist. On the other hand, Cooley, Sorokin, Lundberg, and Merton began and ended their careers as sociologists. But all of our writers won distinction as sociologists, and all wore the label. All of them were members of a department of sociology (in Sumner's case, a department of the science of society), all were active members of the American Sociological Association, and all served the association as president.

The Legacy of Spencer

The work of all of our sociologists, up to but not including Parsons, represents a tradition of social thought, a tradition that stems directly from Comte and Spencer, and especially the latter. All of them except Parsons and Merton were immersed in Spencerian concerns and tried, with greater or less success, to answer Spencer's question, "What is a society?"

> This question has to be asked and answered at the outset. Until we have decided whether or not to regard a society as an entity, and until we have decided whether, if regarded as an entity, a society is to be classed as absolutely unlike all other entities or as like some others, our conception of the subject-matter before us remains vague.[1]

The answers our sociologists gave to this question differ in detail, as is to be expected, but they all fit into the same general framework. The description of society, the discovery of its structure, and the delineation of its component parts—these are the tasks that most of them set for themselves as they pursued their sociological careers. It is not until we come to Parsons that Spencer is explicitly repudiated, and then Parsons himself returned to Spencer's problems and perspectives late in his career. However much they differed on specific issues—Sumner and Ward, for example, on laissez-faire—they were all evolutionary thinkers, Ward no less than Sumner, Ross no less than Ward, Cooley no less than Ross, and so on almost, but not quite, to the end of the list. Evolutionary thought is clearly visible in MacIver's treatment of social change, and although Sorokin's theory of change is one of trendless fluctuation rather than linear or multilinear evolution, the influence of Spencer can clearly be discerned in his conception of the sociological enterprise.

The Normative Taboo

All of our sociologists knew the difference between categorical propositions and normative propositions, and almost all of them subscribed to the view that sociology be limited to the former. None of them was indebted to Max Weber for this position, and none needed the German word *Wertfreiheit* to express his preference for a value-free discipline. Sumner was an opponent of reformers because they tried to meddle with the natural processes of society; Ward specifically distinguished sociology from meliorism and said that for the sociologist *nil admirari* ('nothing is to be admired'); Cooley assumed that everyone would agree with him on the nature of good and evil, but there was no tincture of the reformer in him; and Ross, rife with recommendations on matters of social policy, nevertheless distinguished sociology from ethics on the ground that the latter is normative, whereas the former never goes beyond the laws and causes of social phenomena. All of the succeeding sociologists, from Znaniecki to Merton, with one exception, remained faithful to the principle of ethical and political neutrality in their sociological writing, and there is a special in-

1. *Principles of Sociology*, 3d ed., 3 vols. (New York: D. Appleton & Co., 1898), vol. 1, p. 447.

sistence in Lundberg's advocacy of it. Science does not take sides on questions of value. The exception is Sorokin, whose admiration for an ideational culture and contempt for a sensate one is bruisingly evident.

This is not to say that these sociologists did not have political predilections. They were, after all, citizens as well as sociologists. On the political spectrum we find them at various points, none perhaps relevant to their sociological theory. None, except possibly Ward, was an enemy of capitalism, and none a friend of socialism. Sumner was a staunch champion of capitalism; to him it was a visible sign of the truth of Social Darwinism, and he believed that under capitalism the American working class enjoyed a better life than any working class in history. He was probably right. One cannot otherwise explain the rate of European immigration to the United States during his lifetime. All of our sociological writers, it goes without saying, would have supported the principles enunciated in the Bill of Rights, especially in the First Amendment. But there are shades of gray in the spectrum, and accordingly there are liberals and conservatives among them. Thus, we would find on the liberal side Ward, Ross, MacIver, and Parsons, and on the conservative Sumner, Cooley, and probably Sorokin and Lundberg. Ward's views on sex and sexual equality were a century ahead of his time. Ross and MacIver both served on the Board of Directors of the American Civil Liberties Union, the former as chairman. Parsons, indicted steadily by his critics for paying more attention to social order than to social conflict, was nevertheless always on the liberal side on social and political issues. Sumner, on the other hand, was active in the Republican party and for some of his views might even merit the label of reactionary. Sorokin and Lundberg are difficult to classify. Sorokin, of course, was a revolutionary in his youth and was often arrested for subversive activity. In later years, however, his utterances became increasingly conservative, and he took great delight in referring to himself as "a conservative Christian anarchist." He, Cooley, and Parsons, incidentally, are probably the only ones who retained throughout their lives their original religion—Sorokin, Greek Orthodox, and Cooley and Parsons, Protestant Christian. Lundberg, a socialist in his youth on the midwestern prairie, became increasingly conservative and in his later years often expressed reactionary sentiments. The political predilections of Znaniecki and Merton are not apparent.

American References

Our sociologists, again up to but not including Parsons, are generous in their references to their American predecessors and contemporaries. Ward knew Sumner's work well and reviewed some of it. Cooley wrote an article on Sumner and praised him almost effusively. Ross was especially impressed by Ward, chose him as the model for his own career, and indeed the Ross–Ward correspondence continued until the latter's death. Znaniecki mentions most of his American predecessors and contemporaries and was, of course, indebted to W. I. Thomas, as Thomas was to him. Znaniecki and MacIver, colleagues and friends, held each other in high esteem. MacIver, trained in a European tradition of political philosophy, cites Sumner, Cooley, and Ross with approval and appreciation. Indeed, he uses some of Sumner's own language in discussing the social codes. He paid no attention, however, to Parsons. Sorokin's scorn for all of his predecessors, both European and American (except possibly Ross) is well known, but he was intimately familiar with their work. He is especially critical of MacIver, excessively harsh with Lundberg, consistently hostile to Parsons, and seriously negative about Merton.[2] MacIver wrote unfavorable reviews of several of Sorokin's books, but they both constructed systems of sociology—systems, moreover, that exhibit interesting similarities. Lundberg and MacIver clashed on a number of issues, some of them basic, and, to the delectation of the profession, carried their controversies to journals and books. Lundberg fully accepted Sorokin's view of sociology and quoted him at length. He was also indebted to Cooley. There is, in short, an American tradition of sociological theory, and the first eight of our ten writers, including the "foreigners" Sorokin, MacIver, and Znaniecki, not only subscribed to it but also built upon it and carried it forward.

The first break in this tradition occurs in Parsons. Ellsworth Faris, in his caustic review of *The Social System*, indicts its author for the almost total absence of American names, the names of those in the American tradition who gave us our concepts, the concepts that are the very tools of our trade.[3] He could have written similarly of *The Structure of Social Action*. It is true that Parsons mentions Znaniecki in the latter work because Znaniecki preceded him as an action theorist and thought of action as the central concept in sociology. But the discussion is brief. There is a brief mention of Sorokin also, but only in disagreement with Sorokin's interpretation of Pareto—an interpretation, we may say again, that is much

2. For his treatment of Merton, see *Sociological Theories of Today* (New York: Harper & Row, 1966), pp. 445–456. He regards many of Merton's propositions as "trivialities dressed up as scientific generalizations" (p. 452).

3. *American Sociological Review* 18 (February 1953): 103–106. He notes, in addition to the English Spencer, the omission of Ward, Giddings, Sumner, Park, Mead, Dewey, Cooley, Thomas, Ogburn, Burgess, Znaniecki, MacIver, Lundberg, Barnes, and Odum.

closer to the mark than Parsons's is. We have observed that, so far as mutual awareness is concerned, Parsons and Lundberg might as well have lived on different planets. The observation needs one important qualification. It was the determinism and the behaviorism, as represented preeminently by Lundberg, but not mentioned by Parsons, that Parsons resisted with the full weight of his work. Indeed, his pen became a cudgel with which to attack the positivistic view of man and society.

Parsons, curiously, has little interest in Spencer's question and lacks the sense of society that we find in Sorokin and MacIver. He is interested instead in a construction of his own, the social system, itself a subsystem of action systems in general. In short, Parsons is no part of the American tradition of sociological theory. He tried instead to create a tradition of his own, a tradition whose origins he unsuccessfully sought in Pareto, Durkheim, and Weber. Indeed, these three are treated as pre-Parsonians in the discovery of the voluntaristic theory of action.

Merton overtly appreciates the insights of Sumner and Cooley. In addition, he has many references to Sorokin, MacIver, and Parsons and some criticism of Lundberg. On the other hand, there are few signs of an influence of Sorokin, MacIver, and Parsons in his work. Although Sorokin was his teacher at Harvard, there is no attempt to emulate Sorokin's comprehensive system of sociology, as in *Society, Culture, and Personality*, or his massive assault on the problem of social change, as in *Social and Cultural Dynamics*. Merton's essay in one Sorokin Festschrift, written in collaboration with Bernard Barber, is devoted to Sorokin's sociology of science, which is not one of Sorokin's central themes.[4] Merton's essay in another Festschrift, written in collaboration with Elinor Barber, is on the concept of ambivalence, which is a subject of no concern to Sorokin.[5] Nor is there much evidence of the influence of MacIver, who was for many years Merton's senior colleague at Columbia. He has no apparent ambition to write a new and superior *Society*. In fact, Merton alone among our American sociologists has made no effort to construct a system of sociology.[6] For him and some of his younger contemporaries, the construction of such a system seems to be a sterile and possible disreputable enter-

4. "Sorokin's Formulations in the Sociology of Science," *Pitirim A. Sorokin in Review*, ed. Philip J. Allen (Durham, N.C.: Duke University Press, 1963), pp. 332–368.

5. "Sociological Ambivalence," *Sociological Theory, Values, and Sociocultural Change: Essays in Honor of Pitirim A. Sorokin*, ed. Edward A. Tiryakian (New York: Free Press of Glencoe, 1963), pp. 91–120.

6. This observation is in no way intended to denigrate the quality and magnitude of his other accomplishments.

prise, one that can be relegated to the authors of textbooks.[7] Because textbooks carry no intellectual prestige, this prejudice unfortunately deprives sociology of an inner core and encourages its abandonment as a general inquiry into the nature of society.

Even more interesting perhaps is the relationship between Parsons and Merton. Parsons was Merton's mentor at Harvard, and the label of structural-functionalism is attached to both of them.[8] But there are few similarities or "correspondences" in their writing. It is not surprising that the younger man did not influence the older. Parsons's paper in the Merton Festschrift has more to say of Parsons than of Merton, and in it he complains, somewhat disingenuously, that "to my knowledge Merton has never seriously attempted to achieve theoretical closure of the set of primary functions of a social system."[9] It merits attention, however, that there is so little of Parsons in Merton. Merton makes no use of the pattern-variables, the general "system-variables," or any of the other elaborate paradigms to be found in Parsons. Nor can one discover in Merton any trace of a voluntaristic theory of action. In fact, action is not a category in Merton. Parsons concludes that Merton has no theory in the Parsonian sense. And of course he is right. But the claim of Parsons that he was constructing not *a* sociological theory but *the* sociological theory for his own and future time is confounded close to its source. Ross, incidentally, was content with the more modest claim that he was offering not *the* but only *a* sociological theory.

The Holy Trinity[10]

Our American sociologists have a striking feature in common. None of them, up to Parsons, was influenced by Marx, Durkheim, and Weber—"the Holy Trinity"—who by 1980 had reached a pinnacle of fame and

7. In the revised and enlarged edition of his *Masters of Sociological Thought* (New York: Harcourt Brace Jovanovich, 1977), Lewis A. Coser treats Sorokin's theory of social and cultural dynamics but not, except for a few words, his systematic sociology.

8. Although they prefer the term *functional analysis.* See Talcott Parsons, "The Present Status of 'Structural-Functional' Theory in Sociology," *The Idea of Social Structure; Papers in Honor of Robert K. Merton,* ed. Lewis A. Coser (New York: Harcourt Brace Jovanovich, 1975), p. 67.

9. *Ibid.*, p. 76. Parsons's conception of sociology is clearly exhibited in this language. As always, he is more interested in a social system than he is in society. In this essay, however, he makes a strong defense of his preference. See pages 71–73.

10. I am indebted to Howard S. Becker for this expression. He uses it in an article entitled "What's Happening to Sociology?" *Transaction: Social Science and Modern Society* 16 (July–August 1979): 24.

whose work was regarded as the sine qua non of sociology. None of them, including Parsons and Merton, was or is a Marxist, and Marxism plays no role in their theory. Sumner, as we have seen, stressed the importance of the economic factor in the formation of society, supported a labor theory of value, and noted the significance of class conflict.[11] But these were doctrines of his own, presented neither in the context of Marxist theory nor with any reference to Marx. Ward, like Sumner, subscribed to a labor theory of value ("All value is the result of labor"), but rejected the economic interpretation of history—a doctrine he attributed not to Marx but to De Gréef and Seligman. There is no mention of Marx in his treatment of either subject. Indeed, he regarded Marx as a politician and reformer rather than as a sociologist. In Cooley there is a single mention of Marxian socialism, but Marx does not appear in his discussion of class and class consciousness. Nor did he need Marx in order to argue against the economic interpretation of history. Ross noted on a number of occasions the impact of economic conditions on social change and strongly emphasized the "strife of social classes." Indeed, class conflict is for him the most important and serious of all kinds of conflict. But he does not refer to Marx on these occasions, nor does he need Marx in order to treat the subject of alienation, which he calls "estrangement." In short, Marx is often given credit, and sometimes sole credit, for ideas that, whether accepted or rejected, were commonplace in the history of American sociology.

MacIver does refer to Marx. He is unhappy with Marx's dogmatism and critical of Marx's conception of social class. Furthermore, in his opinion Marx was unable to comprehend the intricate relationships between economic and political power. He concedes, however, that despite their exaggerations Marx and Engels are correct in their view that in all societies of any size there is always a ruling class. Sorokin attends to Marx in detail in *Contemporary Sociological Theories*, but there the treatment is a demolition project rather than a scholarly discussion. For Sorokin the economic interpretation of society is as old as the history of social thought itself, and Marxism is only an almost demented expression of it. In his view Marx and Engels hindered rather than helped the progress of social science.

For Lundberg Marxism suffers from serious terminological faults and the economic interpretation of history is as arbitrary as any other. The assumption of an inherent priority of any factor in the social process is incompatible with science. Science can take any variable, regard it as an in-

11. Indeed, as Lewis A. Coser has written, "Sumner's doctrine involved a kind of economic determinism considerably more dogmatic and unbending than that of Karl Marx." "American Trends," *A History of Sociological Analysis*, ed. Tom Bottomore and Robert Nisbet (New York: Basic Books, 1978), p. 295.

dependent variable, and regard all others as dependent variables. The economic interpretation of history is solely a matter of methodological convenience. Parsons wrote papers on Marx and was intimately familiar with his thought, but Marx did not win inclusion in *The Structure of Social Action*, and Marxism played no part in the Parsonian system as it developed. Nor can a Marxist influence be detected in the work of Znaniecki and Merton.

It might be remarked that, as Donald MacRae has pointed out, there is more than one Marx.[12] There is Marx the philosopher, Marx the economist, and Marx the reformer. But there is no Marx the sociologist until after the middle of the twentieth century, when some sociologists began to claim him as part of the sociological tradition and sometimes to confuse him with the tradition itself. In at least one university (identification intentionally omitted) a course on the history of sociology dealt almost entirely with Marx, and by the late 1970s there was a section on Marxist sociology in the American Sociological Association. What this latter might mean is not altogether clear, unless there is also a Marxist botany and a Marxist astronomy. It has even been claimed that all social thought antecedent to Marx is in anticipation of Marx and all subsequent social thought is a dialogue with Marx's ghost—that Marx, in short, is the great pivot around which the whole creation moves. This claim, as the history of American sociological theory shows, is as foolish as it is false. No really distinguished American sociological theorist has been a Marxist.

Ordinary canons of criticism, of course, do not apply to Marx. The reason is that Marxism, through no fault of Marx himself (*"Je ne suis pas un Marxiste."*), has become a religion. It has a prophet (Marx), a holy book (*Das Kapital*), a redeemer (Lenin), a hymn ("The Internationale"), a church (the Communist party), a heaven (the classless society), an Apostles' Creed (the Communist Manifesto), and a body of believers. The believers view the doctrine with reverence and regard deviations from it as apostasy. Our American sociologists, however, did not get the Word, and in any event they were not churchgoers.

If there is no Marx in the history of American sociological theory, neither is there much of Durkheim or Weber. Until Parsons placed their statues in the pantheon in 1937 they were simply two names, of no more importance than many others. They were not unknown. On the contrary, American sociologists referred to them much more often than they referred to one another. All of them were familiar with the work of Durkheim and all of them have references to him. Sumner includes Durkheim's essay on

12. "Karl Marx," *New Society* (January 28, 1965): 22–23, reprinted in Timothy Raison, ed., *The Founding Fathers of Social Science* (Baltimore: Penguin Books, 1969). This is the best brief treatment of Marx in the sociological literature.

incest in the bibliography of *Folkways* and *The Science of Society* and in the latter place also includes *The Rules of Sociological Method* and *The Elementary Forms of the Religious Life.* Cooley praises Durkheim for his discovery of altruistic suicide but otherwise pays no attention to him. Ross often mentions Durkheim, but usually in series with others. He pays special tribute, however, to "the genius of Gabriel Tarde." Znaniecki is critical of both Durkheim and Tarde, whose conceptions of sociology he regards as unfortunate. MacIver approves of Durkheim on suicide but criticizes his "quest for origins." Sorokin uses *Suicide* as a superior example of what sociological research should be. On the other hand, he says that Durkheim's sociology in general is hopelessly one-sided and "monopolistic," and he has no respect for the "fictitious entity" that Durkheim made of society. As noted earlier, in *Contemporary Sociological Theories* he devotes more than twice as much space to Le Play as he does to Durkheim and Weber combined. Merton, as I have also noted, chose Durkheim as his model sociologist. But Durkheim comes into his own, so to speak, with Parsons's strenuous effort to rescue him from positivism in *The Structure of Social Action* and to transform him into an action theorist.

The story of Weber is somewhat different. Although as a recognized academic figure he was invited to lecture at the Saint Louis Exposition of 1904, and did so, he was not regarded as a sociologist by his American contemporaries. He was certainly not regarded by Ross or by anyone else as one of the founders of the discipline. Not until we come to Sorokin and MacIver do we find treatments of his work. Sorokin, as we have seen, discusses him briefly in *Contemporary Sociological Theories* but makes no use of him in developing his own theories. MacIver approves of Weber's concept of the ideal type but is critical of Weber's conception of social class. He is critical also of Weber on the Protestant ethic. The relationship between capitalism and Protestantism is more complex than Weber supposed: Capitalism can grow and thrive without Protestantism, as the example of late-nineteenth-century Japan discloses. Finally, as mentioned earlier, all of our Americans insisted upon a value-free sociology, and none of them relied on Weber in making the point. In short, the history of American sociological theory up to Parsons is as independent of Durkheim and Weber as it is of Marx. To most of our Americans the holy trinity is neither holy nor a trinity.

Style

Style is part of the measure of a man, and I have accordingly commented throughout on the literary grace and facility of our sociologists. Now that we have them in one place, so to speak, we can indulge in some comparative judgments, even though they will not elicit universal agreement. For trenchant, lively, and even beautiful prose Ross probably deserves the palm. He wears his erudition lightly and pleases his readers with deft turns of phrase. MacIver's prose is serene and stately. Both *Society* and *The Web of Government* contain numerous quotable sentences. The prose of Ward, Cooley, and Merton is always lucid and free of jargon. Znaniecki is altogether to be admired for his mastery of the English language, a mastery exhibited best, perhaps, in *The Social Role of the Man of Knowledge.* Sumner is slovenly and often dull in *Folkways* but exciting and provocative in his essays. One remembers Lundberg for an occasional bright polemical thrust, but on the whole his prose is undistinguished and even careless. Sorokin, of course, is full of vituperation. He was fond of saying that he had forgotten his Russian and never learned English, and one is bound to agree with at least the latter half of his jest. Parsons plods along at the bottom of the list, his words, his sentences, and his paragraphs often sinking into the slough of unintelligibility. To anyone who respects the English language his prose can only be offensive. It has done harm to the discipline it was designed to serve.

Despite Parsons, the indictment frequently laid upon sociologists by literary critics and journalists that the language of sociology is jargon-ridden cannot be sustained. Among our ten sociologists a jury would find only Parsons guilty of the charge. The prose of the others, Sorokin and Lundberg excepted, is superior to that of a number of literary critics, including, for example, F. R. Leavis.[13]

Znaniecki and Merton comment on the importance of taxonomy, the former suggesting that every classification is already a theory and gives us systematic knowledge of some area of reality, and the latter saying that although taxonomy is not the whole of theory it is nevertheless an important part of it. There is, however, a wide variation of taxonomic talent among our writers. Sorokin, most conscious of the canons of classification—even to the point of discussing them—is easily the worst offender. As we have seen, his classification of groups, for example, is a golden treasury of taxonomic errors. He is devoted to the number three, and his categories

13. Consider the following:

> For to insist that literary criticism is, or should be, a specific discipline of intelligence is not to suggest that a serious interest in literature can confine itself to the kind of intensive local analysis associated with "practical criticism"—to the scrutiny of the "words on the page" in their minute relations, their effects of imagery, and so on: a real literary interest is an interest in man, society and civilization, and its boundaries cannot be drawn; the adjective is not a circumscribing one.

This sentence appears in an essay entitled "Sociology and Literature," Leavis, *The Common Pursuit* (Harmondsworth, Eng.: Penguin Books, 1962), p. 200.

therefore tend to appear as triads. Parsons, heavily dependent upon the number four, is an expert and indefatigable taxonomist, but the end results are less than satisfactory. This is especially the case with the pattern variables, which, in any case, are an extension of Tönnies's *Gemeinschaft* and *Gesellschaft* to a redundant degree. Ross, incidentally, did not need pattern-variables to invite attention to the antithesis between the professional and the commercial spirit. It is difficult to find a consistent *fundamentum divisionis* in any of Sumner's classifications. On the other hand, Ward, MacIver, Znaniecki, and Merton are sensitive to the logical requirements of classification, and Merton's typology of modes of individual adaptation to the norms of society deserves—as it has received—special commendation. Merton and MacIver, however, sometimes slip, and their treatment of groups—in Merton's case reference groups—leaves something to be desired.

If we ask how well organized our writers are we again perceive some differences. Ward, MacIver, Sorokin, Znaniecki, Parsons, and Merton are all well organized. Parsons, especially, is systematic in every way even though, as we have said, there is finally more organization than content. Cooley's chapters have no logical order. Ross tried to construct a system of sociology but his enthusiasms interfered with his efforts. Few would compliment Lundberg on his organization. He is clearly more interested in the philosophy of science than in the structure of society. Sumner intended to build a system, of which *Folkways* was to be the first part, but *The Science of Society*, put together by Albert Galloway Keller from Sumner's notes, does not qualify. Of the ten, in fact, Sumner displays the least organization, especially in *Folkways*. One is reminded of Montesquieu's *The Spirit of the Laws*, another classic without any organization whatever. Montesquieu, incidentally, was aware of the defect and made candid confession of it in his Preface.[14]

Mater Scientiarum

The attitudes of our sociologists to philosophy, the mother of the sciences, are not only interesting but they also shed some light on the

14. "I have followed my object without any fixed plan—I have known neither rules nor exceptions; I have found the truth, only to lose it again." Montesquieu, "Montesquieu's Preface," *The Spirit of the Laws*, with an Introduction by Franz Neumann. (New York: Hafner Pub. Co. 1949), p. xix.

nature of their work. Sumner was openly hostile. He regarded philosophy as an anachronism, "a complete fake," and seriously advocated its abolition at Yale. For him science begins when inquiry emancipates itself from metaphysics. Ward, a polymath, could have written on any philosophical subject—indeed, he published a paper on the antinomies of Immanuel Kant. On the other hand, he regarded much of philosophy as no more than "intellectual gymnastic" and referred slightingly to the barren systems of the metaphysicians. Metaphysics and epistemology, by their own admission, made both Cooley and Ross uncomfortable. Ross especially foundered on Hegel, for whose philosophy MacIver also had an antipathy. Both would have agreed that it is a "ghostly ballet of bloodless categories."[15]

Znaniecki began his career as a philosopher and developed a philosophy of his own named cultural realism, in which he found for the realm of culture an ontological significance. He argued that this philosophy would conquer and transcend the faults of both idealism and materialism. It has been said that all Scots are philosophers, and MacIver clearly fits the facetious stereotype. Although I have judged his *Social Causation* as something less than a success, no one unfamiliar with the history of philosophy could have written it. Sorokin struggled to extricate himself from the coils of the sociology of knowledge in order to protect his own theory of social and cultural dynamics from the fluctuations that afflict "systems of truth." He struggled in vain. The problem has no solution. It brings to mind Comte's assertion, *"Tout est relatif; voilà le seul principe absolue."*

Lundberg dealt primarily with methodological—that is, philosophical—matters, but his elementary logical errors led him to unfortunate positions, such as the denial of the difference between cardinal and ordinal measurement. In addition, his empiricism is so radical that it has solipsistic consequences. Like Sumner, he had no use for philosophers and in one of his polemical moments permitted himself to characterize them as "semantically deranged." Parsons, like Znaniecki, attempted, albeit briefly, to develop a philosophical position of his own, which he called "analytic realism," but he did not elaborate it and no one has subscribed to it. As I have emphasized, his voluntaristic theory of action presents formidable metaphysical difficulties, especially in the dualism involved in the sharp separation of actor and organism. Merton frowns on the philosophical systems of the past and comes close to suggesting that the history of philosophy might well be forgotten. Indeed, one of the misfortunes of

15. An Oxford student, his tongue twisted, once recited this expression as a "ghastly ballet of bloody categories."

sociology is that its history resembles the history of philosophy. Each of the "founders" presented his own theory, in competition with all of the others, and for this kind of effort Merton has no sympathy.[16] Although he has himself discussed the many senses in which the word *theory* is used, he tends to conceive of it not as a set of concepts that lucidly, logically, and parsimoniously delineate the structure of society but either as a group of cumulative inductions from middle range research or a master conceptual scheme from which subsidiary theories can be derived. For the second of these, he says, we are not yet ready—another indication, shall we say, of a certain lack of enthusiasm for the Parsonian enterprise.

Now it may be, to invoke the spirit of Francis Bacon, that a little philosophy is a dangerous thing. It would surely be unwise for sociologists to tarry too long with philosophical puzzles to which twenty-five centuries of speculation have brought no wholly satisfactory answers. On the other hand, a sociological theorist needs enough philosophical sophistication to recognize that the positions he takes have metaphysical, epistemological, and logical antecedents and consequences. In this respect Lundberg and Parsons are both at fault—and at fault precisely on the broad philosophical issues that separate them—behaviorism versus voluntarism, positivism versus "analytical realism." Both "stand squarely on the platform of science." But the platforms are different platforms. They stand at a considerable distance from each other, and their carpenters used different blueprints.

L'Envoi

Ross and Sorokin both wrote chapters entitled "Retrospect and Prospect." The retrospect, of course, is easy; the prospect difficult. We shall eschew all prediction here except for the single suggestion that the sociology of the future may resemble the sociology of the past more closely than Merton, for example, would like to think. Surely the works of the men represented in the chapters of this book, whatever their faults, have given us enlightening glimpses of the social order. For anyone afflicted with the itch of curiosity and the love of wisdom society itself will always be a fit and dignified subject of inquiry. Just as men have always "cast their eyes into the heavens and pried into the entrails of the earth,"[17] so also will they

16. Actually, he exaggerates the degree of competition. Sumner's concepts, for example, have been absorbed in the theories of his successors. There are signs that some of Merton's will be too.

17. The words belong to George Berkeley.

continue to peer at society, examine its contours and dimensions, and tell us what they have seen. In the telling they will be giving us their sociological theories, and it may be, as Ross thought and Parsons did not, that many theories are better than one.

Appendix

Franklin Henry Giddings

Because of the prominent position of Franklin Henry Giddings (1855–1931) as longtime chairman of the department at Columbia University, where he was professor of sociology and the history of civilization, I had originally planned to include a chapter on him. After reading his principal sociological works, however, I decided that a few brief paragraphs would suffice.[1]

The Principles of Sociology[2]

Giddings's principal, and only well-known, contribution to sociology appears in his first and probably most important book. It is the concept of "the consciousness of kind," a consciousness that distinguishes social from nonsocial phenomena and is the cause of social conduct. He characterizes it as follows:

> The original and elementary subjective fact in society is *the consciousness of kind*. By this term I mean a state of consciousness in which any being, whether

1. Omitted from the discussion are his *Inductive Sociology* (1901) and *Civilization and Society* (1932). The first is a syllabus of principles and problems, and the second, a collection of lectures delivered at Teachers College during the two academic years 1924–1926, arranged and edited by Howard W. Odum (New York: Henry Holt & Co. 1932). For a bibliography, see *Bibliography of the Faculty of Political Science* (New York: Columbia University Press, 1931).
2. (New York: Macmillan, 1896). There is a third edition, also 1896, and numerous reprintings. References are to the 1907 reprinting.

> low or high in the scale of life, recognizes another conscious being as of like kind with itself. Such a consciousness may be an effect of impression and imitation, but it is not the only effect that they produce. It may cause contract and alliance, but it causes other things as well. It is therefore less general than impression and imitation, which are more general than association. It is more general than contract and alliance, which are less general than association. It acts on conduct in many ways, and all the conduct that we can properly call social is determined by it. In short, it fulfils the sociological requirement; it is coextensive with potential society and with nothing else.[3]

He makes heavy use of the concept, and definitions of it recur in subsequent volumes. Incidentally, he distinguishes between psychology and sociology on the ground that the former is the science of the association of ideas, the latter, the science of the association of minds.[4]

Giddings's distinction between ethnical and demotic societies has also been put to an occasional use.

> Ethnical societies are genetic aggregations; a real or fictitious blood-kinship is their chief social bond. Demotic societies are congregate associations. They are groups of people that are bound together by habitual intercourse, mutual interests, and coöperation, with little or no regard to origins or to genetic relationships.[5]

This, of course, is Giddings's contribution to the familiar dichotomies in the literature.

There are four stages in the synthesis of social phenomena: (*a*) aggregation and association, (*b*) the evolution of the social mind, (*c*) the social composition, and (*d*) the social constitution. To these correspond four kinds of sociology—the zoogenic, the anthropogenic, the ethnogenic, and the demogenic. There are also four social classes: the social, the nonsocial, the pseudosocial, and the antisocial. In the first the consciousness of kind is well developed; in the second it is only partially developed; in the third (made up of paupers) it is degenerate; and in the fourth (made up of instinctive and habitual criminals) it approaches extinction.[6] Giddings's concepts, like those of Parsons, seem always to walk on four feet.

---

3. *Ibid.*, pp. 17–18. In the Preface to the third edition he defends his concept from four criticisms:

> First, that the phrase, "the consciousness of kind," is only another name for "fellow-feeling," and that, therefore, no new discovery has been made in sociology; second, that the consciousness of kind is a biological rather than a sociological fact, and that it therefore does not differentiate sociology from biology; third, that the consciousness of kind is only a metaphysical notion; and fourth, that even if the consciousness of kind is a social fact of some sort, it is at any rate not a social force, and is therefore not a true cause of social phenomena.

4. *Ibid.*, p. 25.
5. *Ibid.*, p. 157.
6. *Ibid.*, pp. 126–127.

Among many definitions of sociology, Giddings offers in this book the following: "Specifically, sociology is an interpretation of social phenomena in terms of psychical activity, organic adjustment, natural selection, and the conservation of energy."[7]

The Elements of Sociology[8]

In this book, "a text-book for colleges and schools," Giddings tells us that a society is "any group or number of individuals who cultivate acquaintance and mental agreement"[9] and distinguishes four kinds—the natural, the integral, the component, and the constituent. The unit of sociological investigation is the socius, because society is a group of socii. We are offered another definition of the consciousness of kind: "The consciousness of kind, then, is that pleasurable state of mind which includes organic sympathy, the perception of resemblance, conscious or reflective sympathy, affection, and the desire for recognition."[10] The book also includes a number of "laws," such as, for example, the law of sympathy: "The degree of sympathy decreases as the generality of resemblance increases."[11] Another example is the law of the social force of tradition: "Tradition is authoritative and coercive in proportion to its antiquity."[12] The book contains a number of "laws" like these, all italicized and presumably intended to be implanted in the memories of students of sociology.

What Giddings has to say about institutions is at least interesting:

> There is no word in any language that is more carelessly used by writers who should know better than this word "institutions." An institution is a social relation that is established by adequate and rightful authority. The ultimate source of authority is the social mind. Consequently, those forms of organization, those relations and arrangements which the social mind has reflected upon, which it has accepted, allowed, or commanded,—and these only,—are institutions.[13]

7. *Ibid.*, p. 419.
8. (New York: Macmillan, 1910). The first edition appeared in 1898.
9. *Ibid.*, p. 6.
10. *Ibid.*, p. 66 (italics omitted).
11. *Ibid.*, p. 67.
12. *Ibid.*, p. 154.
13. *Ibid.*, p. 175. He immediately confuses us, however, by continuing: "A band of robbers may be an organization, but it is not an institution. [So far so good.] The social arrangements of a community of savages are modes of organization, but they are not institutions. [Now the confusion.]"

Inasmuch as Giddings refers here to a social mind—a concept he uses frequenty—it should be said that for him it is a concrete, not an abstract, phenomenon, and that it can be found only in individuals, individuals who are directing their attention to the same thing at the same time. There is no suggestion that a group or a society can think or that there is in some sense a group mind that transcends individual minds.[14]

Studies in the Theory of Human Society[15]

This book is a series of essays on various sociological subjects, some at least, and possibly all, reprinted from original sources. One of them, "Social Theory and Public Policy," was his presidential address to the American Sociological Society in 1910. In another, "A Theory of History," he presents a typology of philosophies of history (there are five different kinds) and then presents his own: "History, then, is adventure, *and the urge to adventure is the cause of history.* This proposition is the kernel of my theory."[16] This "kernel" seems excessively small and simplistic. In fairness to Giddings, however, it should be said that he arrives at it after a long and elaborate discussion.

In a chapter entitled "The History of Social Theory," he says that the first strictly sociological treatise was the *Social Statics* of Spencer (1850) and writes that the book "challenges comparison to an extent that perhaps no other writing does, with both *The Republic* of Plato and *The Politics* of Aristotle."[17] In a chapter entitled "Social Self-Control" he pays tribute to Ross's "admirable book" on this subject and expresses "a generalization of significance": "Society is a type or norm or mode, which in a measure controls the variations from itself."[18] In his final chapter, "Further Inquiries of Sociology," he offers a curious definition of sociology: "In the same large sense in which economics is the science of the production and distribution of wealth, *for* man, sociology is the science of the production and distribution of adequacy, *of* man and *in* man."[19] He comes to the conclusion indeed

14. See *Principles of Sociology*, p. 134.
15. (New York: Macmillan, 1922).
16. *Ibid.*, p. 92.
17. *Ibid.*, p. 111.
18. *Ibid.*, p. 202.
19. *Ibid.*, p. 291:

> Adequacy comprises endurance, health, reproductive vigor, intelligence, self control, ability to make adjustments with others and to get on helpfully with others in cooperation. Society produces these factors of adequacy in the same sense in which the breeder produces desired qualities in animals, namely, by selecting them and providing the conditions under which they can survive.

that his definition is not at all idiosyncratic, that "without explicitly telling us so the founders of sociology have, in fact, it would seem, without exception conceived of the science of society as a systematic study of the increase and distribution of human adequacy to exist and achieve."[20] For interested students, Giddings summarizes, and reprints in his Preface, his system of sociology in four brief paragraphs, all pointing to the concept of adequacy. As a last matter of interest he refers to Sumner as "perhaps the most consistently sociological if not the greatest of sociologists."[21]

The Scientific Study of Human Society[22]

In this, his last book, various portions of which also appeared elsewhere, Giddings emphasizes the importance of scientific method in sociology and in particular the importance of statistics. His own examples of statistical method are relatively primitive in contrast with the versatile and powerful methods in use today. He offers an elaborate classification of societal facts that is now as obsolete as Parsons's diagrams are destined to become. It has two parts, one entitled "Categorical Scheme of Societal Genesis," and the other, "Categorical Scheme of Societal Variability."[23] He sometimes descends to simplicities. For example, in discussing the service that sociology can perform for social workers he says that although it cannot give them rules of technique it can and should give them "poise and balance, a comprehensive view, a sense of relative values, an apprehension of proportions and of probabilities."[24] In a chapter entitled "Societal Telesis" he pays high tribute to Ward. He begs us to measure societal energies and trends. He gives us another definition of society:

> Society is any considerable number of human beings living and working together, and more or less enjoying themselves with one another; and a lot of ways, more or less organized into arrangements, and more or less made orderly by precedents and rules, in which we, human beings, carry on and help one another to make life secure and desirable.[25]

Definitions such as these unfortunately carry more sentiment than logic.

20. *Ibid.*, pp. 292–293.
21. *Ibid.*, p. 293.
22. (Chapel Hill, N.C.: University of North Carolina Press, 1924).
23. *Ibid.*, pp. 70–78.
24. *Ibid.*, p. 99.
25. *Ibid.*, p. 198.

Conclusion

There are those who have had a high opinion of Giddings. Howard W. Odum, for example, wrote in his Introductory Note to *Civilization and Society*, "Here he appears again as the great teacher with much of his charming style, keen analysis, inimitable humor and satire, logical thinking, lucid presentation."[26] And Harry Elmer Barnes declared that he was "probably the ablest sociologist that the United States has ever produced" and that his *Principles of Sociology* is "probably the most important single volume yet to be published in the sociological field."[27]

My own opinion is a contrary one. Despite a penchant for classification—and many awkward examples of it—Giddings's work in general exhibits little sophistication. He has a degree of erudition, but no penetration, no profundity. His writing is straightforward but dull. One searches in vain for an epigram. His emphasis upon society as something that "selects and perpetuates the adequate" is, shall we say, inadequate. Inadequate also is his theory that adventure is the cause of history. The final judgment must be that his sociological theory lacks distinction.

---

26. P. v.

27. Barnes, ed., *An Introductrion to the History of Sociology* (Chicago: University of Chicago Press, 1948), pp. 764, 175. See also Clarence H. Northcott, "The Sociological Theories of Franklin Henry Giddings," *ibid.*, pp. 744–764; John L. Gillin, "Franklin Henry Giddings," *American Masters of Social Science* ed. Howard W. Odum (New York: Henry Holt & Co. 1927), pp. 191–228; Frank H. Hankins, "Franklin Henry Giddings, 1855–1931: Some Aspects of His Sociological Theory," *American Journal of Sociology* 37 (November 1931): 349–367; and Leo Davids, "Franklin Henry Giddings: Overview of a Forgotten Pioneer," *Journal of the History of the Behavioral Sciences* 4 (1968): 62–73.

Name Index[1]

1. Note: This index includes the names of all persons mentioned in both text and footnotes, except those of editors and translators and those of a purely biographical interest.

Subject Index